3 WEEK LOAN

Please check all items for damages
before leaving the Library.
Thereafter you will be held
responsible for all injuries
to items beyond reasonable wear.

1918

WAR AND PEACE

Gregor Dallas

THE OVERLOOK PRESS
WOODSTOCK & NEW YORK

First published in the United States in 2001 by
The Overlook Press, Peter Mayer Publishers, Inc.
Woodstock & New York

WOODSTOCK:
One Overlook Drive
Woodstock, NY 12498
www.overlookpress.com
[for individual orders, bulk and special sales, contact our Woodstock office]

NEW YORK:
386 West Broadway
New York, NY 10012

Library of Congress Cataloging-in-Publication Data

Dallas, Gregor.
1918 : war and peace / Gregor Dallas.
616 p. cm.
Includes bibliographical references and index.
1. World War, 1914–1918—Peace. 2. World War, 1914–1918—Armistices. I. Title.
D644 .D35 2001   940 4'39—dc21   2001021104

Manufactured in the United States of America
1 3 5 7 9 8 6 4 2
ISBN 1-58567-157-6

1918

By the same author

The Imperfect Peasant Economy: The Loire Country 1800–1914
At the Heart of a Tiger: Clemenceau and His World 1841–1929
1815: The Road to Waterloo

To Max Dallas Shaffrath

Contents

WINTER 1919

SPRING 1919

EUROPE, EUROPE

Illustrations

Movements (between pages 168 and 169)

Cities (between pages 328 and 329)

The author and publishers would like to thank the following for permission
to reproduce illustrations:

Plates 2, 5, 8, 11, 13, 29, 41, 42, 43, 44, BDIC Musée; 18, 19, 20, 23, 24, 25, 26, 27, 28,
Deutsche Kriegzeitung; 31, Mary Evans Picture Library; 51, Hoover Institution of War,
Revolution and Peace, Stanford, California; 39, Hulton Getty; 10, 30, 33, 36, 40, 45,
48, 53, 57, 60, *Illustrated London News*; 1, 3, 4, 6, 7, 9, 12, 15, 16, 17, 21, 22, 46, 47, 54,
55, 56, 59, *Illustration*; 35, Harry Kessler, *Walther Rathenau* (New York: Howard Fertig,
1969); 52, David King Collection; 37, 58, *Kladderadatsch*; 32, PA Photos; 14, Popperfoto;
38, US Army Signal Corps; 34, Woodrow Wilson Papers (Princeton University Press);
49, 50, Mikhail Zolotarev Collection.

Preface

How do wars end? This question has intrigued me for more than ten years. In his remarkable book *The Soldiers' Tale*, Samuel Hynes notes that soldiers' stories of the First World War almost never finish with the Armistice of 11 November 1918, which for most people today represents the last day of the war. Either their narratives conclude in the middle of the war or they run on beyond the Armistice. As examples of wartime endings, Hynes cites Siegfried Sassoon (who ends up in a London hospital) and Max Plowman (who returns to England with shell shock); he also quotes the last terrifying paragraph of Hervey Allen's *Toward the Flame*, where American troops are attacked by German flame-throwers – Allen himself described his book as 'a moving picture of war, broken off when the film burned off'. On the stories which go beyond the Armistice, Hynes observes that they nearly all end with some trivial detail about post-war civilian life. 'The story trails off here,' says Robert Graves in the final chapter of *Good-bye to All That*. The narratives 'fizzle out', they lose their momentum 'like runners who have passed the finish line but can't stop running', says Hynes.[1]

'Burned off', 'trailing off', 'fizzled out', 'can't stop running' – these are the soldiers' memories of how the Great War ended. Their conclusions are indecisive and tantalizingly incomplete.

In every European family there is a story buried somewhere on the Great War. The one which I cherish most is that of my wife's grandfather. Henri Heiberger's family came from Alsace, a contested province. He went to school in the Vosges, and then went to war at the Chemin des Dames, participating in Nivelle's disastrous offensive of April 1917; he was nineteen and a half years old. Because his name sounded German, the commander of his battalion placed him, at every 'push', in front of all the other assault troops. Heiberger, who was no shirker, decided to volunteer for the new French air corps; it had the highest casualty rate of all the armed forces. But Heiberger was still alive when he turned twenty-one – on Monday, 11 November 1918. When the astonishing news of the Armistice came through, he celebrated his birthday by performing a little aerobatics, and crashed his coloured biplane in a dung heap. He was pulled out of the wreckage unharmed. Lieutenant Heiberger's war had a tragi-comic end.

There is, in fact, a multitude of memories about how the Great War ended, many of them contradictory. Historians of the war only add to the muddle, for they often *do* conclude their story on 11 November 1918. Well . . . if the war suddenly ended on 11 November, then how was the peace made? The historians answer that the peace was a complicated affair and must be relegated to a separate chapter, or even a separate book. The continuity of the story is thus lost.

But it is this continuity that matters. For instance, if a reader is not aware of the developing disequilibrium during the war between the military power of the Western European Allies on the one side, and the economic power of the United States on the other, the tensions that appeared during the Paris Peace Conference in 1919 make no sense at all. Or take another example: if a reader has not followed the way Germany's Imperial Army was squeezed up against the Ardennes in Belgium by Allied armies in the autumn of 1918, Germany's 'revolution' of the ensuing winter and spring – which was made up of fragments of that old Army – seems a complete absurdity. The Bolshevik Revolution in Russia and the subsequent civil war; the Soviet–Polish war of 1919–21; the famine of the southern Volga in 1921–2: all these are also sequels to a war that began when Germany's armies began marching across Europe's northern plain in August 1914. The whole succession of events, from 1914 to 1922, is one great historical epic that is too often told in parts.

I am a local historian by taste and training, and it may be thought that this would make me easy prey to the perils of too narrow a focus. But I actually believe that it is world historians – with their analysis, methods and systems – who are more likely to impose limits on the tale. The shape of the hills, the bends in the rivers, the shape of the coast, the way in which villages and towns are settled are what fascinate me. It seems to me that when historians abandon these basic facts for abstract global systems of economy, of politics, of social class or of military manoeuvre they open themselves to error.

An anecdote well illustrates this. Marc Bloch, who was a most distinguished French rural historian, tells how Frederick Seebohm, the specialist of rural England, wrote in 1885 to Fustel de Coulanges, the great historian of medieval political systems, to ask him whether the 'open-field system' of cultivation, with its long furlongs, had ever been common in France. Fustel replied that he could find no trace of it. Fustel, said Bloch, 'was not a man on whom the external world made much impact'. When travelling 'it is quite probable that he never took any special notice of the characteristic pattern of ploughlands visible all over northern and eastern France which so irresistibly call to mind the open-fields of England'.[2] The landscape of Europe contains tell-tale signs which are essential knowledge for a rural historian, and he will not find this in documents and theories.

And so it is for the historian of the Great War. Familiarity with the lie of the land is just as important for anyone wanting to understand the manoeuvring of the armies, the flood of the refugees, and the kind of peace which followed.

There is a singular epic movement behind all of this; the war of 1914–18 and the peace of 1919 cannot be separated. In tracing a narrative, I have followed the same three time-lines that guided my *1815: The Roads to Waterloo*, which was also about a transition from war to peace: the developing drama of the daily events, the cycle of the seasons, and the quasi-timelessness of place. It is this schema – hardly my invention – that enables a local historian to open up vistas on the world. I have focused much of my attention on the experience of five capitals: London, Paris, Washington, Berlin and Moscow. Not only are these cities the sites of major decision-making; they also represent in a very graphic, physical, way evolving popular attitudes as the war gives way to the peace. Furthermore, with the obvious exception of Washington, they all lie on Europe's great northern plain which so much shaped the whole epic cycle.

Many people have assisted and encouraged me in my project. I am most impressed by the young historian Frank Gilson, a native of Compiègne, who led me like an American Frontier scout across the fields and forests of southern Picardy, into quarries and caves, down human tunnels, and into other such terrifying places unknown to the public and untouched in eighty years. Through bramble thickets we followed the zigzag of the trenches. We discovered exquisite carvings in the white limestone rocks. It is probably perverse to say that these abandoned, silent places are beautiful. But as a matter of fact they are. As we emerged in a spatter of rain from the remains of one German machine-gun post, Gilson said to me, in his lovely quiet way, 'Listen, these fields are singing.' They were: it must have something to do with the way water runs down the stem of the grasses; these places are haunted.

I have exploited several libraries in the last two years, the most important being the Bibliothèque de Documentation Internationale Contemporaine. Its brightly coloured tower, winking like a Florentine palace at a desert of ugly university buildings in Nanterre, houses one of the world's finest collections of books, memoirs, periodicals and newspapers published in the last hundred years; practically every source cited in this book, including the newspapers, can be found in the BDIC. Geneviève Dreyfus-Armand, its director, cheerfully defends the library's tradition as a working 'historical laboratory', and her staff – Martine Lemaître, Catherine Penin, Anne-Marie Blanchenay, Gianni Carozza, Thérèse Blondet-Bisch, among others – have made my research a pleasure.

Caroline Dawnay continues to guide me through the maze of modern publishing. My publishers, John Murray, have brought together a small and most efficient team: Grant McIntyre, Gail Pirkis, Bob Davenport and Stephanie Allen.

My wife, Christine, supports my strange moods and delights. We both like to look across frontiers. We talk about peace. We talk about nations and language. And we talk a lot about the future of Europe.

I dedicate this book to my American cousin Max Dallas Shaffrath, who many years ago, when I lay on my back in a hospital in San Francisco, brought me books on every subject under the sun. My reading became obsessive – and has remained so ever since. Max Shaffrath changed my life, and for that I am most grateful.

But my subject today is a story. It begins with a rumble in the night.

G. D.
Anet (Eure-et-Loir)
1997–2000

Maps

EUROPE
BEFORE 1914

Helsingfors

St Petersburg

Sea

Riga

Moscow

RUSSIAN

Kaunas

Vilna

Minsk

EMPIRE

Warsaw

POLAND

Kattowitz

GALICIA

Kiev

Lvov

HUNGARIAN

Rostov

Budapest

Odessa

Sea of Azov

EMPIRE

ROMANIA

Sevastapol

Belgrade

Black Sea

SERBIA

MONTE-NEGRO

BULGARIA

ALBANIA

Constantinople

OTTOMAN

Salonica

EMPIRE

GREECE

Dardanelles

Sea

CYPRUS

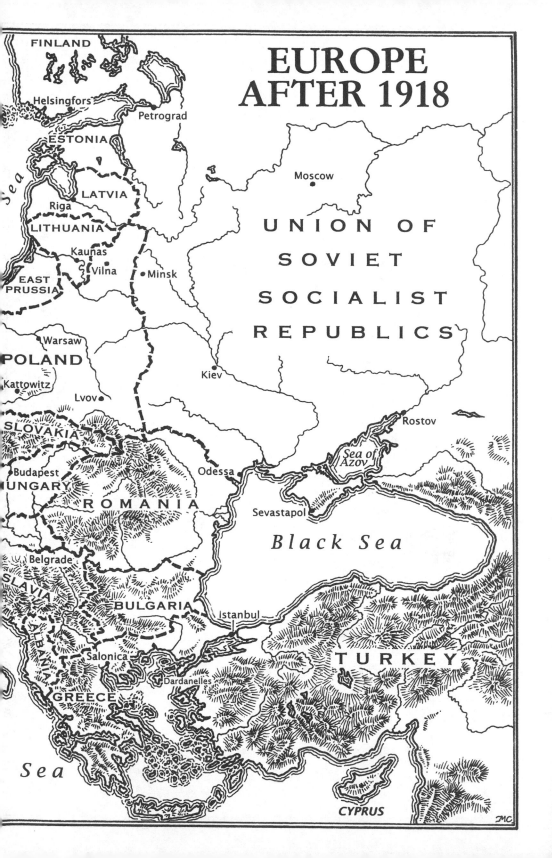

EUROPE
AFTER 1918

North Sea

THE

The Hague

NETHERLANDS

Dusseldorf

Bruges

FLANDERS

Ghent

Antwerp

Cologne

R. Rhine

Ypres

Maastricht

Aachen

BELGIUM

Brussels

Liège

Loos Lille

Namur

Verviers

Spa

Koblenz

Vimy

Mons

Valenciennes

Maubeuge

R. Mosel

Mainz

Cambrai

le Cateau

la

Capelle

Amiens

Hirson

R. Somme

St Quentin

Mezières

LUXEM-

BOURG

Trier

Roye

PICARDY

Sedan

Compiègne

Laon

Soissons

Villers-

Cotterêts

Reims

R. Aisne

Senlis

Château-Thierry

Verdun

Metz

Paris

R. Marne

St

Mihiel

Nancy

Strasbourg

R. Rhine

F R A N C E

~~~~~ Furthest extent of German
armies, March to July 1918

——— Armistice Line of
11 November 1918

- - - Hindenburg·Line

+++++ Railway lines

WESTERN FRONT

Movement of armies
and the occupation
of Germany

NETHERLANDS

GERMANY

BELGIAN

FRENCH

BELGIUM

BELGIAN

R. Rhine

BRITISH

BRITISH

AMERICAN

R. Rhine

FRENCH

LUXEM-
BOURG

FRENCH

LORRAINE

AMERICAN

R. Rhine

FRENCH

ALSACE

R. Rhine

FRANCE

〜〜〜〜〜 Furthest extent of German
armies, March to July 1918
– – – – – Hindenburg Line
ooooooooooooo Front, 26 Sept 1918
• • • • • • • • • Front, 31 October 1918
———— Lines separating Allied army
zones on Front and separating
Allied occupied zones in Germany,
including 'bridgeheads'

MC.

POLISH BORDERS AND RUSSIA, 1919

SWEDEN

Murmansk

FINLAND

MILLER

Archangel

Stockholm
Helsingfors

Petrograd

ESTONIA

Vologda

Viatka

Riga
Pskov

Libau
COURLAND LATVIA

R. Volga

Ural Mountains

Kovno

Königsberg Vilna

Moscow

Kazan

Omsk →

LITHUANIA
Smolensk

Simbirsk

KOLCHAK

Bialystock Minsk

BELORUSSIA

Warsaw
Brest

DENIKIN

POLAND

R. Bug

GALICIA

Kiev

UKRAINE

Lvov

R. Don

Tsaritsyn

R. Volga

Odessa

Rostov

CRIMEA

Kuban
Steppes

Caspian Sea

Novorossiisk

Black Sea

GEORGIA

German 'Ober-Ost'

ARMENIA

AZERBAIJAN

Baku

mls 0 500
kms 0 800

The Eleventh Hour

Beginnings

1

Soldiers on the front believed in phantoms. They had been seen in the march up the line – fleeting, jeering spectres, weird sisters, their leathery faces grinning like gargoyles. They had appeared in the wastelands where no man trod – bearded bandits shambling in rags; ghosts who pillaged corpses and stole food and drink. They had been noticed at the quiet of dawn, old comrades who wanted to talk – for they had hardly been dead a year. Visions and shadows like these did not surprise men who had been forced to watch their friends die. Every rank of every nation had witnessed the same thing. Weren't angels seen protecting British forces in their retreat from Mons? Couldn't lucky coins, buttons, dried flowers and hair cuttings deflect the power of bullets and shells? Hadn't it been predicted that, when the leaning gilt Virgin on top of the ruined church tower of Albert eventually tumbled, the Great War would end? She came crashing to the ground – amid an explosion of smoke – in that last year of fighting, 1918.[1]

Even today in a late autumn evening the road from La Capelle to Rocquigny, some seven or eight miles west of the French–Belgian border, has the look of a haunted corridor. On the night of 7 November 1918 it carried no traffic, and emitted no sound. Clouds of vapour rose from the sodden soil where the men of the French 171st Infantry Regiment lay waiting.

They had taken La Capelle that morning and had been preparing to pursue the enemy when Commandant de Bourbon-Busset – a trimly dressed count with a drop of royalty in his blood – had driven in from First Army Headquarters at Homblières with the astonishing order to suspend fire and simply hold their positions. The front line at that moment ran through the hamlet of Haudroy, just east of La Capelle. The pock-marked road had a slight bend in it, and what lay beyond a shadow of distant ruined houses, still in German hands, was unknown. A broken wooden signpost at the crossroads bore French village names in Gothic script; there was a gaping hole at the corner where a mine had exploded a few hours earlier, scattering across the fields the limbs of the poor devils who had stepped on it. Now silence. And a fog that typified the whole war.

A halo of light arose from one side of the wrecked buildings. There was the blare of a lonely trumpet, intermittent, like a ship's horn in the night. Gradually the air filled with the rumble of engines. The first thing the French soldiers could make out in the night was a flapping sheet of white linen.

On its approach they could see it flew from a pole fixed to the running-board of a Mercedes open tourer – cream yellow with German imperial eagles emblazoned on its doors. It slowly drew to a halt before Captain Lhuillier, company commander, now standing in the centre of the road. Four other vehicles – one high-backed saloon and the rest tourers also equipped with white flags – pulled up behind.

The silhouettes of several men could be seen through the beaming head-lights as they descended from their cars. One of them – a tall, pale-faced man in a neat grey uniform – clicked his heels, made a short bow and said in perfect French, 'General von Winterfeldt, of the parliamentarians' mission.' 'Captain Lhuillier, front-line batallion commander,' the twenty-five-year-old French officer responded without as much as a nod. In the artificial glare one could notice, sure enough, that his coat was covered with the white mud of the Thiérache.

'Please excuse me, Captain, for being so late,' continued the General, who had been expected by First Army Headquarters several hours earlier. 'It was because of the bad state of the roads. I wonder if I may make some introductions?'

'No, General,' the Captain crisply replied, 'I am not in a position to receive you officially. Please return to your cars and follow me and I will introduce you to our forward command.' He immediately turned round to face his troops, who had risen like the dragon's teeth of Cadmus from the ground. As the five motors revved up, Captain Lhuillier jumped up on the running-board of the first car to give directions. Progress was slow as inquisitive soldiers crowded around to catch a glimpse of these strange visitors from beyond the line. Corporal Pierre Sellier, who had served throughout the war, was ordered to join the first car and play on his bugle a refrain that had not been heard in over four years – *le cessez-le-feu*, the ceasefire.

Commandant de Bourbon-Busset had in the meantime set up temporary headquarters in a red-brick villa on the other side of La Capelle. He had arrived there at nine o'clock that morning to find hot chocolate and buttered rolls which a German division command had generously left behind barely an hour before; the sign 'Kommandatur' remained tied to the iron railing above the front porch for the remainder of the day. Bourbon-Busset, sur-rounded by officers, was standing on the steps as the five German Mercedes rolled into the driveway. The delegates got out and General von Winterfeldt, after presenting himself, introduced Bourbon-Busset to three other men:

'*Son Excellence* Erzberger', Secretary of State and head of the mission, a small frock-coated figure with a stiff black bowler hat; Ambassador Count von Oberndorff, also in civilian dress; and Captain Vanselow, whose uniform with golden braid descending to his cuffs indicated that he was here to represent the German Admiralty and the High Seas Fleet. Bourbon-Busset invited them to enter the villa.

They walked past a billiard table, requisitioned during the German occupation, to a long brightly lit conference room dominated by a portrait of Emperor Napoleon in his green chasseur uniform. 'Now the scene', ran the Army's official report of the events, 'really had an air of grandeur.'

Bourbon-Busset's attitude was cold but correct. 'Excellency,' he pronounced the word slowly, 'I must first clear up a misunderstanding.' The German delegates were almost certainly already aware of the problem. Earlier that day German troops in this sector had attempted to fraternize with the French. '*Kameraden! Kameraden!*' they had shouted across the line (though this had, in a few cases, been followed up with the burst of machine-gun fire), '*Die guerre ist fini!*' A German officer and five soldiers had actually presented themselves at a French outpost claiming that they wanted to say '*bon jour*' to their French *Kamaraden*; they were promptly arrested and sent to the rear as prisoners of war.

'We've received several parliamentarians from a German division', continued Bourbon-Busset, 'saying that they believed an armistice had already been signed.' He paused. 'It is of course agreed that military operations shall continue.'

The German delegates nodded. 'This is an error on the part of the division,' confirmed Winterfeldt.

It was agreed that the delegates would leave their own cars where they were parked in the driveway and be driven by the French to an undisclosed destination where a meeting with the Supreme Commander of the Allied forces, Marshal Foch, would take place. Bourbon-Busset, disconcerted by the way Erzberger kept on pronouncing the Marshal's name with a hard German 'ch', pointed out that the name was 'Fosh' and was Breton in origin.

It was by now around midnight. A crowd of civilians had assembled in the driveway. As the delegates emerged there were cries of '*Vive la France!*' while a few mockingly cried out '*Nach Paris!*'[2] None of the delegates thought this very funny.

The temporary ceasefire had apparently already ended. Not far away rockets were throwing flares into the night sky, creating periodically an eerie red glow. A journalist attempted to take a photograph, but his magnesium lighting failed. Some accounts say it was pouring with rain; Erzberger remembered a gloomy moon. Visibility must have been poor. The small procession of cars had not got far out of La Capelle when brakes were suddenly applied; Bourbon-Busset and Erzberger, in the first of the cars, were both thrown out of their seats. Erzberger's stiff bowler was dented.

They had nearly collided with an abandoned German cannon: two dead horses could be seen lying to the side of the road.

The jagged shape of broken walls could be made out in the headlights as they drove through Guise, which the French had entered only two days before; the cars swerved from left to right to avoid white heaps of rubble or the occasional black pit of a bomb crater. Near Saint-Quentin they stopped at the small vicarage of Homblières where General Debeney, commander of the French First Army, had set up headquarters; it was one of the few houses still standing. In the bare dining room the delegation supped; then, after a brief meeting with the General, they continued their journey into the night.

At about 4 a.m. they arrived at a railway station. 'But there are no buildings here,' said Erzberger, astonished.

'Yet this was once a busy town,' replied Bourbon-Busset.

Tergnier was one of those strategic railway junctions for which thousands had given their lives. What had not been destroyed during the fighting had been dynamited by the Germans in their retreat. The delegates clambered across broken brick and stone, past girders and rails curling up into the night's haze like antediluvian reptiles, to a torchlit platform where a French rifle company saluted them and a train with two carriages awaited. The window curtains had been firmly shut.

For three hours the German 'parliamentarians' mission' were rattled across unknown country while they sipped French brandy; no one felt like sleeping. Eventually, at about 7 a.m., their engine shuddered to a halt and let out one last long gasp of steam. Matthias Erzberger daringly lifted the corner of a curtain to discover trees shrouded in mist, a railway wagon on a parallel line about a hundred yards distant and duckboards laid out for the walk.

'Where are we?' he asked.[3]

2

The first step on Erzberger's long road to that forest clearing had been taken under the sun of August 1914, when seven German armies swept through neutral Belgium and Luxembourg into the northern plains of France. It was the largest armed force yet assembled in the history of the world: one and a half million men equipped with breech-loading rifles and machine-guns, in the company of heavy howitzers, bulbous siege guns, 38 airships and 800 light aircraft.

France had just elected the most pacific parliament in a generation; the President of the Republic and his Prime Minister were on a state visit to St Petersburg when the crisis broke. Britain's government and parliament were likewise populated by men for whom the whole idea of war was anathema and who were deeply suspicious of militarism and Continental involvement; the government was still discussing the parish borders of Fermanagh and Tyrone in northern Ireland in late July.

There can be no doubt about it: Germany had placed herself hopelessly in the wrong and the government of the day admitted it. 'Our invasion of Belgium', said the Chancellor, Theobold von Bethmann Hollweg, to the deputies of the Reichstag on 4 August 1914, 'is contrary to international law, but the wrong – I speak openly – that we are committing we will make good as soon as our military goal has been reached.'[4]

Matthias Erzberger, as leader of the Catholic Centre Party and parliamentary reporter of the Military Affairs Committee, had become one of the Chancellor's closest associates and gave the deputies the same message. A month later he was writing to the Minister of War, 'Don't worry about undermining the rights of peoples or violating the laws of humanity. Such sentiments are now of secondary importance.' Or, as he put it publicly in an article in *Der Tag*, 'If one could find the means of entirely destroying the town of London it would be more humane than letting the blood of a single German soldier flow on the field of battle. Sentimental weakness during war is the most unforgivable stupidity.' The idea was simple: get the dirty business done as quickly as possible and then worry about human rights and international law.[5]

One hundred years earlier France's Foreign Minister at the Congress of Vienna, the prince de Talleyrand, had warned of a special kind of revolutionary ferment that could one day reign in Germany. He had called it German Jacobinism. German Jacobinism, he had said, would develop there 'not like in France in the middle and lower classes, but among the wealthiest and highest placed nobles'.[6] In fact it followed a long and complicated route, but Talleyrand was basically right. By 1914 the 'German Jacobins' were ready for their 1789, when German ideas, German science, German culture – and German armies – would burst beyond their national limits and radicalize the course of world history.[7] The assumption was that, just as invaded Germany in the 1790s had provided no effective resistance to the French, now France would fall before the Reich's massive, violent, revolutionary waves of field grey. But France fought back.

Long after the war had ended – over four years later – historians and writers, people with the noblest of intentions, sought to achieve a 'balanced' view of the appalling attitudes that had developed in Germany. They ascribed them to 'historical conditions' that could be compared with those in any other nation – to racism and nationalism, to Social Darwinism, to capitalism or its opposite, the persistence of a 'feudal-value system', to the arms race, to commercial rivalry, to imperialism and, more recently, to masculine sociability – and they produced a picture of something inevitable, fatal, a situation which gave the statesmen and the military leaders in Germany no room for manoeuvre.[8]

No room for manoeuvre: that sense of Germany being hemmed in actually dominated thought at the time. It was what would lead Max Weber, one of the founders of modern sociology and one of the most humane spirits of the century, to write in 1916, the year of the Somme and of Verdun, 'Had we not been prepared to risk this war, then we should never have bothered to found the Reich and should have continued to exist as a nation of small states.'[9] The tiny Central European princedoms, electorates, kingdoms and archbishoprics of Napoleon's day had forged themselves into a nation, and were now marching on the rest of Europe to prove it. It was as if the only way in which Germany could establish the freedom of national expression was by shedding blood.

Prince Metternich, the Austrian Chancellor, had worried about this in 1815, when 'Germany' was still a collection of small states, and it was why he had opposed Prussian plans for a new, centralized Reich. Ironically, a descendant of his, a certain Count Metternich, was the ambassador in London of just such a Reich shortly before the war broke out. In the summer of 1911 he invited to dinner his old friend Winston Churchill, who was then Britain's Home Secretary.

It was Churchill who started the conversation by saying what a pity it was that in 1871 the Reich's first Chancellor, Bismarck, had allowed himself to be forced by his soldiers into taking Lorraine; Alsace-Lorraine lay at the root of all the rival alliances. Metternich replied that Alsace and Lorraine had been German provinces until Louis XIV had, in the seventeenth century, 'pranced over the frontier and seized them'. Perhaps, remarked Churchill, but their 'sympathies were French'. Metternich said they were 'mixed'. Churchill responded that the Alsatian problem anyhow kept antagonism in Europe alive; 'France could never forget her lost provinces, and they never ceased to call her.'

That led directly to a discussion of the formation of rival alliances in the last decades of the nineteenth century and the problem of Germany's lack of room for manoeuvre. Metternich complained that 'people' – he meant the Triple Entente of Britain, France and Russia – 'were trying to ring Germany round and put her in a net, and that she was a strong animal to put in a net'.

Churchill thought this an odd thing to say about a nation that had two first-class powers as allies, Austria-Hungary and Italy, and added that Britain had for a long time been alone 'without getting flustered'. Metternich said it was a very different business for an island. When 'you had been marched through and pillaged and oppressed so often' – though the last to do this was Napoleon, a hundred years earlier – and 'only the breasts of your soldiers' provided the barrier to invasion, 'it ate into your soul'.

Churchill registered little concern about Germany's 'soul', but he did remark that 'Germany was frightened of nobody, and that everybody was frightened of her'.[10]

*   *   *

One can be, as people frequently were at the time, overly abstract about national souls and historical processes. The whole problem was in fact geographical, and could be explained with an atlas.

Europe is not a continent but a peninsula jutting westward out of mainland Asia. Its south is bordered by a barrier of mountains; but across the entire northern flank there stretches, from the Pyrenees in France to the Urals of Russia, one huge open plain. Europe's history is constructed on that fact.

The northern plain had been created by an ancient geological struggle between earth and water. Long ago trees had dominated the landscape; then, for a few million years, it had been the turn of swamp; then the sea had swept in, until finally it withdrew. It was a delicate game of nature; the frontier between land and water was never certain. Every age left its deposit.

In the last twenty thousand years men had marched over the plain; practically every native of Europe could trace his ancestry to the people who crossed its flat surface. They had travelled chiefly in armies, but there were trading routes, too. The cultivation of the plain's soils was based on ideas imported from the East, not Rome. For well over a millennium nature's struggle between land and water provided energy (wind and running streams) for human industry; then man dug beneath the fertile loam to discover the remains of the ancient forest – coal.

So, Europe's wealth lay on an industrial belt built on an agricultural belt which followed the route of old armies.

French troops marching east of industrial Nancy in August 1914 noticed a stone marker by the side of the road: 'Here in the year 362 Jovinus defeated the Teutonic hordes.' Soldiers of the British Expeditionary Force at Mons could recall Marlborough's victory over Louis XIV's Army at nearby Malplaquet. Germans moving out of Aachen into Belgium must have thought of Blücher's advance before and after Waterloo; French-speakers in the area still called rabid dogs 'Blüchers'. The Europe that went to war in 1914 was an old world governed by an old system of armed might and diplomacy.[11]

But how life on the plain had been altered by the energy of coal, the temper of iron and the marriage of agriculture with industry in the century since Blücher's terrifying march on Paris! More goods, more wealth, more people. Growth dominated every aspect of existence, from its most banal, material forms like food and clothing to the most abstract realms of thought in science and philosophy. All were guided by the same recurring theme: progress.

And yet, in every area, that sense of expansion was accompanied by the opposite: a confinement, a restriction. This place of limitless horizons had, paradoxically, fixed frontiers. Local identity, pride – and hatred – had never been stronger. Henry Cochin, an administrator from one of the French departments under German occupation during the war years, referred to this in a speech he made in Paris in 1917 when he said, 'We are a frontier. But what kind of frontier? Nothing really marks it. It is drawn on a map. It is not a creation of nature. This makes it only the stronger and the more real. It is marked in our hearts.'[12] Though he was speaking of northern France in the war, Cochin's words could have pronounced by anyone of his generation about the frontiers that criss-crossed the map of Europe's vast plain. The lines were drawn in men's hearts.

If there was a single reason why Germany felt like a strong animal put in a net it was that the country, with a rate of economic growth comparable to the island of Japan and the isolated United States, was placed right in the middle of this European plain. 'The German race brings *it*,' the nationalist Friedrich Naumann had propounded before the war. 'It brings army, navy, money and power' in a way made possible when 'an active people feels the spring-time juices in its organs'. And they brought 'it' with all the subtlety of an angry adolescent: Germany lost every friend she had in Europe, besides Austria-Hungary, thanks to her inept diplomacy with the people whose frontiers she shared.[13]

After the creation of the Reich in 1871, Chancellor Otto von Bismarck had declared his intention of securing peace to construct a 'solid house'; he had assured his neighbours that, as a 'saturated power', Germany no longer sought territorial aggrandizement. Germans, like Count Metternich or Matthias Erzberger, would later argue that it was the formation of peacetime military alliances that put a ring round Germany and led, with the mechanical inevitability of a clock, to war in 1914. But it was Bismarck himself who created the first of the peacetime military alliances in Europe. It was formed between Germany and Austria-Hungary with the aim of controlling Vienna's foreign policy. In 1883 Bismarck extended the alliance to include Italy.

France and Russia were then faced, despite all the professions of peace, with a formidable military coalition led by the most powerful country in Europe. Bismarck even attempted to re-cement relations with Prussia's old ally Russia through a Reinsurance Treaty in 1887. Thus the larger part of Europe – the plain and the mountains from the Urals to the Rhine, and from the Baltic to the Adriatic – fell within Berlin's sphere of influence. The system of a 'balance of powers', which had maintained the general peace since the Congress of Vienna of 1815, no longer existed.

After Bismarck's forced resignation in 1890, Germany, formerly so dependent on the policy of one man, lost her sense of orientation. She threw caution to the wind. One heard no soothing voice now of her 'saturated power'. Germany began to seek a 'place in the sun', but without method and without a thought as to how her neighbours might react.

This was due to a breakdown, in Berlin, of collective government responsibility. While the Reichstag (the lower house of Germany's parliament) amused itself with long political debate, each department and every interest group pursued its own private aims unchecked. Nothing closely resembled the British Cabinet or the French *Conseil des ministres*. The Reich, which remained an agglomeration of petty states that formally paid homage to Prussia, in fact had no centre. But she brought blind 'army, navy, money and power'.

Germany's General Staff was a world unto itself; no politician interfered with its arcane procedures; the Kaiser himself, though saluted as the All-Highest Warlord, always complied with its decisions.

This formidable military organization had been the brainchild of General Gerhard von Scharnhorst, who had decided, in the early years of the nineteenth century, to emulate Napoleon's staff system. He had been mortally wounded at Lutzen in 1813, during Germany's 'War of Liberation', but a generation of soldiers continued his work, among them the military theorist Karl von Clausewitz. Perhaps the influence of Clausewitz on Prussian military thinking has been exaggerated; he left few practical guides on the management of war, and if his ghost walked the corridors of the new Reich's General Staff it would have shivered at what the new men were up to.

Just as politicians did not interfere with the workings of the General Staff, so the General Staff maintained its distance from the politicians. The chiefs of staff simply turned their backs on politics. For chiefs like Schlieffen and the younger Moltke, the only problems Germany had were military; politics and diplomacy had no place in their plans. Yes, the phantom of Clausewitz shivered in these modern corridors. 'When the thinking about war is divorced from political life,' he had warned, 'the many links that connect the two elements are destroyed and we are left with something pointless and devoid of sense.'[14]

That was the German Reich before the Great War: huge, increasingly wealthy, dominating the centre and east of the peninsula of Europe, but 'pointless and devoid of sense'. When republican France entered into an alliance with tsarist Russia in 1894 they were hardly consigning Europe to the war that broke out twenty years later;[15] their odd partnership merely provided them with a degree of security in the face of a giant that lay between them and did not know where it was going. Far from seeking a political or a diplomatic solution to the tension she had herself created in Europe, Germany turned her back on the 'foreigners' and started talking in anger to herself. 'We cannot allow any foreign power, any foreign Jupiter to tell us "What can be done? The world is already partitioned,"' Chancellor von Bülow exclaimed famously to the Reichstag in 1899. The generals turned their backs on the politicians, and developed military plans that might provide an outlet for Germany's 'spring-time juices' – without the slightest concern for their diplomatic consequences. It cannot be said that the gradual build-up of defensive military alliances against Germany was the cause of war; it was the other way round: by the early years of the new century all Europe was reacting to the German General Staff.

Only one power actively sought war. Only one power believed it was inevitable. With every diplomatic crisis, Germany was testing the ground. Would it be war with France in 1905 while Russia was conveniently out of the way? Or war with Russia in 1909 over the Balkans, which had not yet attracted the attention of the West? Or with France again in 1911, over the crisis in Agadir? On each occasion Germany stepped back from the brink: her problem was in finding someone else to blame.

The Balkans, hidden on the other side of the southern mountains, provided an ideal location for beginning a general war on the northern plain. Germany would not be directly involved, while Russia, linked ethnically and sentimentally to Serbia, had always had suspect motives in the area. So push Austria, which had annexed Bosnia in 1909, ever further down into the hills (the process had been going on ever since Napoleon had marched across Europe), encourage her with arms and a diplomatic pat on the back, and when the Slavic keg of powder finally explodes blame it on Russia. Blame it on Russia and immediately march westward on her ally France: that was the logic of the German General Staff.[16]

The ideal occasion was unintentionally provided by the heir to the Habsburg Empire, Archduke Franz Ferdinand, on a visit to the recently annexed province of Bosnia-Herzegovina. On his arrival in the capital, Sarajevo, on 28 June 1914, young Serb conspirators provided a reception by throwing a bomb at the royal car – for Serbs regarded Bosnia as their territory, and this was the sacred day of Vidovan, a commemoration of their late victory over the Turks, in 1389. Twenty people were injured, but the Archduke and his morganatic Czech wife were untouched. He visited the town hall and then ordered his chauffeur to take him round to see the wounded. The poor driver got lost in the old town's winding streets and pulled up – by pure chance – by a bridge opposite one of the Serb conspirators, Gavrilo Princip, who took not a moment's hesitation to draw his revolver and shoot the Archduke and his wife at short range.

The beginning of world war? Most Westerners sighed at the prospect of yet another crisis and returned to more interesting matters like Madame Caillaux's trial for murder, the fantastic performance of the Baron de Rothschild's horse at the Grand Prix, or the shape of the parish borders of Fermanagh and Tyrone.

But the men in Berlin were busy. A major review of Austrian and German policy in the Balkans had taken place only the previous spring: Austria was seeking the occasion for a localized war to get even with Serbia, while Germany was ready for a more general settling of accounts; if a European war became inevitable, noted the Chancellor, Bethmann Hollweg, at the time, 'then the present moment would be more favourable than a later one'.

Austria was assured of German support in the case of war with Serbia, provided she did not flinch from the consequences. Thus it was Austria that took the initiative in drafting an ultimatum to Serbia on 7 July – an ultimatum with terms so damaging to Serbian sovereignty that it could not possibly be accepted. Delivery to Serbia was delayed because the French President was in St Petersburg and the German authorities did not want the French to co-ordinate activity with Russia; but on 23 July it was handed over to the Serbs, who were given forty-eight hours to reply. There was an uncomfortable moment when Serbia accepted every term save one, which would effectively have led to the abandonment of her sovereignty. Austria eventually found this reason enough to declare war on Serbia on 28 July, and within two days she was bombarding Belgrade. It was after this that Russia mobilized.

On hearing the news of Russian mobilization, the Bavarian military attaché in Berlin ran into the War Ministry. 'Beaming faces everywhere,' he reported in his diary. 'Everyone is shaking hands in the corridors: people congratulate one another for being over the hurdle.' Russia guilty! Austria had perhaps been touched by a spot of blood, but Germany's hands were pristine.

Luxembourg was occupied on 2 August. The invasion of Belgium began on the 4th.[17]

3

It is possible that the nuns of Louvain were not raped.[18] It is most doubtful that Catholic priests were hung upside down to serve as clappers for church bells. Were prisoners of war really crucified? One would do well to look again at the evidence.

Today the atrocities of the Second World War are readily recalled, but our collective memory of those of the First has faded. The conviction remains that the massacre was on the military front; whatever went on behind the line is dismissed lightly – too lightly – as the rumours of propaganda. Such selective memory does those who suffered a disservice.

Nowadays, few tourists on the autoroute from Liège to Maastricht will turn off to see the village of Visé, on the borders of Belgium, Holland and Germany. If they do, it is for the famous restaurants that serve roast goose in a garlic sauce, or to look at finely crafted old crossbows, arquebuses and muskets. In August 1914 Visé was burnt out and completely gutted not by front-line troops but by a rearguard that had seen no fighting. It would become a common practice: '*Man hat geschossen*,' the troops would cry, and in the name of some phantom *franc-tireur* – or sniper – they would round up hostages to be shot, evacuate the population, and put their homes to the torch. The residents of the Dutch town of Eysden could hear, on 23 August, the shooting in Belgian Visé, and the next day they were flooded by 4,000

refugees – but not the 700 men and boys who were deported to Germany
for labour. Who could imagine today that Dinant, with its picturesque high-
gabled houses, its bulbous black church tower and its citadel atop a sugar-
loaf hill, was the site of similar horrors? Over 600 hostages were herded into
the main square and in the evening were lined up in two rows, the women on
one side, the men on the other, one kneeling before the other. The firing squads
were marched into the square's centre, from where they shot, their backs to
each other, until no one was left standing. Reconstruction has hidden the scars
of 'medieval' Louvain, the university town. On 25 August an 'incendiary column' of German soldiers, using phosphorus, started a fire by the railway
station, then turned on the Old Market, the University Library, with its price-
less collection of rare books and art, the Cloth Hall, the college houses. After
six days of plunder and burning, the only area left largely untouched was the
suburban borough of Heverlee, which contained the property of the Duke of
Arenberg, a German citizen. Over 200 citizens were killed – mostly shot, but
some strangled and burned – while at least another 600 were deported in cattle
wagons to Germany. Mock executions were held, and sham bombing was
employed to empty the houses and shops of inhabitants so that troops could
help themselves to the contents.[19]

A similar system of terror accompanied the German troops into France.
Notices would be posted in towns warning that prestigious persons, such
as the mayor and leading magistrates, had been taken hostage and would
be shot in the case of *franc-tireur* activity. Sometimes there were not enough
prestigious personalities available, so a random selection of hostages would
be made, street by street. Summary executions were frequent – railway
stations were a favourite site. Reasons could be bizarre, as in the execution
of at least sixteen pigeon fanciers in northern France on suspicion of their
using the birds for communication with enemy armies across the line. Forced
labour was introduced: the workers came to be known as the *brassards
rouges*, from the colour of the armbands they wore. Deportations to Germany
were conducted by the trainload; German authorities explained this as a
means of solving the 'unemployment problem'. Forced indemnities and
requisitions resulted in inhabitants watching their homes being emptied, as
a shopkeeper in Roubaix put it, of 'the latches, the name plates for houses,
the hangers of wardrobes, the coat stands, the door knockers, the coffee
mills, etc.'. Leather, copper, wood and wool became much sought-after
items; after four years of war there was barely a mattress left in the three
neighbouring towns of Lille, Roubaix and Tourcoing.[20]

Officialized brigandage in occupied territory was aggravated by shortages that developed in Germany itself; the terror against citizens, on the
other hand, dated from the day Belgium was invaded. This could be partly
blamed on a certain war mentality that had grown in Germany. For example,
the myth of the *franc-tireur* – '*der Franktireur*' – had been spread by veterans
of the Franco-German war of 1870–1. A novel, which sold 130,000 copies

in 1907, told the story of an attack on Belgium, where fanatical Catholic priests roused the local population, aided and abetted by socialist terrorists, and women poured burning oil from windows and castrated wounded German soldiers. The *franc-tireurs* at Louvain in fact turned out to be the Germans themselves, when the rearguard fired on their own retreating spearhead they had mistaken for the Belgian army. But far more important was the fact that terrorism had been adopted by government and military officials as a policy of war. Clausewitz had taught that the civilian population of the enemy, far from being exempted from the pressures of war, should be made to feel its severest effects so that they would force their leaders to sue for peace; the object was to place the enemy 'in a situation in which continuing the war is more oppressive to him than surrender'. The same message was repeated by Schlieffen, by the younger Moltke, and by the parliamentary reporter of Berlin's Military Affairs Committee, Matthias Erzberger.[21]

So Germany, pursuing the idea of a swift war of terror, marched westward into Belgium and France in order to punish 'guilty' Russia.

The reasoning lay, again, in the geography of Europe. Europe's military sciences had always claimed to be of universal validity, but they would prove to work less well on the continents of America, the deserts of Africa or the jungles of South-East Asia than in Europe's funnelled peninsula of plain and mountain. Europe provided a model for outmanoeuvring and entrapment. The rivers, flowing northward across the plain like ribs of a fan, provided further opportunities. Ever since French revolutionary and imperial armies had poured across the plain, military schools had been studying the tactics of the flanking attack, the strategy of enveloping the enemy's line of communications: probing for the flank, isolating the foe, and then defeating him in detail or starving him into submission. Napoleon's armies showed what could and could not be done. Forcing a military decision in the East, on the Continental steppes of Russia was difficult; how much easier it had been in the centre of the peninsula to push Austria's back up against the mountain, or Prussia's back against the sea! Flanking attacks won battles and wars; frontal attacks were expensive and lost them. That had been the lesson of Waterloo.

Small wonder that Count Alfred von Schlieffen, chief of the German General Staff from 1891 to 1905, had formulated a plan for a swift military decision in France that would isolate Russia. If, like Schlieffen, one ignored all political and diplomatic consequences of such a brutal act it made sense. The seven German armies would advance across the whole plain like a mechanical blade pivoting about an axis fixed in the mountain of Switzerland; 'let the last man on the right brush the Channel with his sleeve'. The blade would sweep across Paris and push the French armies, concentrated on the German frontier of Lorraine, up against the mountain: the ultimate envelopment.[22]

State secrets never remain secret for long. By 1911 the Western Allies had got wind of the plan and developed their response to the German General Staff. The only error they made was to imagine, generously, that the Germans would not advance west of the Meuse through neutral Belgium – one of the ribs of the fan – but would instead advance into France down the east bank of the river. The French General Staff developed the plan of a counter-attack across neutral Belgium. But France was governed by civilian authorities who vetoed it. The generals were thus obliged to cobble together, in 1913, the famous Plan XVII that limited a counter-attack to the French–German border, in Lorraine.[23]

Germany's war aims, like her civilian 'foreign policy' before the war, were tailored to the needs of the General Staff. On 2 September 1914, less than a month after the invasion of Belgium, they were neatly summed up in a memorandum to the Chancellor drafted by, among others, Matthias Erzberger.

After the sweep of the blade across France and the defeat of Russia, Germany would enjoy control over Europe for 'all time'. The neutral states on Germany's borders would be abolished, and a Confederation of European States would be created, governed from Berlin. England's hegemony over world affairs would be ended, and the Russian Empire would be partitioned, with Poland and the Baltic states being annexed to Germany, while Belorussia and the Ukraine would be granted independence. Germany would retain military control over all Belgium, Luxembourg and the French coast as far as Boulogne, and would annex the Lorraine iron-ore basin of Briey-Longwy and Belfort in Upper Alsace. Erzberger made no mention of the fate of British colonies, but the French ones would go to Germany. Heavy reparations would be forced from the conquered nations to pay both for Germany's war expenses and for her national debt. Germany's aims, as initially expounded by Erzberger and his collaborators, remained virtually unaltered until the autumn of 1918.[24]

Allied war aims were, in the beginning, quite simple: the freeing of occupied territory. 'France is a history, it is a life,' wrote the future premier Georges Clemenceau in his newspaper in September 1914; 'we cannot sacrifice it without laying down the tombstone on ourselves, on our children and on the generations which would be born to them.'[25]

General von Moltke, isolated in his headquarters in Luxembourg, became worried about the situation in East Prussia, where the Russians were advancing more quickly than expected; he detached two corps from his right wing in Belgium and sent them east along with a new army commander, General Paul von Hindenburg, and his deputy, Erich von Ludendorff, the hero who had destroyed Liège. A third corps was shorn off to attack the Belgian town of Maubeuge, which was still holding out.

Was the detaching of the two corps an error? What looked on a map flat and easy to sweep with a blade was one of the most industrialized and most densely populated areas of Europe. British cavalrymen, trained on the wide rolling downs of England, were amazed, when sent forward to Mons, to discover a land 'full of little smoky villages, coal mines, railway embankments, endless wire, and a population that seemed as dense as that of a London suburb'. The advancing Germans had the same surprise.[26]

French troops, in easily targeted blue coats and red trousers, launched an offensive on Lorraine and Alsace; more French were killed and wounded than in any other battle of the war. But General Lanrezac, commander of the left French army, turned in a complete wheel and marched north to cut off – as it was said – the menacing German right arm from its shoulder. But the arm was too mighty, and the British and French forces retreated back on to Paris and the Marne.

The Germans were astonished at the resistance they met; Mons, Le Cateau, Charleroi, Guise, Néry and Villers-Cotterêts were no small skirmishes. It was not the Kaiser that called the British Expeditionary Force a 'contemptible little army' – that was an invention of the War Office in London.[27] A detailed map of the German advance across the plain shows a series of crooked little pathways of exhausted men moving into hostile territory by foot, inadequately equipped by supply lines that had to be defended. Gaps developed between the German armies. The right wing moved more slowly than the plan intended. Moltke, constrained to concentrate his force, decided not to envelop Paris – the biggest fortress in the world – but to bypass the city to its east. An army in Paris attacked the Germans in their flank.

The 'Battle of the Marne' involved the collision of thirteen or fourteen armies, each one of them a city on the move. Historians do not agree on the day it began or ended. Many combatants were not even aware they were in it. While some fought, others ate, slept, relaxed or marched. It was fought under both rain and sun. French historians say the battle raged from Paris to Verdun; the Germans claim that all seven of their armies were involved, down to the initial mountain axis of the Vosges: it was the battle of the plain – Europe's plain.

'I will never forget 10 September 1914,' wrote the future historian Marc Bloch in a hospital bed a year later. But then he couldn't really remember it either. The events, he said, 'formed a discontinuous series of images, very lively but poorly co-ordinated, like a torn roll of cinematic film': the panicking horses, the machine-gun bullets humming like hornets in the leaves, the dead corporal who had knocked over a bowl of potatoes in his fall. 'How long did we remain in this fold of land? How many minutes, how many hours? I have no idea.'[28]

Moltke lost his job. The German armies retreated to what highland areas they could find, and then attempted to outflank the Allied armies to the right in a desperate attempt to gain control of the French Channel ports. They failed.

By December the line of the Western Front had been drawn. On the map it resembled a top-heavy drunken 'S', following the low ridges to which the Germans had withdrawn, a line tracing the folds of the plain and the wasted human energy of an invasion that had gone wrong. On the ground it developed into 400 miles of stinking ditch, running from Neiuport in Belgium down to Héricourt on the Swiss border.

Places recovered a terrible significance. Geography was transformed into a sinister new dictator. The whole war became local.

In January 1915 the retired Count von Moltke had a long conversation with Matthias Erzberger, now a chief of propaganda. Moltke confessed that he had thought, right from the start, that the massive advance on the West had been a mistake and that Germany should instead have concentrated its forces against the 'Russian steamroller'. The Schlieffen plan, he thought, was out-dated because it was based on the premise that Russia would take two months to mobilize – which by 1914 everyone knew was wrong. The Minister of War and Moltke's successor as Chief of Staff, General von Falkenhayn, had earlier told Erzberger that, after the Marne, 'in reality the whole war was lost'.

As Erzberger would later comment, 'Military successes might enlarge it, but they would never shatter the prison into which the German people were now locked.' War was no way to get out of the net they had drawn around themselves.[29]

4

Between 1915 and 1918, with the exception of Falkenhayn's desperate offensive on Verdun in 1916, Germany in the West was on the defensive. She was on the defensive, but she was unwilling to sue for peace. Like Napoleon and his troops after 1812, Germany's government, the Army and, indeed, most people in the country believed that the gains won in blood could never be forfeited.

A military situation had developed that had never before existed in European history. The entire northern plain was blocked at the point where it funnelled into France; no flanking manoeuvre was possible. Italy's adhesion to the Western alliance in 1915 (she had abandoned her alliance with Germany the year before, on the grounds that the agreement had been defensive in purpose, not aggressive) proved to be of little help because of the technological difficulty of conducting an offensive through mountains – the sort of operation that the fiasco at Gallipoli, that same year, had done little to encourage. Gallipoli had also demonstrated the limits of British sea power: there was no 'soft point' behind the front. Passchendaele in 1917, an offensive initially designed (before it ended in the mud) to be co-ordinated with a landing operation on the German-occupied Belgian coast, confirmed this.

Historians are sometimes criticized for being too parochial when they concentrate on Western Europe in a conflict that did indeed touch many parts of the globe. But the naval war, the submarine war, the African campaigns, Mesopotamia, Palestine, Syria, and even the war on the Eastern Front were never at the heart of the struggle. None of them could decide the war. They were, as was said at the time, 'sideshows'.

What made the Western Front so important was the same as had counted for most in Europe's earlier wars: strategy and the nature of coalition warfare on the great peninsula. Germany's hope was to separate the Western Allies. This could be achieved only on the western plain; Russia was fighting in isolation, and no German drive to the East, however successful, could shatter the combination against the Reich. The Allies were obliged to focus on the Western Front because that was where German forces were concentrated; as Clemenceau commented, shelling water would not defeat the German Army. Germany's great weakness was that, even if she exhausted one enemy power, there was always another that could move, financially and militarily, in behind.

Germany's formidable wall of defence in the West – one huge bastion of concrete, barbed wire and earth – left the Allies three alternatives: to negotiate a peace; to penetrate the wall and thus re-establish their freedom to manoeuvre; or to wear down the Reich by attrition – a twentieth-century version of siege warfare.[30] Negotiated peace has always relied on each side presenting war aims that are then thrashed out until agreement is reached; if one side withholds its war aims, insistence on continued talks by the other side will in the end lead only to its negotiated surrender. Germany on several occasions announced her 'willingness to make peace' but, understandably, never made public her ambitious war aims; the Allies had no intention of surrender. Negotiated peace was no alternative at all.

The laboured efforts over the remaining two military alternatives – penetration and attrition – have given the West's 'château generals' a black name:

> Good-morning, good-morning!' the General said
> When we met him last week on our way to the line.
> Now the soldiers he smiled at are most of 'em dead,
> And we're cursing his staff for incompetent swine.
> 'He's a cheery old card,' grunted Harry to Jack
> As they slogged up to Arras with rifle and pack.
>
> . . . .
>
> But he did for them both by his plan of attack.[31]

That was Siegfried Sassoon, after being wounded during a famous attempt at penetrating enemy lines in April 1917. Sassoon was expressing a sentiment that was widespread in the junior ranks of the armies.[32] The rational criticism came later, from people who believed there were other alternatives to penetration and siege. Basil Liddell Hart argued in 1934 that Douglas Haig, the British Commander-in-Chief, and his staff were not fighting 'the British way in warfare': with naval blockade and light commitment on the Continent.[33] Liddell Hart was a great military historian who knew his Napoleonic wars well; but Wellington did not defeat Napoleon with the Navy.

With the entire European plain walled off, penetration could be achieved only by frontal attack – 'over the top' – which the military schools for the last generation had taught would cost heavily in casualties. Napoleon had achieved it in the early nineteenth century with the help of his six-pounders; his enemies at the time had neither the roads nor the rails to bring up reinforcements. Now they did. Official Allied accounts of their attempts at break-through up to 1918 often glowed with stories of initial success, followed by the deadly phrase 'then German resistance stiffened'.

A passive siege alone could not defeat Germany's huge armies, for there was a greater chance that the Allies would fall in the process. So the Allies developed a strategy of pinching the upper grand salient of the drunken 'S'. That idea eventually won the war, but at enormous cost. Haig – no 'cheery old card' but a dour Scotsman – would sweep his hand across the map through Belgium to Germany. General Robert Nivelle, the Allied Commander-in-Chief in 1917, with a pleasing smile, spoke so confidently of creeping barrage and infantry infiltrations that even Lloyd George, the British Prime Minister, who was not usually so committed to the Western Front, was convinced that the French would break through north of the Aisne. And it was a tactic that worked – in the Second World War.

Life for the generals, forced into a war of offensive siege, was not so comfortable. Nivelle was retired to an obscure post in Africa. Haig fell back on religion, as did Foch. Pétain tumbled into bouts of depression and pessimism.

But the war was harder on the men.

5

Sophocles once wrote a play in which he reversed the cosmology of life and death. King Creon ordered Polynices' body to be left exposed beyond the city walls, while he condemned the dead man's sister Antigone to be buried alive. Thus he inverted light and shadow, day and night. Death and the sun stared each other in the face. Antigone, by her own will, looked forward to a buried life, alone.

This is the image we have of the First World War: the dead on the surface, the living buried underground. In the valley and the hills of the Aisne one can still find today caverns which housed up to 60,000 men. These are the so-called *creutes*, hewed out of the rock by medieval stonecutters in search of the material that made Picardy's towns and graced the façades of the cathedrals. But the elaborate carving inside dates only from the Great War: an underground chapel with the names of men who had died; exotic land-scapes etched in relief; or designs in an art-nouveau style of strange monsters and curling serpents. The outline of noble cavalrymen from Napoleon's wars can be caught in the beam of a modern torch. The figures of many women decorate the walls – women in dresses, in robes or in nothing at all – while a few tall phalluses provide a column to the roof, a corner to a room, or might even serve as a fountain. There is a place for rest; a place for eating; and a two-storey house for the captain. There are sinister things, too, down in these unlit damp holes – like the stacks of now petrified sacks of cement, a few rusted munition boxes, and the reels and reels of decayed barbed wire stuffed up the ventilator shafts.

Technology had made the long defence wall possible; it had permitted the mobilization of millions of men, and had driven them all underground. Technology had created the misleading emptiness on the surface – the vast spaces of churned-up soil manured with the dead, a 'garden full of strange plants' – below which whole armed cities lived. A fantastic technology had given birth to the odd shapes and horrifying sounds of 'toffee-apples', 'whiz-bangs' and 'coalboxes'. Yet the technology could never separate itself from nature. Indeed, in some parts, it was as if the old primeval swamps of the European plain had actually been restored by the violence, as if the delicate equilibrium between land and water had once more been upset.

Gunner William 'Mac' Francis described how his tank got stuck outside Ypres one day in August 1917: 'shells were dropping all around us and we were rocking like a small boat on a rough sea'. Men leapt into the shelter of bomb craters and were sucked down into the mud; others slipped off the log 'corduroy' roads and drowned in the quagmire. 'Hell is not fire,' wrote an anonymous contributor to one of the French trench newspapers, 'it would not be the worst form of suffering; the real hell is mud.'[34]

Mud and rain: nature's contribution to the war. That one word 'rain' pretty much summed up the war as experienced by the soldiers. Their nastiest memories are coated in a 'grey palsied weather' in which the sky merged indistinguishably into the stench of the soil.

> ... Curse the Wood!
> It's time to go. O Christ, and what's the good?
> We'll never take it, and it's always raining.[35]

Though technology had transformed Germany's thrust down the plain into world war, it was that unlovely marriage of technology with nature which made the same world war seem so very local. Globalization involved localization.

Right next door to the trenches – sometimes within a matter of yards –

were the most bucolic scenes of hornbeam alleys and the leafy canopies of chestnut rows. Soldiers' memoirs are filled with such contrasts: one day in the stinking ditch, and the next spent wandering through quaint villages or talking with the humble folk – the north of France, which had a reputation for friendliness in 1815, had not lost it in a hundred years. Even the rain, which defined hell at the front, could within a mile become bounteous and tender. Memories were local, and memories were fragmented.

The eager quest of later generations to know 'what the soldiers really thought' will probably never be satisfied. There were ten million soldiers and ten million thinkers – who frequently changed their minds.

Some actually enjoyed the fighting. A case always cited is that of Corporal Adolf Hitler, who volunteered for every hazardous mission, captured French soldiers single-handed with only a pistol, and damned pacifists and shirkers back home who threatened to spoil the fun. But there were, on either side of the line, many others who were fascinated, even found something sublime, in the destruction and the killing, though this could be mixed with feelings of humane gentleness and a revulsion from what was happening to one's friends. It is a perverse thought for those who generalize, for those who were not there; but it has some meaning when it is borne in mind how parochial the experience of war was, how limited horizons had become for the soldier.

'I can't tell you how *muddling* it is,' Julian Grenfell wrote home before he was killed by a shell splinter in his head at the Second Battle of Ypres. 'We did not know what was our front: we did not know whether our own troops had come round us on the flanks ... Four of us were talking and laughing in the road when about a dozen bullets came with a whistle. We all dived for the nearest door, which happened to be a lav, and fell over each other, *yelling* with laughter ... I *adore* war. It is like a big picnic without the objectlessness of a picnic. I've never been so well or so happy.'[36] One needs to recall that England's tender war poets kept on returning to France, even when they were not obliged to.

The war was local and the war, if it had initially been designed to work like a vast impersonal machine – Schlieffen had envisaged the commander-in-chief, the modern Alexander, directing the war 'from a house with roomy offices where telegraph, telephone and wireless signalling apparatus are at hand, while a fleet of autos and motorcycles ready to depart, wait for orders'[37] – did not in reality operate in that way, for either the generals or the men. Georges Clemenceau, as chairman of the French Senate's Army Committee, kept noting how the Army had changed since his own struggle with it during the Dreyfus Affair less than twenty years earlier; today's Army was a citizens' army that did not fit easily into the old hierarchical chain of isolated professionals.

That break in the chain caused terrible tension. After the failed offensive of 1917, the French citizens' army was in revolt. It was, outside Russia, the largest mutiny any of the belligerents experienced. But it was not for peace that the vast majority of mutineers demonstrated: they were protesting against the way the war was run. In May, Philippe Pétain replaced Robert Nivelle as French Commander-in-Chief, and over the next year France refrained from any further major offensive.[38]

The main burden of the Allied effort now fell on Britain. It is amazing that British forces did not experience the kind of mutiny that had occurred among the French, especially after the disasters of Passchendaele in the wet summer and autumn of 1917. The transformation of a tiny professional army into a citizens' force, including the introduction of conscription in 1916, was an experience a great deal more radical for the British than it had been for the French. But the only major revolt to occur was at the base camp of Etaples in September 1917. As in the case of the French, this did not involve demands for peace or questions about the aims of the war; the anger was directed by seasoned troops against military police and instructor NCOs who were treating them like raw recruits. Disciplinary procedures, more strictly enforced than among the French, and Britain's regimental tradition, which encouraged local loyalties, are probably the main reasons for the general absence of protest.[39]

Was innocence lost with the Great War? Had the thread of memory been dropped? Did the course of history change for ever? The people who lived through it would tell you so, would even insist on it, regarding any other opinion as heresy.

Churchill, who spent some time in the trenches, discovered the strange literary and pictorial value of this apparent break in the rhythm of history and exploited it to the full. Like many of his contemporaries, he set his picture of the last July days of peace on an easel and dashed out with a brush his brightest colours, so different from the greys, blues and khakis of war. 'The world on the verge of its catastrophe was very brilliant,' he applied with a touch. 'Nations and Empires crowned with princes and potentates rose majestically on every side, lapped in the accumulated treasures of the long peace.' Then he mixed in the quieter tones of a 'polite, discreet, pacific, and on the whole sincere diplomacy'. But a few jagged strokes of black showed that 'national passions, unduly exalted in the decline of religion, burned beneath the surface of nearly every land', so that when one stepped back to regard the painting as a whole there was a sense of discomfort: 'Almost one might think the world wished to suffer.'[40]

One of the reasons why people were tempted to look upon the war as a natural catastrophe – 'the breaking of the storm', 'the unfurling hurricane' – was that the weather during those years was so awful. And yet it did not rain on every one of those 1,568 days: there were summer weeks when the sun did shine. Not every prince and potentate lost his throne; the anthems rang out in all seasons. The music halls were filled, and the dancing floors were never abandoned. In every European capital the diplomats were kept busy, and what is striking about their dispatches is how polite, discreet and pacific they remained – even those from revolutionary Russia. Step back into the Europe of 1918 and one is astonished by how much of the old world still stands – an old world of little details. Not far from the war front the windmills still turn. In the evenings the peasants still sit in their lamp-lit rooms; next morning they will ride to the fields in their wooden wagons. The roads are tiny rural tracks, many even lacking cobbles. By the railway's level crossing the keeper's little red house stands guard; in the town, the complicated crooked street withdraws into the artisan's courtyard hiding behind arches. The old world is perceptibly old.

That it should have been so was an intolerable thought for a generation of citizen soldiers who had, because of the war, been cut off from their own ordinary lives. They were scandalized that other lives should still be so ordinary: French troops scorned Paris; British troops poked fun at the 'Home Front'.

They could add a caustic joke on the absurdity of life in an army which stubbornly hung on to 'tradition'. The honour of the regiment and its proud record in the Napoleonic wars or the Crimea, in India or South-East Asia – past feats used to mould the professional soldier – all that was hardly a compensation for the shattered individual memories of the uniformed civilian. In his isolated local war, history had made a break, a radical break: there was no past, either personal or professional.

And the future? It was difficult to conceive of anything other than war. Perhaps it would go on for ever. The idea of actually returning to civilian life was, for some, almost as bad as the thought that the world had not changed – indeed, almost as bad as death.

One citizen soldier was a witness to that. On a night at Molancourt, in February 1916, Siegfried Sassoon of the 1st Battalion, Royal Welch Fusiliers, watched his machine-gun officer in his blankets on the quartermaster's floor; he had taken a drink or two, so he was 'in the pink' and for this brief moment 'his blood ran warm':

> To-night he's in the pink; but soon he'll die
> And still the war goes on – *he* don't know why.[41]

'But soon he'll die/ And still the war goes on . . .' As a matter of fact he did not die, and the war did not go on for ever. The man was suffering from 'alcoholic poisoning', and Sassoon's own footnote tells us that he 'departed for England, never to return' – as if the front were the only reality. He 'departed for England' – comfy old Blighty. To a civilian life? To peace? To madness? Which fate was worse?

One year later Sassoon was wounded and he himself departed for

England to convalesce. He wrote a letter of protest for peace that was read in the House of Commons and was immediately published in *The Times*: 'I am making this statement as an act of wilful defiance of military authority,' he famously said, 'because I believe the war is being deliberately prolonged by those who have the power to end it.'[42] Some have argued that he had merely fallen under the influence of the London pacifists, Bertrand Russell and Lady Ottoline Morrell. The official army line was that he was temporarily insane, and he was sent to Dr W. H. R. Rivers's mental-health clinic at Craiglockhart, near Edinburgh. This way he avoided court martial.

But did Sassoon really want to avoid court martial? His motives were ambiguous; he was one of England's war poets who in 1918 returned willingly to the war after being offered an office job. Pacifists attacked him for his hypocrisy. Patriots attacked him for his pacifism. But the greatest hostility lay perhaps within himself, a civilian in uniform at war with civilians.[43]

In 1918 there were tens of thousands of Europeans like him.

Movements

1

On Friday, 4 January 1918, a short grey-haired Texan walked into the White House in Washington DC. Two things were on his mind. In the first place, he was seeking a way of keeping the new Bolshevik regime in Russia in the Western alliance. Second, he hoped that his country's unrivalled economic power would provide the means of bringing the war to a close. Edward M. House, at fifty-nine, belonged to the select club of 'those who have the power to end it'.

There was a lot of talk about peace in the first week of January 1918. The Bolsheviks, on signing a ceasefire with the Central Powers (Germany and Austria-Hungary) on 15 December, had presented a six-point programme for a peace without annexations or indemnities; it could appeal to an American president who, before going to war with Germany the previous April, had called for 'peace without victory'. The civilian authorities in Berlin had answered the Russians with a 'Christmas Declaration' that appeared to accept the Bolshevik terms. There was some doubt that Germany's Supreme Command – the *Oberste Heeresleitung* (OHL) would go along with this, but the Eastern and Central European initiatives demanded an immediate response from the West. A political deadlock of nearly four years seemed to be breaking.

House was among those who believed, like a soldier on the front, that the war had created a totally novel situation, an international configuration of forces that had no precedent in history. So the response had to be radical. House, who served a most unusual president, believed he had the wherewithal to give it.

He was himself no ordinary man. Most citizen soldiers who survived would shed their military titles as soon as they re-entered civilian life. House, on the other hand, was a civilian who delighted in military title. He was addressed as 'Colonel', though he had never been a soldier and had seen no battle; the honour had been bestowed on him in Houston for his sage advice to four successive governors of Texas. He was voted to no office, he held no post; but an inherited fortune had given him the power of influence, and a keen political mind did the rest. His talents were appreciated on the two continents. Clemenceau would regard him as a 'super-civilized man out of the wastes of Texas, who saw everything, understood everything and, acting on his own sense, knew how to be heard and respected by everybody'.[1] The young English diplomat Harold Nicolson called him 'an affable Athena'.[2]

Woodrow Wilson, twenty-eighth President of the United States, spoke of him as his 'privy counsellor', and it was in that capacity that he had been called to the White House. Wilson wanted House to help him draft a speech on America's war aims which would answer the Russians, rally the Allies and drive a wedge between the rulers and the ruled of Germany. But above all it had to show the world that the American initiative that January represented a complete break with the past.

House had come to Washington equipped with information and recommendations from a body of scholarly advisers known as 'The Inquiry'. (A strange vocabulary would be one of the marks of the New Diplomacy.) Under House's aimiable chairmanship, this group of 150 learned men had been meeting, in great secrecy, within the premises of the American Geographical Society of New York since September. Wilson's instructions to them had been to prepare data for a 'diplomatic offensive' and for an eventual peace conference structured in accordance with the new ideas.

That Friday, House managed only to present the materials gathered; the drafting of the speech began the next morning. 'We actually got down to work at half-past ten,' House recorded in an impeccably kept diary, 'and finished remaking the map of the world, as we would have it, at half-past twelve o'clock.' They laboured alone, behind closed doors. Wilson himself typed up the final version and read it aloud to House on the Sunday afternoon. Both men were very moved. House told Wilson, 'You will either be on the crest of the wave after it's delivered or reposing peacefully in the depths.' This would be America's entry into Europe.[3]

Across the ocean, another speech on war aims was delivered that weekend. The British Prime Minister, David Lloyd George, was also under pressure to lay out his terms as a result of the developments in Eastern Europe. Well aware that the Americans were about to make a statement, he wanted to get his word in first. He did, in a speech made on Saturday, 5 January, not in Parliament but in nearby Caxton Hall, where trade unions were holding a conference on the problem of manpower shortages – a serious issue in 1918. Lloyd George was deliberately addressing his peace plan to the representatives of British labour.

The previous November the Liberal Lord Lansdowne had published a letter calling for a peace of conciliation based on the *status quo ante bellum*, and a month later the Labour Party had issued a memorandum which, echoing aims enunciated in Russia, repudiated secret diplomacy and refused to distinguish enemies from allies. Casualty figures from the recent Passchendaele offensive had had a sobering effect on the most hawkish members of the government.

In total contrast to Woodrow Wilson, Lloyd George had consulted everybody – the Cabinet, the opposition, the Labour Party leaders and representatives of the Dominions. His speech itself was largely drafted by the South African Minister of Defence, Jan Smuts, and his own Under-Secretary to the Foreign Office, Lord Robert Cecil. When Lloyd George stood up in Caxton Hall he had the whole British Empire behind him.

'We are not fighting a war of aggression against the German people,' he said. 'Nor are we fighting to destroy Austria-Hungary or to deprive Turkey of its capital, or of the rich and renowned lands of Asia Minor or Thrace.' The speech focused mainly on territorial problems. It tended towards intransigence on Britain's extra-European goals and to compromise on the Continent. Beyond retaining Asia Minor and Thrace, for example, Turkey could expect nothing; the old Ottoman Empire would be dismembered. German colonies would be disposed of on 'a basis acceptable to their inhabitants'. But Britain's only absolute commitment in Europe was limited to the withdrawal of German forces from occupied France and to Belgian independence. 'We mean to stand by the French democracy to the death in the demand they make for a reconsideration of the great wrong of 1871'; in other words, the status of Alsace-Lorraine would be subject only to a 'reconsideration'. For the Italians he merely pledged 'satisfaction' of their 'legitimate claims' for 'union with those of their own race and tongue' – hardly what had been outlined in the secret Pact of London of 1915. An independent Poland would be desirable, but Lloyd George's remarks made it clear that Britain would not prolong the war to gain it. Even the establishment of democracy in Germany was considered a matter best decided by the German people themselves; they could keep their imperial constitution if they wanted it. He spoke of the secret treaties between the Allies, recently published by the Bolsheviks; these, he said, had been made under the stress of war necessity and would not 'prevent a free discussion between Allies as to their future, as the Russian collapse had changed all the conditions'. Austria-Hungary might be required to grant self-government to the nationalities who sought it, but Lloyd George did not equate this with a break-up of the Habsburg Empire. The Prime Minister actually seemed harsher on Russia: he thought the country could be saved only by its people; he showed little sympathy for the Bolsheviks' recent espousal of 'open diplomacy'; and he noted that Britain could provide little help if the present rulers were bent on destruction.

Lloyd George called for reparations to be paid to the victims of the violations of international law – he was thinking principally of Britain's merchant seamen. He concluded with an idea that had frequently come up in Cabinet meetings and had been popular with the political Left. 'A great attempt', he said, 'must be made to establish by some international organization an alternative to war as a means of settling international disputes.'

The speech was warmly applauded by the trade unionists, and they agreed, in response, to conduct a more vigorous comb-out of the factories so as to maintain the strength of Britain's armies abroad. The press was enthusiastic. But it certainly did not satisfy all partisans of Labour, or the more radical elements of the Liberal Party. They were waiting to hear word from their prophet, President Woodrow Wilson – 'a figure', as The Inquiry's secretary, Walter Lippmann, described him, 'of mystical proportions, of really incredible power'.[4]

Woodrow Wilson – an American president who resembled no other, a university professor who stood neither within nor without academia, a Southerner who was not a 'Southernist', a 'mystic' who spent his entire life damning abstract thought and metaphysics – was certainly one of the most curious public personalities of the twentieth century. 'Why should anyone be particularly concerned with my personality?' wondered Wilson, somewhat perplexed. 'I am charged with a great work to do. The work and not I is the important matter for consideration.'[5] But there was no escaping it: friends, foes, journalists, chroniclers and historians would never let go of Mr Wilson's personality.[6]

Wilson himself would have willingly abolished personalities. They obstructed his vision. The task of 'remaking the map of the world' required an understanding of the structure of things; he wanted to get behind the rough surface phenomena of people and events to touch the grander causes that motivated them. Wilson's New Diplomacy, which responded so well to the popular quest, in the fourth year of the war, for a complete break with the past, was backed up with a New History. As a young professor of jurisprudence, he had explained his view of the New History at the Universal Exposition of St Louis, Missouri, in 1904. What was important, he said, lay 'not so much in what happened as in what underlay the happening; not so much in the tides as in the silent forces that lifted them'. He had baffled his colleagues with the same thought when he was an even younger practising lawyer in Atlanta, Georgia. For his fellow lawyers it was sufficient to know that a law was on the statute books. They would stare at Wilson 'with uncomprehending eyes' as he would attempt to explain that for him it was a matter of supreme interest how such a thing got on the statute books, and 'what process of social and political development had led to the making of laws'.[7]

It was not that Wilson was woolly or verbose. His language was sharp, direct, yet distinguished. If it moved crowds, it could also send thinking men into flights of imagination. He also had the physical appearance to do this. One of his colleagues at Princeton University had said, 'The Lord set out to make Woodrow ugly, but he turned round and made himself hand-some.' He stood almost six foot and had a remarkably long jaw counteracted by an occasional shy smile which saved his face from severity. Wilson himself had always been convinced he was ugly, and he liked to quote the ballad, 'For beauty I am not a star.' Yet he had an illuminated, mobile countenance which convinced people there were lofty things going on in his mind. 'It was a remarkable face,' said his friend Mrs Edith Reid of Baltimore, 'the caricature of a Scotch Covenanter.'[8]

He had suffered in childhood from what our prosaic, scientific age would call 'developmental dyslexia'. He did not learn the alphabet until he was nine, and he did not read a book before he was twelve; he had only eight years of formal schooling before he entered Davidson College, in North Carolina, at the age of seventeen – it was an unusual route for a future university professor to follow, even in the nineteenth century. This made him an outsider. Though he lived at a time when team sports were being advocated as a part of a man's education, Wilson stuck to bicycles, billiards and golf. As a child in Augusta, Georgia, his life somewhat resembled that of Tom Sawyer, playing hide-and-seek among the cotton bales of the warehouses, laying two pins crosswise on the railway tracks for the locomotives to press into scissors, making friends with the drivers of streetcars, inventing his own games and amusements; he was known as 'Tom' and the name stuck, even as an undergraduate at Princeton. 'I wonder if I am the slowest reader in the world!' he exclaimed when a professor of history and economics at Bryn Mawr College in Connecticut. His younger brother-in-law, Stockton Axson, said it was *non multa sed multum* with Wilson: he was an intensive reader rather than an extensive reader; he was always reading the same thing, just as he enjoyed repeating the same rides on his high-wheel bicycle, the same walks, the same recreations, the same trips abroad. In these activities he discovered his own version of history, the 'silent forces' that lifted the waves. Too much talking and debate caused too much surface agitation and confused the basic issue. Wilson would instinctively strip from his thought all that was unessential.[9]

But Wilson, who was sixty-two in 1918, was ill. He had headaches and constant stomach disorders; he suffered from a severe neuritis which at times rendered his right hand useless; and as a young man he had developed a tic under his right eye. The cause, it seems, was a serious form of hyper-tension that would lead to a number of minor strokes, the first perhaps occurring at Dickinson College when he was only eighteen. In 1906, shortly before he turned fifty, he woke up in bed, 'casually passed his hands over his eyes and suddenly discovered that he was unable to see out of one of his eyes'. The cause was a retinal haemorrhage, and for the remainder of his life he had only peripheral vision in his left eye. People would often describe a strange feeling when they looked into Wilson's large, luminous, blue-grey eyes; it arose from the fact that the man was half blind.[10]

Wilson's ancestors were Scotch-Irish and Scotch (it was always 'Scotch' in America). His grandmother came from the borderlands of Scotland and England, the land of Robbie Burns and Thomas Carlyle, but also the region that gave birth to the poetry of Wordsworth. When Wilson, before the war, took his pleasure trips 'to Europe' it was always here that he came, landing in Glasgow and then travelling by train and bicycle to the Lake District. Mrs Wilson often wondered why voyages 'to Europe' never involved France, Italy, Germany or Spain. 'Are you never going to understand', he would reply, 'how I do not need to do a variety of things but how I love most to do the thing I love best again and again?'[11] A 'healthy and robust' Scottish Presbyterianism had given Wilson the directness of his language and a determination to build his beliefs on rational principle rather than metaphysics. He inherited this from his father, Dr Joseph Ruggles Wilson, who was born in Ohio but established himself early as a distinguished minister of the Southern Presbyterian Church. His sermons had always been plain and to the point. One of his models had been the great Northern orator Daniel Webster, whom he had once seen speak in Washington under a blazing sun. Webster had stepped to the front of the platform, slowly extended his hand towards the sun, and, in a deep, sonorous voice, opened his address with the phrase 'Hail, thou, sun of liberty.' 'And do you know,' said Dr Wilson, 'I thought the sun winked back at him.'[12]

A teaching career would bring the younger Wilson into the small college towns of the North-East. But he never lost his sympathy for the South: that touch of grim melancholy upon his brow was due to the Civil War. If he had been old enough he would have fought for the South. Yet, typically, he saw the tragedy on both sides: as lawyers, he explained to his students, Southerners were right, but as statesmen they were wrong. Even then, his views on statesmanship could also be traced back to the South and his upbringing in Presbyterian 'plain talk'. This was what drew him like a magnet to the writings of Edmund Burke. 'There is no page of abstract reasoning to be found in Burke,' he noted in an essay on the eighteenth-century Anglo-Irish statesman. The same taste led him to distrust Thomas Jefferson and to detest all German thought, dismissing it as 'metaphysical'.

While Wilson read Burke and wrote good books on constitutional government, reform and reconstruction, a massive economic transformation was taking place in America. Growth in her agricultural and industrial production was so fast that the United States not only was surpassing every rival state in Europe, but by the second decade of the new century, was on the point of overtaking all Europe put together. She was easily the largest producer of coal and oil in the world, and the greatest consumer of copper; her pig-iron production was ahead of that of Germany, Britain and France combined; her national income was more than three times greater than that of Britain or Germany, and more than six times that of France. By the beginning of the twentieth century the United States was far and away the greatest economic power in the world. But she was not yet a part of Europe's Great Power system.[13]

Some of the United States' new wealth came into the pockets of Woodrow Wilson's graduates. After earning their degrees, they had gone out to the great industrial centres of Boston, Philadelphia and New York to make their fortunes. Some of them then returned to set up residence in Wilson's pretty little college town, Princeton, fifty miles from New York. It was through the ensuing conflict between Wilson and Princeton's rich graduates that Wilson came into national prominence.

Though so close to New York, the former College of New Jersey had, until some years after the Civil War, catered largely to the sons of the South – to people like Woodrow Wilson. A graduate of 1879, Wilson had joined the faculty in 1890 to teach jurisprudence. He was Princeton's most popular professor, lecturing with his father's voice and his Southern reliance on facts and simplicity. He was also an able administrator, and in 1902 became president of the university. Wilson was no monk in an ivory tower. 'I have had sight of the perfect place of learning in my thought,' he concluded in one famous speech to the faculty: 'a place . . . to which you may withdraw and use your youth for pleasure, where windows open straight upon the street, where many stand and talk intent upon the world of men and business. A place where ideals are kept in heart in an air they can breath; but no fool's paradise.'[14]

So, a place where windows opened upon the street and no fool's paradise. When America's new wealth moved into Princeton, the life on the streets outside began to change. Smart-looking traps and horses replaced the old college buggies, the automobile made its first appearance, women wore fine accoutrements imported from Paris; the tone of the *monde* made itself felt. The students themselves abandoned the old 'horse style' of dressing, which allowed the son of a blacksmith to eat with the son of a millionaire; now the mode was black ties, stiff collars and jackets, for those who could afford them. Small and exclusive undergraduate clubs proliferated. The senior class never addressed the sophomore class, and freshmen lived in their own tiny world, apart.

At first all this was a mere distraction to the goals of education and learning, but by the time Wilson became university president these exclusive cells of affluence had become the mainstay of life in Princeton. Wilson determined to change this; he took up his first fight for democracy. What was the role of the university in the world? To improve the life of the mind. He introduced a series of radical reforms: a change in the curriculum that laid down the line of courses to be followed; a 'preceptorial' system of teaching that created guided discussion groups after lectures; and a new 'plan of college life'. This last, with its organization of living space into 'quadrangles', came into head-on collision with the clubs – not only the university clubs, but the alumni clubs of Boston, New York and

Philadelphia, with the privileges, earned and unearned, of the rich.[15] For Wilson, the clubs were extra-collegiate institutions, absorbing the minds of undergraduates yet beyond the control of the college authorities; Wilson wanted the college itself to absorb minds. That singularity of purpose corresponded exactly to his vision of leadership in a democracy – casting aside the superfluous, cutting his programmes to the essential. That was the way Woodrow Wilson read books.

'It is my lonely privilege to find that on Princeton academic occasions I seem always to be the only person who talks about the things of the mind,' said Wilson at the annual dinner held by the college paper, the *Princetonian*. Three of his most tenacious opponents had just spoken of the dear, lifelong male friendships formed in the clubs; nobody knew how the silent students were going to react. The president's speech, recalled Stockton Axson, who was present, was 'twelve minutes of shrapnel shot'. Friendships, Wilson said, wonderful and beautiful as they are, were not the reason for the college's existence; the college existed for education and for leadership in national affairs. There was not a sound in the hall as he pronounced his finale: 'I summon you men to follow me!'[16]

The applause was deafening. The traditional college yell, 'The Locomotive', was called an unprecedented three times. Wilson's enemies skulked out. The battle was won with the students.

The battle was won with the faculty. Even the trustees' board, filled with rich alumni, went along. But in 1910 Isaac Wyman of Massachusetts, Princeton Class of 1848, died leaving a bequest that would preserve the old system. The trustees accepted both the donation and its conditions. Wilson was defeated by a dead man and money.

He resigned from the university and ran, on a progressive Democratic ticket, for the governorship of New Jersey, which he won with a handsome majority. Two years later he was elected President of the United States.

2

Wilson strove to open a democratic window upon a world at war in much the same way as he had learned Burke and administered Princeton: stripping the issues back to the essential and sidestepping annoying details, particular interests, the 'clubs'. In the same way as he had broached a new plan for college life, Wilson was determined to recast the inherited world order. He knew there would be a sector of world opinion behind him – beginning with Europe's suffering citizen soldiers, who sought a complete break with the past. World war and revolution had changed all the rules. The Old Diplomacy would give way to the New. The Old History of uncomfortable details, personalities and events, of Balances of Power and Concerts of Europe, would have to yield to the New History of principle and structure, the 'silent forces' that lifted the tides. The results of applying the New over the Old would be as different – Elihu Root, elder statesman of the Republican Party said it – 'as are the results which flow from the American Declaration of Independence compared with the results which flow from the Divine Right of Kings'.[17]

Wilson knew what was the essential matter even before the war broke out in Europe – indeed, even before he had entered the White House in 1913. He had discovered it at Princeton: it was the fight for democracy. But the world came to know this only when America entered the war in April 1917. America, said Wilson in his address to Congress, was going to war not for conquest but for peace and justice; her quarrel was not with the German people but with 'autocracy' – the German autocracy was guilty of 'throwing to the winds all scruples of humanity'. America's mission was clear: 'The world must be made safe for democracy.' This was the central matter, the force that lifted the waves: democracy against autocracy.

In Princeton, Wilson had devised his system of 'quadrangles' to enhance the community of intellectual lives. Something similar was needed to promote and extend the community of democratic nations. Again, he had his answer before America went to war. It dawned on him when he returned to the White House after burying his first wife in the grounds of her home town, Rome, Georgia. That was in August 1914, as Germany marched into Belgium. Stockton Axson was with him. 'I have been thinking', declared Wilson, 'a great deal about a remark of Napoleon Bonaparte's that "Nothing was ever finally settled by force."' Not a very reliable source, one would have thought, for that particular moment. But then Bonaparte was a man who also reduced politics to its simplest principles and who also told the world he was fighting for democracy against the 'Divine Right of Kings'.[18] Wilson then developed four points that he regarded as absolutely necessary for the ordering of the globe in the future: there must never again be a foot of ground acquired by conquest; it must be recognized that small nations had an equality of rights with the great nations; ammunition must be manufactured by governments and by not private individuals; and there must be 'some sort of association of nations wherein all shall guarantee the territorial integrity of each'.[19]

It was this last point that became the keystone to Wilson's New Diplomacy. Within a year he had put it into practice, establishing a Pan-American Pact in which the nations of the Western Hemisphere agreed to a mutual guarantee of their independence and their territorial integrity under republican forms of government. Reviewing the agreement in 1918, Wilson admitted that his ambition was 'to have the states of the two continents of America show the way to the rest of the world as to how to make a basis of peace'.[20]

This required a diplomatic offensive, and it was for that reason that The Inquiry had been set up in New York – and deliberately not in clubbish Washington, where the professional diplomats of the State Department might divert the scholars' attention from their cause. On 22 December 1917

The Inquiry set out the objectives of the diplomatic offensive: to play upon the hopes and fears of the German people by holding out the temptation of belonging to a world community; to attain American terms of peace through the use of America's economic might – 'this is our strongest weapon'; and to establish the main object of their desires: an association of democratic nations. The embryo of such an organization, the memorandum suggested, already existed within the anti-German alliance.[21]

But Wilson wanted to maintain his distance from this alliance for the same reason that made him keep the State Department at arm's length. Clubland Europe could prove to be a distraction. He distrusted the Supreme War Council in Versailles, where government delegations and military representatives of the alliance had met since November 1917. Even though America was in the same war as they, she had only an 'observer' there. America had actually refused the status of 'Ally'; she was an 'Associate', and as such she would guard her independence and assure that her intentions in the war were pure.

Lloyd George's speech on Britain's war aims had been prepared over a period of six months in consultation with the committees of a varied empire. Wilson's speech on America's aims was prepared by himself and his Southern friend Colonel House behind closed doors in the White House. This secrecy was another feature of the New Diplomacy.

The centrepiece of the speech was fourteen 'provisional' points that defined what America sought in the peace. House tells how they were divided into two parts: 'general terms' and 'territorial adjustments'. House's account, as well as later comments from Wilson, makes it clear that – in total contrast to Lloyd George – the general terms were considered more important than territorial matters. The Inquiry might have been housed in the headquarters of a geographical society, but geography was not the principal concern of the Americans. The points Wilson would describe as 'essentially American' were the first four – 'open covenants of peace, openly arrived at'; 'absolute freedom of navigation upon the seas'; 'the removal, so far as possible, of all economic barriers'; the reduction of 'national armaments' – and the final, fourteenth, point, that called for 'a general association of nations'.[22]

House insisted on the first point, concerning open diplomacy, saying that nothing would better please the American people and the democracies of the world and 'that it was right and must be the diplomacy of the future'. The irony that this was decided in strict privacy did not apparently strike Wilson. 'Treaties' seemed by their nature secret, so they became in the parlance of the New Diplomacy 'covenants'. House wrote the paragraph on the 'absolute freedom of navigation upon the seas'; Wilson added the cautionary phrase 'except as the seas may be closed in whole or in part by international action for the enforcement of international covenants' because he knew the British would never accept the article without such a loophole permitting naval blockade when her sovereignty was threatened (this had been the cause of war between the two countries back in 1812).

The other points, concerning 'territorial adjustments', were quite similar to those outlined by Lloyd George, which was hardly surprising. Since the outbreak of war in Europe, House had been conducting what we would today call a 'shuttle diplomacy', visiting the various capitals and assessing the different territorial demands. Britain, which was now bearing the main military burden of the Allies in Europe, got favoured treatment in that her demands were introduced by the verb 'must', whereas everybody else got 'should'. Thus, Point VII stated that Belgium 'must be evacuated and restored', while Point VIII said that all French territory 'should be freed' and that the matter of Alsace-Lorraine 'should be righted'.

In January 1918 the United States still had nothing resembling an army in Europe and was dependent on the military effort of the Allies; in no way could she take an independent line where territorial matters were concerned. Yet there were already differences. Like Lloyd George, Wilson did not call for the break-up either of Germany or of the Austro-Hungarian Empire (though his speech laid a great deal more emphasis on the need for national 'self-determination' and 'democratic' solutions). But nor did Wilson call for the break-up of the Ottoman Empire, which for Lloyd George was going to be an area for partition.

Even more noteworthy were their differences over Russia. Lloyd George answered the recent Russian armistice with Germany with a threat: he said that if the Russians did not themselves combat their 'economic and political enslavement to Germany' the Western powers would leave them to their fate. Wilson answered with flattery: he welcomed the new Russia 'into the society of free nations under institutions of her own choosing'. His speech contained a most sympathetic portrayal of a Soviet diplomacy shaped 'very justly, very wisely, and in the true spirit of democracy'. This is not how his own Secretary of State, Robert Lansing, would have phrased it.

Tuesday 8 January 1918 was one of those bright American winter days when every colour stands out on its own; white buildings were silhouetted against the deep blue of the sky, naked sycamores rose stubborn, alone and erect, and each blade of grass on Washington's Mall seemed to call out its identity. In the morning Wilson played golf, returning to the White House only at 11.30 a.m. He instructed his secretary, Joseph Patrick Tumulty, to inform the Vice-President and the Speaker of the House that he would be at the Capitol in thirty minutes to address a joint session of Congress.[23]

Nobody was expecting him, because he had addressed Congress only four days before. Senators and representatives were rustled up, a few members of the Cabinet rushed in without the first idea of the subject at hand, while only one ambassador – the British – managed to get to the diplomatic gallery before Wilson, at noon, stepped up to the speaker's stand.

He was right on form, his tone calm and measured. If his compliments to the Bolsheviks caused little enthusiasm, his declaration 'to assist the people of Russia to attain their utmost hope of liberty and ordered peace' brought a crackle of applause. Late visitors continued to file in. The basic American war aim, he went on, was unselfish. All nations would be assured of justice and fair dealing. 'The program of the world's peace, therefore, is our program; and that program, the only possible program, as we see it, is this . . .'

There was complete silence as Wilson began reading his Fourteen Points. The evacuation of Belgian and Russian territories caused not a stir. But when he spoke of France and Alsace-Lorraine the senators and representatives jumped on their chairs and waved their arms 'as if they were at a football game'. Wilson gave a sheepish smile, waited for the applause to die down, then continued to his fourteenth point – on the 'general association of nations' that would guarantee the 'independence and territorial integrity to great and small nations alike'. Americans would devote everything to this principle of justice for all peoples: 'The moral climax of this the culmination and final war for human liberty has come, and they are ready to put their own strength, their own integrity and devotion to the test.'

Right across America there was applause for this speech. Even his most ardent opponents complimented him; they compared it to Lincoln's Emancipation Proclamation.

But the British were did not look forward to 'absolute freedom of the seas' and had doubts that a moral climax was at hand. The Italians did not relish readjustment of their frontiers 'along clearly recognizable lines of nationality'. And when Clemenceau read the Fourteen Points in Paris he exclaimed, 'Even the Lord Almighty limited himself to Ten!'

3

The Germans replied with their guns. Negotiations with the Bolsheviks at German headquarters in Poland, at Brest-Litovsk, broke down on 10 February 1918 and a week later the German Army resumed its march into Russia. The Bolsheviks finally sued for peace, signing a treaty on 3 March by which Russia lost 34 per cent of her population, 32 per cent of her agricultural land, and the major part of her industry (73 per cent of her iron-ore output and 89 per cent of her coal). Less than three weeks later, just before the misty dawn of 21 March, the British sector before Amiens was subjected to the greatest artillery barrage ever witnessed in the war – it would even dwarf all those launched in the Second World War. Lieutenant-Colonel Georg Bruchmüller, known by the troops as *Durchbruchmüller* ('Breakthrough Miller'), orchestrated 6,000 guns along a forty-mile front, mixing large quantities of mustard and tear-gas shells among his high explosives. 'Machine-gun posts were blown sky-high – along with human limbs,' remembered a British gunner; 'men were coughing and vomiting from the effects of gas, and men were blinded'. It sounded 'as if the world were coming to an end', recorded one German artilleryman. On the British side entire battalions disappeared; after five hours of bombardment and ten hours on the offensive, the Germans broke through to open country.[24]

The two offensives, in the East and the West, were a mirror image of the war of manoeuvre in 1914: this time the Eastern opponent was to be knocked out first and then the war would be swiftly concluded in the West. Once more military considerations took priority over politics.

Could it have been otherwise? The time for Germany to make peace with her neighbours was surely now, while she still held a strong bargaining position. All her principal opponents had outlined their aims and had thus laid the base for serious negotiations. For Germany to seek a military solution this late in the war was to put at risk not only her own national existence but also that of her allies.

Though not strong, there were political forces in Germany which understood this. One of the aims of Wilson's speech in January had been to exploit them by setting them against Germany's military Supreme Command that was so oblivious of political considerations. For a moment it looked as if the idea might be working. On 28 January the new Chancellor, Georg von Hertling, in a speech to the Reichstag, made a guarded acceptance of Wilson's general Points while dismissing all concessions on Belgium and Alsace-Lorraine and leaving Germany's options in the East open. The speech caused bitter disappointment within the German Left, and the socialist press started a radical campaign for peace. The shape of that peace was determined by the demands from strikers in the key munition factories of Berlin, Hamburg, Essen and Leipzig for the Bolshevik programme of December – a peace without annexations and indemnities. The total number of strikers amounted to a little over half a million, and 250,000 workers demonstrated in Berlin alone. The strikes became violent.

But, unfortunately for Wilson, the strikers were not the German nation. 'German public opinion', Matthias Erzberger later wrote, 'was not ripe for steps in favour of peace and the politicians responsible had not prepared it in any way.'

That was something that had haunted propagandist Erzberger for the previous two years, ever since he had come to realize that there was no way that Germany and her allies could win the war. 'Right up to the end, to the moment of disaster, Germany's military leaders understood nothing about the psychology of war,' he recalled; all they could do was talk about victories. 'The great mass of the German people wondered why there was not peace because a victory was reported every day.' All references to food shortages, undernourishment and suffering were rigorously censored in the press: 'Our enemies were better informed on the situation than was the mass of German people.'[25]

Erzberger, was a southern German, a Catholic from Wüttemberg, a man however who had developed an intense admiration for what he regarded as the moderate policies of Bismarck. One would often hear him quoting elegant Prussian phrases from the wise Iron Chancellor.

What really decided Erzberger to seek a political solution to the war was the failure of 'unlimited submarine warfare' to bring Britain to her knees in 1917. Germany, he thought, would die of starvation long before Britain, and his great regret was that Germany had not built more U-boats before the war. The generals kept deceiving the public that Britain would be knocked out of the war within six months; Erzberger felt that Germany would be lucky to escape simply with 'a black eye'.

Erzberger's work as a chief of propaganda in the Ministry of Foreign Affairs took him to many countries in Eastern and Central Europe. He was therefore much more exposed to what foreigners thought about Germany than were the generals of Supreme Command, whose view of the world was only as wide as their military plans would allow. Late in April 1917 Erzberger had travelled to Vienna to discuss Austria's role in the war. He had interviews with both the Foreign Minister, Count Ottokar Czernin, and the young Kaiser Karl, who had ascended the throne just four months earlier on the death of his grandfather, Franz Josef. What Erzberger learned had appalled him.

First he discovered that Czernin had the same doubts about the effects of 'unlimited submarine warfare' as he. But far more worrying was what Czernin had to say about Austria's domestic situation. The Austro-Hungarian Empire, he said, was engaged in 'a veritable race between war, revolution and hunger'. Kaiser Karl elaborated on this point. A revolutionary republic in Austria-Hungary, he told Erzberger, would mean the dissolution of the empire, because only two things held it together: the dynasty and Roman Catholicism. Karl concluded that it was absolutely essential to arrive at a peace 'by next autumn' – autumn 1917.[26]

The Austrian interviews turned German assumptions about the nature of her alliances upside down. It was not her allies that were contributing to Germany's war effort, but the other way round: Germany was not only helping them in a moment of severe crisis, she was providing them with the means to survive.[27]

A vote for war credits was coming up in the Reichstag in the summer of 1917. Erzberger decided to use this opportunity to realign the political parties and win a majority vote on a peace resolution that would unite the parties of the Left with his own Catholic Centre Party. The move met with startling success. Erzberger's resolution was adopted on 19 July 1917 by 212 votes to 126. But adoption revealed to the world two crucial weaknesses in German politics: the feeble authority of the Imperial Chancellor and the ambiguity of the peace programme itself.

The Peace Resolution was one of the main reasons for the resignation that same month of the man who had been Chancellor since the onset of the war, Bethmann Hollweg, for he had opposed it. Supreme Command pushed a new candidate; Erzberger and his friends also had a candidate. However, in the end it was neither Supreme Command nor the new 'peace' majority in the Reichstag that picked Bethmann's successor, but Kaiser Wilhelm, whose choice fell on an unknown Prussian civil servant, Georg Michaelis, an Imperial Commissioner of Food. The stage was now set for an open struggle between Supreme Command, which had much power but no policy, and the new Reichstag majority, which had much policy but no power.

The Peace Resolution itself indicated the kind of settlement Germany's peacemakers were seeking. Most remarkably, it contained no territorial clauses at all, so absolutely nothing could be ascertained as to what Germany's genuine war aims were. Its overall content was based, as its opening statement affirmed, on the parliamentary declaration of 4 August 1914 that had announced, as German troops streamed into Belgium, that the Reich was 'not motivated by the will for conquest'. If this was hardly of much comfort to Germany's enemies, the vague clauses that followed could, and would, be seen as being in accord with Wilson's 'general terms', pronounced in January 1918. 'The Reichstag hopes for a peace of understanding and a durable reconciliation between peoples. Forced territorial acquisitions and political economic or financial oppressions are irreconcilable with such a peace' – with imagination, one could read this as an endorsement of the principle of 'self-determination'. The resolution called for a lifting of the economic blockade, 'freedom of the seas', and even the creation of 'international juridical organizations'. In brief, it contained all of Wilson's future 'general terms' save the call for open diplomacy and the reduction of national armaments.

The course of events over the next eighteen months would demonstrate how very perverse the parallel was. Wilson, naive and isolated as he was, genuinely stood for a peace without conquests. In contrast, Erzberger and his colleagues in the Reichstag were seeking a political means of reducing the costs of war while holding on to the territories won by it. The key lay in their interpretation of 'self-determination'.

It was Russia that won the race to 'revolution and hunger', but Austria-Hungary was not far behind, and the situation in Germany itself was, by January 1918, critical. The average German citizen was living on a diet of one thousand calories a day, consisting almost entirely of ersatz commodities like 'bread' made up of sawdust, chalk and potato peel, and a meat regime of dogs and cats ('roof rabbits'). 'The rounded contours of the the German nation have become a legend of the past,' wrote Princess Blücher in Berlin, with the irony of the Englishwoman she was. 'We are all gaunt and bony now.' The world talked about Britain's losses at Passchendaele, for the casualty lists had been published; nobody mentioned the devastating effect the same campaign had had on Germany's forces. Ludendorff described the British offensive as 'almost irresistible'; it demonstrated Allied superiority in the air and what seemed to the few Germans who could examine the results an almost unlimited supply of material and manpower. A solution had to be found – and found fast.[28]

One faint glimmer of hope lay on the eastern horizon. The Russian collapse could at the very last moment deliver Germany from catastrophe like a divine intervention by one of the Fates. For Supreme Command it offered the chance of more troops on the Western Front, more food to nourish them, more material to arm them; for deputies in the Reichstag it opened the way to a political solution of the war, an endorsement of German expansion since 1914 couched in the terms of a humane peace.

The new German Foreign Secretary was Richard von Kühlmann. Like Erzberger, he was well aware of the new limits of German power. After long discussions with the Austrian minister, whose ambitions in Poland far exceeded those of Germany, he arrived at a formula that would, first, goad Russia's new Bolshevik regime into signing a separate peace with Germany and, second, safeguard German interests in the East through a series of 'declarations of independence' among the eastern nationalities, thereby creating a strip of subsidiary states that would be wholly dependent on the Central Powers. The process was already begun in the autumn of 1917: a 'council of regency' was set up in Poland, Courland got a nominally representative body that was soon appealing for the Kaiser's 'protection', local 'independent' assemblies were organized in Livonia, Lithuania and Estonia, and the Finnish Diet voted a 'declaration of independence' that would be recognized by both Germany and Russia in 1918. In the agriculturally and industrially rich Ukraine, elections were held in November 1917 to the Kiev 'Rada', during which Ukrainian nationalists overwhelmingly outvoted the Bolsheviks.

So the Germans opened their arms to the Bolshevik programme of peace with 'no annexations, no indemnities'. Kühlmann drafted a 'Christmas Declaration' which accepted the programme on condition that the Western Allies accepted the same and joined in negotiations by 5 January 1918. Kühlmann knew full well that, without specific territorial terms laid down, there would be no response from the West. Thus Russia was waltzed by Germany into signing a separate peace.

But the political calculations of Kühlmann and his friends in the Reichstag were far too complicated for the generals of Supreme Command: they wanted outright annexation. At a Crown Council held in Kreuznach in December 1917, Kühlmann, exasperated, demanded that Hindenburg tell him why he was so keen on occupying the foreign lands of Courland and Lithuania. 'I need them', Hindenburg responded with a grunt, 'for the manoeuvring of my left wing in the next war.'[29]

Germany signed a separate treaty with the 'independent' Ukraine on 9 February. The Russians, headed by Trotsky, walked out of the negotiations at Brest-Litovsk the next day. On 18 February, German armies marched into the Ukraine and across Estonia until they were within seventy-five miles of Petrograd.

Ludendorff drafted the final terms of the Treaty of Brest-Litovsk, which was signed by the Russians on 3 March. When it was presented to the Reichstag for ratification, Erzberger stood up to announce that the treaty would comply perfectly with the Peace Resolution of 1917 if 'genuine self-determination' were applied to the new borderland states. Apart from the Independent Socialists (who voted against) and a few Social Democrats (who abstained), the Reichstag's peace majority all voted in favour of Supreme Command's dictated treaty. The world was now warned of what to expect from a German-imposed peace.[30]

4

It was through no accident that Supreme Command came to be dominated by two men: Hindenburg and Ludendorff – the 'terrible twins' as they were dubbed by the Western Allies. Wellington had dealt with a similar partnership at the top of the Prussian Army during the Waterloo campaign, in the persons of Blücher and Gneisenau – one old and respected, the other young and doctrinaire; a conservative force balanced by a certain spirit of radicalism. So it was with Hindenburg and Ludendorff. They embodied the character of the German Army. Of course it was conservative and represented a famous 'moral' force which opposed, tooth and nail, all efforts at political reform and every decadent sign of 'democratization'. At the same time, no army in Europe was so flexible in doctrine, so swift to change from a defensive to an offensive stance, from a 'war of manoeuvre' to a 'war of positions' and then back again – so quick to adapt to the opportunities of the moment. Hindenburg, now seventy, with his square head and burly figure, was the image of stability – a bedrock for doubting, starving Germany. Ludendorff, fifty-two, whose neatly trimmed blond moustache was perhaps designed to distract attention from the double chin and slight bulge in the neck (which, however, Western cartoonists never failed to depict), was all movement, all thought – no statue for worship. His memoirs demonstrate the clear, independent military mind that had impressed his superiors and would for long remain innocent of cloudy politics. Together, the old aristocrat and the merchant's son, both from Prussian Posnania, were a fair representation of what made up the high command in the German armies.

Their appointment as Chief of Staff and First Quartermaster General had been made in late August 1916, at the height of the Verdun battle, which had been designed to bleed France white; it did, but achieved much the same for Germany. Britain's offensive in the Somme was at that time entering its third month. On their visit to the front in September they were appalled by the condition of the troops and so executed their first about-turn in strategy, to a defence in depth that relied on powerful rear 'positions' – *Stellungen* – to which the Germans eventually retired in late winter, 1917.

The Allies referred to the new emplacements collectively as the Hindenburg Line, after their new object of hate, but, as one German general pointed out, 'We have no line, but a complicated system of redoubts and fortifications extending from Cambrai to La Fère' – all patterned by the weaving contours of France's northern plain. The Germans named the positions, romantically, after the old folk *Nibelungenlied*: the Kriemhilde Stellung was in the southern hills of the Argonne, the Brunhild Stellung in Champagne, the Alberich Stellung overlooked the Aisne, and opposite the British armies of the Somme was the Siegfried Stellung: the top half of the drunken 'S' had been willingly blunted by the invaders of 1914. At first, the long and deep belts of wire before the trenches and machine-gun posts created, at a distance, a flickering blue sheen in the afternoon, but by 1918 this had turned to an organic brown, producing mock scenes of autumn in winter and spring and even under the heat of that summer.[31]

Nineteen-seventeen was an expensive year for the Allies; so it was for the Germans. 'As our best men became casualties, our infantry approximated more nearly in character to a militia, and discipline declined,' wrote the First Quartermaster General. This would lead to a second shift in strategy. With American entry into the war it became clear that Germany could not win a war of attrition, and anyway the prolonged period of defence was not helping morale. This, at any rate, was Ludendorff's view: 'In the West the Army pined for the offensive, and after Russia's collapse expected it with the most intense relief.'[32]

Ignoring all political considerations, Hindenburg and Ludendorff began planning a co-ordinated series of offensives on the Western Front within a fortnight of the Bolshevik takeover in Petrograd. Troops were being transferred to the West before the end of the month. The Bolsheviks signed their armistice with the Central Powers on 15 December, but already, on 3 December, Ludendorff had sent his list of eastern annexations to Kühlmann. If Wilson's Fourteen Points of January 1918 excited some opposition in Germany, his 'Four Principles' of 11 February – which promoted the new creed of national self-determination over the old-fashioned European notion of the 'balance of power' – fell absolutely flat. Heaven-sent reinforcements and food from Eastern Europe had fallen into Germany's lap and the country was gearing up for the kind of swift victory that had been the hope in 1914. It was a moment of grace. It was fate – but fate hitched to the wax wings of Icarus.

There was something remarkably Napoleonic about Ludendorff's planned offensives for 1918. There was the same aim at the 'hinge', or point of contact, of the Allied opponents; the same jagged lightning attacks to left and to right to knock out first one opponent and then the other; the same idea of cornering the foe against some physical barrier – all these had been features of Napoleon's campaigns of the Danube, of Prussia and Saxony, and of Waterloo. Like Napoleon, on 21 March Ludendorff launched his initial offensive against the 'hinge' – the weak point where the British sector joined the French – with the aim of driving his two enemies apart, and ultimately of pushing Britain's forces up against the Channel, 'with our backs to the wall' as Haig would put it in his communiqué of 11 April. In this sense, Ludendorff was rehearsing a classical war of manoeuvre on the great northern plain.

But the full width of the plain was his field. The scale of the fighting was unprecedented. 'The transformation from static to mobile warfare demands unbelievable accuracy and farsightedness,' reflected the artilleryman Lieutenant Herbert Sulzbach in his diary as he prepared for Ludendorff's third offensive; yet he found it 'enormously exciting'. Nobody in history had ever seen such huge armies on the move along the rural tracks of Picardy and Champagne. 'My God, where have all these people come from?' wrote Albert Sagewitz to his family back in provincial Hesse. 'It looks like the migration of a nation.' Ludendorff's violent swings to the left and the right included Flanders and the Aisne, as well as the Somme. And yet, like every campaign in the war, the wider it got the more local was the field of initiative. That indeed was the new doctrine, based on an opportunistic philosophy that let infantrymen, not artillery, determine the pace and even the point of attack. Teams of well-trained foot soldiers, organized around light machine-guns, would penetrate the enemy lines, bypassing pockets of resistance; they were to be known as 'storm troopers'.[33]

But, as they ranged left and right in nature's mists and man's own poisonous fogs, there was a danger of losing sight of Supreme Command's general strategic aim. On the field, the movement of the German armies became a wicked parody of trackless German politics: in the March offensive they lurched southward, not north to the Channel. The open land looked like the steppes of Russia; there was a 'lack of any definite limit', as a worried Ludendorff himself put it. Each subsequent offensive fanned the German armies further afield, to left and to right, so that, on the map, the northern loop of the drunken 'S' took on a well rounded form once more. In April it was Flanders. In May, June and July it was the Aisne, initially designed to be a feint for the ultimate *coup de grâce* dealt to the British in Flanders. But that operation never materialized. It was, ironically, code-named 'Hagen', after the figure who killed Siegfried by a stab in the back. A stab in the back: the image would haunt Germany for two decades.

Ludendorff's *Blitzkrieg* of 1918 was conducted on foot. He had no tanks or armoured cars worth speaking of; he even lacked cavalry. 'It was a crowning mercy that they had not cavalry,' declared Sidney Rogerson, who was in the British military rabble when the Germans broke through a twenty-five-mile front on the Aisne at the end of May. 'How many times during the retreat did we thank Heaven for this!' Ludendorff's own accounts of his five offensives invariably concluded with tales of troop fatigue, pillaging and, more ominously, 'poor discipline': 'The absence of our old peace-trained corps of officers [they were all dead, wounded or missing] was most severely felt. They had been the repository of the moral strength of the army.'[34] On the night of 14–15 July 1918 – Bastille Day had just been celebrated in Paris – Ludendorff launched an offensive on the river Marne, along the same line where Moltke had led his armies in September 1914. On the third day of battle he fatally exposed his right wing, just like Moltke. The Allies were waiting for him under the cover of a wood. But on this occasion they had not been brought to the field in Parisian taxis: they came at him on the 18th with tanks and an air force.

5

The military science of manoeuvre and envelopment was born on the plains of Europe. So was a certain kind of international association: the coalition, the combination, the league. These groupings were not abstractions invented in remote ivory towers; they were created to counter whatever power was dominant on the European peninsula and they had, like military science, a geography of their own. Lord Castlereagh, Britain's Foreign Secretary at the time of the Napoleonic wars, had recognized this in the formation of the last coalition against France; he sometimes referred to the alliance as the 'United Nations', and, in a horse-drawn carriage, he followed it as it developed across Germany into Switzerland, to France and then on to Vienna. The Congress of Vienna of 1815 had devised the 'Concert of Europe', built upon an eighteenth-century notion of equilibrium, the 'balance of power'. A century of peace proved its practicality and also showed that it was not as unfavourable to parliamentary government and national identity as its more violent detractors – like that famous saviour of democratic nations, Napoleon – had imagined.

Russia aside, the coalition against Germany, formed in the years before 1914 because of Germany's persistent threats to the peace, remained united throughout the war. That was something else that made the Great War unique in European history. There was no 'diplomatic revolution', no 'second' or 'third coalition', no case of an isolated power heroically holding out against a conquered Continent: the conquest never happened; the chains of the alliance never broke.

And yet, if the Allied leaders now travelled by steamboat and rail, they tackled problems that would not have been entirely foreign to statesmen brought together in Vienna by horse-drawn carriages. As in the Napoleonic wars, the international institutions born out of the alliance took their shape only in the last year of the conflict. As in the Napoleonic wars, they were the product of discord between allies rather than agreement. And, as in the

Napoleonic wars, the men who created them would not be popular – in the decades that followed, history would in both cases censure them.

The first of these international institutions of the Great War was the Supreme War Council, set up in November 1917 ostensibly to co-ordinate Allied strategy. It sat in the luxurious Trianon Palace Hotel in Versailles, where it was thought (under the same sort of illusion as had inspired King Louis XIV's house move in the late seventeenth century) it could escape political intrigue. Political representatives of the member governments sat on the Council alongside 'permanent military representatives'. Each ally had its own idea of the Council's purpose. The French wanted to increase the power of their armies' General Staff. The British wanted to decrease theirs. The Italians simply wanted a voice. The Americans, who sent only an 'observer', wanted no voice at all, though they were deeply offended if decisions were made without their being consulted.

For four months the Council served as a forum for political argument. Clemenceau complained that the British would accept the idea of a 'unity of command' only under the threat of German cannon.

Ludendorff's cannon fired in the Somme on 21 March 1918. On Tuesday, 26 March, political and military authorities – including Clemenceau, the French President Poincaré, Field Marshal Haig and the British War Minister, Lord Milner – assembled in the town hall of Doullens. From it they could watch an endless column of khaki retreating west down the main street; a line of tanks to the east of the town kept the Germans at bay. Just before lunch they signed a note charging General Ferdinand Foch 'to co-ordinate the action of the Allied armies on the Western Front'. On 9 April Ludendorff's cannon thundered in Flanders. Five days later Foch was named 'Commander-in-Chief of the Allied armies in France'. 'Well, you've got what you wanted,' Clemenceau remarked during their small lunch at Doullens (they had not been invited to join the British). 'A fine present you give me,' replied Foch; 'you give me a lost battle and tell me to win it.'[35]

Foch's staff was tiny. At no time did he have more than twenty officers working for him, and on any given day many of them would be away on liaison duty. Foch commanded by exhortation, combined with a certain talent for hint and persuasion that usually won his powerful subordinates round. He laid down principles and goals. The details were left to the army commanders, the corps commanders, the division and regimental officers: this would remain to the end a local war.

Foch could be found, always confident and usually cheerful, sitting in his office at Beauvais or the Château Bombon, dressed in blue with brown gaiters and boots while he puffed a cigar and occasionally glanced at the large map on the wall. He would do all the talking, gesturing with a punch or a kick in the air: *'Je les attaque . . . Bon'* – it had been his philosophy ever since he had been a lecturer at the Ecole de Guerre – *'Je dis, allez à la bataille. Tout le monde à la bataille. Bon. Je ne les lâche pas, les Boches . . .'*[36]

War mathematics dominated discussions in the higher echelons of Allied command. Each nation had its own way of counting casualties. The total killed was, in normal circumstances, about one fifth of the total casualties. Between 70 and 80 per cent of the wounded returned to fight again. But prisoners would never return. So it was with some pride that, in the later months of 1918, the British staff could record two and a half British casualties for every German prisoner taken.

In Ludendorff's five spring offensives the German Army had suffered no fewer than 963,300 casualties. But the French were losing men at a rate of 112,000 a month, and the British armies were declining by 70,000 a month. The British were now conscripting men up to fifty years of age. 'There are many things that show the approach of the end of England's manpower,' noted General J. G. Harbord – charged with securing American supplies – when he visited an army camp in Brentwood, Essex. The men were 'physically poor, runts, crooked, underdeveloped, a sad contrast to the splendidly set up Tommies of peace times'. 'The strength of the British Army is decreasing day by day,' reported Foch in a formal memorandum to the Supreme War Council on 1 June. 'It even decreases more rapidly than that of the American Army increases . . .The result is a decrease in the total strength of the Allies. This consequence is exceptionally grave: it may mean the loss of the war.'[37]

Foch may have belonged to the old French school of *l'attaque à outrance*, but in nearly four years of war he had learned to respect barbed wire, machine-guns and rapidly firing artillery. The Americans had not.

There were about a quarter of a million American troops scattered around new training camps in France at the time when Ludendorff launched his first offensive in March. The slogan 'Wait for America' was becoming a sore joke among the Allies. 'Is there the slightest reason to imagine it will come next year, or the year after, or even the year after that?' a frustrated British officer wrote of the 'American army' to his brother that trying spring. The German offensives goaded Woodrow Wilson into promising an American army in Europe of eighty divisions made up of 3.3 million men. 'There is but one response possible from us,' said Wilson in a speech in Baltimore that April: 'force, force to the utmost, force without stint or limit.' By the end of May there were over 600,000 American troops on French soil. By July there were three quarters of a million. The American First Army was formally inaugurated on 13 August 1918. 'History awaits you,' Clemenceau had written to the American commander, General John J. Pershing, three weeks earlier; 'you will not fail it.'[38]

Pershing's instructions from his government had been clear: 'The underlying idea must be kept in view that the forces of the United States are a separate and distinct component of the combined forces, the identity of which must be preserved.' The Allies would have preferred to incorporate American units into the existing armies to strengthen the weak – the desperately weak – points on the front as they developed. Pershing, 'maddeningly mulish', would continue to insist on his great self-contained American Army: 'The principle of unity must prevail in our army. It must be completely under its own command.' Eventually, after Ludendorff had already launched three offensives, it was agreed, that American units could be deployed in Allied armies until the Americans had set up their own. The first American unit to see action was, appropriately, the 1st US Infantry Division. Supported by French tanks, flame-throwers, aircraft and artillery, on 27 May just south of the river Somme, outside the ruins of Cantigny, it gained 1,600 yards for the Allies.[39]

The Americans, in fact, *were* very different. Crowds would weep with joy at the sight of them. 'One who knows his history can well imagine what it meant when Napoleon rode in from wars,' recorded General Harbord when first exposed to Gallic enthusiasms. Compared to the exhausted troops of the other armies, the Americans seemed so tall and magnificent. They sat in tight rows in their army lorries, with their feet up, singing out loud songs that lifted the soul of the whole country. In their turn, the Americans – most of whom had not travelled beyond the county borders of their own home towns until they had joined up – found their new environment very strange. 'All the houses both in England and here are made of stone or bricks,' wrote Private Everett Scott to his mother in Iowa. 'There are very few wooden buildings, and all of the people wear wooden shoes.' The young women wore short skirts and silk stockings – unknown in America's Mid-West. Meals in the cafés were cheap. For a few francs you could have soup and a slab of meat, accompanied by another novelty, 'French fried potatoes'. 'About all the French use water for is to wash clothes in,' Elmer Sherwood told his family in Indiana. 'If one asked for it the waitress might have to make a special visit to the town pump.'[40]

The Americans were confident that, along with their New Diplomacy, they could bring a different style of war to tired old Europe. Machine-guns and rapid artillery fire didn't worry them. Their 'independent character' and innate feel for 'open warfare' would break the deadlock. American military doctrine was drawn from the 1917 Field Service Regulations, which were a barely altered version of the classic 1911 edition: battles were won by powerful 'infantry rushes', which established their superiority with 'accurate rifle power'. The tactic had been proven in the campaigns against Plains Indians, the Moros of the southern Philippines and the Mexican *bandidos* of Pancho Villa – battles where General Pershing had made his reputation.[41]

When the US Marines began their counter-attack at Bellau Wood on 2 May, the German defenders were at first amazed. They admired the accuracy of American rifle fire, but expressed pity that so many enthusiastic young men were slaughtered. The scene reminded Germans of another age: the Somme in 1916, when they had mowed down British infantry as they advanced in waves.[42]

6

The sun and the night added their own particular ingredients of terror to the war in the summer of 1918: fighting took place in a world of shimmering whites and unfathomable black. Thus Ludendorff's final offensive upon the Marne pushed his armies, on 15 July, across a chalky wilderness where all the topsoil had been blown off by previous bombardment. It was a treeless, waterless zone, with no shade, no paths; the only landmarks that remained were the crumbling white embankments of abandoned trenches, infested by rusty snakes of broken barbed wire. Three days later Allied counter-attacks, west of Soissons, advanced through fields of ripe corn, wheat and white barley that stood over two feet high: enough to conceal enemy infantry and machine-guns. The soldiers looked out upon a threatening, quivering sheet of heat that extended, in ripples, to the horizon. And all advancing armies faced the peril of bombardment, which, when it came, threw up great geysers of hot earth – and cut out the light of day.[43]

The erratic association of colours was only one element in a growing pool of violence. There was also the strange mixture of the new with the old, which confused the generals and gave many citizen soldiers a feeling that they lived outside time. No neat patterns of progress emerged in the fighting. No one could point a finger at a specific place at a particular moment and say, 'This was new' or 'This was old.' No theory worked; no process could be detected. Some soldiers did manage to put their faith in novel technologies, but others turned to God, while many simply stared into the empty night. Over 200 tanks gave General Charles Mangin's French Tenth Army the victory when they came rumbling out of the Forest of Villers-Cotterêts on 18 July to startle the right wing of Crown Prince Wilhelm's German Army Group. But it had been a Canadian mounted cavalry that took Moreuil Ridge at the end of March and saved Amiens for the Allies. American Marines at Villers-Cotterêts on 18 July were astonished when they saw emerging from the woods to their left uniformed French dragoons, lancers and armoured cuirassiers to mop up the isolated German positions they had bypassed: it was a scene from Napoleon's century. The prophets of novelty had a few surprises. Scottish soldiers of the British 15th Division were shocked to discover the results of America's 'new' version of 'open warfare': when they came in to relieve the American 2nd Division in the evening of 19 July they found several thousand of the Marines lying dead in swaths where the German machine-guns had caught them.

In the rarefied atmosphere of some staff offices one could hear the debate go on between 'Ancients' and 'Moderns', but the argument was never resolved. The technological enthusiasts of warfare by tank, like the British Minister of Munitions, Winston Churchill, were not entirely aware of what exhaustion meant for the crews of Mark Vs and 'Whippets' in the summer of 1918. Mark Vs advanced on the hard open road at a maximum speed of

4.6 m.p.h.; Whippets, at full throttle, roared ahead at eight. Under the sun the ammunition swelled and thus jammed the guns; the steering was impossible to touch: some engineering genius had lodged the radiator of the Mark V Star inside the steel armoury, with no compensating ventilation. The men inside, during a summer's battle, lost their reason, became delirious and, on occasions, had to be overcome by force. And, of course, slow-moving tanks made easy targets for the German field guns.[44]

The 'war of movement' of 1918 advanced yard by yard, foot by bloody foot. White, red and yellow aeroplanes buzzed overhead.

The future Catholic theologian and biologist Pierre Teilhard de Chardin was a stretcher-bearer in Mangin's army when he watched, from a high observation post, the counter-offensive take place on 18 July. 'There was something implacable about all this, above all; it seemed *inanimate*,' he wrote to his sister. 'You could see nothing of the agony and passion that gave each little moving human dot its own individual character and made them all so many worlds. All you saw was the material development of a clash between two huge material forces.' Teilhard's theory of evolution would one day contain a wry smile of optimism. That was more than could be said of the summer thoughts of the German lieutenant Rudolf Binding: 'This generation has no future, and deserves none. Anyone who belongs to it lives no more.'[45]

Ludendorff's offensives had knocked the top half of the drunken 'S' further out of skew. The Allies' first task was to recover lost ground and reduce the most menacing German salients, especially outside Paris. The strategic significance behind Mangin's counter-offensive of 18 July had been that Allied guns had managed to dominate the important railway junction and main road connecting Soissons with Château-Thierry. This sort of fact was the vital concern in the weeks and months that followed. It was the roads and rails that fanned the plain which determined Allied military plans for the remainder of the war.

The reason was simple. In August 1914 some fifty-four German divisions had passed between the Belgian–Dutch frontier to the north and the French town of Metz to the south. By the spring of 1919 the Germans had over 200 divisions stationed along a great arc about 350 miles in length. They were supported by field guns, mortars, machine-guns, aeroplanes and every other instrument the war had invented in four years. Behind them lay the plain – but also the great Belgian ancient massif of the Ardennes, which in places was a veritable mountain range.

In no way would the Germans be able to retreat at the speed at which they advanced, even if that were their intention (which it was not). There were only two routes of escape: to the north and to the south of the Ardennes. If the Allies could manage to block these two 'points' (though these formed the greater part of the plain), then they could destroy the German Army.[46]

Vague plans had been presented by Foch as early as May. But it was only after Mangin's offensive that the Allies met – on 24 July in Foch's gabled Château Bombon (Poincaré, who had no sense of humour, insisted on calling the place 'Pomponne') – to lay down their intentions. There was the usual discussion of war mathematics. Thousands of troops were being hospitalized and dying not as a direct result of combat but because of the 'Spanish flu'. (What the generals did not know was that the Germans were suffering more.) Foch pushed for an all-out offensive, along the whole front. Haig had his doubts. Pétain said it was impossible. The Americans did not yet have an army. But the general idea of a pincer movement at the north and the south was accepted; both areas were rich in industry and minerals, and both were the sites of railway junctions – Germany's only routes of escape.

This set the positions of the armies. British armies would apply the pinch in the north; the new American Army would push in the south. How exactly this would be achieved was, again, left to local initiative. In July 1918 it was thought that the task of clearing out enemy salients at Château-Thierry, Amiens and Saint-Mihiel would be enough on the agenda for that year. The pinch would begin in 1919. *'L'édifice commence à craquer,'* Foch cheerfully repeated at Bombon; *'tout le monde à la bataille!'*[47]

The point of juncture between the French and the British on the Somme would be critical, for here the two Allies would advance together and thus eventually tighten their grip on the trapped enemy. Oddly, that point of juncture was found near a town called Roye, where Louis XVIII had stopped to form his government after the Battle of Waterloo. Roye, where the front turned from south to south-east, carried some significance in the troubled history of Anglo-French relations. Co-ordination was essential here if the Allied 'hinge' was to be successfully converted into a hammer.

There was, of course, a lot of argument. Should the main thrust be made from the south (as Foch desired) or from the north (as Haig demanded)? The two armies involved were Henry Rawlinson's British Fourth Army and Eugène Debeney's French First. Rawlinson thought the French general lacked fire in his stomach. Harbord described Debeney as 'a typically provincial Frenchman' who, as Debeney himself admitted, found staff work a 'heavy burden' and preferred to be in the company of his troops.[48]

But, whatever the temperamental differences, Foch eventually agreed to place Debeney's army temporarily under Haig's command and to concentrate on a northern attack – a combined offensive upon German positions that still threatened the vital railway junction at Amiens. On 7 August Foch issued one of his exhortatory orders of the day: 'Yesterday I said to you: Obstinacy, Patience, your American comrades are coming. Today I say to you: Tenacity, Boldness, and Victory must be yours.' Before dawn the next morning a British barrage opened up that sounded 'like a colony of giants slamming iron doors'. Two thousand of Rawlinson's guns had started with a single crash; over 400 tanks moved ahead in the mist, along with the British 1st Cavalry Brigade. In the sky there was a constant buzz as fleets of aircraft of the recently formed Royal Air Force flew in to provide cover.

'As the sun set on 8th of August on the battlefield,' ran the official German report, 'the greatest defeat which the German Army had suffered since the beginning of the War was an accomplished fact. The positions between the Avre and the Somme, which had been struck by the enemy attack were nearly completely annihilated.'[49]

7

On the other side of the Belgian Ardennes the August sun shone as brightly as it had before the war. The thermal resort of Spa – with its arcades and open markets, its casino, its great neoclassical bathhouse, its rococo hotels and private pavilions stringed with wrought-iron balconies – was a picture of the world 'very brilliant' abandoned in 1914 by the violence. The town was both vulgar and beautiful, popular and noble; above all, it was still peaceful. Up the steep cobbled south end of the Rue Royale, beyond the fountain of laughing cherubim, lay the Hôtel Britannique. Since March 1918 this imposing structure of black-striped walls and art-deco bay windows had housed Germany's Supreme Command.

Behind the hotel wound a narrow mountain lane; to follow it was like climbing into an eagle's nest. Soldiers guarded it. Trees hid the nineteenth-century villa at the summit, along with its garden and fish pond. Underneath the building, army engineers had constructed a concrete bunker and passages which could provide quick routes of escape – for here was the residence of Kaiser Wilhelm II.

Even at the beginning of the war the Kaiser was complaining that his General Staff was giving him no information. 'If people in Germany think I am the Supreme Commander,' he had whispered to one of his dinner guests in November 1914, 'they are grossly mistaken. I drink tea, saw wood, and go for walks, which please the gentlemen.' His life had become increasingly remote as the war progressed. In March 1918, Supreme Command had insisted on the dismissal of the Chief of the Civil Cabinet for no apparent reason; the Kaiser fought desperately to maintain his right to choose the members of his own household, but he eventually capitulated. His wife suffered a stroke in late spring. Since the Allied counter-offensive of 18 July he had spoken of himself as 'a defeated War Lord' and asked his dinner companions to 'show consideration'. He had no appetite, he refused conversation; during his sleepless nights he had visions of all his English and Russian relatives and all the ministers and generals of his own reign marching past and mocking him (only Queen Maude of Norway showed some sign of friendship). Admiral Georg von Müller, Chief of the Naval Cabinet, tried to cheer him up with news of sinkings in the Atlantic, but when he wanted to introduce the Kaiser to the brilliant U-boat Captain von Nostitz und Jänkerdorf, who had 'just returned from a trip to the North American coast', the Kaiser retorted that 'his house was not a hotel' (though he later relented). The Kaiser had his own peculiar way of turning defeat into victory. 'A very unpleasant evening with His Majesty,' recorded Müller in his diary on 2 August; he 'terms our defeat on the Marne as the greatest defeat the enemy has ever suffered. Piles of American corpses, etc . . .'[50]

On the evening of 8 August came disastrous news from the Somme: French, British and Canadian troops had broken through the German front to a depth of seven miles. 'It's very strange', remarked the gloomy Kaiser, 'that our men cannot get used to tanks.'[51]

But on this one occasion he took the initiative. To find out what had happened, he made a quick trip to Ludendorff's forward headquarters in France, where he arrived on 10 August. Ludendorff immediately offered his resignation, which both the Kaiser and Hindenburg refused. Ludendorff confessed that he could no longer guarantee military victory. The Kaiser became quiet and meditative, then said, 'I see that I must balance accounts. We are at the end of our ability to do anything. The war must be ended.' And he concluded before the shocked silence of the General and the Field Marshal, 'I will expect you, gentlemen, at Spa in the next few days.'[52]

So, by will of the Kaiser, a balance sheet of the world war was to be drawn up at Spa by the military authorities, in front of the Kaiser and in the company of civilian representatives of the Reich. It was a moment when the relationship of the powers which governed Germany could have changed.

The two military chiefs arrived in Spa by train at 8 a.m. on Tuesday, 13 August.[53] Rumours had been going around in Berlin that Ludendorff was a 'completely broken man', but this was far from the truth. The Allied success of the 8th had, for one who had counted on the weakness of British forces following the German offensives of spring, been a serious shock. Even worse had been the reports of breakdown in German military discipline. 'I was told of glorious valour but also of behaviour which, I openly confess, I should not have thought possible in the German Army,' recalled Ludendorff in his memoirs; this was why, looking back, he called August 'the black day of the German Army'. However, during the weekend, the remains of General von der Marwitz's Second Army had managed a remarkable withdrawal: German forces were not trapped by the action of 8 August, for the formidable defences of the Hindenburg Line still lay behind them. At Spa, Hindenburg and Ludendorff would argue for measures of improved discipline and for a new strategy of defence. Those who saw them found nothing broken in their spirits at all.[54]

Ludendorff is commonly regarded as the 'dictator' of Germany by the summer of 1918. He was, but this was by default of political authority – a phenomenon that had developed in Germany long before the war, had been one of the chief causes of the war, and was now seriously aggravated by the war. Ludendorff held the initiative in German policy in 1918 because there was no one else to. By 1918 the Army controlled practically every aspect of German life. It ran local administration, it was responsible for newspaper censorship, it organized the main economic and industrial forces in the country, it set down rules of assembly, and, of course, it laid down the policy of running the occupied territories – including sinister racial plans for German 'living space' in the East. But the soldiers were acting in a vacuum, performing only the duties for which their narrow professional formation had prepared them. When one of the Kaiser's relatives, Prince Max of Baden,[55] first met Ludendorff in February 1918 he found a man who 'shook inwardly'; 'it was like the quivering of a man's frame after a bodily effort which has gone beyond his strength. His mood was much rather "I must" than "I will."' Prince Max was convinced that a grand act of statesmanship would have overcome Ludendorff; indeed, it was what he was half waiting for. But 'this assault was not made'.[56]

The two representatives of civilian authority who arrived in Spa on 13 August were not the kind of personalities who could lead such an assault. One was the Chancellor, an old man, Count Georg von Hertling. As Prime Minister of Bavaria he had proved himself to be a person of independent mind, and it had been for this reason that in the previous October the parliamentary majority in the Reichstag had pushed his candidature as Chancellor in the place of the bumbling Michaelis; Hertling was Supreme Command's man. The other representative was the Foreign Secretary, Rear Admiral Paul von Hintze, a naval officer, who astonished everybody by his diplomatic skills but nevertheless proved no substitute for his predecessor, Richard von Kühlmann. Kühlmann, in June, had made a speech to the Reichstag which concluded with the perfectly sane comment that 'given the enormous extent of this war of coalitions and the number of powers involved in it, an absolute end is hardly to be expected from military decisions alone, without recourse to diplomatic discussions'. As Admiral von Müller noted in his diary at the time, it might have been the truth, but it was not exactly tactful 'in view of the mood of the German nation'. There were howls from the benches of the Conservatives, the National Liberals and the Fatherland Party, all claiming that Kühlmann was undermining army and civilian morale; the press took up the issue, and then Supreme Command stepped in. Kühlmann – the man who had opened negotiations with the Bolsheviks at Brest-Litovsk – was dismissed on 8 July.[57]

It is incredible that, at the moment of the nation's great crisis in mid-August 1918, Germany's parliament remained in summer recess. Again, this could not be wholly blamed on Supreme Command: there were party leaders, including those of the Catholic Centre and the Social Democrats, who were hoping to benefit from the Reichstag's temporary inactivity.

Extraordinarily complicated political manoeuvres were going on in Berlin at this time. One of the men involved – he had ambitions of becoming Foreign Secretary – was Prince Max of Baden, the advocate of statesmanlike 'assault'. As heir to the throne of the Grand Duchy of Baden, Prince Max could boast of contacts that no member of the Reichstag could claim. Some of his cousins were army commanders who wrote regular reports on conditions at the front. He had important friends in business and industry. He had links with America. He knew the pacifists in Switzerland and the pacifists in Holland. He had uncles, aunts, nephews and nieces who reigned in neutral and Allied kingdoms. He even enjoyed contacts with the British Conservative Party. But, unlike Matthias Erzberger, he was not a party man. He had in fact opposed Erzberger's Peace Resolution of July 1917 on the grounds that it was untimely and undignified and would 'have got on the soldiers' nerves'. Many of the leaders of the moderate and centre parties had hoped that Prince Max would then become Chancellor – he would be able to use his name and yet, at the same time, 'stand apart from the parties' and thus give Germany, for the first time since Bismarck, a true 'statesmanlike' policy.[58]

There was a genuine element of *Realpolitik* in the foreign policy he proposed. A 'peace of understanding' he argued, could be established only at the right moment – when German military power was at its height. In the meantime Germany would have to establish its good name by a systematic use of the 'psychological method' – what we would call propaganda – to weaken the enemy behind the front. Prince Max advocated a declaration that would guarantee Belgian independence, not for the sake of the Belgians but because this would drive a wedge between Britain and France. His interests in the 'psychological method' had led him to propose his candidature as Minister of Propaganda in May, when there had been a short lull in the fighting. By summer his banker friend Max Warburg, from Hamburg, was campaigning for him to be named Foreign Secretary.[59]

But there were those in Supreme Command who had other plans for him. On 12 August two General Staff officers presented a memorandum that proposed to make Prince Max Chancellor for the 'new mobilization' and the 'revival of our inner force'. The Prince was perhaps not as innocent of this manoeuvre as he claims to have been in his memoirs, for three days later he was writing to his 'cousin', the Kaiser, 'The Battle of Ideas is now raging, and in the battle we must be victors, if we are to emerge as victors from the war.' This kind of radical departure from complacent politics would have served Germany better in the years before the war, but now the hour was late.[60]

In the end, Prince Max was not invited to Spa. But his close associate Colonel Hans von Haeften did accompany the current Foreign Secretary, Admiral von Hintze, on his journey from Berlin. At Spa, Haeften managed to speak to Ludendorff before any of the civilian authorities had a chance for an interview. He found the General 'calm, but very grave'; it was not the loss of the territory on the Somme that worried him so much as the morale of the troops and the effect that pacifist elements in the rear were having. Ludendorff urged Haeften to accept the post of Minister of Propaganda that had been offered him in Berlin. He assured Haeften that the front could hold out until late autumn, which would give the government enough time to 'take all necessary measures' to establish a peace.[61]

Hintze met Hindenburg and Ludendorff at the Hôtel Britannique early in the morning of 13 August. The confidence of the two men surprised him. Ludendorff, however, admitted that it would no longer be possible to compel the enemy to accept peace 'by the offensive', though he abruptly added that 'we should be able, through a strategic defensive, to weaken the enemy's spirit and gradually bring him to terms'. Clearly, Ludendorff was thinking as a soldier; diplomacy was not his problem.[62]

Another meeting, in the presence of Chancellor von Hertling, began at 10 a.m. Hindenburg and Ludendorff began by outlining the military situation, which, if it 'had changed for the worse', could still be turned 'to break the enemy's will' and force him to sue for peace. Ludendorff returned to his obsession with German morale and the need to counter enemy propaganda that was aimed at German civilians.

Hintze, obviously more concerned with the actual way in which diplomatic overtures to the West could be made, spoke of Germany's war aims and particularly the future of Belgium and Poland.

'Why bring up Belgium?' interrupted Ludendorff. 'That question has been settled in black and white.'

Hintze carried on regardless. He pointed out the weakness of Germany's allies: Austria-Hungary was on her last legs; Bulgaria was ready to desert; and Turkey was launching her own campaign against Armenians in the Caucasus which was of no value to Germany at all.

There were no hard feelings. The meeting was adjourned with no conclusions drawn; the civilian and military authorities went their own ways, like ships that had passed in the night.

The next morning Hintze woke up in a sweat. He realized that Supreme Command had nothing that even approached a political programme, while the military situation was hardly as reassuring as the chiefs seemed to make out. He telephoned Chancellor von Hertling to say that he was going to ask the Kaiser directly for permission to make peace overtures to the West, and he announced that if the Kaiser did not support him he would resign.

'I am an old man,' replied Hertling. 'Let me go first.'

But they had no time for a private interview with the Kaiser. The Crown Council was due to begin at 10 a.m., so they immediately set off for the meeting. Kaiser Wilhelm entered and took his chair. He was accompanied by the Crown Prince and three members of the imperial suite. Hindenburg and Ludendorff also attended.

The Chancellor opened with a devastating report on Germany's internal situation, describing the shortages of food and clothing, along with clear evidence of war-weariness. Ludendorff interrupted with a demand for measures that would establish more civilian discipline.

Hintze, with tears in his eyes, outlined the international situation. The enemy, he said, were expecting victory and were more willing to fight than ever because they knew that time was working in their favour. The neutrals had by now lost all sympathy for Germany's cause. And no help could be expected from Germany's allies. But Hintze had evidently lost his resolve of a few hours earlier and concluded rather lamely that 'we are compelled to bear the military situation in mind in deciding upon the political course we should take'. In other words, he was leaving the decision to others.

The Crown Prince, who in late July had been demanding the opening of negotiations 'through neutral channels', merely endorsed Ludendorff's call for 'stronger discipline' at home.

The Kaiser pointed out that English harvests had been bad and that many enemy vessels had been sunk, so that 'it is possible that England will gradually begin to think of peace'. But he agreed with Hintze's assessment of the deteriorating international situation. 'We must find a suitable moment in which to come to an understanding with the enemy,' he concluded, and he suggested that the King of Spain or the Queen of the Netherlands might be of some help here.

'A suitable moment': that became the chief refrain in the meeting. The old Chancellor immediately took it up. 'Such a moment', he said, 'might present itself after the next successes with the enemy.'

'I hope in spite of everything', remarked Hindenburg in conclusion, 'that we will be able to stay on French soil and thus eventually enforce our will upon the enemy.' Those present felt that no enterprise to which this calm, dignified and steadfast man had given his blessing could possibly go wrong.

The civilian and military authorities once more separated, all hoping that 'a suitable moment' would soon come when diplomatic overtures to the enemy could be made.

But one man, biding his time on Baden's shores of Lake Constance, was not happy. When Colonel von Haeften reported back to Prince Max, the Prince became furious over the inaction. 'What the balance sheet of the world war on 14 August demanded', he recorded, 'was a change in programme, in other words, a change of government.' He was thinking in terms of a 'Government of National Defence' – such as the French had set up in 1792 and again in 1870. Why couldn't Germany do it?[63]

On the same day that the Crown Council met, Wilhelm received at Spa an important guest, young Kaiser Karl of Austria-Hungary. Karl had come to plead in person for an end to the war; his empire was collapsing under the effects of starvation rations and nationalist demands. Karl's birthday was celebrated in Wilhelm's villa the following Saturday. One cannot imagine it being a very festive occasion.[64]

The German government, in the meantime, was not totally inactive on the diplomatic front. Negotiations were kept open with the Russian Bolsheviks, who by August were only too grateful to have at least one power recognize them. On 27 August 'supplementary treaties' were signed in which Russia ceded sovereignty over Livonia and Estonia, and recognized the independence of Georgia. The Bolsheviks also agreed to pay an indemnity of 6 billion marks for damage done to German property and for Soviet. nationalizations; in addition they promised to deliver to Germany one-quarter of the production of the Baku oilfield.[65]

German ambitions had not yet been quelled by the defeat of 8 August.

8

General Debeney, whose French First Army would remain at the right wing of British forces until the end of the war, was envious of the way the British reported fighting on the front. They divided operations into 'battles' – like the 'Battle of Amiens', the 'Battle of Cambrai' or the 'Battle of the Sambre' – and 'the public understood'. French reporting, on the other hand, was 'presented to opinion with a greyness [*une grisaille*] that provided no landmark to attract one's attention'. British reporting presented the story in nice simple stages. But was it the truth? The more one explores conditions on the front, the more one is tempted to accept French *grisaille* as the reality.[66]

The 'war of movement' may have begun with Ludendorff's first offensive in spring 1918; all the same, old-style trench campaigns were still going on in the following autumn. Will Holmes of 15th Battalion, the Hampshire Regiment, remembered the day he lost his leg: 'On September 4, 1918, we marched to our front line trenches near the villages of Meteren and Wyteschaete by Messines Ridge. After liberal rum rations we went "over the top" at dawn.' His kneecap was shattered by a machine-gun bullet; others were killed and maimed. 'The cries of the wounded for stretcher bearers were pitiful.'[67]

Horrors that would have been incredible to anyone before 1914 were the daily dose for soldiers on the front in 1918. Down the straight old Roman road from Amiens to Vermand the German dead lay everywhere, their white faces staring glassily to the sky, a chest blown out, a head disfigured:

> You love us when we're heroes, home on leave
> Or wounded in a mentionable place . . .[68]

Men fell from the air in flames; others were torched to death on the ground, died neglected, were gassed, stabbed by bayonets, or machine-gunned down. The manhood of the Western world was bled white. French soldiers, with gaunt faces, still travelled in boxcars to the front through the *gares régulatrices*. Half the British Army was now under nineteen years of age.

But a certain macabre logic did lie behind it all: Germany was retreating, the rivers and the contours of the northern plain always determining her position. The winding river Somme and its associated canals provided one barrier to the Allies; 'the Boches are trying to get behind water', it was said after Amiens. Beyond that lay the eternal autumn shades of barbed wire on the Hindenburg Line. Further east still, the Germans were building a new system of fortifications: the Herman Stellung, the Hagen Stellung and the Freya Stellung. Then, if the situation really became desperate for Germany, the river Meuse could become the site of a prolonged winter battle – or a winter's pause.

Germany supplied her armies by road and rail. The most critical line ran from the munition factories of Westphalia through Cologne to martyred Liège and then, across the north of the Ardennes, to Namur and the occupied French fortress town of Maubeuge. Day and night the freight wagons rumbled on. Through Maubeuge ran a lateral line that supplied the whole German western front – northward to Ghent and Bruges, southward to Hirson, Mezières and Metz. Allied commanders were aware of this line, but few of them dreamed – until 8 August – that this could in 1918 be the place of battle. No specific plans had been laid down to take it.

Even after 8 August, locally led armies fought for locally defined aims. It was *la grisaille* for anyone who lived it. In typical fashion, the great success of 8 August before Amiens was followed, on the 9th, by a 'stiffening of German resistance' and Allied slowdown; then mounting casualties. The disagreement between Foch and Haig over the town of Roye became serious. After further fruitless action on the 11th, Haig called off his joint frontal attack with Debeney and waited for heavy guns to be brought in for a full artillery battle. Foch insisted by personal telegram and directive that the assault on Roye not be delayed, though even Debeney, reportedly in a state of tears by the 14th,[69] was beginning to have his doubts.

In the meantime Haig – unknown to Foch and both the General Staff and the government in London – transferred some of his forces northward to reinforce his his First and Third Army fronts between the Ancre and Scarpe rivers; he would unlock the south by a thrust in the north. It was one of the great military manoeuvres of the war.

On Thursday afternoon, 15 August – a sacred day for the Catholic Foch – Haig drove out to the Commander-in-Chief's new headquarters at Sarcus. 'I spoke to Foch quite straightly,' recorded Haig in his diary, 'and let him understand' – he underlined his words – 'that *I was responsible to my Government and fellow citizens for the handling of the British forces.*'[70] Foch, to his credit, was ready to listen. Nevertheless, Debeney's First Army reverted to French command the next morning.

The following three weeks must count among the most extraordinary moments in the history of the British Army. Haig had, without the beat of a drum, supplied reinforcements to the northern sector of the Somme, between Monchy-le-Preux and Miraumont; Haig's initiative was picked up by local command and local units – most notable among which were the Canadians, the New Zealanders, and the Australians. A blow was dealt here, then there; the German counter-attacks were often swift and brutal, but at other times whole divisions simply melted away. Fighting developed along a thirty-five-mile front, then for forty miles, north to south; then the French First, Third and Tenth Armies joined in a terrible fray.

No one had ever seen battle on such a scale. No grand strategic scheme lay behind it. No single commander controlled it. The 'Battle of Bapaume'? the 'Battle of the Scarpe'? It was a widening, deepening whirl of violence, pushed on by men many of whose names are unknown. Roye fell to the Allies on 26 August; the ruins of Bapaume were entered on the 29th. A thousand Australians, without the support of tanks, crossed a hidden bend of the Somme and took the bare but heavily fortified Mont Saint-Quentin on 31 August – that opened up the flattened town of Péronne and a bloody contest to its south, along the so-called 'Drocourt–Quéant switch'. Heroes and cowards alike were drawn into the tempest; the slaughter was indescribable. By 3 September Germany's armies were back where they had started in March, at the fearsome Hindenburg Line.[71]

Part of Foch's problem with Haig arose from the military intentions of the 'Associate Power', the United States. By August there were over a million and a half American troops in France, most of them still in training in preparation for the decisive campaign of 1919. No one doubted the significance of the American contribution to the future Allied success. No one, except possibly Haig, thought that that success would arrive before 1919. In August, when asked when he thought the war would end, Foch replied, 'about next autumn – in twelve months'.[72]

The new American First Army had been positioned in what was by now the quiet front of Verdun, to the right and south of French forces, in accordance with the vague plan of a 'pinch', as enunciated at Bombon in July, but more particularly so that it could play its part in the task set for 1918: that of clearing out German salients.

One of these salients was Saint-Mihiel, to the south of Verdun. During a minor sideshow in the great 'Battle of the Marne' of September 1914, the Germans had seized this small town on the left bank of the Meuse. The action had created a protrusion in the Western Front that the Germans would hold for the next four years; it pointed at Paris, and it cut off French railway communications with the north-east. The aim of the American First Army – perfectly in accord with Allied plans in July – was to reduce it.

But the Allied situation had dramatically changed by late August. The Americans seemed unaware of the fact. Thousands poured into the ports of western France to prepare for the great campaign of 1919 and lend a hand to

President Wilson's Great Abstract War for Democracy; if their army had been placed on the Pyrenees, on the Atlas Mountains or next to Mount Kilimanjaro it would have been the same war for them. Why should even General 'Black Jack' Pershing, from Missouri, worry himself with the shape of tiny Europe's plains? The critical issue for him, as it was for his crusading President from Georgia, was the maintenance of an independent American army.

By August nine American divisions had been involved in fighting on the British and French fronts. Pershing would have preferred to pull them all out and integrate them into his growing American Army; he eventually agreed to leave two divisions in the northern Belgian sector, but the rest were pulled out in August.

An utterly illogical situation thus began to develop: American troops were being withdrawn from the area that was rapidly developing into the war's epicentre, in order to reinforce the by then silent southern sector of Verdun. Moreover, an offensive upon Saint-Mihiel would lead the American Army eastward towards Metz and the blue Vosges of Lorraine – not an easy terrain for battle in the best of circumstances. If the Americans were to converge with Allied forces, they would now have to change orientation by ninety degrees, heading northward up the Meuse and across the heavily fortified Argonne Forest to Mezières and a city of sinister memory for the French, Sedan: thirty miles of terror. The American Army had locked itself in a dilemma.

On 31 August, with an eighty-mile front now blazing between Lons and Soissons, Marshal Foch (he had received his baton that month) visited American Army Headquarters in an attempt to persuade General Pershing to abandon his useless offensive on Saint-Mihiel and, instead, shift several American divisions north to join the French Second Army in a joint attack up the Meuse on 15 September. Pershing was furious at any idea of splitting his forces. Foch was furious at the American refusal to assist in the huge combat developing to the north: '*Voulez-vous aller à la bataille?*' spluttered the Marshal.

The interpreter was so embarrassed that he hesitated to translate; but Pershing understood the question. 'Most assuredly,' replied the General, 'but as an American army and in no other way.'

'That means it will take a month!'

'If you will assign me a sector I will take it at once,' said Pershing; and when Foch wondered aloud which one that could possibly be, Pershing responded, 'Whatever you say' – whether it was the Pyrenees, the Atlas Mountains or Kilimanjaro was a matter of total indifference to the General.[73]

Nevertheless, the exchange set afoot a practical, if terrifying, programme for executing a pincer movement across northern France, beginning in late September. It was designed to break down the whole Hindenburg system and shatter Germany's supportive lateral rail line. If it worked, Germany could be defeated within a month.

*　　*　　*

The plan was put together by Haig and Foch, and consisted essentially of a series of attacks mounted first in the south towards Mezières, then in the north behind Cambrai, and then upon the Hindenburg Line itself in the centre. Haig referred to the opening of the operation as 'Z-Day'.[74]

Z-Day would begin with an offensive launched on 26 September by the Americans northward on the Meuse–Argonne sector. In order to accomplish this and at the same time preserve the unity of their army, the Americans proposed the worst possible solution: they would go ahead with their Saint-Mihiel offensive, as planned, on 10 September and then turn their whole army around in a fortnight and march north sixty miles along hill tracks designed centuries earlier for peasants and pedlars. It was, even for an experienced army, a complicated manoeuvre. But the Americans were not experienced.

The operation was more absurd than any of the Allies then realized: unknown to them, the Germans, exhausted by the heavy combat in the north, were already planning to pull their forces out of the Saint-Mihiel salient. They started the movement on 10 September. Their big guns were rolled away, the reserves were withdrawn; none of the barbed-wire obstacles were maintained. The troops that remained were chiefly Austro-Hungarians, who had no intention of continuing the fight (some of the national minorities openly sympathized with the Allies). A complete withdrawal was to take place on the 12th – the very day the unexpected American attack came (after the Americans had been delayed two days for supply reasons).[75]

The offensive is recorded as having been an immense success. The Americans cleared the whole salient in under forty hours, liberated 200 square miles of French soil, and opened up French rails to the north-east. The popular American racing-car driver Eddie Rickenbacker made news by shooting down, from a French one-seater plane, several German balloons and aircraft that flew with Hermann Goering, the successor to the 'Red Baron'. Casualties had apparently been light: the Americans announced only 7,000 lost. Pershing explained to Brigadier General Dennis Nolan that the victory was due to the superior nature of the American character: that of immigrants who had left old Europe behind and forged a great nation out of the wilderness; men with a will-power and spirit that Europe lacked. Nobody at the time mentioned that a rate of loss of 3,500 men a day was the equivalent of rates that Haig had sustained at Passchendaele in 1917.[76]

Colonel George C. Marshall, a master planner, was given the task of transferring over half a million Americans and a quarter of a million Frenchmen to the new sector of the Meuse–Argonne. An immense traffic jam developed, aggravated by a complete lack of co-ordination between French and American staff. Ninety thousand horses were required to haul ammunition, fuel and medical supplies across a land turning to mud under the kind of misty rain which had dogged most of the war. Though the engineers worked day and night, hundreds of horses were left to die by the side of the tiny roads, and whole convoys of food and supplies were abandoned. The men trudged on, mile after mile, by foot.

But Z-Day, 26 September, arrived and at dawn, as scheduled, the American First Army with the aid of General Henri Gouraud's French Fourth Army on their left, led an attack up the left bank of the Meuse and into the tangled landscape of the Argonne Forest with the hidden fortifications of Germany's Kriemhilde Stellung. The next day they came up against the machine-gun nests on the heights of Montfaucon; 'enemy resistance stiffened'.

That same Friday the British First and Fourth Armies attacked positions south of the Arras–Cambrai road. German defences in this northern point of the Somme were made up not only of the wide and deep Canal du Nord, but also of marshes liberally peppered with armed concrete fortifications. In the Argonne, the Americans faced five enemy divisions; Haig's two armies advanced on fifty-seven.

On 28 September the Flanders Army Group, under the command of King Albert of Belgium, pushed across the old battlefield of Ypres, beyond Bellewarde and Westhock Ridges, and on to the Zonnebeke Redoubt. It was grey, it was raining; the land turned to bog. There must have been a regret or two among British troopers when they learned that the village of Passchendaele had been taken that day – by the Belgians.

On 29 September Rawlinson's British Fourth Army led an assault on the Siegfried Stellung, the most awesome of all the positions on the Hindenburg Line. Its most formidable obstacle was the Canal Saint-Quentin, which the 46th Territorials – the 'Terries' did not have a reputation for heroics – crossed with lifebelts, floating piers, collapsible boats, mud mats, lifelines and scaling ladders under the cover of fog. Scarlet-painted German Albatross triplanes swooped over the lines 'like huge red birds diving down on the look-out for their prey', but they found it too late: the Hindenburg Line had been breached.[77]

Photographs of a multitude of British citizen soldiers on the steep banks of the Canal Saint-Quentin – some cheering, others simply exhausted by the combat – indicate the first hint of a growing but still incredible thought; the Great War might be ended in the year 1918.

Ends

1

On 27 September, from the steps of the New York Metropolitan Opera House, President Woodrow Wilson delivered a speech about his notion of 'impartial justice'. He spoke in handsome generalities about the need for a balanced peace, administered 'with no discrimination between those to whom we wish to be just and those to whom we do not wish to be just'. Individual or specific group interests would not provide the base for the final settlement, made under the aegis of a new world organization, the 'League of Nations': 'There can be no leagues or alliances, or special covenants and understandings within the general and common family of the League of Nations'; nor would there be 'special, selfish economic combinations'. All treaties would be known to the entire community after this 'final triumph of justice and fair dealing'.[1]

Ten days earlier, from the tribune of the Senate in Paris, the French Prime Minister, Georges Clemenceau, had also made a speech. It too was built upon generalities, but its tone was very different. Clemenceau used the language of earlier French war leaders, Danton and Gambetta; he employed the rhetoric of the French Revolution of 1792 and the Paris siege of 1870. He made no reference to any kind of international order. He placed his faith on military force. 'I hear it said that peace cannot be brought by a military decision,' he remarked, and then he paused to hammer out the words 'That's not what the Germans said when they launched upon the peace of Europe the horrors of war.' He spoke of the countryside devastated by war, the towns and villages ruined, the pillaging, and the institutionalized system of slave labour imposed by the occupier on the north of France. 'The most terrible accounting of people to people is opened,' he said. 'It will be paid.'

Clemenceau had been fighting French nationalists throughout his long political career, but he would not deny he was a patriot. He concluded with lines borrowed from the 'Marseillaise': *'Allez donc, enfants de la patrie*, go on and free the people from the last furies of blatant force! Go on to victory untainted! All France, all thinking humanity is behind you!'[2]

It was easier to speak of 'impartial justice' from the steps of a New York opera house than it was in either London or Paris, where war had been a part of life for four years.

Peace could not be brought by military decision? The advance of Allied armies on the Western Front transformed the state of politics in Germany. That change occurred the day that British forces breached the Hindenburg Line.

Until the last days of September 1918 the policy followed by the German authorities, both civilian and military, remained essentially unaltered; their aims had barely shifted, and the faith that these could eventually be brought about by their armies had hardly wavered. On 12 September the German Vice-Chancellor, Friedrich von Payer, offered the West his version of the *status quo ante bellum*: Alsace-Lorraine would remain German, and Belgium would be granted independence on the guarantee of a 'parallelism' between German and Belgian interests (i.e. Germany would maintain economic and political controls). The German Reich, the Vice-Chancellor was also pleased to announce, would no longer demand war reparations from the West. It was another matter in the East: 'In the East we have peace, and that remains for us peace, whether this pleases our Western neighbours or not.'

The Chancellor, Count von Hertling, continued to speak of Germany's 'maximum interest' in the Lorraine coal-mining basin of Briey and Longwy. The Foreign Secretary, Admiral von Hintze, limited himself to non-binding conversations with Dutch and Swiss agents that yielded nothing. In general, the government's policy was to avoid major diplomatic initiatives until the enemy 'frenzy' had subsided; it waited, as in August, for 'a suitable situation' to develop. In other words, the German government had no policy at all.[3]

Prince Max of Baden, in the meantime, continued to receive the attention of his vast private network of dukes, counts, soldiers and prominent politicians. He was still an advocate of the 'psychological method', which he hoped would provide 'the German spirit to help the German sword'. As he put it in a speech before the Duchy of Baden's Chamber of Deputies on 22 August, his kind of national government would act as the 'guardians and physicians of the people's soul'. On 6 September the Prince, with the help of Colonel von Haeften, drew up a government programme that promised 'no peace offer, but a proclamation of war aims and a call for national defence'.[4]

But it was too late to think of such programmes now. The German sword suddenly showed serious signs of buckling. Austria-Hungary, with the 'cry of a drowning man',[5] offered a separate peace to all the enemy powers on 14 September. On 29 September – the same day the Hindenburg Line was breached – Turkey's army in Syria was put to flight and Germany's weak partner in the Balkans, Bulgaria, signed an armistice with an Allied army after barely a fight; this opened up a back to door not only to Austria-Hungary but to Germany itself.

However, it was the break on the Western Front that proved fatal. An eerie kind of ping-pong match, between several players, followed. The play began among the German authorities themselves, between the military men in Spa and the civilians in Berlin. Then Washington was drawn into the match. Then London and Paris. Different plans for stopping the killing bounced from one capital to another, between military councils and civilian councils, between generals, prime ministers and presidents. No umpire was there to mediate; no kind of international organization existed that could weigh the pros and cons.

Did Ludendorff panic? That was the opinion in Berlin. Conflicting reports on peace, armistice offers, collapsing allies and the calamitous state of the army caused all sorts of rumours to spread through the German capital in the first days of October. Inevitably attention turned to Ludendorff, far away in Spa, and a cry of alarm was raised: 'Ludendorff must go; he has lost his nerve.' Yet very few people who actually saw the First Quartermaster General at work during these critical days thought this to be the case. Colonel Bauer, who made several trips between the two towns, did complain about Ludendorff's health – but as an Austrian and a Social Democrat he had every reason to do so. In his memoirs, written only months later, Ludendorff of course vigorously denies panicking; there was, he claims, the 'customary tension' on the front, which he deliberately exaggerated in order to get the slow politicians to act. Historians have since argued that Ludendorff was conducting a shrewd manoeuvre which would get Supreme Command off the hook and saddle the parliamentary Left with responsibility for the war's end.

It was more likely a combination of all these factors – a temporary nervousness, a desire for political aid, linked with a touch of cunning – that lay in Ludendorff's sudden decision to seek an immediate armistice with the enemy. He was, as Prince Max had said of him earlier in the year, a man who 'shook inwardly' over the responsibilities that had fallen upon him. With news arriving of, first, the American offensive in the south, then the Somme, then Flanders, he must have realized that his intention to bring the battle to a standstill on rearward lines – of holding off the enemy to 'dispose them to peace' – was not going to work. A retreat to the Meuse would expose his rail supply lines. A retreat to German frontiers, behind the Ardennes, could be achieved only by a pause, a ceasefire, an honourable armistice.

Ludendorff developed a visionary's kind of faith in this route of escape, as if the old rules of knights' warfare and chivalry still applied in 1918. The question of why the Allies should let Germany withdraw to the Rhine and there regroup her armies was never posed. The war for him had now become too perilous to continue; it had deteriorated into an ignoble 'game of chance'. 'I want to keep my army intact,' he repeated religiously; 'the army requires a breathing space.'[6]

Ludendorff admitted defeat on Saturday morning, 28 September. At 10.30 he telephoned his representative in Berlin, General von Winterfeldt, to inform the Chancellor that the military situation required an immediate demand for peace. He suggested that the government making this demand be of a 'wide national base'. The Foreign Secretary, Admiral von Hintze, on receiving this message decided to leave at once for Spa, having consulted with his colleagues on the means of setting up a government on 'a wide national base'. Before even boarding his train for Spa, Hintze had decided that the request for peace would be sent to President Wilson and that the 'programme of negotiations' would be founded on an acceptance of the Fourteen Points the American President had outlined in his speech of 8 January.

An 'Inter-Party Committee' had been meeting in the Reichstag for the opening of parliament, which, amazingly, was still in summer recess. The Committee passed a resolution criticizing the Chancellor's inactivity. Count von Hertling thought this an opportune moment to resign, for he had no intention of presiding over a 'parliamentary government'. So he too, later that Saturday, boarded a train for Spa, in order to present his resignation to the Kaiser.

Thus Berlin, at this critical moment, had neither the Chancellor nor the Foreign Secretary to provide information. This was felt, throughout a city verging on panic, as an abandonment.

In Spa, at six in the evening, Ludendorff entered Hindenburg's office and said that a request for peace would not be enough; to convince the Americans of Germany's serious intention to end all hostilities, it would have to be a demand for an 'immediate armistice'. Hindenburg agreed, and the decision was formally recorded for the General Staff twenty minutes later.

Kaiser Wilhelm had been spending a few days at his autumn residence, the Schloss Wilhelmshöhe, near Kassel, at the time. He had no idea what was happening on the front, in Spa or in Berlin. He passed that Saturday evening in 'trivial conversation' with his wife, the Kaiserin, who was dressed in 'full regalia, studded with pearls and diamonds'. The next morning, at Supreme Command's request, he set out for Spa, still under illusions about the eventual success of his noble armies.[7]

It was a day of 'glorious sunshine', and the forested hills glowed with every shade of red and yellow. The Kaiser was driven from the station up to the Hôtel Britannique, where he found Admiral von Hintze in grim conference with Hindenburg, Ludendorff and a secretary of the General Staff. Hintze had begun the meeting, as in August, with a summary of the diplomatic situation, and he was thoroughly stunned when Ludendorff interrupted to demand an 'immediate armistice'. Hintze remarked that this would be tantamount to unconditional surrender and could well lead to a revolution in the country and the overthrow of the imperial dynasty. With the arrival of the Kaiser, a Crown Council was immediately held. The Kaiser showed 'sovereign dignity' as the argument for an immediate armistice was repeated before him. Hintze suggested that that His Majesty had to choose between democratizing the government or setting up a dictatorship that would suppress a revolution. 'Nonsense,' replied the Kaiser.

Ludendorff, a professional soldier, showed no willingness to become Germany's dictator at this point, and there was no other candidate, so they launched a new policy of 'revolution from above'. A parliamentary government would have to be set up, just in time to sign an armistice. But, whatever government was created, it would be offered little scope in defining war policy, because the main decision had already been taken at Spa.

As if to ensure this, the next day, in the Kaiser's villa, Hintze and von Hertling (though the latter had already officially resigned as Chancellor) decided to inform the Austrians and the Turks that they were proposing to President Wilson an 'immediate cessation of hostilities' on the basis of his Fourteen Points. With their allies thus informed, there could be no backing out.

Berlin knew nothing of this. A representative of Supreme Command, Major Hilmar von dem Bussche, was hurriedly dispatched to the capital to explain to the party leaders the sudden decline in German military fortunes. The Kaiser and Hindenburg prepared to follow him. In the meantime, a new Chancellor had to be found. The political manoeuvres of the last two months made the choice clear: it would be Prince Max of Baden.[8]

2

'*Der Bademax*', as the Prince was then nicknamed, was neither a pacifist nor a liberal. Later he might be known as the 'Pacifist Prince' or 'Max the Pax', but that was not the case in the first week of October 1918. He had stood out clear and strong against Matthias Erzberger, who had pieced together the left-leaning majority in the Reichstag with the Peace Resolution of July 1917. Prince Max had pressed for a public declaration on Belgium only to prise Britain away from France. 'Belgium', he wrote in January 1918, 'is the only pawn for compensations that we possess.' His speeches and writings give no hint of pacifism. On the day that Ludendorff launched his first offensive he had sent copies of his pamphlet *Ethical Imperialism* to Spa and Berlin. In it he presented moral justification for the 'tremendous strength which we have displayed' and explained that the war had created a new type of German 'who had never before known heroism except in the life of thought'. 'The fortune of war', he mused, 'has done us a service in making this new type of German known all over the world.' No pacifist ever wrote like that. Not realizing the 'meaning of our defeat', he sent further copies of *Ethical Imperialism* to the Kaiser, Ludendorff and Crown Prince Rupprecht after Mangin launched his counter-offensive of 18 July.[9]

It was the military situation that would eventually change his views.

Central to Prince Max's thinking was that 'control of popular psychology is part of the art of war'. 'Today words are battles,' he remarked the first time he read Wilson's Fourteen Points. He was convinced he was involved in 'the spiritual struggle of a thousand years' and, in the process, was determined to remove every hint of German 'war guilt' – '*die Kriegschuld*'.

Prince Max became obsessed with this idea of 'war guilt'. As early as 1916 he was talking about the need to 'keep on hammering certain facts about the origin of the war into the mind of the world, facts which must end by demolishing the dogma of a German attack'. In his view, Poincaré's presidency in France had, from the very start, been aimed at 'the recovery of Alsace-Lorraine'. Russia was, of course, the real guilty power, while Britain turned the conflict into a world war by not remaining neutral. '*Gott strafe England!*' – 'God punish England!' – was the war slogan of Germany, and it was the earnest desire of Prince Max. 'I can never forget the satisfaction with which England pictured the Russian steamroller crushing Germany,' he remarked in an interview in February 1918. Germany had committed no evil; German expansion to east and to west was justifiable. 'We can honestly inscribe on our banners the principle of Right; we need do no wrong in order to extend our power,' he wrote in *Ethical Imperialism*. Prince Max was sure this would one day be proven by 'the incontrovertible result of historical research'. The 'Verdict of History' became Prince Max's guiding angel.[10]

It was Ludendorff who called the Prince a liberal. 'He is a Prince and a Liberal,' the First Quarter Master had told one of Supreme Command's officials in May, 'and when you have said that you have said everything.' But Ludendorff was not a reliable political judge. Prince Max was a defender of aristocracy and monarchy, and he objected strongly to any attempts to set up any form of Western parliamentarian regime, either in his home state of Baden or in Berlin. 'Aristocracy', he wrote, 'is the salt by which democracy shall be salted.' He had very little respect for 'soulless and decrepit parliamentary groups', and regretted that Germany had not yet found a 'born leader' who would give the country's chaotic politics a direction. Such a leader should, he thought, be chosen by 'an authority which stands above party, not with the parties'. He had in mind the Kaiser, to whom he wrote on 15 August and again on 7 September urging a government programme which would make it clear that 'German freedom is better than Western democracy.' The government he was proposing, he claimed, would be 'the last chance for the monarchical idea in general. In the East it has collapsed miserably, in the Western democracies it is long since there has been any room for the free decision of a leading personality.' On 11 September the Kaiser wrote back, 'Our views are essentially one.'[11]

In hindsight, Prince Max's thinking looks sinister: the 'new German' evolved from war, the 'struggle of a thousand years', the control of the masses by propaganda, the battle over 'war guilt', the dislike of 'decrepit parliamentary groups', the yearning for 'German freedom' and the 'born leader'. Certainly the conventional view of Kaiser Wilhelm's last Chancellor as a pacifist and liberal is wrong; but it would also be a mistake to portray him as a proto-Nazi. He was a prince – and an enormously cultivated one at that. He genuinely loved nature, which one can understand, for Baden was one of the most beautiful of the Reich's remaining twenty-three states; his greatest pleasure was to take long walks in the Black Forest. He considered himself a friend of humanity, and had devoted the first years of the war to the well-being of Allied prisoners of war. Now, at fifty-two, he would roll his romantic eyes up to the decorated ceiling of his Karlsruhe palace, soliloquize on the 'advance of humanity' and the 'internal freedom' of the Christian German, the ultimate creation of 'one great human community given to us to realize', damn the 'new paganism' in France and Britain, and then sigh that things could have been better.

He did not like Matthias Erzberger. Erzberger represented for the Prince the very worst of parliamentary politics: a party man, a manipulator without scruple, one who had no experience of the countries and peoples he wished to influence, a character of unlimited confidence, ambition and guile, an ignorant busybody, a commoner. It was with almost a physical repulsion that he had rejected Erzberger's Peace Resolution – 'the misbegotten child of fear and of the Berlin dog days'. But when the Reichstag reassembled in October he would be faced with Erzberger's Majority, an alliance of the Catholic Centre and the parties of the Left.

The programme Prince Max had formulated with Haeften in early September was designed to offer an alternative to a parliamentary government under Erzberger and his Socialist ally Philipp Scheidemann – a 'much feared' ministry. This parliamentary government, warned the Prince, would call into question 'the powers which have governed Germany up to now'. Erzberger, he further accused, was preparing a new peace step in the Reichstag that would amount to 'hands up' to President Wilson and the Americans. Germany, argued Prince Max, faced a choice between an abject peace made by Erzberger 'at the end of the month' or a government that would 'say not a word about peace at this hour and yet visibly strengthen the peace atmosphere in the enemy countries'. But by September Germany had no such choice at all.[12]

The irony of the moment was that Prince Max was forced to seek an alliance with the Reichstag majority. He had been preparing the way since at least July, with the idea that, if open annexationists in his new government suddenly started pleading for peace, the enemy powers would regard this as a bid for surrender. The Prince anticipated that the political Right would go into 'loyal opposition' while the Left would participate in his government. He himself would stand above and apart from politics: his authority would come from the Kaiser.

It is tempting to compare the strange partnership which developed between Prince Max and Erzberger in the last weeks of the Great War with that between an equally odd couple who joined hands at the conclusion of the Napoleonic wars, Talleyrand and Fouché. Talleyrand was a prince, Fouché was a commoner. Talleyrand was the philosopher, Fouché the manipulator. Their relationship was governed by a cordial mutual hatred. But here the parallel ends. Talleyrand's philosophy was founded on economics, and its source of authority was 'the people'. Prince Max's philosophy, on the other hand, was guided by an 'inner freedom' designed to bring life to the 'soul' and 'community' of Germany; not a phrase of economics ever passed his fair lips or even touched his fine pen. Prince Max's authority was innately imperial. As for Erzberger, he had not half the wiliness of a Fouché.

In the second half of September political tensions rose in Germany as news and rumour spread of an approaching military disaster. It was the Progressive deputy (and Prince Max's friend) Conrad Haussmann who had remarked that, when military events developed unfavourably, public morale descended in the same direction, but in geometric relationship.[13] His analysis was amply fulfilled. The press – though heavily censored – complained of hunger rations, the Kaiser fell into silence, Supreme Command drew the curtains across their thermal spa, while the political leaders in Berlin locked themselves up in their 'Inter-Party Committee'. There were calls for Ludendorff's head.

'This dreadful era of scruples must come to an end,' said Haussmann when the first announcements of the Allied general offensive percolated down the Reichstag's corridors. On 30 September Chancellor von Hertling resigned and the Kaiser published his proclamation of a 'Revolution from Above'.

So the old government was gone and there was nothing there to replace it. As British troops crossed the Canal Saint-Quentin, the Inter-party Committee went on debating.

In Dessau, Prince Max – like Talleyrand in Mons after the Battle of Waterloo – was awaiting his hour. He was staying with his sister, the Duchess of Anhalt. He had already drafted a new government programme: there would be no peace offer, but an attempt would be made to enunciate war aims; in foreign policy he would attempt to play on British fears of America; the question of 'war guilt' would be submitted to an international commission once hostilities had ended. The call came in the evening,[14] from one of the Kaiser's advisers: 'to come to Berlin at once'. 'You can expect anything of me but a peace offer,' he assured the Duchess as he set off.

His programme lay in tatters before dawn. On his arrival in Berlin, his friend from Supreme Command, Colonel von Haeften, told him of the decision to appeal to President Wilson, to accept the Fourteen Points and to request an armistice. For a long while Prince Max remained stunned and silent, then he asked, 'I cannot even have till November?' The Colonel replied, 'No.'[15]

The sun did not rise over Berlin on Tuesday, 1 October; it was a cold and grey day, its mysterious heavy and oppressive atmosphere hovering over the large cafés of the town's centre. Dense crowds pressed together outside the telegraph rooms of the newspaper buildings to catch a glimpse of the latest telegrams. 'How pitiful it is,' muttered old men in black bowlers. Morale was below zero.

Walking down the Wilhelmstrasse with Haeften, Prince Max discovered that his old friend was a changed man. His brisk confidence was gone, and in deep gloom he kept on repeating, as if it were a formula, 'The army needs rest, the armistice offer must be issued at once.'

Over the next two days, several of the Prince's closest advisers and associates urged him not to accept the chancellorship. His cousin the Grand Duke of Baden, during a telephone conversation, warned him of the black name any responsibility in the liquidation of the war would give his house. Max Warburg, the banker, told him bluntly, 'Let the soldiers cross the line with a white flag.' But when, late on Tuesday evening, the Prince found himself alone in his hotel he felt that old 'inner freedom' return with a surge and his faith in his programme revived: 'Our situation is not such as to justify this act of despair,' he thought to himself. 'The projected offer makes our situation worse; there is another and better way.'

On Wednesday morning Major von dem Bussche made his report on the military situation to the Reichstag party leaders. Friedrich Ebert of the Social Democrats went as white as death and could not utter a word. Gustav Stresemann of the National Liberals looked as if he had been struck by lightning. The Prussian Minister mumbled as he left the room, 'There is only one thing left now, and that is to put a bullet through one's head' (though he did not do so).

Meanwhile, in Spa, Ludendorff kept up the pressure on the civilians by telegram, telephone and letter. Without a government the note to Wilson could not be sent, but that note, Ludendorff insisted, had to be sent in twenty-four hours. He called Haeften at midnight on Tuesday and demanded that he wake up the exhausted Prince, have him named Chancellor, and then get him to sign the note. 'I want to save my army,' said Ludendorff.

Prince Max, in Berlin, became stubborn. He refused to sign. He clung to such fragments of his programme as remained. If the military situation was so bad, he reasoned, it could hardly be saved by an armistice offer. 'The Offer', as he scornfully called it, was a 'fatal mistake', which would have the most disastrous political consequences. It would advance enemy 'chauvinism'; it would be an admission of defeat. He objected to having his name linked to it; he objected to being summoned when matters had reached such a state of bankruptcy. He said he would need at least a fortnight to create the proper psychological atmosphere for peace. He would first make a speech before the Reichstag announcing 'war aims' corresponding to Wilson's Fourteen Points. He would address the question of 'war guilt'. If the enemy did not accept these terms, then there would have to be an appeal for a *levée en masse*, as in France in 1792 – 'the German people will be called upon to summon up all their powers of willing sacrifice for a last life and death struggle'.[16] In the Inter-Party Committee, Prince Max's candidature for chancellorship was initially supported only by the Progessives (who were not progressive at all), but the other parties could not agree on an alternative candidate. By Thursday, 3 October, Prince Max, as he had foreseen, was making serious inroads into Erzberger's majority. He eventually set up a government on Friday, almost four days after his arrival in Berlin. A notable development was when Friedrich Ebert of the Social Democrats agreed to join, despite Scheidemann's warning that he was entering a 'bankrupt concern'.

Thus for three critical days, 1–3 October, Prince Max was acting as Chancellor without a government. He was alone. His only counsellors were Haeften, who was depressed, and another Berlin representative of Supreme Command, the elegant General von Winterfeldt – the former military attaché to Paris, whom fate had marked out for a historic role. It was a fearsome game. Prince Max liked to quote the famous comment of a Reichstag deputy: 'If you are lying on the ground and someone has got his foot on your stomach, you don't say anything likely to annoy him.'

The Prince, nevertheless, continued to resist pressure from Supreme Command. Did Ludendorff really think he would be able to order around Wilson and Foch in the same way he was attempting to impose his orders on the new Chancellor? Did he honestly imagine the enemy would willingly grant the German Army a rest? Prince Max placed his hopes on the Kaiser and Hindenburg.

They arrived in the capital on Wednesday, 2 October, at midday. The Prince found Hindenburg more optimistic in tone than Ludendorff; and in truth the Allied advance was slowing down. There were some almost comic scenes in Berlin's General Staff building, where the Prince and the Field Marshal sat across a table from each other and stiffly read out prepared statements – often reported in history books as 'conversations'. It soon became clear to Prince Max that Hindenburg's position in fact differed not one jot from Ludendorff's. The most galling experience of them all was the Crown Council held that Wednesday afternoon in the Chancellery. The Kaiser walked in with an imperial air. 'What a state of nerves Berlin is in,' he said. Prince Max then outlined his objections to an immediate armistice offer. The Kaiser interrupted: 'The Supreme Command considers it necessary, and you have not been brought here to make difficulties for the Supreme Command.'

Prince Max eventually abandoned his initial project for a speech in the Reichstag, and had a team of experts prepare another one in which 'every word that might irritate Wilson and give him an excuse for refusing was avoided'.

But before that came the note itself, *the* Note. It was prepared on the night of 3–4 October and sent off at 1.10 a.m. The Prince, at that time, had not yet pieced together a government. He would later describe the note as 'a bolt shot at random'. When asked why he had signed it and not left the responsibility to Supreme Command, he explained that the note signed by anyone else but the Chancellor would have been read as a capitulation. Prince Max of Baden had still not abandoned his programme. The wording was made as vague as possible. 'The German Government', it began, with the assumption that by the time Wilson read the note there would be one, 'requests the President of the United States of America to take in hand the restoration of peace.' The German government – though, because it did not yet exist, it had obviously not yet been consulted – formally accepted the American President's 'programme' as announced on 8 January and in his 'subsequent announcements' (the Fourteen Points were not mentioned). And the German government, the note concluded, 'requests the President to arrange the immediate conclusion of an armistice on land, by sea and in the air'.

3

Throughout most of October northern Europe was wrapped in a wintry blanket of mist and rain. It created everywhere a steely light that would colour people's memories of the final act of the war. On the front, the Western armies painfully pushed Germany's forces back from where they had come. In the national capitals and in the army headquarters, 'those who have the power to end it' worked day and night on their incompatible answers as to how the Great War should be concluded. It was complicated table tennis. After tossing the ball between Spa and Berlin, Prince Max had been cornered and, in desperation, he thrust the ball across the Atlantic. Washington, for a while, played a private game with Berlin and then pitched the ball to London and Paris. Within a fortnight half the world was involved in the great match for peace. Ultimately, however, its result would depend upon the position of the armies – and, in particular, the armies on the northern plain of Europe.

The most curious feature of the match lay in the private game between Berlin and Washington. Whole armies were involved; every single day the world's press was reporting on the march of events, and the diplomats scrutinized them; but above all that played two extremely isolated men: one a German prince who philosophized about the 'psychological method', the other an American university professor who philosophized about 'democracy'. In his revised speech to the Reichstag on 5 October, Prince Max emphasized that his ideas and those of President Wilson were 'completely in harmony'. On ideas, the proposition could be contested. But the two lonely men certainly had something in common: they were both guiding the destiny of the world.

President Wilson deplored 'clubs' and 'secret diplomacy'; but he acted behind closed doors. He defended with passion the concept of a 'League of Nations'; but he put no faith in the Supreme War Council, although this was the 'League of Nations' in formation.

As the war neared its conclusion, Wilson became increasingly determined to impose the ideas outlined in his speeches of 1918 – his Fourteen Points, Four Principles and Five Particulars – on the eventual peace settlement. The more determined he was, the more withdrawn he became; he had shown the same tendency when president of Princeton University. His ideas lost touch with reality. He was fighting a war of his own construction, a war of 'Democracy' against 'Autocracy'. More and more his addresses sounded like sermons to a Southern Presbyterian congregation – grand in style, weak in detail. He praised 'humanity' and the 'peoples' of the world; he damned Germany's 'military masters' and their 'selfish ambitions'. Germany, he had announced from the steps of the New York opera house, would 'have to redeem her character'. These were the words of his father: an appeal to rise above the blood feuds of the Old Testament and adopt the new promise of the Gospel.

The excitement of his talk could lead him into serious contradictions – no more so than in the case of his policy towards Austria-Hungary. Point X of his Fourteen Points had committed him to maintaining the integrity of the Habsburg Monarchy. But the future of 'Democracy' in the area appeared increasingly to lie in the hands of Thomas Masaryk of the Czechs, Ignace Paderewski of the Poles, and other leaders of the 'oppressed nationalities'. By June he had no trouble in adopting the notion that 'all branches of the Slav race should be completely freed from German and Austrian rule'.[17]

These words had actually been drafted by Robert Lansing, the Secretary of State, whom Wilson regarded as 'flat footed', a dull man. But then Wilson had no great respect for anyone in his Cabinet.

His principal adviser remained Colonel House, who held no office and thus had no obligation to report to Congress or to submit himself to its interrogations. Yet even House kept his distance from Wilson. He lived in New York City, where he continued to preside over his private research commission, The Inquiry. In his apartment building there lived a young Englishman, Sir William Wiseman, who was regarded by those with access to House's closed circle of associates as a spy. The British officially referred to him as a liaison officer between the Foreign Office and the White House – which hardly explained why he lived in New York. 'I think he [House] shows me everything he gets, and together we discuss every question that arises,' wrote Wiseman confidently to the Foreign Office in April. Wiseman looked on House as a 'father figure'.

Lord Balfour, the British Foreign Secretary, thought this relationship 'most unorthodox', but, as he explained to one of his high civil servants in London, 'anything that helps us to work with the President and the President with us is helping to win the war'. Wiseman became a key link between Lloyd George's government and President Wilson. 'The American nation is making its first appearance as a great world power,' wrote Wiseman. 'We must remember that after peace is signed we shall by no means have finished with America. We shall not even have finished with President Wilson.'

Wiseman may truly be regarded as the father of what later came to be known as Britain and America's 'Special Relationship'. It was established behind closed doors.[18]

President Wilson received Prince Max's request for an immediate armistice on Sunday, 6 October. He at once telephoned Colonel House. House's first thought was to refuse it, though in a way 'as to leave the advantage with you'. 'With Foch hammering in the West and you driving the diplomatic wedge deeper, it is within the range of possibilities that the war may be over by the end of the year,' he added.[19]

On Monday House was summoned to the White House, where he arrived late in the evening. Wilson had already composed a draft answer. To House it seemed 'mild in tone and did not emphasize the needs for guarantees'. The Colonel was uncomfortable with the independent line Wilson was following, and advised him to reply to Prince Max's note merely by signalling that the American President would confer about it with the Allies. They spent what remained of the evening arguing.

The following morning, 8 October, Wilson cancelled his golf and worked on a new draft. When he joined him in his study, House was pleased to discover that the tone of the reply was somewhat harsher. But Wilson was still bent on independent action, arguing that the German note was too vague to justify consultation with the Allies.

The final draft, signed by Robert Lansing, stated that the President 'deems it necessary to assure himself of the exact meaning of the note of the Imperial Chancellor'. It asked three questions: Did Germany agree to base negotiations on the principles the President had outlined in his speeches that year? Would Germany consent to immediate withdrawal from Allied territories? And did the Imperial Chancellor speak 'merely for the constituted authorities of the Empire who have so far conducted the war'?

'It is not a reply,' remarked Wilson when he handed it to the press that afternoon, 'but an inquiry.' The European Allies would read about it in the newspapers.

4

The progress of the American First Army in the southern Meuse–Argonne sector was so slow that Marshal Foch, on 1 October, sent his Chief of Staff, General Weygand, over to Pershing's headquarters to suggest introducing another French army between Gouraud's French Fourth and Pershing's First – with the implication, of course, that it would absorb several American divisions. For Pershing this was just another attempt by the Europeans to break up his army. He sent Weygand back from where he came. Then he ordered his left wing, held by the 77th Division, to push ahead, 'without regard of losses and without regard to the exposed conditions of the flanks'.[20]

True, the American northward thrust between the Meuse and the Argonne Forest had encountered obstacles with which few of the other armies had had to contend. After only three days of fighting, the first offensive had ground to a halt under fire from massed batteries of enemy artillery to the left, behind the Argonne wood line. But the Americans had also created their own problems. In order to fulfil his desperate timetable, Pershing had thrown his most available and least experienced units north to the Argonne while his best men were still far south of Verdun, clearing up the Saint-Mihiel salient. Only four of his attacking divisions had had any combat experience; the other five had not even completed their training. Many of the troops who led the offensive of 26 September had been in uniform for only four months. Since the Somme and Verdun, European commanders had learned that divisions had to be rotated out of the front to maintain morale, rest and feed them. The American Army's burgeoning staff of 2,500 men found themselves with too few replacements and a transport system incapable of carrying them even if they had been available. Three tiny roads in the area ran in the direction of the American attack. Over half a million men had to be moved up them, under constant rain, along with munitions and food. With the unanticipated halt in the offensive, these thin arteries of supply simply blocked, creating mile after mile of total anarchy. 'They wanted an independent American army,' wrote Clemenceau, recalling his visit to this sector at the end of September. 'They had it. Whoever saw, like me, the terrible traffic jam of Thiaucourt will bear witness that they can be congratulated for not having had it earlier.' Clemenceau argued that the chaos cost the Allies a good deal in blood.[21]

It cost the Americans 75,000 combat casualites in just over a week's fighting – among the worst figures recorded by any army in any period of the war. The poor conditions under which the troops were forced to live were probably among the causes of a fresh outbreak of the Spanish flu: American hospital admissions climbed to nearly 40,000 in the month of September; 2,500 died from the deadly disease – many more than had died at Saint-Mihiel. In the Argonne, the American 1st Division incurred a further

9,000 combat casualties in the first eleven days of October No army – not even the American – could replace that kind of loss.

In the Argonne, the Americans suffered their Somme, their Verdun, their Chemin des Dames. Mezières, the crucial junction in Germany's lateral railway system, looked as far away in mid-October as it had when the offensive was launched on 26 September. The war began to look as if it might end without the Americans – at the very moment when President Wilson was determined to impose his own kind of peace.

The American Army, however, was not the only one to be held up in the first fortnight of October. Heavy rain had halted the Flanders Army Group before soggy ridges east of Ypres. Behind them lay the nightmare swamps of Passchendaele; tanks, lorries and the four-horse-drawn supply wagons had difficulty making it through. The continental-sized 'pinch' on Germany's lateral lines was not yet working. Both Prince Max in his speech of 5 October and the Kaiser in an army proclamation the same day announced with pride that 'the front was holding.' It was no idle claim. After crossing the Canal Saint-Quentin in late September, Haig's Third and Fourth Armies in the Somme soon discovered what the Germans meant when they insisted that the Hindenburg Line was not a 'line'. It was only on 5 October that the British forced their way through the final *Stellung*, and even then the Germans clung on to Cambrai, to the north. A genuine tank battle followed, with the Germans using British Mark IVs they had captured in earlier action. The next day, 9 October, Cambrai collapsed. When British forces entered it that afternoon, they discovered only the shell of a town. Every house had been demolished, many of the streets had been ploughed up and mined, the churches were destroyed; there was an eerie silence interrupted only by the clatter of broken Gothic signposts against stone walls and flames belching out of empty windows. Haig was amazed at the sudden quietness. 'It was only yesterday that the enemy was driven from this great fortress,' he recorded in his diary, 'and yet I was able to walk about today, 24 hours later, almost out of hearing of his guns.'[22]

Thus two British armies and one French – Debeney's First – broke out, during the second week of October, into a landscape of open fields, copses and hedgerows that had, until then, been virtually untouched by war. This was the country campaigning for which the professional armies of 1914 had been trained; it was the kind of warfare the citizen soldiers of 1918 had hardly known. Haig had foreseen some of the problems involved when, on 24 September, he had appealed to London to 'send me some Yeomanry, cyclists, motor machine guns, motor lorries, etc. In fact, anything to add to our mobility.' An advance of four or five miles a day was considered good; eight or ten miles very good. On 9 October, outside Le Cateau (where Wellington had made his first halt after his victory at Waterloo, and where the British Expeditionary Force had fought in retreat in 1914), mounted Canadians launched a cavalry charge. They captured 500 prisoners, 10 guns and 60 machine-guns and lost only 168 men, killed, wounded or missing; but they 'had done nothing that the infantry, with artillery support and cyclists, could not have done for itself at less cost', as the official history put it.[23]

The central 'hinge' of the Allied armies was indeed being turned into a 'hammer'. But it was a slow process. As for the two great flanks of the Front, they were wounded and static. Germany was not about to surrender.

It just so happened that the prime ministers of Great Britain, France and Italy were meeting in Paris when news of the German demand for an immediate armistice was announced – the weekend Cambrai was surrounded.

Everyone in Paris was talking about the German note, according to *Le Matin*, 'on this day of Sunday rest'. In the streets, in the cafés and in public places, the general opinion was that it was a crude manoeuvre; 'The hour has arrived when we grasp by the throat a bandit who wanted to strangle us. We shall not let go of our hold, because we know with whom we are dealing and we also know what an act of thoughtless generosity would cost us.' The remainder of the article was censored.[24]

Summit meetings of the Allied leaders in Paris were almost a matter of routine now; they were a way of circumventing diplomatic red tape and arriving at decisions quickly. Informal conversations would take place in the morning, either at the Foreign Ministry on the Quai d'Orsay or in Clemenceau's offices, and then, in the afternoon, there would be a more official discussion, including the military representatives, in the Supreme War Council out at Versailles. These meetings were an innovation of the war, but in format they drew upon a long European tradition: the morning's conversation and the afternoon's round-table discussion had been the practice of statesmen at the Congress of Vienna in 1815.

The initial purpose of this particular meeting in Paris had been to formulate conditions for an armistice with Turkey, which, cut off from Germany after Bulgaria's capitulation, appeared to be on the point of collapse. Since the Americans were not at war with Turkey, no Americans were involved in the discussions. But, with news of Prince Max's note, swiftly followed by Wilson's astonishingly independent response, minds became concentrated on Germany.

The Allies decided that Wilson would not be immediately informed of their Turkish terms – they were eventually passed on to him on 19 October, five days after Turkey's expected appeal for armistice was received. The British were furious with the President. The Chief of the Imperial General Staff, Henry Wilson (who would mockingly refer to Woodrow as his 'cousin'), thought that 'a few good *straight* home truths would do *that vain ass* of a President good'. Sir Henry's view was 'let the Boches get behind the Rhine and then we can discuss'. What exasperated Lloyd George was

Germany's implied acceptance of the Fourteen Points as a basis for negotiations. For Britain there could be no 'Freedom of the Seas' in wartime, and
the territorial points especially regarding Alsace-Lorraine – were too vague.
And of course Germany would accept 'evacuation' of occupied territories
as a condition of the armistice; she was already evacuating them. Clemenceau, for his part, remarked that Woodrow Wilson was isolated and
superior, 'He is Jupiter.'[25]

But Clemenceau liked the tone of the American response. It committed
the Allies to nothing while it stipulated that Germany would have to pull out
of occupied territory in France, Belgium, Luxembourg and Italy. Already,
following early notification of the German request, he had asked Foch to
draw up his own terms for a military armistice. These the Marshal presented
to the Supreme War Council on 8 October: in addition to the liberation of
invaded territories, he demanded Allied occupation of the whole left bank
of the Rhine 'as security for reparations' with bridgeheads on the right
bank in case negotiations broke down. Though Foch insisted that the occupation would not be the equivalent of annexation, the British and the Italians
thought the terms too severe.

Eventually it was agreed to send Wilson a formal note pointing out that
an armistice was a military accord that required military experts to fix the
conditions, and that the evacuation of invaded territory was an insufficient
guarantee against renewed German hostilities. Little did they know that
evacuation and recuperation were exactly what Ludendorff had in mind.[26]

Woodrow Wilson, who put no trust in the Supreme War Council, was
reportedly 'very shocked' by the action taken by the Allies, and he asked
their embassies in Washington for an explanation. On grounds of seniority,
the French ambassador, Jules Jusserand, acted as their spokesman. He went
round to the White House almost immediately after the Allied note had
been received by telegraph. Wilson was friendly enough, but he continued
to express his regrets. When Jusserand suggested that the US send an agent
to Paris who could take an effective part in decisions, Wilson replied that
such a man would be too much influenced by his surroundings and, conse-
quently, would be unable to speak as an American. Wilson's lonely pride
was incurable.

Lord Balfour, the British Foreign Secretary, cabled a personal note from
London claiming that what had just happened in Paris was merely the
routine usual as wars reached their conclusion. That kind of historical reference lay outside the President's moral world of political science. It was
Wilson who complained to Colonel House about not being consulted by
the Supreme War Council. It was Wilson who argued that the Council was
wrong in discussing armistice terms right now. The President, wrote House,
was 'much exercised'.[27]

5

The slowdown in the Allied advance changed the nature of the match between Spa and Berlin. On 29 September, Supreme Command, acting out of desperation, had forced the creation of a new government and a demand for immediate armistice. Already by 3 October, the day Prince Max's note was finally sent, it was beginning to think that the front could hold for a while longer. Ludendorff, reading out his answers to one of Prince Max's questionnaires (these rare encounters between the Government and Supreme Command made quite a contrast to the procedure of the Allied Supreme War Council), mumbled in grave tones that 'a general collapse might be averted'.[28]

Ludendorff then started to complain about the tone of Prince Max's note to Wilson, though it was based on a draft he had himself composed. 'I regarded the Note as somewhat weak in tone,' he recorded in his memoirs, 'and proposed a more manly wording, but no attention was paid to my demands.' The patriotic press went further. Walther Rathenau, the great industrialist responsible for mobilizing Germany's economy for total war, wrote in the *Vossische Zeitung* on 7 October that this was no time for negotiation and appealed to the people to rise in defence of the nation. That was also the view of the main conservative parties in the Reichstag. Could not Germany hold out for six more months? 'If you make a man put off suicide for an hour,' Rathenau pleaded with Prince Max, 'he gives up the idea, and it never comes back to him.'[29]

The line was holding. The military situation, at least as viewed from Spa, appeared to provide the breathing space Ludendorff wanted, so perhaps the call for an armistice had not been necessary. It was the peculiar turn of events – day by day, week by week – rather than a deliberate plot that led Supreme Command to pin responsibility for the negotiations with the enemy on Berlin. This would have fatal consequences for Germany after the war.

The Prince was beside himself; he had never wanted to make the armistice offer in the first place. When his old friend Colonel von Haeften told him that, from a military point of view, the request was unnecessary, he was stunned. 'I can hardly describe what a blow this admission was to me,' he recalled. 'Why did they not grant me the eight days' delay which I demanded?' Prince Max blamed his dilemma on particularism, 'which lurks like an inborn curse in the German character' and which had 'taken refuge in the Departments – among the admirals, among the generals, among the diplomats'. The Social Democrat Gustav Noske referred to it as the 'cult of Expertness'. Each expert took care of his own department, his own little room, but bore no responsibility for the whole building. 'Particularism' and 'expertness' characterized the relationship between Spa and Berlin. They forced Prince Max down a road he had never intended to follow.[30]

You could find elements of the phenomenon within the Chancellor's own government, which he had pieced together only after the first note had been sent. Prince Max scathingly referred to some of its members as the 'parliamentary ministers', because their only concern seemed to be the welfare of their parties. Among the very worst, according to Prince Max, was Matthias Erzberger, who became a minister without portfolio only because he was 'less dangerous in the Government than in Parliament'.[31]

Tensions built up as Prince Max's motley team awaited Wilson's reply. Comments in the Allied press had not been encouraging. What if Wilson laid down terms that were unacceptable? Prince Max continued to speak of a 'life and death struggle' and, in his first Cabinet meeting, discussed the idea of a *levée en masse* as had been called by the French in 1792. He also prepared another of his questionnaires for General Ludendorff, who was expected in Berlin within a few days.

Great relief was felt when Wilson's note, in its form of an inquiry, finally arrived on Wednesday morning, 9 October. But then the note did demand evacuation of occupied territory, and it made the Fourteen Points a condition, not a basis, of negotiations.

Ludendorff was in Berlin that afternoon. Contrary to the rumours in Berlin, he did not look the slightest bit shaken in health. The First Quartermaster General reported that the danger of a break-through on the front still existed, but he gave the overall impression that the crisis of the previous week had passed. No, he put no faith in a *levée en masse*; he recommended a still more rigorous combing-out of recruits to solve the manpower shortages. His continual refrain remained 'The army needs respite.'[32]

So it was hardly a time to stand up to Wilson. Berlin's second note to Washington, forwarded on 12 October, was a simple 'yes' to the three questions posed by the President. It agreed that the sole purpose of discussions would be to define the practical details of applying the Fourteen Points, assuming the Western European Allies also accepted them; it suggested that a 'mixed commission' be set up to arrive at an accord 'necessary for the evacuation'; and it confirmed that the new German government had been created by agreement with 'the great majority of the Reichstag' and that the Imperial Chancellor 'speaks in the name of the German Government and the German people'.[33]

But in the days that followed – and more particularly in the nights – Prince Max suffered Faustian nightmares of foreboding. This was not the note he would have liked to have sent. He was cornered. 'I believed that I had been summoned at five minutes to twelve, and find out that it is already five minutes past,' he wrote despairingly to his cousin the Grand Duke of Baden at midnight, 15–16 October. The 'Old Prussian System' had broken down, the 'old belief in authority is past and gone', parties on the Right and Left were openly calling for the abdication of the Kaiser, Germany was wedged in between 'merciless enemies on the West and the Bolshevik Plague on the East'. 'We are already in the middle of a revolution,' averred the Prince[34]

And it was not one in which he would be able to play much of a role. The Social Democrats had been whipped up into a fury against the Chancellor after the press had published a letter proving he had no sympathy with their policy for peace; this was why Wilhelm Solf, the Foreign Secretary, and not Prince Max, had signed the second note.

The Prince was totally isolated in Berlin. As advisers, he still had only Colonel von Haeften and General von Winterfeldt. How could he speak for the German people? Evidently, the Chancellor did not have the 'great majority of the Reichstag' behind him.

The creator of that majority, Matthias Erzberger, much regretted his own absence from the capital. He was in Karlsruhe at the time, watching his wounded son die.

On 10 October a mail packet, the *Leinster*, was struck by two German torpedoes as she plied the seas between England and Ireland. Of the 527 lives lost, many were Americans, several were famous British figures, and over 130 were women and children. For days, relatives stood on the shores to identify the corpses as they were washed up. A howl of indignation buried all charitable thoughts in Britain and the United States when Germany's second note was published.

On the Western Front, the armies began to move again. Mangin's French Tenth Army, which had been pushing painfully north-eastward ever since it had surprised the Crown Prince's right wing at Villers-Cotterêts in July, took the old Picardian citadel of Laon on Sunday, 13 October. Mangin, typically, wanted to be among the first to enter. It was said that the 'Boches' had been too stupid: they had spent all their energy blowing up châteaux and cutting down fruit trees, and had not had time to destroy the roads. Nevertheless, Mangin was forced to abandon his open-top car and proceed by foot; he arrived at the gates of the town that evening, with a cane in his hand and accompanied only by his batman.[35]

The movement had begun on the plain, north of the river Oise. The greatest advances were made where the land lay low, on the left wing of the Allied armies, in reverse parody of the German invasion of 1914. As Foch put it in his memoirs, between the 'hilly sides of the Meuse' and the 'wide plains of Flanders' the way forward became, by grades, relatively easier; 'here the great destinies of Europe had been settled in the past, up to Waterloo'.[36]

But the movement remained local, agonizing. This was still a 'platoon commanders' war' that followed no tactical rule. A blow here, a blow there; soon, somewhere, the Allies would stand astride the German Army's lateral rail west of Ardennes.

The Americans were floundering in the hills of the Argonne. At dawn on 4 October they had launched a second great offensive, but it petered out in four days. Pershing reluctantly dismantled two of his divisions and on

12 October set up an American Second Army to hold on to their gains at Saint-Mihiel. This did not provide much help to the First Army, now placed under the command of General Hunter Liggett, but it did make Pershing a group army commander, which theoretically placed him on an equal footing with Haig and Pétain. On 14 October Liggett ordered a third massive attack northward into the heavily fortified Kriemhilde Stellung; 'enemy resistance stiffened'. By the 16th he had secured objectives Pershing had set for 26 September. Clemenceau, increasingly irate at the lack of American progress, had composed a letter to Foch on the 11th stating that 'the immobility of your right wing could not be among your plans', telling him to overcome Pershing's obstinacy by appealing to Wilson if necessary, and concluding with a trumpet call; 'Commandant, *la Patrie* commands you to command.' The staid French President, Poincaré, shocked by the wording, persuaded his Prime Minister not to send the letter. But the affair did not end there. Clemenceau knew perfectly well that Wilson and Pershing were at loggerheads, and at this critical moment in the exchange of diplomatic notes he was possibly thinking that he had found in this a way to persuade 'Jupiter' to talk.[37]

There was much more success in the central sectors of the front, where on 17 October the British Third and Fourth Armies, having taken Le Cateau, launched an attack along the line of the river Selle, thus menacing the middle section of the rail link between Lille and Mezières. Debeney's French First Army, astride the river Oise, moved upon another significant rail junction at Guise. To the north, in Flanders, a furious six-day battle – the term itself is insufficient – opened up the whole industrial zone occupied by Germany since 1914. General Sir Herbert Plumer's Second Army entered Lille itself on the 17th, finding the town in amazingly good condition; Crown Prince Rupprecht had even left food behind for the Allies. The Germans had also been conducting with the inhabitants a lucrative last-minute trade in Allied flags, and these were hanging out of the windows before Plumer's first troops arrived.

In Douai, taken the same day, it was a different story. The walls were still intact, but there were no inhabitants. They had all been forcibly 'evacuated'. Their homes had been destroyed. What could not be removed had been smashed to atoms. The photographers, who were brought in as witnesses, studied the effects of sunlight upon the smashed mirrors, the slashed canvases, the machine-gunned walls, the broken crockery lying upon the floor; their silent portraits in black and white, their tales of anger without a human figure present, little Vermeers of ruin, are fearfully exquisite. That is the irony of war.

The Belgians entered Ostend that same day. Their cavalry galloped up the beach, Admiral Sir Roger Keyes brought his destroyers in sight, and an airman landed in town as the last Germans withdrew.

Two days later, on Saturday, 19 October, King Albert's Belgians were in

Bruges. Its medieval squares and buildings were, thank God, untouched, though men had been deported, industries had been destroyed, and looting had been widespread. But there was plenty of cheering when the King rode into this old Flemish centre.

The whole Belgian coast was now in Allied hands.

6

Woodrow Wilson was having dinner in the Waldorf Hotel in New York on Saturday evening, 12 October, when the second German note arrived. New York was a city that usually supported the Democratic Party, and Congressional mid-term elections were coming up in November. A concert for the benefit of blind Italian soldiers had been organized at the Metropolitan Opera; Wilson needed the Italian vote, for these elections were going to be close.

The news of German acceptance of America's terms had already spread by the time the President arrived at the opera house in the company of his new wife, Edith, as round and radiant as Wilson was slim and stern. They were met by tremendous applause. Indeed, the pitch of excitement was so high that an uninformed stranger could have been excused for thinking the war was over. Few listened to the music – least of all Colonel House, who left in the middle of the concert and went home to worry. As for Wilson, he spent the rest of the night in his hotel talking with his secretary, Joseph Patrick Tumulty, about what to do. The next day Wilson and House were on their way to Washington to work on their answer to Germany.

Beyond his determination to press ahead with his Fourteen Points, Four Principles and Five Particulars, Wilson was absorbed by two issues. First, he was not going to be able to hold off Allied involvement in the German exchange of notes for much longer. In their note of the previous week, the European premiers had reminded him that they were not satisfied with a mere evacuation of occupied territories and that, in the case of a military armistice, they did expect military experts to be consulted. Second, the American campaign had revealed a popular undertow running against the very idea of an armistice. Republicans, in particular, were being drawn to the old Civil War call of General Ulysses S. Grant: 'unconditional surrender'.

Late in August, Senator Henry Cabot Lodge, principal spokesman for the Republicans, had presented his own 'Ten Points'. On territorial matters they were not very different from Wilson's Points, but they were totally silent on the League of Nations and they showed no sympathy at all for a compromise with Germany's Reich; Lodge demanded that 'we go to Berlin and dictate the peace'. A month later Teddy Roosevelt – a former President and a famous defector from the Republican Party who, outraged at Wilson's failure to declare war on Germany in 1915, had returned to the fold – had gone on a speaking tour attacking the idea of a League of Nations as a sop to the Germans. 'We are not internationalists,' he said; 'we are American nationalists.' In the election campaign, Lodge and Roosevelt presented a combined front on the theme that 'negotiated peace' was not what the American people wanted; what they sought was unconditional surrender 'on German soil'. On 9 October letters from the electorate that called into question the intention of Wilson's first note were read out in the Senate. Why was the evacuation of Alsace-Lorraine omitted? Why were no conditions for the evacuation spelt out? A heated debate was held on Saturday, the 12th. Lodge tabled a resolution for 'unconditional surrender'. Among the senators supporting it was one who argued that to conclude an armistice would be 'to lose the war'. The resolution failed by a margin. Roosevelt published in one of the nation's leading Sunday newspapers an article expressing the hope that the President 'will instantly send back word that we demand an unconditional surrender and that we refuse to compound felony by discussing terms with the felons'. That Sunday was Columbus Day, which had a special meaning for Americans.[38]

That was the day the American First Army was awaiting orders for its *third* attack on the Kriemhilde Stellung. That was the day Mangin walked into Laon. The European Allies were advancing; the Americans were not.

According to House, Wilson had never been more disturbed. He wanted 'to make his reply final so there would be no exchange of notes'. The problem – the dual problem of pressure from the Allies and the vicious opposition he was facing at home – made him think of a 'maze': 'If one went in at the right entrance he reached the center, but if one took the wrong turning it was necessary to go out again and do it over.'[39]

Wilson's long reply to Germany gave the impression of several voyages in and out of this mental maze. Its essential features included a warning that neither the United States nor the Allies would consider an armistice if German armed forces continued their 'illegal and inhuman practices' of sinking passenger ships and the 'wanton destruction' in their withdrawal from Flanders; an announcement that armistice conditions would be set by military experts to maintain 'the present military supremacy of the Armies of the United States and of the Allies in the field'; and a demand for 'the destruction of every arbitrary power anywhere that can separately, secretly and of its single choice, disturb the peace of the world'. Wilson forwarded his note to Berlin on 14 October without consulting the Allies or even his own Cabinet.[40]

But he did make a step towards improving his relations with the Allied governments. That same day he asked House, who had already been on several missions to Europe, to act as his personal representative in Paris. A secret code was devised for transatlantic communication (though British Intelligence had managed to break it before House had set foot in France). 'I have not given you any instructions,' said the exhausted President, 'because I feel you will know what to do.'

So, like Castlereagh when he crossed the North Sea in January 1814, House set out for Europe with no brief, no plan, no hard policy on how to conclude a terrible war. The significant difference, however, was that, whereas Castlereagh had been Foreign Secretary, House had no credentials save a personal note from the President addressed 'To Whom It May Concern'. House's boat left New York on 18 October. He was accompanied by his young British friend Sir William Wiseman.[41]

7

'A black day,' recorded Admiral von Müller in his diary on 16 October. 'The papers have published the details of the reply note. All prospects for peace have been ruined. There remains a life and death struggle. Perhaps a revolution!' Prince Max, who had received Wilson's second reply shortly after five o'clock that morning, was of the same opinion. 'Not a word in this terrible document', he wrote, 'recalled the high office of Arbitrator to which the President had aspired.'[42]

To gauge Germany's capability to conduct the 'life and death struggle', the Prince prepared another of his questionnaires; but this time he had Ludendorff appear before his entire War Cabinet. The meeting took place in the Chancellery the next day.

It is often said that there occurred at this moment a 'swing in the pendulum' between German military authority and civilian authority, between Spa and Berlin. German government officials themselves used the expression. But it was not an accurate analogy. Pendulums don't work where there is no centre of gravity. In late October 1918 there was virtually no authority left in Germany. The situation resembled more the disintegration of a complex galaxy, with each cell of power retreating into itself.

This was occurring at an increasingly rapid pace as one major event swiftly followed upon another. Yet there was always a slight delay between the event and the event's effect on the principal figures involved. During the third week of October, Ludendorff, the professional soldier, was thinking in terms of the Allied slowdown of the first week of October. In fact he was becoming increasingly optimistic: he was retreating into his professionalism.[43]

Could one count on the Western Front holding? 'A breakthrough is possible but not probable,' replied Ludendorff. Was the country able to provide the Army with the necessary 'human material'? 'Reinforcements always come in time,' he assured. But wasn't the fact that the Americans always received bigger reinforcements than the Germans something to worry about? 'We should not exaggerate the value of the Americans,' thought Ludendorff; 'our men have no fear of the Americans as they have of the English.' Ludendorff was counting on a 1919 campaign fought behind the Meuse–Antwerp line, despite Allied superiority in planes and tanks. 'Some formations,' he said, 'such as the Jaeger battalions and the Rifle Guards, treat tank-shooting as a regular sport.'

For the Foreign Secretary, Wilhelm Solf – whom Prince Max described as a 'broken man' – Supreme Command's change in attitude since the first days of October was 'a riddle'. 'What', he asked, dumbfounded, 'is the real reason why things are now possible which were then declared impossible?' Because, said Ludendorff, the War Minister, Lieutenant-General Heinrich Scheuch, had just informed him that 600,000 men could be supplied within a reasonable amount of time and the 'enemy's power of offensive is weakening'. He recommended that the government keep the armistice negotiations going if possible, and not accept terms that 'make a resumption of hostilities impossible'. Ludendorff still had a fantasy of an honourable settlement between jousting knights.

On Belgium, the hero of Liège was impenitent: 'Belgium must be told that peace is still far off, and the horrors, which are inseparable from war, may befall Belgium once again, so that 1914 will be child's play compared to [what she can expect now] ... Belgium must wake up from its peace dreamings and will then be quite a good ally of ours. The more it experiences the horrors of war, the more it will feel the need for peace.'[44]

As Ludendorff sat at the Chancellor's table, the Allies were entering Lille and Douai. Crown Prince Rupprecht, whose soldiers were defending Flanders, warned Prince Max the next day that Ludendorff did not fully realize the seriousness of the situation. 'The morale of the troops has suffered seriously and their power of resistance diminishes daily,' he reported. 'They surrender in hordes, whenever the enemy attacks, and thousands of plunderers infest the districts round the bases.'

Prince Max had only to gaze down one of Berlin's streets at the queues for food, the women worn to skin and bone, the hobbling men, and the armed police patrols tramping the cobbles to know that Germany's 'life and death struggle' was already spent. Yet he remained defiant. By instinct, he opposed the 'hands up' policy pursued by several of his ministers and he hung on to the idea of eventually negotiating a peace through strength. Constitutional reform was rapidly pushed through parliament; on the day when Germany abandoned Belgium's coast the Reichstag was debating Article 11, the right of parliament to declare war. That pleased Erzberger, just back from Karlsruhe, but it was hardly to the Chancellor's taste.

The Prince composed, in private, a lengthy challenge to Wilson's note with the aid of a legal adviser, Geheimrat Walter Simons. In answer to the President's charge of 'arbitrary power', Prince Max answered that 'the Government of Germany was up to now based on Authority' and that the 'great mass of the people' had accepted this 'without feeling any desire for full responsibility of its own'. This caused an uproar in his Cabinet, and he eventually decided to let the ministers write another draft – a short note, sent to Washington on 20 October – that announced the end of the torpedo attacks on passenger vessels, the future responsibility of government to parliament, and an acceptance of the principle that Allied military advisers should decide the armistice terms on the basis of 'the actual standard of power on both sides in the field'. It was little short of surrender.[45]

8

Now the surrender document had to be drafted. Without House by his side, Wilson was more isolated than ever. He regarded his Secretary of State, Robert Lansing, as an idiot and went to the foreign diplomats for advice. In a conversation with Jusserand he weighed up the pros and cons of a 'Bolshevist' Germany over the Kaiser's Germany – they seemed to him equally evil. Three weeks after receiving Germany's first note, he at last called his Cabinet.

Under the pressure of public opinion, their mood was pitiless. The Secretary of the Interior wanted negotiations postponed until German troops had been pushed across the Rhine. The Agriculture Secretary didn't think Germany's constitutional reforms were sincere. The Secretary of the Treasury said it was up to the military to set the terms. The Postmaster General simply demanded unconditional surrender.

Wilson said that the force of public opinion might take him to a 'cyclone cellar' for forty-eight hours. When somebody remarked that the publishing of the peace notes without the consent of the Allies might seem to them coercion, Wilson replied that they needed coercion.

So, incredibly, Wilson wrote his third note to Germany alone. It was almost as long as his second, and was even stronger in tone. The armistice would have 'to make a renewal of hostilities on the part of Germany impossible'. Germany would also have to conform better to Wilson's vision of the new world order: if the United States 'must deal with the military masters and the monarchical autocrats of Germany now, it must demand, not peace negotiations, but surrender'. Thus Wilson sought military capitulation and a transformation of Germany's institutions. Wilson wanted a revolution in Germany.[46]

His note also outlined the course to follow to end the hostilities. All his correspondence with Germany would be passed on to the Allied governments. If they were ready to negotiate peace on the basis of Wilsonian principles, then their military advisers would be asked to submit terms for an armistice that would assure their people 'unrestricted power to safeguard and enforce the details of the peace'. Thus, while the basis of peace negotiations was to be laid by the Americans, the immediate military terms of the armistice were going to be set, as a technical preliminary, by Allied military experts. Somehow Wilson imagined there would be no conflict between the two.

The note was forwarded to Berlin on 23 October. Wilson, in accordance with his plan, opened his entire correspondence with Germany to the Allies, deliberately avoiding any recommendations for the actual terms of the armistice.

House was still at sea when he received the text of the note by telegram. He thought it was a 'long and effusive discussion', a 'reckless and unnecessary gamble' that could push the Germans into further resistance. He very much regretted he had not been in the White House to guide his master. Now he was sailing for Europe with no real credentials to defend the Fourteen Points, Four Principles and Five Particulars before Allies who had not yet been consulted.

House was suffering from indigestion.[47]

In London, Lloyd George's War Cabinet had spent almost a week discussing what to do about the exchange of notes. Lloyd George deeply resented Wilson's refusal to talk with the Allied governments: 'We have borne the heat of the burden of the day and we are entitled to be consulted,' he said. Sir Henry Wilson continued to note widespread feelings of scorn for his 'cousin'. 'Everyone angry and contemptuous of Wilson,' he wrote. 'A vain ignorant weak ASS.' The Cabinet noticed that there had been no mention of Alsace-Lorraine, nor had anything been said about 'salt water' – in other words, what to do about Germany's fleet. Few in Britain were fighting for the 'democratizing of Germany'. There were hard, unresolved issues in this war that 'Cousin' Wilson was simply ignoring.

London resented Wilson's procedure.[48]

In Paris, on 21 October, Clemenceau finally decided to send Foch a modified version of his letter about Pershing's 'immobility'. He warned that if Pershing continued in his 'invincible obstinacy' then it would be 'high time to tell President Wilson the truth and the whole truth concerning the situation of the American troops'. There were already rumours circulating in Washington that Pershing had gone 'glory mad', was responsible for unnecessary American casualties, and had ambitions to run against Wilson for the presidency.

Paris was hoping to tame Wilson's independent policy with a few uncomfortable home truths.[49]

It took House eight days to cross the Atlantic. He landed at Brest on 25 October, and was in Paris the next day – a windy, cold Saturday. He had lunch with Haig and the British Secretary for War, Lord Milner, and was surprised to find Haig insisting on moderate terms for the armistice. At the Elysée Palace, the French President, Poincaré, gave him a cold reception; Poincaré did not think House had proper credentials. (Poincaré later said that Wilson's letter was 'a kind of circular addressed by President Wilson to the whole world and couched in the most autocratic terms'.) House spoke of Poincaré as a 'bitter ender'. It was very different with Clemenceau, who literally threw his arms open and kissed the astonished House on both cheeks. 'He genuinely seems fond of me,' House confided that evening in his diary, and reciprocated, 'Clemenceau is one of the ablest men I have met in Europe.' Clemenceau warned him that Lloyd George and the British in general did not tell the truth. 'Lloyd George sends his orders to me from time to time,' said Clemenceau: 'I wonder how I keep my temper.' House wrote in secret, 'It was news to me that he did.'[50]

House did attempt to see Pershing, but he was ill in bed with flu.

The Supreme War Council, which was to be the main forum for the discussion of the peace terms, had by now become a major international institution. Twenty-four military and civilian leaders from Europe and America sat over blotting pads and baize at a long table on the ground floor of the Trianon Palace Hotel. *The Times* referred to it as the 'first Parliament in the Society of Nations', or, with a memory going back further than that of most of its participants, as 'the Congress'. If the discussion concerned Japan, Serbia, Belgium or Greece, representatives of these countries would enter and join in the conference. Thus the same distinction between the Great Powers and the Secondary Powers developed within the Supreme War Council as had existed at the Congress of Vienna.

When the prime ministers were present, Georges Clemenceau would sit at a central point of the table with Marshal Foch and his generals on his right and Lloyd George, Lord Milner and Andrew Bonar Law, the Chancellor of the Exchequer, on his left; the American 'observers' sat just opposite. Numerous secretaries and staffs would be accommodated at side tables. In heated debates, Clemenceau would shake his shoulders and wave his arms about, brandishing in one of his grey-gloved hands a paperknife, which he would then bang on the table while demanding silence. Long speeches were not tolerated and would be cut off with a word or two pronounced in his sharp, high-pitched French. The gentle and courteous British Foreign Secretary, Lord Balfour, would walk around the table in an attempt to hear what the participants were saying, while the British Cabinet Secretary, Sir Maurice Hankey, kept records, prepared resolutions, and remained convinced that he was running the whole affair.[51]

In this kind of place the neat partition Wilson had raised between political principles and technical military preliminaries soon collapsed. It quickly became evident that, in handing armistice terms to the Allies, Wilson had lost a major part of the initiative in the peace process. This was proved with the fall, at the end of October, of Turkey and Austria-Hungary, allied 'props' of Germany that depended entirely on Germany's strength. The European Allies set the terms of the armistices; the United States played no part in the discussions at all.

Haig might have clung to the distinction between military and political considerations, but this was largely owing to his ongoing battle with the members of his own government. Unlike most members of Britain's War Cabinet, Haig thought the German Army still showed considerable powers of resistance. This also brought Haig into conflict with the other com-manders-in-chief. On 25 October Foch brought them all together at his headquarters in Senlis to present a new variation of his plan to occupy the left bank of the Rhine, with bridgeheads on the right. Foch justified the project on two grounds: it would prevent Germany from renewing hostilities; it would also make sure that the indemnities to which France laid claim would be paid. Haig complained that this second aim was 'political' and did not fall within the Council's military competence.

None of the other commanders present, including Pershing, seemed very concerned about this subtle point. Together, with Haig dissenting, they drew up their armistice terms, which, in addition to the occupation of the Rhineland, included the surrender by the enemy of a large quantity of armaments and railway rolling stock, the delivery of submarines, the with-drawal of the enemy fleet to the Baltic ports, and the maintenance of the Allied blockade until all these conditions were fulfilled. Eventually it was agreed that the naval terms would be set by an Allied Naval Council sitting in London – these terms would turn out to be even more drastic. The 'military experts' had, in effect, drawn up a programme of unconditional surrender before the plan even went before the Supreme War Council.

On the day House arrived in Paris, Clemenceau handed him Foch's final draft on the land terms. House now had to attempt to harmonize Wilsonian political principles with aims already established in the Allied military terms.

House's solution was simple. He decided to stay clear of all territorial issues and to concentrate on the most abstract elements of the Fourteen Points. To achieve this, he sought the collaboration of Professor Walter Lippmann, one of the leading scholars of The Inquiry, and an American journalist, Frank I. Cobb, to compose an 'interpretive commentary' on each of the Points. This commentary virtually gave the Allies a free hand. Point I, for example, concerning 'open covenants', was shown to mean that, as long as treaties were eventually published, they could be negotiated in secret – a principle with which Prince de Talleyrand would have felt perfectly comfortable. The Cobb–Lippmann Memorandum, forwarded by cable to the President for his 'correction and revision', made the initial Points more abstract than they had ever been.[52]

Wilson's reply pushed them into the stratosphere. The commentary, he said, was satisfactory, but its details were to be regarded as 'merely illustrative suggestions and reserved for the peace conference'. Thus, having abandoned 'military' terms to the Allies, did Wilson defer explanation of his 'political' principles.

Without House, he was becoming increasingly absorbed with his grander visions of politics and history, with the changes he wished to effect in the world's system, the justice and democracy he wanted to spread, the pursuit of the hidden structures, the grander causes, the silent forces of time, the wider view – in brief, the American way of looking at things. He told his Cabinet that the quest for 'an absolutely and rigorously impartial peace' was 'growing less and less on the other side of the water'.[53] Too many details. Old Europeans were pursuing old selfish gains. Like House, Wilson was not overly concerned with territorial matters. It was his general principles that had to be pressed – the 'essentially American' Points: open diplomacy, freedom of the seas, the removal of economic barriers, armaments reduction and the League of Nations. On these, Wilson's cables to House became evermore stubborn as discussions got under way in the Supreme War Council.

These discussions – which finalized the terms of the armistice, decided on how they would be physically presented to the Germans, and also laid the foundations of the peace that followed – opened on Tuesday, 29 October, and ran on through the weekend to the following Monday, 4 November.[54]

Lloyd George and Clemenceau were present from the start. The Italian Prime Minister, Vittorio Orlando, a liberal within his sunny Sicilian heart, even if the war had made him a touch tyrannical, did not arrive in Paris until Wednesday afternoon; until then Italy was represented by her Foreign Minister, the high-minded Baron Sonnino. House, on Tuesday morning, was again suffering from indigestion. He was lying on his couch under a blanket when one of his secretaries came in with the announcement that Austria-Hungary had accepted all of Wilson's harsh conditions – including the break-up of the Habsburg Empire. He suddenly sat up. 'That's it!' he exclaimed. 'The war's over!'[55]

But Germany had not yet been defeated. The Allied meetings followed the established pattern that mixed informal encounters in Paris with sittings of the larger assembly out in Versailles. Several of the discussions took place in the large parlour of Colonel House's grey seventeenth-century residence on the Rue d'Université, behind the Quai d'Orsay.

For the Colonel it was of the utmost importance to get the Fourteen Points accepted as the basis of peace negotiations, with the result that most of the debates revolved around this question. When Lloyd George and Clemenceau 'bandied words like fishwives' over the terms of the Turkish armistice, House just sat back and watched. The Italians were left to sign the armistice with Austria. In both cases, it was merely a matter of military surrender.

Germany was the only Central Power for which the armistice conditions were linked to the Fourteen Points. The debate in Paris focused on two issues. One was reparations – not mentioned in any of Wilson's Points, Principles or Particulars, but on the minds of everyone in Paris. Posters were plastered on all the streets: '*Que l'Allemagne paye d'abord.*' Foch, at Senlis, presented restitution as a military aim. At the Supreme War Council, France, backed by Belgium, put it forward as a political aim. Whether military or political, it was hardly an unreasonable demand, given the enormity of the destruction dealt by Germany on these two countries. When Great Britain in a memorandum also claimed 'compensation' from Germany for damages done to Allied civilians 'by land, by sea, and from the air', it became clear to House that a provision for reparations would have to be included in the armistice terms. So he agreed to it.

The second issue, the Freedom of the Seas, raised old phantoms. America argued for the right of neutral vessels to sail the seas; Britain argued for the right to impose blockade. Most of the Allied discussions in Paris were devoted to this disagreement. House spent his entire leisure time talking about it. He threatened a separate American peace with Germany. Wilson, in his cables, resorted to the language of war: he would use American equipment, he threatened, 'to build up the strongest navy that our resources permit and as our people have long desired'. At Versailles, Clemenceau confessed that he could not understand the meaning of the 'doctrine'; 'War would not be war if there was freedom of the seas,' he said.

The 'Freedom of the Seas' debate had no base in reason. It was a patriotic conflict between Britain and America, the insane War of 1812 revisited. Sir William Wiseman cemented over the cracks and Colonel House added the paint. 'The President does not object to the principle of blockade,' he explained in his parlour. 'He merely asked that the principle of the Freedom of the Seas be accepted.' Lloyd George at once grasped at this strange piece of logic. He scribbled on a piece of paper, 'We are quite willing to discuss the Freedom of the Seas and its application.' He handed it to House. 'Will he like something of this kind?' he asked. House was delighted.[56]

Diluted beyond recognition, Wilson's Points, Principles and Particulars were thus formally adopted by the Allies as the basis of peace negotiations. But the military experts' recommendations for the armistice conditions had not yet been approved.

Conditions on the land were outlined by Foch on Thursday morning, 31 October. Beyond a few details, they were essentially those recommended by the commanders-in-chief the week before. If these conditions were accepted by Germany, he explained, 'nobody has the right to shed one drop more of blood'. That was also Clemenceau's view. Lloyd George thought them 'rather stiff' and went on arguing until Friday, then suddenly announced he would abide by them.

When the Allied Naval Council presented its recommendations for conditions on the sea, it was Clemenceau's turn to complain. 'They have left the breeches of the Emperor and nothing else!' he exclaimed. It was Lloyd George's more 'moderate' proposal that was finally adopted, against the opposition of the British Admiralty: all German submarines were to be surrendered and brought into Allied ports; designated warships were to be interned in neutral ports under Allied surveillance, their ultimate destination being decided at the peace conference.[57]

*   *   *

So Wilson's general political principles had been accepted by the Allies and their military experts had defined the conditions of the armistice. 'Wiseman and many other friends have been trying to make me believe that I have won one of the greatest diplomatic triumphs in history,' House recorded in his diary after the Supreme War Council's final pre-armistice session on Monday, 4 November. Gordon Auchincloss, the Colonel's son-in-law, was even more exuberant in his diary: 'Before we get through with these fellows over here, we will teach them how to do things and to do them quickly.'[58]

As Commander-in-Chief of the Allied armies in France, Marshal Foch was instructed to prepare to receive 'properly accredited representatives of the German Government'and to communicate to them the terms of an armistice. Wilson was cabled a brief memorandum that indicated the Allies' readiness to make peace on the basis of the principles agreed in the previous notes exchanged, with two qualifications: that 'Freedom of the Seas' would be discussed at the peace conference, and that the evacuation of invaded territories meant not only restoring the freedom of those lands but also 'compensation' for all damage done to Allied civilians and their property 'by the aggression of Germany by land, by sea, and from the air'.[59]

Wilson forwarded the memorandum to Berlin on Tuesday, 5 November 1918.

9

Events in Germany were still guided by the tension between Spa and Berlin. The sinking of the *Leinster* and Wilson's harsh note of 14 October had brought their differences to breaking strain. Supreme Command wanted the submarine war continued, though it did agree to recalling 'our U-boat cruisers' (two ancient vessels) from the American coast to spare the feelings of the American nation'.

Inside Prince Max's Cabinet, Erzberger proved a very keen advocate of submarine warfare, until it was explained to him that the issue could be exploited to prove that political power now belonged to the government. Erzberger had also been arguing that Supreme Command be forced to sign the notes to Washington, since Supreme Command had started the whole process off. Then suddenly, on 21 October, 'the scales fell from Erzberger's eyes'. 'It can only be good for the world to know that we are really and truly masters in our own house!' he exclaimed, and he launched into 'an impassioned speech'. He abandoned both his struggle for further submarine warfare and his insistence on Supreme Command signatures.[60]

The government's new independent line was not well received in Spa. Behaviour there began to resemble that of a medieval city under siege, cut off from the country, cut off even from its own army.

Meanwhile, in Berlin's Reichstag, the debate on constitutional reform continued. For the first time since the annexation of 1871, an Alsatian was placed at the head of Alsace's administration instead of a Prussian civil servant. The Alsatian deputies were hardly satisfied: they said the whole sad effort at reforming their province was now obsolete. The Poles present openly rejoiced at the prospect of German defeat and celebrated Wilson as a man inspired by God. If it was going to come to a plebiscite on sovereignty, said one of them, 'the dead would have to be allowed to vote too'. The Dane Hansen demanded that North Schleswig, snatched by Prussia in 1866, be returned to Denmark.

Prince Max gave a speech on 22 October. 'In case the enemy Governments desire war, we have no other choice but to defend ourselves,' he said, and then retired to bed with the Spanish flu. He would not re-emerge until the end of the month.[61]

Wilson's third note, denouncing 'the military masters and the monarchical autocrats of Germany', was received simultaneously in Spa and Berlin on the 24th.

Spa made a unilateral bid to break off negotiations by means of a telegram, composed by Ludendorff, addressed directly to the German armies. 'Wilson's answer', it read, 'is a demand for unconditional surrender. It is thus unacceptable to us soldiers.' The field commanders, knowing that their troops had neither the desire nor the means to carry on the fight, persuaded Supreme Command to withdraw the message, but a wireless operator who supported the Independent Socialists had already picked it up and passed it on to the Party in Berlin. There was an uproar in the Reichstag. Prince Max, in bed, offered his resignation.[62]

Berlin's attitude was set by an all-night Cabinet session presided over by the Vice-Chancellor, Friedrich von Payer. Ugly scenes had been witnessed in the last call-up of conscripts; even the Minister of War admitted that in their transportation 'excesses had occurred.' No one felt confident about the idea of a *levée en masse* or Prince Max's more recent calls for 'National Defence'. In Berlin, Karl Liebknecht, an Independent Socialist recently released from prison, had been seen being carried shoulder high by soldiers decorated with the Iron Cross. No, negotiations could not be broken off. Nor could the next answer to Wilson bind Germany to continue the struggle.

The next afternoon, 25 October, both Hindenburg and Ludendorff turned up, uninvited, in Berlin. Defying the government, they went straight round to the Kaiser's residence at Schloss Bellevue to demand an immediate end to the negotiations. The Kaiser refused to make a decision and referred them to his Chancellor. But he was still confined to bed. At nine in the evening they were received at the Ministry of the Interior by Herr von Payer. Hindenburg and Ludendorff spoke of the 'soldiers' honour' and the need to inspire the morale of the nation, and noted that the Army stood still undefeated on enemy soil. 'All I can see is people who are starving,' said Payer. It was a dialogue of the deaf.

Ludendorff had already written a letter of resignation before he joined Hindenburg the next day, the 26th, to report before the Kaiser at Schloss Bellevue. He realized that the government was not prepared to make any defiant stand against Wilson and that he 'was regarded as the one who would prolong the war'; now was the time to go. But the meeting was stormy. Ludendorff railed against the government and against the Kaiser's Chief of Civil Cabinet, and even made insinuating comments about the Kaiser himself. 'You seem to forget that you are addressing your monarch,' remarked the All-Highest Warlord.

Hindenburg stood like a statue of stone, silent. That was the unkindest repudiation of them all: the Field Marshal, who retained his post, gave Ludendorff not a word of support. He did offer to accompany him back to the General Staff building. 'I refuse to drive with you,' said Ludendorff sharply: 'I refuse to have any more dealings with you because you treat me so shabbily.'[63]

General Wilhelm Groener, Ludendorff's successor, knew a lot about railway systems, and two years' service in the War Ministry had won him the support of Germany's trade unions. But he was not a replacement. It was too late to replace Ludendorff. Supreme Command, without Ludendorff, was drained of power.

As was another old centre of influence. On Sunday evening, the 27th, a grim-faced Austrian ambassador, Prince Hohenlohe, came to Prince Max's bedside to announce that Kaiser Karl had taken the irrevocable decision to request a separate peace. Both men must have known that this meant the end of the Danubian monarchy. 'People will spit at me,' admitted Prince Hohenlohe. 'I can show my face no longer in the streets of Berlin.'[64]

In the meantime, Prince Max had instructed Geheimrat Simons to prepare a 'dignified note' in answer to Wilson, including the comment, 'The German Government awaits proposals for an armistice, not suggestions of surrender.' But the German government would have nothing to do with Prince Max's suggestions. 'He [Wilson] will break off! He will break off!' shouted Philipp Scheidemann. Erzberger proposed a much more humble reply, arguing that Germany might get bad armistice terms and yet conclude a good peace.

The final text of the note was decided over a dinner that Saturday evening, held by Solf, the Foreign Secretary, with federal councillors and former government ministers. The general feeling was that one could not risk Wilson breaking off. The note, sent to Washington on the 27th, insisted on the 'far-reaching changes' being carried out on the German constitution and concluded that 'the German Government now awaits proposals for an armistice, which shall be the first step towards a just peace'. If it did place responsibility for the 'just peace' on the shoulders of the American President, there was no hint here that Germany was not prepared to surrender.[65]

In the next few days – as the Supreme War Council met in Paris –

newsreels were shown in German cinemas announcing Ludendorff's dismissal. It was reported that the soldiers were cheering.[66]

10

The grey skies of late October 1918 might not have provided much in the way of comfort to Prince Max in his bed or to Colonel House under his blanket. But it was far worse for the soldiers.

Foch, in a 'directive' of 19 October, had set Brussels as the aim of the Allies' left wing. But the Flanders Army Group got bogged down on the banks of the Scheldt. It was in the centre, beyond the wasteland of the Somme, that the greatest gains were made. Once again, Rawlinson's British Fourth Army took the lead, yard by yard.

In the 'open country', trees lost their leaves because of autumn, not the guns. There were rolling hills, deep vales, high, thick hedges, small enclosures for the cattle, sturdy farmhouses and several flowing streams – grim obstacles for an advancing army.

Along the river Selle the battle raged for over a week. Tanks were employed, but it was the infantry that took the burden. While the Hermann Stellung and the Hunding Stellung could hardly be compared with the great fortresses of the Hindenburg Line, they made a fearsome sight. Barbed wire was laid out in aprons on the defender's slopes and hidden in the hedgerows; machine-gun nests and anti-tank guns were placed in the copses and among the farm buildings.

'You must not imagine when you hear we are "resting" that we lie in bed smoking,' wrote a rather grand twenty-five-year-old British officer to his cousin back home. 'We work or are on duty *always*. And last night my dreams were troubled by fairly close shelling. I believe only civilians in the village were killed (Thank God).' He had just moved up with the Manchesters – the 96th Brigade – to Busigny, about six miles south of Le Cateau and a mile or so east of the Selle; an important section of the railway to Maubeuge lay behind him.

Wilfred Owen's letters home illustrate the difficulty of describing the 'soldier's attitude'. He mocked Clemenceau, he felt London and Berlin bore equal guilt for the violence, he had little sympathy for civilians – although there is no more articulate example of a uniformed civilian than he.

Owen's poems must count among the most acute expressions of the horror, outrage and pity of war in the English language. No one brings one closer to the tragedy of the soldier boys killed or mutilated on the front; no one gives a more intimate view of their smiles, of their pain, of their shattered limbs – of their wounds. What did the other soldier boys think? 'Do you know that little officer called Owen who was at Scarborough,' wrote one of his men disparagingly that October; 'he is commanding my Company, and he is a toff I can tell you. No na-poo. Compree?'

Owen wanted a 'negotiated peace'; he was horrified that the slaughter was allowed to go on; he was indignant at Rawlinson's order that 'Peace Talk must cease in the Fourth Army.' Yet he could have stayed in England, and had to struggle to get posted on the front.

The Manchesters moved forward again when the 'Battle of the Selle' was done. In the very last days of October they were at Saint-Souplet, less than a dozen miles from the next great obstacle, the Sambre Canal. But this time the Germans were in fast retreat. 'Splashing my hand, an old soldier with a walrus moustache peels & drops potatoes into the pot,' Owen wrote to his mother from 'The Smoky Cellar of the Forester's House' on Thursday, 31 October. 'By him, Keyes, my cook, chops wood; another feeds the smoke with the damp wood. It is a great life. I am more oblivious than alas! yourself, dear Mother, of the ghastly glimmering of the guns outside, & the hollow crashing of the shells.'[67]

The task of clearing out the enemy from the Hunding Stellung had been largely left to Debeney's French First Army on its approach to Guise. Its front line lay between the Oise and the Serre, crossing a mournful plain upon which were scattered isolated stone farmhouses. Debeney launched a major offensive on Friday afternoon, 25 October, in relatively dry weather, but that night there was a downpour of rain and by Saturday morning the army was bogged down before the wire of the Hunding. From then on it was individual action which counted: the search for 'chicanes', or passages between the wire, the exchange of rifle fire, the assault on a farmhouse, the surrounding of a hill – all actions that in previous wars would have been recorded as grand heroic deeds but in this one are remembered by a mass graveyard called La Désolation, on the slopes of Mont Pourri.[68]

The First Army finally marched into the ruins of Guise on Monday, 4 November. Even today one finds, in every street in the town, walls scarred by shrapnel. Eugène Debeney, who was known to weep, had a few proud sentiments that day. 'They have created in my life a spot of light so intense', he wrote twenty years later, 'that at the moment of my death my sight shall be serene.' Debeney's army stood right at the head of the Sambre Canal.[69]

This was now the critical point on the front. But, although by that time there were over a million and a half Americans in France, Pershing brought no fresh reserves to relieve it: his men were needed for the formation of his American Second Army down in the hills of Saint-Mihiel.

The idea of an eastward offensive along the Moselle into Lorraine, Luxembourg and the Saar was actually becoming attractive to French commanders, particularly Pétain. Foch – convinced that the whole American effort had to be concentrated northward up the Meuse on to Mezières and Sedan – initially ignored it. But the discussion of territorial matters in Paris evidently changed his mind, so that by 20 October he was actively pressing for a joint Franco-American offensive in Lorraine.

Pétain developed a plan. Then Foch, recognizing that rail transport in the supply zone was already overcrowded, changed his mind again. A more limited operation, advancing up the left bank of the Moselle towards the Saar, 'which the enemy considers as national territory', was therefore put into effect with the launch date set for 10 November. With just a little luck they could occupy the Saarland by the 15th. It was rich in coal and was an old territory of King Louis XIV – which was why the French called it 'Saarlouis'. But the plan was overtaken by events.[70]

American floundering in the Meuse–Argonne sector was one of them. After receiving Clemenceau's letter, Foch issued a directive that called on the Americans to 'stop using up their forces in costly wood fighting unlikely to bring any result'. Costly it was: in October, one army alone had suffered battle casualties of over 50,000. Another 70,000 Americans were hospitalized with the flu, which killed 32 per cent of the men who contracted it. At the end of October, Pershing, confined to bed himself, had the humiliating task of having to break up seven divisions in order to reinforce the rest.[71]

Nobody who lived among the Allied, and American, armies in the 'open country' could be sure that Germany was facing defeat in late October 1918. Although enemy divisions might 'melt away,' as the official histories would later put it, their defensive positions – shrouded in mist and protected by barbed wire and trench mortar bombs – looked awesome.

'While their politicians waffle on, the German soldiers are "holding", and holding hard,' wrote a correspondent in *Le Matin* on Sunday, 27 October. When the following week Foch presented his armistice conditions to the Supreme War Council, Lloyd George, who thought them 'very drastic', asked if he thought the Germans would sign. Foch replied that he didn't think they would, but added that the Allies in any case 'would be able to overpower the Germans by Christmas.'[72]

So perhaps the boys would be home before the fifth Christmas.

11

The Kaiser, on his return to Berlin in early October, had been laid up in bed with sciatica. He found every single decision distasteful.

The Chief of the Civil Cabinet started putting around the rumour that the All-Highest Warlord was playing with the idea of abdication. But after the sinking of the *Leinster*, and with the whole submarine war put in question, the Kaiser got on his feet again and became a good deal more assertive. Kaiser Wilhelm's relationship with his Navy had been since his youth a passionate affair – 'a matter of to be or not to be', as he had put it to Chancellor von Bülow back in 1898. He had lent his name to one naval port as well as to the canal that linked Germany's Baltic to the North Sea. The Kaiser looked upon the Navy as a personal possession – unlike the Army – and any tinkering with it by the Reichstag, by the government, or even by the generals would raise his imperial ire. This had given the Navy a degree of independence in Germany that not even the Army enjoyed.[73]

But October 1918 was not a good time to start asserting independence and imperial prerogatives. The Kaiser's insistence that the submarine war be continued created powerful opponents for himself, not only among the civilian authorities but also inside Supreme Command itself. The ensuing quarrel forged a fatal link between the future of the U-boats and the future of the Hohenzollern dynasty. This link already existed in the minds of Germany's enemies: the outcry among the Western Allies over the *Leinster* sinking rallied people – particularly in the United States, where an election campaign was under way – to the call to oust the Kaiser before making peace.

Starving Germans, confronted with the choice between peace and the Hohenzollerns, were quick to forget their imperial loyalties. In mid-October the press began to howl for abdication, first the papers of the Left, but soon right across the political spectrum. A popular feeling developed that the Kaiser had only to abdicate and peace would dawn. In Berlin, among the middle classes as well as the workers, there was a general revulsion against 'Kaiserism'. In Bavaria there was panic at the prospect of an Allied invasion through weak Austria and an appeal to separate from Prussia and join the new republican movement developing in German Austria. The one loyal element in southern Germany was the Catholic trade unions. In Prussia's docile civil service and in the Army the Kaiser's authority remained unshaken.

Prince Max had not forgotten his letter to the Kaiser of 7 September, pledging that his government would be 'the last chance for the monarchical idea in general', but he was now subject to 'daily growing pressure from below'. The Prince had always held that his job as Chancellor would be to bring the Kaiser and the people together again. Once in office, however, he discovered, as with his 'psychological method' of war, that history was heading in another direction.

On 20 October the Kaiser capitulated on the question of the U-boat war, and the next day he summoned the whole government to the Schloss Bellevue, where he read a short address. 'The New Times shall give birth to the New Order,' he said, welcoming his 'collaborators in the sacred task of bringing the German Empire out of this troublous time'.

'If only this speech had been made three months ago!' exclaimed Haussmann on his return to Berlin. Prince Max thought that the tone of the speech was impressive and reflected 'the natural graciousness' of the Kaiser's personality. Erzberger appreciated the Kaiser's private words of sympathy for his lost son but thought it absurd that, at such a grave moment for Germany, he did not tackle the main political issues: 'the audience lasted only half an hour.'[74]

Prince Max clung on to the monarchical principle. Instinctively, he consulted the federal princes and discovered – not surprisingly – that they too were opposed to the Kaiser's abdication. Then, just after he had contracted flu, a telegram arrived from a cousin and old colleague earlier in the war, Prince Ernst zu Hohenlohe-Langenburg. He was living in Berne, Switzerland, where he had been negotiating with American delegates over prisoners of war. Prince Ernst claimed that Wilson's note of the 23rd 'can really only mean that the only way to obtain even moderately reasonable conditions leads through the abdication of the Kaiser'. 'Now we stand alone, bleeding from a thousand wounds, deserted by our allies, hard-pressed by enemies, whose superiority grows daily,' he wrote in a follow-up letter. He pleaded that the Kaiser be made to abdicate 'for the sake of his people's future' – 'I have a firm belief in the future of Germandom; the world needs our ideals and our character.'[75]

Prince Max, on his sickbed, was pondering the meaning of this letter – which had more effect on him than all the appeals from his ministers or a hundred articles in the newspapers – when news came through that the Italians had crossed the Piave and the Austrian Army had surrendered; 30,000 Austrians had been killed in this final six-day battle, with another 427,000 taken prisoner.

But this was still not enough for Prince Max to make up his mind: 'I still had the feeling that the last hope for the Kaiser lay in maintaining a close reserve,' he admitted in his memoirs. Typically, he selected three 'confidential agents' – General von Chelius, a former imperial aide-de-camp, Count August Eulenberg, Minister of the Royal Household, and the court's chaplain, Herr von Dryander – to go to the Kaiser and ask him if he would abdicate by his own 'free choice'. The agents all refused the mission, believing – understandably – that this was the Chancellor's job. But the Chancellor would not commit himself.

Then the Kaiser suddenly announced that he was leaving Berlin for Spa to be 'in the midst of my generals'. The Prince thought at first it was a 'bad joke'. He made a personal telephone call to the Kaiser, pleading with him not to leave: 'We are now entering on the most difficult time of all,' he implored; 'at such a time Your Majesty cannot be absent.' 'If you do all I have told you to do,' His Majesty cryptically replied, 'all may still be well.'[76]

Kaiser Wilhelm had developed a new theory for peace: a European Monroe Doctrine.[77] He exposed it that afternoon, 29 October, to Admiral von Müller just before boarding his train for Spa. The Kaiser looked 'hollow-eyed', but his behaviour was tranquil and gay. 'Well, this is a strange reversal of the situation,' he exclaimed. 'The English are at loggerheads with the Americans.' And so they were – though not in quite the way his Dutch agent had explained it. The Kaiser recommended that Germany make her peace offer to England, not the United States; then sign a treaty with the Japanese to throw the Americans out of Europe: he already saw the Japanese divisions arriving via Serbia to join with the British and the Germans on the Western Front against America. This was the way to obtain a good peace and also – an important consideration – maintain the Navy along with its submarines.

'We are living through a very interesting era,' he cheerfully concluded, 'first with the development of the Fleet, and then the war years.' He gave his regards to Müller's family and disappeared. Müller never saw him again. The Kaiser never saw Berlin again. But the idea of an anti-American Anglo-German alliance was reborn in the German capital twenty years later.[78]

Prince Max rose like Lazarus from his bed on Thursday, 31 October, to attend a Cabinet meeting. One of his main concerns now was to assure himself that he still had a Cabinet. The Social Democrats were threatening to withdraw their support over the issue of abdication, and no government could survive without them – a fact that was due less to their control of the vote in the Reichstag than to their influence on the hungry crowds outside it.

This was beginning to worry him more than a collapse on the front. The need for an armistice was therefore doubly urgent. If there was to be an abdication of the Kaiser, it had to be used to this end. The Prince defined in his mind two deadlines: the American congressional elections on 5 November and the presentation of Foch's armistice terms, which no one expected to be tender. To strengthen Wilson's hand, the abdication would have to be announced before either of these took place – in other words, within a matter of days.

But the Chancellor again wavered. He could not take on his princely shoulders the responsibility of demanding that the Kaiser abdicate; it had to be the Kaiser's own 'free choice', a 'splendid gesture'. There was much argument in the meeting and even more analysis. Scheidemann pressed hardest for the abdication. The Catholic southerner Erzberger violently opposed it, warning that this would lead to the Reich breaking up just like Russia and Austria-Hungary. The Chancellor made his plea for imperial free will, and the meeting came to an end with no decision having been made at all.[79]

Prince Max returned to the idea of sending 'confidential agents' to the Kaiser with the polite request that His Majesty abandon his throne. The Grand Duke of Baden was asked to carry out the mission, as were Friedrich Karl of Hesse and August Wilhelm of Prussia. They all refused. Prince Max's legal adviser, Geheimrat Simons, lost his temper with Prince Friedrich Karl when the latter backed out at the last minute. He told the Hessian Prince that if he could not bring himself to look his Kaiser in the eye he made a poor comparision with Luther, who in front of the Diet of Worms had announced, 'Here I stand, I cannot help myself, God help me!'

They all refused save one: Herr Drews, the Prussian Minister of the

Interior, 'the embodiment of the best traditions of Prussian officialdom'. Drews consented to leave for Spa the next day and to telegraph immediately the results of his encounter to Berlin with one word: either 'agreement' or 'disagreement'.[80]

'How comes it that you, a Prussian official, one of my subjects, who have taken an oath of allegiance to me, have the insolence and effrontery to appear before me with a request like this?' asked the irate Kaiser on hearing the polite request. Drews made a deep bow. 'Very well, then, supposing I did,' continued the Kaiser. 'What do you suppose would happen next, you, an administrative official? My sons have assured me that none of them will take my place. So the whole House of Hohenzollern would go along with me.' Drews, according to the Kaiser's own account, took fright.

'And who would then take on the regency for a twelve-year-old child, my grandson? The Imperial Chancellor perhaps? I gather from Munich that they haven't the least intention of recognizing him down there. So what would happen?'

'Chaos,' replied Drews, and bowed again.

'All right then,' said the Kaiser, 'let me tell you the form chaos would take. I abdicate. All the dynasties fall along with me, the army is left leaderless, the front-line troops disband and stream over the Rhine. The disaffected gang up together, hang, murder and plunder – assisted by the enemy. That is why I have no intention of abdicating. I have no intention of quitting the throne because of a few hundred Jews and a thousand workmen. Tell that to your masters in Berlin!'[81]

It is not recorded what word Drews sent back to Berlin. Events were moving fast now. Each cell of power continued to retreat into itself. The High Seas Fleet, the Kaiser's proud creation and sign of independence, took matters into its own hands. Admiral Scheer, without even consulting the government, issued an order to the Third Squadron, anchored at Kiel, to set out on a raid to force an exit to the Channel and relieve evacuation operations in Belgium. The sailors of Kiel dubbed it a 'Death Cruise' – and they refused to move.[82]

But the Imperial Chancellor knew none of this. He had not yet recovered from the flu. Exhausted by the ceaseless debate and worry, he returned to his bed on Friday evening, 1 November. His doctor administered a drug that would ensure him rest. It did. Prince Max fell into a two-day coma.

12

The following Sunday, orders were received by the US 3rd Brigade, 2nd Division, to push out a reconnaissance north of American lines in the direction of Baumont, a small town on the left bank of the Meuse about ten miles south of Sedan. The previous Friday Pershing's First Army had launched its fourth offensive in the Argonne, with about as much success as the previous three. Troops were sent forward with their rifles, wave after wave, against German machine-guns; America's entire fleet of eighteen tanks gave the right wing a temporary advantage; Colonel George C. Marshall had had the good idea of using messenger pigeon to keep in touch with the front battalions – but when they ran out of pigeons the contact was broken. The advance slowed. Then the familiar traffic problem developed in the rear; not even the motorcycle couriers could get through. By Sunday the situation was looking as grim as ever – indeed, worse than ever, for the number of combat troops available to Pershing was now in serious decline, despite the huge reinforcements being supplied from across the Atlantic.

So one can understand why the 3rd Brigade proceeded that evening with caution. An ugly, dark strip of woodland lay in front of them. The commander called up artillery to give it a preliminary pounding before ordering his troops in. The road was so narrow that they had to form in single file. They met surprisingly little resistance. They ran into retreating German infantry, who gave themselves up and were simply passed down the American column. They overtook German artillery; the gunners surrendered without a shot being fired. German-speaking Americans had to be brought to the head of the column in order to deal with this novel problem. They came to a farmhouse with the lights turned on and arrested its inhabitants, a full complement of German officers. By dawn the next morning they had already reached Beaumont. For the 3rd Brigade, exhausted by the weekend's stern battle, front-line warfare was transformed that night into a police raid.[83]

It would not be so easy for the rest of the American Army. By Tuesday evening the major part of the American forces had moved up to within twenty miles of Sedan, but there still lay before them the belts of forested hill which, like the breakers of an ocean, bordered the western edges of the great Ardennes massif of Belgium. On Friday they finally joined with Gouraud's French Fourth Army at Wadelincourt on the outskirts of Sedan. That was the day it was announced that German parliamentarians, with their white flags, had crossed the line at La Capelle.

The war correspondent Philip Gibbs was with Horne's British First Army 'in the light of a golden All Souls' Day' – Friday, 1 November – when the Canadians moved on Valenciennes. An uproar of gunfire rose from the coloured woods, women and children from the recently liberated villages were on the roads, holding in their hands bouquets of autumn flowers; around Saultain and along the sides of the little Rhonelle river there were a large number of German dead – the Canadians, it was said, were not taking prisoners. 'They have lived amongst and talked to the French people here,' wrote General Currie of his 'fellows'; 'they have become more bitter than ever against the Boche.' On Saturday – 'a foul day with wet mist steaming through the shell-pierced walls' – they took the old city. 'There was hardly a living soul about, except odd figures like shadows in the wet fog lurking under the walls – our soldiers, by the shape of their steel hats,' recorded Gibbs. In the distance could be seen the black slag mountains, 'like Egyptian pyramids', which had marked the nineteenth century in this northern corner of France. Over the years, Anzin and Valenciennes had manufactured coal and lace, poverty and wealth.[84] But now the place was empty. Gibbs wandered down a street of vacant shops. He found an old couple at one corner. 'Monsieur,' sighed the husband, 'they have stolen everything, broken everything, and have ground us down for four years. They are bandits and brigands.' Up the Rue Saint-Jacques lay the station, 'this great junction of German traffic', now an elaborate ruin; 'Liverpool Street Station would look like this if it had been smashed into twisted iron and broken glass by storms of high explosives.'[85]

It was the seizure of the station, the river Scheldt, the Sambre Canal and the railway line running parallel which broke the German Army during All Souls' weekend, 1918.

Retreat turned into a rout. On Sunday and Monday the RAF conducted a massive air assault on the congested roads south and east of Valenciennes. Because of the low cloud, the aircraft came in at a hundred feet to drop their bombs and open up their machine-guns. Horse-drawn wagons were torn apart, motor trucks, cannon, machine-guns and trench mortars were smashed, while the columns of grey-dressed infantry were split up and massacred. Whole army divisions were destroyed in a single day. Without the railway, their only route of escape was along the country tracks that led into Belgium.

That Monday at dawn the New Zealand Rifle Brigade, the 'Diggers', of Byng's British Third Army began an assault on the walled citadel of Le Quesnoy. Even the normally staid official history described the battle as 'an episode of the age of Agincourt'. In fact Le Quesnoy had fired some of the first cannon in European history upon the English Army during the Crécy campaign of 1346.

In November 1918 its German commander refused to yield. With Stokes mortars and medium trench mortar batteries and machine-guns, the New Zealanders managed to drive the Germans back from the outer ramparts and then, using a thirty-foot ladder, scaled them single file to tackle the precipitous inner bastion. The ladder barely reached its top. Two second lieutenants sprang from its last rung to discover a handful of Germans, who immediately took flight. The city surrendered. Every building suddenly bloomed with tricolours; people came rushing out of the houses and cellars and showered the Diggers with autumn flowers. Here and there could be heard the crack of a rifle. The brigade's young captain, a revolver in one hand, garlands in the other, led the way to the main square, where, before a cheering crowd, he received the German commander's surrender.[86]

No scene on the front in those first days of November was representative of the soldier's experience'. It was not a week of the 'typical'.

The belt of wooded hills to the south of Le Quesnoy lay along the Sambre Canal: the forests of Nouvion, of Rignaval and of Mormal. These now formed the 'hinge' of the French and British front. The first two were left to Debeney's French First Army, which, after taking Guise, forged a way through to the mined crossroads at La Capelle. The larger Forest of Mormal was in the sector of Rawlinson's British Fourth Army. Between Aulnoye and Landrecies, the canal, which included a whole network of parallel ditches exploited by the market gardeners of the Thiérache, formed the eastern border of the wood. A little further on was a farm, 'La Folie'; the village beyond was called Ors.

'Look here, you fellows,' declared a new brigadier a little ingenuously when he visited the 37th Division that Sunday. 'The division will attack in three days' time, right into the Mormal Forest.' He sat down and the men listened to his impossible pledge: 'we are promised from above that it is the last attack we shall ever be asked to make'. Everyone looked at him stupidly. He was perfectly serious. The men called for a drink.[87]

It was actually the 32nd Division which launched the 'last attack' the next morning, 4 November, at dawn – across the Sambre Canal at Ors. Among the assailants were the 96th Brigade, the Manchesters, and the poet Wilfred Owen.

Rain had poured until midnight, then a screen of dense fog had descended, enclosing the fields and trees in wetness. Planks, duckboards and wire-linked wooden floats were heaved across the sodden soil to positions behind the canal. When the whistles blew at 5.45 a.m. the British barrage belched out fire and thunder, sending up great geysers on the opposite side of the canal. Owen led his own platoon down the bank and across a parallel ditch. But, when they reached the towpath by the canal, men were already falling to the stutter of machine-guns that had been brought up after the barrage had lifted. Soon the machine-guns were joined by enemy artillery. Still the men worked on constructing a bridge, the wood splintering in their hands and sparks flying from the wire. One by one they fell. James Kirk, a nineteen-year-old second lieutenant, paddled across the canal on a raft and with his Lewis took on a German gunner at ten yards. The bridge was built and two platoons managed to cross before a shell cut it off – the same shell that killed Kirk. Volunteers went in to repair the bridge and enough of them survived to complete the job, but their commander was killed as his men moved across.

Owen remained on the east bank, walking backwards and forwards congratulating the troops. He was just giving some help with duckboards at the water's edge when he was shot and killed.[88]

At midday the rest of the Manchesters crossed the canal south of Ors.

Byng's Third and Rawlinson's Fourth Army pushed across the Forest of Mormal in the following two days. By Wednesday evening, the 6th, they were within three miles of Avesnes and the main road that linked Maubeuge through La Capelle to Vervins, which had been recently liberated, amid scenes of joy, by the French Third Army.

Tragedy, comedy; cruelty, tenderness; the sun, the cloud and the rain – there is no single true story of the Great War of '14–18.

13

Around midday on Sunday, 3 November, Prince Max awoke from his coma. Colonel von Haeften came almost immediately to his bedside and whispered, 'You need not bear the horrible responsibility any longer.' He had thoughtfully prepared with the Vice-Chancellor a press notice that stated that the Chancellor had suffered a relapse and that Payer would take charge of affairs until further notice. Prince Max found the idea tempting, but then began to reflect on the issue of duty and, in particular, on his obligations to the Kaiser. The press notice was not released.

During his first few hours of consciousness he worried exclusively about the abdication problem. If the Kaiser does not abdicate, he thought to himself, then how is Germany going to resist the other conditions of what will undoubtedly be a harsh armistice? The Prince still put his faith in the 'life and death struggle', and he thought this would be best achieved without the Kaiser. But the Kaiser would have to abdicate voluntarily.

He was unaware of the disasters on the Western Front. In the evening he learned that Turkey had signed an armistice on 31 October, and that Austria had just that Sunday accepted the enemy's armistice terms. Prince Max's principal concern was that this could open up a military front in Bavaria; the Allies were expected to be in Innsbruck by 15 November.

The Chancellor was suffering once more from early-morning premonitions when he got up on Monday. The first thing he did was to telegraph General Groener in Spa, instructing him to come to Berlin as soon as possible, not only to report on the situation on the Western Front but to explain what was going on inside Germany. 'Four weeks ago', recorded Prince Max, 'the question every morning had been: Has there been no catastrophe at the Front? Today our worst fears were focused on the dangers at home.' Groener agreed to be in Berlin the next day.[89]

Virtually the whole of Monday was devoted to the developing mutiny in Kiel. News came through early in the day of bloody conflict between the mutineering sailors and the soldiers still loyal to the Kaiser; there were dead and wounded, and the troops' commander had been severely injured.

The Cabinet decided to send Conrad Haussmann, Prince Max's friend and Progressive deputy, along with Gustav Noske, a leading Social Democrat, to Kiel to find out what was going on and to try to calm the rioters. 'Throughout

4 November,' recorded Prince Max, 'telegraph and telephone connections functioned badly. We waited in a state of extreme tension for the first news from Noske and Haussmann.'[90]

As a matter of fact, the sailors were waiting for some form of government representation. During the weekend, in the dark of night, an officer had crept aboard one of the rebels' battleships and, to a crowd gathered around the forward gun battery, had cried out, 'Tell me what it is you want!' He got none of the expected answers, like amnesty, shore leave, or the cancelling of the 'Death Cruise'. Instead there was a long silence, followed by the scream 'We want Erzberger!' A roar of applause broke out, with the sailors banging their metal mugs together.[91]

Matthias Erzberger was an odd choice for the mutineers. In the Cabinet meetings on Monday and Tuesday the leader of the Catholic Centre Party took a tough stance against the mutineers. He objected to the granting of amnesty, he wanted the ringleaders rounded up, he suggested that proclamations threatening severe punishments be dropped over Kiel by aeroplane, and in the end he joined the Minister of Marine in a call for an armed invasion of the port, combined with bombardment from the sea.[92] But by Tuesday, 5 November, the government was beginning to worry about other things.

General Groener arrived on schedule. Prince Max liked Groener. One has the impression that, given the chance, he would have put him in Ludendorff's place long ago, because, unlike his predecessor, after years of service in the Ministry of War Groener had developed a political mind. He could work with the trade unions. He was appreciated by the Social Democrats. What is more, Groener had long been on outpost duty in the East, where, as Prince Max put it, he had been 'filled with the consciousness of our power and of the responsibility which was laid upon us'. In other words, he – like Prince Max – had a sense of political *duty*; 'these Eastern soldiers had "Ethical Imperialism" in their bones'. Many members of Prince Max's government also respected General Groener.[93]

But ten days in Spa – the bastion and cloister of Supreme Command, a refuge for the Kaiser – had already affected Groener. His military report, which he read out to the Cabinet, carried the familiar musty odour of unreality. Germany was 'encircled'; withdrawal from the Flanders coast had involved the loss of *matériel*, of wounded men and of a 'close-meshed network of railways'. 'Our first duty is and remains that of avoiding under all circumstances a decisive defeat of the army.' Payer followed with the ritual question 'How much longer do we have before we will have to capitulate?' Groener gave the ritual reply: 'We can certainly manage to hold out long enough for negotiations. If we are luckier the time may be longer, if we are unlucky, shorter.' Groener thought the danger point now lay north of Verdun, where the Americans were attacking, and 'he begged us to be patient a few days till the operations in question were concluded'.[94]

The slight delay between the event and the event's effect was again at work here. Groener's report would have been an accurate enough account for late October. It had nothing to do with the situation on 5 November.

That evening Noske telephoned in his report from Kiel. Naval authority had completely collapsed, red flags were flying on the mastheads, the mutineers were demanding amnesty and the Kaiser's abdication; and they had just named Noske as governor of the region.

On Wednesday morning Prince Max invited Groener to join him in the Chancellery gardens. Groener had just been in touch with the Kaiser, who had told him that a direct channel would now have to be established in order to determine exactly what the Allied terms of armistice were. That meant somebody was going to have to cross the lines with a white flag. He said as much to the Chancellor.

'But not for a week at least?' asked Prince Max.

'A week is too long a time,' answered the General grimly.

'Anyhow, not before Monday?' asked the Prince again.

'Even that is too long a wait, it must be Saturday at the latest.'

Inside the Chancellery the Cabinet had already assembled. On entering, Prince Max immediately disclosed what the General had said. 'I too had hoped we should be able to wait eight or ten days till we had taken up our position on the new line,' added Groener swiftly. It was not the fault of the Army, it was not the situation on the front; it was the 'state of feeling at home' – and particularly the problems developing in Kiel and in Bavaria – which had forced him to the conclusion that, 'painful as it is, we must take the step of asking Foch'.

But Groener insisted that ascertaining the Allied armistice conditions did not mean accepting them. If the worst came to the worst, a last resistance would be organized on the Rhine.

At around midday, as had been arranged, a meeting took place between Groener and select leaders from the Social Democratic Party and the trade unions. The Social Democrat leaders were demanding the immediate abdication of the Kaiser. Groener said it was out of the question; with the Army engaged in such a critical struggle, he politely explained, it was 'impossible to deprive it of its Supreme War Lord'.

Philipp Scheidemann came in at that moment, white with excitement, to announce that he had just heard that the mutineers had seized Hamburg and Hanover. 'Gentlemen,' he exclaimed, 'the present is no time for discussion; now it is time to act. We cannot be sure that tomorrow we shall still be sitting in these chairs.'

But Groener remained adamant: there would be no abdication. With tears in his eyes, Friedrich Ebert of the Social Democrats pleaded that the Kaiser's abdication did not necessarily mean the abolition of the monarchy. For Groener it did, and he stood firm: no abdication.

'Under the circumstances, any further discussion is superfluous; events must take their course,' replied Ebert, addressing the whole assembly. Then he turned to Groener and continued, 'We are grateful to you, Your Excellency, for this frank exchange of views, and shall always have pleasant recollections of our work with you during the war. We have reached the parting of the ways; who knows whether we shall ever see one another again.'

He thereupon left the room, and the others filed out in silence.

During the meeting, a report had been picked up on the wireless concerning Wilson's final note. The Allies had apparently accepted the Fourteen Points as a basis for peace negotiations, with the two provisos that 'Freedom of the Seas' was still open to discussion and that 'evacuation' of occupied territories also meant 'compensation'. The note concluded that 'Marshal Foch has been authorized by the Government of the United States and the Allied Governments to receive properly accredited representatives of the German Government, and to communicate to them the terms of an armistice.'

Ludendorff had set up an Armistice Commission during the crisis of early October, but its members were all military men. Before boarding a special train back to Spa, Groener agreed that a civilian would have to be included. 'I could only welcome it if the Army and the Army command remained as little involved as possible with these unfortunate negotiations, from which nothing good was to be expected,' Groener later commented. Wilson had insisted on 'democratic' representation. Furthermore, Prince Max had to face the real possibility that a purely military commission would simply break off negotiations.

The choice fell on Matthias Erzberger. Why Erzberger? Prince Max would have preferred his own friend Conrad Haussmann. But Haussmann was not a member of the parliamentary majority. It could not be a Social Democrat; there had just been a 'parting of the ways'. There was no one else available but Erzberger.

'I was suddenly called, on 6 November 1918, at midday, to direct the negotiations of the armistice,' Erzberger recalled in his memoirs. Groener recorded that the poor man was 'pale with shock' when he arrived at the station to take the same special train to Spa. They had to wait for the delivery of papers granting Erzberger 'full powers' – the Office of Foreign Affairs had never heard of such a document.

It was well after dark when the train blew a whistle and at last shunted out of the station. Groener was heading for Spa and his Kaiser. Erzberger had no idea of his final destination.[95]

14

In the early hours of the following morning an army radio operator at the top of the Eiffel Tower picked up a message from the German Supreme Command addressed to Marshal Foch. It announced that five plenipotentiaries had been selected to conclude an armistice on the Western Front and asked that 'one communicate by wireless the place where they can meet the Marshal'. The astonished operator immediately radioed the message on to Senlis, where Foch now had his headquarters. Foch was woken up. He did not hesitate to send his reply: 'If the German plenipotentiaries wish to meet Marshal Foch and request from him an armistice, they should present themselves at French forward posts on the road Chimay–Fourmies–La Capelle–Guise. Orders have been given to receive them and drive them to the place fixed for the meeting.'[96]

Monsieur Louis Roux-Durfort, inspector of the Chemin de Fer du Nord, was also raised from his slumbers and instructed to hitch up some vintage company railway carriages – if possible dating from the Second Empire – and have them delivered as soon as possible to Chantilly. It was not too tall a demand, since nearby Compiègne had been the favourite residence of Emperor Napoleon III, and several of his carriages were still in the company's rolling stock. Roux-Durfort found two sleepers, a restaurant carriage, two second-class passenger coaches and a saloon. The saloon was a prize – built in 1860, with the interior fitted up in green satin adorned with golden Napoleonic bees and one handsome capital 'N' embroidered in laurels.[97]

A police platoon was awaiting the train when it pulled into Chantilly on Thursday evening, 7 November. As they loaded it with victuals – canned food, crates of Bordeaux wine and a magnum of cognac, vintage 1870 – Roux-Durfort suddenly realized the significant role his train was to play. There had been much speculation in the press about an armistice. The train was obviously designed to receive a German delegation. No German entering it, at the very moment when French and American forces were preparing an assault on Sedan, would be allowed to forget France's humiliation outside the same town in September 1870.

Roux-Durfort was told to continue on to Senlis. There he recognized the familiar profile of Marshal Foch, who boarded in the company of four high-ranking French staff officers and three British naval staff officers. One of them was the First Sea Lord, Vice-Admiral Sir Rosslyn Wemyss.

There was no question of receiving Germans in Senlis. The Germans had shot the mayor and and several citizens during their brief occupation of the town in September 1914. So once more the train set off, past Compiègne, to halt in the middle of the forest, north of the village of Rethondes, where the trees had been cleared for an artillery park. But in the dark hours of Friday morning, 8 November, it was silent and empty.

Finally, at dawn, a second train pulled into a siding a hundred yards away.

15

At Spa, Supreme Command had accepted the idea of civilian representation on the Armistice Commission with some relief. Its chairman, the venerable General F. G. W. T. von Gündell, was removed to make way for Erzberger, who thus became Germany's first plenipotentiary. Erzberger's friend Count von Oberndorff, former minister to Bulgaria, joined him. Erzberger insisted that 'the appearance of a large number of officers would be at this moment, to say the least, inopportune', and the generals couldn't agree more. Eventually the military side of the delegation had been whittled down to two men. One was an obscure naval captain named Vanselow (the British press mistakenly referred to this representative of the German High Seas Fleet as 'Captain von Seelow'); the other was General von Winterfeldt. Winterfeldt knew France well. He had been the German military attaché to Paris before the war, and his father had helped draw up France's terms of surrender at Sedan in 1870. ('I wonder why they sent him,' one of the British delegates later remarked.)

After the meeting, lunch was served in the Hôtel Britannique. Field Marshal Hindenburg said it was the first time in the annals of war that a military armistice was to be concluded by civilians. But he did not regret it. Supreme Command, after all, 'no longer had responsibility for political directives'.

The Field Marshal saw the delegation off in their high-backed saloons and open tourers. 'God be with you and try and obtain the most you can for our Fatherland,' he said.[98]

The sad procession had barely reached the outskirts of Spa when Erzberger's car hit a kerbstone and was thrown against the neighbouring house; the car behind him also collided into it. 'Neither Count Oberndorff, seated next to me, nor myself were wounded by the shattered glass,' recorded Erzberger, 'but the two autos were seriously damaged.' With the remaining cars they continued over the high hills in the direction of 'Chimay–Fourmies–La Capelle–Guise'.

For the first time Erzberger saw what the reports about the Army's 'retreat' meant. The plenipotentiaries ran into a tide of broken humanity. The whole world was on the move. In the remotest hamlets, across isolated plateaux and fields, ragged columns of soldiery tramped: a sea of desperate faces.

As evening fell the party reached Chimay. The commanding general there told them they couldn't possibly get through that night since the road west had been barred by trees thrown across it by his own men. Erzberger telephoned the General Staff, further on at Trelay. A special detachment of

Pioneers was brought in to clear a path and defuse the mines. At 7.30 they were in Trelay. At 9.20, German time, they crossed the line.

An old sheet was cut up to provide flags. Erzberger had brought along a trumpet, and a single note was blown regularly as they passed a village cemetery, a café at the crossroads, down a slope clammy with the night's fog, and round a slight bend to join the misty corridor of a road at Haudroy. Figures rose from a field. They looked, at a distance, as though they were dressed in white.

'C'est fini la guerre?' asked someone in the crowd that gathered round them. The little town of La Capelle was decked in tricolours, though the French had entered only that day. A French car was provided for each one of the delegates. Before leaving, they were photographed under 'the glimmer of rockets'.

Erzberger, accompanied by 'a Prince de Bourbon', was stunned by the destruction he saw. He remembered one village: 'Not a house was standing. It was a succession of ruins. Under the moon, the broken walls had a spectral allure. Not a living being for miles.'[99]

They were served 'French cognac' in the train that took them from a town with no buildings to a place with no name. The carriage curtains were kept closed. At dawn they came to a halt in the middle of a forest. 'I asked several times where we were, without ever getting an answer.'

There was another train nearby.

Shortly after their arrival the French Chief of Staff, General Weygand, entered their carriage and announced that, if they wished to see Marshal Foch, he would receive them in his train opposite at nine o'clock precisely. The last stage of the German delegates' long journey was the hundred yards of duckboard linking the two spurs of track, originally designed for long-range railway guns. They walked in single file, the two civilians in dark suits, the two military men in simple combat dress. Inside the saloon car a long table had been installed and four places, with their names, had been reserved for them. No civilians were present on the Allied side. 'There were no Americans there, or Italians, or Belgians,' observed Erzberger. 'Only the Allied Supreme Command took part in the armistice negotiations.'[100]

From the Allied point of view that was the whole point: this was a purely military affair, designed not to negotiate but to communicate to the enemy Allied conditions for a ceasefire. 'The Bosches evidently wish to make it principally a civilian affair,' Rear Admiral Hope wrote to his wife that Friday, 'and the French and we are very angry with them for only sending military and naval officers of a rather subordinate rank.'[101]

Once the four German delegates had taken their places, in came Marshal Foch and Admiral Wemyss, representing the Allied war effort on the land and on the sea. Foch struck Erzberger as 'a little man with energetic features, who betrays on first sight a habit to command'.

There was a brief introduction and then Foch asked, 'What has brought these gentlemen here? What do you want of me?'

Erzberger replied in German that his delegation had 'come to receive the proposals of the Allied Powers regarding an armistice on land, on sea and in the air, on all the fronts, and in the colonies'.

'I have no proposals to make,' Foch answered categorically.

There was some murmuring over the translation, and then Count von Oberndorff stated that they did not stand on form: the German delegation 'asked for the conditions of the armistice'.

'I have no conditions to *offer*,' said the Marshal.

Erzberger read out Wilson's last note, which stated clearly that the Marshal had been authorized by the United States and Allied governments to communicate to accredited German representatives the terms of an armistice.

Foch said he was authorized to make known the armistice conditions if the German delegates asked for an armistice. 'Do you *ask* for an armistice? If you do, I can inform you of the conditions subject to which it can be obtained.'

Both Erzberger and Oberndorff said 'Yes.' Foch had set the tone; these were conditions, and not a matter for negotiation.

Weygand read out the principal clauses of the armistice. Not a single person sitting in that tiny carriage was unmoved by the event. Foch was 'as calm as a statue', but every now and then he made a telling tug at his moustache. Admiral Wemyss affected indifference, but it didn't prevent him from either toying with his monocle or fiddling with the tortoiseshell spectacles which lay in front of him. Tears could be detected in Winterfeldt's eyes. Captain Vanselow openly wept.

The German delegates expected conditions that would demand evacuation, repatriation of the former residents, the delivery of armaments and rolling stock, along with a tight timetable – initially, twenty-five days for the evacuation. They were not surprised at the demand for reparations. What did shock them was the announcement that the whole left bank of the Rhine would be occupied, along with bridgeheads at Mainz, Koblenz, Cologne and Strasbourg, while a 'neutral zone' would have to be established along the length of the right bank. The requirement to surrender all submarines and a major part of the surface fleet was unexpected. And they were dismayed by the Allied intention to continue their naval blockade of Germany until all these conditions were met.

There was a brief exchange of words. Erzberger, having just witnessed the retreating military mob in Belgium, asked for an immediate suspension of hostilities; German army discipline had broken down, he said, and a revolutionary situation was developing in Germany itself. With Bolshevism installed in Central Europe, he went on, 'Western Europe would find the greatest difficulty in escaping it'.

Foch was not impressed. No one in Western Europe was impressed by this sort of argument, because no one knew, beyond second-hand newspaper reports on Kiel and Munich, what was going on inside Germany. Fierce resistance at some points on the front had led Westerners to overestimate the strength of the country. Would Germany be defeated like Napoleon's France in 1814, fighting to the bitter end? Or would it be like Prussia after Jena in 1806, a rout and collapse within days? Many cautious Westerners, including Foch, thought they had Napoleon in front of them and were preparing for two winter campaigns: one across Lorraine and the other through the Ardennes along the Sambre–Meuse line. But Erzberger could have let them into the secret: it would be Jena on a grander scale.

'It is impossible to stop military operations until the German delegation has accepted and signed the conditions which are the very consequence of those operations,' replied the Marshal. He dismissed the dangers that Erzberger had just pointed out. German indiscipline? That is 'the usual disease prevailing in beaten armies'. The menace of Bolshevism? That is 'symptomatic of a nation completely worn out by war'. 'Western Europe', he assured the Germans, 'will find means of defending itself against this danger.'

General von Winterfeldt appealed for the 'numerous victims who will die in vain at the last minute' if hostilities continued.

'I am entirely disposed to arrive at a conclusion and will help you in as much as I can,' said the Marshal, but 'hostilities cannot cease before the signing of the Armistice.'

The meeting lasted only three-quarters of an hour. Foch explained that his hands were tied by decisions made by the Western governments and their general headquarters. There might be some problems of practical application to discuss, and perhaps even a few modifications to the secondary details would need to be made. But, as for the essential conditions, Germany would have either to accept them or to refuse them. Foch gave the delegation seventy-two hours to reflect. Erzberger's attempt to extend the deadline by another ten hours was not accepted. So the Germans had until eleven o'clock on Monday morning, the eleventh day of November.

First they had to inform Supreme Command of the conditions. Such an important document could not be read over a telephone. The Allies would not allow them to telegraph it 'in the clear', and the delegation had not brought with them their ciphers. So they had to find a courier who would physically carry the document to Spa. It took Captain von Helldorf five hours to reach the advancing French lines and another five hours to get through them, the Germans firing on him 'like devils'. The document was finally delivered in Spa on Saturday morning, 9 November, the beginning of one of the most turbulent days in German history.

Erzberger had given Helldorf a personal message to pass on to Hindenburg. While no counter-proposals to the essential clauses could be made, he would attempt to mitigate some of the material demands with the specific aim of maintaining order in Germany and avoiding famine; he said he would declare it impossible to execute all the demands placed on the country. In other words, the question now was simply one of national survival. Ludendorff's old chivalrous thoughts of honourable withdrawal, regrouping and defence – still alive a fortnight earlier – had been blown to the winds.

In the meantime, on Friday afternoon in the forest (the German delegates had not yet discovered their whereabouts), technical discussions were held. That night the Germans had made a fruitless effort at drafting their own counter-proposals. They wanted the occupation of the Rhine bridgeheads deleted and the naval blockade ended. They rested their case on the collapse of their own armed forces, the threat of Bolshevism, and the prospect of famine. Erzberger argued that the Allies were committing the same error now, in the face of Bolshevism, as the former German government had done when it had signed the Treaty of Brest-Litovsk. It was not a very convincing line to follow. In the first place, Erzberger and his majority had endorsed the treaty. Second, the treaty had permanently dismembered the Russian Empire, while the armistice terms relative to the Rhineland were limited to a temporary military occupation.

The Allied side was worried that the civilians in the German delegation would give the discussions a political tone that nobody, not even Wilson, wanted. That Friday there was a constant exchange of telephone calls between Paris and Foch's train. Clemenceau kept on repeating that the 'conditions of peace' were an affair of government and not the Army. The sole purpose of the meeting was to grant a suspension of hostilities on the basis of the outlined conditions. 'Tell them, once and for all,' Clemenceau urged, 'that no suspension of arms will be accorded until they have signed the armistice.'[102]

Pershing, Poincaré and even the recently promoted Marshal Pétain were all insisting that the Allies continue their march into Germany. On Saturday, Clemenceau met Foch at Senlis. Foch had the German 'counter-proposals' in hand. Clemenceau asked him if he saw, 'as a soldier', any disadvantage to signing an armistice with Germany now. 'I see only the advantages,' replied Foch. 'To continue the struggle any longer would be playing too high a risk. Perhaps another fifty or a hundred thousand Frenchmen would be killed for a moot result: I'd reproach myself for it all my life. Enough blood has flowed. That's enough.'

'I am entirely of that opinion,' said Clemenceau with a nod of his head.[103]

Clemenceau reported immediately to Lloyd George that the Germans 'appeared much depressed' and that the signing of the armistice did 'not appear doubtful'. German pleas over famine were not entirely ignored. 'My personal view', wrote Clemenceau to Lloyd George the next day, 'is that we must honour this signature while making a marginal note relative to revictualling, which we cannot to my mind refuse to discuss ultimately.'

On Saturday evening the German delegates were in their carriage, still wondering in which corner of the world they were stationed, when a French captain requested entry. At last, they thought, Foch has replied. But what the captain carried was a brief telegram from Prince Max of Baden announcing that Kaiser Wilhelm had abdicated and that the Crown Prince, after him, had renounced the throne. Negotiations were under way for a regency. Prince Max remained Chancellor.

At midnight, another of Job's messenger's arrived. It was a French staff officer with a press notice: a new 'popular government' had been set up in Berlin under the direction of the Social Democrat Friedrich Ebert.

Was Germany an empire or a republic? Three German officers from Supreme Command turned up on Sunday morning to report that there had been such vast political changes at home that one might wonder whether the new government would be in a position to fulfil the armistice conditions. 'We found ourselves before an embarrassing question,' recalled Erzberger in his inimitable deadpan manner. 'The Army demanded armistice at any price. On the other hand, we did not want to sign a contract with terms we could not fulfil. We ended by agreeing on this point: if the Government authorized us to sign the armistice it meant it also had the power to fulfil its engagements – at least in so far as these were materially possible.' Had any civilian government in Germany during the war exercised such power, such responsibility? Erzberger must have been wondering.[104]

A devout Catholic, he asked if he might attend Sunday mass. A railway employee unwittingly remarked that he should have expressed this wish earlier, since Marshal Foch had already attended mass at Rethondes and there were now no more priests in the neighbourhood.

Rethondes? So that's where they were – in the Forest of Compiègne.

Most of Sunday morning was spent in further technical discussions. It became clear that the Allies were not bending, despite the vague reports of upheaval in Germany.

At lunchtime, workers let the Germans see the headlines in the newspapers: 'Abdication of the Kaiser'. There was little else to do now. The sun had come out, so Erzberger and Count von Oberndorff took a walk in the woods, but they soon came up against fences – the whole area had been cordoned off.

Foch's reply to the counter-proposals was finally delivered that evening, along with a note from General Weygand reminding the delegates that the offer for armistice would expire the next morning at eleven. The delegates awaited the authorization of the new government.

Between 7 and 8 p.m. two notes in fact arrived. The first was from Supreme Command, warning of revolution and of famine if 'the limitation of transportation is maintained and the blockade continued'. The second read simply, 'The German Government accepts the conditions of the armistice communicated to it on 8 November.' It was signed 'REICHSKANZLER SCHLUSS'.

'Who is this Chancellor Schluss?' the French interpreting officer had to ask. 'This gentleman is known neither to General Staff nor to the Government in Paris.' Erzberger had to explain that '*Schluss*' in German meant 'full stop',[105] and added 'This will probably be the Chancellor's full stop.'

A final plenary session, with Foch present, opened at 2.15 a.m., Monday, 11 November. Most of the discussion concentrated on the continuation of the naval blockade. Count von Oberndorff complained that it was not, as he put it in English, 'fair'. 'Not "fair"!' exploded Britain's First Sea Lord. 'Don't forget you have sunk our ships without making any distinction.' It was finally agreed that, though the blockade would be maintained, the 'Allies and the United States contemplate the provisioning of Germany during the Armistice as shall be found necessary'. The quantity of lorries and of freight wagons to be turned over to the Allies was reduced. A few other minor concessions were granted.[106]

The Armistice was signed at 5.12 a.m. This was amended to read 5.00 a.m., so that the ceasefire could be put into effect six hours later. Foch declared the meeting closed, and the Germans withdrew to their carriage. No one shook hands.

Foch immediately sent a message along the whole front by radio and telephone to the commanders-in-chief: 'Hostilities will cease on the entire front on 11 November at 11 a.m. French time.'

16

Shortly before the eleventh hour of the eleventh day of the eleventh month there arrived in the forest clearing outside Compiègne two generals from Supreme Command and two representatives of the new German 'Central Purchasing Society'. The generals wanted to be assured that the fighting was ended: Allied troops were actually penetrating the Ardennes, and Supreme Command knew perfectly well that German frontiers could not be defended with a non-existent army. The two civilians were seeking guarantees for Germany's food supply lines: they were aware that a significant proportion of the country's population was starving. But it was too late for any action: the Armistice had already been signed. Was there a government in Berlin? It was difficult at that moment to be sure. Erzberger learned from the two generals that 'Reichskanzler Schluss' had in fact been Supreme Command in Spa, because nobody could be found in confused Berlin that Sunday to sign authorization for the accord.

It was around eleven o'clock when the delegates' train pulled out of the clearing. This time the curtains were left open. They followed the same line they had taken three days before. All the stations 'were filled with people,' a 'liveliness and joy reigned everywhere', but 'some threats were addressed to the Germans'. They descended at the same desolate site of Tergnier, with its reptilian curled girders and piles of white stone, which the party had left on Friday morning before dawn. It was already evening when French cars drew up to take them to the lines, which they did not reach until two the following morning. Erzberger records nothing about the front during its first hours of peace. All he says is that they crossed it with seven cars, 'of which we lost five during the night'. They found each other again the next day at Spa.[107]

In general, memoirs, diaries and letters are astonishingly discreet about what happened on the front on 11 November 1918. It was spitting with rain along most of the line. Gunner B. O. Stokes of the New Zealand Field Artillery was a dozen miles from where Erzberger crossed in the night, on the 'hinge' of the French and British armies. 'We heard the announcement of the Armistice', he recalled, 'when we were still in the Forest de Mormal on a cheerless, dismal, cold misty day. There was no cheering or demonstration. We were all tired in body and mind, fresh from the tragic fields of battle, and this momentous announcement was too vast in its consequences to be appreciated or accepted with wild excitement. We trekked out of the wood on this dreary day in silence.' It was near the point where Wilfred Owen had fallen one week before. Gunner Stokes still had his horses and guns to look after.[108]

An artillery officer at Le Cateau wrote that men read the news of the Armistice 'without the least show of pleasure'. Was it a 'deep thankfulness deep buried in their hearts'? Fears and misgivings? 'I'm sure I don't know.'[109]

If the Canadian 42nd Battalion entered Mons playing its bagpipes amid 'tremendous enthusiasm', the Queen's Westminster Rifles were engaged in road clearing – 'the glad news caused no demonstration'.[110]

Down in the French lines it was a similar story. 'I am persuaded that those who read me would be absolutely astonished at the calm that reigned in the regiments on learning the war had ended,' wrote the chaplain, Marcellin Lissorgues – a man who knew the *poilus* well. 'Not a cry. No drinking. They approached one another to shake hands.'[111]

There was apparently some cheering on the German side. The French trench newspaper *L'Argonnaute* reported music suddenly breaking out in German trenches and troops rising out of them as if from a jack-in-the box: '*Kameraden,*' they cried, '*la guerre est finie!*' 'My word,' exclaimed the reporter, 'these defeated men seem happier than us.'[112]

That was on the front of the French Fourth Army, which had just entered Sedan. To their right were the Americans, who, according to one newspaper correspondent, let out a 'roar of voices' as if they were 'at some great college contest' – then to be joined by the Germans until 'the rolling plain was alive with cheering men, friends and enemy alike'. Sergeant T. Grady recorded in his diary on 11 November how firing continued until '11.00 sharp'. Then his captain turned up to tell the men the war was over; 'we were dumb-founded and finally came to and cheered – and it went down the line like wildfire'. But Grady had to report at the same time 'Jones' death'. The captain 'conducted a prayer and cried like a baby'.[113]

The Abbé Lissorgues said that the sudden peace provoked in soldiers on the front a 'kind of stupor' – 'I think of those who, in the course of the last two nights, ended with their own blood a long series of massacres.'[114]

Stupor, relief, bitterness, joy: those who wanted to carry the fight on; those who wanted to return home; those who were glad it was over; those who thought it would never be over. All these sentiments can be found in the rare comments made on the day when peace broke out on the Western Front. They are private thoughts and they are quite contradictory. They are literally voices crying in a wilderness – the wilderness of a war ended, a place outside time. The Eleventh of November 1918 is one of the great silences in history.

Autumn 1918

Berlin in autumn

1

The silence of the front found an odd echo in Berlin: virtually no newspapers were published in the *Reichshauptstadt*, the capital of the Reich, on 11 November 1918.

Theodor Wolff's trusty old *Berliner Tageblatt* on Jerusalemer Strasse managed to get out one sheet printed on a single side; it announced the formation of 'a purely socialist cabinet', briefly outlined the terms of the armistice, and printed in bold type at the bottom of the page, 'Because of the strike the Monday number of our newspaper can only appear in this form.'[1]

Evelyn, Princess Blücher – the former Miss Stapleton-Bretherton of Rainhill Hall in Lancashire[2] – came out of a hiding place she had taken that weekend in Dr Mainzer's clinic by the Tiergarten. She was curious to see 'what the world looked like after the deluge of the last two days'. She walked towards the Linden, heard 'a little desultory shooting now and again', and decided that the best thing to do was to go and have lunch in Countess Larisch's nearby hotel. 'Truly, a great storm is passing over the land,' she wrote in her diary that Monday evening, 'princes are falling from their thrones like ripe fruit from a tree.'

Through the Tiergarten – Berlin's version of Hyde Park – ran the long straight alley of the Charlottenburger Chaussée up to the Brandenburg Gate, which had been set up in the late eighteenth-century city customs wall (long since demolished) and had become the traditional site of welcome for high officials and victorious troops. Beyond the Gate the road continued eastward as Unter den Linden, a procession of mostly late nineteenth-century 'baroque' and 'feudal' hotels, cafés and shops, ending in the royal Schloss on the island of old Cölln. Here was the centre of Berlin. Here was where most of the weekend's fighting had taken place.

'Curiosity', warned the *Vossische Zeitung* (printed the night before), 'not only endangers life, it also hinders the work of the services of order.'[3] The events of Monday proved this to be only too true, though heaven only knew who the 'services of order' referred to. At any rate, unlike the Princess, a large number of Berliners were willing to risk a walk in the streets to reconnoitre the world 'after the deluge'.

The shattered glass on the Linden crunched under their feet, from windows smashed by machine-gun fire. You could see a couple of those machine-guns alongside the copper chariot and four chargers on the top of the Gate; others had been placed upon the roofs of hotels, or peeped out from the top-floor window of the odd palace. Red flags, torn out of curtains and blankets, flew from the Opera House, the Guard House, the University building, the Crown Prince's Palace and at the pinnacle of the State Library.

Now who was it who robbed all the cigars from the shop on the corner of Pariser and Fasanenstrasse? 'Looting will be repressed with the utmost vigour,' cautioned the large poster signed by Otto Wels, military governor of Mark Brandenburg. Who could have shot Anna Schneider, a teenage worker, as she stepped out of a shop on Landsberger Allee at four that afternoon? Or the sixteen-year-old schoolboy Kurt Gasse, standing innocently nearby? Both were killed instantly. That 'desultory shooting', popping off all day, was wicked.[4]

The pillar posts on the pedestrian thoroughfares were the only source of news for most Berliners on 11 November. Torn remnants of the previous week's placards could still be seen depicting towns on the Rhine devastated by bombs and fire – a reminder of what to expect from the 'Entente' powers if Germans weakened their resistance on the front. Most of the new notices, carelessly plastered on top, were red, like the flags. They told of further rationing, ways of tackling the milk crisis caused by the train stoppage, and what 'A', 'B' and 'C' cards could purchase (as long as one was first in the queue).

Several bulletins hinted at the shape the 'New Regime of Workers' and Soldiers' Councils' was taking. There had apparently been, the previous evening, a large meeting of council representatives in the Circus Busch on the north side of the Spree, where famous Socialist leaders had spoken. And it could be read that the 'Volkskommissar for Public Security', Emil Eichhorn, had set himself up in the Police Presidium on Alexanderplatz, along with his 'Agents of the Crime Police'; Eichhorn assured Berliners that their old identity papers were valid 'until the new ones are introduced'.[5]

Berlin's traffic seemed to be returning to normal. The shops were open, if bare. People were going back to work. The trams were functioning. There were even a few trains coming into and going out of town.

That had been the worst part of the weekend's crisis, the train stoppage. The electricity had been cut off, the postal services had failed, no telegrams were delivered, and the telephones worked only for local calls. But the trains! Berlin relied on its trains. If it had been the Kaiser's ancestors who had transformed this town from the 'sandpit of the Holy Roman Empire' into the *Reichshauptstadt*, it was trains that had made it a great human machine, a *Weltstadt*, a 'world city'. Berlin was nothing without its trains.

Several people must have read the editorial in the *Rote Fahne*, organ of the radical Spartakusbund, which had temporarily taken over the offices of the conservative *Lokal-Anzeiger* during the weekend. 'The *Weltstadt* has become a lonely island and every one of us has been turned into a little Robinson Crusoe; now that's a real novelty!' Haggard, shipwrecked Robinson Crusoe – an apt model for the new Berliner? Yes, but there were differences, noted the editorialist: Robinson Crusoe had found fish to fish, fruit to pick; he domesticated wild goats and he cleared the land for their pasture. But what can a Berliner do on asphalt? 'Through a thousand little nerve strands the *Weltstadt* is linked with the rest of the Reich. If most of them are cut there is not only pain, the source of life is affected.'[6]

'The source of life'. Berliners on 11 November 1918 knew what that meant. Vast numbers of them were in mourning.

Nobody who reads today the fragile, yellowing pages of Berlin's newspapers for the week of 11 November can fail to notice them: the 'Family Announcements', all framed in black. '*Statt besonderer Anzeiger . . .*' 'Make special announcement that my beloved son, my dearest brother, my brother-in-law, my nephew, was lost in the last battle . . .'; '*Statt besonderer Anzeiger* . . . that my youngest son, our beloved, dear brother, on 5 November, in the last great struggle . . .'; '. . . my only son, my brother, my nephew . . .'

But how astonishing it is to find so many 'special announcements' to 'my beloved youngest daughter, my sister, my niece . . .' These women had died of *die Grippe*, or *Blitzkatarrh* as it was known on the streets: the influenza epidemic which was sweeping through Berlin with a vengeance. Young women were particularly vulnerable. They were exposed in the factories where they now toiled, in the trams they operated, the wagons they drove, the hospitals where they nursed. The macabre joke told at the time was that God had invented the new plague to even out war's imbalance between the sexes.[7]

Autumn had its flowers, but they were grown for graves, not conquering heroes. As Princess Blücher had been noting in her diary for more than a year, among Berliners 'the heroic attitude has entirely disappeared'. In this military city, where every district had its exercise yard and barracks, the Princess had watched, month after month, the people losing their respect for authority and turning 'more and more democratic'; they even seemed prepared to accept defeat if this brought peace.

The massive demonstrations and strikes of the previous January no doubt had some responsibility for this. But not all Berliners were strikers. When Ludendorff's offensive was launched in sunny March, the black-white-and-red imperial flags had flown from the housetops, the flower girls offered bunches of violets and snowdrops to the crowds, and the newspaper boys bawled out victory. 'Now we've got them!' The Reich's armies, it seemed, had already crossed the Channel.[8]

None of that could be groped from the dull, grey impenetrable mists of

11 November. If the newspapers of the following days were anything to go by, there was very little interest even in the Armistice. When the story did make a front page, it consisted of a few paragraphs shoved into a secondary column (accompanied sometimes by a fanciful map showing 'our current position' – as if there were one – and the Entente's definition of the 'evacuation zone'). The international politics of peace had no popular following.

Nevertheless, on 11 November 'streams of people'[9] poured into Berlin's wide eastward alley, the Linden, microcosm of everything the city represented on Europe's plain. Shootings and public warnings had no effect. They wanted to see. They wanted to witness with their own eyes the buildings, the actual sites of the last two days' battle, the stone buildings, the monuments, the palaces, the guard houses, the granite government headquarters into which the collapsing powers of the Reich had suddenly retreated.

Streams of inquisitive persons – what the educated middle classes, the *Bildungsbürgertum*, were always calling 'the masses'. Yet there was something special about Monday's crowd. It included a 'multitude of field grey never known before'.[10] At every crossing one could see big lorries and wagons filled with raggedly dressed soldiers, armed with rifles, flying the red flag and sporting in their caps red cockades which, at a distance, seemed like patches of blood on the forehead. Odder still was the presence of so many sailors: sailors in Berlin, a city that had no major port and was famously set on no major waterway (Humboldthaven hardly compared to 'the Docks'; the Spree – 'a shabby excuse for a stream'[11] – was not exactly the Thames or the Seine).

The sailors had begun to appear on Berlin's streets the previous Thursday. They were from Kiel, Wilhelmshaven, Cuxhaven, Schwerin, Hanover, Lübeck and Hamburg, the towns of the 'Water's Edge', the towns that lived by their bond with the sea.

The soldiers came from Germany's occupying armies in the East and from the so-called *Etappe*, the intermediary zone that had supplied the men and the weapons to the West. But they were not the soldiers of the Western Front. These began arriving only on the next day, the 12th, as, for example, the *Berliner Morgen-Zeitung* noted: 'At the the Anhalter and Potsdamer stations the first flock of returning soldiers made itself felt. Around [Tuesday] midday the two stations presented a picture that was entirely in field grey.' An atmosphere developed that was like former 'holidays in distant peacetime'.[12]

It was the first trickle of a month-long flood. Would it blend with the field grey of the city? There were hints it would not. Berlin in autumn would be coloured by different shades of grey.

2

That peculiar ping-pong match between Berlin and Spa had continued right up to the eleventh hour. Wilhelm Groener, who had replaced Ludendorff as First Quartermaster General on 26 October, was Spa's last main player. He was a southerner, from Württemberg ('He won't be as loyal as a Prussian,' berated his critics) and he had spent the last months of the war running operations in Eastern Europe ('He is ignorant of the Western Front,' they moaned on). He had spent two years in an office in Berlin administering railways – so he knew how the trains ran and was close to the union men who operated them, along with their party bosses, the Social Democrats. But professional barriers were crossed only at one's risk and peril in imperial Germany; Groener was above all a soldier who occupied himself with soldierly matters.

He knew he could not win the war, but he thought he could save his Army. 'The moral quality of the troops', he had written to the Vice-Chancellor, Friedrich von Payer, on 1 November, 'depends on certain imponderables with which one must not meddle; it is based on officers and those men who up to now have been, in their innermost hearts, ready to sacrifice their lives out of joyful loyalty to Kaiser and Reich.' The soul of the Army was loyal sacrifice. Its backbone was the personal presence of 'their All-Highest War Lord'; Groener was convinced the Army would dissolve without Kaiser Wilhelm.[13]

But he worried about the Kaiser's narrow court circle, and was not happy to learn of his presence in Spa. In particular, he deplored the hold the Crown Prince and his friends had over the sovereign. On a visit to the Crown Prince's headquarters outside Namur on 2 November he found the Prince and Count Schulenburg, his Chief of Staff, utterly unaware of the political dangers that threatened the monarchy. 'Here in the Crown Prince's headquarters one lived at ease in the war, all other considerations playing no role at all; [for them] Berlin was only a terrible nest in which politicians prattled over useless things.' In Spa, the Kaiser was rather too close to the Crown Prince.[14]

Groener had been called to Berlin the following day to consult with the prattlers and give an assessment of the military situation. Before Prince Max, the leaders of the Majority Social Democrats and the trade unions, he fiercely defended the Kaiser's person against the calls for abdication. But the news was bad. It was while in Berlin that he got news of the American late breakthrough in the Argonne. It was in Berlin that he first heard of the mutiny at Kiel. The First Quartermaster General knew it was over. 'Come along with me, Your Highness,' he suggested to Prince Max before taking his train back to Spa. 'Speak yourself with the Kaiser and explain the urgent necessity of his abdication.' Prince Max promised he would visit Spa the next day.[15]

Groener took the same train out of Berlin as Erzberger's Armistice Commission. They had been obliged to stop at Hanover to telegraph Foch that the Commission was now on its way to France. 'Many sailors loitered around the station, though they did not dare draw near us,' Groener recalled. 'It was my first sight of the Revolution and my impression was reinforced that the epidemic was spreading and could no longer be localized.'[16]

While Erzberger and his team continued their lonely journey into France, Groener held a number of desperate meetings in Spa to stave off the plague. His first thought was to build a 'protective barrier between the Army and the homeland', between the birthplace of the troops and the lands they had invaded;[17] but, with news that insurrection was spreading to the Rhenish towns of Cologne, Koblenz and Mainz, it was already too late to execute such an illogical project. When Groener reported on his Berlin trip at a Crown Council on 8 November – with clear outlines of the American advance and the spreading mutiny – the Kaiser announced his intention to march at 'the head of the Army' on Berlin. The invaders were to invade their birthplace. Wilhelm instructed his First Quartermaster General to organize the operation.

Groener knew it was impossible. At 9.30 p.m. he held a confidential meeting with Hindenburg and General von Plessen, the seventy-seven-year-old commander of the Kaiser's private guard, in the Field Marshal's room at the Hôtel Britannique. 'I must reject this operation,' scribbled Groener in the final minutes of the meeting, 'because of the overall foreign and military situation, as well as in view of the events at home.' Hindenburg nodded his wooden head.[18]

Thus a night's private meeting of the generals effectively deprived the Kaiser of his function as Supreme Commander, the All-Highest Warlord.

Prince Max of Baden all of a sudden started speaking of himself as a 'democrat', though there was nothing in his heritage, his life or his actions that could in the least way merit such a label. His real problem now was that he was caught between furthering a parliamentary government based on the existing party line-up in the Reichstag or simply yielding to Supreme Command in Spa by setting up a military dictatorship; for the Prince, it was a choice between two evils. The Majority Social Democrats in his government started describing themselves as 'socialists', though the Independent Socialists (who had made their breach in 1916) could legitimately wonder what had been genuinely 'socialist' about their actions during the last two decades. The problem of the Majority Socialists was that they found themselves caught between their commitment to parliamentary government and the demands of the 'masses'. Every political 'faction' (as parties were appropriately termed in Germany) was faced with such dilemmas at the approach of peace. Real socialists – the Independents and the members of the Spartakusbund – were caught between the demands of the 'masses' and the demands of the Soviet Embassy, which had established itself, after the Treaty of Brest-Litovsk, in the wealthiest, most bourgeois section of town, on the Linden, under a mammoth hammer and sickle and a cheeky banner proclaiming, 'WORKERS OF ALL COUNTRIES – UNITE!'

The 7th had been the first anniversary of the Bolshevik seizure of power in Petrograd. Anniversaries such as this were important for those who sought the total break, the complete upheaval, the realization of the Heavenly City on earth. They served as lessons in 'historical consciousness'. They were used as models of the revolutionary action which set society in motion and defined the radical dream: 1917 was regarded as a part of the same process as 1792 and 1871, the Paris Terror and the Paris Commune. When the story was emptied of people and places it could be made to fit the neat historical, radical line, perpetually rising to heaven, upwards and upwards – but always a struggle.

For Prince Max's government the situation had begun to look sinister early on the 7th with a report that Hamburg had fallen into the hands of mutineers and insurgents from the 'Water's Edge'; they had compelled the dispatch of a train with thousands of armed men to 'get things going in Berlin'. This was shortly followed by news that in Hanover an attack by reserve troops on the railway station, held by sailors, had been a 'total failure'; the General Commander had been captured and 'trainloads of insurgents' were on their way to the capital.[19]

Civil Guards were posted in the old Hansa towns of Mecklenburg and Brunswick, but, as the local commanders warned, these could never be regarded as a substitute for the military. 'When is help coming from the front?' asked harassed town representatives at the Ministry of the Interior that morning. Groener, at the time, was still considering his plan of isolating the invaded western territories from the infected homeland; a few troops were belatedly transferred to the insurgent towns in the afternoon.

It was too late for Mecklenburg. Too late for Brunswick. Worse news for the government came from Bavaria. By evening, Munich was held in the sway of 'workers' and soldiers' councils'.

The war, the Great World War that had shown from the start a strong localizing trend, was now turning into itself. The *Reichshauptstadt* was facing invasion from its own countrymen. The origin of the war had lain in Germany's weakly developed political centre – government had been relinquished to the professionals. On defeat, these various professional cells of power shrunk and were isolated from one another. Each of these little cells – the national government, the municipal government, the local army units, the sailors who had come in from the port towns, the police, and the various trade unions – prepared to defend its own interests.

Prince Max ordered the closure of the Russian Embassy; the ambassador, Adolf Joffe, left for Russia with his diplomatically immune 'staff' of three hundred. Troops and machine-guns were posted at the grand Lehrter station, where the armed mutineers from Hamburg and Hanover were expected. Train traffic was stopped. The rail tracks were even torn up. Berlin had become an island.

Much fear was expressed of the city's 'masses'. Indeed the whole political drama of the next four days was built upon a myth of the 'masses'. Every political faction in town sought survival through the Social Democrats, who appeared to be the one group that could, amid the havoc, 'control the masses'.

If even the Social Democrats spoke of the crowds that appeared in the streets as the 'masses' rather than the 'working class', it was because, like the dictionary definition of the word, these crowds consisted of 'matter not yet moulded or fashioned into objects of definite shape'.

In the half century that preceded the war, 'Athens-on-the-Spree' had become 'Chicago-on-the-Spree'. Huge, burgeoning Berlin made the writer Karl Sheffler think of 'American or Australian cities that arose deep in the bush'. Walther Rathenau, the industrialist who had organized the first year of the war effort, called the place 'Parvenupolis', the 'parvenu among the capitals of parvenus'. If it was the homeland of AEG, AGFA, Siemens, Pflug's train carriages, Egells's ironworks and Schwarzkopf's torpedoes, it was also where the tenement barracks reached out to Prenzlauerberg and unromantic Wedding, where the developers had managed to squeeze two families to a room, where one toilet served for ten flats – well, explained the Prussian city official, none were needed for the men, who were away during the day 'when most stools are passed', while for women 'one sitting takes an average of 3–4 minutes or five including time to adjust one's clothing'. By the time the war broke out, two-thirds of Berliners were immigrants or the children of immigrants. As another writer, Kurt Tucholsky, put it, Berlin was really a Silesian city: 'most Berliners come from Breslau'.

Berlin, capital of the Reich, was the creation of its trains and the receiving station of the greatest peacetime migration in the history of Europe: since the foundation of a united Germany in 1871 a constant torrent of Bohemians, Moravians, Russians, Poles and poor Saxons had appeared at the gates; most of them dreamed of America but had been trapped by poverty at the sandy borders of the *Reichshauptstadt*. In no way could Berlin's 'masses' present a united political force in 1918; they didn't even speak the same language.[20]

It is true that the Social Democrats had built up a following in the poorest parts of Berlin. In a district like Wedding they were all that politics had to offer. The Sozialdemokratische Partei Deutschlands, as it was officially known – or SPD – organized cycling, rambling and singing groups, centres for the youth, and funerals for the dead; women earnestly discussed their rights at SPD sewing parties. Such a wide-ranging social network was the SPD's strength and weakness. With its million members and finances exceeding 20 million gold marks, it was, at the outbreak of the war, not only the largest party in Germany, but the largest political party in the world – and international socialists recognized it as the leading force in the Marxist labour movement.

But, with such a varied base, it had difficulty defining a political line; in the 1890s a violent debate had developed between 'evolutionists' and 'revolutionists'. Worse, due to Germany's poorly developed parliamentary system, Social Democrats lacked a public forum in which to smooth out their quarrels. Like so many other professional groups in the Reich, the SPD's political leaders turned in on themselves; they became introspective and isolated. 'You have neither revolutionary action nor parliamentary action,' chided Jean Jaurès, the French socialist leader, at the Amsterdam congress of the Second International shortly before the war. 'You do not know yet, in practice, what road you shall take.'[21] Like the 'masses' they claimed to represent, the Social Democrats did not show a united front.

With the war, all semblance of coherence collapsed. The sacred triad of class struggle, revolutionary republicanism and anti-militarism, inscribed in the Party's founding Gotha Programme of 1875 and supported by the supposedly paralysing action of the 'general strike', was abandoned two days after Germany's invasion of Belgium, when SPD members voted in the Reichstag for the war credits, pledged not to desert the Fatherland 'in the hour of danger', and accepted the principle of *Burgfriede*, or truce. ('I no longer know any parties,' said the Kaiser on a balcony of the Schloss; 'I only know Germans).' And with not as much as a sign of regret from the 'masses'. Then the armies dug in and the casualties went up.

When the fifth vote for war credits came before the Reichstag, in December 1915, twenty members of the SPD voted against and another twenty-two abstained. Within a month the rebels had founded the Independent Social Democratic Party, or USPD, and by April 1916 they had been written out of the mother organization. But neither 'Majority' nor 'Independent' Socialists managed to form a solid party, even if by November 1918 it had become a habit in the press to speak of 'two strains' of Socialism. 'Majority' and 'Independent' Socialists fought among each other as much as they did against each other; colleagues became rivals; the splinters were splintered.

In 1916 Rosa Luxemburg, a Marxist theorist and pacifist, began distributing her 'Spartacus Letters', named after the leader of the first-century Roman slave revolt, while Karl Liebknecht made inflammatory 'Little Interpellations' in the Reichstag. Together, within weeks of the creation of the USPD, they founded the Spartakusbund. 'Spartacist and Communist chatterers who in order to blossom upwards must push everything down and down,' spat out the 'Majority' leader Philipp Scheidemann.[22]

Scheidemann, much more than Friedrich Ebert, the other Majority

Socialist in Prince Max's government, had a sense of the disaster overtaking both his party and his country. He also possessed a wicked wit – rare among Social Democrats – which hardly worked in his favour. His deeds contained as much humour as his speech; one wonders if it was his own play with irony that had led him to join the Prince in October. At any rate, the Chancellor did not like him. 'I maintained my trust in Ebert,' wrote Prince Max, recalling the last days of the war; but Scheidemann, he had this 'temperament'.[23]

On Friday morning, 8 November, Scheidemann was in 'high spirits' as he spoke before the Cabinet about the situation in Berlin. 'My party will see to it that Germany is spared the horrors of Bolshevism,' he assured his colleagues. But his colleagues, paralysed by the prospect of Berlin rising to the support of the advancing mutineers, knew there was a catch. 'We will keep the masses in hand', warned Scheidemann, 'only if the Kaiser abdicates.'[24]

After the publication of Woodrow Wilson's harsh second note of 14 October, the Reichstag had rushed through a series of measures which had, at least on paper, laid the foundations of a German democratic, parliamentary regime. On the face of it, one could now argue that 'arbitrary power' had been abolished in the Reich. All that was left to do, if one really wanted to send out a signal that Germany had reformed herself, was to force a change in the 'all-highest function'.

But up to now Scheidemann had been hesitant. Only a week earlier he had been assuring Prince Max that he did not want to provoke the collapse of the government – dependent on the support of the Social Democrats – by demanding the Kaiser's abdication; he wanted the decision to come from the Kaiser himself. That was the opinion of most Cabinet members, including the Chancellor. But there was never any discussion in the Reichstag of the matter. No sessions were held at this crucial point. Instead, there were meetings of the 'Inter-Party Committee', while a separate special party caucus was held for the SPD. In their private meetings the Social Democrats showed not the slightest concern for the role of the Reichstag in the reformed regime. Jaurès had been right: the Social Democrats proved to be neither revolutionaries nor parliamentarians – what a contrast they made to the Girondins and Jacobins of 1792, or the French Republicans of 1870, who were supposedly a model for the German Left!

They were very much influenced by calls in the press for abdication. Scheidemann even accused the bourgeois press of exciting the 'masses' with its campaign, intensifying day by day and even hour by hour, demanding the Kaiser's departure. 'We have done all we could to influence the masses,' Scheidemann told the Cabinet. 'If the masses have grown restive on the question of the Kaiser, it was in the first instance bourgeois papers like the *Frankfurter Zeitung* which have brought this about.' Prince Max was warned that the 'mass suggestion' that 'the Kaiser is to blame!' was providing a point of contact between mutineers and the most radical elements among Independents. Majority Social Democrats feared that 'control of the masses' could be lost to the Independents.[25]

Groener's refusal even to consider the Kaiser's abdication, when the question was raised before his departure to Spa, pushed the Majority Socialists into a corner. Ebert warned that his party could not remain in the government if the Kaiser did not go. While Prince Max struggled with entrenched attitudes at Spa, Scheidemann and Ebert were balancing their choice between the government and the 'masses'. They were not worried about parliament.

News of the overthrow of the Wittelsbach dynasty in Bavaria came in as Scheidemann, in party caucus, presided over a debate on an ultimatum: Either the Kaiser quits his throne or we quit the government. One moderate in the circle expressed concern that this might 'break up' the existing Reichstag Majority. Scheidemann laughed: 'Aren't you aware that we are standing directly before the break-up of the Reich, and here you worry about the break-up of the Reichstag Majority!'[26]

The five-part ultimatum was first presented to the government at 5 p.m. on Thursday, 7 November. It demanded that public meetings not be outlawed; that the police and military forces remain 'discrete'; that the Kaiser and the Crown Prince renounce the throne by Friday, midday; that 'the Social Democratic influence in the Government' be strengthened; that the Prussian government (which had not yet been reformed) be brought into line with the reforms rushed through the Reichstag in October.

'No one on whom the idea of the New Age has dawned can help feeling his solidarity with the masses,' commented the party's paper, *Vorwärts*. 'You ought to be thankful to us that we took action,' Ebert told Prince Max. 'Your soldiers have everywhere surrendered.' Then he added, 'It is only the time limit that has enabled us to quiet the masses.'[27]

But Friday was pay day. Berliners did not demonstrate on pay day. So the deadline was extended by twenty-four hours: if the Kaiser and his son had not renounced the throne by Saturday midday, 9 November, the Majority Social Democrats would quit the government and march in the capital's streets at the head of their 'masses'.

For Prince Max, a convinced monarchist, the room for manoeuvre was now very slim. Either he would persuade the Kaiser to abdicate by Saturday in favour of some kind of regency (as Napoleon had attempted after Waterloo). Or, without a parliamentary majority, he would declare a military dictatorship (again, as Napoleon had considered). But the latter course was not really an option. Soldiers with red cockades in their caps were already in the streets by Friday.

Scheidemann had heard rumours that conservative forces were planning to take matters into their own hands under the leadership of the

military governor, General von Linsingen. 'I don't know whether the
younger men will shoot,' he had told the Cabinet on Thursday; 'the old
soldiers certainly will not.'[28]

Linsingen had put his faith in a few crack troops – three battalions of a
Jaeger regiment – but they didn't amount to much. On Friday morning
Linsingen gave orders to the Inspector-General of Aircraft to bomb the trains
carrying sailors to Berlin. The War Ministry intervened and stopped the
operation on the grounds that the trains 'were carrying a large number of
peaceable travellers as well as insurgents'. The military option was thus
closed.[29]

The ultimatum made Prince Max's proposed trip to Spa hopeless; the
foundation of his chancellorship had been undermined. If he could not
persuade the Kaiser to abdicate by Saturday's deadline, the government
itself would collapse.

Frantic calls were put through to Spa. Prince Max proposed a solution
'still more democratic than that of the ultimatum'. One had never heard
language like this from the Prince before. The Kaiser would appoint a
'Deputy' (the Prince seems to have nourished an ambition for the role) and
abdicate; then a 'Constituent National Assembly' would be called. Thus 'the
fighting temper of the masses will be diverted from the streets to the polling
booth'. But, with Erzberger's commission negotiating surrender in Compiègne and the Social Democrats promising revolution the next day, Friday
was a little late for such considerations.[30]

Groener reports that telephone connections between Berlin and Spa were
very bad: 'we either heard indistinctly or nothing at all'. Vague messages
came through about the Social Democrats' ultimatum, 'but nothing on its
deadline'.[31]

This might explain why Prince Max's account of his telephone 'conversation' with the Kaiser on the desperate night of the 8th includes almost
uniquely his own words, that read like a professor's lecture down the crack-
ling line: 'Your abdication has become necessary to save Germany from
civil war and to fulfil your mission as the Peacemaking Emperor till
the end. The blood would be laid upon your head. The great majority
of the people believe you to be responsible for the present situation . . .'
Throughout he addressed the Kaiser with the second-person singular, 'du',
which Germans used when speaking to God or to a close relative, but not
to the Sovereign.

There was another crackle on the line. His Majesty replied that he had
just given orders to head his army into Germany and 'reduce the country
to order'. (Groener, in fact, was about to sit down at his meeting with
Hindenburg and von Plessen at the Hôtel Britannique.) Prince Max asked
to be dismissed as Chancellor. 'You sent out the armistice offer,' replied the
Kaiser; 'you will have to put your name to the conditions!'

The Prince followed up the conversation with a telegram that listed the

German kings and dukes who had lost their seats in the last two days and concluded by pointing out the likelihood that, in the next few hours, 'the Reich will find itself without a Chancellor, without a Government, without any compact Parliamentary Majority'; it would thus be 'utterly incapable' of negotiating a peace with its enemies.[32]

3

After a misty dawn, Berlin awoke on Saturday, 9 November, to beautiful sunny weather – a remnant, no doubt, of the cloud break and those rare and brilliant rays that had coloured the Canadian attack on Valenciennes the week before. A nice day for a revolution! The right weather for a republic! Wasn't it under a glowing autumnal sun that Parisian rebels, after the defeat of Sedan, had invaded the French National Assembly and overthrown an Empire? Why not in Berlin?

Princess Blücher looked out her hotel window and watched the people standing about. She sent her servants down to ask them if they were going to make a riot. 'No,' they answered, 'but as the Government could not put an end to the war, they were going to show them how to do it.'[33]

Admiral von Müller checked his army revolver, in case he had to defend himself. He had quit his post as Chief of the Kaiser's Naval Cabinet and was now living in retirement in Berlin. For lack of anything better to do, he sat down at his desk and started to write a 'Commentary on the Story of the Outbreak of War'. It was not long before the heavy lorries with red flags appeared.[34]

Philipp Scheidemann hadn't slept all night, but he was up at six 'ready to march'. After enjoying with his wife some nondescript 'German tea' and a dry lump of bread, he called up the Chancellery. It was around seven o'clock.

'Has the Kaiser retired?' he asked.

'Not yet,' was the answer. 'But we are waiting for news of his retirement any moment now.'

'I will wait just another hour,' said Scheidemann; 'if he's not gone by then, then I go!'[35]

It was a grey day at the top of the mount, in the Kaiser's villa at Spa. His Majesty had left his wife in Potsdam. He spent his breakfast, in the white dining room, going over the night's telegrams and messages. 'The Reich will find itself without a Chancellor, without a Government, without any compact Parliamentary Majority,' he read, and then furiously wrote in the margin, 'That's what has already happened!'[36]

In an attempt to calm himself, he went out into the garden with young Commandant Alfred Niemann, who had recently joined his staff. The steep lawns vanished into fog; little silvery beads of water fell from golden leaves clinging to the branches and a last moment of glory; the plants in the flower beds and the high wooden pots were either blackened or shrivelled by frost; it was cold, very cold. Commandant Niemann recalls that the Kaiser found it so invigorating he couldn't stop talking. He spoke principally of Bolshevism. 'In the face of a peril which threatens all Europe, it would be absurd to continue the war,' he said. Surely the enemy could see that. 'A solid dyke has to be built against these follies.' The Austrian Empire had collapsed. Germany was menaced. The whole of European civilization was threatened. Of course the enemy would understand. 'We will overcome these difficulties with rapid military action.' The Kaiser already saw himself 'at the head of a crusade against the red peril'.[37]

A guardsman came tearing out of the mists to announce that the Field Marshal and General Groener had arrived. It was just before eleven o'clock.

The Berlin 'masses' were beginning to take on physical shape in the form of a 'general strike'. By eleven o'clock, most of the city's major factories – all of the AEG plants, the munitions works of Ludwig Loewe, Daimler's line at Marienfelde, Siemens, Argus Motors, the Siler Works, and virtually every factory in Weissensee – had come to a halt. Most paralysing was the workers' seizure of control of the S-Bahn depots on the north side of the city, shutting off the electricity. Suddenly all the overhead trains in the centre of town ground to a halt. When the management turned on an alternative circuit, which supplied only a few of the lines, gangs of men attacked the train drivers and derailed the carriages. In late morning, Berlin offered the spectacle of rows and rows of metropolitan trains stopped dead in their tracks.[38]

By then the marches into the centre of town had got under way. Women and children were placed at the head of the columns. They sang 'The Internationale', or the 'international Marseillaise' as the *Morgen-Zeitung* put it. They carried huge red flags and placards reading, 'Freedom! Peace! Bread!' and 'Brothers don't shoot! Join us!' All reports tell how peaceful they were. And how well ordered.

Berlin's poor suburbs were quiet. Berlin's 'revolution' of November 1918 showed nothing comparable to the boiling troubles in Paris's *sans culotte* 'Sections' of 1792 or to the uproar in Paris's artisanal districts, like Montmartre and Belleville, during the Commune of 1871. Berlin's revolution signalled a new, twentieth-century, version of the 'rise of the masses': halt work in the big factories, switch off the electricity, stop the trains, and march in tidy procession to the city centre.

But most of the 'masses' stayed at home. At the heart of the civilian movement was a tight-knit group that identified itself with what Scheidemann called 'fully disciplined, class-conscious workers', the 'real pioneers of the German working class', the 'silent heroes'. Ebert gave some idea of their size when, with what was supposed to sound a threat, he told Prince

Max just before the ultimatum was announced, 'This evening there are twenty-six meetings taking place in all the big public halls. This evening we must announce the Ultimatum from every platform or the whole lot ['*die ganze Gesellschaft*' or, literally, 'the whole of society'] will desert to the Independents.' Habel's Brewery on Bergmannstrasse and the municipal hall in Neukölln might each have been able to pack in a thousand, so perhaps, at a generous reckoning, the 'whole of society' consisted of 26,000 persons. But this was not Berlin's four million.[39]

In the final Cabinet meetings of Prince Max's government (the Prince himself was rarely present) the the two Majority Socialists, Ebert and Scheidemann, based their claim to 'control the masses' on 'men of confidence', or *Vertrauensleute*, who represented the SPD on the factory floor. What worried them, as the deadline for the 'general strike' approached, was not so much the multitudes of Berlin's tenements: it was the attitude of the 'men of confidence' who might turn their support to the Independents or even to the tiny, but highly radical, Spartakusbund. Many of them already had – like the Revolutionary Shop Stewards (*Revolutionäre Obleute*), who had broken with the Majority Social Democrats at the time of the Russian Revolution in the spring of 1917. They probably numbered in the hundreds rather than in thousands. But they knew how to switch off the electricity and stop the trains.

Berlin's 'drift to the Left', during the last week of the Great War, was not the responsibility of vast crowds.

There was another peculiar feature about Berlin's 'revolution' of 9 November. The crowd converging on the city centre actually changed in composition during the day: from civilian black to field grey. The *Berliner Morgen-Zeitung* speaks of soldiers, after ten o' clock, 'catching up' with a procession that had started its march on the southern periphery of town; it was shortly 'joined' by troops from barracks in the centre. It was in the town centre that the first violence occurred, at around 11.30, when an officer at the 'Maybug'[40] barracks pulled out his revolver and ordered his soldiers to shoot a group of mutineers; instead, they shot him – he was 'seriously wounded'. The whole barracks then began to 'fraternize' with the crowd outside.[41]

At approximately eleven, mutineering troops from Hamburg began arriving in Berlin. The attempts by the government to isolate the city had achieved little, save starving the inhabitants. The mutineers included corps of engineers who relaid the tracks that the government had only partially torn up (one must bear in mind that tearing up a railway track is hard work; bombing had been refused). Many arrived by foot. Then the sailors poured in. Among the first to appear were those who had commandeered a Zeppelin outside Kiel earlier in the morning; their slender silver vessel, with red flags flying, came in to land on the Johannisthal airstrip, to the cheers of an occupying force of 'workers'.

'Workers' and soldiers' councils' – first introduced into Germany during the strikes of January and based on the model of Russian 'soviets' – were apparently being organized on the streets. And contemporary reports laid special emphasis on the soldierly side of the councils – the soldiers and sailors with red armbands and red cockades.

Up to midday the main sounds were those of the milling crowd and the clatter of automobiles on cobbles, accompanied by a chorus of eructating army lorries. A wide circle around the Schloss, extending as far east as Alexanderplatz, had been closed off to the public by the three Jaeger battalions brought in on Friday. It was from somewhere around there that the first vague tat! tat! tat! of rifles could be heard.

Prince Max spent his morning with what remained of his Cabinet. Scheidemann records that he had sent in his own resignation by telephone before eight. The Prince claims that, having agonized over a 'senseless, inexplicable wait,' he heard about the resignation of the two Social Democrats only sometime after eleven. It didn't make much difference. From a library window the Prince watched the growing crowd; the Reich's government was on its knees.

The Minister of War, General Heinrich Scheuch, remained ever the optimist. 'We in Berlin are garrisoning a besieged fortress,' he remarked; ' everything depends on our holding Berlin.' He was expecting dependable soldiers from the front to relieve the capital of the home enemy.[42]

Geheimrat von Schlieben came in from the Ministry of the Interior to report on the 'masses' descending on Berlin in processions from the north; he was not smiling when he said that 'Everything depends on whether the police, in conjunction with the troops, remain at our disposal.' Would they resist?[43]

After news of the 'Maybug' mutiny, a devastating report came in that the whole of the Naumberger Battalion – the most trusted of all the Jaegers – had gone over to the insurgents.

A press attaché to the Foreign Office, Lieutenant Colin Ross, entered the Chancellery and spoke in vivid terms of the huge processions and the fraternization between troops and civilians. Quite obviously the few formations left guarding the Schloss were not going to shoot on the crowd. He warned that, if an attempt were made to order disaffected troops to fire, then victory would almost certainly go to the radicals – to Herr Liebknecht and his *Bund*. That was what the choice seemed to be to Prince Max: either Ebert as Chancellor, or victory to the Bolsheviks.

Who made the decision not to shoot? It was one of the great questions during the *Dolchstoss*, or 'stab-in-the-back', trials of 1925. Prince Max always denied giving the order. But it was certainly received in the barracks. Probably it was Lieutenant Ross who telephoned the order from a Chancellery that seemed on the brink of chaos.[44]

News of the Social Democrats' resignation was telephoned in from the Reichstag. Prince Max decided to announce the abdication of the Kaiser, though no such message had come through from Spa. Admiral von Hintze, now acting as the government's observer at Supreme Headquarters, had telephoned at 9.15 to report that Groener and Hindenburg had decided, the evening before, not to support the Kaiser's project to march with his army on Berlin. 'In, these circumstances there is no alternative left to the abdication,' responded Arnold von Wahnschaffe, an under-secretary of state who was to spend his entire morning sitting by the telephone attempting to get definite confirmation of this. There were two telephones in the Kaiser's villa at Spa; one was always engaged, the other was disconnected. At sporadic moments Spa would ring up Wahnschaffe to say 'the decision is imminent,' 'events are taking their course,' 'you must wait a little . . .' Shortly after eleven came the almighty news: 'The matter has now been decided in principle; they are now simply engaged in the formulation . . .' That was not enough for Prince Max. He decided there and then to make a public announcement that Kaiser Wilhelm II had abdicated.

'The Kaiser and King has resolved to *renounce the throne*,' read the text handed to the Wolff Telegraph Agency. 'The Chancellor remains in office until the questions connected with the abdication of the Kaiser, the renunciation of the Crown Prince of the German Reich and of Prussia, and the setting-up of the Regency have been regulated . . .' The news was on the streets at midday.[45]

At this point, a delegation of five Social Democrats, led by Herr Ebert, was shown into the Chancellor's library. With their black bowler hats, they looked very solemn.

On hearing the guard's urgent message, the Kaiser returned immediately from his misty garden. The Chief of the Military Cabinet, the commander of his private guard and General Count Friedrich von der Schulenburg were standing in the round, colonnaded entrance hall. Nobody explained exactly what the seventy-seven-year-old Count, the Crown Prince's chief of staff, was doing there. Wasn't he supposed to be in Namur? The three men accompanied His Majesty into the grand salon, where a very formal meeting had been prepared. Groener and Hindenburg rose to their feet.

Hindenburg was in a profoundly emotional state. 'Your Majesty,' he began in a heavy tone, 'I humbly request you to accept my resignation for, as a Prussian officer, it is impossible for me to say to my King what the situation would oblige me to say.'[46]

The Kaiser was visibly shocked. He demanded how he could be thus abandoned by 'the man who, for both me and the people, represents the highest authority' – he paused – 'to which even myself, the Kaiser, feels subordinate'. There was a terrible silence. The Kaiser walked over to the fireplace, where a few flames flickered, and turned. 'Well? Let us see,' he muttered and, waving his right, healthy, arm, invited an explanation from Groener – Groener the Württemberger.

Groener delivered a long report on the conclusions reached at the Hôtel Britannique the night before. A military expedition across Germany was impossible. The rebels had seized the bridges across the Rhine; they held the railways, the telegraph stations, the supply depots, and the towns of Verviers and Aachen, which were virtually next door. Germany's Western enemies would be on their heels. It would take weeks to march on Berlin, through country in a state of civil war.

Hindenburg maintained his wooden silence. Eventually old Schulenburg interrupted.

In the Count's view, General Groener's assessment was a mite pessimistic. Out of the good troops from the front one could piece together a new army in eight or ten days – 'the time to sleep and get rid of their lice'. One was not talking about attacking the whole of Germany, anyway: just a few select points. One could start along the road of Verviers, Aachen and Cologne. Send in elite troops equipped with the 'most modern weapons': smoke bombs, gas bombs, cluster bombs and flame-throwers. There would be no problem with supplies: our men still occupied rich Belgium. 'Order would be re-established.'

Schulenburgs[47] had over a hundred years of provincial anger flowing in their blood. Old Count Friedrich, grandson of Count Friedrich: the one who had denied Prussia the pleasure of forcing the King of Saxony's abdication in 1814. But Saxony, in the process, had been diminished, while Cologne and Aachen had gone to Prussia. Bomb Cologne and Aachen!

Groener knew the danger. 'I've got other news,' was all he said.

The Kaiser, his eyes 'sparkling with fury', ordered Groener the Württemberger to put that in writing. Then he seemed to hesitate. Schulenburg took up the offensive once more. Groener was resolute: 'The Army will return home in good order under the command of its chiefs, but not under the orders of Your Majesty; it stands no longer with Your Majesty.' Schulenburg protested. But wooden Hindenburg at last confirmed the First Quarter-master's opinion: the Army's loyalty to His Majesty could not be guaranteed.

The Kaiser, not knowing which party to listen to, dismissed the meeting. 'Interrogate all the commanders-in-chief on the morale of the Army,' he said, waving his arm once more; 'if they tell me the Army is no longer behind me, I am ready to go. But not before!' He winced, and then left for the garden.

Unknown to the Kaiser, thirty-nine commanders were at that moment being interrogated in the Hôtel Britannique. From the villa, Admiral von Hintze put a call through to Berlin: 'The matter has now been decided in principle . . .' The problem was with the formulation.

The discussion continued in the garden as small groups conversed with the Kaiser, talked among themselves, returned to the villa. The Crown Prince appeared. He found his father gesticulating energetically with his right hand to a dozen men in grey uniform; 'I was struck by by the way he had changed: his face pallid and thin, his manner crisp; it was painful to see.'[48]

He went back to the salon. Groener introduced him to Colonel Wilhelm Heye, who had been charged with the interviews at the Hôtel Britannique. Though not yet completed, his inquiry into the attitude of the Army's field officers (as opposed to isolated group commanders like the Crown Prince) was showing a clear pattern. Could the Kaiser, at the head of the troops, 'reconquer the Fatherland in battle'? No. Were the troops prepared to fight 'the Bolsheviks in the interior'? No. 'The troops will remain loyal to His Majesty,' reported the Colonel with a 'sonorous voice'; 'but they are tired and indifferent. They will not march against the country, even with Your Majesty at their head. They will not march against Bolshevism. They only want one thing: the armistice, without delay. For that armistice, every hour gained counts.'[49]

Groener summarized the situation with a phrase for which he would be condemned for eternity by the Kaiser's supporters: 'Oath to the colours? Warlord? Today these are only words, nothing else but an idea.'[50]

Admiral von Hintze remarked that His Majesty did not need an army 'to go for a walk' but an army that would 'fight for him'. His Majesty was silent, his lips pinched and pale, his face white. Hintze, 'in the name of the Chancellor', pleaded that he abdicate in order to save a desperate situation.

Schulenburg came up with the magic formula. Wilhelm would abdicate as Kaiser of the Reich, but remain King of Prussia; he would return home in triumph with his Prussian troops. Even if it was constitutional nonsense, it was a wonderful way – while Erzberger desperately negotiated an armistice in Compiègne – of putting the blame, and the pressure, on Berlin. In the final draft, composed by the greatest minds in Supreme Command, Wilhelm named Hindenburg commander of the German Army *'in the case of abdication as Kaiser'* and concluded that 'the army chiefs and the commanders-in-chief are of the opinion that the abdication of the Kaiser, the supreme sovereign of war, is of a nature to provoke the greatest disturbances in the Army, and they are unable to take responsibility for order among the troops'. So even the abdication of the Kaiser was made conditionally, while responsibility – a key issue in the months to come – was placed squarely on the shoulders of the government: a government that no longer existed.[51]

While Schulenburg, Hintze and the Chief of the imperial Military Cabinet, General Count von Marschall, worked on the document, the Kaiser, the Crown Prince and a few intimates had lunch – 'this silent assembly' – in the white dining room. Fresh flowers decorated the table.

Lunch did not last long. The Kaiser rose and returned to the salon, where he signed the document; Hintze telephoned the text immediately to Berlin. But what a shock he received. Prince Max's announcement of a complete abdication – of both father and son – had already hit the streets.

The door of the salon opened and a timid voice asked, 'Sire, could you come here a moment?'

It had just turned two.[52]

Exactly what happened at midday in the Chancellor's library will probably never be known. The accounts of two of the witnesses, Prince Max and Philipp Scheidemann, differ on significant points. In fact they do not even agree on who was present.

What is clear is that the delegates were not the choice of a parliamentary assembly. They had been selected, according to Scheidemann, by *Vertrauensmänner*, 'shop stewards', and consisted of three deputies to the Reichstag (including Scheidemann and Ebert) and two trade-union leaders. After his initial call to the Chancellery, at 7 a.m., Scheidemann had rushed over to the Reichstag to join a meeting organized by the SPD. He found the meeting hall 'very lively', with numerous people present: parliamentary deputies, the Party's leaders, 'shop stewards from Berlin organizations' and 'a deputation from Berlin's trade unions'. It must have been quite chaotic. Scheidemann describes the Reichstag as already looking like a 'huge army camp', with 'workers and soldiers going in and out; several carried weapons.' Somehow a discussion got moving and, in one way or another, a delegation to the Chancellery was selected.[53]

Before the delegation arrived on Wilhelmstrasse, Prince Max, it seems, had already decided to hand over the chancellorship to Friedrich Ebert. In his public announcement of the Kaiser's abdication, Prince Max also declared his intention to appoint 'Herr Ebert to the chancellorship'. Several have suggested that a secret meeting between the two men had taken place earlier in the morning.[54]

In Prince Max's account, the meeting with the delegates began with Ebert demanding the chancellorship – 'We have been instructed by our party, for the preservation of peace and order [and] the avoidance of bloodshed that the Government be now entrusted to men who possess the full confidence of the people.' According to Prince Max, this was supported by the delegation.[55]

For Scheidemann, quite the opposite happened: Prince Max demanded that Ebert take on the chancellorship. 'If anyone is actually in the position to protect our Fatherland from the worst it is your party,' he supposedly declared; 'You have the largest organization and the greatest influence. Herr Ebert, accept the chancellorship!' Herr Ebert then expressed concern that his party should first be consulted. The delegates agreed. They were highly annoyed at the suggestion that the decision was already taken and that their mission effectively served no purpose.[56]

Ebert, all the same, did accept the job. Two unconstitutional acts had thus been accomplished within half an hour: the 'declaration' of the Kaiser's abdication and the 'handover' of the chancellorship. A third, even more momentous, act would take place in the next forty-five minutes. Ungovernable Berlin, compelled by events, was abandoning the law.

The disappointed delegates rushed back to the Reichstag, leaving Ebert behind with the Prince in the Chancellery. It must have been close to two.

A newspaper reporter for the *Morgen-Zeitung* was at that moment standing with the crowd outside Berlin's unloved parliament building – what one city architect had called a 'first-class hearse', though 'tombstone' might have been more apt after 1916, when the inscription *'Dem Deutschen Volke'*, 'To the German People', had been carved beneath its high grey pediment. That Friday afternoon it was the crowd's banners that stole the attention: 'Freedom! Peace! Bread!' Armoured cars rattled about. The reporter noticed two automobiles drive up to the front of the building: one with a large red flag waving before it, the other filled with 'different sorts of soldiers and sailors'. A man clambered to the roof of the first car and delivered 'a fiery speech' to an audience 'growing by hundreds'. No one could hear the exact content of what was said, but the gist of it was that the price of achievement was calm and level-headedness; workers and sailors would soon have all they wanted. The speaker 'finally invited those present to give three cheers for the German Republic and proclaim the German Social Republic'.[57]

The reporter did not identify this man, but he sounds like Karl Liebknecht, who had been making such impromptu speeches all over Berlin since early morning. This particular appearance suggests that the Spartacists had an edge on the Majority Social Democrats. But how many people actually heard Liebknecht's declaration in front of the Reichstag?

Scheidemann and his colleagues were hungry when they got back to the 'armed camp' of parliament, so – after instructing the printing department to distribute immediately a poster guaranteeing the city continued food supplies – they went to the Reichstag's restaurant. A vague parallel might be made with pot-bellied French revolutionaries preparing the Republic's constitution of the Year II at Procope's; revolution and food have never been been served at separate tables. Scheidemann's company were just sitting down to a nice dish of armistice gruel when 'a horde of workers and soldiers stormed into the room'. 'Fifty' men all yelled at once, 'Scheidemann, come along immediately!' 'Philipp, you've got to come out and speak!' 'Dozens' persuaded him to join them. In the Reichstag's grand lobby he saw weapons stacked in pyramids; 'it presented a dramatic and moving picture'. He could hear trotting horses and neighing outside in the courtyard, even though inside 'a thousand' men were screaming. Up the stairs rushed Scheidemann to the Reichstag's reading room. 'Liebknecht's going to declare a Soviet Republic!' exclaimed someone. All power to the Workers' and Soldiers' Councils? Germany a province of Soviet Russia? Scheidemann clambered up on the window sill, wobbled a bit, then shouted, 'The Old and Decayed have fallen! The Monarchy is shattered! Long live the New!

Long live the German Republic!' And the masses, of course, threw up their hats and cheered. Scheidemann returned to his gruel.[58]

Herr Ebert was now to be seen at the table, fuming. 'You have no right to proclaim the Republic!' he stamped a fist and roared.[59]

When the Kaiser walked out of the salon for 'a moment', the Crown Prince and Count Schulenburg looked at each other in wonder. The Kaiser returned. There was silence. The circumstance forbade words. The enormity of the shock paralysed. 'The ground', recalled the Crown Prince, 'just fell from our feet.'[60]

The Kaiser made a gesture. Schulenburg spoke. 'It is a *coup d'état,*' he said, 'an act of force to which Your Majesty must not yield. Your Majesty still has the Crown of Prussia and it is absolutely necessary that you remain with your army as Warlord. I guarantee that the troops will remain loyal to Your Majesty.'

'I am and will remain King of Prussia,' muttered His Majesty, 'and in that capacity I shall stay by my troops.'

Second by second, notch by notch, his nerves tightened. He could hardly breathe. His teeth chattered. Tears welled up in his eyes. It was like a seventeenth-century drama – and the language, indeed, was amazingly archaic. Nineteen eighteen? At the conclusion of such a mechanized, modern holocaust? After the Marne? Verdun? the Somme? It was 1618 – the start of the Thirty Years War.

'Treason!' exclaimed the Kaiser. 'Vile, outrageous treason!'

Schulenburg continued to urge resistance. The Kaiser ordered that arms be immediately brought to his villa.

The Crown Prince bid a tragic farewell and, outside the villa, made a short speech to the Rohr Battalion, which at least appeared loyal. Then he set out for his new headquarters in Luxembourg to carry on the war – less than forty-eight hours before the armistice was signed.

Schulenburg took his leave, and was never to see his Kaiser again. He had been called to attend a meeting, chaired by Admiral von Hintze, in the Hôtel Britannique. There, two questions were discussed: Did Supreme Command possess the material means of annulling Prince Max's proclamation in Berlin? And could it guarantee the Kaiser's personal security? The conclusion on both was no. Groener reported that workers' and soldiers' councils were being set up at that moment in Spa itself. The Kaiser could not contemplate returning to German even as a private citizen. Nor was he safe in his villa. The meeting decided that the only option left open to him was escape to neutral Holland.

Groener and Hindenburg drove back to the villa. 'Lord Jesus!' cried the Kaiser. 'It's you again?'

He refused to listen to Groener, on the grounds that Württemburgers, following the partial abdication, no longer had a warlord. So the Prussian

Field Marshal was obliged to speak. He made a brief summary of the conference that had just taken place: 'I have to advise Your Majesty to lay aside your crown and depart for Holland.' Or did he omit the phrase about the crown? One can never be certain with Hindenburg.

By 8 p.m. the Kaiser had crossed town to board his private train. But he did not give the order to move, and nobody could be sure whether he intended to leave for Holland or to join with retreating troops from the front and return home 'at the head of his army'.[61]

News of the Kaiser's abdication – first announced in the form of Prince Max's statement to the Wolff agency – utterly altered the mood of the crowd gathering in central Berlin. They had come to force the removal of the Hohenzollerns; now they demanded the suppression of every symbol of the Reich and of Prussian royalty: its black-white-and-red flags, its buildings and monuments – particularly the Schloss – and its insignia, carried by army officers. What had been an ideal goal in the morning turned into physical objects for attack in the afternoon.

Parallel to the change in mood was the change in the composition of the crowd, from civilian to military. Thousands of mutineering sailors arrived by foot from Kiel at around three in the afternoon. 'A Social Democrat, member of parliament, went out to meet them, in order to put himself at their head.' They joined the mutineering soldiers. It was then that the violence escalated.[62]

Princess Blücher had been watching the developments from her ground-floor apartment at the Esplanade Hotel: 'We, of course, had all our iron blinds pulled down and the doors of the house locked, and only kept one window open to be able to see what was going on.' The first news of the Kaiser's abdication caused tears in her household, but outside 'there could hardly have been a greater air of rejoicing had Germany gained a great victory'. It was just 'after luncheon' when 'a perfect avalanche of humanity' began to stream by. More and more people appeared – men, women, soldiers, sailors, French and Russian prisoners of war, 'and strangely enough a never-ceasing fringe of children playing on the edges of this dangerous maelstrom'. In less than two hours around two hundred 'great military motor-lorries, packed with soldiers and sailors' had passed. The Princess was convinced that these were the source of violence. The occupants of the lorries seemed to be no more than eighteen; they were all armed, and were 'constantly springing off their seats and forcing the soldiers and officers to tear off their insignia'. The whole crowd was headed in a single direction: Pariser Platz, Unter den Linden and the royal Schloss.[63]

Admiral von Müller also took note of the attacks upon military insignia. 'From 3.30 to 4.30,' he recorded in his diary, 'I walked with Helfferich [a wealthy banker who had served as Vice-Chancellor and then as ambassador to Moscow during the war] in the Tiergarten in uniform. This was very imprudent. Helfferich overheard several passers-by remark: "They won't be strutting about like that for long."' On his return home he noticed that the Naval Cabinet, just opposite, had been taken over by 'revolutionaries', who had 'insisted that the officers should sport red cockades and remove their badges of rank. This was rather a fiasco because nearly all the officers in the building were in mufti.'[64]

The Adlon Hotel – 'the best address in Berlin', at No. 1, Unter den Linden – was also attacked 'after Scheidemann had proclaimed the Republic from the steps [*sic*] of the Reichstag', by 'revolutionaries' in search of officers. All the personnel were assembled in the lobby at gunpoint; then 'a young lad with a sailor's cap' stood on a chair and ordered them to raise their right arms, clench their fists, and shout three times, 'Long live the Republic!' A girl, who had been selling newspapers in the lobby, jumped upon a table and sang 'The Internationale'. When this ceremony was finished, interrogations regarding the whereabouts of 'officers' began. Louis Adlon, the acting director, said there were none in the hotel; he was marched out into the 'palm garden' and told he would be shot in front of the statue of Hercules if any were found. Fortunately for Adlon, Fräulein Hartmann, the personnel director, had just wheeled the only officer present, a wounded colonel of the cavalry, out of his room and hidden him in the laundry lift, with a bottle of Henessey's brandy.[65]

The violence of the weekend of 9–10 November was essentially limited to this rich central section of Berlin. The suburbs were silent.[66] This was an unusual phenomenon for a 'revolution' that supposedly involved the 'masses'.

The shooting seems to have begun on the cobbled banks of the Friedrichsgracht, the main canal of the Spree, which the painter Otto Nagel succeeded in making look quaint even in Hitler's day.[67] Just south of the Schloss, it was the oldest part of Berlin. Rifle fire rang out from the top of a building belonging to the company Heimann & Vittner; the rumour spread that the place must be occupied by 'officers and cadets'; soldiers in the crowd fired back; the building was stormed.[68]

The same thing occurred on nearby Behrenstrasse, where one of the large banks was taken over by an arms-bearing crowd on the grounds that it was occupied by 'officers'. There was fighting around the Reichsbank. They fought with pistols at the Halleschen Gate. Then, to the east, a battle broke out on Alexanderplatz; 'its origin could not be ascertained'. For twenty minutes an exchange of fire took place between men on the ground and a machine-gun nest on the tower of St George's church. The Police Presidium, on the south side of the square, was taken over, 650 prisoners (according to the *Rote Fahne*) were released, and Emil Eichhorn, Independent Social Democrat, set himself up as Berlin's new police president.[69]

The *Morgen-Zeitung* describes the change of atmosphere in central Berlin as something abrupt: 'At different points in the city huge numbers of people were suddenly fleeing in great haste through the streets. At the same time one heard the firing of machine-guns and rifles.'[70] This happened between two and three in the afternoon – in other words, within about half an hour of Scheidemann's declaration from a window sill. By all accounts, he was reacting to a situation, not creating it.

But what of Karl Liebknecht, touring the centre in his automobile? By four o'clock, when he arrived before the Schloss, red flags were flying from its towers. The takeover was theatrical. Requisitioned imperial cars blared their horns, making a sound that most Berliners equated with the arrival in town of the Kaiser. After the armed band entered, there followed the usual search for 'officers'. This time they found them. One of them later recounted how, 'with tears in his eyes' he 'had taken off his badges and thrown them on the flagstones, and then [the officers] were told they were free to return to their barracks'. A rider on horseback dashed out of the great gateway waving a red flag, and at the same moment Liebknecht appeared on a balcony – the very same balcony where the Kaiser had spoken to the jubilant crowd on 4 August 1914 – and proclaimed the 'Free Socialist Republic of Germany': 'The day of liberty has dawned. A Hohenzollern will never again stand at this place.'[71]

The worst of the fighting occurred in the dark hours of the following morning as competing forces struggled for control of the Brandenburg Gate, the Linden and areas westward towards the Reichstag. On Sunday there were running street battles to the south of the Tiergarten, down the Friedrichstrasse and on Potsdamer Platz and Alexanderplatz, as well as at the Lehrter and Stettiner railway stations. By Monday, 11 November – as the Western capitals of Europe celebrated the great Armistice – the fight had been reduced to 'a little desultory shooting now and again'.

At dusk on Saturday evening, Prince Max came to bid farewell to the new Chancellor, Friedrich Ebert. 'Herr Ebert,' said the Prince, as he turned at the door, 'I commit the German Reich to your keeping!' Herr Ebert replied, 'I have lost two sons for this Reich.'[72]

The Kaiser's train eventually chugged out of Spa's station at half-past four on Sunday morning. Only two red lanterns placed at the end of the last wagon gave the signal that the All-Highest Warlord was leaving his Reich. The rest of the train was plunged in darkness, for there was great fear of encountering mutineers on the tracks.

At dawn the Kaiser was in Holland.[73]

4

Despite its official title, the 'Summer Detention Barracks for Officers', inside Magdeburg's ancient citadel, had been open for all four seasons during the war. The first floor, reserved for prisoners of high standing, contained a bedroom, a dining room and a reception hall, though the resident had not much use for this. Outside there was a little garden with fruit trees and bushes. Downstairs, on the ground floor, lived the prisoner's guardians; an armed soldier always stood by the closed fence of high wooden palings in the garden. In winter the apartment got cold, but the administration did its best to correct that evil.

The Belgian commander of the fortress of Liège had been housed here after being wounded and captured in August 1914. Since autumn 1917, however, the three rooms were occupied by a man of much greater interest to the Germans: Józef Piłsudski, commander of the Polish Legion.

'It seems to me that I was born for a prisoner's life,' remarked Piłsudski a few years later. 'I put up with solitude very easily and do not feel its whole burden as others do.'[74] In 1885, when he was nineteen, the Russians had sent him to Siberia for his involvement in an anti-tsarist plot. In 1900, for another, they had imprisoned him in the famous Warsaw Citadel, from which no one escaped; Piłsudski feigned madness, was transferred to St Petersburg, and from there escaped to London. But soon he was back in Poland, organizing new terror in Austrian-held Galicia. Russians were his enemies, not Germans or Austrians. He founded 'riflemen's clubs' and an 'officers' school', and when Central Europe went to war with the world he put the lot together as a 'Polish Legion' and marched it into Russian Poland. It was the most effective arm of the Austrian Army, but hardly the most loyal. After the Russians had, in 1915, been pushed out of Poland, the Polish Legion lost interest in Austria and Germany. In November 1916 German Supreme Command proclaimed in occupied Warsaw an 'independent Poland', limited in area to former Russian Poland. Few Poles celebrated. Unperturbed, the Germans went ahead in their aim to recruit a Polish army. The oath they proposed was 'I swear to serve my Polish Fatherland, to preserve brotherhood in arms with the German and Austro-Hungarian armies, to obey the Kaiser of Germany as the Commander-in-Chief in the present war, and the Kaiser of Austria and King of Hungary as likewise all other military superiors.' Over 5,000 of the 6,000 Legionaries refused to take it; they were sent into internment camps. On 22 July 1917 Józef Piłsudski was arrested.[75]

Piłsudski overcame the anxieties of solitude by turning the 'flowers of memory' – the intense sensual images that came to his mind as he walked alone in the garden – into analysis. He became a writer.

But it was hard. 'I was so tired by what I had gone through, and by my work in which, besides describing events, I unconsciously poured out my longing for everything that makes up Poland – the muddy road, the dilapidated village, the people, the landscape, my dear colleagues . . .'[76]

'The muddy road, the dilapidated village . . .' Where did it begin, where did it end, this Poland? Piłsudski, who was actually a Lithuanian, did not know the answer.

Nobody knew the answer. The military decision of the world war was eventually made on the Western Front, not on the endless plain of Poland. Until Russia dropped out of the war, neither the British nor the French could make up their minds whether the Poles were friends or enemies; they populated both the Allies' prisoner-of-war camps and their fighting armies. In his address at Caxton Hall in January 1918, Lloyd George had made no commitment on Poland. The professors of The Inquiry, in their geography offices in New York, were already having a problem locating Poland; it came out in Wilson's speech that month: in the thirteenth of his Fourteen Points, the President (who was superstitious about the number thirteen) committed himself to the insoluble puzzle of 'an independent Polish State' made up of 'territories inhabited by indisputably Polish populations' but also with 'free and secure access to the sea'. If the Allies' armistice terms outlined in detail the western territories Germany had to evacuate – along with the number of locomotives, rail carriages, guns, boats and submarines she had to surrender – they were vague on Germany's eastern frontiers; and, most particularly, they did not demand the evacuation of Poland.

Poland, as Napoleon had once said, was the 'key to the vault'. It was also the key to Europe's problem.

Germans, in their hearts, might have admitted defeat on the Western Front in November 1918; but they were not so sure about Poland. Foreign affairs were not the first concern of the press during the turmoil that surrounded the abdication, but in the third week of the month a small 'Save our East' campaign was getting under way.

It had long been a subject for discussion in government circles. When Prince Max proposed to Spa the formation of a 'Constituent National Assembly' he was thinking in terms of a 'nation' that would include German Austria and would be open to an affiliation with Poland. On 6 November – the day he ordered Erzberger to set off with his Armistice Commission to France – he sent another government official to Magdeburg to release Piłsudski and immediately negotiate an accord over Poland.

Prince Max's representative was Count Harry Kessler, a master of many trades – a patron of the arts, a collector, a publisher and a writer as well as a soldier and diplomat. His Irish mother, the former Miss Alice Bosse-Lynch, had been the last love of old Kaiser Wilhelm I – 'True,' the Count would admit, 'but in the same way as Marianne was the last love of Goethe in his old age.' Wicked mouths spread the rumour that the Count was Wilhelm II's uncle.[77]

Kessler and a fellow officer arrived in Magdeburg from Berlin on Thursday, 7 November. They were pleased to discover that the soldiers in the streets still saluted 'promptly and smartly', but they were under no illusion about what the future held: Hamburg, Lübeck and Cuxhaven had already been seized by naval mutineers. By the next morning there were demonstrations in the streets, with officers having their epaulettes torn off;

it was announced that rail traffic to Berlin had been interrupted. Kessler decided to take Piłsudski back to the capital by car. He ordered a military vehicle to be taken out of town and parked on the far bank of the river while he and his colleague went to fetch Piłsudski. Dressed in mufti (Kessler simply borrowed a civilian hat and coat), they slipped through the town's narrow sidestreets to the citadel. They found Piłsudski with one of his Polish colleagues, General Sosnkowski, 'pacing the garden together'.[78]

The two Poles were delighted to learn of their sudden freedom, but surprised at the conditions. 'When we looked at the officers' mufti in aston-ishment,' recorded Piłsudski, 'they told us with embarrassment that a revolution had broken out in Magdeburg, and we were to leave in motors, not as soldiers, but as ordinary mortals . . . I don't know what I would have decided then if the officers' statement had not contained a promise that at six o'clock that evening, I should be already sitting in a train carrying me to Warsaw.'[79]

Piłsudski left the fortress 'with the most necessary toilet articles wrapped in a piece of paper'. They crossed the bridge over the Elbe by foot, 'as if we were out for a walk.' On the other side, two cars roared up and 'quickly carried us away from the revolted town'. On the road to Berlin they were held up at one railway crossing where 'two tightly packed trainloads of sailors' passed on their way to the capital.[80]

Piłsudski was put up in the luxury Continental Hotel in the city centre. Saturday morning seemed quiet enough. He was treated to a lunch at Hil-ler's Restaurant on Unter den Linden. A private room had been prepared, where several members of Germany's Foreign Office were awaiting the honour of meeting him. Germany, he was told, was entirely committed to Wilson's thirteenth point, and, since Piłsudski, commander of the Polish Legion, was obviously going to play a major role in the new independent state, they hoped they could reach some accord on frontiers now. It was two o'clock. A fearful clamour broke outside. Piłsudski stood up and demanded that he be provided immediately with a train for Warsaw. The German Foreign Office, at that moment, had no choice but to oblige.

On 10 November, Piłsudski was in Warsaw. On Armistice Day, Monday the 11th, three days after his release from Magdeburg, he was named Chief of the Polish State.

'An extraordinary thing happened,' said Piłsudski of himself in a speech delivered five years later. 'In the course of a few days, without this man making any efforts, without any violence on his part, without any bribery, without any concession, timber or otherwise, without any so-called "legal" occurrences, something most unusual became a fact. This man became Dictator.'[81]

5

So next door, in new, frontierless Poland, a dictatorship was established, while in imploding Germany the central government collapsed. This was what made nonsense of Oswald Spengler's complaint that Ebert's Majority Socialists, having found 'what they had been working for for forty years, full power', now 'regarded it as a misfortune'.[82] The future author of *Decline of the West* should have known the truth: there was no political power in Germany. In his grand trilogy *November 1918*, Alfred Döblin described this shrivelling of power as part of a peculiarly 'German Revolution': 'Revolution, which in other nations behaved like a fury, setting fires and driving terrified people from their homes, wanders through Germany, across this wide land unravaged by war, grows ever smaller and smaller, becomes a flower girl in a ragged skirt, shivering for cold, fingers turning blue, looking for shelter . . .'[83] In fact, it wasn't a revolution at all; it was the Great War turning into its source.

'The Revolution was, in the first place, a military revolution,' concluded the *Morgen-Zeitung* on 16 November, as it surveyed the 'council frenzy' which followed upon the events of the previous weekend. All these 'workers' and soldiers' councils', after all, seemed to be run by soldiers and sailors, not workers. To Princess Blücher, young soldiers seemed to be operating everything; 'it seems that they are all respectful enough in business hours, but out of them there is no saluting, and they attempt to treat their superious as equals, needless to say not very successfully, as old customs and habits cannot be changed in one day'.[84]

True, the Revolutionary Shop Stewards had set themselves up in the Royal Stables, next to the Schloss, but they were guarded by sailors. Comrade Eichhorn ran 'Public Security' from the Police Presidium – also under the surveillance of sailors. The Workers' and Soldiers' Councils of Greater Berlin sat in the Reichstag surrounded by their armoured cars; no point in discredited conservative deputies approaching the place – one's identity papers were closely examined.

The Chancellery, behind its big iron gates, was one of the few government buildings left that was run by civilians; but Ebert and his colleagues had little control of the rest of Berlin and they knew virtually nothing about what was going on in whole areas of Germany – like Bavaria, which was now an independent Soviet Republic.

Ebert was Reichs Chancellor for just one day. His efforts to establish a provisional government were blocked by the Independent Socialists, who would only join a Cabinet transformed into a 'Council of People's Commissars' that had the approval of Berlin's workers' and soldiers' councils. So on Sunday, 10 November, a huge assembly of representatives of these councils, supposedly elected on the factory floor that morning (despite the street fighting), met in the Circus Busch to approve the new executive council.

The meeting was chaotic. There was a lot of cheering when it was anounced that there would be peace, an end to the mass slaughter. Ebert spoke in favour of a Socialist Republic and promised the election of a constituent assembly. Liebknecht and another Spartacist, Richard Müller, argued that a constituent assembly would be 'the death warrant of the revolution'. Ebert's Council of People's Commissars did, none the less, manage by voice vote to win approval from those present.[85]

Fritz Ebert, ex-saddler, thus became Chairman of the People's Commissars; he was addressed in German as *'Volksbeauftragte* Ebert' (or People's Commissar Ebert), a title that denied him even the position as first among equals. What legal argument was there to justify this? What were its constitutional grounds? Every regime – revolutionary or reactionary – requires some degree of legitimacy to survive. That essential 'principle of legitimacy' had been defined by Talleyrand a hundred years earlier when the Napoleonic Empire had collapsed. Legitimacy required, he had said, a founding act 'acceptable to the people' along with institutions capable of being 'consolidated and consecrated by a long succession of years'. The test of the people and the test of time: these were the basic challenge, whatever the system of government, 'whether monarchical or republican, hereditary or elective, aristocratic or democratic'. In 1918 the principle could be applied as well to Soviet Russia as it could to Great Britain; and it had its relevance for Berlin's Council of People's Commissars.[86]

Ebert's problem was that he had been handed the chancellorship, in a library, during a moment of crisis; without his approval, a Republic had then been proclaimed from a window sill; the authority of his 'Council of People's Commissars' was subsequently confirmed not by the Reichstag or the Kaiser, but by the applause of 'elected' workers' and soldiers' representatives gathered in a circus. There had been no founding act, there was nothing to show that this strange regime was acceptable to the people, and no institution which had stood the test of time supported it. To establish his legitimacy, Ebert had only one course left open: to delay all significant acts of government until a constituent assembly had been elected by the people of Germany.[87]

In two areas, however, there could be no governmental delay: the economy and demobilization.

Both the size and the shape of Germany's economy had been radically altered by the war. By November 1918 something like 95 per cent of her industry was geared to war production. Estimates of the size of Germany's disintegrating Army in early November are obviously very rough; there were in October about 6 million German soldiers on active duty, of whom about 2.5 million were on the Western Front and another 2.9 million in the so-called *Besatzungsheer*, or army of occupation. Germany had a population of between 58 and 64 million, depending on which territories were included in the calculation. In the course of the war, industrial production had slumped to about 57 per cent of what it had been in 1913, and in the process it had been diverted away from the satisfaction of consumer needs. Coal production was 61 per cent of what it had been, steel 40 per cent, cement 30 per cent. Inflation was showing its first signs.[88]

By the armistice terms signed on 11 November, Germany had fifteen days in which to evacuate all occupied territories in the West, including Alsace-Lorraine, and she had thirty-one days to evacuate the whole left bank of the Rhine and retreat to a line ten kilometres to the east of the river. In other words, Germany's economy would somehow have to accommodate six million soldiers by 11 December.

The extraordinary fact of the next few weeks is that, despite the abdication, the revolution, wartime impoverishment and the impending invasion by her own Army, Germany's social and economic substructure held together. This was in large part because Germany had already established the machinery of an advanced industrial economy. Whatever the political situation, and despite the government's paralysis, the huge wheels of the economy just kept on turning: Germany was not Russia.

By Tuesday, 12 November, all the trains in Berlin were running again, the cafés and *Kneipen* had never closed, the restaurants were doing a thriving business, the shops were open, and factories were operating. The Kaiser was to blame for all of Germany's difficulties. And after the Kaiser had gone the government was to blame, along with all the politicians. Germans had never really been interested in politics: they let the professionals do the work and complained only when things went wrong. In November there were plenty of meetings. As it was cynically said, 'The shorter the rations, the more the party platforms.' There were plenty of posters and plenty of songs in the streets – 'The Internationale,' 'Brothers, Onward to Sunlight and Freedom', 'Deutschland, Deutschland über alles'. But the songs were often quite contradictory in their political orientation, or contained no politics at all.

A 'revolution', after all, is a return to the point of origin. As old Comrade Eduard Bernstein, socialist revisionist and Independent, reminded his colleagues, 'We still have a bourgeois economy.'[89]

The great wheel kept turning. The propertied remained in control of their properties, party leaders remained at the head of the parties, army officers maintained their ranks, the same civil servants ran the administration, no peasant stopped farming his land, industrialists managed their industries, and the trade-union leaders never let go of their unions.

'A few days have elapsed since the overthrow of the old authoritarian regime in Germany,' wrote Herr Professor Doktor Hugo Preuss in the *Berliner Tageblatt* on 14 November; 'this drastic change has at least up to now taken place in order.' That is how many Berliners perceived things, despite all the shooting. The next day Preuss, a civil servant, was named to a ministry along with his colleague Eugen Schiffer. Neither was a socialist;

they were both already famous for their liberal economic doctrine of non-intervention by the state.[90]

On the very same day, 15 November, German big industry and big labour reached an accord known as the Stinnes–Legien Agreement, by which the principle of mandatory collective bargaining was accepted by both parties, the unofficial, hated 'yellow' unions would be excluded, and a series of measures on work conditions, such as the eight-hour day, were laid down. They also set up an independent Central Working Community (the *Zentralarbeitsgemeinschaft*, or ZAG) that would implement the agreement over the critical period of demobilization and on into the future.

So at the moment of the great proletarian revolution in Berlin – with red flags flying atop the Reichstag, the Schloss and the Royal Stables – labour and industry were establishing an alliance. Walther Rathenau, the industrialist and war organizer, who had a talent for being on every side at once, asked the unionist Carl Legien if he was not worried about 'forming what is more or less a coalition with the employers in the midst of such a movement'. Legien shrugged his shoulders: it didn't worry him at all – he wanted order and to keep the economy going.[91]

The fascinating thing about this accord is in the way it so suddenly revealed hidden economic structures in Germany, which had certainly existed throughout the war but which emerged only with the peace and the disappearance of central government. The accord was based on secret meetings between industry and labour that had been going on since 1917. The one thing that infuriated Germany's industrial and commercial leaders during the war – more so than SPD incantations to Marxian and proletarian theory – was the national planning of Rathenau and his successor Wichard von Moellendorff. And, oddly, the unions agreed with them. What they all feared was, as the shipowner Albert Ballin put it during an angry meeting in Hamburg in June 1918, the 'dangerous intention of driving the national economy and the world economy into the barrack square'. An increasingly audible rumble of voices which opposed national planning accompanied Germany into the last years, months, days and hours of the war.[92]

At the very time that Germany's armies lost the war on the Western Front, Germany's economic centralizers lost their battle in Berlin. Their Economic Office (the RWA) had no credibility by October. The hero of their opponents was Hugo Stinnes, the industrialist who had led the negotiation with the unions. He came under strong pressure to set up a new Demobilization Office and become the 'dictator of demobilization'. But Stinnes refused. Nevertheless, as a result of this non-interventionist lobbying, a Demobilization Office was established on 7 November by Prince Max, who named Colonel Joseph Koeth its director.

Stinnes and Koeth were of like minds. Stinnes wanted, in co-ordination with labour, to determine the basic policies of demobilization and to get 'rid of Berlin's tutelage relentlessly and forcefully'. Koeth defined the way to do it: not with 'grand ideas' or 'far-reaching thoughts'. As he would put it before Ebert's Council in December, 'I have only a small idea: how to get from one day to the next.'[93]

The order of the day was to muddle through without bothering about politics or government.

6

Much the same sort of self-sufficent, professional philosophy was to be found in Germany's defeated Army. General Groener had spent two years of the war in Berlin, organizing with the civilian authorities the resources for the war. The experience not only introduced him to the operation of rail networks, he also met the men who ran the economy – the traders, the industrialists and the trade unionists. Before he became First Quartermaster General, Groener knew how Germany worked. The news that big labour and big industry had decided to collaborate, independent of the government, would have caused him no surprise, for this was Germany's way of getting things done.

The professional centre of the Army was the officer corps. Clausewitz, its founder, had defined it a hundred years before as 'a kind of guild, with its own laws, ordinances and customs' – thus already establishing the parallel with Germany's economic structure.[94] The officer corps was well suited to Germany's little worlds of petty states and kingdoms, of competing orders, courts and hierarchies, soldiers, professors, guildsmen and administrators. Bismarck's Reich had been imposed on them all. But the little worlds did not disappear – any more than the officer corps. When the centralized Reich disappeared in November 1918, they were still there.

Groener understood the meaning of this. To preserve his Army – and in particular the officer corps – he would have to forge some strange alliances, just as industry and labour had done. It was all now a question of muddling through.

Groener identified his ultimate aim in a phrase: 'to bring what remains of the Army back to the homeland [*die Heimat*] on schedule, in order, but above all in inner good health'. Just like in a guild, the maintenance of order in the profession depended on a strict, internal code of morality, taught and enforced by the officer corps. Thus, to ensure the 'inner good health' of the Army, Groener hoped 'to enable the officer corps, as the bearers of the ideas of the Army, to cut a way through the novel situation'. For Groener, these officers had an inner commitment to Germany; they understood a national identity that went deeper than the superficial business of politics and temporary alliances; and, whatever the apparent outcome, they could show that the immense effort and sacrifice made during the war had been worthwhile. Despite the Kaiser's comments, there was a lot of German 'soul' in the Württemberger Groener, and he used it to work out a policy of demobilization.[95]

The schedule of the Army's return home was set by the Allies' armistice conditions. These arrived by aeroplane in Spa on Saturday evening, 9 November, just as the Kaiser was leaving for his train. The deadline for a German signature was Monday morning, so Groener spent the whole of Saturday night and most of Sunday morning working on an answer. He had the help of Colonel Heye and the field commanders who had come to Spa to be interviewed on the loyalty of the Army to the Kaiser. In addition, all divisional commanders were sent a questionnaire on the possibility of further resistance to the enemy. The results, collated by Colonel Heye on Sunday morning, proved that there could be none. In his memoirs, Groener claims that a final report was forwarded to Berlin; 'the regime arrived at a conclusion and accepted the conditions'. Groener knew perfectly well that there was no 'regime' in Berlin on Sunday morning; it was his own Supreme Command that telegraphed, in the evening, acceptance of the conditions to Compiègne, signed 'REICHSKANZLER SCHLUSS'. On Sunday evening, Germany no longer had a Chancellor.

All previous plans for further resistance and a gradual demobilization had now to be abandoned – including Groener's own idea of isolating the front from the homeland, as well as the programme devised by Walther Rathenau, national planner par excellence, for a great last effort on Germany's frontiers. Within a month, all of Germany's armies had to be moved east of the Rhine.

This immense forced migration was made still harder by the conditions of Germany's defeat: in the last weeks of the war the chief points of railway access to the front had been seized by the Allies as they pushed the German armies back on the Ardennes. The evacuation of the occupied territories would therefore have to be accomplished on foot, across hills and steep valleys.

Spa itself would have to be evacuated. The final paragraph of the Armistice set up a 'permanent International Armistice Commission' that would 'ensure the execution of the present convention'. The Allies decided that the Commission would occupy the buildings formerly employed by German Supreme Command at Spa.

So, without any general plan, Groener had to cobble together an enormous administrative machine that would rely, even more than during the war, on private initiative and local talent. Not surprisingly, it was made up of odd cogs.

If he was going to get his Army across the occupied territories and a large part of Germany within a month, there was no way of avoiding the workers' and soldiers' councils. Groener simply decided to follow the trend, in the hope that, by so doing, he could maintain some element of control. On Sunday, 10 November, he therefore sent out a directive calling for the election of a soldiers' council for every battalion, squadron and company. He later claimed that this initiative was based on an 'accidental order' by a subordinate who had never had his approval; but 'one had to make the best of disaster once it had occurred'. He immediately began a campaign to get reliable officers placed in the councils, and forwarded mountains of pamphlets appealing for order on the rail lines and in the supply depots, recommending army collaboration in early elections for a National Constituent Assembly (the opposite of what Independent Socialists and Spartacists wanted) and warning returning soldiers not to allow 'our victory over our former dictators to be abused by the creation of a new dictator, which would lead necessarily to Russian conditions [*russischen Zuständen*]'. *Russische Zustände* became the catchphrase for misery in November and December 1918.[96]

One odd cog in the machine was Commissar Fritz Ebert. Groener had got to know Ebert during his two years of war work in Berlin. But it was only after a conversation on Sunday morning with the conservative Reichstag deputy Friedrich Naumann, in Spa after touring the front, that Groener had the idea of directly contacting Ebert by telephone; the secret line to the Chancellery (No. 988) had not been cut since Prince Max's departure. He put a call through that Sunday evening. Groener, in his own words, 'informed' Ebert that 'the Army would put itself at the disposal of his regime in return for the regime's support for the Field Marshal and the officer corps through the maintenance of order and discipline in the Army'. In addition, 'the officer corps demands of the regime a battle against Bolshevism and is ready for such an engagement'.[97]

Thus, just as proletarian revolution drew industry to labour, so did military defeat lead Germany's officer corps into an alliance with the council movement and Commissar Ebert. Throughout these delicate negotiations Field Marshal Hindenburg, of course, remained as silent as a statue.

But it was Hindenburg who became the figurehead of co-operation between the workers' and soldiers' councils and Supreme Command during those critical weeks of November. When, on 14 November, Supreme Command moved to the royal castle of Wilhelmshöhe, outside Kassel – where Jerome Bonaparte had kept his fairy-tale court of 'Westphalia' under the watchful eye of brother Napoleon, and where Napoleon III had been imprisoned after Sedan – Kassel's Workers' and Soldiers' Council announced that 'Hindenburg belongs to the German people and the German Army.' 'His person stands under our protection!' they exclaimed.[98] Groener appreciated the talent some of the Council members showed for chess.

The Field Marshal and the First Quartermaster General would walk together every morning in the Hawk's Forest to discuss the turn of events. 'How beautiful it is here!! and how sad things appear in our Fatherland!!' wrote Groener's wife shortly after their arrival. The collapse, she thought, was a greater misfortune than the entire war, for it signified the disappearance of 'individual courage'; it was 'the saddest phenomenon in the history of the German people'. For four years the German people had stood

unbroken against a world of enemies; now they were letting themselves be
'turned over like a corpse' by a handful of sailors, 'injected by the poison
of Herr Joffe [the exiled Russian ambassador] and his comrades'. And who
was pulling all the strings? 'Jews here as there.'[99]

Groener and his colleagues got to Kassel none too soon. When Matthias
Erzberger and his commission arrived in Spa on Tuesday morning, 12 November, he was pleased to hear the Field Marshal thank him 'for the extremely
valuable services he had rendered the Fatherland' (a compliment he would
never again receive in his life), but noticed mobs tearing epaulettes from the
shoulders of officers, soldiers who refused to salute, and every automobile
carrying red flags. Having persuaded anover's Workers' and Soldiers' Council not to continue their trip to Brussels, where he told them they would
not be very welcome, he asked them to let him board their 'special train'
and drive him back to Berlin. Thus, brave, bespectacled Erzberger reached
his capital in a Council locomotive on 14 November, one week after he had
left, and five days after the German Revolution.[100]

On Thursday, 15 November, the first Allied members of the new International Armistice Commission arrived in Spa. The Kaiser's villa was
assigned to the French; the British were put up in Ludendorff's (and, briefly,
Groener's) villa, lower down the hill; the Belgians moved into the Crown
Prince's villa; the German mission was somewhat surprised on being
assigned rooms in the Hôtel Britannique. When Colonel Samuel G. Shartle
arrived on 17 November with the American mission in a caravan of cars,
they were immediately directed to Field Marshal Hindenburg's former residence. 'Von Hindenburg's departure had evidently been a hasty one,'
recorded Shartle, 'for he left us several cases of German champagne, and
Rhine and Moselle wines, all boxed ready for shipment. This acceptable
booty of war supplied our table for several months.'[101]

Naturally enough, tension soon developed between Supreme Command
and Germany's motley array of workers' and soldiers' councils. Groener in
his soul, which echoed most front-line officers' contempt for the rear, had
never abandoned the notion of isolating the best army elements in Germany's former occupied territories from the corrupting influences back
home. All through November he insisted that the soldiers' councils of the
field army could not compared with the workers' and soldiers' councils of
the *Heimat*. But gradually the realist in him took over: he noticed that even
in Kassel's soldiers' council there were elements not entirely in sympathy
with his own high moral goal of preserving the officer corps as 'the bearers
of army ideas'. There was, for instance, an NCO named Weckerle, 'a crafty
fellow who pushed against our will in the council and aimed at radicalizing
it'.[102]

To counter such insubordination, Supreme Command organized at Ems
– another thermal resort – a 'Congress of Soldiers' Councils of the Field

Army' for 1 December. Groener prepared a programme that would have disbanded the workers' and soldiers' councils, suppressed all armed forces in the country besides the German Army, firmly established the authority of the officer corps, and convoked the old Reichstag (which had never actually been dissolved). The soldiers' councillors politely assembled in rows, and then, to the alarm of every officer present, up stood the ferocious little Emil Barth, head of the Revolutionary Shop Stewards and the best public speaker radical Berlin had on offer. Groener's programme sank within a minute.

The collaboration of November was thus transformed into the struggle of December: Supreme Command was not going to submit to the will of the councils.

Nine divisions of the regular Army were collecting outside Berlin; Groener demanded that they enter the capital and 'disarm the citizens'. Ebert resisted. Hindenburg wrote him a pompous letter. 'If I address you the following lines' – which were, naturally, of Groener's composition – 'I do so because it is reported to me that you, as a true German, love your Fatherland before everything . . .' To rescue 'our people from threatening collapse', Supreme Command would be willing to co-operate with 'the regime' on condition that the workers' and soldiers' councils be abolished, that officers be saluted, that the Army restore order, and that military commands come uniquely from military authorities.[103]

With literally millions of troops returning to the heartland of Germany – many with their weapons – such a monopoly of arms, authority and public order remained a fairyland dream: the kind one might expect out of Schloss Wilhelmshöhe. But Groener was a man who could face reality. Groener knew how industry worked. Groener understood the private little worlds that actually governed Germany. The local soldiers' councils had not been a success. So he would elaborate on another idea that had first occurred to him in Spa: he would encourage the growth of small voluntary forces, 'Free Corps', that not only might restore order in Germany's cities but also perhaps might solve the little problem developing next door, in Marshal Piłsudski's new Poland.

7

The *Berliner Morgen-Zeitung* had dispatched a reporter to Frankfurt to watch the trains go by. 'Day by day', he recorded on 18 November, 'the demobilization of the Western Front is becoming more impressive in appearance.' The number of military trains passing through the main station alone had swollen to eighty a day. Each carriage compartment was crammed with twenty or more men; the corridors were stuffed full of humanity; men clung on to the footboards outside, and on to the brake frames – they even lay crowded on the roofs, appearing as they passed like a collection of 'colourful little cubes'. Boxes, packets and broken old trunks were tied to whatever space remained. The reporter estimated that over a hundred thousand men passed through Frankfurt every day. 'And yet', he noted cautiously, 'it is worth considering that these troop transports are not yet from the heart of the field army, but are rather from the *Etappe-* and *Heimat-*zones.'

More impressive still were the *Räumungzüge*, or 'evacuation trains', which transported war matériel, heavy artillery and stock. At least twenty of these were passing daily: 'I saw many on the tracks laden with artillery and goods picked up in Mainz.' The accompanying personnel lay on straw in cattle trucks, though they appeared 'affable', in 'a comradely way'. Sometimes a particular individual would catch the eye: 'On the side of an uncovered guard's van I saw an officer standing on the brake frame of a passing *Räumungzug*.'[104]

Erzberger, returning to Berlin, was another witness of these trains. They were crowded with soldiers on the footboards and the roofs, he observed – 'as in Russia'.[105]

The numbers were not given, but newspapers of the day noted there were 'many mortal accidents'. Roofs were the most dangerous place to travel: men were killed as the trains passed through tunnels or under girders. Or, after the march across Belgium or Luxembourg, they were so exhausted that they fell from the sides and the tops of the carriages as they slept. The deadliest track ran from Liège to Aachen, for on its way lay several tunnels.

It was the largest, the most organized, the most rapid migration of men in the history of humankind. Within a period of just over four weeks between 4 and 5 million soldiers – there were not four cities in the world of this size, and several nations were smaller – had to be moved eastward across the Rhine. For the men on the front, the first part of the voyage was by foot. 'Two huge armies, the Sixth and the Seventeenth, will soon be tasted here,' wrote the *Morgen-Zeitung*'s correspondent in Cologne on 19 November. 'To each of them are attached no less than 400,000 men, between 140,000 and 150,000 horses with countless wagons and cannon.'[106] So as to maintain morale, triumphal arches in wood and canvas were set up in the Rhineland towns, and from the buildings and monuments hung flags – the black-white-and-red flags of imperial Germany, not the red of the 'council regime'. Allied occupation of the left bank of the Rhine was due to begin on 5 December.

Groener, who repeats the impression of most of the generals at Schloss Wilhelmshöhe, speaks of his gradual disillusionment as the Imperial Army disintegrated: 'In the very first days after 9–10 November we at Supreme Command harboured the dream that we would have enough reliable troops to build a protective barrier on the Rhine. This proved to be a false hope.' The soldiers, he said, proceeded 'in the fullest order' to the Rhine, and then entered the 'revolutionary atmosphere' of the *Heimat*. In an attempt to

counter this, through a series of orders dating from 12 November, 'inocu-
lators' ('*Serumspritzer*') – 'efficient, skilful officers that would immunize the
troops against the spirit of revolution' – were sent out on to the routes of
march. 'Inoculation' did not work.

One can trace here the evolution of thinking at Supreme Command, from
the first hope placed in the soldiers' councils to the new notion of control
through the 'Free Corps', from a policy of co-operating with 'other ranks'
to a lesser ambition of maintaining the professional 'ideas of the Army'
wherever they could still be found. More generally, one might note the
process of the war turning in on itself – collapsing into its origins and not
exactly ending. It was 'localizing': the war was coming home.

The story Supreme Command presented – of the Army retreating in
order until it met revolution on the Rhine – has often been repeated. But it
is not the truth. The disintegration began in the face of Allied armies; it was
not the product of revolution at home. The defeat of the German Army was
total: Germany signed her defeat at Compiègne, and she signed because
her critical rail links to the Western Front had been broken and her forces
were cornered. That is why the grand Imperial Army had to walk across
the Ardennes to the Rhine.

Colonel Shartle, the American commissioner at Spa, had first encountered
the so-called 'retreat in order' at Dinant on 17 November. Setting out from
American Headquarters at Chaumont two days earlier, he and his colleagues
had crossed battlefields in the moonlight and the areas behind La Capelle
and Maubeuge where Germans had been bombed and machine-gunned
from the air the week before. 'All day', he said of his journey of 16 November, 'we saw evidence of the German retreat – helmets, overturned trucks,
equipment scattered around and destruction of wire lines.' After passing a
night in Givet, at the Belgian frontier, he left the French lines outside Chimay
and in the morning, on a high barren plateau, ran into the German Army,
'this bedraggled mob . . . plodding along in the mud towards home'. 'There
was not a single instance of disrespect,' Shartle wrote in a letter on the 17th.
The German soldiers were indifferent to the Belgians, who had their national
colours flying from every roof; a few officers saluted the American procession as they managed to find a way through. Shartle noted that 'they
are abandoning war *matériel* everywhere', and when his car broke down,
in Liège, German soldiers helped push-start the motor – a technique they
had never seen before. For ten days Shartle and the residents of Spa watched
column after grey column wind its way back home to Germany. 'There
were all kinds of vehicles, some loaded with provisions, others with para-
phernalia, and a few with furniture.' Many of the soldiers led cows, and
ponies, chicken and horses were also noted in the slow-moving crowd. True,
the bands were playing, and there was a lot of singing: the favourite song
of the day was '*Meine Normandie*' – not exactly appropriate, given the direction of march. 'The music was rather sweet,' wrote Shartle on the 18th, and

'produced a feeling of pathos'. But, for all their singing, these people were 'really down and out'.[107]

The last Germans left Spa on 26 November. For a day the Belgians washed the streets with fire hoses and decorated the town. At noon on the 29th a brigade of British cavalry appeared. The flags and the decorations were impressive. But among all the colours the most striking of all were the black crosses painted on so many of the windows: Belgians did not want the world to forget that they had really suffered in the war.

Shartle went to see King Albert and his Queen enter Liège on 30 November: 'There were immense crowds and very enthusiastic, but they didn't make as much noise as a similar crowd in America would have made.'[108]

The first real effects of the returning field army were felt in Berlin on Tuesday, 19 November. Long trains pulled up in the great nineteenth-century station halls at Friedrichstrasse, by the Zoo Garden and in Charlottenburg. Members of the Red Cross were there to welcome them, along with a number of volunteers; so were the security guards, with their white armbands, and the officials of the station Kommandatur. The orders from Otto Wels, military governor, were that all troops who were not residents of Berlin or who had not received specific permission for leave in the city were to be immediately transferred to 'collecting depots' outside the city – where nine army divisions were assembling. One of the most infamous depots was at Döberitz, about six miles west of the city limits; the novelist Alfred Döblin would describe the barracks there as 'absolute pigsties'. The execution of Wels's orders 'was not accomplished without some tense scenes', according to the *Berliner Lokal-Anzeiger*, 'but disturbance was avoided'.[109]

Every day after that Tuesday the trains arrived in swift succession. All theatres and cinemas in the centre of Berlin and around the stations were appropriated by soldiers' and workers' councils, for the problem among the city's competing authorities was not just to keep troops in transit off the streets, but to provide them – poorly clad and exhausted – with some warmth.

'The traffic is greater than ever,' reported the *Morgen-Zeitung* on Thursday, the 22nd. By the weekend, Supreme Command in Kassel had started dictating its terms for a formal, honourable entry of the Army – its nine divisions – into the capital of the Reich.

8

As a matter of fact it was getting very cold; and the coal supplies were running low. Rations were reduced. Gas and electricity were frequently cut because the plants did not have enough fuel to keep going. The rich got accustomed to eating their dinners under lamps and candles; the poor shivered in their tenements; troops in transit had nowhere to go. On 21 November the Spartacists organized a 'Council of Deserters, Stragglers and Furloughed Soldiers', while the armed 'People's Naval Division' would send men out of their headquarters at the Royal Stables to 'expropriate' goods from stores in the neighbourhood. There were occasional gunfights in front of Comrade Eichhorn's Police Presidium, and an odd corpse or two would be left lying on Alexanderplatz.

On 28 November all the Siemens works went on strike. Then the Daimler plants struck. Respectable newspapers began to complain that Bolsheviks were running German factories and that the workers' councils had created a dictatorship.[110]

On 5 December the International Armistice Commission in Spa announced that, with both the old occupied zones of the West and the left bank of the Rhine successfully evacuated, the armistice terms would be extended for another month. That also meant at least another thirty days of Allied blockade. The British entered Cologne on 6 December; French troops filed into Aachen, before the Kaiser's statue draped in black, the next day – the Belgians had already been there a week.

In Berlin, an extraordinary feature of this period was the way in which the rich continued celebrating in their clubs, bars and restaurants, despite the threat of 'expropriations'. Members of the famous gambling casino, the 'Klub von 1880' on Viktoriastrasse, had all their cash taken from them by armed soldiers. In another club, on Lennéstrasse, sailors also took watches, rings, necklaces and bracelets. An extraordinary act of 'expropriation' was that carried out by the ex-convict and sailor Otto Haas, who, posing as one of Ebert's commissars, managed to take over a whole hospital train; he lived off the proceeds in the Hotel Adlon for a month until he was found out.[111]

Quite obviously, it was getting difficult to distinguish Berlin's proliferating authorities – Ebert's Council of People's Commissars in the Chancellery, the *Vollzugrat* of Workers' and Soldiers' Councils in the Prussian Landtag, the Workers' and Soldiers' Councils of Greater Berlin in the Reichstag, Eichhorn's Agency of Criminal Police in the Police Presidium, and the Revolutionary Shop Stewards in the Schloss and the Royal Stables – from regular bandits and crooks. Political terms like 'Left' and 'Right', 'revolutionary' and 'counter-revolutionary' carried little meaning in December 1918. Moderate politicians kept silent.

But some of Berlin's respectable civil servants were in too much of a hurry. On Friday afternoon, 6 December, three high officials in the Foreign Office – Count Matuschka, von Rheinbaden and von Stumm – persuaded several hundred soldiers and sailors to join in a demonstration outside the Chancellery and declare Commissar Fritz Ebert 'President of the Republic'. A soldier named Spiro stood up on 'a rough block of wood' and warned of 'total catastrophe' if the power of the *Vollzugrat* of Workers' and Soldiers'

Councils was not ended and free elections for a National Constituent Assembly were not held before 20 December. He raised his right arm and proclaimed, 'The German Social Republic and its first President Fritz Ebert! Hurrah! [*Cheers*] Hurrah! [*Cheers*] Hurrah!'

By this time the small crowd was roaring. The drums rolled. Moved by the din, Commissar Ebert came out on the balcony and, in a very brief speech, shouted out that 'We stand before immense difficulties that war and the armistice conditions have imposed on us.' 'The economy is the basis of life,' he added, and advised his new friends to concentrate on this rather than embark on 'unauthorized measures' and 'individual experiments'. He saluted the rule of law and exalted 'united will', then disappeared behind the French windows to get back to his office.[112]

This small event is what Spartacist editors of the *Rote Fahne* would call the '*Putsch* of 6 December'. Terrified of the possibility of national elections before they had definitely established council power in Berlin, they immediately organized a counter-demonstration of 'the masses'. 'The masses', it just so happened, were attending two Spartacist meetings in the halls of Germania and Sophia on the north side of town, so they were at once invited to join in a procession across the Hackescher Markt, down Oranienburgerstrasse into the twilight mists of Chausseestrasse. There, by the corner of Invalidenstrasse, they were surprised to encounter a row of machine-guns.

The machine-guns were handled by the military residents of the nearby 'Maybug' barracks, where, ironically, Berlin's violence of 9 November had begun with the shooting of an officer. What the politics of the Maybug barracks were in December remains to this day a mystery.[113] So does the origin of the order to open up the guns.

The shooting lasted five long minutes. People took shelter in Fabisch's coffee house. Horses were shot; wagons splintered. Men and women lay on the ground, dead and wounded, some screaming into the fall of the night. While the guns went on chattering, the No. 31 streetcar clanged its bell at a corner and – horrifyingly – turned into Chausseestrasse: straight into the line of fire.[114]

9

'Down with Wels, Ebert and Scheidemann!! All power to the workers' and soldiers' councils!' That was the slogan when the *Rote Fahne* held its Saturday rally on the Siegesallee in support of a general strike. 'To work, to the ramparts, to battle!' The meeting was surrounded by a ring of Spartacist lorries, all equipped with machine-guns.[115]

Rallies were held all that weekend. Independent Socialists organized one in front of the Reichstag; Liebknecht spoke to other crowds in the Treptow Meadow as well as before the Chancellery ('There they sit, the traitors, the *Scheidemänner*, the social patriots,' screamed Liebknecht, pointing up to the grey walls from the roof of his car); meanwhile, Ebert and the Majority Socialists were bravely conducting a meeting in the Lustgarten, right outside the Schloss. Rain kept the numbers down.

Some were busy preparing for the grand entry of the field army on Tuesday. Ebert – on his secret telephone with Kassel as well as through the good offices of Prince Max's old liaison officer, Colonel von Haeften – had persuaded Supreme Command to agree that it was the civilian government's responsibility, and not the Army's, to disarm the various paramilitary groups in Berlin. In return, all nine army divisions would be granted an honourable entry. They could even march with their arms – provided they left their ammunition behind.

So, to the sound of falling rain, cheering rallies and the odd gunfight on Alexanderplatz, the decorations for the parade went up: Herr Sandkuhl designed the crowned fir columns by the Brandenburg Gate and the large transparency with the inscription 'Peace and Freedom'; the painter Adolf Sommerfeld was responsible for the ornamentation of the Friedrichstrasse station; Gardener Vergson had arranged rows upon rows of flowers leading from the Potsdamer station to the square. All these decorations – the high masts, the transparencies, the wreaths, the garlands, the fronds of palm, the ribbons – reflected strangely the adornment of Europe's cities in the summer and autumn of 1814, following Napoleon's first abdication. The motifs had barely changed.

Were they, as in 1814, to celebrate victory? The newspaper campaign which began that weekend claimed that the troops had never been defeated, that they had returned 'in good order', that 'their bodies had held the line of defence to the very last minute', 'their shield of honour is not stained'; 'they are welcomed to the *Reichshauptstadt* by warm hearts with warm thanks as true conquerors'.[116]

The parade began shortly after dawn on Tuesday, 10 December, in the western district of Wilmersdorf. Schoolgirls had been brought out to throw flowers; on nearly all the trees hung flags – the black, white and red of the Reich, not the red of the councillors' Republic. Women with baskets were there to hand out apples, nuts, cigarettes and cigars.

Soon the troops arrived. Many were dressed in new uniforms. They wore a sprig of fir in their lapels. Most were in soft caps; some had battered steel helmets. The artillery wagons were covered with fir. The horses, too, were decorated with evergreen and flowers, though they showed 'the strain of life in the field'. Many of the soldiers carried flowers in the barrels of their rifles – just as had the soldiers who marched out of Berlin in August 1914. There were cavalry, machine-gun companies and the *Minenwerfer*. Behind each company came the baggage wagons.

Shortly before midday the procession approached the Brandenburg Gate. The trams and the buses had all been stopped. No cars, besides the official military vehicles, could be heard. Around a hundred thousand spectators

had gathered on Unter den Linden and in Pariser Platz, before the Gate –
and according to the *Berliner Morgen-Zeitung* there were between eight and
ten policemen. Incredibly, no way had been cleared for the Army. As the
troops came through their arch of triumph, they simply mixed with the
crowd. It was not the Army which disarmed the population, but the population which disarmed the Army. There were other things that were
unexpected: 'Women and children were torn from each other and trampled
by the growing masses. Cries and screams for help could be heard, and
heard without end.'[117]

The officials of Berlin and the government had great difficulty getting to
their stand before the Hotel Adlon. Lord Mayor Wermuth made a short
speech which nobody heard. Then Chairman Ebert made a long speech
which certainly nobody heard. But both speeches were printed in the newspapers the next day.

One of Ebert's reported phrases was repeated with fury in every Western
capital: 'No enemy has vanquished you,' he said to the troops.

He spoke of the opening new age: 'You will not find our land as it
was before, as you had left it. All has become new. German freedom is
established.'

He welcomed them to their 'Socialist Republic', claiming that 'work is
the religion of socialism'.

And he concluded with a salute to 'our German Fatherland, German
Freedom, the Free People's State of Germany – long may they live!'[118]

The soldiers had come home.

1　A rare view of the trench war from an altitude of 600 feet: the French Tenth Army assaults German positions before Vermandovillers in the Somme, 17 September 1916

2　The view from below: French troops lay barbed wire above a new communications trench in the Aisne. The photo was taken shortly after the German retreat to the 'Hindenburg Line' in 1917

3 (*above left*) The open war of spring 1918: French troops dig in under apple trees lining a road

4 (*below left*) Rifle pits are dug outside Villers-Bretonneux, near Amiens, in the Somme

5 (*right*) The famous 'leaning virgin' atop the basilica at Albert. It was said that, when she fell, the war would end. She came crashing to the ground in the year 1918

6 (*below*) Lorries, horsemen and cyclists of Rawlinson's British Fourth Army pass by what is left of the basilica on 22 August 1918

7   (*left*) The armies of 1918 were cities on the move: German prisoners captured by the British on 21 and 22 August

8   (*above*) Men of the North and South Stafford regiment on the banks of the Saint-Quentin Canal, Bellenglise, on 2 October

9   (*below*) One of the first British patrols to enter Cambrai on 9 October

10   A German Mercedes tourer, carrying a white flag, crosses Allied lines in November 1918

11   A French soldier stands guard in the Forêt de Compiègne on the morning of 10 November. Through the trees one can just see Foch's train (*left*), and Matthias Erzberger's train (*right*)

12   The only existing photograph of the Armistice at Compiègne. Foch leaves for Paris on the morning of 11 November, carrying the signed text in a briefcase. Admiral Rosselyn Wemyss (*centre*) stands beside him

13 Armistice Day in Paris: an American 'doughboy', a British 'tommy' and a French 'poilu' are carried down one of the *grands boulevards* on the shoulders of the crowd

14 Armistice Day in London: citizens take over a lorry

15 Armistice Day in Berlin: mutineering sailors take over the Kaiser's Schloss

16　The Kaiser (*right*) chats with the King of Saxony in his villa at Spa in June 1918. This photograph, found in German baggage, was widely diffused by the Western press shortly after the Armistice – it gives a rare view of the Kaiser's withered left arm

17　At dawn on 10 November 1918, the Kaiser (*fourth from left*) and his followers wait on a railway platform at Rijsden, on the Belgian-Dutch frontier, for the train to take them into exile

18 Mealtime for retreating German troops in November 1918 at a station outside Liège, in Belgium, where Germany's western invasion began in 1914

19 German troops retreating through the streets of Cologne in December 1918. A few citizens are present

20 (*above*) German troops retreat across the Hohenzollern Bridge at Cologne in December 1918

21 (*left*) British troops advance across the same bridge less than a week later. An equestrian statue of the Kaiser gazes down upon them

22 (*above right*) The citizens of Trier watch American troops enter their city

23 (*below right*) German U-boats are lined up in the port of Kiel for delivery to the British Royal Navy

24   The first column of returning troops advance through the Brandenburg Gate on 10 December 1918

25   Friedrich Ebert, on Pariser Platz, hails the troops. 'No enemy has vanquished you,' he proclaimed. The crowd includes civilians

26   Civilian victims of a Bolshevik massacre in Wesenburg, Lithuania, are put on view by German forces in February 1919. Atrocities of this kind were not uncommon in Eastern Europe after the signing of the Western Armistice

27 A Free Corps flag in February 1919: black, with a white skull in the centre, and written around it in white 'Free Corps Brüssow from Berlin to the East'. Sometimes the flag bore only the skull, sometimes the skull-and-cross-bones. One can see how this circular design, with a cross in the centre, would evolve into a swastika flag within the year

28 General Georg von Maercker, founder of the first Free Corps, and defender of Weimar

Paris and Washington in autumn

1

A traveller heading west from the front on 11 November 1918 would have been struck by the contrast in mood between soldiers holding the line and people to the rear. Say he had begun his journey in the outskirts of Mons at precisely eleven o'clock when 'our scattered troops' – according to a *Times* correspondent that day – 'were told to unfix bayonets and unload magazines and stand for further orders'. It was grey and drizzling, and the order received was to clear the road leading back across the French border.

Progress would have been difficult past the rubble, broken wagons and abandoned cannon; one would have run into a stream of refugees returning to what was left of their homes. 'Silent thankfulness is the prevailing sentiment today in the war area of Northern France,' reported the same correspondent. Yet in just a few miles the change in mood could be noticed: 'amongst the troops in rest there is more jubilation'. One imagines the traveller reaching Amiens at some time in the afternoon; there soldiers were dancing with civilians, hats were being thrown in the air. He could easily have reached Paris by nightfall; in the capital, sunset had been a golden glow and, as another *Times* reporter put it, the city 'went charmingly off her head'.[1]

The contrast could not have been greater: silence on the front, carnival in the capital. Paris was caught up in a mad whirl of festivity, drawing in every district and every class, military and civilian. People described it as a physical, almost erotic, experience – '*Ce soir, la France est comme un lit sur une cime/ Où tu te livres nue à nos baisers ardents,*' penned the poet Fernand Gregh at the Odéon as the day neared its end – just as it was a visual one: for the first time in over four years, Paris literally turned on her lights.

No one had expected such an extraordinary release of energy. To speak of the phenomenon as a 'celebration of victory' would be quite insufficient; it was something more profound, its roots reaching down into hidden, contradictory sentiments. Worry was one of them. Less than four months earlier, in darkness, Parisians had watched from roofs and balconies the eastern night sky become a sea of fire as Germany launched her final offensive on the Marne. Since 1915 bomb alerts had been spreading alarm. First it was Zeppelins, whose bombs 'sounded like one motor tyre, or two, or three, or as many as seven exploding in the street'; then Gothas and Taubs, their engines reverberating like flying tractors; and finally the daytime shelling, without warning, from 'Big Bertha'. Total casualties from air raids amounted to hundreds rather than thousands, for Paris had developed a very effective system of defence against bombers, including anti-aircraft guns and barrage balloons around the city. The effect of the raids was less physical than psychological – not a factor to be underrated: in March 1918, at Métro Bolivar, sixty people were trampled to death in a panic.

It was because of the threat of bombing that many of the street lights had been turned off; those that remained on were covered with glass shades which lit the streets in a blue glimmer; blinds were drawn on all shop windows; the cafés closed their doors at eight; there was not much nightlife in Paris. Foreigners spoke of wartime Paris as a 'city of shadows', the districts 'darkened and deserted'. The cobbled roadways and alleys looked particularly empty when the air-raid sirens were wailing. Church bells gave the all-clear. Then people, like ghosts, would come out of their cellars and 'one could see through the darkness the flicker of candles and matches, also the rapid, sudden lightning from an electric lamp'.[2]

After the Allied offensive of summer 1918 had got under way the air raids had dwindled to nothing. But Paris remained dark at night.

Clemenceau, the Prime Minister, had had the idea of displaying on the Place de la Concorde weapons captured as the armies moved forward. So field guns in their dozens, mortars in hundreds, machine-guns in thousands, along with a few pieces of heavy artillery, were spread out on the most public of public squares in the city, overlooking a bridge on the Seine and the Chamber of Deputies. At night, they too had the air of phantoms. The purpose of the show had been to raise a 'Victory Loan', for the government was in desperate need of money. But the symbolism of captured German cannon on the Concorde could not have escaped Clemenceau; forty-eight years earlier, after the announcement of France's defeat at Sedan, he had been among the crowd in the square that had marched on the parliamentary palace and overthrown the Second Empire. It was on the Place de la Concorde that the celebrations of 11 November began.

There were many corners of Paris where events would repeat themselves like this. Paris had her continuities: this was not shifting, radical Berlin. True, journalists went on about changes since the outbreak of war – the closing of the night restaurants, the disappearance of elegant dresses, the silence of the demi-monde, the banning of absinthe. But these were superficial things, part of a world that had catered mainly to the pleasure of foreigners and outsiders. It was true, too, that social commentators would insist on longer, more profound, transformations – the mechanization of industry, the decline of the artisanal classes, the opening of the great department stores, and, with the factories, the appearance of a new kind of poverty on the city's periphery. But, while Berlin's population had more than quadrupled since the war of 1870, Paris had increased her number only by one-half; while all of Eastern Europe seemed to appear at Berlin's gates, France as a whole contained only a million foreigners in 1910.[3]

'All this has escaped!' exclaimed Arnold Bennett, standing on his balcony near the Louvre in 1915. For the novelist, who had been observing Paris for more than three decades, the city had somehow been miraculously preserved, through peace and war.[4]

Continuity was what gave Paris such a mythic power over her own inhabitants as well as foreigners: Paris was the one fixed star in the universe. Paris still had her *quartiers*, different, but weaving into one another, thus making the city manageable, walkable, comprehensible to native and stranger. The municipal tax inspector would still clamber into trams, trains and buses to collect *l'octroi*, the city toll, from those who crossed the urban frontier (though for a century tradesmen had been campaigning to abolish it). And Paris, significantly, was still surrounded by walls: those massive fortifications – '*les fortifs*' – defined where Paris began and Paris ended.

The great novelty of the war was the absence of the men. This, like the air raids, was a major factor in the psychology of Paris in 1918. In a collection of women's essays published that year, an anonymous contributor, 'SM', described the 'drama of a tight anxiety and of a stirring humility that will never find a poet: that of waiting'. Everywhere sad, single women could be seen in the city – in the stations, in the streets, in the cafés at the end of the day: 'they wait.' They waited 'for a formidable event which will revive and rejuvenate the world'. They waited for revenge: 'they will kill war! . . .They will no longer bear children for the horrors of slaughter!'[5]

Mourning was another novelty. The heavy black crêpe that the widows wore as veils was said to be the only item in the war not rationed. John Macdonald, a correspondent who lived (and died) in Paris in 1916, was struck by the sight of 'the new widows of Paris, widows young and old . . . yes, widows and widows and widows in the deepest of mourning'. Then the dull 'stump, stump on the pavement, [here] comes the mutilated soldier on crutches. Here comes the soldier with the empty sleeve. Here comes the soldier with the sunken cheeks, and the dark and deep red-and-blue scars.' In every administrative building, in every school, in every hospital, and even in the banks and in the railway stations, there was a stone slab in the entrance reading '*Morts pour la France*', with a list of names that grew longer every year – and enough space left for the next. Teenage boys, attending their *collèges* and *lycées*, passed by that stone every morning.[6]

'Composure', 'darkness' and 'tension' were the words that summarized best the atmosphere in Paris up to the very last days of the war.

*   *   *

The celebrations of victory actually began in the presence of death. In the early morning of 11 November a procession of dilapidated old hearses, requisitioned because of the flu epidemic, had descended the Champs-Elysées. Women were still dressed in mourning. Henry Muller remembered how, on the announcement of the Armistice at the Collège Tannenberge, one of his school friends behind him bowed his head in his hands and wept – he had lost his brother a few months earlier. Roland Dorgelès, author of *Croix de bois*, climbed to a high point on the Place de l'Opéra and shouted 'Vive les morts' to the crowd. Gustave Téry printed on the front page of *L'Œuvre* a sketch of a *poilu* on his knees, his head bowed before a cross marked '1914' and the soldier's cap of that year hanging on it. The caption, 'Eh! vieux! Ça y est!' captured the feeling of many, even though they cheered.

'One shouldn't say we have lost a *fifteenth* of our population,' said Téry in his editorial, written on 11 November; 'one should say: we have lost *more* than a quarter, almost a third of our arms and our muscles, a good quarter of our labour . . .' Young Jean Cocteau was mourning the loss of his male lover, Jean Le Roy; 'The concept of *patrie*?' he said. 'My fellow citizens are in heaven.' His friend Guillaume Apollinaire, the symbolist poet, died of the flu at the age of thirty-eight just after the announcement of the Kaiser's abdication. 'A bas Guillaume! A bas Guillaume!' screamed the crowd outside his window at Montparnasse; the poet's last thought was that they were calling for his death.[7]

The authorities had worried about how officially to announce the Armistice. Clemenceau simply wanted to read aloud the terms to the Chamber of Deputies, but the President, Raymond Poincaré, insisted that nobody would be able to keep the secret between eleven, when all firing stopped on the front, and mid-afternoon, when Clemenceau was expected at the Chamber. Sirens? Cannonfire? Church bells? In restrained, anguished Paris, sirens might have caused alarm, cannon made the sound of bombardment, and church bells were now associated with funerals. The suggestion that the job be done by a town crier with a drum was dismissed as a bit quaint. During the weekend, a municipal councillor came up with the idea of a peeling of all the city's church bells combined with cannon fired in series of three: thus the voice of spiritual joy would mix with the voice of triumphant warriors. That was the formula adopted.

The newspapers in the weekend of 9–10 November had downplayed the possibility of an armistice. The arrival of Germany's plenipotentiaries had made headlines on Friday; but no one could be certain that this meant peace – talk of peace had been going on for weeks. The movement of the armies, on the other hand, took on a special meaning for Parisians. With the crossing of the Sambre and the Meuse, the German forces were divided in two: the British advanced on Mons, where they had first engaged the enemy in August 1914, while the French and the Americans moved on to Sedan. 'La Revanche de 1870 à Sedan' ran *Le Matin*'s headline on the 8th; 'L'heure du *châtiment'* on the 9th; *'Le Kaiser, symbole du destin, a abdiqué'* on the 10th. That the German Emperor should lose his throne as a result of defeat at Sedan was music almost too sweet to a Frenchman's ears after four years of war.[8]

There had been celebrating on Saturday afternoon. A clamour broke out on the boulevards – *'Il a abdiqué!'* *'Vive la France!'* *'A bas Guillaume!'* But Paris still maintained her proud reserve, and the demonstration was relatively restrained. There was news that the German courier had not been able to deliver the Allied conditions to Spa: 'That's the German way!' said cynical voices. 'Don't expect peace yet!'

Paris on Monday morning, 11 November, was cold, misty and as ordinary as any Monday. There were few people on the Place de la Concorde when, at five minutes past eleven, two 75 mm cannon on the banks of the Quai d'Orsay were fired; 'Bombs!' said the pupils of the Collège Tannenberge. The brass bells of Notre-Dame began to toll; then the bells of Saint-Louis, the bells of Saint-Julien, the bells of Saint-Gervais and the bells of Saint-Germain. More cannon blasted off. More bells. Shutters and windows were thrown open. The flags appeared.

Thousands upon thousands of people swept into the streets and gathered in groups, waving their little paper flags and singing. Traffic came to a standstill. Factories were shut. Shops were deserted. Schoolmasters cancelled their classes, saying *'La guerre est finie!'*

Late risers were just having breakfast when the noise on the Place de la République penetrated the British Army and Navy Leave Club, which overlooked the square. Its director, Miss Decima Moore, abandoned all attempts to maintain order as every flag of the Empire was yanked from its socket and carried outside – along with Miss Moore herself, held shoulder high. A procession was formed and, led by the Horse Guards band (that had been billeted in the club), headed westward down the boulevards to crowds that cheered and sang and danced and cried.

On the Place de la Concorde, Parisians mixed with Portuguese, Italians, Belgians and Americans. Besides, the ebb and flow of national anthems came an eddy of popular airs: different versions of 'Tipperary', 'Home, Sweet Home', *'Ah! il fallait pas'*, 'Over There' and a song about a barmaid that a man called Bach had composed before the war, had become a rage in the year of Verdun, had in 1918 followed the Allied armies into French villages which had never before heard it, and was on everyone's lips on that 11 November – 'Madelon! Madelon! Madelon!'

There was no lunch hour. Central Paris became a mass of civilian black, horizon blue and khaki. Workers came in from the suburbs, dressed in their *costumes de dimanches*. They gathered on the sides of the stalled buses, on barrows and charabancs; the branches of the trees were weighed down with cheering people; they clambered on to the German guns, which hefty youths then hauled up the Rue de Rivoli, up the quays, up the boulevards, up narrow alleys and passages as far as Montmartre and Belleville. Those people had a sense of history.

The cannon still boomed. The church bells rang.

Some of the densest crowds could be found around the Chamber of Deputies, where Clemenceau was expected to make a speech. A few wealthy ladies, in capes and furs, had found tickets to the visitors' gallery. The tambour of the Republic rolled, a uniformed usher entered, followed by Monsieur Clemenceau, 'President du Conseil, Ministre de la Guerre'. When the tumult in the Chamber had died down, he read out the terms of the Armistice. The cannon still sounded outside.

After he had finished reading, he raised his trembling head and said, 'Honour to our great dead who have brought us this victory! Through them we can say that, before any armistice, France has been liberated by the power of her armies.' As for the living, 'we await them for the great work of social reconstruction'. Clemenceau lifted up his arms. 'Thanks to them, France, yesterday the soldier of God, today the soldier of humanity, will always be the soldier of the ideal!'[9]

Here were the three themes that would dominate French concerns in the peace, won by a citizens' army: the sacrifice, the power of arms, and 'the great work of social reconstruction'.

The crowds in Paris never stopped growing. Peasants poured in from the countryside. Every vehicle in town – buses, trams, pedlars' wagons, ancient *fiacres* and the shivering, rattling old taxis that had been the curse of city traffic since the outbreak of war – was taken by assault for the view of the spectacle provided from tops and running-boards. 'Never again would I have the same feeling of bodies pressed upon me by other bodies and stifling me, so gaily, with kisses on my hair, my nose, my ears, of hands shaking my shoulders, of voices crying "Long live America! Bravo the Teddies!"' said Lieutenant Cabeem of the US Army, recalling the moment he was cornered under Joan of Arc's statue. 'I thought I was dying, but what a pleasant death!'[10]

Nature itself seemed to share in the goodwill, for the sun appeared in the evening and – rare in that cold, wet year – would shine for the next five days, creating what the French called a 'St Martin's summer'. As evening gathered, the lights were turned on: the Eiffel Tower had not been illuminated in over four years; the restaurants and cafés in the Latin Quarter seemed suddenly to dazzle, while people in strange costumes and odd headgear chanted in the streets.

But the greatest show that night was at the Place de l'Opéra. For the last three days the opera house had been on strike; that evening it was announced that Marthe Chenal would at nine o'clock sing the national anthem from the steps of the empty house. Tens of thousands crammed into the square. Searchlights in red, white and blue scanned the ground, the buildings and the roofs as Mademoiselle Chenal walked out in a robe of equally striking red, white and blue, with a black Alsatian cap on her head. The crowd joined in the refrain.

2

When the young English diplomat Harold Nicolson arrived in Paris a couple of months later, he found the whole town in a morbid state: 'The brain of Paris, that triumphant achievement of western civilization, ceased to function. The nerves of Paris jangled in the air.' Drunk on victory in November, Paris by early January 'had withdrawn to lick her wounds'; within weeks, despondency had replaced the joy of armistice: doctors had seen this on the front – exaltation and grief, they were the two symptoms of shell-shock.[11]

A shell-shocked capital was not perhaps the best place in which to hold a peace conference. But the speed of events had made the choice of Paris inevitable. On 11 November people, including many of those in government, had the impression that peace would be negotiated in the next few days.

All the machinery for an international conference was at hand in the Supreme War Council, which sat in Versailles. All the Allied and Associate powers had a military base in Paris, and through their embassies in Paris they had co-ordinated their war effort. Only two weeks had passed since the premiers of Britain, France and Italy had met here to set the terms of the Armistice – when it was also decided that Paris would be the location for negotiations on the terms of the peace. So, while Berlin limbered up for invasion by an army of defeated soldiers, Paris prepared for the invasion of the diplomats.

Clemenceau had insisted on Paris because he wanted to preside over the conference. In his one year in office he had seen France's fortunes turn from defeat to victory; now he had hopes of 'winning the peace'. But not everyone agreed with his choice of venue. 'I never wanted to hold the Conference in his bloody capital,' Lloyd George later admitted to Sir William Wiseman. 'Both House and I thought it would be better to hold it in a neutral place, but the old man wept and protested so much that we gave way.'[12]

All the same, for those who awaited the dawn of a new age – and plenty of them were present in the crowds of 11 November – Paris seemed the right place to establish the peace after the *'der des der'*, the war to end all wars. Paris was, after all, the home of the Enlightenment, the Rights of Man, and the Revolution. As capital of the Republic, Paris could be regarded as a city of the liberal world – such a nice contrast, thought its champions, to little-minded, aristocratic Vienna, site of the hated, reactionary Congress of 1815!

But one didn't have to be an Arnold Bennett to notice what a conservative place hid behind the fortifications built seventy years earlier. The walls, over six feet thick and pierced at regular intervals with gun ports, symbolized so well the politics of Paris: defiance in the face of the invader, commitment to security, and a determination to block the flow of armies across Europe's northern plain. Moreover, if French security was at stake, Paris would halt the exchange of trade, too; Paris would bend the laws of economics if she had to.

That was the crux of the matter. Central to the whole complex issue of peace was the immense disparity that had developed between military force and money. With Germany's collapse, France now had the most powerful army in the world. But she did not have money. The greatest economic power in the world was the United States. But the United States did not have a military force that corresponded to it.[13]

This imbalance between armed power and economic power was among the most significant outcomes of the war. The United States paid the Allies' war bills, but she did not – until the very last week – make a decisive military contribution to the victory. Indebted France paid for her victory in blood: 1.4 million killed in action. If one adds to this the rise in civilian mortality rates and the dramatic decline in fertility ('We will no longer bear children for the horrors of slaughter') one arrives at an overall loss of 2.9 million lives, or a shortfall of 7 per cent of what the total population would have been if there had been no war. No other belligerent paid so dearly. '*Plus jamais ça!*' was the cry in Paris.[14]

'Death has passed by here and we see everything through our tears,' wrote Maxime Leroy, one of the many young reformers who could be found in the French civil service at the time of the Armistice. For France, the sooner the peace settlement was signed the better; it was the only way she could press her short-term military advantage. A tragic kind of urgency thus motivated French statesmen. As Leroy warned, the world was moving out of an old political age, where France still had the advantage, into a new era of economics, dominated by 'producers' and moulded by science and industry. This could not be to France's benefit. But it could be to Germany's.[15]

So urgency was coupled with fear: a fear that the nation – economically weakened – could be caught alone next to a powerful, vengeful neighbour. The walls around Paris furnished, once more, a potent symbol of this: they had been built at a time of diplomatic isolation. 'We must be prepared to find ourselves faced with an unknown Germany,' wrote an editorialist in *Le Temps* on 10 November. Perhaps Germany had lost her Army, 'but she will be a power just the same'. Peace, for Paris, required maintenance of the alliance.

As the army of diplomats gradually took over Paris's hotels, apartments, private houses, restaurants and cafés, as the languages multiplied and the streets became ever more cosmopolitan, it became clear that real national interests were at stake in the forthcoming negotiations. Many of them were incompatible. Several conflicted directly with Wilson's Fourteen Points, Four Principles and Five Particulars.

Inevitably, the grand visions of the future began to narrow as the national issues emerged. This is what 'winning the peace' had common with 'winning the war': the conflicts became local. The wider the vision, the more provincial the debate. The greater the interest, the more detailed the argument. One began with a view of a new world order; one ended with a discussion of an enclave in the Balkans, or the bend of a river in Poland, or a headland in Istria, or a coalfield on the Rhine. As in the war, globalization had a tendency to lead to localization. This was the terrible logic of both the war and the peace.

Among the major nations represented in Paris, the Italians seemed only concerned with Italian matters; born of city states, they remained the masters of local issues. The British still sought a European 'balance of power' – a self-adjusting Continental engine that, once put in order, would tick away without any intervention, leaving Britain free to withdraw to the more important matters of her island. The Americans, with two oceans, a desert and polar ice to protect them, were attracted to the same insular principle of a self-adjusting Continent. But they also had a republican ideal to defend: their peace would be just – and if it were not just they only had to threaten, with money behind them, to withdraw to their republic.

The French, with Germany on their doorstep and foul trenches to clean up, were less concerned with Continental self-adjustment and justice. They wanted security. The only card they had to play was their Army. And what an Army it was: France did not demobilize; in April 1919 she still had 2.3 million men serving under her colours.[16]

The French put no faith in 'so-called German democracy', a product of military defeat; there had been no sign of it the previous August. Yet Paris, in peace as in war, was against interfering with Germany's domestic affairs. The secret hope was that 'the federalist movement' would lead to a division of the Reich and counter 'the centralist tendencies which were those of Prussia'.[17] 'National self-determination' might be a fine ideal, but it should not be pushed too far with the Germans. French strategy on Germany's western frontiers was to control, directly or indirectly, as much territory as possible.

'Que l'Allemagne paye d'abord' – the posters were still plastered up on the streets of Paris as a hint to arriving diplomats of what was expected of them. For the French, the payment of 'compensation' – an issue which had taken up a large part of the pre-armistice discussions in Versailles – was more a military question than an economic one: it provided a reason for prolonging the occupation of the Rhineland. The conviction in Paris was that a military frontier on the Rhine was the only guarantee against another surprise attack from Germany.

This was France's policy of the wall across the plain. It conflicted with the Wilsonian principle of 'self-determination'. It flew in the face of economics. But it helped Frenchmen sleep at night.

3

If anyone had told Georges Clemenceau in September 1893 – when he lost his seat in the Chamber of Deputies – that he would one day be the most celebrated premier of the French Third Republic, he probably would have laughed and told that deluded person to go and read Cervantes' dream of noble grandeur. At the time, he admitted to a friend, 'I am unrecognized in my home, betrayed by my friends, dropped by my party, ignored by my electors, suspected by my country . . . I am riddled with debts and have nothing, nothing, nothing.'[18] At the age of fifty-two, the future did not look too bright for the former Radical deputy of the Var.

There *was* actually something of Cervantes' Don Quixote in Clemenceau, a kind of lone soldier-philosopher tilting at what he always took for the same evil giant: barbarism. What is more, he was always tilting for the same mistress: civilization, a majestic but fragile creature.

Barbarism's giant could appear in several forms: it was ignorance, poverty, injustice, the fanaticism of a party, the prejudice of a class, the sudden violence of a crowd, the arrogance of an emperor, the sullen indifference of a people. And it was always there, ready to strike down civilization, the creation of the millennia.

Clemenceau frequently lost his tournaments and would have admitted himself that the exercise was not entirely rational. But then reason was not his goddess; he let sentiment be his guide. This explained the difficulty he had had with the late socialist leader Jean Jaurès, who, Clemenceau felt, had got carried away with reason. He had had a similar problem with General Pétain, as he one day admitted to his private secretary, Jean Martet: Pétain, he said, 'is always full of reason. Too full of reason. He lacks a grain of folly.' Too much reason, argued Clemenceau, leads one inevitably to defeat.

The fight against barbarism was what had led him, in 1897, to take up the cause of Alfred Dreyfus, a Jewish captain imprisoned on a false accusation of treason. To break the silence of the government and the Army, Clemenceau published in a newspaper he edited a series of manifestos in favour of Dreyfus, signed by prominent writers, artists and scientists – the civilized people of France. They came to be known collectively as the 'Manifesto of the Intellectuals'.

It was Clemenceau who popularized the French term 'intellectual'. But, for Clemenceau, 'intellectuals' were not members of a university caste, a political grouping, or a professional association: they were isolated figures, hacking their way through the dark primeval forest of indifference; they were pioneer road-builders, the solitary engineers of human communication. Clemenceau described them at the time as 'these great monks in revolt, for whom the right to live implied the right to think'. Charles Péguy, one of Clemenceau's 'great monks', described Clemenceau as a 'lonely Socrates'.[19]

Dreyfus was eventually 'pardoned' and 'amnestied' for a crime he had never committed. For Clemenceau this proved that there was no general process of historical progress; the only eternal law was the law of the jungle, the repression of the weak by the strong – one could always count on that. History, he believed, if left to impersonal forces, would in all probability end in victory for the powers of evil and repression, not of good. It was the duty of the 'intellectual', the 'great monks in revolt', to stand up to this.

The struggle for Dreyfus had led to the creation of political formations, interest groups. Clemenceau did not like this at all. When his own Radicals set up a political party in 1902, Clemenceau refused to join them.

For a long time he described himself as a 'Radical Socialist', but he was not attracted to Marxism, which for a long time he regarded as a temporary aberration that would soon fade away. (He would later hold the same view of Russia's Bolshevik Revolution.) He very much opposed the idea of a state-controlled economy – what he called the spirit of 'collectivist barracks and convents'. Again, the problem with Marxism lay in reason: it relied too much on reason.

Clemenceau had joined the Senate in 1902, and in March 1906 he eventually became a Cabinet minister. Seven months later, at the age of sixty-five, he formed his own government. It survived for three years, making it the second-longest government of the Third Republic. Because of a series of violent strikes, it was also one of the most controversial – and Clemenceau came to be known as 'the Tiger'. For revolutionary syndicalists of the Confédération Générale du Travail (CGT) he was 'Clemenceau-*le-rouge*', 'Clemenceau-*le-tueur*', the 'cop', the 'dictator'; the sketches in their newspapers of Clemenceau's 'death's head' were later imitated by German cartoonists during the war; 'The Clemenceau ministry cannot live without corpses, it needs them,' declared *L'Humanité* in June 1908.[20]

But it was the nationalists of the Right, not the socialists of the Left, who threw him out of office in July 1909. A remarkable feature of his first government was that it ushered in a short era of conciliation with Germany: though Clemenceau had lived through the Paris siege and the Commune of 1870–1, he was no *revanchard*, who sought revenge for defeat. What the nationalists had against him was that he had committed the unpardonable error of allowing French military force to decline during his premiership.

So the defender of Dreyfus, 'lonely Socrates', the politician who refused parties, entered the war with the cause of civilization behind him – 'The life of the whole world is playing itself out: everything that man wanted, everything that he tried to attain is going to be torn from him...'[21] The darker side of human nature had revealed itself once more, this time with unprecedented violence. The talk at the time was of the 'technological' war, the 'industrial' war, even the 'democratic' war. For Clemenceau it was the bureaucratic war, a nightmare.

In 1915 he was elected chairman of the Senate Army Committee, which several at the time likened to Robespierre's Committee of Public Safety of 1793; government officials appeared before it, terrified. With parliamentary debate restrained for 'reasons of security', the Committee's hearings provided the only way of interrogating government.

The Committee's members regularly visited the front. They became highly critical of the way the war was being administered – *'cette incurie!'* – and expressed shock at the appalling, senseless waste of life. If soldiers felt contempt for *les gros* – the generals and the decision-makers – they at the same time developed a certain admiration for the old man, chairman of the Army Committee, Clemenceau. As Jacques Meyer, who in 1915 had left the prestigious Ecole Normale to join the Army, put it, 'one single politician escaped [the soldiers'] unanimous reproach: that was Clemenceau ... His numerous interventions against *everything that didn't work* were a direct echo of the recriminations of the combatants.'[22]

Ministers were accused in Clemenceau's Committee of 'criminal negligence'; 'one hundred thousand dead,' lamented Clemenceau after hearing a report on an offensive in Champagne – 'one hundred thousand dead, naturally for nothing, for the communiqué.' 'It's not the commanders who command,' growled his colleague Paul Doumer, 'it's the *bureaux*.' Henry Béranger, after collecting massive evidence on France's bungling response to German gas attacks, paid an unusual compliment to the enemy: 'Everything is organized in an intelligent fashion among the Germans, no stupid improvization; they are scientists,' he remarked; 'while here it's a *rond de cuir parisien* that decides everything.' For Clemenceau, the worst aspect of war was its isolation, its silence, its sinister indifference.[23]

The Committee had no faith in President Raymond Poincaré's 'Sacred Union', which had officially put an end to partisan politics at the outbreak of war and united all France behind the defence of her frontiers. Poincaré was a nationalist and a conservative, the kind that Clemenceau – a 'Radical Socialist' of the centre – could not tolerate. But during the first two years of the war, under the 'Sacred Union', Poincaré's government was socialist. Clemenceau's Committee did not trust these socialist politicians who on one day had been 'international anti-militarists' and the next were committed to the 'national war effort'. After the fiasco of Chemin des Dames and the mutinies of 1917, the socialists began to pursue 'another style of politics'; they returned to the principle of 'internationalism'. They believed that an international socialist congress held in neutral Stockholm would usher in a new era of world peace; Russia was already showing the way. 'Stockholm', proclaimed Pierre Laval (later, Vichy's Prime Minister), 'is the star of the north.'

There was a fundamental difference in temperament here. Socialism was a school of optimism that could attract a following when times were bad: its hopeful message of inevitable, step-by-step historical progress appeared 'reasonable'; its method of study seemed 'scientific'; its claim was to be 'democratic'. Clemenceau's politics did not cater to it. For him, human history was not governed by reason; his speeches and writings took heed of sentiment; and he knew, through experience, how quickly 'democratic' politics could turn 'demagogic': Clemenceau maintained a healthy distance from crowds.

Socialist adherence to the Sacred Union owed a great deal to the work of one man: Louis Malvy, the Minister of the Interior. When Malvy's wartime career came to an end, so did socialist co-operation. Clemenceau despised Malvy. He represented everything bad about the professional *politicien*. His life was built on connections and compromise. A Radical Socialist, he was only thirty-nine when he received his portfolio in 1914, but he already knew all the newspaper editors, the business leaders and the trade unionists; he was on friendly terms with every parliamentary deputy from the centre to the extreme Left. He was also on excellent terms with the pacifists: instead of arresting them, he subsidized them, and when their public comments became too compromising for government support he let them seek funds elsewhere – from Germany. A whole series of financial dealings, through Switzerland and through German banks in America, many of them aided and abetted by Malvy, was revealed in the spring and summer of 1917. Malvy resigned on 31 August. The socialists became a block of opposition to the continued war effort. Clemenceau became Prime Minister in November.

Controversy rages on to this day over who followed the right policy. The ultimate question is: Could France have made peace with Germany in 1917? She could, but it would have been surrender. Germany's war aims had not altered one jot a since her invasion of Belgium three years earlier – and they remained the same until her military collapse in November 1918. France, suing for peace in 1917, would not only have had to sign away the independence of Belgium, but also all her northern coalfields, the cities of Toul, Verdun, Belfort and Briey, and a coastal zone stretching as far as the mouth of the Somme; in addition, she would have to have paid a crippling 'war indemnity'. 'Today', wrote Clemenceau in an article in June 1917, 'the word *pacifism* has no other sense than that of submission to the master of brutality.'[24]

Clemenceau's government left no room for ambiguity. 'We present ourselves before you with the unique thought of a total war,' he said when he stood before the Chamber of Deputies on 20 November 1917. Gone was the distinction between front and rear: 'Let every zone be a zone of the Army.' Gone was all compromise with pacifism: 'All the guilty to the court martial. The soldier in the court, in solidarity with the soldier at combat. No more pacifist campaigns, no more German intrigues.' One, unique goal: 'Neither treason, nor demi-treason: war. Nothing but war . . . The country shall know it is defended.' Winston Churchill, Britain's Minister of Munitions, was sitting in the visitors' gallery. Clemenceau, he recalled, 'looked like a wild animal pacing to and fro behind bars.' Churchill never forgot the lesson, nor the words.[25]

Guy Pedroncini, historian of the French mutinies, records that, in the French Seventh Army during the first month of Clemenceau's government, dissatisfaction at the lack of action taken over the dealings and political scandals being reported from Paris dropped from 86 per cent to 20 per cent. The soldiers trusted Clemenceau.[26]

4

The Prime Minister was seventy-seven years old when Germany collapsed twelve months later and France, exposed and in debt, faced the uphill task of 'winning the peace'.

Two days after the Armistice, Clemenceau requested Washington to notify the German government that it should henceforth address its communications to all Allied governments as well as that of the United States. The American State Department complied, adding, in response to a German request for the creation of a 'central diplomatic agency', that such an agency already existed: it was called the Supreme War Council, and it sat in Versailles.[27]

Clemenceau's move achieved three things for France. In the first place, it broke the divisive strategy Germany had been pursuing since October of playing Washington off against the Allies. Second, it established the priority France would give to maintaining the military alliance into the peace. Clemenceau's call in the Senate Army Committee and during his year in government had been for the 'unity of command'; now it would be for the unity of the alliance: France did not want to find herself isolated, as she had been in 1870. Third, by assigning such a central role to the Supreme War Council, Clemenceau's early initiative defined the legal basis of the peace: the Supreme War Council's *acceptance* of Wilson's Points, Principles and Particulars, and *not the principles themselves*. It was clear that the Council had in late October, during the last premiers' summit, accepted Wilson's principles under very special conditions – Colonel House's extremely broad 'interpretations'.

At that time, Clemenceau had insisted not only that the forthcoming peace conference take place in Paris, but also that he be its president. 'What if Wilson comes to Paris?' snapped President Poincaré, thinking that a head of state took precedence over a mere prime minister. 'Well, if Wilson comes,' retorted the Prime Minister, 'I'll preside all the same.' He told Poincaré that Wilson would arrive not as head of state but as head of his government. 'In a meeting of this kind, I represent France; and I shall not cede precedence to anyone. If Wilson comes, we'll give him an ovation. But he will not preside.' One might wonder why the job did not go to the President of the French Republic. Clemenceau had provided the answer back in 1913, when

Poincaré had succeeded to the post. 'There exist two useless organs,' said Clemenceau (shortly after undergoing surgery): 'the prostate and the presidency of the Republic.'[28]

A more functional organ, the Supreme *War* Council, the co-ordinating limb of the Allied powers, maintained its name. This was because, as far as Clemenceau was concerned, Europe remained in a state of war until peace had been established. 'Winning the peace' was a part of 'winning the war', not a separate chapter.

The same principle was applied to French government. Unlike in the United States, where elections were held according to a mathematical timetable, or Britain, where Lloyd George demanded a mandate, it was decided that there would be no poll in France until after the peace had been signed and ratified.

Because there were no elections, Paris, after reaching a fever pitch during the week of the Armistice, was actually a calmer place than either London or Washington. There was less political debate. There was less invective in the press – still censored. While in London and Washington angry words were pronounced against President Wilson and his principles, Paris remained diplomatically mute: Paris hung on the policies of her economically more powerful allies. Paris, with an army but no money, would have her peace tomorrow if she could convince her allies and friends. But she could do this only by stealth. Like women in the war, the spirit in Paris was that of awaiting action; it was the same silent drama of 'tight anxiety and of a stirring humility that will never find a poet: that of waiting'.

Clemenceau governed France with a hushed authority. He worked at Rue Dominique, in the Ministry of War, where, unlike his predecessors, he chose one of the smallest offices – the one that had no telephones. 'This government,' proclaimed *Le Canard enchaîné* when first presented with the Clemenceau phenomenon in November 1917, 'it's Clemenceau in all the ministries.' Lord Derby, Britain's ambassador, said as much in his report to London a fortnight later: 'It is practically a one-man ministry.'[29]

In fact Clemenceau left the detail (and not a small part of the policy) to others. A notable feature of his government was the unprecedented number of non-parliamentarians it contained. Several of the ministries were headed by specialists. Professionals of the civil service found they had more access to this government than under previous administrations. This was particularly true in the case of foreign affairs, where two high civil servants exerted enormous influence: Philippe Berthelot and André Tardieu.

Berthelot remains an enigma in history. Like Clemenceau, he left no memoirs and he burnt all his private papers before his death. Unlike Clemenceau, he was a poor public speaker, so he made no advance in and had no ambition for a political career. His name never appeared in the public record. His words were never set down in the minutes. Yet his athletic, handsome profile – Colette, the writer, called him 'Seigneur Chat' – had been noted at every Allied conference during the war, just as it would adorn every peace conference after the war. Only the initiates knew it: this was the man to question if you wanted to know the secrets of French foreign policy; he was the mind of the Quai d'Orsay, the power behind the power, an emblem of Parisian continuity. His father, Marcellin Berthelot, had been one of the founders of modern chemistry and, for a brief period in the 1890s, Minister of Foreign Affairs. That was how the son entered the French foreign service. For years he kept in the background, gathering information in his civilized, encylopedic brain. Then suddenly, when the crisis of July 1914 broke, he found himself formulating French foreign policy, for no other major figure in Paris was present: President Poincaré, Prime Minister Viviani and the leading officials of the Quai d'Orsay were all in St Petersburg.

A wicked man might say it was Berthelot who had brought France into the war. Berthelot believed in the Entente with Britain and the alliance with Russia, and he distrusted Germany's motives. He believed Austria-Hungary provided Central Europe with economic and geographical unity, but, early in the conflict, he abandoned this notion as he realized that the old multi-national empire had, through its own acts, become a political impossibility. He became France's specialist of the 'successor states', the new nations struggling to arise out of the rubble of Reich and Empire; in November 1918 the war had not ended in their part of the world. Berthelot was wor-shipped by the Poles, the Czechs and the Yugoslavs. Berthelot formulated the complex network of friendships and alliances that could guarantee France's future in the face of 'unknown Germany'. Clemenceau, recognizing his power, kept him at arm's length – but only at arm's length. Berthelot had made himself indispensable.[30]

The Prime Minister felt much closer to and had more admiration for André Tardieu. 'You're Napoleon; but I warn you I'll have you shot after Marengo,' said Clemenceau jokingly in reference to the battle that had pushed the French Emperor into the political forefront. Poincaré thought Tardieu's influence on Clemenceau was total, that 'Clemenceau simply says what Tardieu whispers to him.'[31]

Tardieu was a great public speaker and also a combative journalist. Like Berthelot and many other high civil servants of the Quai d'Orsay, he was born into a world of immense privilege and fortune, a child of the VIIIe arrondissement, the wealthiest corner of Paris. 'Bourgeois I am, and I don't hide it,' he would happily admit, sucking on a long cigarette-holder, an elegant silk waistcoat glistening beneath his jacket. Though everyone who served at the Quai d'Orsay had entered by stiff, scholarly competition, private distinctions were made between *héritiers* ('heirs') and *boursiers* ('grant holders'); Tardieu, first in the class of 1898 at the Ecole Normale Supérieure, was a *héritier* who rejoiced in the fact.

In thought, he was a 'neo-capitalist': he was part of a generation of reformers, acutely aware of the imbalance developing between the economic world and the political world, and the difficulties this was going to pose for France. Having worked for the diplomatic service for more than a decade, he was elected to parliament in April 1914 and joined the Army at the outbreak of war. He thus became one of several soldier-deputies in the Chamber that collaborated with Clemenceau's Army Committee in its criticism of the way the war was run. What worried Tardieu was that France, unprepared for the war, would now be unprepared for a peace that promised to be economically hard to implement. The best way for France to overcome her potential weakness, thought Tardieu, was through the adoption, in both the private and the public sectors, of systems of 'scientific management'. He spoke of a 'policy of prosperity'. His model was the United States.

Tardieu's thinking so impressed Alexandre Ribot, Prime Minister at the moment of America's entry into the war, that he sent him to Washington to head a 'high commission' charged with co-ordinating the war effort of the two countries. In Washington, Tardieu set up an enormous administrative machine – Ribot called it 'a veritable ministry'. He also established contact with a number of influential Americans, such as William G. McAdoo, Bernard Baruch and Herbert Hoover. He became a close friend of Colonel House, and it was Tardieu who introduced House to Clemenceau.

In June 1918 Clemenceau brought Tardieu back to Paris to head a 'Commission des affaires de guerre franco-américaines'. At the same time, he became chairman of a 'Comité d'étude' that had been set up the previous year at the Quai d'Orsay to study economic and territorial questions in preparation for the peace. It was the French equivalent of The Inquiry. But the basic French policy was not to prepare too much, because – as Paul Cambon, the ambassador to London, warned Clemenceau – this could 'obscure the major points' on which the Allies and Associate America ought to agree. Clemenceau and his diplomats sought *adhésion de principe*, not scholarship.[32]

Four days after the signing of the Armistice, and two days after Clemenceau's request that German correspondence be directed to all the Allies, France produced a plan for peace. It was an extraordinary document – one which, in its breadth of vision, could be favourably compared to Talleyrand's famous 'Instructions', written before the Congress of Vienna. Behind its suggestions for procedure played the science of Tardieu. Behind its territorial proposals lay the mind of Berthelot.[33]

Its argument was historical, founded on an analysis of all the major peace congresses that had taken place in Europe in the last century. Its purpose was to end, at the earliest date possible, the state of war still legally in effect throughout most of Europe. With this in mind, it listed the outstanding international problems in order of urgency and proposed a timetable for their discussion at the Supreme War Council. To speed matters up, it recommended a two-step procedure (founded on historical precedent) of a 'peace conference' followed by a 'general congress'. At the 'conference', the Allied and Associate Powers would lay down the terms of a 'preliminary treaty' with Germany that would be limited to the essential matters of disarmament and territory that would make a German renewal of hostilities impossible. Germany would not participate in the 'conference'; the preliminary treaty would be imposed. All other questions pertaining to peace would then be discussed in the 'general congress', with German representation included.

In its territorial proposals, the plan included several of Wilson's Fourteen Points, but it did note that some of the Points – those that Wilson considered 'essentially American', such as the freedom of the seas and the removal of economic barriers – 'are not sufficiently defined in their character to be taken as a basis for a concrete settlement of the war'. Instead, they were to be regarded as 'principles of public law' and, like the whole notion of the League of Nations, were to be left to the 'general congress' to discuss, once peace had been established.

Even in matters of territory, the document was not in complete accord with Wilson's Points. The latter, for example, said nothing about the future constitution of Germany, whereas the French plan showed a clear preference for the current 'federalist tendency' that appeared to be weakening the centralized institutions Bismarck had set up after 1871. (It was for this reason that France did *not* want to interfere with German domestic affairs.) The plan also took note of the collapse of Russian power and the chaos and continued war in Eastern Europe, and placed hope in the establishment of new states – Poland, Czechoslovakia and Yugoslavia – large enough to be reckoned as powers. It admitted that broad frontiers for these states would conflict with the principle of 'national self-determination', an idea it did not consider wholly practical. The 'successor states' were not designed as a bulwark against Bolshevik Russia, which still looked very feeble; they were a substitute for the collapse of Russia on the Eastern Front of 'unknown Germany'. Clemenceau's government knew that this plan was not in perfect harmony with the wishes of their allies. It was therefore passed with great discretion through diplomatic channels. At the same time, an enormous effort was made to reinforce Allied links. Clemenceau proposed that the premiers immediately come to Paris to prepare for the 'peace conference', and carefully avoided any statement that could ruffle the sensibilities of President Wilson. House reported to Wilson that Clemenceau had promised 'he would never bring up any matter at the Peace Conference that he had not first discussed with us, and the inference was clear that if we disagreed he would yield to our wishes and judgment'.[34]

Clemenceau's government placed priority on the alliance but, acutely aware of the country's economic weakness, sought a swiftly settled preliminary peace.

5

On Tuesday, 5 November, while Allied armies marched on Sedan and Mons, as the pre-armistice negotiations came to an end in Versailles and Colonel House announced his 'diplomatic victory', Americans went to the polls. America's mid-term congressional elections usually involved issues no more exciting than local roads, bridges and sewers. Only two of them have had a major impact on the country's history. One was in 1866, just after the Civil War. The other was in 1918, during the last week of the Great War.

In the White House, Woodrow Wilson was expecting to win. He wrote that day that 'the results will be very unusual and surprising to our opponents'. The chairman of the Democratic National Committee predicted that their party would win an easy majority in the House of Representatives and maintain their strength in the Senate.

'The impending Republican defeat', his most recent report concluded, 'will be converted into a rout.'[35]

The very opposite happened. In the Senate, Republicans turned a minority of six into a majority of two; in the House, their former minority of five became a majority of forty-five; their popular votes exceeded those of the Democrats by two million – an enormous figure for a mid-term election. The victory brought Republicans a coveted prize: the powerful Senate and House committees, which had been dominated by Southern Democrats for a generation. But it was one of the peculiarities of the American constitution that the new Congress with its new committees would not sit until after the following March. Thus, during the four critical months following the Armistice, the United States would be governed by an electorally wounded President and a lame-duck Congress.

In the week when German plenipotentiaries negotiated with Foch at Compiègne, the mood in the White House was understandably grim. Advisers to the President spoke of being 'deeply grieved', 'depressed', 'dismayed', 'sick to heart'. Their bleak spirits were made yet bleaker by the happy mood in the streets: because of a series of bungled news announcements, half of America started celebrating the Armistice on Thursday, 7 November, before Erzberger's commission had even crossed the line into France. 'We have been deeply distressed down here by the false news of the last day or two,' the President wrote to a friend that Friday.[36]

Wilson had placed high stakes on a Democratic success in the congressional elections, appealing to voters on 25 October to 'express yourselves unmistakably'. They did. A year later, after Wilson's peace programme had suffered many other setbacks, House reminisced in his diary that the appeal had been a 'great political blunder' and that, instead of calling for a Democratic Congress, Wilson should have asked for the election of candidates pledged to his war aims 'regardless of party'. A lot of Republicans thought so at the time. Were Republicans any less patriotic than Democrats? The appeal set off a tidal wave of resentment.[37]

Passions deep and distant, some going back to the Civil War and beyond, were what drove America's election of 1918. Traditionally, it was Republicans who stood for the unity of the nation; Democrats were Southerners and confederate. Historically, it was Republicans who defended the country with economic protection for northern industrialists and the farmers of the Mid- and Far West; Democrats were 'sectionalists', demanding free trade for cotton. The forces that combined against Wilson in 1918 were part of the continuing civil war of wheat against cotton – the comparison with the congressional elections of 1866 is an apt one: both were fought against a President too soft with the South, and for Congress's power to 'reconstruct' the peace.

Democrats were the minority party. Wilson had been elected President in 1912 because of a split vote among Republicans. In 1916 he was re-elected President on the slogan 'He kept us out of the war'; even then, the Repubican presidential candidate won half a million more votes than Wilson – it was the division of the vote that prevented a change. Why did a wheat state like Nebraska turn Republican in 1918? According to the defeated Senator Dan Vorhees Stephens, it was due not only to the campaign for protective tariffs but also to the 'anti-war vote', derived mainly from the large German-American community – 'we lost about half of it two years ago and this year we lost it all'.[38]

The old Republican call for the right of Congress to advise and consent in the reconstruction of the peace found an echo in the Republican's economic platform and in their foreign policy. On 26 October four Republican congressmen put together a statement claiming that the Senate's role was 'equal to that of the President in the consummation of peace by treaty'. If in the West the emphasis of the campaign was on protection, in the East it was patriotic; the new Republican majority was made up of a most complex alliance.

'I most earnestly hope', said the patriotic New Yorker Theodore Roosevelt in a published telegram to Senators Henry Cabot Lodge, Miles Poindexter and Hiram Johnson, 'that the Senate of the United States, which is part of the treaty-making power of the United States, will take affirmative action as regards peace with Germany and in favor of peace based on the unconditional surrender of Germany.' He put his faith in the force of arms – 'let us dictate the peace by the hammering of guns and not chat about peace to the accompaniment of the clicking of typewriters' – and wondered why Wilson insisted on calling the United States an 'associate' rather than an 'ally' of the Western nations whose troops were brigaded in battle; to play 'umpire' like Wilson was to cater to the desires of Germany and create suspicion among the Allies.[39]

Yet there were also Republicans who showed sympathy with Wilson's aims once the campaign was done and won. The former President, and Mid-Westerner, William Howard Taft was not going to protest against Wilson's trip to Paris. And, though Lodge and Wilson mutually detested each other, Lodge did not actually oppose the idea of a League of Nations. The line of agreement between Republicans was that neither the League nor the more general terms of the Fourteen Points could make a practical basis for peace. In other words – though they had never seen it – they were generally in accord with the ideas outlined in the French plan of 15 November: a preliminary treaty imposed on the enemy, followed by an international discussion of the 'principles of public law'. If the League of Nations could be separated from the treaty, many Republicans could accept them both. Furthermore, in November 1918, Republicans regarded the United States as an 'ally', not an 'associate'. Clemenceau, who had sympathized with the Radical Republicans of 1866, would have appreciated that.[40]

For gloomy Democrats the picture of the world was altogether more simple. As the results poured in on Wednesday, 6 November, Senator Key Pittman was sitting in the Democratic National Committee room in Washington when 'the window curtain was blown aside' and Wilson's portrait 'which was hanging on the wall was flooded with sunlight'. For loyal Democrats Wilson was sunshine and hope, a torchlight in the battle against the forces of darkness. The problem, in their view, was that the Democrats had not yet built up a party that was liberal enough: 'If we have not destroyed the reaction in this election we will rearm the fight immediately and pluck victory from [it] in 1920.' They were certain they were on the right side of history; they were sure the 'progressive and democratic elements' of the nation would eventually rise against the 'patriotic dollar-a-year men', the spokesmen of 'a reactionary trade-imperialistic war'. George Creel of the Committee of Public Information reflected the mood: 'It seems to me if the defeat is to be repaired, the issue as between the imperialists and the democracy will have to be stated.' Recovery could be achieved by rallying the 'liberal, radical, progressive, labor and socialist press' to the cause of the President. 'The recoil is sure to follow,' forecasted Senator Stephens. Even the Republican majority, under the light of Wilson's leadership, would not dare disapprove of his liberal peace programme. For the moment, one would have to rely on the people of Europe; 'The situation as it is now', wrote Pittman, 'is better understood in Europe than it is in the United States.' Wilson would 'lick' the reactionaries by seeking his support in Europe.

It was Athens against Sparta, freedom fighters against oppressors, civilians against militarists, a liberating culture against the old repressive order. From Paris, Wilson would let the sun shine on the world.[41]

In the days immediately before and after the Armistice, Wilson spent long periods alone in his office. Homer Stillé Cummings of the Democratic National Committee came in to see him on Friday 8 November, and found him aggrieved that the people had not responded to his appeal for support. There was a gentleness about him, a refusal to blame anyone for the defeat: his conversation expressed more the idea that this was 'simply one of those things'. His mind had already shifted from American problems to world problems. But these elections, he admitted, 'made his difficulties enormously greater'.[42]

He wrote several letters to friends and supporters. He spoke of his 'pang', his 'distress', but declared that 'the stubborn Scotch-Irish in me will be rendered no less stubborn and aggressive'; 'my Scotch-Irish spirit has rallied [and] I accept the additional burden with demur'.[43]

Washington was still celebrating the 'false armistice' on Saturday, the 9th. But Sunday was quiet, after Americans realized that the war was still raging. Wilson went to church with his new wife and her family. 'I do wish you would go right to bed,' said his mother-in-law that evening; 'you look so tired.' 'I wish I could,' he replied, 'but I fear The Drawer.' 'The Drawer' was where code cablegrams to the White House were collected. Wilson did the decoding himself; it was a time-consuming task. His wife volunteered to help, so she remained with him while the in-laws returned to their hotel. At three the next morning the teletype stuttered out the news: the guns had stopped firing; the war had ended. Mr and Mrs Woodrow Wilson stared at each other in silence.[44]

Wilson penned a statement: 'A supreme moment of history has come. The eyes of the people have been opened and they see. The hand of God is laid upon the nations. He will show them favor, I devoutly believe, only if they rise to the clear heights of His own justice and mercy.'[45]

At instances like this one is reminded of Tsar Alexander of All the Russias at the end of the Napoleonic wars. Tucked away in his palace of Tsarskoë Selo, he also fretted about the 'rights of the peoples', he too dreamed of a peaceful world system. Of course, Wilson would have deplored Alexander's mysticism, especially its German romantic influences; the President thought of himself as a practical man, whose ideas were designed for a 'worka'day world'. But Alexander would have retorted that he was just as reasonable a man – and a man, moreover, who drew his ideas from the same source as Wilson: the European Enlightenment. He might not really have had All the Russias behind him, but he was convinced he represented the will of the peoples, more so than those other illiberal European statesmen – Castlereagh, Metternich, Talleyrand. Wilson's attitude was similar. Though in November 1918 he might have lost All the Americas, he still regarded himself – not Lloyd George, Clemenceau or Orlando – as the liberator of the 'people'. It is amazing, in fact, how far the parallel between Wilson and the Tsar did go: Alexander's project for world peace, dating back to 1804, would have set up a league of the nations, international law and a system that would have abolished war for ever. And both Wilson and the Tsar were isolated, secretive men, who had their hours of torment.[46]

* * *

Washington was again in a state of pandemonium when at midday, 11 November, the President was driven up to Capitol Hill to read out the terms of the Armistice. 'The war thus comes to an end,' he concluded, emphasizing each syllable. Though there was no suggestion of it in his address, which focused on the collapse of 'armed imperialism' and the 'hazardous task of reconstruction', Wilson's private thoughts were turning religious. The electoral defeat, followed so swiftly by the cessation of hostilities, animated the preacher within him – Daniel Webster's 'Hail, thou, sun of liberty!' that had so inspired his father. On 16 November, for instance, he made a Thanksgiving Proclamation: 'God has in His good pleasure given us peace. It has not come as a mere cessation of arms, a mere relief from the strain and tragedy of war. It has come as a great triumph of right . . . A new day shines about us.'[47]

Friends and religious leaders played up to this. Bernard Baruch, in a personal letter of encouragement, complimented him on his 'Christian patience and sublime courage'. 'In happier days to come,' he wrote, 'countless millions will always be thankful to God for having given us Woodrow Wilson, in, perhaps, the greatest crisis of all times.' A Vatican memorandum spoke of the Pope's praise for 'the Wilsonian peace terms' and warned that a second's hesitation could jeopardize his programme. The president of the Jewish order B'nai B'rith presented the President with the organization's gold medal and hailed him as 'the champion of permanent peace'. In accepting the reward, Wilson noted that 'if we truly intend peace we must truly intend contentment, because there cannot be any peace with disturbed spirits'.[48]

Along with such pious pronouncements came the inspiration for a great voyage – a crusade – to Paris.

But the Allied premiers did not want the President, a head of state, participating in the conferences. 'This seems to be neither desirable nor possible,' Clemenceau cabled Lloyd George in the week of the Armistice. Lloyd George agreed. The Americans in Paris, having watched the political sniping at Versailles in the pre-armistice negotiations, also started to worry. Frank I. Cobb – the journalist who had composed the incredibly elastic 'interpretations' of the Fourteen Points for presentation to the Supreme War Council – was convinced that seasoned prime ministers and foreign secretaries would wear Wilson down with 'endless contraversey' [sic]; 'it has been the game of European diplomacy', he warned, 'since the days of Metternich and Tallyrand' [sic]. He thought the President ought to stay in Washington as a kind of 'court of last resort of world democracy'. House put it rather more diplomatically: yes, Wilson certainly could come to the French capital – preferably as quickly as possible, so as not to hold up proceedings – but it would be best if he kept out of the actual conferences, as the kings and princes had done in Vienna in 1814.

The objections of the European premiers and the Americans in Paris fed into the opposition to the trip in Washington. Wilson's enemies on Capitol Hill claimed the voyage was unconstitutional (no president, during his term of office, had ever left the country before), while many of his own supporters openly expressed concern that, by embroiling himself in the politics of the Old World, he would lower his dignity and 'lose the moral support of peoples'.[49]

Each comment added salt to the President's electoral wound. He became irritated. He did not welcome opinion. When Secretary of State Robert Lansing came into his office to suggest that he could practically dictate the terms of peace if he stayed in Washington, Wilson's face became harsh and obstinate; 'he said nothing but looked volumes'. Wilson did cable House to tell him that the reaction in Europe upset every plan he had made. If he were kept out of the conferences he imagined he would become 'a sort of sublimated lobby'; and he particularly resented Clemenceau and Lloyd George for seeking 'a way of pocketing me' – it confirmed his worst suspicions about European statesmen. 'It is universally expected and generally desired here that I should attend the conference' – a masterly phrase if one reads it twice.[50]

It was just at this moment – Saturday, 16 November – that he received the first draft of Tardieu's plan for the peace. House had doctored it, cutting out the infelicitous remarks about the Fourteen Points and omitting all references to European diplomatic congresses of the nineteenth century, universally reviled by historians in the United States. All the same, Wilson bridled at the proposal that the preliminaries begin with an 'unofficial examination by the Great Powers (Great Britain, France, Italy, United States) of the questions to be discussed'. 'This has the old element of danger which existed in the Concert of Powers,' he wrote in the margin. 'It smacks of "secret diplomacy" and will doubtless invite that criticism by the smaller powers.'[51]

France might have been in a hurry; but Wilson wasn't. The French position was that, historically, no peace conference had taken place without a preliminary treaty, which had given it a legal definition. House, who sympathized with the idea of a swift 'preliminary', would later speak of this as the 'customary method'. Wilson was not interested in custom. He wanted to break all precedent; he wanted to proceed in the reverse order: first the conference, which would define the shape of the League of Nations, then the treaty – whether he meant the 'preliminary treaty' or the 'final treaty', he never made clear. As he admitted in a letter to an American cardinal in Rome on 30 November, 'I have formed no plans.' He hadn't even decided whether he would sit in on a part of the conference, the whole conference or none of the conference. Nor did he have much of an idea what this 'conference' was or who its members would be.

In the meantime, the European premiers, under the urging of Clemenceau, decided to hold an 'Inter-Allied Conference' in London on 2 and 3 December to define first points of procedure – before Wilson had even boarded his boat. This drove the President into a tsarist fury against the reactionary spirit of the Europeans.

It was actually only at the London Conference that the number of delegates (or 'commissioners', as the Americans called them) assigned to each power for the conference and the congress was finally determined. However, at the end of the pre-armistice negotiations within the Supreme War Council, House had suggested that the Great Powers – including Germany – 'should each have 5 places at the table', while the other belligerents would have between one and three 'according to their relative importance'.[52] The principle had been generally, though informally, accepted. Because the accord was not official, House advised Wilson not to make any public communication about his choice of 'commissioners'. The President took this more than literally: he didn't consult anybody. Though recommendations came pouring in, Wilson ignored them all.[53]

Like House, Wilson's commissioners were picked as 'executive agents', men not subject to approval by the Senate. 'The Senate must take its medicine,' Wilson confided to the French ambassador. Two of his choices were already determined: himself and Colonel House. The third would have been difficult to avoid: Secretary of State Robert Lansing was the formal head of American foreign policy. The fourth was made on the basis of his brilliant performance on the Supreme War Council over the previous year: General Tasker H. Bliss was a Republican in sympathy who had resisted Pershing; he was a scholar and a linguist, but he was not well known in America. Wilson's fifth choice was an experienced diplomat, Henry White, who also had Republican sympathies – Roosevelt said he was 'overjoyed' at the appointment – but, because he had spent most of his time abroad, was unknown to the party operators in Washington. In any case, it was clear who was running the show. As House himself later admitted, 'there was but one Commissioner at the Conference and that was President Wilson'.[54]

Behind the commissioners were teams of specialists drawn from the diplomatic corps and from academia. Some of them were already in Paris; others would join Wilson on his boat. Many were young and idealistic. Very few had links with political Washington.

As for the date of departure, Wilson announced he could not leave 'before delivering my annual message to the Congress on the second of December'. His 'State of the Nation' address on that cold Monday contained nothing on his plans for the peace conference, save vague comments such as the promise that it would be 'a peace against the violence of irresponsible monarchs and ambitious military coteries'. He gave no suggestion that he would ever be asking Congress for either its advice or its consent. As a matter of fact he spent more time lecturing on the future of American railways than on the peace. 'I shall be in close touch with you and with affairs on this side of the water, and you will know all that I do,' he concluded, pointing out that American press censorship had just been lifted and that two direct cables now lay between Washington and Paris. 'I shall make my absence as brief as possible.'[55]

'Surely he must have felt the chilliness of his reception,' recorded Senator Henry Fountain Ash in his diary. 'Two or three times his friends attempted to incubate an ovation for him but it was impossible.'[56]

The following afternoon Republican senators launched a vicious attack on the President for leaving the country to attend a peace conference about which they had never been consulted. Senator Lawrence Sherman introduced a resolution declaring that during Wilson's absence 'the office of President is vacant'. The offensive was successfully parried by the Democratic majority. But the countdown on the days remaining to them had started.

6

The USS *George Washington* was actually a German passenger boat that had been seized and converted into a troop transport. When its high black form backed out of the army pier at Hoboken shortly after 10 a.m. on Wednesday, 4 December, every whistle in New York harbour bellowed out a farewell. 'Sail on, Thou, too, O Ship of State . . .' One newspaper correspondent was put in mind of Horace's ode to the ship that bore Virgil to Athens.

The President's suite was huge and comfortably furnished, though Mrs Wilson thought the green curtains in the bedroom had a 'gloomy look'. Her husband did not enjoy the meals, prepared by the best chefs of New York's Belmont Hotel: he could not understand why good food had to be constantly 'dressed in pajamas'. He was suffering from a cold, he was dead tired, and his doctor – Rear Admiral Cary T. Grayson – noticed that his half-blind eye had begun to twitch.[57]

'I can't help but feel that he is beaten out in America,' noted his social secretary, Miss Edith Benham, in her diary on the 5th. As at Princeton ten years earlier, defeat only made Wilson more determined. In particular, he was not going to let the European Allies deform his ideals. He became highly suspicious about the content of their discussions in London, which had opened on the same day as the Republican debate in Congress – he cabled House to have all arrangements postponed until his arrival. He made no response to the French plan, and prepared to do battle with 'the English' over Freedom of the Seas. Just before boarding ship he had told reporters, with a husky voice, that Americans had won the war at Château-Thierry and that if England refused to reduce naval armaments 'the United States should show her how to build a navy'. A couple of days later news arrived by wireless of Winston Churchill's announcement that Britain had no intention of reducing her naval armaments. 'Mr Wilson', thought Miss Benham, 'is very bitter always against the English and their demands, and in fact about England and her part in the war generally.'[58]

None of this was calculated to cheer his associates in Europe. Nobody there, for example, would have denied how important was the aid of the US 2nd Infantry Division at Bellau Wood, north of Château-Thierry, in early June 1918, When Duchêne's French Sixth Army was retreating before Ludendorff's third spring offensive. Many Allied leaders, however, were convinced that American insistence on a separate US army caused needless delay in the Allied advance after July: the epicentre of the fighting was in the Somme, not the Argonne. It was certainly a gross distortion to say that Americans had won the war in 1918: they had financed it, not won it.

The ship which sailed to Europe that December was a divided vessel. The State Department hogged all the best berths – 'I don't know where all these boll weevils come from that are on ship,' Grayson complained to Tumulty, who had stayed behind in Washington. As a result, all members of The Inquiry were sent down to D Deck, below the waterline, where they discovered what conditions had been like on a transatlantic troop carrier. In a frank discussion with the President on 9 December, William C. Bullitt reported that 'most men with brains on board had been treated like immigrants and felt entirely left out of the game'; it was clubland, Princeton, on water. The mood of those on D Deck became sceptical and cynical. 'Even Mr George Creel, who is supposed to know as much as anybody, complained that he "did not know a God-dam thing about what the President was thinking".'[59]

Raymond Blaine Fosdick caught sight of Wilson on deck, a half gale blowing, on Thursday, 5 December: 'He looks well in spite of his weariness.' He walked with his wife at a brisk step, a covey of Secret Service men running after him. 'There is continual saluting. I think it bothers the President a bit.' Through the spray, his party could count a dozen American destroyers in formation.[60]

Most of the time the President was confined to his suite. Grayson worked hard at clearing up his cold, and by Friday he was beginning to get results; in the evening Wilson went upstairs to watch a moving-picture show in the main dining salon. The convoy entered the Gulf Stream during the weekend and the weather became almost summery. On Monday Grayson triumphantly recorded that the President had 'fully recovered from his cold and was in splendid shape.' He started going over his papers, including the last draft of the French plan. Then, true to style, he launched a campaign against clubland *George Washington*.

On Monday evening Wilson descended below the waterline to attend a show at the 'Old Salt Theatre'; he appeared unannounced. The show began with a 'sing'. The words of 'Pack Up Your Troubles', 'Keep the Home Fires Burning' and 'Over There' were thrown up on the screen. The President sang along with the others; he had a good voice. This was followed by a film, 'a fearsome movie with ladies losing their clothes and gentlemen likewise – but not in unison as it were'. When it was over, Wilson insisted on shaking hands with every man in the auditorium; 'You never saw such a lot of happy faces as those waiting to be greeted.'[61]

On Tuesday and the days that followed (the ship passed the smiling hills of the Azores on the 10th) Wilson laid out his ideas in a series of conferences with members of The Inquiry and the three newspaper correspondents aboard. His comments were influenced by an intelligence report on Britain and France he had just received from a certain Edward P. Costigan. Throughout Europe, Costigan reported, 'there is extraordinary and unmatched faith among the masses of the people in you, your insight and leadership'. Because Britain had not been invaded, the government in London tended to be 'more liberal and less bitter than in Paris'. Nevertheless, 'much pressure continues to be exerted by certain influential Englishmen in support of aggressive French efforts to impose conditions of future economic servitude on the defeated enemy'. Costigan told Wilson to expect the Allies at the peace conference to complain about American simplicity and democracy in their attempt to push forward their 'discredited practices of the old diplomacy'. The President, however, should stick to his ideals: 'Your own powerful and outspoken leadership is the most hopeful and least dispensable factor of the situation.'[62]

All this was music to Wilson's ears. He was in a playful spirit at the conferences, colouring his remarks with literary allusions and quotations. Members of The Inquiry were impressed. 'His personal magnetism is very strong,' wrote Charles Seymour, a professor of history at Yale who had once been his student; 'I realized it as I had years ago in college.'[63]

The United States, explained the President, was 'the only nation which was absolutely disinterested', while the leaders of the Allies – the men his audience were about to meet – 'did not represent their own people'. It was 'our troops who had turned the war'. If this was to be a just peace, the League of Nations would have to be incorporated into the treaty, thus doing away with the notion of 'Great Powers and of balance of power' – the Old Diplomacy, which had 'always produced only aggression and selfishness and war'. The people which he represented 'are heartily sick of such a course'. 'If it won't work, it must be made to work,' he concluded, for this was the way the United States did business; 'it is a protest against the way in which the world has worked'.

Demanding that Germany be treated 'in the fair way', he spent much of his time attacking England's control of the seas. 'If England holds to this course, it means that she does not want peace,' he declared.[64]

The reporters cabled the Wilsonian message to the capitals of the world. Members of The Inquiry admitted among themselves that they now had a cause worth fighting for.

On the morning of 13 December the happy passengers of the *George Washington* could make out on the horizon the rocky capes of Finistère, 'land's end'. Thirty American warships appeared as escorts; French aeroplanes wheeled over their heads; British and French warships joined them. The destroyers formed a big outer ring to the harbour while the battleships created a lane through which the President's vessel passed. To the sound of bands thumping out 'The Star-Spangled Banner' and the cheers of sailors, the New World chugged into the Old.[65]

7

Poincaré had his chance to speak in public of the French victory when, on Sunday, 17 November, every league, society, association and committee in the nation – or so it seemed – marched down the Champs-Elysées under their federative banners to welcome Alsace-Lorraine back into the fold. Between the statues to Lille and Strasbourg, on the north-east corner of the Place de la Concorde, a wooden stand had been set up for government and officials. A photograph taken at the time shows them all listening attentively to the French President with the exception of Clemenceau, who, his top hat slightly askew, stares out into a middle space. The weather had turned chilly and grey. The next day it was freezing; 'around 3 p.m.', reported *Le Matin*, 'several light flakes of snow fell with melancholy'.[66]

Paris had not shaken off the presence of war, its hardship, its fascination. Within days of the Armistice the Western Front had become a tourist site. At first, Parisians would drive out to inspect the lunar landscape of the Somme and the North. Then, after a few weeks, a special train service was organized by the Chemin de Fer du Nord. One could be on the battlefields in a couple of hours; 'MM les voyageurs would do well to bring along a few nibbles to eat during the trip,' recommended the railway company's guide.[67]

Reports on the advance of the Allied armies into Belgium, Luxembourg and Alsace-Lorraine bore a resemblance to the announcements made in the last months of the war. There was the same element of triumphalism: Metz was liberated on 19 November (though the celebrations were marred when General Mangin was thrown by his horse and hospitalized); Strasbourg received Marshal Foch and King Albert of Belgium on the 25th. It had been a poignant moment four days earlier when, at dawn, in preparation for the solemn entry into Brussels, British troops had met the French on the old battlefield of Waterloo. A white hoar frost covered the ground and fog hung in the air.[68]

In the third week of November, prisoners of war released from German camps began to appear on the roads of Lorraine and along the frontiers of Belgium. They had been left to their own devices, without food and without decent clothing. Many wore the black cloth uniforms and German caps that had been distributed in the camps; several Frenchmen were dressed in the red pantaloons and blue tunics of 1914; others, desperate for warmth, had clad themselves in women's clothes they had found in dumps. Ragged, emaciated, their faces 'frail like phantoms', they had walked day and night to reach the Allied armies. British prisoners, exposed during their internment to particularly harsh treatment ('*Gott strafe England!*'), were in an especially poor condition. 'They are, in the majority, no longer men but shadows clothed in torn rags, and so thin!' declared a French reporter stationed at Nancy.[69]

Most prisoners of war were first lodged in army division rest camps and then transferred to Paris, with the result that the city's military hospitals were probably fuller in the first month of peace than they had been at any time during the war. The main receiving centre was the Grand Palais on the Champs-Elysées, which had served as a hospital since 1914.

The condition of the former prisoners, along with the spread of stories about the forced transportation, during the war, of French civilians to camps in northern Germany, Poland and Lithuania – no mere myths – created a new rage for reparations and indemnities. Jean Poiry, municipal councillor, moved that the City of Paris demand from Germany 'not only just reparation for the damages caused by her crimes since 1914, but also that our enemy return us the 200 million francs they insolently extorted from us in 1871'.[70] Within days, the Parisian newspapers were evoking the 'immanent justice' Gambetta had called for in the 1870s. Parliamentary deputies started putting about the idea that Germany should pay for the entire cost of the war, and not simply for the reparation of damage inflicted – as had been agreed during the Allied pre-armistice negotiations.

Added to anger was disappointment. '*La guerre est finie!*' had been proclaimed from the rooftops on 11 November. The lights had been turned on. But at the end of the month Paris still looked and felt as if she were at war. New ration cards were distributed. Restaurants and cafés closed early. ('There will be no celebrations of the New Year this year,' joked *Le Matin*.) Sandbags, designed as protection against bombardment, still hid most of the monuments and churches; the stained-glass windows remained covered by wooden panelling: work to remove them began only in December.

And there was the flu. Paris was one suffering part of what was the only truly worldwide phenomenon of the 'World War'. It is now estimated that as many as 40 million people may have died throughout the globe from the influenza epidemic of 1918–19, almost twice the number of total combat-related deaths between 1914 and 1918 – and a larger figure than for the victims of the Black Death in the hundred years following 1348. The flu was one of the greatest and most rapid killers of humankind. And, contrary to popular wisdom at the time, it probably had no direct relationship to the war. The subcontinent of India was the hardest hit. In the West, the highest mortality rates were to be found in the United States and Switzerland, which had been barely touched by the war. In all probability, the agent that spread the 'Spanish flu' was the virus A°, which had its origin in China, not Spain. Why Spain should be blamed for the disease is unknown, though a rumour went round that German secret-servicemen had been injecting pathogenic bacilli into Iberian fruit and vegetables, which were then canned and shipped off to the Allies.[71]

The disease came to Europe in two waves: in the late spring of 1918 and, in a more virulent form, in autumn. In Paris, as in Berlin, deaths from the flu peaked at the end of October; in the week of 27 October to 2 November alone it accounted for 2,566 deaths in the French capital. Nationwide, it killed a total of around 200,000 people, compared to 187,000 in Germany and 112,000 in Britain. A large proportion of the victims were young: there is a theory that the older generation had been immunized by the epidemic of 1889. At the time of the Armistice the press announced the happy news that only between 100 and 150 a day were dying in Paris, as opposed to around 350 a day the previous week. By 17–23 November the weekly toll had declined to 352. Then, in December, the numbers picked up again.

The symptoms could be terrifying. The disease might begin with a violent nosebleed, followed by high fever, wheezing and finally a choking rattle that sounded like strangulation – for the sick person was indeed being strangled. French doctors described this last stage of the illness as '*l'asphyxie bleu*' – a 'most frightening feature where the patient becomes blackish in the face'. People died within a few hours of the first symptoms. Hospital corridors and entrances were filled with patients lying and dying on mattresses. There were cases of entire families being wiped out in their homes. 'We really are faced with a huge epidemic,' reported one doctor at the Hôpital Saint-Anne, 'before which we feel quite powerless.'[72]

Colonel House's secretary and son-in-law, Gordon Auchincloss, wrote in his diary on 23 November that the atmosphere in Paris was the 'most depressing' he had ever known in his life: 'Everyone around seems to have something the matter with him.' The Americans seemed to be particularly vulnerable to the flu. Nearly all the embassy staff, as well as the the group working for House, fell ill. Major Willard Straight, a young prodigy who had been appointed executive officer, died. Ambassador Sharp was incapacitated for a couple of weeks. House himself was sick throughout most of November.[73]

On the 24th the French government requisitioned the grand hotels for the foreign missions that were beginning to turn up in Paris for the 'Peace Congress': The Hôtel Crillon was handed over to the Americans, the Majestic went to the British, the Lutetia was reserved for the Belgians, while the Hôtel du Louvre was left to the Italians. The British and the Americans, mindful perhaps of the spying that had gone on in Vienna a hundred years earlier (as well as the French habit of dressing up food 'in pajamas'), insisted on having their own cooks, waiters and chambermaids. So, within days, guests and personnel of the Crillon and the Majestic found themselves in the street. The situation at the Crillon, the grandest hotel of them all, was particularly scandalous. Lying ill in his room overlooking the Place de la Concorde was the veteran French diplomat Jules Cambon. He had just been named one of France's five delegates to the conference, and he simply refused to move. Foreigners, complained his brother Paul, ambassador to London, 'are going to turn Paris into a bawdy-house . . .What a mess they make and what future wars they will prepare!' Jules managed to hold on to his room until January.[74]

The Crillon proved to be too small for the Americans. By early December, there were already over 1,300 of them – new 'economic men' representing the dawn of the new era. 'They are the hosts of minor retainers,' recorded Adolph Berle, one of the young Americans present, 'gold-plated secretaries swaggering in splendid and unused uniforms, charges drawn in from our legations, State Department officials and the like . . .The surroundings are luxurious.' On 7 December Joseph C. Grew, secretary-general of the United States Commission to Negotiate Peace, cabled the State Department that three buildings had already been filled and that more would almost certainly be needed. The civilized Athens of modern men's dreams was being turned into an overcrowded imperial Rome.[75]

Late in November and throughout December the sovereigns and princes of Allied Europe made triumphant entry into Paris. 'This itching to be acclaimed is assuming unhealthy proportions,' complained Paul Cambon. It was cold and poured with rain on 27 November, the day that King George V descended the avenues, though the crowds were full and jubilant. 'Together we have suffered, together we have fought, together we have conquered. We are united for ever,' said Poincaré when he toasted the King at the evening's banquet. 'I pray all those of you present to drink with me to the health of the President of the Republic and to the happiness and prosperity of the French people,' replied the King in French; but he said nothing about being united for ever. After the King's departure a brief public notice was issued that Monsieur Clemenceau was leaving for London to meet the other Allied prime ministers; 'one of the subjects will probably be the date of the opening of the peace conference'.[76]

The preliminary 'conference' or the final 'congress'? It was never made clear in the press, and the discussions in London would not clarify the matter. The French plan of November was fading into the fogs of December.[77]

Clemenceau returned to Paris to hear the reports 'circulating like wildfire' on Wilson's mid-Atlantic comments. Worried, he asked House if Wilson was coming to Paris 'in a hostile spirit'. House reassured the Frenchman, telling him that Wilson was the most charming, easy person with whom to work. But that did not prevent House from cabling the President, requesting him to state, in his first speech in Paris, that 'the United States understands and sympathizes with the heavy trials and suffering which the Allies have undergone for the past four years'.[78]

Trade unionists, who expected a lot from Wilson, planned a demonstration on his entry into Paris. The government, meanwhile, proposed that on his third day he visit 'the devastated regions of France and Belgium'.[79]

Paris had mixed feelings – some hopeful, others apprehensive – as she awaited the arrival of the representative of the new era, the dispenser of world justice, the protector of the oppressed.

8

Even after the neighbouring restaurant, Maxim's, had been annexed to the Hotel Crillon, the Americans – swarming into Paris by mid-December – still did not have enough working space. The 'economic men' proved to be as numerous as the diplomats, and they all required offices. On 10 December Herbert Hoover, the US Food Administrator, took over a whole apartment block on the Avenue Montaigne. Asked by some of his European colleagues what Hoover's functions actually were, General Pershing replied, 'Mr Hoover is the food regulator of the world.' Lord Derby, the British ambassador, called him 'the food dictator'.[80]

America was beginning to show her economic might, now equivalent to that of the whole of Europe combined. She might not have won the war on the battlefield, but she was about to prove that she counted in the shaping of the peace. This worried some people. Edward N. Hurley, chairman of the US Shipping Board and one of Hoover's most bitter rivals, had become quite sensitive to the concerns of Europe: 'It is not the League of Nations, nor an International Court, nor even the Freedom of the Seas that is feared by Lloyd George, Clemenceau, Orlando or their associates,' he explained in a letter to Wilson on 12 December. 'What they are thinking about, as you are probably already aware, is the increased power of our shipping, commerce and finance.' Hurley's impression, after seeing both London and Paris, was that 'the European nations are really suffering from an attack of "nerves". They have had a bad night, and the morning finds them depressed and worried.'[81]

Nobody had even drawn the curtains yet. The officials gathering in Paris had little idea of conditions in Eastern and Central Europe; they were not sure of the situation in their own Western countries. From the Baltic to the Mediterranean, from the Rhine to the Urals, vast tracts of chaos were spreading amid the ruin of four empires. Industrial activities had been diverted into war production, labour had been taken off the land, fertilizers had been converted into explosives, the grain crops of Europe as a whole were 60 per cent of their pre-war levels, there was one-fifth the number of horned cattle and half the number of swine; and the farmers were hoarding what they had. Children were dying. Millions were facing starvation.[82]

At the same time, the North American continent was suffering from surplus. It was the glut in the grain market – artificially sustained by government price guarantees and buttressed by loans from tiny private banks –

that had created the swell of Mid-Western agricultural discontent in the congressional elections of November. The United States food surplus at the end of 1918 was estimated to be about three times the amount exported in an average year before the war. Much of this consisted of perishables.[83]

Studies of food surplus and famine in our own time show that the transfer of essentials from the world of abundance to the world of want is no simple matter: it involves marketing mechanisms, complex linkages between regional needs and systems of production, local culture and, of course, politics. It demands knowledge. In the autumn of 1918 that knowledge was lacking.

The man who was determined to solve the problem of the world's food disequilibrium, Herbert Hoover, described himself as an 'administrative engineer', and his travels across the six inhabited continents had put him in contact with people's daily life and work. In the eighteen years before the war he had been managing large industries in Russia, China, India, Australia, New Zealand, South Africa, Canada, Britain, Belgium, Mexico and the United States – 'my relations with their peoples were not as a tourist or a diplomat'. Hoover hated diplomats as much as he despised their 'power politics'.[84]

The adjustment of food policies to fit post-war needs may not seem material for romantic adventure; Hoover himself admitted that 'food admin-istration is hard stuff, involving little drama'. But for those involved in his programme it quickly developed into a religious mission. Hoover would refer to it as America's 'second intervention'; Wilson called it the 'Second American Expeditionary Force to Save Europe'. 'America is the only nation since the Crusades to fight other people's battles at her own gigantic loss,' said Hoover, thinking in terms of the money spent over the following months. As a man raised on the Bible, he regarded this as a combat against the Four Horsemen of the Apocalypse – War, Famine, Pestilence and Death – though Hoover would argue that the sixth chapter of Revelation actually mentioned five, the last one carrying a great sword and riding out on a red horse: Revolution. Moreover, 'if [the Prophet] had lived another two thousand years he would have added seven more to his five – Imperialism, Militarism, Totalitarianism, Inflation, Atheism, Fear and Hate'.[85]

These might be the general evils of war, but in Hoover's mind they were particularly Europe's: the New World was engaged in a crusade against the Old – the whole of the Old: allies and enemies lumped together. By beating these evils, America would save the Old World from its 'balances of power', its 'empires', its religious and racial persecutions. In Europe, Hoover had discovered twenty-six races 'cheek by jowl in an area two-thirds the size of the United States. Through them surge the deep seated tribal instincts of nationalism, imperialism, age-old hates, memories of deep wrongs, fierce distrusts and impellent fears.' The difference between the New World and the Old was greater than the ocean and greater than the three hundred years that distanced them. 'We separated from them because we did not like them.'[86]

Hoover – who in all his time in Paris never went to the theatre, rarely accepted an invitation to dinner, sat a few times for Sunday service in Notre-Dame and took a couple of motor trips into the countryside – was not a smiling man. He was not yet forty-five, and his smooth-shaven cheeks, his straight nose and his round, hard chin revealed grim determination; a face 'full of curves', said Will Irwin, a journalist who knew him, is the mark of a man of ability. There was affection in him, and an epic poem yearning to get out. He read a lot. Before leaving the United States, he spoke to the employees of the Food Administration in Washington about the novels of Frank Norris. Norris had planned a trilogy on the miseries involved in Mid-Western wheat production, but had got only the first two completed: on the dreariness of the farmer's life, and on the manipulation and violence that existed in the Chicago wheat market. Hoover said he planned to live the third, unwritten, volume: the triumph of 'the honest and fair treatment of the farmer, the lifting of his level of life, the abolition of speculation, the honest and economic distribution of our daily bread'. It would be the story of a 'royal sharing' – 'if Norris could have lived he would have found this, "The Song of Wheat", a theme in the world's regeneration'.[87]

He set about the task sternly. 'If you want to get the glummest view of any subject on earth,' said his wife, Lou Henry Hoover, 'ask Bert about it.'[88]

Herbert Hoover was a Mid-Western Quaker, orphaned at ten. Out on the rolling prairies of eastern Iowa, 'sickness was greater and death came sooner', as Hoover put it when recalling his first decade of life in West Branch, by the banks of the Wapsipinicon. His father, a blacksmith, died of 'rheumatism of the heart' in 1880, and his mother, a preacher in the Society of Friends, succumbed to typhoid fever less than four years later. Both sides of the family were descended from frontiersmen, constantly on the move. The Hoovers were initially the Hubers of the Swiss Alps, until they left for the German Palatinate in the late seventeenth century to escape religious persecution. They were in Lancaster County, Pennsylvania, in the 1730s, in the mountains of North Carolina in the 1760s, in the Western Reserve of Ohio in the early 1800s, and they crossed the Mississippi in covered wagons in the 1850s. The Minthorns, on the mother's side, sailed from England in 1725; they trekked from Boston to Ontario, to Detroit and on to Iowa, where they settled in 1859 at the Lone Tree Farm between the Quaker settlements of West Branch and Springdale. Both the Hoovers and the Minthorns were caught up in missions of good works to the South (the anti-slavery Friends of Springdale had provided refuge to John Brown as he plotted his raid on Harper's Ferry) and to Indians (Hoover's guardian was an Indian agent and author of *Our Red Brothers*). They were all supporters of sobriety and temperance; 'There is not a saloon in the place,' read the directory of West Branch, 'and the moral influence is such as to recommend it to those seeking a good locality to educate their children.' But it wasn't the heritage, the ancestry or the background that was considered important: what mattered was the end product, the man. When asked whether she was related to John Wesley, the founder of Methodism, Hoover's maternal grandmother, who lived to be ninety-nine, replied, 'Begone with thee. What matter if we descended from the highest unless we are something ourselves. Get busy.'[89]

At ten, Hoover was moved out to the frontier village of Newberg, Oregon, another Quaker settlement. His stern uncle was a doctor and a man of enterprise – he made a small fortune in fruit farming. But the heart of this little universe was religion. On the wall hung the motto his mother had given Hoover: 'Leave me not, neither forsake me, Oh God of my salvation.' Though he lay awake at night, Quaker discipline prescribed silence in his suffering, for, as his mother had taught him, 'If thee has nothing to say, then hold thy peace.'[90]

By his teens Hoover was already earning a good wage from the Oregon Land Company: the boy had a flair for business. He entered Stanford in 1891, the year in which that Californian university opened its doors. There he studied mechanical engineering and geology, and became treasurer of the *Daily Palo Alto*. From then on his career went only one way: upward.

As a geologist and mining engineer he worked in the gold mines of Nevada and Western Australia. On his first visit to London he found British propriety disconcerting and was shocked when his manservant commented on the poverty of his wardrobe: in London, everyone wore silk hats and formal evening dress after the clock chimed six. British inefficiencies in the gold mines troubled him. But his harshest judgements on European mores came when he moved out to China to study the antracite mines of Tientsin; that was in 1901, the moment of the Boxer Rebellion. 'The constant encroachment by the European empires – Britain, Russia, Germany, France – on the independence and sovereignty of China had at last touched off hidden mines in the Chinese soul,' commented Hoover. Tientsin was under siege for a month, and there then followed the most appalling reprisals. Hoover remembered a 'British naval bully named Captain Bailey' with a 'pompous judge' conducting a trial under torchlights 'and various hysterical wharfers testifying to things that could never have taken place'. Hoover, who was an authority in town, managed to stop some of the executions. British Tommies, aware of corpses floating in a nearby canal, painted on the water carts 'Boxeril', after the popular beef extract 'Bovril'.[91]

Thereafter, Hoover's contempt for all things European never ceased to grow. He was in London when the war broke out. Though he had no official standing, his wealth and his reputation as an 'administrative engineer' counted for something among the staff of the American Embassy in Grosvenor Square. Hoover was driven by his old Quaker sense of mission, justice and commitment to peace; he declared his own war on the Horsemen of the Apocalypse.

As a first self-assigned task he helped a hundred thousand stranded American tourists return home. Unaware of it at the time, this act brought his engineering career to an end and, as he later confessed, set him on 'the slippery road of public life'.

On 25 September 1914, as the European armies desperately attempted to outmanoeuvre each other in the 'race for the sea', an eminent American engineer, Millard Shaler, arrived in London from Brussels to report that he had been able to cross German lines with money to buy 2,500 tons of food for the City of Brussels. A little over three weeks later the Commission for Relief in Belgium (CRB) was born, to get food past the navies at sea and the occupying armies on the land to feed an entire nation. 'I was not bothered over administrative matters such as the purchase and overseas shipment and internal transport of large quantities of materials. Any engineer could do that,' recorded Hoover. 'But there were other phases for which there was no former human experience to turn for guidance.'[92] It was an extraordinary venture, which had no precedent in history. Hoover supplied food to 9 million civilians trapped between the German armies of occupation and the British naval blockade; when its doors eventually closed in 1919, the CRB had spent almost $1 billion raised privately in America – an incredible amount for that day, and one inconceivable outside the United States.

Between 1914 and 1917 Hoover spent many days on old Dutch steamers crossing the North Sea – 'seldom a pleasant trip'. He suffered from sea-sickness; but, as he explained in his memoirs, with numerous German submarines running about and the waters mined, a 'semi-comatose condition has its advantage'. When not unconscious, he read. He read about revolutions and peacemakings in Europe, 'and especially the political and economic aftermaths'. Hoover realized that famine was the rule. Perhaps because of his own ancestry, the aftermath of the Thirty Years War particularly interested him: 'one third to one half of the population of Europe died'. In all history, he concluded, 'there had never been such a thing as relief'.[93]

The troubles he encountered in crossing armed frontiers reinforced all his old prejudices about Europe. To board the Dutch vessels he had to join the queues 'for inspection and general inquisition by British Intelligence officials'. There was an 'equally vigorous disrobing process by the Germans at the Belgian frontier'. He described Belgium as a 'land of imprisonment', though it is remarkable how lenient he was on German atrocities – war, he explained, is 'not an afternoon tea party'. In the summer of 1916 he watched the Battle of the Somme through powerful field glasses from the German side, 'under the thunder and belching volcanoes of 10,000 guns. The horror of it all did not in the least affect the German officers in the post. To them it was pure mechanics.' Hoover, the Quaker, thought it was all horrible, a 'devastating reality, no romance, no glory'.[94]

Hoover's politics never stooped to murder. On the contrary, he saved several million lives. In the process, he built up a reputation as the 'rudest man in London'.[95]

In his memoirs, Hoover speaks of the Armistice as a time when 'idealism burned brightly', a time that celebrated 'the end of mass murder, freedom of men, the independence and safety of nations', a time that would witness the 'rebirth of mankind'. On 21 November he arrived in London from Washington, and on the following day he attended a meeting of the Allied ministers. There he came in for 'some disagreeable surprises'. All he could see about him was 'national intrigue, selfishness, nationalism, heartlessness, rivalry and suspicion, which seemed to ooze from every pore'. A multitude of inter-Allied councils had been created, a 'movement' to pool Allied and American economic power was well under way, a plan to reduce American food prices by releasing to the world 'the dammed-back supplies in the Indies and the Southern Hemisphere' was being considered, and the food blockade was to be continued, thus 'closing the outlet for our surpluses'. Hoover became involved in a 'blockade battle' and a fight to defend American resources from control by foreign interests. At stake was the American effort to relieve 'the greatest famine since the Thirty Years' War'.[96]

'Disillusionment' was a popular literary genre in the post-war years, and the theme was well suited to Hoover's story of adventure. But here he was distorting the truth.

Hoover had been combating the British blockade of Central Europe since 1914. He had always defended a complete independence of American action. He had never had any sympathy for Europe's inter-Allied councils. When Germany declared unlimited submarine warfare in February 1917 (and immediately torpedoed three CRB food ships), Hoover had been obliged to leave London for Washington, where he became Food Administrator and a member of Wilson's War Council. The CRB was henceforth administered by neutral Spanish and Dutch officials. Even before the United States declared war on Germany, Hoover was pleading that the country refuse all political alliance with the Europeans and that it build up its military forces so as to counter European proposals for peace – Hoover's war was fought against the whole of Europe, not just Germany.[97]

A major reason why the US government guaranteed food prices to farmers was that it was expecting the war to continue into 1919; the warehouses of the Atlantic ports were filled to bursting point with supplies for the huge US armed forces being put together for the campaign. Then came the German notes pleading for an armistice, coinciding uncomfortably with the election campaign. 'Peacemaking might catch us suddenly,' the Food Administrator warned the President on 24 October 1918. He pointed out that 'considerable accumulations have taken place in the Far East and the Southern Hemisphere as the result of short shipping'. He also noted that 'some members of the Allied Food Council are putting forward suggestions for international control of world distribution of food after peace'. Stay clear of this, advised Hoover: 'If peace arrives at any time during the next few months, we will have the dominant supplies and my own view is that we should maintain a complete independence.'[98] The Armistice was signed less than three weeks later. Hoover's voice became shrill.

Urgent action was needed to convert the war's food programme into one of 'European relief and reconstruction' – and to do this without consulting the Europeans. Hoover cabled House, in Paris, a long note informing him that 'this government will not agree to any programme that even looks like inter-Allied control of our economic resources' and once again confirming that American assistance to foreign nations 'will revolve around complete independence of commitment to joint action'. The State Department thought the note so blunt that it asked House not to communicate it to any of the Allies.[99]

'Hunger does not breed reform; it breeds madness and all the ugly distempers that make an ordered life impossible,' said Wilson in his Armistice address to Congress. Millions of Europeans were facing starvation, and there was no man on earth more qualified to solve the problem than Herbert C. Hoover. Wilson instructed him to set sail immediately for Europe and there organize a relief programme – America's 'second intervention'.

But many American officials were worried about Hoover's qualities as a diplomat. Franklin L. Polk, presidential counsellor, urged Hoover, before he left, not to ignore Europe's existing organizations; then he wrote to Hugh Gibson, liaison officer, warning that 'Hoover has got a great job but he cannot play it alone', and to House, advising him 'you will have to calm Hoover down a little'. Hoover's own counsel, Norman H. Davis, described the Food Administrator at the time as 'a very impulsive man'.[100]

During the voyage across the Atlantic, Hoover set about planning his new relief programme. There were, he reckoned, 400 million people in Europe, and they lived, as a result of war and revolution, in twenty-eight nations. Among them were the three major Allies and two minor ones; these had ships and would be able to obtain credit to buy supplies in the United States; they could also get supplies from the Southern Hemisphere. Then there were the thirteen neutral countries, which had actually made money out of the war. By contrast, the thirteen liberated countries – Belgium, Poland, Yugoslavia, Albania, Czechoslovakia, Romania, the Baltic States, and Armenia, Georgia and Azerbaijan – were destitute of everything and were suffering from assaults by the Communists. The situation, he thought, was equally bad, if not worse, in the five enemy countries – Germany, Austria, Hungary, Bulgaria and Turkey – that were also threatened by Communism and the spread of unemployment; they had some gold resources, but their ships had been taken away from them. Finally, there was Bolshevik Russia, which was in a state of total chaos.

By the terms of the Armistice, the Allies continued to blockade the twenty-three neutral, liberated and enemy countries, as well as Russia, though it had been agreed at Compiègne that 'the Allies contemplate the provisioning of Germany during the Armistice as shall be necessary'. This policy was extended to the other enemy states. Furthermore, the blockade of the liberated and neutral countries had proved to be quite ineffectual.

'To cope with this demoralized and divided Europe and the world's scarcity of supplies there must be rapid, decisive organization and executive authority,' concluded Hoover.[101]

Hoover and his idea of an independent American executive authority got a cool reception from the three Allied-government representatives – Lord Reading, Clémentel and Crespi – assembled in London to discuss the organization of relief. During the war the Allies had established in London an Allied Maritime Transport Council, which acted as the naval branch of the Supreme War Council in Versailles. But, with their ships torpedoed and their own supplies short, the Allies' ideas about relief, especially in enemy territories, were not very advanced. What Hoover perceived as the 'movement' to pool economic power probably went back to a suggestion made on 13 November by Sir Maurice Hankey, the British Cabinet Secretary, that the Allied machinery for food distribution serve as a base for the construction of the League of Nations. The Allied Maritime Transport Council seemed the natural organ through which to achieve this.[102]

The so-called Allied plan to release into the world 'the dammed-back supplies in the Indies and the Southern Hemisphere' was pure fiction. Economists, even in those primitive days, could calculate the costs of transportation by ships in short supply. Speculation in food soon drove the prices of food imported from the Southern Hemisphere way above those of North America. Hoover should have been comforting himself: American food products were not only competitive, they were dominant.

But Hoover, in the gloomiest mood, rushed over to Paris to consult with House and get American 'executive action' moving. Within twenty-four hours they came up with a full American plan for 'the relief of the civilian populations of the European countries affected by the war'. Somewhat artfully, they argued that 'there be a unity of direction similar in character to that which has proved so successful under French and British Chief Command in the operations of the Allies on the land and on sea respectively' – the United States had never accepted the idea of a 'unity of command', insisting instead on the independence of its Army. The plan proposed the creation of the office of Director-General of Relief, which 'must be held initially by the United States Food Administrator', although he would be responsible to the Supreme War Council, 'to whom he should report'. The plan urged that enemy tonnage be brought under his service rather than, as initially planned, being under the control of the Allied Maritime Transport Council, which could lead to 'many embarrassments'. Wilson added his signature, and on 1 December the plan was forwarded to the Allied foreign ministers.[103]

The French were too preoccupied with maintaining the military alliance – and America's 'association' – to make much of a fuss. The Italians were concentrating on their northern frontiers, though they hoped they would have some say in the supply of food to Austria and the 'Kingdom of the Jugo-Slavs', which was taking shape to their east. But the British were getting worried. Lord Reading, reporting on 28 November to the Imperial War Cabinet about the conference with Hoover, said that everyone agreed that if there were to be a meeting with German delegates to discuss the food situation it would take place in London – everyone agreed, that is, except Hoover, who had just announced to the press that it would take place in Brussels. Reading thought it would be most unfortunate if America started playing a lone hand. Lloyd George, who was ready to provide aid to German civilians, added that this insistence on American independence was an ill omen for the League of Nations. How strange it was that the land which preached international order refused to participate in international councils and accepted the principle of 'unity of command' only when she herself commanded.[104]

Hoover attended two meetings in London in December: the premiers' conference of 2–3 December (which had so infuriated Wilson as he prepared to disembark from New York) and, following on that, another meeting of government representatives on relief. By this time the inevitable stories were appearing in the Allied press about the American 'surplus', a determination to dump it on European markets, and the curious sympathy the Americans were showing for the Hun.

Hoover remained as aggressive as ever. He suggested that management of food supply should be in proportion to the national contribution; given the depleted state of Allied stocks after four years of war, this meant the Allies would manage virtually nothing. He maintained that 'the United States would not countenance the use of food, medicines and clothing for political pressures', while announcing his intention to send independent American 'mission specialists' into Central Europe to investigate the food situation. It was news to no one, except perhaps Mr Hoover, that such agents would exert enormous political pressure – as events would prove. Consultation with the Allies over such missions was quite out of the question for Hoover: 'Do nothing else,' he advised House, who wanted to discuss the matter with the British Foreign Office. 'That is, simply inform them.' Hoover wanted the naval blockade ended immediately; he argued that it no longer served any military purpose. For the Allies the war was not technically over: they had signed an armistice with the enemy, not a treaty, and, as Churchill later explained in the Commons, 'We are holding in readiness all our means of coercion in full operation or in immediate readiness for use. We are enforcing the blockade with vigour. We have strong armies ready to advance at the shortest notice. Germany is very near starvation.'[105]

American ships, loaded with supplies, were already steaming into neutral ports by the first week of December. On the 10th Hoover opened his head-quarters on Avenue Montaigne. 'By the opening of operations,' he recorded, 'I had done away with the pool and Allied control of American resources in one act.'[106]

Four days later the President of the United States entered Paris.

9

The Allied armies were still marching east in December. While Berlin was receiving her soldiers on behalf of the German nation in 'its eternal glory', British forces were moving from the Belgian frontier of the Meuse on to the Rhine bridgehead at Cologne. A new American army, the Third, liberated the Duchy of Luxembourg and followed the valley of the Moselle in the direction of the second Rhine bridgehead at Koblenz. To their right marched the French Tenth Army from Saarbrücken across the Palatinate to the third bridgehead at Mainz. An advance British cavalry division crossed the three-hundred-yard Hohenzollern Bridge, beneath a high statue to the Kaiser, and entered Cologne on the evening of 6 December. 'It seemed to me to be the culminating point of the soldiers' life of every one of us,' Brigadier General Bonham-Carter wrote home to his family a week later.[107] All reports suggest that the inhabitants accepted the occupation with a sense of quiet resignation. By the 13th the Allied and American armies had attained a line on or just west of the Rhine, stretching from the Dutch frontier down to newly incorporated French Alsace. The American Third Army penetrated Koblenz that afternoon; the French Tenth occupied Mainz the next morning.

On Friday, 13 December, as Wilson sailed into Brest, Marshal Foch met Matthias Erzberger and his fellow German plenipotentiaries in a railway saloon car at Trier (or Trèves), now occupied by the Americans. Foch read out the terms of the renewal of the Armistice, which had been agreed upon by the Allies at the premiers' conference in London earlier in the month. To the original terms the Allies added a condition that gave them the right, at six days' notice, to occupy the ten-kilometre neutral zone on the right bank of the Rhine between the Dutch border and Cologne. Erzberger signed, and the ceasefire was thus extended to 5 a.m. on 17 January; 'This month's prolongation shall be extended until the conclusion of the peace prelimi-naries, on condition of assent by the Allied governments,' stated the accord. Erzberger declared that his government had, to date, loyally fulfilled the original terms; that the prisoners of war had been repatriated, though 'unfor-tunately, in freeing themselves in the turbulence of the German revolution, [many] had brought on a result that could not possibly have been avoided'. However, he claimed that the provisions promised in the Armistice of 11 November had not yet been delivered – 'take full account, gentlemen, of the responsibility that you assume in further delaying the importation of food products'.[108]

On the same day that Wilson entered Paris, Saturday 14 December, general elections took place in Great Britain and Ireland.

Poincaré and Clemenceau had just returned from a tour of Alsace and Lorraine. At Metz, Philippe Pétain had received his marshal's baton. 'You have obtained from the French soldier all that you demanded of him,' said Poincaré to the man who had ended the crisis of 1917. 'You have understood him, you have loved him, and he responded with loyalty and devotion to all that you gave him in concern and affection.' Pétain, who would always be the hero of the soldiers of *quatorze–dix-huit*, was in tears. There followed an embarrassing scene as the President of the Republic attempted to kiss an astonished Prime Minister. But the crowds cheered. 'The plebiscite has been made,' Poincaré remarked at Strasbourg's town hall as he looked out on the people waving thousands of handkerchiefs and flags from the streets and windows and roofs. William Sharp, the American ambassador to Paris, reported it was impossible to describe in words the enthusiasm he had encountered in Strasbourg 'by members of a family reunited after a long separation'.[109]

In Paris, the French Socialist Party (the SFIO) and the Confédération Générale du Travail were preparing a reception for President Wilson. Militants of the CGT, unhappy over the lack of political results in the strikes of 1917 (when munition workers had simply accepted a pay rise and gone back to work, losing all interest in the 'pacifist' campaign), were pushing for a reformed, more centralized, organization of the trade unions; they frequently cited Bolshevik Russia as an example. But, in December 1918, Woodrow Wilson was their idol. They plastered red posters all over Paris, addressed to 'Worker and Peasant France!' and to the 'Workers of Paris!' and announcing that 'President Wilson is an audacious statesman who knows how to place rights above interests.' Workers would gather in the streets on Saturday, 14 December, to welcome him.[110]

Demonstrations in Paris required a government permit. The government did not refuse it. Instead they proposed that the socialist leaders telegraph the American President, still on the high seas, and ask his consent – the radio transmitters on the Eiffel Tower were made available to them. In the meantime, House cabled Wilson to say that 'a committee of labouring men and Socialists, headed by Albert Thomas, Renaudel, and Cachin, wish to present you with an address . . . and hold a monster parade in your honour'. Lansing cabled from the *George Washington* the next day that the President 'wants to avoid a demonstration of labouring men and socialists'; he did not want to be identified with 'any single element'. For their part, the socialist leaders thought a request for the President's consent would be discourteous; they called the formal demonstration off and, instead, asked their followers to line Wilson's route into Paris and 'salute him with their acclamations'.[111]

Wilson, in his black overcoat and doffing a silk top hat, was received in Paris like a king. He towered over the bearded Poincaré, sitting next to him in the victoria which led the procession down the Champs-Elysées, across the Pont Alexandre III, past the Chamber of Deputies, and across a bridge again to the Place de la Concorde. Mrs Wilson, in a second horse-drawn vehicle, also wore republican black: black dress, black tricorne hat and a black feather coyly pointing at an angle towards the crowds. Hers was a wagon of statesmen's women that included Mme Poincaré, Mme Jusserand and Miss Margaret Wilson, the unmarried daughter. Behind rode the Prime Minister and a couple of French generals.

Aeroplanes flew in low formation above their heads. Wounded soldiers stood on the steps and waved from the windows of the military hospital at the Grand Palais. Huge French and American flags, formed in banners, draped the buildings from top to bottom. Across the entry of the Rue Royale hung in six-foot-high letters a *'Vive Wilson!'* A transparency covered the façade of one hotel reading *'Honneur à Wilson le Juste'*.

Crossing the Pont de la Concorde the procession encountered a group of Royal Engineers, who, perhaps feeling somewhat outdone, held up a banner in red letters: 'British – your allies since 1914'.[112]

At the Elysée luncheon, Poincaré, with no intention of being ironic, began his toast with the remark, 'Paris and France have been expecting you with impatience.' 'Upon the misery and sorrow of yesterday must follow a peace of reparations,' he added, 'and, what is more, a guaranteed defence against the dangers of yesterday.' Wilson's reply did include the comment 'I know that the contemplation of the ruins left by the armies of the Central Empires would inspire in me the same repulsion, the same profound indignation that the people of France and Belgium feel in their hearts.'

But Wilson did not want to contemplate these ruins. The French government had initially planned a three-day visit to the devastated regions immediately following his arrival in Paris; Wilson spent that week in his residence – a palace by the Bois de Boulogne designed for Napoleon's marshal Joachim Murat – listening to House and Hoover, and negotiating with foreign officials. It was then hoped he would make the tour after Christmas; Wilson left for London on the 26th. Wilson, unlike his French hosts, was not a man in a hurry.

The press began to speculate over the cause of Wilson's refusal to see the destruction just outside Paris. Wilson never gave a public answer. However, one of his private counsellors, Mr A. H. Frazier, did hear him say, 'The French want me to see red. I could not despise Germans more than I do already.'[113]

10

So much rain fell in December that there was serious concern that the Seine and the Rhône would flood; landslides were reported in the Côte d'Or, Burgundy. 'The atmosphere is not particularly Christmasy, for it is typical of Paris winter, grey, rather raw drizzle,' wrote Professor Charles Seymour to his parents on Christmas morning. He could at least enjoy the luxuries of the Hôtel Crillon – white, crusty bread; butter and sugar available on demand – while the 'doughboys', as they called the American soldiers, were disconsolate and homesick. 'I wanted to say "Merry Christmas" to the orderly outside my room, but was afraid that he would kill me if I reminded him of the season.'[114]

However, in the afternoon the clouds cleared up and Seymour went out for a walk. 'I have never seen the Place de la Concorde so beautiful; it was glistening with the sun on the wet pavement, with a rosy haze over everything, the pennants streaming from the great flagstaffs they have erected around the Place.' Thousands of people were looking at the big guns and tanks. Children played soldier with the 75s and trench mortars. He walked down by the quays; the river was in a torrent.

He spent the next few days unpacking boxes and preparing his offices above Maxim's. Occasionally he would go out, and see the French queuing up outside an *épicerie*, a tobacco shop or a confectioner 'who had put up a placard saying that he would have a limited amount of chocolate at such and such an hour'. There were lines of *poilus*, 'round-shouldered, squat, mustachioed, unshaven, and very dirty'; they spent their whole time munching at pieces of bread, even when attending mass. Seymour told his parents that relations between American and French troops were not good. The Americans disliked the dirt, and were angry at being constantly overcharged; the French were angry at the Americans for driving up prices. 'I think the sooner we get our troops home the better for our national relations.'[115]

On Sunday – it was the 29th – he attempted with some friends to get into the Chamber of Deputies 'and see the big men'. It was not easy without a special card, but when they proved they were members of the American Peace Commission they were guided to a gallery reserved for generals. He was surprised how small the French 'hemicycle' was. He could see all the faces. Despite the heckling and denunciation, Clemenceau, seated in the centre on the government bench, showed not the slightest concern. The socialist deputy Albert Thomas made a speech. Then 'to our delight Clemenceau got up'.[116]

Seymour was witnessing the conclusion of a marathon debate. It had begun the day after Christmas and it continued, morning to night, for the next four days – French Republicans ignored weekends.

The debate was prompted by the government's desire to settle pressing budget problems, particularly those connected with military indemnities, pensions and widows' allowances. The socialists at once protested that the government had never made known the war's casualties. Abrami, the Undersecretary of State for War, answered that this had been done systematically every month of the war; then, to a house in total silence, he read out the statistics of casualties suffered by France up to 1 November 1918:

Killed:	31,300 officers	1,040,000 men
Missing:	3,000 officers	311,000 men
Surviving prisoners:	8,300 officers	438,000 men

Most of the missing in action would turn out to be dead. Swiftly the debate moved on to the question of how to prevent such a destructive war from ever occurring again. At issue was France's policy for the peace.[117]

For the first three days the debate was dominated by deputies from the extreme Left, though they occupied only eighty seats. They built their argument on a defence of the Wilsonian peace programme, and specifically upon the first of his Fourteen Points: 'open covenants openly arrived at.' As Marcel Cachin, their leading spokesman, put it, it was the beginning of a new era: 'This war must not be concluded like the wars of former times, like the wars of the old regime.' He pointed out that 'class war' now extended from the Rhine to the Urals, and that the revolutionary movement was likely to spread still further. 'In this deeply troubled Europe, this Europe in turmoil, you have to establish the peace. No parallel can be made with the wars of the past.' Over fifty million people had been drawn into battle. He quoted Wilson: 'It has been a war of the peoples; one must therefore establish a peace of the peoples.'

In fact, references were made several times to 'the people'. From their eighty seats, the deputies of the extreme Left felt they had a special claim on 'the people'. Wilson, though he had just lost the most recent elections, was also identified with 'the people' – one should not merely applaud his name, said Cachin, but also 'sympathize with his spirit and his thought'. They spent many hours speaking of the 'Russian people' and the Bolshevik government that so manifestly represented them – the aristocracy had been expelled, no bourgeoisie existed to replace them, so power had been seized by 'men of socialist doctrines'; 'the Government of the Soviets has demonstrated its ability to acquire the sympathy of the Russian people,' affirmed Alexandre-Blanc. There was even talk of the 'world's people', united in peace under the League of Nations – or the 'family of nations' as Cachin preferred to call it.

The people's peace would have to be an open peace – no secret treaties; no selfish annexationist policies pursued behind closed doors. The deputies wanted to know what the government's intentions were in the occupied west bank of the Rhine and in the Saar, and most especially they wanted to know what Allied troops were up to in the former Russian Empire.

Throughout these debates Clemenceau remained silent, though several deputies at the tribune had challenged him to speak; some even had the impression he was sleeping. Then on Sunday Stéphen Pichon, the Foreign Minister, mounted the tribune to defend the government's policy.

Pichon agreed that the entire world – 'Europe, Asia, Africa, America and Oceania' – would be affected by the peace conference about to be held in Paris. But, he argued, for that very reason the government could not answer every question in a public debate, for this would 'compromise and betray the secret of negotiations which are not our property'. As for France, the central issue was the future of Germany. 'Germany', he said, 'is defeated, but not fallen.' Out of the chaos, the country would attempt to save every element of power it could. 'Its old military oligarchy, which has been the scourge of Europe . . . maintains, under deceitful appearances, an important part of power' – no one with a knowledge of Germany in December 1918 could deny it. France's first duty was to take this fact into consideration. Allied troops were in Russia because, in March 1918, the Bolshevik government had signed a 'shameful treaty' with Germany and with Austria-Hungary: 'How could we, our allies and us, have remained impassive in the presence of such an act?' Allied troops were still there because, with Germany withdrawing, the new nations to the east of Germany, who were the potential allies of France, had to be protected. Pichon made it clear that the French presence in Eastern Europe was not designed to overthrow the Bolshevik regime: it was there to build up a countervailing power to a future, strengthened, Germany – 'We are simply defending ourselves.' Pichon's comments were a confirmation of ideas first presented in the French plan of 15 November.

In a long and eloquent speech Albert Thomas, who had been the Munitions Minister before Clemenceau came to office, demanded that the Prime Minister outline his policy for peace. Clemenceau rose and, without mounting the tribune, spoke from his bench for about three-quarters of an hour. It was a memorable moment.

'Monsieur Albert Thomas asks me when I intend to return to the rigorous method of the parliamentary regime. No, I will not return to it, because I have never left it.' He spoke of the number of interpellations he and his ministers had faced since coming to office, and added that 'the government has the right to choose its hour to speak'. The opposition's claim that the government was silent was simply a manoeuvre; 'I disapprove of, I repudiate this tactic.'

The situation facing France, he admitted, was indeed novel. 'This question of peace is a terrible question, it is one of the most difficult that has ever been submitted, I don't mean just to a parliament but to a nation, and I can say in all time.' Do not think, he went on, that because President Wilson – 'who arrives from America with his high thoughts and desire to realize them in Europe' – has expressed himself 'that I am obliged immediately to express my own'. France was in a particularly difficult position: 'She is the closest country to Germany. America is far. She took her time in coming.' He recognized Britain for being there since the start; he recognized America for making, in the end, 'a prodigious effort'. Everyone was saying that such a war should never be repeated. But how could this be achieved?

'There was an old system, which appears condemned today and to which I am not afraid to say I remain today partly faithful: the countries organized their defence.' A stir began on the Left. 'It is very prosaic,' the Prime Minister continued. 'They attempted to maintain good frontiers; they armed themselves. It was a terrible burden for all the populations.'

'The system is bankrupt!' exclaimed some. 'This is abominable!' cried others.

'It is me who is abominable?' responded Clemenceau. 'Let the Chamber and the country be the judge!'

'It is a scandal to hear such things said,' came up another cry.

The old man carried on regardless. He argued that if the system of balance which had developed spontaneously during the war had been observed before the war – if Britain, the United States, France and Italy had openly announced that an attack on any one of them would be regarded as an attack on them all – the war would never have begun. Someone on the Left announced that this was the principle of the League of Nations. But it wasn't. The League of Nations involved all the nations. Clemenceau, true to the November plan, gave priority to an alliance of the 'Big Four'. 'For this entente I will sacrifice everything,' he declared. He reported that 'conversations' were currently under way with the United States; they would be 'laborious and redoubtable, and I say "redoubtable" because if we do not arrive at an accord our victory will have been in vain'.

He explained that President Wilson, coming from a country distant from the frontiers of Germany, did not have the same preoccupations as 'a man who has seen his country devastated during four years by an enemy who was within several days of Paris'. Yes, Mr Wilson 'has a broad mind, open and elevated. He is a man who inspires respect by the simplicity of his words and the *noble candeur* of his spirit.'

The French word *'candeur'* is a *faux ami* meaning 'naivety' or 'guilelessness', not 'candour'.

'It is abominable!' screamed out Paul Renaudel from the extreme Left. 'It must be a joke!' A joke that the socialists and militants of the CGT would never let Clemenceau forget; for months their newspapers would repeat the phrase the Prime Minister 'had irreverently used in speaking of Monsieur Wilson'.[118]

Abominable or not, the debate ended with a vote of confidence in the government of 398 votes against 83 – the largest parliamentary majority Clemenceau had won in his life.

Professor Charles Seymour hoped the official record of the remarks on Wilson would read *'noble grandeur'*. He went home thinking, 'I do not believe that Clemenceau really represents France.' For Hoover, Clemenceau's speech merely confirmed the wicked European spirit of 'power politics' and the need for an American policy of total independence. House, reflecting on the event the next day in his diary, wrote: 'The situation strategically could not be worse'; he wanted Wilson to bind the Allies more stringently to the Fourteen Points. But nobody in Paris knew how Wilson would actually react, for he was still in London.[119]

London in autumn

1

On 11 November 1918 Britain's Grand Fleet lay at anchor off the east coast of Scotland. News of the signing of the Armistice had come through in early morning; the naval clauses, which required Germany to surrender all her submarines and to hand over for internment the bulk of her High Seas Fleet, were announced in the afternoon. The odd quietness that had been observed among the troops on the Western Front was also witnessed on the assortment of grey iron vessels off Scotland: a thirty-mile line of battleships and cruisers, torpedo boats, minelayers, minesweepers, 'stunt' ships, motor patrol boats, coalers and trawlers rolled and pitched in the heavy, cold swell. In the evening a light mist descended upon the waters.

Then, all of a sudden, with a roar, the Fleet gave 'voice' to victory. It seemed as if the night sky were being torn apart. Star shells were thrown up, fireworks scrawled across the heavens, searchlights played patterns in the clouds; myriad signal lights dazzled the eyes; sirens wailed and the big hooters bellowed; a repeating 'whoop! whoop!' from the torpedo boats penetrated the ears: 'It was a volume of sound, never of its kind, perhaps, equalled in its intensity before, and it must have been heard over a radius of a hundred miles.' After an hour, at nine o'clock, the sirens just as suddenly stopped, the lights were snapped out, and, in autumn's night chill, the Fleet resumed its silent watch.[1]

The Grand Fleet was as much a symbol for Britain as Paris's fortified walls were for France – perhaps a little more so. Four hundred years of history lay behind it. 'The British Navy has preserved, for the third time in history, the freedom of the world against a military tyrant,' Winston Churchill reminded his constituents in the old seaport of Dundee that same month. 'The great victories on land could not have been won had the Allies not had behind them the power of the British Navy,' asserted the current First Lord of the Admiralty, Sir Eric Geddes, in London on 9 November. 'We must have our Navy,' exclaimed David Lloyd George. 'It has saved us for centuries, and we should be guilty of a great folly if we gave it up.' The

Prime Minister's argument was that the Navy was a defensive weapon: 'You cannot take the Navy to Berlin . . .The Germans could not have invaded Belgium with their navy.'[2]

President Wilson's determination to disarm the Navy and enforce the 'Freedom of the Seas' made no sense to the British. The Navy was the ally of liberty: not only did it counter the forces of Continental despotism, it had abolished the slave trade, it had wiped piracy from the seas, it was the guarantee of the free movement of merchandise during peace, and it thwarted the ambitions of military conquerors. Few but a handful of idealists could accept Wilson's proposal that an as yet non-existent League of Nations could act as a substitute for an armed force which had maintained world peace for a century and, in fifty-one months of war, had made the destruction of German military power possible. Yet, within a month of the Armistice, reports were coming through that Wilson, sailing for Paris, was threatening to launch an American naval programme to 'lay two keels to Britain's one' if the British government did not accept his doctrine of the 'Freedom of the Seas'. Even before he had set foot in France, there was a feeling in Britain that the American President had 'a chip on his shoulder'.[3]

Early in December an inquiry was sent by the United Press of America to leading figures in Britain asking them what they understood by the expression 'Freedom of the Seas'. H. G. Wells and Bernard Shaw – long advocates of a League of Nations – were as vague on the matter as Wilson's Point II had been in his address of 8 January. Lieutenant-Colonel Charles Repington, the *Morning Post*'s famous war correspondent, answered, 'I have not the faintest idea what the freedom of the seas means, nor have I met anyone here who can tell me.' Most pointed out that the British blockade had won the war, and thought Americans would understand this; some even expressed the hope that America would join Britain in her policing actions. 'Freedom of the seas German version means sinking without trace,' replied Mr J. St Loe Strachey. 'The British Fleet ensured victory,' responded Admiral Lord Beresford. 'Without the British Fleet the whole world would have been under the domination of Germany. The German view of freedom of the seas would have been parallel to their view of the freedom of the land.' Several said that there could be no such thing as freedom of the seas during a war. The most pertinent point was made by Sir Frederick Maurice, who had been directing operations in France and was a famous defender of Haig: he argued that no government could bind itself to such an abstract principle, because 'the unexpected is the rule' in war and 'war methods change rapidly with mechanical developments'.[4]

For centuries the Navy had defined Britain's relations to the peninsular Continent. But technology had changed the rules of the game. At the end of the Napoleonic wars Castlereagh had interpreted Britain's national interest in terms of two principles: Maritime Rights and what his master, William Pitt the Younger, had called a 'just equilibrium' in Europe – what most historians would subsequently refer to as the 'balance of power'. The former was written into the Treaty of Paris in 1814; the latter provided a working basis for the Congress of Vienna, which completed its 'Final Act' in the week of Waterloo, June 1815. What Britain meant by 'Maritime Rights' was her right, in time of war, to visit and search neutral vessels on the high seas. Britain's initial understanding of a European 'just equilibrium' took the form of constructing barriers on the Continent to future French expansion; this explained why Castlereagh had followed a policy of 'bringing Prussia forward' to the Rhineland. But by the summer of 1815 Castlereagh was having nightmares about Prussian military expansion. It was not, however, something that worried his government back in London. The reason was that, with Napoleon defeated and a Continental equilibrium apparently established, London lost interest in Europe and turned its attention to its fleet sailing across the seven seas and opening Britain's horizons to world trade. It was a fleet driven by sail and guided by tactics of war that had not changed much since the days of Francis Drake.

Though they continued to play lip-service to the concept of European balance, few of Britain's nineteenth-century leaders took an active interest in developments on the Continent. Britain played no role in the mid-century movements of national unification, no role in the political debates that rocked dynasties after 1848; when Prussia invaded France in August 1870, Britain sat by and watched. The only major area of concern was Europe's south-east – for this was a zone that cut across trade routes.

It was an exceptional period in British history. In the previous half of a millennium no major European war had been fought without Britain eventually getting involved – save the Thirty Years War in the seventeenth century, when Britain was at war with herself. In the anomalous nineteenth century there were no major European wars, partly as a result of British policing of the seas.

But the technology of travel by sea changed, and so did the nature of naval guns. This transformation coincided with the collapse of one of the two supporting pillars of British foreign policy; the European balance of power. Its demolisher, Bismarck, was a wily enough engineer to realize that, while he could hack away at the European balance – indeed, could throw it completely askew by marching into Austria and then into France, and follow this up with an alliance with Russia without any interference from Britain – he could not menace Britain's supremacy on the seas. It was only after his dismissal, in March 1890, that Germany began to batter at this. It led to the greatest arms race the world had yet known.[5]

No major naval war had been fought since 1815; there had been no major naval battle since Trafalgar. Yet the naval experts in Britain sought, in the case of conflict with Germany, the same tactics as in the earlier war with France: a strangling blockade and a decisive battle.

Under Admiral Sir John Fisher, First Sea Lord in the years before the

Great War, the Grand Fleet was prepared for the twentieth-century Trafalgar along the lines of three principles: rapid concentration, speed and firepower. Fisher was convinced that the decisive battle would occur in the North Sea, so the old naval ports of Portsmouth and Plymouth were run down, while the ports of the east coast were developed: Britain's guns now faced east to Germany, not south to France. Fisher was acutely aware of the menace of enemy firepower, which would render the old tactic of close blockade obsolete. After his retirement in 1910 a new concept of distant blockade was introduced: the whole North Sea would be transformed into a flexible barrier. Fisher's plans, however, overlooked one technological innovation: underwater explosive devices – they would count more than surface firepower.

Fisher's reforms had an important side effect on the distribution of British power in the world – an effect that would be magnified during the war years: they reversed a hundred-year trend towards dispersal. The Grand Fleet was moved back to the home waters and the North Sea. Britain, almost despite herself, was moving back into Europe after nearly a century's absence.

It was part of a larger European pattern of concentration, based on the movement of trade, of peoples and, eventually, of armies across Europe's northern plain, which became the whole drama of 1914–18. And the whole problem of the peace that followed. Britain could not escape it. That was why Britain went to war in 1914. Maybe she could have delayed the declaration. It is conceivable that Britain could have sat by as Germany slaughtered civilians and transported others in cattle wagons into forced labour; it is inconceivable that Britain would have tolerated the German colonization of Belgium and the occupation of the Channel ports: at some point Britain would have gone to war. One imagines a history of Britain entering the war at a later date: it would not only have been less dignified, it would also have proved more expensive in men, money and equipment.

For the idea of Britain standing aside and letting the Navy do the work was a pipe dream. Within months it became clear that Britain would require a huge Continental army: an army that invaded by the plain had to be met on the plain. The greatest illusion under which British leaders laboured was the myth of Trafalgar. It was wrong from the start. Trafalgar might have destroyed Napoleon's fleet, but Napoleon enjoyed his greatest successes on the Continent in the months that followed; and it took a decade to defeat him, by massed armies on the plain.

The 'decisive sea battle' in the Great War never took place. It was expected within the first weeks of the war but, instead, Britain in 1914 suffered a series of setbacks.

The moment of 'Trafalgar' appeared to arrive in late May 1916, as the Battle of Verdun was raging. Off Jutland, the two fleets steamed towards each other at forty knots; capital ships fired at each other at ranges of up to 16,000 yards. 'I had no real idea of what was going on,' reported poor Admiral Jellicoe four days later, 'and we could hardly see anything except flashes of guns, shells falling, ships blowing up, and an occasional glimpse of an enemy vessel.'[6] The British lost 14 ships sunk and 6,000 men dead, while the Germans lost 11 ships and 2,500 dead; the rest of the German High Seas Fleet sailed back to its harbours. One month before the Battle of the Somme, British opinion was already in a state of shock. On 5 June the *Hampshire* hit a mine off Scapa Flow; nearly all aboard were lost, including the Secretary for War, Lord Kitchener.[7]

Worse was to come. Since February 1915 German U-boats had been periodically torpedoing without warning both Allied and neutral shipping; over a million tons were sunk thus in 1916. Within two months of Germany's declaration of unrestricted submarine warfare in February 1917, one in four ships approaching British shores was being sunk; a million tons of shipping was lost in April alone. Britain was left with only six weeks' supply of wheat, and no timber at all was getting through from Norway – critical for the supply of pit props in Britain's coal industry. 'There is absolutely no solution that we can see,' ruefully admitted Admiral Jellicoe, who became First Sea Lord in December 1916.[8] But there was a solution: the convoy system, which was forced on the Admiralty by the new Prime Minister, Lloyd George. Of all ships convoyed since the summer of 1917, less than 1 per cent were lost from any cause.

As on the land, defensive strategy and tactics held the advantage over the offensive. The concentration of forces proved more effective than their dispersal. It was a hard lesson for an island nation at war with Continental powers to learn; it was always tempting to search for a weak point behind the line, to deliver a small force by navy and attack in the back, to put up a 'side show'.

The Prime Minister himself never accepted the term 'side show'. 'You heard a good deal of the side shows,' Lloyd George said mockingly to a crowd in Leeds in December 1918. 'Well, I will tell you what these side shows were: Mesopotamia, Palestine, that is, the East. The British Empire to these gentlemen was a side show.'[9] The bitter conflict between 'Easterners' and 'Westerners', between Lloyd George and his generals, was more than mere polemic: it was a clash between those who still followed the old trend of dispersal and those who favoured concentration; between the champions of a naval British Empire and the new defenders of a Britain in Europe. In the Dardanelles campaign of 1915 British and Dominion forces suffered total casualties of 145,000 men in establishing a new line of trenches on a narrow, rocky peninsula which they eventually had to abandon. In the spring of 1916 Sir Charles Townshend surrendered in the desert at Kut a force of 12,000 British and Indians to the Turks; the British had to send out another 300,000 to redeem the loss. In the pestilential Greek enclave of Salonica, 600,000 Allied troops, on British insistence, faced trench warfare until

Bulgaria collapsed – out of internal weakness – in September 1918; then, and only then, were communication lines between Germany and Turkey threatened. All in all, over two million men had been diverted to the Eastern side shows.

Britain was drawn into Europe – at times kicking and screaming; but she went in all the same. No huge armies? She enlisted them. No conscription? She installed it. An independent command? Under the guns of Germany she accepted the unity of Allied command. It was a British army under a French generalissimo that broke the back of imperial Germany.

But Britain could not have done it without her Navy. There was no Trafalgar, the amphibious side shows had been no great help, but the block-ade worked. Virtually all seaborne trade and supplies were cut off from Germany – fodder imported into neighbouring, neutral, Holland dropped from 1.6 million tons in 1915 to 4,000 tons in 1918; cereals from 860,000 tons to 82,000 tons; fresh fruit from 105,000 tons to zero[10] – while success in defence against submarine attack guaranteed military and economic supplies for the Allies. When the German High Seas Fleet was ordered out on a 'Death Cruise' in October 1918 it mutinied. A month later it was steaming into British ports for internment.

The British Grand Fleet had every reason to celebrate on 11 November 1918.

2

English war memoirs tend to be silent about the Channel crossing to join the regiment in France, or to return home on leave. On the way out, the woods on the Isle of Wight 'hazily recede'; on the way back, the chalk cliffs of Dover 'appear very quickly, like in a dream'. One writer might casually mention that he went down to the officers' saloon to have a plate of ham, another that he sat on a tarpaulin cover on the bow of the boat. Vera Brittain, who, because of the submarine war, had to return from nursing service in Malta through Italy and France, recorded a smooth crossing from Calais to Folkestone on a hospital boat escorted by destroyers; in mid-Channel they met a transport heading for France, the 'men all waved to us and cheered'. 'Light does not gleam upon the immediately following journey,' wrote Edmund Blunden about his first voyage to wartime France. In fact, for security reasons, many of these Channel crossings were made at night.[11]

For many citizen-soldiers the dark waters of the Channel marked a barrier between them and their countrymen. 'The Front Line was behind us,' said Siegfried Sassoon on a sick leave he took in the spring of 1917; 'but it could lay its hand on our hearts . . . Our minds were still out of breath and our inmost thoughts in disorderly retreat from bellowing darkness . . . We were the survivors; few among us would ever tell the truth to our friends and relations in England.'[12]

London, though it could frequently hear the guns in France and actually shook when the mines of Messines Ridge in Belgium were blown on 7 June 1917, was a different place from Paris. It was the largest port in the world. One approached it both by water and rail; that's what made London so special, in war as in peace.

The port and its accessory services had been the source of extraordinary wealth in the nineteenth century; and an amazing thing was the continued generation of this wealth during the years of trench warfare, the years of the U-boat. In the winter and spring of 1916–17 there had been shortages, but they were never vital. Grain, timber, coal, fish, meat, fruit and vegetables still poured into London; dockworkers were counted among Britain's 'indispensables' who were prevented from going to the front. The most profitable commodity traded in London was money; 'English capital runs as surely and instantly where it is most wanted, and where there is most to be made of it, as water runs to find its level,' Walter Bagehot had once commented.[13] This remained true in 1918: in London it was 'business as usual', and the soldiers returning from the front noticed it.

The railway lines were what had initially caused the nineteenth-century Stock Exchange to turn its attention away from government stock into private investment, for the capital demanded had been enormous. Railways had changed the face of London. Unlike Paris, no walls could be now built around London; the outcrops of Roman and medieval masonry at Cooper's Row and All Hallows were isolated curiosities, not the components of an active fort. Railways had fostered a leapfrogging process in urban residence that bore no comparison to either Paris or Berlin: when the rich discovered their semi-rural retreats were being turned into suburbs and that their employees were becoming their neighbours, they moved further out. In the decades before 1914 hundreds of rural villages became crowded suburbs, while the 'Fever Patch' of the Strand, Covent Garden, Waterloo Bridge, Camden Town and the Borough – Dickens's London – was emptied of residents. Railway building had led to the destruction of 800 acres of central London. England's old Georgian capital had gone, and with it the rookeries, the lodges and the crowded tenements, as well as the street theatres and the Italian musicians; the performers had moved into the city's music halls. Seven million Londoners, governed by twenty-eight municipal boroughs, lived in a sprawl of houses, brick cottage rows, terraces and 'railway villas' that had no equivalent on the Continent. They lived in gentle anarchy, they revolted against central planning, their neighbourhoods were shaped by the clout of money, and their homes were unashamedly bourgeois, comfortable – decorated with patterned wallpaper and patterned carpets, and furnished with settees and ottomans.

Up the meandering Thames the Zeppelins flew, 'long narrow objects of a silvery hue'. Unlike Paris, London was not defended. Responsibility lay in the hands of the Navy, but until the autumn of 1915 it had no guns, searchlights or aircraft; warnings and the all-clear were given by police whistles – it was felt that the ringing of bells or the blowing of hooters would serve as guides to the invaders. Eventually an Anti-Aircraft Corps was formed out of the Royal Naval Volunteer Reserve; they were armed with a few pom-poms. It was the outcry over the inefficiency of London's defence (Pemberton Billing, Independent MP for East Herfordshire, built a political career on it) that led at last to the creation of the Royal Air Force in early 1918. By that time Gotha biplanes were flying over London. Huge anti-aircraft guns were placed in Wandsworth Common, Clapham Common, Green Park and Hyde Park; residents found them more frightening than the bombers. Warnings were given by the firing of maroons, while Boy Scouts on bicycles sounded the all-clear with bugles. Residents were told to stay inside their homes. Some took cover in the Underground. Theatres continued to function; a dozen people standing outside the Lyceum, watching the approach of a Zeppelin, were killed one night in October 1915. Total casualties from bombing during the war were 670 dead and 1,960 injured. Londoners were never seriously exposed to the material violence of the war.[14]

It was the railways that provided the most sensitive link with the front. At Charing Cross, Waterloo and Victoria stations the farewells created an atmosphere so suffocating that it was said they sucked the oxygen out from the high-glassed enclosures. Vera Brittain, in a space of three years, saw her fiancé, his friend and her own brother off to their deaths. 'I had come superstitiously to believe that a railway station farewell was fatal to the prospect of meeting again,' she unsurprisingly confessed in her memoirs. The dull stoicism of the crowds on the stone platforms hardly relieved the pain; rather, it emphasized 'the uncomprehending remoteness of England from the tragic, profound freemasonry of those who accepted death together overseas'.[15]

What really brought the war home to London were the convoys of wounded that arrived in the same stations after a big 'push' or an enemy offensive: 25 September, 1 July and 21 March – Loos, the Somme and Ludendorff's spring offensive – were dates imprinted on the minds of Londoners for a generation. Like the telegrammed notifications of death ('Regret to inform you . . .'), the convoys of wounded began to come in three or four days after the action. On 4 July 1916 there were not enough platforms to accommodate the agonized men, so their trains were transferred to Paddington. Stretcher cases were laid out in rows; ambulances queued up at the main entrance and then slowly moved off to First London General in Camberwell, Second London General in Chelsea, Queen Alexandra's in Millbank, or the officers' hospital in Park Lane. Then the rush was on in the surgical wards; red-cloaked matrons and VADs (nurses of the Voluntary Aid Detachments) stamped up and down the aisles with an efficiency that surpassed human understanding (''Allo, and 'ow are you today?'); scratchy gramophones blared out all morning and afternoon a medley of popular songs – many a soldier groaned and died to the strains of 'If You Were the Only Girl in the World'.

Londoners found plenty to complain about. After the first air raids, the city was 'blacked out'. Outside advertising was forbidden, the illumination of shopfronts was stopped, oil lamps replaced flares in the street markets, street lamps were masked or muffled, trains and buses were shrouded with curtains: but, as numerous reporters discovered when they crossed the Channel, 'Darkest London' was not as dark as Paris. In hotels, clubs and eating houses – the French word 'restaurant' was deliberately avoided during the war – a meatless day had to be observed once a week, and afternoon tea and cake could not cost more than sixpence. There were serious shortages of tea, sugar, butter, margarine and bacon with the outbreak of unrestricted submarine warfare; there was less milk, because cows were less productive, although Britain did not make the same mistake as Germany of emptying the farms of fodder to feed the population. In March 1918 rationing was introduced into London and the Home Counties; by July, National Ration Books were being distributed and one could not even eat in a Lyons' tea shop without producing a 'coupon'; but rationed London never saw the long queues for the *soupes populaires* that had become daily fare in Paris. And it saw fewer women in mourning. This might have been because London was so much more a middle-class town: in Catholic France, peasants and workers wore mourning and their influence spiralled upward; in Protestant England, the Duchess of Devonshire and Mrs Edward Lyttelton refused to wear black and their example percolated downward.

Churchill kept on repeating both during and after the war that well-fed Britain had the Navy to thank, and he was undoubtedly right. But the abandonment of 'Britain's way of war' – Navy, money subsidies to the Continent and few human casualties – for the 'Continental way', with a mass of graves in Picardy and Flanders, had caused a trauma back home. There was no consolation for death, no comfort in loss, so Londoners turned away from the ongoing tragedy in France. They seemed utterly indifferent to 'foreign affairs'; their conversation became trivial. They talked about the food shortages (though, with the rationing of 1918, more food was actually available to the lower classes than there had been the year before); they discussed the air raids (by summer they were non-existent); they complained about the lighting; they bemoaned the shortage of maids. When London's police went on strike for a day (on 31 August) it seemed the whole social order of England was collapsing. 'Will the Home Front hold?' soldiers on the real front asked half jokingly – but only half. Consistent with a trend that expressed itself in different ways throughout Europe, London, with the globalization of war, became provincial.

London developed a hatred of foreigners. This had a history. On 18 May 1900, when it was announced that Colonel Robert Baden-Powell's small force had been relieved at Mafeking after 217 days of siege by a Boer army, Londoners had gone into wild celebration of a kind never seen before. The English language acquired a new word, 'mafficking' – 'to indulge in extravagant demonstrations of exultation on occasions of national rejoicing' (*OED*) – and Londoners were convinced that the war in South Africa had ended in victory. But it went on for another two years – a brutal, debilitating guerrilla war. The final result had come so close to defeat that questions were asked not about South Africa, but about London.

The poor were discovered; recruitment had revealed that huge numbers of young men living in the East End and the South had appalling health. The presence of immigrants and aliens was noted; in Spitalfields and Whitechapel, Houndsditch and Stepney there were whole streets where, it was told, nothing was spoken but Yiddish. In the 'Khaki Election' of 1900 the Conservative (or 'Unionist') candidates for Stepney and Bethnal Green proved that this was a vote-getting issue. A parliamentary inquiry was subsequently held, and in 1905 an Aliens Act was passed which placed such restriction on immigrants that the number entering Britain halved within four years. London did not experience the same influx of foreigners as had Berlin.

During the Great War it was rumoured that the Zeppelins which flew over London were actually built in Battersea; that spies and 'nosy parkers' were working from their bakers', barbers' and tailors' shops in the East End; that a secret syndicate called the Hidden Hand was operating within political, society and business circles to undermine morale. The 'member for air' – Mr Pemberton Billing again – had to be physically carried out of the Commons by four burly attendants after complaining, out of order and against the warnings of the Speaker, about 'the number of damned Germans that are running free about the country'. Male enemy aliens of military age were interned in the Islington workhouse or Alexandra Palace in north London, where, according to Michael MacDonagh, who visited the palace in December 1915, they enjoyed a degree of comfort. Anti-alien riots and demonstrations took on a worrying dimension. After the sinking of the *Lusitania* in May 1915 over 250 people were injured in the East End and Kentish Town; a number of shops were looted and destroyed – woe betide the good Scots publican Mr Strachan, who had his windows smashed because his name sounded German. After German shepherd dogs were stoned, their name was changed to 'Alsatians'. Liverwurst and delicatessen were now advertised as 'Good English Viands'. Many families thought it a good idea to alter their names too: Rosenheim became Rose, Schact became Dent, Siegenberg became Curzon; after Prince Louis of Battenberg was forced to resign his post as First Sea Lord of the Admiralty he transformed himself into Lord Mountbatten. On 17 July 1917, by a proclamation signed at a meeting of the Privy Council in Buckingham Palace, the two-centuries-long reign of the House of Hanover came to an end and the 'House of Windsor' was born.[16]

Lloyd George claimed that the same kind of social conditions existed during the Great War as had scandalized the press during the Boer War. Recruiting statistics, he told an audience in Westminster in November 1918, showed 'a much higher percentage of physical unfitness in this country than in France, Germany, or any other great country'. There were signs of such poverty in London, but its worst ugliness had disappeared because, with the war, its main cause had gone: there was no unemployment. When the Liberal politician and reformer C. F. G. Masterman revisited Dockland, Bermondsey, Wapping and South-West Ham just after the war he found the houses in a poor state but the inhabitants healthy. 'Except for anxiety for those at the Front,' he wrote, 'many would have wished these conditions to continue for ever.'[17]

Throughout the war the lower Thames and the docks were swarming with vessels from every corner of the world, except Germany; the warehouses and sheds of the Port of London Authority were bursting with stock; steamers queued up to unload their cargoes to the overworked dockers. Light work and casual labour relieved the young, the old and the handicapped, so that the Salvation Army's shelters were virtually emptied. The theatres and music halls were packed to the sounds of ragtime and the songs of the Piccadilly Johnnies, while the 'picture palaces' became a regular form of entertainment. 'The Great War gave birth not to a new Puritanism but to the Roaring Twenties,' says one historian. MacDonagh might have complained in his journal of the 'drabness' and 'untidiness' of civilian clothing – 'It is some time now since a man or woman in evening clothes has been seen in the theatres,' he grieved on 12 January 1918 – but that was an older man looking down at the young: top hats were definitely out; soft hats and 'straws' were in. The girl clerks who worked in the ministries and government offices at Whitehall (the term 'secretary' still applied to the minister in those days) did not wear petticoats or bustles. When they were seen in the streets at lunchtime they were known as 'flappers': London's answer to the *midinettes*.[18]

The department stores in Oxford Street did good business. Good teas were served – in exchange for coupons – at Gorringe's in Buckingham Palace Road and Fuller's on Regent Street. Siegfried Sassoon prepared his statement to *The Times* on the war and 'those who have the power to end it' sitting in the Savoy Hotel Grill: 'Watching the guzzlers in the Savoy (and conveniently overlooking the fact that some of them were officers on leave) I nourished my righteous hatred of them, anathematizing their appetites with the intolerance of youth,' he admitted in his customary paradoxical way.[19]

It must have been galling for the men on leave – this richness, this sparkle, this apparent indifference. German soldiers did not find this when they returned to their poverty-stricken homes. Frenchmen faced real shortages and unemployment. But after a short trip by boat and train a British soldier could be in booming London. London was rich compared to Continental cities. If the Roaring Twenties were born here during the Great War, so was the literature of 'disillusionment'. The soldiers left so naive; many returned so bitter.

In Paris, Clemenceau had mounted German guns on the Place de la Concorde to raise a loan for his government. A 'Feed the Guns' campaign for the purchase of war bonds was launched in October 1918 in Trafalgar Square. But, instead of rolling out captured cannon, the authorities reconstructed an entire shell-shattered French village, as if London needed to be reminded of what was going on beyond the Channel. A ruined farmhouse was built on the fountain, the Gordon statue was hidden by a crumbling church tower, next to it were two military lookouts camouflaged as tree trunks, and trenches built of sandbags surrounded the whole village. But Nelson, from his column, stared out to France with indifference.

Six months earlier hundreds of thousands of men were being rushed out from their training camps to face Ludendorff's onslaught at the front. They could be seen tramping down the streets in close formation on their way to the railway stations. Wives and sweethearts joined them, some waving small Union Jacks. But there was no music. Instead of bands, policemen marched at their head. *The Times* published an anxious letter contrasting the scene with the noisy departure of troops for South Africa in 1899. 'Why should we not give the lads a real send-off, instead of smuggling them out of the country?' asked the anonymous correspondent. Nobody answered the question. It made one wonder, if peace with victory ever did come, whether this time round, with London so absorbed with her own domestic problems and the soldiers feeling left outside, there would simply be silence in the place of a 'mafficking'.[20]

3

News of the Kaiser's abdication was reported at five o'clock on a sunny Saturday afternoon, 9 November, just as the crowds in the City were dispersing after the annual Lord Mayor's Show. 'Here and there cheers were raised, but, generally speaking, the citizens remained either unconvinced or remarkably indifferent,' noted the normally fiery and patriotic *Morning Post*. The mood tallied with an observation James M. Black, former US Attorney-General, had made at the Pilgrims' Society a couple of days earlier: 'In New York the bells are ringing, the whistles blowing, and pandemonium reigns' – he was referring to America's premature 'Armistice' celebrations – 'but you remain silent in the hour of your triumph. England sees its most formidable foe at its feet, and never a shout proceeds from its lips. It is perfectly amazing to a stranger.'[21]

Whatever festival spirit existed, it owed more to the City's Show than to the Kaiser's sudden departure. The old pageant had become definitely more military in character over the last four years. Streams of troops from Britain and the Empire had proceeded up the Strand and Fleet Street to the 'sober rejoicing of the people'. A great sausage balloon floated over St Paul's, bands lilted, flying-boats were carried in on lorries, while a uniformed puppet chimpanzee saluted from a howitzer. There was the traditional Ballad Concert at the Royal Albert Hall that evening, where Mr Herbert Cave sang 'The Gates of Sleep' and Miss Carrie Tubb chanted an unintentionally topical ditty called 'Bill'. At the Alhambra the popular singer-comedian George Robey appeared on stage in heavy Teutonic garb, saluted the Kaiser, and then hurled his armour to the floor to roars of laughter and cheering. In the clubs, the eating-houses and the coffee shops there was a lot of talk on the toppled Emperor, 'but nowhere was there any suggestion of "mafficking"'.[22]

The Prime Minister had just returned from Paris, where he had been negotiating the terms of the armistice with the Allies. He appeared at the Lord Mayor's Banquet that night in a Windsor uniform; his hair had turned white in one year, but he still had a glint in his eye. 'As a fairly accustomed speaker,' he told the guests at the Guildhall, their tables aglitter with gold and silver, 'I dislike intensely letting my audience down, but if I have to do so I like to get it over quickly: I have no news for you.' There was lots of laughter. 'Owing to the rapid and temporarily inconvenient advance of the Allied troops and their relentless pursuit the German envoys have not been able to get through' – more laughter – 'and other means have had to be devised for enabling them to cross the lines.'

In the cinemas that Sunday, news was flashed across the silver screens that the British were on the outskirts of Mons, that there was 'revolution' in Germany. A special picture show was organized at the Opera House of 'Men whose Names will Never Die': Marshal Foch ('the man who did it'), Clemenceau ('the Tiger of France'), Admiral Sims ('whose Fleet helped to maintain our dinner-table'), Lloyd George ('He delivered the goods'), Bonar Law ('who found the money') and President Wilson ('champion of liberty'); then the King and the national anthem.

The Stock Exchange opened on Monday, 11 November, in a somewhat dull mood: war loans were firm, consols were down, there was a slight rise in English railways; the greatest gains were made in the Latin American rail issues and Mexican Eagle oil shares. But there were persistent rumours that an armistice had been signed, and when these were confirmed a 'peace demonstration' took place: all dealings ground to a halt. At midday the whole floor sang the 'Doxology', or English *Gloria* – 'Make a joyful noise unto the Lord, all ye lands' – and followed this up with 'God Save the King'. Then, dressed in their top hats and frock coats, the members left in a large group which descended on to the Embankment and up Northumberland Avenue with a band of tin kettles filled with stones and a piercing rattle at their front. It was, said MacDonagh, 'the queerest incident of the day'.[23]

Rumours had led crowds to gather at Downing Street shortly after 10 a.m. They were cheering and singing 'For He's a Jolly Good Fellow' when the door of No. 10 opened and Lloyd George appeared, his white hair fluttering in the wind; he waved his arms upward and said, 'At eleven o'clock this morning the war will be over.' Loud and prolonged cheers followed. 'We have won a great victory and we are entitled to a bit of shouting,' added Lloyd George and promptly disappeared again. A few minutes later the maroons boomed, and at midday Big Ben chimed for the first time in more than four years.[24]

Lloyd George, like Clemenceau in Paris and Wilson in Washington, read out the terms of the Armistice to his parliament. When he had finished, he made an equally brief statement. 'Thus, Mr Speaker, at eleven o'clock this morning came to an end the cruellest and most terrible war that has ever scourged mankind,' he said, his voice apparently shaking with emotion. 'This is no time for words. Our hearts are too full of gratitude which no tongue can give adequate expression to.' He moved that the House immediately adjourn and attend a church service 'to give humble and reverent thanks for the great deliverance of the world from its great peril'.

For London and Paris the war had ended so suddenly. Could the guns really be silenced in a moment? There was more than just singing and joybells in the two Western European capitals – awe, shock, reverence, every emotion spread through their streets and public buildings.

Lords and Commons gathered in St Margaret's to hear the Archbishop of Canterbury read a lesson from Isaiah 61: 'The spirit of the Lord God is upon me; because the Lord hath annointed me to preach good tidings unto the meek.' Then Parliament sang, 'O God, our help in ages past, Our hope for years to come' – not quite the same message as the French 'Marseillaise'. Lloyd George, the Nonconformist, sang as loud as the Anglicans.

Outside, rain was by then pattering down from the grey autumn heavens. Yet it was a day 'unequalled in the memory of man' according to *The Times*. 'In the mile from St Paul's to the Nelson Monument you can see all England,' said the *Morning Post*; 'who thinks of Holborn or the Victoria Embankment?' All London seemed to be crammed into the Strand.

For some later influential literary figures, London's regal mile was definitely not the place to be on 11 November. Siegfried Sassoon had, the previous week, been touring the greats – T. E. Lawrence in London, Thomas Hardy in Dorset, John Masefield and Robert Bridges ('What did you say his name was, Siegfried Digweed?') in Oxfordshire – and was taking refuge in Lady Ottoline Morrell's grand Tudor property at Garsington on the day peace was announced. In a typically contradictory frame of mind, and though he knew the experience would disgust him, he immediately boarded a train for London to get a first-hand glimpse of 'mob patriotism'. He found it, of course, 'a loathsome ending to the loathsome tragedy of the last four years'.[25]

His friend Robert Graves was training cadets in North Wales. News of the death of two companions, Frank Jones-Bateman and Wilfred Owen, sent him walking alone along a mountain dyke, 'cursing and sobbing and thinking of the dead'. Owen's parents in Shrewsbury received the dreaded telegram as the armistice bells were ringing. His brother, Harold, on an African cruiser, dreamed at that moment that he saw Wilfred's ghost.[26]

Vera Brittain was in London, working at Queen Alexandra's Military Hospital in Millbank in an effort to forget her sorrows. She said little of her experience of the Armistice in her memoirs, for, as she explained, 'hardly a memory now remains'. She had passed 'into a permanent state of numb disillusion'. She did, however, remember hearing the maroons crash; going out and struggling through the 'waving, shrieking crowds in Piccadilly and Regent Street; joining a group of elated VADs on a walk to Buckingham Palace; watching, with amazement, all the street lights turn on 'like in a fairy tale'; and detaching herself from the others: 'in that brightly lit, alien world I should have no part . . . The dead were dead and they would never return.'[27]

It was not only the literary and famous who felt their inconsolable losses on 11 November. 'And here – on the night when all are laughing and enjoying themselves,' wrote Phyllis Iliff, in her diary, of the fiancé killed four months earlier, 'left alone I think of what it would have been had you not been taken away and my heart were not slowly breaking. This night when "everyone is happy" as people say. Dear Lord! have mercy it is not in human nature to stand so much.'[28]

Inspired by newsreels which show scenes comparable to those in Paris – open buses and taxis being waylaid, soldiers and citizens clambering up the sides of statues and monuments, and (what scandalized the newspapers) girl clerks standing in the streets *without hats* – some historians have given blood-hot accounts of Armistice Day in London. 'Total strangers copulated in doorways and on the pavements,' claims A. J. P. Taylor; 'they were asserting the triumph of life over death.' 'I believe I should have noticed some of this, especially what was happening on wet London pavements,' commented C. H. Rolph, who had been in the crowd around Mansion House that day.[29]

When the new Lord Mayor, in a violet gown, stepped out on to his balcony the crowd sang the national anthem. Then the chief magistrate shouted out, 'We are a Christian nation, let us sing the Doxology.' So they all bellowed out the 'Old Hundredth'. One heard 'Rule, Britannia', 'Keep the Home Fires Burning', 'Tipperary' and 'Land of Hope and Glory' too. Soldiers and sailors were carried on shoulders. In the East End, all the houses hung out banners. The noisiest quarter was in Pennyfields and Limehouse Causeway, London's Chinatown, where the fireworks crackled until dawn.

In Jermyn Street one man thought the right way to celebrate was to 'roll his trousers above the knees', and several others imitated him. But, as the

Morning Post noted, here and elsewhere in London 'there was much less bold enterprise than on Mafeking Night'.[30]

4

The mother of parliaments, the Imperial Parliament in Westminster, was overdue for an election. The last general election in Britain, in December 1910, had been a tumultuous affair during which the abolition of the House of Lords had only just been avoided. Major constitutional reforms had, however, been achieved through the passage of a Parliament Bill that, among other things, required a general election at least every five years instead of every seven.

The ostensible reason for not holding elections in 1915 was the war. But the real cause was the total collapse of Britain's traditional two-party system – a phenomenon which, like Spanish influenza, had nothing to do with the war, though it would eventually be aggravated by it.

There had been plans for elections in 1915, but both Herbert Asquith, the Liberal Prime Minister, and Andrew Bonar Law, leader of the Conservatives, thought their interests best served by avoiding the plunge and instead, in May of that year they joined hands and formed a national coalition. Their act has been called 'a conspiracy of the front benches against the back', the imposition of a government on Parliament through the force of the chief whips. Yet they could hardly have done this without some tacit support in the House. Significantly, the political feuding which led to Asquith's overthrow in December 1916 ended not with general elections but with another national coalition, this time under Lloyd George. Lloyd George's takeover has been described as 'a long-delayed revolt of the provinces against London's political and cultural dominance' – a rebellion of the backbenchers, and thus the very opposite of what had kept Asquith in power. But the new forces were no more prepared to go to the country than the old ones. For all parliamentarians alike, the electoral waters looked just too dangerous.[31]

An extension of the franchise further encouraged postponement of the elections. The householder and occupancy franchise of 1885 had granted the vote to only three adult men out of five; women were excluded. With the constitutional upheavals of the pre-war years, the rise of the suffragette and, most especially, the war in defence of democracy, the system was looking very weather-worn. The political bargaining for a new system had begun as electoral talk picked up in 1916. But it was only in June 1917 that the Representation of the People Bill – giving the vote to all men over twenty-one and to women, subject to occupancy qualifications, over thirty – went through its first reading in the Commons; it passed the House of Lords in February 1918, and the new voter registers were finally ready the following summer. The argument obviously developed that one could not possibly have an election on the basis of the old system: so one had to wait.[32]

'Can the right honourable gentleman say definitely whether there is to be a General Election before Christmas and name the date of the election?' John Dillon, leader of the Irish Nationalists, asked the Chancellor of Exchequer, Bonar Law, on 7 November 1918.

Dillon, who stood to lose his seat, did not want an 'early' election. Nor did Labour. Nor did many of the Liberals. While there was nothing much these parties could agree on, most of them went along with Dillon's argument that democracy could not work without 'party machinery', and that the only alternative to party machinery was 'secret bureaucracy' – which is what Lloyd George's coalition stood accused of. The two national coalitions – Asquith's in 1915 and Lloyd George's in 1916 – had been established in the face of a national emergency; with peace, it was implied, there should be a return to the good old parliamentary days of party government and party debate. Time was needed for that.[33]

But, unlike in France or even Germany, in Britain there were no parties to fall back on. The eighty Irish Nationalists knew their days were numbered; after the conscription crisis the previous spring, most Irishmen were preparing to vote Sinn Fein, which had already proclaimed a republic and would certainly never sit in Westminster. With only forty seats, Labour was not yet a major force. The Liberals, with 270 seats, were hopelessly divided. One spoke of 'Squiffites', who supported Asquith, and 'Coalition Liberals', who supported Lloyd George, but in fact there were multiple factions that covered virtually the whole political spectrum; some sat on the government side of the House, others on the opposition benches, though the Prime Minister was nominally a Liberal. By-elections had brought the Conservatives, sitting with the government, half a dozen more seats than the Liberals. Having absorbed Liberals opposed to 'Home Rule for Ireland', most Conservatives were calling themselves 'Unionists' and had some reason to feel 'sure that their hour had come'[34] – but after twelve years in the wilderness they were not that sure, and they still relied on the twinkle of Lloyd George as their beacon. Thus there were no parties in the proper sense. They had been fragmented by a constitional upheaval; they held on to power through artifice of coalition; they were disorientated by Britain's evolving position in the world.

It is most significant that on the same day that the Commons was debating the question of elections – and just as Matthias Erzberger was crossing the lines for Compiègne – the Australian Prime Minister, William Morris Hughes, protested at the Australia Club, in the City, that the Dominions had not been consulted on the proposed armistice terms and, in particular, 'President Wilson's Fourteen Points were never agreed to.'[35] This was bad news for Lloyd George's coalition, so dependent on Unionist support, so proud of its 'Imperial War Cabinet' that bound Britain and her Empire together, so keen on the idea of 'imperial preference' – the Unionist dream of a closed system of trade in industrial produce and raw materials, a

British overseas system supported by the Navy. The government responded immediately through its press bureau, claiming that the general peace settlement had been exhaustively discussed by the Imperial War Cabinet. Hughes denied it.

The quarrel exposed the difficulty Britain was having in relating the Empire to Europe; it brought to the fore another version of the strategic polemic that had dogged the whole war between Easterners and Westerners, imperialists and Europeans. There were two loyalties here, two contradictory ways of identifying the national interest. The conflict coloured all of British politics, dividing the parties against themselves and provoking instability in 1918.

The Empire was governed a little like decentralized London and its twenty-eight boroughs: there were self-governing dominions, protectorates, crown colonies, princely states and kingdoms, all in different constitutional relationships with Britain and guided only by one common principle – that they not cost the mother country too much. There was a lot of pomp and ceremony – local equivalents of the Lord Mayor's Show, designed, as Lord Curzon, a member of the War Cabinet, had once put it, to demonstrate 'to ourselves our union, and to the world our strength'.[36] But the Empire had no geographic cohesion and could not even boast of a common language.

In 1918 the Empire was looking more dispersed than ever before. Not only in Ireland was there talk of independence and sovereignty. The old ideals which had shaped Britain's two major parties – a laissez-faire imperialism for the Liberals; a protective imperial tariff ring for the Conservatives – were looking as shaky as the old franchise. But who was going to reform the parties?

The war had raised a question that no one dared answer. It had been won on the Western Front in Europe, most essentially by a British army. What had the Empire contributed? It was the Canadians who had taken Vimy Ridge in a blinding snowstorm in April 1917. General John Monash's Australians broke through the Hindenburg Line at the Saint-Quentin Canal in September 1918. Canadians marched into Mons in November. Ninety-two thousand Chinese labourers lived in huts on the Somme and in Flanders. But looked at coldly, statistically, the evidence indicates that the bulk of the victorious forces came from the British Isles – men of the new battalions attached to the old regiments that had initially made up the tiny professional Army of 1914. By the beginning of November 1918 Britain fielded an army of 101 divisions on the various war fronts. Thirty of these were made up of divisions from the Dominions and India – a substantial figure, it is true. But of the 64 divisions stationed in France, only 10 were imperial. The war was not won in Mesopotamia.[37]

Logically, and purely from the viewpoint of national security, Britain should, at the moment of peace, have committed herself unambiguously to the defence of Western Europe, to the defence of the frontiers of France, whose significance the war had proved. A lot of later problems would have been avoided if a 'Westerner's' policy had been followed: Britain might have adopted the French plan of 15 November – or some variation on it – that proposed early 'preliminaries' and a treaty limited to the essential matters, like frontiers. Wilson delayed because he gave priority to an ideal, not frontiers. Pride, sentiment and Empire-gazing got in Britain's way. But what really paralysed her was the unstable political situation at home.

Lloyd George had been plotting an electoral alliance with the Conservatives since May 1917, so Bonar Law was not the least bit surprised when he received, on 2 November 1918, a long letter from the Prime Minister proposing a joint programme. 'If there is to be an election I think it would be right that it should be a Coalition Election,' wrote Lloyd George. He would ask support for the current coalition 'not only to prosecute the war to its final end and negotiate the peace, but to deal with the problems of reconstruction'. Peace and reconstruction: it was a five-year programme. Lloyd George remained deliberately vague about its content. The Liberal in him was brief: there was 'an imperative need of improving the physical conditions of the citizens of this country through better housing, better wages, and better working conditions'. He was more prolix when it came to his Conservative agenda: he accepted a tariff policy of 'imperial preference'; key industries would be protected, and duties would be raised to prevent foreign 'dumping'; the six northern, Protestant, counties of Ulster would never be coerced into accepting Home Rule for Ireland.[38]

On the day after the Armistice there were party meetings and manoeuvrings. In the Connaught Rooms on Great Queen Street, Bonar Law read the letter to 600 Conservatives, including members from both Houses, candidates and party workers. Then he moved that the 'Unionist Party in present circumstances should stand firm in support of Mr Lloyd George', and went on to elaborate the advantages this would bring to the British Empire. Sir Edward Carson, die-hard Ulsterite and protectionist, seconded the motion, which was passed unanimously and with great applause.[39]

The pledge was made.

In his residence at Downing Street, Lloyd George in the meantime spoke to a smaller meeting of around two hundred Liberals, the majority committed to his coalition, a few still 'sitting on the fence'. It was his usual fluent kind of speech, made without aid of notes and lasting over an hour. 'I am as much a Free Trader as ever,' he assured his audience. He was not so sure the old Liberal policy of Home Rule for Ireland could work 'after the way Ireland had behaved during the war'. He did, however, say that he was very much in favour of the League of Nations, 'without which there could be no reduction of armaments and no guarantee that we could get rid of conscription'. All this was good Liberal policy – none of it mentioned in the letter to Bonar Law. Yet he spoke of his appreciation for the patriotism of the Unionist Party and hoped it would co-operate in the effort to halt 'the spread of a revolutionary spirit in these islands' and, instead, open the way to 'large schemes of social progress'. When he had finished, H. A. L. Fisher, a historian Lloyd George had brought in from Oxford, moved that the Prime Minister be authorized to join forces with Bonar Law in the next election. Lord Leverhulme and Winston Churchill seconded, and this motion too was passed unanimously. It would be a Coalition election.

On Thursday, 14 November, Bonar Law rose from the Treasury bench and, with a casual tone, announced: 'I have something to say to the House.' There was dead silence. The Chancellor went on to say that Parliament was to be dissolved and a general election was to be held. The nomination of candidates would be made in three weeks' time, on 4 December; polling day would take place on 14 December, while the count would be postponed until after Christmas, on the 28th, because of the large number of votes expected from soldiers overseas. The campaign had started.

The Labour Party announced that it was withdrawing to the opposition, but Labour's government ministers, G. N. Barnes, G. H. Roberts and G. J. Wardle, decided to stay on and support the Coalition. They were there when the leaders of the Coalition held a jubilant meeting in Central Hall, Westminster, on 16 November. Lloyd George said it was going to be 'the most important Parliament ever elected in the history of this country', one on which would depend 'the fate and destiny of this country and the Empire, and through the Empire, of the world'. Bonar Law called for an end to party politics. Mr Barnes said, 'Ditto.'[40]

A rather more sober atmosphere could be found in Caxton Hall, where Liberal activists came the following Monday to listen to an address by Herbert Asquith. It was in the same hall that Lloyd George had outlined Britain's war aims the previous January. Asquith, a master of old parliamentary oratory, gave a speech that had the rhythm of a dirge to the long nineteenth century, like a rolling drum in a funeral procession of ancient parties and traditional loyalties, a ceremonal farewell to Victorian liberalism. The call for a general election now, he said, was 'a blunder and a calamity'. 'I tell you frankly for myself that I go into the election as a Liberal' – there were loud cheers – 'without prefix or suffix' – more cheers and hear! hear! – 'without label or hallmark of any sort of description'.

The Liberal Party was split, for ever.[41]

Candidates had great difficulty in getting the electorate interested. The weather was a factor, for campaigns were still run in halls, in the streets from the tops of taxis, trucks and carts, in city parks from a few planks cobbled together, from 'the hustings'. Winter was creeping in, and it was not easy to get the people out; in London there were days on end of showers, fog, mist – 'a very dirty day in the Metropolis . . .', 'the damp wind deposits its moisture, all round . . .', 'Rain had fallen during the night in London, and throughout the day the air was like a wet blanket, with a dismal gloom at times.' Added to that was the threat of flu: one put one's life at risk in attending overcrowded places. London's flu epidemic peaked, like that in Paris, the week before the Armistice, when 2,458 died from the disease – almost double the number in the preceding week and six times more than in the week before that. Thereafter the death toll gradually declined in London, but the epidemic continued 'with unabated virulence' in the provinces; in most of England and Wales the deaths increased; Birmingham, Nottingham and Manchester were in the worst of their crisis during the first fortnight of December, as the election campaign reached its conclusion. The death rate for the whole of England and Wales in the week of the Armistice was 55.5 per 1,000 – a rate compatible with the seventeenth century, though 'The present epidemic has no relation to plague, as some have suggested,' readers of *The Times* were told on 12 November. Gargling was recommended as both a preventative and a cure. 'Nose and throat' drill was introduced into all the schools; Wellington and St Paul's cancelled their football matches.[42]

But the main problem in the elections was the confusion caused by the break-up of the parties. There had never been so many candidates. People didn't know whom to vote for. 'The London electoral campaign is, generally speaking, being carried on in a remarkably dull and unexciting fashion,' noted a correspondent for the *Morning Post* on 29 November. 'Things have been so rushed that there must still be large numbers of electors who are unacquainted with the names of all the candidates from whom they will have to make their choice.' In most of the London constituencies there were at least three candidates running, and in the few cases where there was a straight fight between two it was rarely between Left and Right, between what nineteenth-century commentators would have considered 'progressive' and 'conservative' candidates. Lloyd George would argue that voters faced three clear alternatives: either Ramsay MacDonald's pacifists in the Labour Party, or Mr Asquith and his friends, or the forces for the present government. To make matters easier for the electorate, Lloyd George and Bonar Law had sent a joint letter to the candidates they approved – a letter which Asquith Liberals immediately referred to, like the rationing tickets, as a 'coupon'; and the election came to be known as the 'Coupon Election'.[43]

Down in the constituencies the alternatives were not so clear. In South Kensington and Putney, for example, voters had a choice only between the Coalition Unionist candidate and the National Party, made up of a motley collection of generals, brigadiers and colonels who went to the polls under the slogan 'Make Germany Pay'. Shoreditch, on the other hand, suffered from an 'embarrassment of riches' with a National Party candidate, a Coalition Liberal, an 'Opposition Liberal' (who had been during the war an outspoken pacifist), a Labour candidate and an Independent.

The reform of the franchise had contributed to the variety of choice by bringing into the electorate insecure small tradesmen, who made up a large part of the population in the East End. Contrary to a popular myth, the new franchise did not help Labour, which drew most of its support from members of the trade unions already enfranchised before the war. Since 1900 most of the East End had been Conservative country, on account of the anti-foreign vote. In Stepney–Limehouse by the river's bank, where the fireworks had spat on Armistice Night and where the flags hung out from every window, Captain D. D. Sheehan ran for Labour. He had surrendered his old seat in Mid-Cork to a Sinn Feiner, and was now hoping to build on his support from the dockworkers and resident Irish in the constituency – but these hardly constituted the majority. Charles Rodwell of the Nationalist Party stood a good chance of winning: he was born in Limehouse, and 'as nobody would live in Limehouse if he could live elsewhere it follows that he comes from humble stock'. He had built up a profitable business in footballs, boxing gloves and cricket bats. 'If all the people who have promised to support me would vote I should be sure of getting in,' he declared. His main opponent was Sir William Pearce, one of the Liberals swept into Parliament by the landslide election of 1906. Sir William was in receipt of Lloyd George's 'coupon'; he had been born in the West End, and he ran a factory in Limehouse that supplied the chemicals for shells. So, in Limehouse, it was a race between two businessmen. That is the way it was throughout much of the country – one might have called it the 'Businessmen's Election'. In Limehouse, it did not cause a great deal of excitement: 'there is great apathy among the heterogeneous crowd which forms the population of dock and riverside labourers, employees in a host of small factories, and home-workers in the clothing trade'.[44]

Voters proved to be indifferent to what the politicians called 'reconstruction'; Lloyd George might well call for 'homes fit for heroes to live in', but he had to devise a better slogan than that to get people, first, out of their homes. 'Foreign affairs' did not excite much interest either. The whole purpose of the election had ostensibly been to give Britain a popular mandate in Paris, but few candidates were willing to talk about the peace conference. 'With regard to peace,' said Lloyd George in his opening campaign address, 'I am not going to dwell upon it today, because there are so many other matters which I have something to say about.' Over the next four weeks he never did give a full accounting of the subject. Asquith also maintained a healthy distance from foreign affairs: 'I have not the time,' he remarked in Caxton Hall. Labour was probably the party that dwelt most on the topic – because it couldn't agree on anything else. In its meeting in the Albert Hall on 30 November it passed a very long resolution calling for 'the abolition of conscription, total disarmament, open covenants, and the self-determination of all peoples, including Ireland and the other subject peoples of the British Empire'. It also demanded 'withdrawal of the Allied armies from Russia', protested against 'capitalist intervention in any foreign country', and called for the 'immediate restoration of the workers' International'. 'No punitive indemnities is what Trotsky said!' exclaimed Mrs Philip Snowden in a fiery speech. 'Leave peace to the capitalists and you will have no peace!' confirmed Ramsay MacDonald. With a waving of red flags and a singing of 'The Internationale' the resolution was carried. Labour Party foreign policy was almost identical to that followed by the socialists in Paris.[45]

In the second week of the campaign Britain's prisoners of war began returning home. The steamships arrived in Hull, Dover and Southampton, packed with men. For the prisoners who had come in through Germany, Holland, Denmark and Norway a special reception camp was set up in Ripon, North Yorkshire; most of the remainder passed through another vast camp outside Dover. From the camps, men would take the trains home: London's railway stations were once more crowded with khaki. Cannon Street station in the City was the main destination of the Dover trains; every returning soldier wore a small Union Jack in his cap; the platforms were decorated, and military bands would strike up as the trains steamed in; the authorities of the YMCA were there to provide assistance. On 27 November around four hundred 'Old Contemptibles', who had been captured during the retreat from Mons in August 1914, arrived at Waterloo station; there were sixty-four cot-cases among them.[46]

The prisoners of war brought tales of a revolution in Germany. They had seen German officers shot, and others 'stabbed in the back' – those officers, you know, 'were brutal to the last'. The men had been employed under shell fire. The food was appalling. 'Our one day's ration consisted of pieces of bread and some watery soup,' said a trooper of the Royal North Lancashires, and then pulled out a hard black-looking object from his haversack: 'This is German bread.' When the men were released – often by revolutionary guards – they were just told to find their own way home.

The stories were widely reported in the press, and there was a wave of charity appeals made to help 'our prisoners'. Lord Curzon, President of the Council and a member of the War Cabinet, was obliged to make a statement in the House of Lords. 'The question of dealing with the Germans who had been responsible for these crimes and atrocities was engaging the close attention of His Majesty's Government,' he announced on 21 November.[47]

It did not take long, of course, for the subject to be raised on the hustings. George Barnes was having the fight of his life in the Gorbals, the poorest division of Glasgow, against William Gallacher of the British Socialist Party. 'Well,' declared Barnes, 'I'm for hanging the Kaiser.' The phrase resounded with a vibrance in the Gorbals.[48]

Looking back ten years later, Churchill wrote that the election of 1918 'woefully cheapened Britain'. He argued that political leaders were caught up in the passions of their constituencies – passions first sparked among a people that 'had suffered too much', and then fanned 'by the popular press into fury'.[49] Churchill, whose life, like Picasso's, went through many phases, was in the late 1920s entering his undemocratic phase. The British people had suffered less than most in Europe, and reports of the time suggest that the main problem candidates were facing in the electorate was indifference, not passion. As for the press, it was responding to a major event, the return of the prisoners – a tiny fragment of the epic movement afoot on the Continent, it is true, but one (the arrival, in three weeks, of the equivalent of a fairly sizeable town) that must count as a major chapter in the history of British immigration, the immigration of her own people. In Germany and on their journey back through the lines, the prisoners had seen and experienced horrors which were quite unknown in the islands. The press, forever accused of exaggeration, was in fact probably not reporting enough: war-torn Europe remained a mysterious place.

Moreover, most of the candidates responded with restraint, considering the scale of the event. Asquith's comments were limited to the need to maintain the alliance. Most Labour leaders had by now adopted a pacifist line. A few exclamations arose from the ranks of the Nationalist Party, but it hardly commanded a majority. From the start, that majority lay with the Coalition, and Coalition candidates trod with caution where foreign affairs were concerned. 'Justice must be stern,' said Churchill in Newcastle. 'It would not be in the interests of the future of the world if the guilty nation and those who have instigated its criminal actions are to escape from the consequences of their crimes unpunished and unchallenged.' But he did not call to hang the Kaiser – something that was far from his private thoughts. 'It must be a just Peace, a sternly just Peace, a relentlessly just Peace,' repeated Lloyd George. 'Justice must not be merely vindicated in the victory; it must be vindicated in the settlement as well.' No mention here of a hanging. In public it was stated that the possibility of the trial of the Kaiser had been referred to the Attorney-General; in private, the matter was discussed in Downing Street when Clemenceau visited London on 2 December. As the campaign drew to a close, Coalition leaders were speaking of the whole war as a crime. 'The men responsible for this outrage on the human race must not be let off because their heads were crowned when they perpetrated the deed,' wrote the Prime Minister in a statement published by all the press on 5 December. There was a hint of the old constitutional reformer in this.[50]

Lloyd George called for the expulsion of enemy aliens ('they spied and they plotted, they assisted Germany in the forging of plans for the destruction of the country which had offered them hospitality'): that theme had always won votes in popular quarters. He promised that Britain had no intention of maintaining that foreign thing, a conscript army. Indeed, on the eve of the election he moved for the abolition of conscript armies everywhere: 'these great military machines are responsible for the agony the world has passed through and it would be a poor ending to any Peace

Conference that allowed them to continue'. But, as he had said in Bristol two days earlier, 'We must have our Navy.' Lloyd George was a reformer and a British traditionalist.[51]

In the British tradition there was the Navy – and money. Who was going to pay for the criminal war? The answer that it would be the German lemon, 'squeezed until the pips squeak', was derived from a speech made by the First Lord of the Admiralty, Sir Eric Geddes (a businessman), at a rally at the Drill Hall in Cambridge on 9 December. Geddes was prepared to 'strip Germany as she has stripped Belgium'. But even Geddes recognized that too much squeezing could hurt British industries.[52]

In Cambridge such reservations were wise, for there were men at the University who had a better understanding of the new science of economics than Sir Eric. One of them was now down in London, preparing a long memorandum for the Treasury on the 'Indemnity Payable by the Enemy Powers for Reparation and Other Claims'. His ideas were already making a stir in government circles. Lloyd George referred to them in his speech at Newcastle on 29 November, and again at Bristol on 11 December. For a 'sternly just Peace, a relentlessly just Peace', Germany would have to pay an indemnity – in Newcastle he said 'for the costs of the war'.

'We have consulted our financial advisers,' he reported in Bristol, quickly adding for the sake of a Liberal audience that did not like bankers, 'not international financiers – these are not our financial advisers – I mean the financial advisers you get in every Government Department'. The advisers had expressed doubts about Germany's ability to pay for the full 'costs of the war', and to the end of the campaign Lloyd George said that Germany should pay – yes, she should pay to 'the last penny' – but he always added 'up to the utmost limit of her capacity'. Lloyd George also mentioned the existence of a committee – 'a strong Committee', a 'British Imperial Committee' – that 'you will be glad to hear' took 'a more favourable view of the capacity of Germany than the officials of the Government Departments'. What, of course, he did not note was that he had set up this 'Imperial Committee' to make war on the adviser at the Treasury.

Some fantastic estimates of what Germany would pay Britain were quoted in the last week of the election. What nobody seemed to notice at the time was that a certain confusion about indemnities was developing. What were these figures supposed to represent: 'costs', 'reparations' or 'indemnities'? And what was the source of these magic numbers?[53]

On Saturday, 14 December, Britain went to the polls. The electors had never had so many candidates to choose from. Candidates had never faced so many electors. Women voted for the first time. Ireland voted in the United Kingdom for the last time. The sun shone in northern England. It poured with rain in London.

5

'I have been put in principal charge of financial matters for the Peace Conference,' John Maynard Keynes, adviser at the Treasury, wrote to his mother on 21 November. He was only thirty-five. To his mother he was 'John'; to his friends he was 'Maynard'. He was was the subject of much contention: Lloyd George called him 'mercurial and impulsive', and the Americans in London spoke of him as 'rude, dogmatic and disobliging'.[54] Since 1915, when he had been promoted to the Treasury's No. 1 Division, he had played a leading role in in the country's war finance: he reported directly to the Chancellor; he spent weekends with the Asquiths; he sat for the Treasury in key interdepartmental discussions; he bargained with the Americans; and when the Inter-Ally Council for War Purchases and Finance was eventually set up under American chairmanship in December 1917 it was Keynes who travelled to Paris to represent Britain. Keynes chaired Britain's Wheat Committee (until it was transformed, in early 1918, into the Wheat Export Company), and it was he who devised the methods of purchasing and financing cereals for the Allies. Keynes was the central figure in the establishment of the whole complicated system of inter-Allied war credits – from the initial decision in February 1915 to set up loans to France and Russia, to the transfer of Allied gold to the Bank of England, the centralized buying system, the financing through New York, the bargaining with the Americans, and ultimately the debts. Keynes was a member of the 'Tuesday Club' which, since the spring of 1917, had met every week at the Café Royal to discuss post-war finance. He had a staff of seventeen at the Treasury to help him in his manifold tasks. He produced elegant memoranda at a legendary speed; he would read dozens of official reports on a Sunday afternoon and was known as the man 'who can quote figures at you'. He was Britain's obvious spokesman for financial matters at the peace conference. Yet his position was contested.

Keynes was an elitist, but no aristocrat. Like Herbert Hoover, he came from a family of Low Church Protestants: his father's side had been Baptist since the early eighteenth century, while his mother's family included two noted Congregational ministers, one of whom, John Brown of Bedford (Keynes's grandfather), had published a popular biography of John Bunyan, the town's most famous churchman. There was also a tradition of trade in the family. Keynes's grandfather John Keynes had made his fortune from the flower nursery he ran in Salisbury; Mr Keynes, reported the *Gardener's Magazine* in 1878, knew how to 'squeeze rent out of glass'.[55]

Low Church and trade were a common background for the new 'economic men' of 1918. But there the parallel with Hoover ends. Trade did not carry the same prestige in Britain as it did on the other side of the Atlantic; the first concern of many families which had got into it was, then, how to get out of it again. The best route available was through academic success.

In this the Keyneses were stars. Keynes's father, John Neville, laid the way by taking a degree at University College, London, in logic and moral philosophy – an ideal subject for Nonconformists in an age of doubt. He headed for Cambridge, where he studied mathematics and moral science, won a fellowship, married one of his undergraduates – the Baptist Miss Florence Ada Brown – and eventually settled down at 6 Harvey Road as a well-paid university administrator. His three children – Maynard, Geoffrey and Margaret – were academic prodigies. Maynard himself was a College Scholar and was elected to 'College Pop', the prestigious debating society, at Eton; he was a scholar, then fellow, at King's College, Cambridge, where he was elected to the selective and secret society of the Apostles when still only a freshman. 'We're really a wonderful family,' he wrote to his father on learning of Geoffrey's first prize in a scholarship examination at St Bartholomew's Hospital, thus opening up his career as a surgeon. 'If only the examination system lasts, another two or three hundred years, we shall end, I'm sure, by being the Royal Family.'[56]

The Keyneses had put base trade behind them. At the same time, their most famous son elevated the study of the creation of wealth to a noble university science; as a lecturer at King's College, Maynard Keynes expanded the programme of the Cambridge Economics Tripos, which had been established only in 1903, while as editor of the *Economic Journal* he gave the subject intellectual discipline. Keynes showed just how far he had moved on from Grandfather John's nursery business when he assessed the great human qualities of the artist and the scientist in a paper he read to the Apostles in 1909. 'Putting moneymaking and capacity aside, is there any brother who would not rather be a scientist than a business man, and an artist than a scientist?' he asked rhetorically. The scientist, he argued, was lower than the artist because he spent most of his life 'busied with preparations'; but, with occasional beauty in his arguments, he was way ahead of the businessman, whose life was 'partly one of irksome toil and partly one of bridge'. Businessmen, in Keynes's view, held roughly the same low rank as politicians, of whom he later said, 'They're *awful* ... Their stupidity is inhuman.'[57]

Keynes had become a part of what his most recent biographer calls 'Cambridge civilization'. It was very small. Most undergraduates at the university would have been unaware of it. The Kantian joke among Apostles was that their secret society was 'real' while the rest of the world was 'phenomenal'; non-Apostles were referred to as 'phenomena'.

Apostolic Cambridge did, however, extend as far as Gordon Square and the neighbouring Gower Street in London, where its denizens, in a bed-hopping frenzy ('The society of buggers has many advantages – if you are a woman,' declared Virginia Woolf) and in the patronage of the most exquisite new arts, declared a war on Victorians and came to be known to the phenomenal world as the Bloomsbury Group.

Apostles and Bloomsberries had their own particular way of looking at Europe. In the opening chapter of his popular post-war book *The Economic Consequences of the Peace*, Keynes describes 'Europe before the War' – where 'the inhabitant of London could order by telephone, sipping his morning tea in bed, the various products of the whole earth', where 'he could secure forthwith, if he wished it, cheap and comfortable means of transit to any country or climate without passport or other formality, could despatch his servant to the neighbouring office of a bank for such supply of the precious metals as might seem convenient, and could then proceed abroad to foreign quarters'.[58] Keynes had been enchanted by many of the places he had visited before the war. 'It must be the loveliest spot in Europe,' he wrote from Aragon. 'It will be to this valley that I shall retire, to live amongst trout and strawberries and Spanish shepherd boys.' In April 1911 he crossed the seas to Morocco: 'The Arabs are wonderful – very beautiful and the first race of buggers I've seen.'[59] This was 'Cambridge civilization' on the move.

There was, in all of it, much that calls to mind the equally small-scale aristocratic eighteenth-century vision of civilization – which had peaked at the Congress of Vienna in 1815: its material pleasures, its preciousness, its scorn for the populace, its worldly scepticism, its radical tastes in the arts. It was Beethoven in Vienna, Russian ballet in Bloomsbury. Bloomsberries and Apostles regarded themselves as the avant-garde, but they maintained at the same time a strong *arrière-garde* that did not want to let go of the world which had passed. They might have declared confidently in public that they stood at the brink of a new civilization, but in private they kept one fearful step back from the edge; and they never looked over it.

In the years before the war, Keynes had developed a philosophy that spurned forecast and crystal-ball gazing. Like his father before him – and like Adam Smith in the eighteenth century – the subject which had prompted his most creative thought was moral philosophy. It was an important field of investigation in the land where they sang 'O God, our help in ages past' and where they were losing hope in his divine presence for the years to come: the search had begun for an alternative to religion as a base for morals. The most important book in Keynes's life, G. E. Moore's *Principia Ethica* (1903), had opened the way to an introspective approach, shifting attention away from public matters to private relations by arguing that 'actions which do good' were more important than 'actions which are good'. There was less concern here with social and political affairs than with friendship and intimacy, but Moore had concluded by stressing the need for 'general rules of conduct', which corresponded to a Christian ethic. Keynes accepted the introspection, but rejected the 'general rules'. He did this in his thesis, an investigation into the meaning of probability. Keynes began with Moore's premise that rational ethical judgement could be based only on reasonable probability: we can never be sure of the ultimate outcome of our actions, but we can calculate their immediate probabilities. Upon this he built a philosophy of expediency, a 'doctrine of means', a counter to grand abstract systems. Ironically, he had arrived at a position close to the conservatism of another eighteenth-century thinker, Edmund Burke, whose writings Woodrow Wilson so admired.

The thesis had a profound effect on the development of his economic theories. It might be argued that his rejection of 'general rules' ultimately led to his rejection of the gold standard and other absolute values of the Victorian system; his famous 'multiplier effect' was built on the mathematics of probabilities. But in 1918 the Keynesian revolution had not yet happened – not even to Keynes. His administration of finance at the Treasury was governed by caution. His theory of probability and his refusal to forecast influenced his attitude to the war: you could argue that there had been wars in the past that had ultimately proved to be of general benefit to mankind, but there was no way of knowing where you were going as you launched into war in the present. Our causal knowledge, and hence our power of prediction, would always be inadequate.

Keynes's twice-born elitism, his intellectual discipline, his private concerns and extravagances, his respect for the Establishment, Eton and the old universities, along with his fears for an unknown future, all affected his attitude at the Treasury during the war years. In 1921 he translated his attitude into words when he delivered a lecture on 'The State and Finance' to the Society of Civil Servants.[60] It reads like Asquith's farewell to Victorian Liberalism, like Churchill's depiction of a pre-1914 'world very brilliant'. It is a song to a quality of pre-war government finance that Keynes ascribed to 'Treasury control', the 'Treasury which can say No'. The Treasury was always fighting against the odds, because there was nearly always a good case for expenditure. The Treasury was, however the only government department which was responsible for providing a balance between the other spending departments, for establishing the 'truth', for judging relative urgencies. All the other departments, in their struggle for money, played a kind of blind man's buff – they tampered with the truth; they closed their eyes to the general view. 'Treasury control', said Keynes, was unique to Britain: in the United States the Treasury had little authority 'beyond looking after the collection of taxes'; in France too it was 'more or less a tax-collecting institution'; the German Reich – he astutely pointed out – was made up of virtually independent departments, which fought with each other as much as they did with the enemy. But control made the Treasury unpopular. The Treasury's weapon was its 'prestige', founded on an array of rituals. For Keynes, the Treasury embodied 'the age of efficiency and incorruptibility in the civil service which was introduced in the Gladstonian epoch'. 'I think', said Keynes, 'Treasury control might be compared to conventional morality'; it possessed 'certain aesthetic elements', and also attributes of institutions 'like a college or City company, or the Church of England'. It defended itself, like the eighteenth-century sceptics, as 'a bulwark against too much enthusiasm'. The Treasury stood for continuity. 'My Lords' had a long life and could reasonably hope to outlast the passing enthusiasms of individual ministers and governments. The great chair in the Board's room, in which the Chancellor did not sit, in which nobody sat, was the visible symbol of 'My Lords', eternally present – and eternally in control.

But eternity had ended with the war. 'The old system was swept away.' The 'experimentalists' of a new war regime moved in. The importance of husbanding resources was thrown to the winds. Everything was improvised. There were 'innumerable enthusiasts who believed they could win the war if only they could spend unlimited sums of money'. 'Truth' was lost. The general vision became blurred. Department expenditures were let loose. Among the worst of the 'enthusiasts', the 'man who did the foul deed', was the Prime Minister, David Lloyd George; he 'had no aesthetic sense for the formalisms [of the pre-war Treasury], and no feelings for its institutional aspects'.

This was the true voice of John Maynard Keynes, who is depicted in so many textbooks as a revolutionary. Like the Bloomsberries, he was an elitist and a defender of the old order. Few of them were pacifists, and Keynes certainly was not. The war threatened their world. They were conscientious objectors not out of opposition to war per se, but because conscription and large Continental armies did not fit the old Liberal way, the British way, of making war. Let the Europeans fight; let Britain maintain control. This was the ethic of the Treasury.

Though he had actually been exempted from the Army because of the national importance of his work, in February 1916 Keynes insisted on registering with the Holborn Local Tribunal his 'conscientious objection to surrendering my liberty of judgment on so vital a question as undertaking military service'. 'I work for a government I despise for ends I think criminal,' he wrote to his lover, the painter Duncan Grant, in December 1917. Even more significant was what he wrote on 11 March 1918 to an acquaintance at Cambridge, the famous socialist activist Beatrice Webb: 'It is hard to over-emphasize the importance of *prestige* attaching to the Treasury.' Conscientious objection to Lloyd George's war of conscripts and defending the prestige of the Treasury were part and parcel of the same thing.[61]

It is striking how much two major features of Europe's Great War are evident in Keynes's own war experience. On the fighting front, globalization had been accompanied by a localization; Keynes's defence of the Treasury, worldwide in its vision, was also very parochial. The fundamental problem of trench warfare had been that the military were caught in a technological limbo; so too was Keynes's economics – it lay somewhere between the noble age of cavalry and the mass age of the tank.

6

In 1910 Sir Norman Angell, a newspaper manager and journalist, published a book called *The Great Illusion*, which argued that wars in the modern world could not be sustained, because the resulting fiscal burden would swiftly lead to the ruin of international banking and finance. Wars would prove counter-productive even to the victor: Angell attempted to demonstrate that the indemnity that Prussia imposed on France in 1871 actually had an evil effect on German finances. The book was read by the whole Liberal Establishment, including Keynes. It was one of the factors behind the hesitations of Asquith's government in August 1914. 'War would be accompanied or followed by a complete collapse of European credit and industry,' the Foreign Secretary, Sir Edward Grey, warned the Austrian ambassador in the last days of July. A Continental war would involve such vast sums of money that industry would be laid to waste and the power of capital destroyed.[62]

The war demonstrated that it was Angell and the Liberals who were living in 'the great illusion': industry continued to produce and the capital markets went on functioning. There was no serious financial constraint on war – it eventually came to an end because Germany was defeated militarily, not financially. Pre-war economists had underestimated the degree of adaptability in the world's money supplies. An enormous quantity of money was released for use by the belligerents through the suspension of gold convertibility, moratoriums on public debt, new forms of paper currency, and the more rapid circulation of existing funds. Government bond markets, already well developed before the war, opened up another avenue for credit. The supply of money might not have been inexhaustible, but with European government expenditures averaging, before the war, only 5 per cent of national incomes (as opposed to about 50 per cent today) it began to look as if it could never run dry. With the war, the money supply ceased to have any relationship to the gold and silver ingots held in the vaults of the central banks.

No economist at the time could explain this. Keynes himself was convinced that dire financial constraint would force an end to the fighting. There was much wishful thinking in this. At Christmas 1917 he was feeling 'buoyantly bolshevik' when he wrote to a friend to rejoice that 'our rulers are as incompetent as they are mad and wicked' – they never listened to his warnings. In August 1914 he had forecast that the clearing banks, the accepting houses and the discount houses would crumble, and he was convinced the powers would be forced to make peace within a year. In September 1915 he predicted financial catastrophe for Britain by the following April. In February 1917 he claimed Britain would be able to carry on the war for only four more weeks. In every case he was wrong.[63]

Ironically, Keynes was one of the agents responsible for this. It was

Keynes and his colleagues at the Treasury who established the complicated chain of loans and credit that would set the expansion of the world's money supply in motion. The pattern was laid down at a conference in Calais early in 1915, when it was agreed to centralize Allied credit in London, site of the largest money market in the world. The ethic of 'Treasury control' probably explains why London granted a single New York banker, J. P. Morgan, a monopoly over British import finance – creating immense profits for the bank but, at the same time, making it depend on Britain and her Allies not defaulting. There was even an element of the old 'British way of war' in the operation: Britain would pay her Allies to fight the war on the Continent. Only, unlike during the Napoleonic wars, Britain was providing loans, not subsidies; she soon found herself forced to build up her own Continental army; and almost the entire line of credit was now being channelled through a New York banker. This was not initially viewed as an abandonment of Britain's sovereign power: even the pessimistic Keynes continued, right up to the end of the war, to refer to Britain and the United States as the 'joint paymasters' of the alliance.

Keynes was not wrong here. Britain was in fact a net creditor at the end of the war. Britain could have paid for her own war expenses out of her own pocket: the difficulties she eventually faced lay in the credit she had extended to her Allies.

Keynes wanted to turn the burden of the Allied loans over to the rich United States after she had entered the war; the United States baulked at this, preferring British obligations to those of the other Allies. Three important issues grew out of the resulting deadlock: a creeping fear that the United States was attempting to impose her will on Britain and her Allies; the quite vicious Anglo-American discord over food distribution in Europe; and a growing British demand for a German indemnity.

In October 1916 Keynes was already warning that 'in a few months' time the American executive and the American public will be in a position to dictate to this country on matters that affect us more nearly than them'. The following September he actually travelled to America in the company of the diplomat Lord Reading, with the aim of setting up machinery for the transfer of funds from the large proceeds of the American Liberty Loan to Allied claimants. The Americans were not impressed with Keynes, and he sailed home empty-handed. Nor were the Americans ever to show much interest in helping support Allied loans: even at the height of the Ludendorff offensives in spring 1918 the American Treasury insisted on limiting aid to current British expenditures. Keynes's frustration came out in a telegram he drafted for Bonar Law, by this time Chancellor of the Exchequer: 'The US Treasury has been in my opinion small-minded and unreasonable,' it read. 'It almost looks as if they took a satisfaction in reducing us to a position of complete financial helplessness and dependence.'[64]

Keynes was not wrong here either: his suspicions were well founded.

Hoover, for whom Britain represented almost as much an enemy as Germany, was the least amenable member of the American government, but the others were not much friendlier. In July 1917 Woodrow Wilson was boasting that England would soon be 'finally in our hands'. As a means of forcing the Old World to comply with its policy for peace, The Inquiry recommended the employment of America's 'economic weapon'; it was applied, with increasing pressure, into the year 1918.[65]

Keynes and the British Treasury responded by buying up futures in the world's wheat market in an effort to relieve British financing of France and Italy. Observations made in Argentina in December 1917 had led to speculation – which proved to be correct – that the world harvest in 1918 would be very good. The idea was that Britain, through her merchant navy, would supply herself with US wheat paid for in dollars while she would carry wheat from other parts of the world, paid for in sterling, to Italy and France and then ask for a dollar reimbursement from the United States that would be paid into her overdrawn American accounts. It was all done above board. 'Our policy is to lay all our cards on the table and to furnish every scrap of information,' Keynes wrote on 30 January 1918 to the Treasury's representative in the United States, Sir Basil Blackett. The British plan was laid out before the Inter-Ally Council on War Purchases and Finance, chaired by an American, Oscar T. Crosby, who had worked with Hoover on Belgian relief. Bonar Law (whose text was probably written by Keynes) cabled Lord Reading, now ambassador in Washington, on 25 March, 'British and American departments could get together on the infinitely complicated and difficult business of pooling resources without disturbance from the confused currents of self-interest which now darken counsel.'[66]

The scheme was all too clever by half for the Americans. Hoover claimed that 'pooling' was an underhand attempt by Europeans to dominate American markets and destroy the livelihood of hardworking American farmers by flooding the world with the produce of the 'Southern Hemisphere'. William McAdoo of the American Treasury wrote that 'Great Britain is computing claims against the Allies on a basis that we cannot accept.' His problem was, in fact, countering charges from his foes in Congress that he was being outmanoeuvred by the British Treasury. The neo-mercantilist philosophy in Washington was that if you get American loans you buy American products, and Hoover intended to relieve Europe with American-grown wheat. As Ludendorff's divisions poured into France, America showed no willingness at all to pick up the British burden of financing the Allies.[67]

As the tide of the war turned in the Allies' favour, Britain began to place some hope, though not a welcome one in governing circles, in a German indemnity at the end of the war. Germany had imposed a heavy indemnity on Russia by terms of the Treaty of Brest-Litovsk and the supplementary treaties of August 1918; one of her negotiating ploys in September, as the

Reich's armies retreated, was to offer cancellation of Western Allied indemnities *owed to* Germany. Throughout the war, French and British demands for war indemnities had, on the other hand, been moderate; it was widely assumed that they would be limited to reparation for physical damage done, on the field, by Germany's invading armies.[68]

Britain's initial reluctance to push for a heavy indemnity could be traced back to Norman Angell's argument in 1910 that war indemnities actually did harm to the victor because the defeated power, in order to pay, would have to diminish its imports and increase exports – not something the victor would want to encourage. It was a theme Liberal Free Traders repeated throughout the war. Lloyd George himself brought up the issue in his campaign speech at Newcastle on 29 November. 'Germany must pay,' he said. 'The only restriction is that she must not pay in such a way as will inflict more damage to the country that receives than the country that pays . . . She must pay as far as she can, but we are not going to allow her to pay in such a way as to wreck our industries.'[69]

But a second difficulty with indemnity tended to push Britain in the opposite direction. These offshore islands had not been invaded and therefore they had no claim to reparations limited to physical damage inflicted on territories overrun by the enemy. Indeed, the issue in Britain was 'indemnity' rather than 'reparation' – which was of little national interest. The distinction meant even more to Britain's scattered Empire, virtually untouched by enemy action. The loudest cries for an 'indemnity' to cover the 'costs of the war' came from Britain's Dominions. The former Prime Minister of Newfoundland, Lord Morris, was one of the first to raise the issue of 'war costs' in a speech he made in October amid the mock French 'ruins' in Trafalgar Square. Canada swiftly followed suit.

But the loudest voice of them all was that of the Australian Prime Minister, William Morris Hughes. When he complained in London on 7 November that the Empire had not been consulted on the proposed terms of the armistice, what he was objecting to was the use of Wilson's Fourteen Points as a basis of negotiation with Germany – and particularly Point III on the freedom of trade. For several months Hughes had been making the case for a post-war settlement founded on economic discrimination against the 'German commercial octopus'. Hughes belonged to the school of Joseph Chamberlain: he was an outspoken advocate of protection. In Hughes's mind, 'imperial preference' and indemnity for the 'costs of war' came together. 'The right of any nation to make whatever tariff it thinks fit must not be impaired,' he said. 'And is Germany to escape bearing at least some share of these frightful burdens?'[70]

It was Hughes's influence that led the director of the *Revue politique et parlementaire*, Fernand Faure, to publish on the eve of the Armistice, an argument for a 'total indemnity', setting off a chain of financial demands in the French press. It was Hughes's intervention on 7 November that made 'indemnity' such an important issue in Britain's election. Lloyd George could not help but encourage it. He had just agreed with Bonar Law to a Coalition programme that included 'imperial preference', 'protection of key industries' and 'empire development'; 'indemnity', Hughes had demonstrated, was the foreign counterpart of protection, and no Conservative was going to let the Prime Minister wash his hands of it.

Lloyd George, who despite his Coalition programme professed to be a Liberal Free Trader, resorted to the old political manoeuvre of offering his critic the responsibility of office – wasn't that what he was asking for? Just as the electoral campaign was getting under way, the Prime Minister set up a 'Committee of Indemnity' and named Hughes as its chairman. It is known in history as the Hughes Committee.[71]

But there was someone in the Treasury who was already working on the problem of indemnity. When Keynes wrote to tell his mother that he had been 'put in principal charge of financial matters for the Peace Conference' he meant war indemnities. He had just had brief 'Notes on an Indemnity' flown out to Versailles for consideration by the Supreme War Council during their pre-armistice negotiations. Now he was working full-time on a 'Memorandum by the Treasury on the Indemnity Payable by the Enemy Powers for Reparation and Other Claims'. It would be presented, along with a report from the Hughes Committee, to the Imperial War Cabinet on Christmas Eve. As L. S. Amery, Parliamentary Secretary to the Colonies, remarked on Boxing Day, the two reports 'seem, both of them, to exaggerate the position in two opposite directions'. The dilemma was perfectly British.[72]

The main concern of the Hughes Committee was to find a solution to imperial budgetary problems; it was not overly concerned with Germany's capacity to pay. Its deliberations were dominated by Lord Cunliffe, who as governor of the Bank of England had been in a vicious fight with the Treasury the previous year over the management of Britain's gold reserves; Bonar Law had forced Cunliffe to resign. Cunliffe did not have much sympathy for Treasury officials, yet he made selective use of a report Keynes had drafted back in 1916 on 'The Effect of an Indemnity', emphasizing its proposal that indemnity did not do harm to the receiving power and could be paid in instalments over a number of years.[73] Keynes was even invited to attend three of the Committee's sessions, though the minutes indicate that he remained largely silent. The Committee also employed data supplied by the Board of Trade.[74] But the Board's figures were vague. The Committee's final report concluded that Germany should be charged the full Allied costs of the war, estimated to be £24 billion, and recommended that these be paid in annual instalments of £1.2 billion. These figures were said to have been revealed to Lord Cunliffe during a church service.[75]

Keynes, both in his 'Notes' and the longer 'Memorandum',[76] paid much closer attention to Germany's capacity to pay. He, too, was using figures supplied by the Board of Trade, as well as a report recently released by the American Federal Reserve. According to Lloyd George, Bonar Law (Cunliffe's foe) had some influence in the estimation of Germany's capacity, though he thought Keynes's final figures far too low. Keynes's main source was documents at the Treasury, many of which predated the war. In response, for example, to a proposal made by a correspondent to *The Times* that Germany be forced to surrender all her mines and mineral deposits, Keynes pointed out that all the mines in Germany, of every kind, had a market value of £300 million – a mere fragment of what war costs represented. This figure was calculated from data on Germany's pre-war national output.

Whole passages from the 'Memorandum' were later transcribed into his book *The Economic Consequences of the Peace* – proving that many of his ideas were already formed before the peace conference even opened (and before he met any German officials, whom, it has been argued, exerted great influence on him). The final pages of the 'Memorandum' were entitled, significantly, 'The Economic Consequences of an Indemnity'.

Keynes took issue with Angell's argument that the French indemnity to Germany in 1871 had done Germany more harm than good. 'This view is contrary to common sense,' he said. An indemnity began to do damage to the staple industries of the receiving country only at the point where it became necessary to stimulate the paying country's exports through the furnishing of raw materials and markets. However, rather than defining this point objectively and mathematically in terms of Germany's balance of trade, Keynes chose the much vaguer distinction between an amount available for indemnity 'without crushing Germany's productive power' and a sum that would crush 'her future economic life' – it was a tacit admission that his figures were not wholly reliable. In his preliminary 'Notes' of 31 October he had estimated that £1 billion 'could be obtained without crushing Germany, half of it immediately . . . and half of it gradually'. In his 'Memorandum', as presented to the Imperial Cabinet on 24 December, this figure had magically risen to a sum 'not exceeding £3,000 million'. Keynes's recommendation at this point was £2,000 million, half of it paid in annual instalments.

It was a figure well below Hughes's £24 billion, and below even the United Kingdom's war costs, estimated at £8.85 billion. Keynes stated that 'the general costs of war . . . could not be met even in part'. Priority had to be given to 'the probable reparation claim' for damage inflicted by the enemy; Keynes argued that Germany's capacity to pay would cover between 50 and 75 per cent of that claim.

The obvious question arising from such a conclusion was: Would Britain be able to claim anything if Germany's payment was to be confined to 'reparations'? Keynes answered yes: 'It might be fairly urged that between the various claims of the different Allies priority should be given to compensation for *illegal acts*, of which the chief would be the *invasion of Belgium* and *unrestricted submarine warfare'* (my emphasis). Arguing that assets in ceded territory 'would probably be more than ample to cover damage done in Belgium', Keynes made it appear that the lion's share of reparations would actually go to Britain in payment for ships sunk.

There was as much an element of fantasy in Keynes's 'Notes' and 'Memorandum' as there was in Hughes's report. What did they have to do with the war that had just ended on the French front? The discipline of the economic argument showed the small presence of 'Cambridge civilization'; the underlying concern for funds that would fill the overdrawn war accounts suggest a continued defence of 'Treasury control'. Between Hughes and Keynes one finds evidence of the great divide in British opinion: 'imperial preference' and 'free trade'. It was an island's argument. Amery was perfectly right to complain in his Boxing Day letter that the two reports were going in opposite directions – while, he added, they 'leave out of account what seems to me almost the most important aspect': how the German sum 'is to be distributed as between ourselves and our Allies'.[77] Keynes gave a hint, but no more. What was certainly so far absent, from these reports and from the entire electoral debate, was anything approaching the international realities of the peace.

7

Legal peace had been established rapidly at the end of the Napoleonic wars. In 1814 the Allies had signed a treaty with France within less than two months of Napoleon's abdication; the Peace Congress at Vienna – a rather more drawn-out affair which dealt with the general problems of the European settlement and at which the French had their representatives – had followed four months later. After Napoleon's Hundred Days in 1815 it took the Allies four months to draft a new treaty with France; the French were not invited to the negotiations, and the treaty included an 'indemnity' of 700 million francs to cover the costs of the war. At the time, there had been much discussion among the Allies about an international system that would prevent further wars. The most ambitious scheme was Tsar Alexander's 'Holy Alliance', which, in its initial form, as drawn up in Alexander's own hand, contained many liberal ideas. It included clauses on the rights of peoples and nations, and it was not designed as an alliance between monarchs. When Castlereagh first saw it in the new British Embassy in Paris he dismissed it as 'a piece of sublime mysticism and nonsense', but he did accept the institution of a new 'Conference System', by which the major powers of Europe intended to maintain the peace in the years to come. What was left of the Holy Alliance – an alliance between Russia, Prussia and Austria – was transformed into the reactionary institution, as history remembers it, after Britain withdrew from the Conference System, leaving the 'powers that be' to their own devices.

Put Wilson in the place of Alexander, rename the 'Holy Alliance' as Wilson's 'Covenant', substitute the 'Conference System' with the 'League of Nations', call 'Britain' the United States, and you have the prime elements of the story of Europe after 1918.

The French November plan for a 'preliminary' conference to establish an early treaty with Germany, followed by a 'general' congress where Germany would be represented, followed the legal precedent of 1814–15. A week after it was submitted to the Americans, a version of it was presented, on 26 November, to the British government by the French ambassador in London. Wilson pocketed the plan; he probably didn't even read it until he was aboard the *George Washington*. Officials in London, on the other hand, appear to have realized its significance. Somewhat garbled versions of it even began appearing in the British press at the end of November.[78]

During the week of the Armistice, Clemenceau had been urging Lloyd George to travel to Paris in order to get the process of peace moving. But Lloyd George would not come. He explained that his time was preoccupied with the election.

So Paris came to London. Clemenceau, accompanied by Foch, arrived in the afternoon of 1 December, along with the Italian Prime Minister, Orlando, and his Foreign Minister, Baron Sonnino. The presence of the three main European Allies made the encounter look very much like the beginning of the 'preliminaries', despite House's reassurance to Wilson – still in Washington – that no important decisions would be made. House himself was too ill to travel. 'It is rather characteristic of President Wilson's suspicious nature', Lloyd George justifiably noted in his memoirs, 'that he would not depute the task of representing his views, or even of reporting the views of the delegates of other nations, to the American Ambassadors in France or in London.' Wilson trusted no one but House.[79]

Clemenceau and Foch were received like heroes by the crowds that lined the streets and squares between Charing Cross and Hyde Park. The street hawkers were out selling portraits of Foch, 'the man who won the war'. Clemenceau, who had come to regard the English as a reserved race, was visibly astonished at the acclaim and waved his silk hat through every street he passed along.[80]

The conference at Downing Street, which lasted two days, was more important than either the press or House, in his reports to the President, suggested. The two foreign issues that were getting attention in the electoral campaign – the 'indemnity' and the trial of the Kaiser – were first and second on the conference's agenda and were discussed in detail. Clemenceau, who would never show the slightest interest in statistics, suggested that each nation ought to prepare its list of claims against the Central Powers and bring it before an inter-Allied committee that would then establish the order in which damages should be recompensed. It was agreed to set up an Inter Allied Reparations Commission. Clemenceau was also one of the most eager in the conference to bring the 'ex-Kaiser and his accomplices before an international tribunal'. He argued that if 'we could get seven or eight persons, and make them responsible before an international tribunal, this would be an enormous progress for humanity'. It was decided that the Allies would await Wilson's arrival before any further action was taken, but, simply by discussing the two issues in this order, the Allies had managed to link war reparations to the matter of legal 'responsibility' – for the first time in world history.[81]

Other important matters – such as the representation of Russia, the future of Constantinople ('ancient capital of the Greek Empire') and the League of Nations – were left open. Clemenceau and Sonnino were the least enthusiastic about the idealism embodied in the last of these. Foch was given authorization to extend the Armistice with Germany by a month, with the possibility of further extensions until the treaty was signed; these were the terms he presented to the German Armistice Commission at Trier on 14 December. As for procedure, it was agreed that the Allied delegates would first thrash out the vital issues between themselves in a preliminary conference – along the lines suggested in the initial French plan – before the opening of the 'Peace Congress'. All present confirmed that preliminaries should begin on the earliest day on which President Wilson would be able to attend.

But another six weeks would pass before the Allies met again. The United States and Britain were principally responsible for the delay.

Wilson did not like to act according to historical precedents, particularly if they were European. On several occasions, following his arrival in Paris, he made disparaging remarks about the elitist Congress of Vienna. It had been a Congress of 'bosses', as he put it to *The Times*: the 'delegates were concerned more with their own interests, and of those of the classes they represented, than with the wishes of their peoples. Versailles . . . must be a meeting of the servants of the people.' 'This is not a war in which the soldiers of the free nations have obeyed masters,' he told American troops on Christmas Day. 'You have commanders, but you have no masters.' Masters, aristocrats, bosses and congresses – all these belonged to an Old World that had disappeared with the war and the entry of America into the affairs of Europe. Wilson wanted to keep the 'preliminaries' as informal as possible and then get down to the task, not of establishing a treaty with Germany, but of setting up the League of Nations. This new League would solve every problem. But Wilson had no specific idea of what the League would be.[82]

When Britain's ambassador to Paris, Lord Derby, first met Wilson he was appalled at the President's lack of plans. 'His views seem to me to be of the most visionary character,' Derby wrote, distraught, to Arthur Balfour, the Foreign Secretary. Derby asked Wilson a few questions about this League of Nations. Wilson appeared to think that the League would somehow magically develop out of the peace conference (which he had not yet defined) – 'he said if you can once start the machinery of a Conference their work would gradually develop'. 'I am afraid you won't think this letter very clear,' Derby closed, 'but honestly I am not clear myself as to what he meant.' Derby wrote like Castlereagh after an interview with Tsar Alexander.[83]

Wilson's subordinates were as much in the dark as Derby. Two days after their arrival, House wrote character sketches of the four peace delegates who had accompanied the President to Paris. Henry White, nominated to represent the Republicans, was 'a well accomplished old gentleman and may be of some service later on', but 'he knows next to nothing about the work we have in hand'. Until he met House he was still arguing that the League should not be formed until after the 'Peace Conference'. Robert Lansing, the Secretary of State, was 'a man that one cannot grow enthusiastic over'; House found him 'completely ignorant of most of the things with which he should be cognizant'. General Tasker H. Bliss was a 'scholarly, statesmanlike, soldier', but 'so little known and understood that he will be a liability to the President'. George Creel's main problem, as chief of the press bureau in Paris, was his intense dislike of Lansing; a 'head-on collision' looked imminent. 'As the matter stands today the President and I are doing everything,' wrote House.[84]

Linked to his faith in a kind of spontaneous generation of the League out of the 'meeting of the servants of the people' at Versailles was Wilson's strange new idea of 'reciprocal feeling' between himself and the crowds he encountered. Wilson started talking about it after his lavish reception in Paris on 14 December. The experience 'in this wonderfully beautiful city' created a 'combination of emotions that one would not have more than once in a lifetime' – and made quite a contrast to bickering Washington, where he had just lost the congressional elections. As he told his friend Herbert Brougham, 'I have been instructed by [the acclaim of the crowd], because I know upon what it is based. It is based upon the trust that I will stand fast to the principles and purposes which I have avowed.' This notion of an 'instructing' people and responding principle and purpose was repeated by many of Wilson's aides during December. Ray Stannard Baker, a young liberal journalist who was named his chief press officer, was one of its most eager proponents; just back from Italy, he contrasted the popular acclaim for Wilson's principles with the lack of enthusiasm for Italy's own stale parliament and government. Wilson spoke at the Sorbonne of 'my conception of the League of Nations' as 'the organized moral force of men throughout the world', exactly as the war had witnessed the organized force of free nations. '*Wilson le juste! Wilson le juste!*' cried a crowd of gowned students in a show of 'reciprocal feeling'.

Wilson and his aides developed immense confidence in the President's strength as a result of such crowd scenes. On Christmas Eve, Thomas Nelson

Page wrote to Wilson from Rome to say that in Italy the President was regarded 'as a sort of Messiah sent to save them from all the ills that the war has brought on the world'. The day before, Thomas Logan of the US Shipping Board in Paris wrote to his boss, Edward Hurley, that 'the peoples of Europe have given to President Wilson the greatest reception ever given to any man'. The governments of Lloyd George and Clemenceau would, he surmised, instantly tumble if they opposed him – 'no man in Europe can challenge the President'.[85]

With this kind of power there seemed no pressing need to act.

During November and December, British diplomats, agents and their domestic servants appeared in dribs and drabs at the Hotel Majestic on the Avenue Kléber. But it soon became evident that Britain was not pushing for an early conference either. Eventually Lloyd George and Balfour agreed to come over to Paris on 21 December for a three-day visit. Then they cancelled at the last minute. Wilson was furious.

The British elections were the most obvious cause of delay. Lloyd George repeated throughout the campaign that the government needed a popular mandate before it could send its representatives over to Paris to negotiate the peace. Without an election, Lloyd George could not depend on the support of Parliament, He had no party organization behind him; he could be faced with the united opposition of Squiffite Liberals and Labour. Added to that was the developing American propaganda on behalf of the 'Messiah'. The results of the poll of 14 December would not be known until the 28th.

After Hughes's fiery intervention in early November, the question of how Britain and her Empire would be represented in Paris had become urgent. It had been discussed during the Allied conference in early December, but no definite decision had been made before Christmas – a fact that must have accounted in no small way for Lloyd George's cancelled appointment in Paris on the 21st. The report of the Hughes Committee had still not been heard by the Imperial War Cabinet. The formula eventually adopted by the Imperial War Cabinet for the representation of British Dominions – 'Canadian losses during the War have been greater than those of Belgium,' thundered the Canadian Prime Minister Sir Robert Borden; 'In men, [American] sacrifices were not even equal to those of Australia,' growled Hughes – was that they should be placed on equal footing at the conference with 'Belgium and the other smaller Allied States'. To achieve this, Britain's fifth delegate to the conference was filled from a rota of Dominion premiers. The other four were Lloyd George, Bonar Law, Balfour, and George Barnes, who 'represented the views of organized Labour'.[86]

Britain had, in fact, no particular reason to rush to a Paris conference. Her frontiers were not threatened. The menace of Germany's battleships and submarines had been solved: they were all now safely interned in British harbours. Germany's former colonies were all occupied by British troops. A large portion of the former Ottoman Empire was also under British occupation.

The unresolved issues for Britain lay not in territorial matters, as for the rest of Europe, but in the areas of finance and shipping – areas which brought Britain directly into conflict with the United States. Gradually a policy developed of building a League of Nations not out of some as yet undefined peace conference, but out of existing inter-Allied councils, for in these Britain, as a result of her war effort, was dominant.

America's unwillingness to share the burden of Allied war finance had irritated London; the internationalism of 'Dr Wilson', as he was coming to be known, seemed hypocritical. 'America has neither given the material nor the moral help which entitle her to come before France,' said Hughes, implying that Clemenceau had more of a right to give lessons in morality than the American President. Just before Christmas a US Treasury official in Paris prepared a list of US loans to the Allies, along with their dates of maturity. It read like a credit note from Uncle Scrooge to a delinquent debtor:

> The Secretary of the Treasury has indicated to the Allied Governments the following generalizations respecting loans to them by the United States: that he is not disposed to establish further credits for purchases outside of the United States; that he looks for an early curtailment in advances for purchases in the United States, which are expected, as a general rule, to be limited to foodstuffs . . . etc.[87]

This was a strange way of addressing Allies who had just emerged from a world war. The United States was demanding immediate attention to the business of the League of Nations, but she did not want the matter of Allied loans discussed in public. Carter Glass, the new Secretary of the Treasury, warned Wilson that the Allies might advocate the cancellation of obligations. Wilson responded that he was working to prevent 'plans and maneuvers on the loans' and there was no question of their being discussed at the peace conference.[88]

Hoover's heavy-handed administration of food relief – which Keynes had hoped would provide a solution to the tangled problem of Allied debt – caused further tension. Hoover was in London in the second week of December to talk with members of the British Cabinet. The British wanted relief administered by the wartime Allied Maritime Transport Council; it was during the meeting with Hoover that Sir Maurice Hankey, the Cabinet Secretary, suggested that such administrative machinery could be used as the basis of the League of Nations. For Hoover, this was a subversive British attempt to control the American economy. He returned to Paris advocating 'direct executive action', independent of all Allies. Wilson granted it when he let Hoover set up his organization on the Avenue Montaigne. Lloyd

George remarked that America's show of independence was 'a bad omen for the League of Nations'.[89]

Because Lloyd George was avoiding Paris, House and Wilson planned a visit to England. Evidence suggests that this was not a friendly overture: the idea was to weaken the British government.

House found an unlikely ally in Lord Northcliffe, who, as owner of both *The Times* and the *Daily Mail*, was the mightiest of the British press barons. Northcliffe sought political power, and his impression was that he was not going to gain it through Lloyd George. In December he was in Paris looking for friends. House opened his Texan heart to him. 'I did something today which has pleased me more than anything I have done since signing the Armistice with Germany,' House wrote in his diary on 17 December. What could this be? A conversation with the President? A dinner with the French premier? A celebration of the peace? No: 'I took Lord Northcliffe for a ride and a walk for an hour.'

House and Northcliffe discovered the common distrust they had in the capacity of the 'Entente Governments' to interpret the aspirations of the people. Wilson was the only statesman capable of doing this. Wilson's reception in Paris was 'an expression of the great body of the people'. A great press campaign was needed to sustain the momentum. House urged Northcliffe to take the lead in England and become there the 'voice of the people'. Northcliffe was already convinced that he was. He agreed to publish in *The Times* a long and favourable 'interview' with the President (the entire text was actually drafted by House's son-in-law, Gordon Auchincloss, and appeared on 21 December). The President would then visit England and 'receive the reception there which we knew awaited him'. After such massive popular acclaim, 'Lloyd George and his colleagues would not dare oppose his policies at the Peace Conference.'[90]

Immediately following his encounter with Northcliffe, House 'sent for' Lord Derby (though House still held no formal position in the US government) and planning for Wilson's trip to England began.

'I hope I may never again have to do with arrangements for a Presidential visit to England,' Derby confessed to Balfour on the 20th. 'The President is treated so like a God that one only gets his views second hand.' The President did not even answer a personal invitation from King George V to stay with him and his family at Buckingham Palace. He nevertheless turned up at the palace on Thursday afternoon, 26 December – Boxing Day.[91]

8

Boxing Day, by tradition, was the first weekday after Christmas, when the ladies and gentlemen of the household, too preoccupied during the festival to worry about business matters, presented servants and postmen with their

Christmas boxes. In the early nineteenth century 'boxing time' extended into the first week of January. It became a 'day' when, in 1871, Parliament instituted bank holidays. 'Boxing' was virtually abandoned with the Great War, because of the dramatic decline in domestic servants and because the postman, the bearer of bad news, was not always a welcome character. London now put Boxing Day aside for digesting the feast, a walk in the park, or perhaps bidding farewell to a son or a husband returning to the war. But, above all, Boxing Day had become the greatest theatre day of the year. It was the day the pantomime season opened.

It was the first Boxing Day of the peace. London's pantomimes proved equal to the occasion. They were democratically vulgar; they used every trick of their sister trade, the music hall; they were magical. *The Adventures of Robinson Crusoe* opened for its fourth year at the Wimbledon Theatre. The director had, of course, made it a hymn to British sea power, with great nautical scenes, wreckage, heroic survival, and constant references to 'Jack' and 'Tommy'. *Aladdin*, at the King's Theatre in Hammersmith, carried the lamp of peace; 'children screamed with delight'. A. A. Milne (inventor of 'Winnie the Pooh') joined hands with Arnold Bennett to create an original piece at the Hammersmith Playhouse that the critics hated but sent the children squealing. The scene of the moulding of the magic slipper in the Lyceum's *Cinderella* made special sense on 26 December 1918, as the Spirit of Evil, Demon Malvino, fought over the heroine's fortunes with the Spirit of Good, a hairy-legged Fairy Godmother.[92]

The relationship between theatre and war has long fascinated literary critics, not only because of the language used (adolescent conscript soldiers wear 'costumes' in the 'theatre' of war), but also because theatre has been shown to have an effect on the way war is described and even perceived on the field. Theatre also had an effect on the way people experienced the transition from war to peace. There is hardly a more graphic example of this than the pantomime.

In the case of war, Paul Fussell has emphasized the particular significance of an an old theatre trick, dating back to Georgian times: the transformation scene. It was achieved by the lighting of a painted scrim which might first appear as solid as a brick wall but then, gradually, magically, would dissolve before a second scene. Fussell shows how the memory of this affected soldiers on the Western Front, particularly at morning and evening stand-to. He quotes Richard Aldington watching at dawn as 'very gradually, very slowly the darkness dissipated, as if thin imperceptible veils were being rolled up in a transformation scene'. And Norman Gladden recalling, 'As the dusk began to fall the landscape towards the town gradually took on a new aspect. It was like a transformation scene on a vast stage.' Every child in England would have known what Gladden meant by a transformation scene; he had seen it in the pantomime.[93]

It affected the way one saw the transition from war to peace in 1918. On

26 December children in London watched in awe as the dark, wicked scene of the magic slipper was transformed into a 'fairy opening' on a forest glade into which Miss Nancy Gibbs, as Cinderella, entered in her russet rags singing a song. Or as the naval wreckage in a vicious sea storm was transformed into the sunny, tropical beach of Crusoe's island.

The transformation scene that got the loudest applause was at Drury Lane Theatre, where *Babes in the Wood*, by Frank Dix and Arthur Collins was being performed. This *Babes in the Wood* was a story of wretched peasants fleeing through a devastated countryside, burning fires lighting them on their way. Then gradually, from behind the scrim, there rose a sun until it reached its noon in a sensational Peace Pageant. It brought a standing ovation. Collins was demanded again and again before the curtain: he had touched the heart of London.

The YMCA, in an appeal for aid to stranded soldiers, had called it the 'Victory Christmas'. The *Morning Post* called it the 'Great Peace Christmas'. Rationing was already on its way out. The Food Controller had revoked controls on cereals and potatoes, and he had increased the purchasing value of the meat coupon, which essentially meant beef – pork, poultry, game, hares, rabbit and horse flesh were coupon-free. Farmers were complaining of a grain glut. Shoppers at the Leadenhall and Smithfield markets grumbled about the scraggy appearance of the geese and turkeys on sale. Charles E. Brooke, Past Master of the Poulterers' Company, admitted that they were only about half the size of the previous years – that is, during the war – because of limited poultry food supply. Jam rationing was still imposed, and it was wise, when going to hotels and restaurants, to bring along one's own sugar bag.

The pavements were thronged with thousands of soldiers, many of them Americans. In the packed railway stations there were signs saying 'Don't be lonely' and inviting servicemen to step into a YMCA enquiry office.

All through Advent it had been squally and overcast, but it had not been cold. On Christmas Eve temperatures fell. If Scrooge had been in his room that night, interviewing the Last of the Spirits, he would have noticed at dawn a blue sky, thrown open his window, and exclaimed, 'Golden sunlight; heavenly sky, sweet fresh air; merry bells. Oh glorious.'

Christmas 1918 in London was glorious.

Because of the storms in the Channel on the 23rd, House had got cold feet and decided not to take the crossing with the President. Derby reported to Balfour that the Colonel was 'very seedy again'. House named his son-in-law as his replacement, but young Gordon Auchincloss – who had no doubt that it was efficient America, and only America, that had saved the world for democracy – was not a great diplomat. In the meantime Wilson had soured relations with Clemenceau by summoning him to Murat's palace and making a long rambling speech on the League of Nations. Clemenceau was not impressed, and he did not like the idea of Wilson departing for England, perhaps with the intention of making some secret deal with Lloyd George. On Christmas Eve his Cabinet issued a formal memorandum pleading with Wilson not to suppress existing inter-Allied councils, which guaranteed supplies to the Allies and maintained a degree of order 'in the social life of nations'; as yet there was nothing else to replace them.[94] Clemenceau spent his days after Christmas attending the great parliamentary debate in the Chamber that concluded with his defence of the 'old system'.

Wilson spent Christmas Day at Pershing's military headquarters at Chaumont; with the exception of one Sunday visit in the following March, this was the closest he ever got to the front. In a quiet field, untouched by war, he paid homage to the American troops for 'the gallant fighting you have done'. He had spent most of the previous night sitting up in his special train, because the French laundry service had made up all the beds with cold, wet sheets.[95]

Early on the 26th his train pulled into Calais. A frosty mist hung over the waters. The sea was flat calm. Outside the town he had passed a gang of German prisoners of war unloading freight wagons on the other side of the tracks; they stopped work and simply watched the President pass by. Wilson and his staff boarded the *Brighton*, which had been one of the glories of the Dieppe–Newhaven ferry run before the war. After being converted into a hospital ship and receiving coatings of blue and grey paint for camouflage it looked quite dowdy. Destroyers joined in convoy. Planes flew overhead. The sun came out.

The brass cannon thundered out a royal salute from Dover Castle, as they had for Francis Drake over 300 years earlier. Princes, kings and emperors, the Kaiser, the Tsar and republican chiefs of state had stepped ashore under these chalk cliffs, but never before had the white star and eagle of the American President's flag been seen there. One might have thought this would have attracted a crowd, but in fact the streets of the port were virtually empty – it was an English Boxing Day.

The Duke of Connaught, the King's uncle, gave Wilson a hearty handshake, and as they advanced down the carpeted gangway of Admiralty Pier, with the Grenadier Guards pounding out 'The Star-Spangled Banner', the daughters of Dover, dressed in white with small aprons of red, white and blue, threw paper roses at their feet. The President responded with a toothy smile. The engine of his train was hung with the Stars and Stripes and decorated with Christmas holly. In a little over an hour it drew into Charing Cross station, where the King, the Queen and His Majesty's entire government stood ready to begin London's welcome.

Admiral Cary T. Grayson thought the enthusiasm of the crowds that lined the streets between the station and the palace 'really surprising'; the warning that 'the average Briton was phlegmatic and loath to show his emotions' was 'not borne out by the facts'. Lloyd George noted the contrast between Wilson's reception and the welcome given Clemenceau and Foch four weeks earlier: Wilson was 'not exactly a popular hero with the ordinary citizen of our country. He did not make the same appeal to their combative instincts as Clemenceau and Foch did. They still remembered his "too proud to fight" speech, when their sons were fighting to the death.' But around Queen Victoria's statue there were a mass of wounded veterans who saluted him. When a group of Americans on St James's Street started chanting there were many in the crowd who joined in. The word 'Welcome' was set out in large letters on the front of the Burdett-Coutts mansion. Outside the gates of Buckingham Palace a throng chanted in unison, 'We want Wilson! We want Wilson!'

The sun, sinking into the icy veiled skyline, gave a golden touch to the air above; silver aeroplanes 'stunted' before the crowds and troops; the gate of St James's Palace 'massed up purple' in the afternoon's light: it was, said the reporter for the *Morning Post*, 'an actual transformation scene in the streets'.[96]

In Buckingham Palace there was a great court dining room that the King had refused to use during the war. He had it refurbished for Wilson's visit. The hundreds of gold and silver plaques and shields on the walls were polished, the pipes of the great organ were cleaned up, and the tables were laid with gold dishes and a solid-gold table service. 'This dining-room is one of the most remarkable in the world,' remarked Grayson. All the other empires in Europe had collapsed by December 1918: what was left of Russia was half Bolshevik and half chaos; Germany had at least two Soviet republics and two competing central governments; the Austrian Empire had fragmented into its non-component parts. Several noted, that Christmas, that no other state in the world could produce such a pageant as the British throne could display. 'I have never witnessed such a dazzling scene either before or since,' declared Lloyd George.[97]

Representatives of the whole Empire were present at the banquet on Friday, 27 December. There was not an official present who could remember such a widespread guest list before. Admirals, field marshals and generals – all in uniform – sat down with princes and prime ministers; the whole ambassador corps had been invited; merchants and financiers hobnobbed with press barons; the whole literary establishment was there, including Conan Doyle and Rudyard Kipling. 'It was a dream of magnificence.' And it was all in honour of Wilson. He sat at the main table in the black dress suit of an American Republican.

King George made a toast of friendship to the great overseas democracy and spoke warmly of the role Americans had played in bringing the war to a triumphant conclusion. Wilson rose and admitted that 'America does love freedom.' Then he embarked on one of the themes of his New History – his history without balancing powers and personalities: he addressed himself to 'the great moral tide now running in the world', the 'great tide running in the hearts of men'. He concluded by lifting his glass to the King and proposing 'your health and the health of the Queen, and the prosperity of Great Britain'.

Not once had he mentioned a general, an admiral, a government minister; he had been silent on the Army and the Navy; he had said nothing on Britain's contribution to the war. When he sat down, a chill spread through the hall.[98]

After dinner, in the Royal Reception Room, Wilson ran into Winston Churchill. 'Well, Mr Churchill,' asked Wilson, 'and how is the Navy?' Churchill flushed and made no reply.[99]

Lloyd George returned to Downing Street late that night and instantly wrote a letter to Lord Reading, Britain's ambassador to the United States, who had been in London since November.[100] Lloyd George pointed out the mischief the President's blundering speech could cause, and emphasized how anxious he was to co-operate with the Americans, especially on issues of the peace where Britain's approach was more liberal than Clemenceau's. Reading – hated by Hoover, but supposedly on good terms with Wilson – replied the next morning that he had been in touch with the President and had been assured there would be cordial references in his Guildhall speech that afternoon.

Wilson was in a festive mood. It was his sixty-second birthday. The King came to his rooms and gave him a set of books on the history of Windsor Castle. Wilson commented that the day was 'the greatest of my life'. There was another pantomime spectacle in the streets as Wilson rode in a state carriage, the King's Household Cavalry before him, to the Guildhall, where the Guards stood in their costumes, 'picturesque in the extreme'. The Lord Mayor and High Sheriff, in their robes and chains of office, came out to greet him. He was offered, in great ceremony, the Freedom of the City. Decorated officers of the Army and the Navy applauded him. Citizens wearing their ribbons of honour stood up and cheered him. Wilson made a speech.

It was an elaboration of his theory of 'reciprocal feeling' between himself and crowds. 'Ceremonies like this have a new significance,' he told the gleaming assembly. He was very honoured by his new title, but he realized it was not personally meant for him, for he was only part of 'a great body of circumstances' – here came Wilson's New History again. 'I do not believe that it was fancy on my part that I heard in the voice of welcome uttered in the streets of this great city and in the streets of Paris something more than a personal welcome. It seemed to me that I heard the voice of one people speaking to another people, and it was a voice in which one could distinguish a singular combination of emotions.' The 'great moral tide' rose again. Wilson admitted that he had not been to any of the battlefields, but 'I have conversed with the soldiers.' 'They fought to do away with an old order and to establish a new one, and the center and characteristic of the old order was that unstable thing which we used to call the "balance of power".' Wilson glanced briefly back at the dreadful European nineteenth century: it was 'maintained by jealous watchfulness and an antagonism of interest'. The plan for today? 'There must now be, not a balance of power, not one powerful group of nations set off against another, but a single, overwhelming, powerful group of nations who shall be the trustee of the peace of the world.'[101]

Not a single personality was mentioned; no reference was made to a soldier, a sailor or a citizen; there was not the slightest hint of a recognition of Britain's almighty war effort.

Wilson had his supporters. After listening to Wilson's speech that day – 'The whisper of grief that has blown all through the world is now silent, and the sun of hope seems to spread its rays' – Viscount Morley turned towards Dr Grayson and declared, 'History will accord only two figures in this war – Wilson, the Statesman, and Foch, the Soldier.' The former Prime Minister, Asquith, the current Archbishop of Canterbury and the Bishop of London nodded in approval.[102]

The President had already received the warm approval of the Bishop of Oxford, who had written to tell him that, though the 'educated' classes in Europe might oppose him, the 'common people are with you'. That was what Wilson liked to hear. Other representatives of the 'common people' confirmed the idea. The Trades Union Congress and the Executive Committee of the Labour Party addressed a long manifesto to the President announcing that 'secret diplomacy has brought European nations near to ruin'. Northcliffe continued to act as the 'people's interpreter'. Lord Bryce encouraged Wilson to think of the League of Nations as an assurance against the restoration of an elitist 'balance of power'. Sir George Paish, adviser to the previous Chancellor of the Exchequer, wrote from Pall Mall, 'never have the hearts of the British people beat in closer harmony and sympathy with their kinsmen overseas than they do today'. Asquith sent the President a collection of his popular addresses, on which he inscribed, 'Like yourself, I have always been a University man.'[103]

All these common people! On the Saturday when Wilson made his 'great body of circumstances' speech at Guildhall the ballots of the December election were counted.

Lloyd George had been moving heaven and earth to please Wilson. Sir William Wiseman, who had been living with House in New York, helped Auchincloss prepare the Prime Minister for his first business encounter with the President, which took place on Friday morning in Wilson's fabulously furnished study at Buckingham Palace. Wiseman had told Lloyd George that behind Wilson's 'stern and dauntless radicalism' lay a hesitant, even timorous, man. Auchincloss got Lloyd George to agree that the first item on the agenda of the peace conference would be the League of Nations. He persuaded Wilson to be non-committal about British aims. Lloyd George, in the company of Balfour, went into the meeting with the idea of letting Wilson have his League of Nations; it would be the first item on the conference agenda. He found the President 'extremely pleasant', with 'none of the professorial condescension towards young learners which I had been led to expect'. Lloyd George told the Imperial War Cabinet three days later that the League of Nations 'was the only only thing that he [Wilson] really cared about' and was to be the solution to all other problems, including the Freedom of the Seas.

The only difficulty was that Wilson 'had no definite formal scheme' for the League of Nations, and there was now talk of the peace conference beginning in Paris within a week. The most specific projects to date had been prepared under British auspices, by Lord Robert Cecil, Under-Secretary to the Foreign Office and General Jan Smuts, the South African Minister of Defence and a member of Lloyd George's War Cabinet.[104] Wilson's policy was apparently to establish 'agreement on the general principles and outlines before forming a plan'. He had the same approach to the whole procedure of the peace conference: he hated the French proposal for formal 'peace preliminaries' (too reminiscent of 'secret diplomacy' and 'balance of powers'), though he did admit to the utility of informal talks between the four Western powers before summoning the Germans to a general congress. At the Imperial War Cabinet, Lord Curzon, on hearing of Wilson's proposed procedure, warned of the danger of 'loose talk' and expressed fear that the 'Peace Conference would be a dreary fiasco'.

On the other issues Wilson remained deliberately vague. Though Freedom of the Seas was to be 'left for further consideration after the League of Nations had been established', both the Prime Minister and the President could agree to the abolition of conscripted armies – Lloyd George had made it an election pledge. On colonies, Wilson agreed that former German overseas territories should not be handed back to the Germans; he favoured Smuts's idea of administrative 'mandates' from the League of Nations. Lloyd George tried to interest him in an American mandate in either Palestine, Mesopotamia or East Africa; Wilson showed himself opposed to any intervention by the United States in 'any of these territorial questions'.

With regard to indemnities, Lloyd George reported Wilson 'stiffer than on any other question'. The President thought priority should be given to 'the claims of pure reparation'. Lloyd George, who had spent his Christmas poring over the reports of Keynes and the Hughes Committee, pointed out that this 'practically ruled the British Empire out, in spite of the enormous burdens it had borne'; France and Belgium, with lesser financial burdens, would get everything. The indemnities question was obviously tied to the American attitude on Allied war debts, but on this matter Wilson remained religiously silent. Wilson's refusal to acknowledge Britain's role in the war must be placed in this context: in the last resort Wilson intended to follow the early recommendations of The Inquiry and impose his policies on Europe by use of the 'economic weapon'. For the moment, however, he relied on popular acclaim.[105]

A large banquet had initially been planned for Saturday evening at Lancaster House. In deference to the President's wishes it was cancelled and, instead, Lloyd George gave in his honour a stag dinner party at 10 Downing Street. As the men sat down to table the results of the election came in.

Lloyd George had won the greatest parliamentary majority that has ever been recorded in British history: the Coalition took 529 seats[106] as against 177 for all other parties – a majority of 352. Opposition Liberals had been swept out: Asquith had lost his seat at East Fife, and nearly all his frontbench colleagues had suffered a similar fate. The most famous pacifists of 1917 – Ramsay MacDonald, Philip Snowden, Arthur Ponsonby, W. C. Anderson and C. P. Trevelyan – had been ejected from Parliament; many of them were among the most ardent supporters of the League of Nations. Labour had increased its strength from thirty-seven to sixty-four seats, but some of its major figures would not be sitting in the new Parliament: Sidney Webb, Arthur Henderson, George Lansbury. The popular turnout, however, was one of the lowest in modern British electoral history: a little over 50 per cent of the expanded electorate had not voted. The large overseas military vote was cited as the technical reason at the time. But undoubtedly indifference and confusion over the breakdown of the traditional parties – which had been noted by reporters during the campaign – were also important factors. And perhaps the British people were not as frenziedly patriotic as some of the commentators liked to think; the last general election with such a low turnout had been the 'Khaki Election' of 1900.[107]

Grayson's diary is notably silent on Wilson's reaction that night at dinner. House, though he kept in touch with the progress of Wilson's English tour, says nothing. Lloyd George left no record.[108]

After the dinner Wilson left by train to visit his mother's church in Carlisle. It poured with rain all night, but at least the President's sheets were dry. At the church he spoke of the need for a great crusade and the 'combination of moral force'. On the advice of Northcliffe he then travelled to Manchester, where he expected to find an American town. On Sunday night Clemenceau spoke in favour of the 'old system'. Wilson replied on Monday from Manchester. The unity of military command in the war (which he had hardly respected) must become a 'unity of spirit' in peace. And a unity on American terms: 'I want to say to to you that [the United States] is not now interested in European politics. But she is interested in the partnership of right between America and Europe.' This was also an answer to the mischievous, unprincipled British electorate. What was the 'partnership of right'? It was the opposite of the 'balance of power', for the United

States 'will join no combination of power which is not the combination of all of us. She is not interested merely in the peace of Europe, but in the peace of the world.'[109]

The next day he crossed a stormy Channel for France. In Paris he played a game of golf and then set off – it was New Year's Day – to conquer the hearts of the Italians.

Wilson had developed an antipathy for Britain. 'You must not speak of us who come over here as cousins, still less as brothers; we are neither,' he had told an American Embassy official in London. 'Neither must you think of us as Anglo-Saxons.' English, he admitted, was a common language for Americans and the British, but that, he thought, was a disadvantage. He understood the American people, he went on: 'They cannot be said to be anti-British, but they are certainly not pro-British. If they are pro anything, it is pro-French.' This was just after he had heard the results of the British elections.[110]

House, by contrast, had a more positive attitude. After talking about the President's trip with Balfour, who had just arrived in Paris, he recorded that Wilson and the British government seemed in 'fairly general agreement'.

Undoubtedly this was partly due to the influence that the last meeting of Dominion prime ministers had had on Balfour as well as Lloyd George. If Hughes was on a war footing against Wilson's 'dictatorship', Borden of Canada warned of his need for friendly relations with his neighbour: Canada, he said, wanted to 'keep clear of European complications'. Britain's sprawling Empire went in every direction.[111]

Curzon, who also emphasized the need to co-operate with the Americans, helped Lloyd George face his dilemma by remarking that 'at the Conference Mr Lloyd George would go with an authority fully equal, and indeed superior, to that of President Wilson's'. Elections were not for nothing.

Winter 1919

Berlin in winter

1

A man who watches his neighbour being killed has a tendency to think things ought to be different. A woman who sees her young husband die has questions to put to the world. That is what makes revolution the hand-maiden of war – people do not accept war's appalling conditions. The tragedy of most of history is that the real revolution never happens. Take the example of Berlin.

The problem in Berlin started when the war came home in the Christmas of 1918.

No Berliner believed that Germany had lost the war. One talked a lot of the 'melancholy atmosphere' in the streets; some spoke of 'catastrophe', especially after the shoot-out on Chausseestrasse on 6 December; but one rarely heard anyone pronounce the word 'defeat'. Lieutenant Knowlton L. Ames, Jr, of the US Army, who arrived in Berlin on 10 December to help supervise the handover of Allied prisoners of war, was struck by the popular street song which ran, 'The war is over now. We are at peace. Let us forget. Comrade.' Every German to whom he spoke told him, 'We didn't win and we didn't lose, but why worry about that, for the war is over.'[1]

No foreign army had appeared on German soil until the 'Entente' occupied the Rhineland – under the terms of the 'Armistice'. For many Berliners the flowery celebrations in spring, with the announcements of Ludendorff's offensives, were fresh in their memory; it was easy to imagine, in the *Reichshauptstadt*, that Germany was actually winning the war until late September, when Supreme Command suddenly began to change its tone. Then Ludendorff was dismissed. The Kaiser abdicated. And after that the troops came home.

They kept on coming home – a strutting field-grey multitude – right up till Christmas. Lieutenant Ames was staying at the Adlon Hotel, from where he would daily watch the troops goose-stepping through the Brandenburg Gate and into Pariser Platz. 'The way Berlin was decorated', he reported, 'and the reception that the people at home gave the soldiers upon their arrival in Berlin might even have led the returning soldiers to think that they had been victorious.' Ames noted how the Allied blockade had introduced a new word into German popular vocabulary: '*ersatz*', or 'substitute'. There had been a proliferation of *ersatz* foods (like acorn coffee) and *ersatz* materials (such as cabbage-leaf cigars), but what seemed most evident in front of the Brandenburg Gate in December were the *ersatz* troops with their *ersatz* victory. Every day, upon the wooden platform by the Adlon, groups of government officials would stand up to address a welcome to 'our heroes' from the new 'German Socialist Republic', to say 'we are proud of you', and to declare that 'the old powers have gone'. The entry of the Jaeger Division, in their green uniforms, received loud applause from the crowds on 11 December. On the 19th the 5th Infantry Guard Division marched in as schoolchildren sang '*Gott grüsse dich*' and '*Ich habe einen Kamarad.*' The 4th Infantry Guard Regiment – made up of boys from Spandau and Berlin – had served at Thiepval, Bapaume, Péronne and Villers-Bretonneux, and, 'in the last months took up defence operations instead of attack'; they were 'sound, battle-hardened troops', and the places where they had fought all had French names. Count Harry Kessler, returning from an unsuccessful diplomatic mission in Poland on 18 December, witnessed a division marching down Unter den Linden. All the troops were wearing helmets, and a number of them had flowers attached to their tunics, rifles and helmets; their limbers and guns were garlanded and decorated with black-white-and-red flags – Prussian and imperial colours; there were no red flags.[2]

After marching through the Brandenburg Gate and along Unter den Linden, many festooned soldiers promptly disappeared. General Groener, who remained with Hindenburg at Supreme Headquarters in Kassel, blamed this on the spirit of Christmas. 'The pressure to be at home for Christmas', claimed Groener, 'proved stronger than military discipline.' There was also the 'revolutionary atmosphere in the capital'. And, to cap it all, one had to contend with 'the muddle of Berliner power and personalities, including Ebert'. Supreme Command's old prejudice against the *Etappe*, the rear, was as marked as ever and its faith in a front-line army had barely diminished, even though there was no longer any front, nor any occupied territories in which to protect its best troops – Groener was still pursuing his idea, first developed in Spa, of a healthily isolated, disciplined volunteer corps that could maintain order at home and defend German frontiers, particularly those to the east. Like Hindenburg, Groener was convinced that Supreme Command represented the sole legitimate power in Germany – a power that it had inherited directly from the Kaiser at Spa on 9 November. But, without the new disciplined volunteer force, it had, at least for the moment, to maintain an alliance with the regime in Berlin 'to save our people from threatened collapse', as Hindenburg had put it in his letter to Ebert on 8 December.[3]

For the Army's commanders Ebert's government was always the

'Regime', not the 'German Socialist Republic'. After their arrival in Berlin, deputations of the various army units would go round to the Reichs Chancellery on Wilhelmstrasse to take a pledge of loyalty – 'oath' would be too strong a word. The 4th Infantry Guard, for example, 'declared that we, standing by Hindenburg's declaration, will remain faithful to the Regime and fulfil our duty fully and completely': thus their first loyalty was to Hindenburg. One dragoon regiment, on 15 December, presented an even more qualified statement: 'The Regiment has pleasure in declaring itself for a united German Reich and stands resolutely behind the current provisional Regime . . . However, regarding the future constitution of the German State the Regiment requests that the decision of the [as yet non-existent] National Assembly will not be anticipated. Not until the regular decision is taken, can the Regiment take an oath for the new form of the State.' The pledge concluded by assuring the regiment's services to either a 'democratic Monarchy' or a 'democratic Republic', whatever the National Assembly decided. This was not a rousing endorsement of Commissar Ebert's 'Regime'. Other units followed their pledge with a statement in the newspapers of what they would not support: 'We have sworn loyalty to the Regime,' declared the Cavalry Guard Division on 13 December, but 'a small band of troublemakers are up to mischief in Berlin'. The statement warned of civil war, and the Division promised 'to protect our citizens from these criminals'. It added, menacingly, 'We demand of the Regime loyalty against loyalty; we demand of it not only the will for order, but also the force to carry through this will.' Their loyalty was basic and raw: 'What drives us is merely love for the Fatherland; we are dependents of the Regime and enemies of any counter-revolution.' All Berliners, whatever their politics, their profession, their class, swore they were against the 'counter-revolution'. Who could dare advocate a return to the Kaiser's war?[4]

The Circus Busch, on the north bank of the Spree and not far from the Schloss, was Berlin's equivalent of the Albert Hall; during the revolutionary days that followed the war it acted as host, on different occasions, to every pressure group in town. The Spartacists had held meetings here, as had the Revolutionary Shop Stewards, and the mutinous sailors from the ports. When the soldiers came home, they too gathered in rows to hear political speeches and listen to the invigorating pomp of their military bands. Hordes of NCOs, who never really knew whether they belonged to the masters or the proletariat, turned up on 6, 14 and 19 December for addresses made by captains and lieutenants who reminded the audience that they were heroes, that the loss of their comrades was not in vain, that their duty was to keep the Fatherland united. Songs from the front were sung. The afternoon meeting of 19 December ended with an exquisite concert in which Herr Professor Hugo Rüdel conducted the choir of the Field Artillery Regiment of 1st Reserve Guard: it sounded like the return of God on earth; the

Fatherland was the home of the Romantic. Shortly before, Captain Erich von Salzmann, in a rousing speech, had warned the soldiers not to allow the Reich to be split by 'the people of the enemy'. 'The current Regime can secure us freedom only if it has power behind it. That power is the Army. The old Army is dead! Long live the new Army!'[5]

From the Circus Busch one might have wandered down the river bank that evening and crossed the bridge to the Lustgarten and the Schloss. For the moment, those buildings looked so immobile, so peaceful; they were the constant creatures of central Berlin, and it must have been a comforting thought that, though the Imperial Army had scattered and the frontiers were threatened, though revolution menaced the centre, those buildings had not been touched by the war. All that had changed were their occupants. Within little more than a mile lay Alexanderplatz, the Schloss, the Guard House, the University, the Reichs Chancellery and the Reichstag – all still there, with the same number of windows, the same gates, the same gutters that they had had in 1914. But during the walk one would have passed by half a dozen centres of power that had turned themselves into virtual sovereign states by now. The papers were full of theory and social analysis on how this had happened: the rise of the masses, the revolt of the proletariat. Yet none of these buildings were occupied by a specific social class; they were held by fragments of the ex-Kaiser's armed forces – some of them on half-pay, most of them on no pay at all – who were hungry and bitter.

The Police Presidium on Alexanderplatz was under the control of Emil Eichhorn's 'Security Service', a medley of around three thousand soldiers and sailors. Eichhorn, the former telegraph chief at the Russian Embassy, was for the moment playing a very underhand part in the events; he even announced on 20 December that his forces would be dispersed once the situation in Berlin had calmed down. Red flags flew from the Kaiser's Schloss and his neighbouring stables, the Marstall, which were occupied by the People's Naval Division, a group of about two thousand mutinous sailors. During their last weeks in the northern ports they had not been paid, but they had persuaded Ebert's government to turn over 125,000 marks in November. Now they were demanding 80,000 marks as a Christmas bonus. In the meantime they lived off 'requisitions' they made in the neighbouring parts of town. Columnists in the *Rote Fahne* wrote of these sailors as the 'heart of the Revolution', but it was never explained why Berliners, so many of them proletarians, required sailors from Kiel to act as their spearhead. Just over the canal bridge from the Schloss, on the northern corner of Unter den Linden, was the Guard House. This was now the headquarters of Berlin's military governor, Otto Wels. He was supported here, in the University next door and across the street at the Crown Prince's Palace, by a force made up mainly of non-commissioned officers under the command of Sergeant Suppe of the 64th Reserve Infantry Regiment. 'Suppe' means 'soup' in German, and the Spartacists referred to these majestic buildings as the 'Suppe Barracks'.

Eight hundred yards down the Linden lay Wilhelmstrasse, where the main government buildings stood, where the decisions of the Reich were made, where Europe's Great War had begun in July 1914. Commissar Ebert, the former saddler, now sat at Bismarck's desk, attempting to administer the affairs of the Reich. There were five other members of the Council of People's Commissars, two of them Majority Socialists, three of them of the Independent branch. In a speech to the soldiers gathered in the Circus Busch on 15 December, Sergeant Suppe had regretted the elimination of the bourgeoisie from politics.

The answer to the lack of 'bourgeois' politics lay at the far end of the Linden, on the other side of the Brandenburg Gate, at the Reichstag. The Reichstag had not sat since the Kaiser's abdication. 'Why not convene the Reichstag?' Groener had asked the Reichstag President, Konstantin Fehrenbach, when he visited Supreme Command on 7 December. 'We would at least have *one* legal institution available that would give validity to bourgeois opinion against the radicals.' Groener, who had a historical mind and was perhaps thinking of Adolphe Thiers establishing a National Assembly in Versailles after the French defeat in 1871, suggested that Reichstag members meet in Kassel. Fehrenbach said no: it would be seen as a rump parliament, and the parties of the centre and Right would almost certainly boycott it.[6]

In the place of a national parliament, a Congress of Workers' and Soldiers' Councils now sat in the Reichstag. Most of the delegates were Majority Socialists with moderate goals. But they were subject to pressure. On 19 December the *Rote Fahne* published an editorial explaining that bourgeois revolutions occurred 'behind walls', and citing the example of the French Revolution, which was guided from the inside of Parisian convents; the 'first proletarian revolution in Germany', on the other hand, had its central organ in the streets. There was a continual cry for mass demonstrations outside the Reichstag: 'Workers! Comrades! Out of your workshops! Down with Ebert–Scheidemann!' The claim that a quarter of a million had turned up on 16 December, when the Congress opened, was no doubt an exaggeration. But Liebknecht was there, speaking like a parson from the top of a truck. On the 19th armed sailors, their faces daubed in mud, charged the entrance, and the Reichstag guards had to use their truncheons.[7]

Inside, the Independent Socialists spoke in numbers out of proportion to their small representation; they persuaded the Congress to adopt the 'Hamburg Points' (after the delegate from Hamburg, who proposed them), which renamed the Imperial Army the 'People's Army', abolished the insignia of rank, called for the election of officers by the soldiers' vote, and passed responsibility for discipline and punishment to the soldiers' councils. Supreme Command's response was immediate. 'I do not accept the resolution passed in Berlin by the Congress on 18 December concerning arrangements in the Army and, in particular, the status of officers and NCOs,' stated Hindenburg in a letter published on the 19th. He claimed the Congress had no authority to make such a reform; he called for a National Assembly 'appointed by the whole people'.

The next day Groener and an assistant, Major Kurt von Schleicher, were in Berlin. They crossed the city centre on foot, in full uniform, their medals glittering, and 'not a soul touched us'. Ebert met them at the Chancellery, and assured them that his government 'needed the support of the Army'. Three of the other commissars confirmed this. On the other hand, Emil Barth, one of the two Independent Socialists in the government, demanded Groener's immediate arrest, and 'if he had been able would have had great pleasure in carrying out his threat'.[8]

In the Congress of Councils the incessant, shrill campaign of the Independents and Spartacists seriously backfired: the Congress voted to hold a general election for a National Assembly. In no way could the 'masses' in Berlin's streets outvote the national masses in the polling booths. Social theory could not save them. Violence outside the Reichstag did not work. Demonstrations in Treptower Park did not provide the number. On the 21st, the burial of the victims of the Chausseestrasse gun battle brought out 'a contingent of Red sailors, then several thousand men and women walking in tidy ranks and carrying large numbers of red flags and banners'[9] – but this was hardly an electoral force in a national poll.

The debate in the Congress had been between those who favoured a constituent parliamentary assembly, which would set up the institutions of a democratic republic, and the partisans of the 'Russian system', the 'council system'. 'All power to the workers' and soldiers' councils!' proclaimed the *Rote Fahne*, echoing the Leninist line. It regarded the Congress of Workers' and Soldiers' Councils as 'the highest organ of legislative and executive power'. But this Congress voted for national elections. Not only did its members approve of the democratic method, but they pushed for an early deadline. '*Mitte Januar – nicht Mitte Februar!*' ('Mid-January, not mid-February!') became the slogan of the Majority Socialists in the Congress. The election date was set for 19 January.[10]

Thus, like the United States and Britain, Germany embarked on an immediate post-war election. France held back because her government, with an easy majority in parliament, wanted the peace settled first – and fast. The United States had elections because of her political calendar. Britain, where the old party system was shattered, was forced to the polls because an election was overdue. Germany chose to have one in the name of the 'November Revolution'. Of the three campaigns, Germany's was the shortest, being limited to less than a month. It would be a campaign stained with blood.

2

The sailors of Berlin, spearhead of the Revolution, had not received their Christmas bonus. On 21 December the government directed the military governor, Otto Wels, to pay the People's Naval Division 80,000 marks, 'but only upon the evacuation of the Schloss and the delivery of all keys to the city commandant'. It further warned that after 1 January payment would be made to no more than 600 men. Wels, in his Kommandatur across the bridge from the Schloss, prepared the sum in cash and waited. Nobody came.

For several days the Spartacists, who had been using the sailors' Schloss and Marstall as headquarters, had been running a campaign against the 'Ebert–Wels blood bond', blaming it for the shooting on 6 December.[11] The People's Naval Division would have nothing to do with General Wels and his 'Suppe guard'. The pavement of Unter den Linden was a kind of no man's land separating sailors from soldiers, though shoppers and promenaders would traipse up and down it, unmindful that their presence was obstructing the progress of the German Revolution. The sailors would deal only with the Spartacists and the Independent Socialists. Instead of going to the Kommandatur, they decided to appeal to Emil Barth at the Reichs Chancellery.

On Monday afternoon, 23 December, a troop of them burst into the conference chamber just as the People's Commissars were discussing whether to stay in Berlin or not. Ebert, like Adolphe Thiers in March 1871, wanted to pull out of the capital and build up his forces at either Weimar or Rudolfstadt. Barth accused his colleagues of attempting to sabotage the Revolution by turning the Reich, with the support of the Army, against Berlin. Then the sailors came in. The commissars assured them they could have the money as long as they delivered the keys of the Schloss. So off went the sailors. They returned, fully armed, carrying a large case that contained the Kaiser's keys, which they placed in front of Barth in his office – and demanded the money. Barth said he didn't have it: the money was held by Wels. The sailors would have nothing to do with Wels. Barth telephoned Wels and advised him to hand over the money. 'First, the sailors must bring me the keys,' replied Wels tersely, 'without which I'm not giving a pfennig.' The sailors left Barth's office furious. Within a few moments it was announced that the Reichs Chancellery was under siege. No one could leave; no one could enter. The sailors took over the telephone exchange.[12]

But they did not know of Ebert's secret line to Kassel, No. 998. Ebert looked at the black telephone for a moment, and then dialled. Major von Schleicher, Groener's assistant, answered. 'Herr Major,' said Ebert, 'you have always said that in such a situation as has now arisen, you would help. The moment has come to act.' Schleicher assured him that General Lequis and his trustworthy troops at Potsdam, south-west of Berlin, would immediately come and deliver him. 'Perhaps, after so many lost occasions, we have at last the chance to deal a coup on the radicals,' he added. Within an hour, as darkness gathered, Lequis's force boarded trains for Berlin.[13]

In the meantime, the sailors decided that they were going to get their money. Around six or seven hundred collected at the Schloss and began to march on the Kommandatur. Passers-by, mindful of the events of 6 December, discreetly disappeared when they saw ranks of mariners, the red cockades in their flat, round caps, tramp across the bridge.

An armoured car trundled out in front of the Kommandatur. *'Nicht schiessen, Kameraden!'* cried out one of the sailors at the head of the column. The armoured car replied with a tat! tat! tat! Machine-gun fire rang out from the University. More than a dozen men fell, wounded or dead, within instants.[14]

The sailors were no longer looking for money: they were looking for Wels. A number of them managed to enter the building and dragged him out, along with two of his assistants. Already looking very battered, the three hostages were pushed into a car and driven up the street, scattered with the wounded and the dead, to the Schloss. A dull, grey night's mist had descended upon the city.

Ebert received a call from Major von Harbou in Potsdam. Lequis's force, he said, was on its way with the intention of dissolving the People's Naval Division – by force if necessary. Ebert responded that the government had given no such order. The major replied with the same formula that governments in Berlin had heard throughout the war: 'Supreme Command is taking action under its own risk and peril. Should the Regime in some way attempt to prevent the planned measures this will now have no effect on the course of events.'[15]

Under the cover of night some of Lequis's forces entered the Chancellery. Others could be heard trooping on the street outside.

There followed a three-way negotiation between the government, the sailors and the soldiers, with fighting threatening to break out inside the Chancellery at any moment. Barth went down to the front gate and ordered the soldiers to withdraw. They told him they took no orders except from Ebert. Their commanders were shown into Ebert's office. 'If you want to do battle,' said Ebert, 'then do it here right in front of my eyes.' The officers were utterly baffled. 'Whatever happens, we have to put an end to this sailors' business,' replied one of them. 'The time for negotiation has passed.'[16]

By eleven that night both the sailors and the soldiers had withdrawn from the Chancellery. Ebert left immediately to take a car to the Schloss, where another battlefield was taking shape. In the square before the front gate he clambered on to the top of the car and, with soldiers on the ground and sailors in the windows, he made another speech in favour of peace. It was a Shakespearean soliloquy before the castle siege – though presented in the unvarnished language of a Schwabian saddler. 'Enough blood has flowed,' he pleaded. 'And there is no just reason for German citizens to tear each other apart in a civil war.' Amid cries and laughter Ebert returned to the Chancellery.[17]

Groener telephoned at around midnight. 'The Field Marshal and I are at the end of our patience,' he said with his slow, southern-German accent. 'This type of negotiation of yours is undermining the fighting spirit of the last troops faithful to the officers.' He affirmed his determination to give these forces the chance to dissolve the People's Naval Division.[18]

As dawn crept in on Christmas Eve the defenders of the Schloss could detect the emerging outlines of troops equipped with machine-guns in the Lustgarten, along with field cannon on the Schloss Bridge and out on the Werdererscher Market. At 7.30, when it was still barely light, five delegates of the government forces came forward, bearing a white flag, to deliver an ultimatum. If the People's Naval Division did not surrender in the next ten minutes, the troops before them would attack.[19]

This was the class war of the German Revolution: soldier against sailor, the forces of the front against the forces of the rear, now both withdrawn to the national capital.

The 'Battle of Christmas Eve' was a baroque affair. Every half an hour or so there would be a pause and sailors would come forward to conduct a little negotiation and then return to their positions to continue the fighting. During the interludes, people would break through the barriers on the Linden and on the east banks of the Spree to inspect the damage or to take part in small political gatherings. Speeches were made as bullets flew about.

The cannon fired their first 7.5 cm shells at around eight o'clock. The first hole was pierced in Portal No. 4, just next to the balcony where Kaiser Wilhelm had told the crowds, at the outbreak of the war, that 'Germany no longer has any political parties.' By 8.30 the cannon had scored about twenty hits. Machine-guns were being fired from the side of the Crown Prince's Palace and the Lustgarten. Sailors replied with machine-guns mounted at the windows; several used rifles from the roofs. At nine o'clock the first white flag was seen, waved by a civilian from the main gate of the Marstall. Streams of women and children, who had been staying with the sailors, came out. By 9.30 the machine-gunners were at it again. Only three of the artillery pieces were at work; with more and more people appearing, the fourth couldn't manoeuvre. Hand grenades smashed down the main gate of the Schloss and five storm troopers entered. They fired their light machine-guns and threw a few bombs, thus destroying the ex-Kaiser's main living quarters, but they found the place virtually empty – most of the sailors had now moved back to the Marstall, where they were receiving reinforcements from Eichhorn's security men (who were, however, officially neutral). The storm troopers took three prisoners and returned to their lines.

At ten o'clock another white flag appeared, and this time there was some serious negotiation with government officials. An agreement was drawn up that the People's Naval Division would receive their 'entitled' 80,000 marks as soon as they had laid down their arms and left the Schloss; that those sailors not resident in Berlin would leave the city in the next forty-nine hours; and that Wels and his two assistants would be released immediately.[20]

The three hostages, their clothes torn, were escorted out of the Schloss by a detachment of Eichhorn's security forces and taken to the University on the Linden. Wels, who had faced three mock executions that night, was a mere spectre of himself; he had lost his military bearing; his hands were trembling.

Thick groups of people gathered before the Schloss. Many sailors were among them. Several well-known figures of the Spartakusbund were also there. At one moment a huge grey truck rolled in from Alexanderplatz. Up leapt a slim, bespectacled figure to commend the mariners of Berlin: they had brought the Revolution into the city, and if they were forced to leave the Revolution would end. He cursed the Scheidemänner and the Majority Socialists for backing the counter-revolution. Red flags were waved and shots rang out.

A full-scale battle was once again under way by eleven. More holes were punctured in the masonry; statues and curlicues were shattered.

At midday there was another pause. Crowds poured in to have a first look at the torn-up asphalt, the splintered trees in the Lustgarten and the ruined façade of the Schloss. A young sailor got up on a makeshift pedestal and shouted, 'They gave us an ultimatum of ten minutes to leave the Schloss and to be led off to jail. But we're still here!'[21]

There was total confusion. On the battlefields of the front, soldiers looked for a gap in the hedges, a dip in the hill; here the obstacle was moving people. A few machine-guns were manoeuvred into positions but the gunners didn't know where to point them. By one o'clock that afternoon most of the government forces had melted into the crowd. 'With that, the effect of the entry of the troops had definitely ended,' wrote Groener in his memoirs.[22] He blamed it on Christmas. Indeed, the traditional Berlin Christmas Fair was doing good business as the battle proceeded. Christmas and battle: it did not presage a secure future for either the Regime or Supreme Command.

3

If Britain's 1920s were born in wartime London, Germany's Weimar culture – with its odd mixture of poverty and wealth, despair and hope, violence and beauty – was already recognizable by the time the soldiers got home to Berlin for Christmas 1918. 'The city looked like a grey corpse made of stone,' thought George Grosz on his return from the front. His descriptions, like his paintings and sketches, epitomized a whole era: 'There were cracks in all the walls. Plaster and paint were crumbling. The dead, dirty, hollow windows seemed still to be mourning those many for whom they had looked in vain.' All the same, 'I threw myself madly into life, and teamed up with people who were searching for a way out from this absolute nothingness.'[23]

It was one of Grosz's friends, Count Harry Kessler, who had noted the lively state of the Christmas Fair while artillery roared before the Schloss. The street traders were selling indoor fireworks, gingerbread and silver tinsel on Friedrichstrasse, as the hurdy-gurdies thumped out their tunes. The jewellers' shops on Unter den Linden – on the boundary of the battle – were 'brightly lit and glittering'. In rich Leipziger Strasse, a few yards away, 'the usual Christmas crowds thronged the big stores'. Anton Fischer, one of the three hostages released that morning, spoke of the madness of the festival season: 'Day and night, senseless shooting, partly from exuberation, partly from fear. Berlin lived, danced, drank and celebrated.' Berlin's school authorities extended the Christmas vacation by a week – to mid-January.[24]

The restaurants remained open. There was the odd armed robbery. On Christmas Day Spartacus held a demonstration in front of the Victory Column and marched down Siegesallee to the Schloss; a handful of men, with their guns, then headed for Belle-Alliance Platz, where they took over the offices of *Vorwärts*, the leading newspaper of the Majority Socialists. 'Long live the revolutionary sailors' division, the revolutionary proletariat, the international socialist world revolution! All power to the Workers' and Soldiers' Councils! Down with the Ebert–Scheidemann government! Arms for the workers!' declared the Christmas number, printed on red paper. The workers at *Vorwärts* did not take kindly to their new managers, and reinstalled the old ones the next day. The consequence of this brief takeover was that *Vorwärts*, which had run socialist propaganda throughout the war, became the most virulently anti-Spartacist newspaper in town. 'The despicable actions of Liebknecht and Rosa Luxemburg soil the Revolution and endanger all of its achievements,' commented one of its editors a few days later. 'These brutal beasts . . . want to demolish and destroy with lies, slander and violence everything which dares oppose them.'[25]

The *Lokal-Anzeiger*, for once left alone by the revolutionaries, called it a 'red Christmas'. 'Berlin celebrates not in golden festive brilliance, but under a red, storm-taunting sky.' On the streets the crowds were shabbily dressed, the men in a semi-military attire that could mix a civilian pair of trousers with an army jacket, a torn sweater with a military cap, or an open trenchcoat with mufti. Many had knapsacks on their backs. Some hobbled along on sticks. 'They stand together in groups with earnest faces'; they had 'the countenance of hungry hyenas'. The advertising pillars were covered with red posters. Christmas trees with red bows stood in the flower-bedecked shop windows. 'Here is a coffin decorated with a red pennant; over there are workers with small red flags in their hands; Christmas trees are on the streets and in the squares.' In the warehouses 'a thousand men queue up to buy a couple of honey cakes or toys for the children'.[26]

The skies *were* red and stormy on Christmas Eve. But on Christmas Day, as in Paris and London, the sun glowed. The first thing Berliners wanted to see was the damage at the Schloss and the Marstall. They swarmed across the bridges and into the surrounding squares to inspect the crumpled pilasters, the pierced walls and most especially the great shell hole above the broken balcony where the Kaiser had addressed the Reich on 4 August 1914. The sailors even gave a few guided tours in the Hall of Pillars, where the large painting had been torn to shreds by an exploding grenade, and through the Kaiser's ruined living quarters, most of whose contents, including private correspondence with Queen Victoria, were now being hawked about the streets.[27]

Street trade had never been so intense in Berlin. The war had taken the hawkers and penny musicians off the streets of London. In Berlin it had had the opposite effect. All the old rules regarding fairs and marketing were broken. The barriers separating residential from commercial zones disappeared. The policing was non-existent. Now even in the richest areas stalls were set up selling army clothes, shoes, women's stockings, garters, sweets and cigars. In the corridors and lobbies of the apartment houses you could buy shaving soap and old wellington boots. The organ-grinders churned out melodies on the corner of the avenue, and kites and coloured paper windmills shimmered in the breeze. 'Street trade has declared itself sovereign and rules Berlin,' reported the *Lokal-Anzeiger* on 24 December.

Was there famine? There was a rapid increase in infant mortality, especially among illegitimate infants (of whom there was an unusually high proportion – Lieutenant Ames, apparently ignoring the natural tempo of human gestation, explained this was due to the attitude 'I am attempting to have a good time, because I am trying to forget').[28] In prisons, orphanages and mental asylums – the institutions where rationing was followed to the letter – mortality soared. But Berlin was not starving. Nor were any of the urban centres in Germany. Contrary to the dire predictions of Herbert Hoover, and several specialists inside Germany, famine in Europe was limited to pocketed, disfavoured regions within Belgium (which had been robbed of her economic infrastructure), to Austria (which had been pushed beyond her limits), to the western reaches of Russia and the Ukraine, and to parts of the Balkans (which had always suffered from a degree of isolation unknown elsewhere on the Continent). Despite the war and the effects of blockade, most people of Europe's great northern plain managed to feed themselves.[29]

The great wheel of the modern economy – as if in defiance of war, huge population shifts and military defeat – just kept on turning. Dislocation there was, but not collapse. The food chain between town and country had been severely strained, but not destroyed. There were markets. The production of goods and services in the cities had been held up, but not halted. There was movement. The agreement forged immediately after the Armistice between Hugo Stinnes, the great industrialist, and Carl Legien, the great unionist, held. There was fighting in the streets, the Revolutionary Shop Stewards spoke angry words, and, under their influence, the big metal industries went on strike. But it was not actually class war. Eduard Bernstein, the socialist 'revisionist' who had scandalized the Marxists of his party in the 1890s, stood before the government on 12 December and stated categorically, 'We still have a bourgeois economy.' It was ill, but hardly dead.

The statistics of that time are not reliable, because the administrative machinery which collected them was not working. If one is to believe the information gathered by law-abiding trade unions of Germany, unemployment in the Reich, at less than 2 per cent of the labour force in November 1918, rose to a peak of 6.6 per cent in January, 1919.

'Given the enormity of the labour-market problem, the formal percentage of unemployed was remarkably low, even during the worst months of January and February 1919,' one specialist of the period has recently observed.[30] The 'labour-market problem', faced by all belligerents but particularly severe in Germany because of the speed at which demobilization was accomplished and because wartime government controls had been stricter than elsewhere, was her reconversion to a peace economy; 'one cannot for instance simply convert a grenade factory to the building of railway carriages', said Colonel Joseph Koeth of the Reich's Demobilization Office.[31] It was a local problem, and it was especially Berlin's problem. Official reports of the time estimated that there were 80,000 unemployed in the city at the New Year; historians today put the figure at over a quarter of a million. The burden of unemployment relief, based on a government decree of 13 November, fell on the municipal authorities. This is what so annoyed Berlin's Mayor, Adolf Wermuth. The Reich authorities, he complained in a letter to Commissar Ebert on 12 December, 'are very free in providing lectures on how the communities are supposed to carry out the tasks assigned them', but were making little effort to redirect workers out of the city to where they were needed – in coal mining and agriculture.[32]

By the standards of the age, the relief benefits handed out by Berlin's municipal authorities were extraordinarily generous. The government had learned a lesson from Russia and the Bolshevik *coup d'état* of November 1917. It took the opposite course from Kerensky's fated provisional government: for the People's Commissars in the Reichs Chancellery it would be peace, bread and work *at any price*. 'The presses are working well,' the Reichsbank assured them. 'I do not believe that the workers will be inclined to hold back in their demands,' Bernstein warned the government in mid-December. 'From where will come the billions demanded? They can only come from an increased use of the printing presses.' He spelt out the danger of a phenomenon called 'inflation': 'We get an unhealthy development of the market, an unhealthy development of wages, and these are things that make the demands, as they are presented, appear extraordinarily question-able to me.' But for the government the risks of a coup from the extreme Left – of a *Putsch*, as the German slang at the time put it – were too awful to contemplate. In the first two and a half months of its existence it had forked out 16.5 billion marks without any legal authorization, for there was no parliament to approve a budget. Prices edged up. Inflation, which had its origin in the way Germany had financed her war, accelerated – just as Bernstein had predicted. By January wholesale prices were, on average, more than two and a half times higher than before the war. There was a lot of talk of tax – on war profits, on capital gains, on higher incomes, on inheritance – but there was no effective tax. Relief benefits, calculated on the basis of the local cost of living, spiralled. The municipal authorities negotiated with the unions and the councils: let the capitalists pay! By January Berlin had the best-paid unemployed force in the Reich. The sailors making demands at the Schloss were representative of workers only in the sense that they headed not a violent labour movement, but an expensive one. Where had the 125,000 marks they had received in November come from? What was the origin of the 80,000 marks Wels kept in his office? The Reichsbank had printed them.[33]

Administrators and economists began complaining of a general disincli-nation to work among the population of Berlin – a perception which, though it hardly corresponded to the usual portrayal of the national character, contained more than a grain of truth. There were 2,000 jobs on offer at construction sites out in Grunewald, but fewer than 500 men turned up. There was no enthusiasm to leave for the mines of the Ruhr or of Silesia, and, Colonel Koeth ruefully admitted, 'The city people do not want to go to the country and the farmers do not want to take the city workers.'[34]

One sector, however, was ready to take them on: their former employer, the Imperial Army. '*Zu den Waffen!*', 'To arms!', one could read advertised at the top and the bottom of the newspaper columns, 'report immediately for entry into the Volunteer Regiment . . .' It could be the Reinhard Regiment in Moabit, the Suppe Regiment on Fasanenstrasse, the Huelsen Regiment in the Potsdam Beer Gardens, or the regiments collecting out in Zossen and Döberitz – one had a luxury of choice by January. Demobilization of the Imperial Army was officially decreed on 31 December, but after the Battle of Christmas Eve the Army had already ceased to exist. The future of the German Army lay in the 'Free Corps'.

Groener had given Ebert another telephone call on Christmas Eve, to find out what his plans were. Ebert replied that he intended to evacuate everyone from the Chancellery except the door porter. As for himself, he was going over to a friend's home to catch a few days' sleep. If the Spartacists took over the building, all they would find would be an empty house.

But the Spartacists celebrated Christmas in the *Vorwärts* building. Ebert slept in the Chancellery. Groener enjoyed a cheerful Christmas Day among his staff at Wilhelmshöhe Castle. All the men were full of hope: 'The volunteer forces were increasing in number.'[35]

4

The war came home at Christmas; it also marched east. News during the week leading up to the New Year was dominated by the fall of Riga, in Latvia, to a Bolshevik army, and of fighting in Posen, or Poznań as the Poles called the town, which most Berliners still assumed to be a part of Prussia.

'Los von Preussen!' 'Separate from Prussia! That is now the battle cry to the south and the west and even in the north,' wrote a reporter on 27 December. '[But] to speak of Prussia is to refer especially to the eastern lands: who knows where these eastern lands of the Reich now lie?'[36] One of the reasons why the Congress in Berlin was in such a hurry to have national elections was to preserve what was left of the Reich – and in particular Prussia, which had brought Germany together in the first place. The west bank of the Rhine, gained by Prussia after the Napoleonic wars, was now occupied by the Allies, and there were fears that, encouraged by the French, the area would declare itself the independent 'Republic of the Rhineland and Westphalia'; but at least the November Armistice had defined the frontiers of the occupied zone. There was a strong possibility that Bavaria might break away from the Reich; but in Berlin this was considered an internal issue. More worrisome was the future of 'old Prussia' itself – the Baltic borderlands, the Polish colonies, Silesia, and Danzig.

The Armistice was not at all clear on the matter. Its convoluted article on the 'Eastern Frontiers of Germany' required that German troops withdraw to frontiers 'as they existed on 1 August 1914' as 'soon as the Allies shall think the moment suitable, having regard to the internal situation of these territories'.[37] Germany's earlier, punitive, Treaty of Brest-Litovsk with Russia was annulled. The word 'Poland' was studiously avoided. In other words: Germany must withdraw from Eastern Europe, but to what point we don't know, when we don't know, and if she could consult the Allies before doing so, that would be useful.

The problem that both the Allies and Germany faced was that Europe east of the Reich's undefined frontiers was still at war. Russia's civil war between Bolsheviks and anti-Bolsheviks was spreading across frontiers. The Baltic states – Estonia, Latvia and Lithuania – reaffirmed their independence, which had been at least officially granted by Germany nine months earlier; they sent their delegates to Paris. A squadron from Britain's Grand Fleet, which had never been so active, cruised off their coast. German Supreme Command set up *Grenzschutz Ost*, or 'Frontier Defence Force East', with its own command system. Observers in Berlin could be forgiven if they thought the Allies secretly wanted them to maintain arms in the East.

Yet the Germans' withdrawal here was as precipitous, and every bit as dramatic, as it had been in the West. The German forces fell apart. Discipline disappeared. Germany had nearly half a million troops to pull out of the Ukraine. The initial plan was to retreat across Poland, but Piłsudski's government in Warsaw – for some very good reasons – forbade them entry. So they had to work their way through Lithuania to East Prussia and the Baltic. As it retreated across the sandy plains and forests of Latvia, the German Eighth Army, which had been within thirty miles of Petrograd the previous March, disintegrated into bands; some of them were run by soldiers' councils, others by local German warlords – 'little Wallensteins' as the new Minister of National Defence, Gustav Noske, called them.[38]

Of the three new Baltic states, the best protected was Estonia, to the north, thanks to a ribbon of lakes that separated it from the advancing Bolshevik forces. So the Russians skirted it and marched instead into Latvia. Latvia's Prime Minister, Karlis Ulmanis, a former high-school teacher in Nebraska, USA, had organized an efficient little group of sharpshooters, the Lettish Rifles, but they were no match for Trotsky's Red Army. Ulmanis appealed to the Allies for help. But, as Lloyd George had pointed out, you couldn't march a navy across the plain; and, anyway, the Allies did not want to be seen fighting on the side of the Germans. Ulmanis was invited aboard the flagship of Britain's Baltic Squadron and the commander explained to him that no help was coming; he would do best to come to some sort of agreement with the Germans. The port of Riga fell to the Russians. Ulmanis signed a treaty with Germany. Its terms, in the Reich's tradition, were crushing: the Germans would serve under their own officers; there would be no increase in Latvian forces without a corresponding increase in German forces; the Germans, after a month's service, would automatically be entitled to Latvian citizenship. The story was even put about that each one of them would receive ninety acres of free land – a great motivation for volunteers in the Fatherland.[39]

To the south and west of the Baltic states lay another new state; undefined Poland, which had succeeded in the past four years in being both an enemy and a friend of the Allies. Since the Armistice terms had not explicitly recognized their claims, the Poles had to act quickly; they did not want the peace in Paris to turn out to be another Vienna. By the end of December they were at war with all their neighbours.

With the aid of his former German jailers, Piłsudski had established a dictatorship in Warsaw. But this was not the only Polish 'government'. Early in the war, Roman Dmowski had set up in Russian Poland the 'Polish National Committee', and after the fall of the Tsar he had moved it to Paris, where it was treated as a government. The four million Polish residents in the United States had also organized themselves. Their leader, Ignace Paderewski, one of the grandest interpreters of Chopin of all time and himself a composer of works for the piano and orchestra, arrived in Posen on Christmas Day 1918 and, under the winter's sun, headed a procession down the main street before cheering Poles and waving red-and-white flags. Posen was the headquarters of the Prussian 5th Army Corps. A regiment of grenadiers, recently returned from the Western Front, demanded that the flags be torn down. There was scuffling. On 26 December the Germans fired on a procession of children that had come to welcome Paderewski. Within twenty-four hours Posen was in a state of siege.

Nobody knew what the answer would be to the Polish problem. 'The German government was paralysed by bouts of impotence,' said Matthias Erzberger concerning policy in Poland even during the war. It was Count Harry Kessler who, having accompanied Piłsudski from his prison in Magdeburg to Berlin, acted as German minister to Warsaw after the Armistice. He found the country in a 'state of gang warfare', where 'our soldiers are living like savages, killing people, committing arson, and so on'. Diplomatic relations between Piłsudski's government and Germany were finally broken off on 15 December and Kessler, in perpetual fear of his own assassination, left as fast as he could for Berlin.[40]

Poland was another nation that held swift post-Armistice elections: it was the only way to solve the dilemma of her three 'governments'. Piłsudski, Paderewski and Dmowski united in the sense that they became, respectively, Chief of State, Prime Minister and Minister of Foreign Affairs. But the Prime Minister ignored the Chief of State, and the Chief of State followed his own policy. As for the Minister of Foreign Affairs, he remained in Paris. Piłsudski by January had built up an army of 100 infantry battalions, 70 cavalry squadrons and 80 batteries of artillery – Lloyd George's promise to abolish all conscript armies would be a hard one to honour.

Wars today are not declared and they are often ended without treaty. Europe's Great War was declared on most fronts and it was concluded with the Treaty; but the difficulty the statesmen of all nations faced was that the war in the East had not ended.

On Monday, 6 January, as Berlin once more stared into the abyss of civil war, Colonel Koeth of the Demobilization Office despairingly concluded one of his meetings with the remark, 'Things will have to come to the point where each person will have to reach for his rifle so that we can at first give ourselves some breathing space in the East.' Worried about the consequences of local unemployment, Koeth had unwittingly hit the nail on the head: the German civil war and the situation in the East were related. The search for a little 'breathing space', the promise of land, the desire for adventure had combined with a determination to stamp out 'the band of troublemakers doing mischief in Berlin' to fill up the ranks of the 'Free Corps'. Its members were ready to fight both the enemy without and the enemy within, to wage a war in which they regarded themselves as the revolutionaries: 'We are simply moved by love for the Fatherland,' declared

the Berlin Horse Guard Rifleman's Division, one of the earliest manifes-
tations of the Free Corps in December; 'we are the dependents of the Regime
and the enemies of every counter-revolution.'[41]

In the weekend that preceded Koeth's troubled remarks, Ebert and his
Defence Minister, Noske, had visited the military camp of Zossen, on the
outskirts of Berlin. Four thousand well-equipped, well-drilled troops strut-
ted before them on the cold parade ground; they were General Georg von
Maercker's Volunteer Rifles, the very best of the early Free Corps and a
model for all that followed. It was as if the Army had sprouted up again
from the snows. Noske slapped Ebert on the back: 'You can relax now.
Everything will be all right!'[42]

The idea of forming voluntary corps out of elite front-line troops came
to Groener in Spa, during the last weeks of the Western war. It was first
put into practice when Supreme Command sent in the 'innoculators' to
preserve order in the retreating army, and had its ancestry in Ludendorff's
'storm troopers', so effective in his spring offensive. But the guiding spirit
of the Free Corps was born earlier, in the generation that grew up in Germany at the turn of the century – the war generation.

Throughout Europe there had been an explosion of new art forms during
this period, but nothing was so radical, so militant in its rejection of liberal
bourgeois society – its 'sham' of religion, its 'triviality' of politics, the 'life-
lessness' of education, the 'sentimentality' of commercialized literature, the
'trashy' art, the 'mechanical' drama, the 'repressed' relationship between
the sexes in and outside marriage – as the German youth movements of
the 1890s and early 1900s. The historian Modris Ekstein has even argued that
at the heart of the Great War was their war of liberation, their *Befreiungskrieg*,
against the Victorian hypocrisy and conservatism of England: that England
was Germany's main enemy, not Russia, or France.[43]

The link between Nordic nudes singing songs and making love in the
forest and the furious volunteers of the Free Corps is not self-evident –
many members of the *Wandervögel* (the 'Roaming Birds') and Mount Cenis
were pacifists, jailed for their activities. And yet they had the same mystic
fellowship of the *Volk*, the same corporative spirit. They called in the same
irrational, fervent manner for a leader, *der Führer*. They sang the same song
of the freebooters, '*Das Landsknechtslied*'. The youth movements despised
the convenient, mechanical habits of the bourgeoisie, *das Bürgertum*; the
volunteers hated the rear, *die Etappe*: 'Yes, and then we have the Rear!! The
Rear lies far, far behind the Front and there is plenty of everything there:
plenty of comfort, food, conveniences, peace – all the enjoyments of life
combined in that one little enticing word: The Rear! ... We called them
"Chair-bound goldbricks" ["*Etappenhengste*"] and the word was never
spoken without an undertone of contempt.'[44] The youth of the forest said
the same of the townsfolk. These were not the bitter words of England's
war poets, raised on Hardy and Kipling; or the French *normalien* who went

to war and returned home disillusioned. They were more radical. More violent. And, if one responds that the pacifist antidote in Germany was Erich Maria Remarque's *All Quiet on the Western Front*, one might read that book again and see in it the very same cult of youth, the cult of the soldier, the cult of death, as in the writings of Ernst Jünger and Franz Schauwecker.

The Free Corps were recruited among the 'new men' from the front, 'strong and packed with purpose'. They were the freebooters, guards, captains, lieutenants and willing mercenaries whom Ludendorff's failed offensives in the West had left standing in the streets wondering what to do next. Maercker, for instance, had had no difficulty at all in finding, and selecting, the men for his Volunteer Rifles. The problem was supplies, for each company had to have its own machine-gun and trench-mortar section, like Ludendorff's storm troopers of March. Maercker had to rush from one military depot to another in order to beat the councils and the Spartacists, who were busy looting them. But he found what he needed, and more; he added heavy and light artillery, flame-throwers, armoured cars and even aircraft. Volunteers would receive daily pay of between 30 and 50 marks, and a daily meal of at least 200 grams of meat and 75 grams of butter; they were guaranteed pensions. The government paid for all of this – by turning to the Reichsbank's printing presses.

Some likened the Free Corps to the volunteer 'training corps' that had grown up in Prussia after her defeat at Jena in 1806. Napoleon in 1807 had strictly limited the number of conscripts Prussia could recruit into her Army, but he hadn't counted on the volunteers.

5

Lest one forget, a national election campaign was under way. In addition to the fighting in the streets, the recruiting in the beer gardens, the Christmas fairs and the trading, a number of political rallies, representing the various parties, took place in Berlin. Theoretical articles appeared in the press, many on the problem of 'socialization' (or 'socialistization' as as some of the more conservative papers called it). Academics played a leading role in the developing debate.

The franchise had been determined by the October reforms pushed through the Reichstag immediately after receipt of Wilson's third note (which had stated that the United States would not deal with 'the military masters and the monarchical autocrats of Germany'); it was a part of Prince Max's 'revolution from above'. All German citizens over the age of twenty-one – male and female – were granted the vote. Ebert's government subsequently introduced a system of proportional representation on a regional level to replace the old system of single-member constituencies. German suffrage was now wider than in Britain, France or the United States.

A tentative draft of the constitution, to be presented to the National

Assembly for approval, was delivered to Ebert on 3 January by Professor Hugo Preuss and his colleagues sitting in the Ministry of the Interior. They were mostly German liberals, not socialists. Their main concern was to save the unity of the Reich. Among the members of Preuss's committee was Professor Max Weber, the Beethoven of sociology. Weber's wonderfully rich studies of ancient religions in the Middle East had revealed to him the idea of 'charisma', the gift of leadership granted by grace of God to certain individuals universally recognized for their talents. Weber would have encouraged Germany's natural, charismatic leader by having a President of the Republic chosen by popular plebiscite and granted 'emergency powers', which he would use if the unity of the Riech were under threat. Preuss, however, was more of a parliamentarian. Even during the war he had opposed the authoritarian nature of the Prussian-German state and urged, instead, a constitution more like that adopted by the French in 1790, which had given primacy to a national assembly and had divided the country into equal administrative regions as an antidote to provincialism. Preuss's draft of 3 January had the President elected by parliament (though keeping his 'emergency powers') and the Reich divided into sixteen equal regions; most remarkably, this included the division of Prussia. Ebert looked across his warring frontiers and asked that all territorial matters be excluded from future drafts. Then a committee of representatives of the twenty-five states of the former imperial Reich was brought in – a guarantee of continuity with the old order. No one would yet dare advocate restoration of the Kaiser (such talk returned only in the months immediately before the rise of Hitler). But Germany's many special-interest groups, unions, corporations, local authorities and administrators pushed for the preservation of their old privileges. Added to *ersatz* foods and *ersatz* troops, one began talking of an *Esatzkaisertum* – a 'substitute imperial regime'.

Much ink has been expended on the nature of the new franchise and the constitution; but Berlin's real problem, like that of all Germany, was the political culture that received them.

There were groups that had no intention of participating in a democratic election. After the Congress of Workers' and Soldiers' Councils had committed itself to the process, and especially after the Battle of Christmas Eve, the various factions of the extreme Left were at open war with the government, though they could not agree on a common policy among themselves. Quite the opposite. By New Year one was left looking at fragments of fragments. The Spartacists split from the Independents. The Independents split from the Majority Socialists. The Revolutionary Shop Stewards decided to go their own way.

The *Rote Fahne* assailed 'Ebert the hangman' for his bloody, counter-revolutionary deeds at Christmas and called out the masses to demonstrate at the funeral of the victims on 28 December: 'Proletarians! Men and women of labour! Long live the world revolution!' The black-and-silver coffins, decorated with wreaths of white and red flowers, were mounted on imperial hearses and driven down the Linden; the red roses stacked on biers before the Schloss looked like the hanging gardens of Babylon.

Vorwärts, on the same day, declared war on the 'bloody dictatorship of the Spartacist League' and asked the people of Germany to fight against 'the terror of a minority'. At the instigation of the Spartacists, eighty-seven delegates and sixteen 'guests' – including Karl Radek, the Russian representative – met in the banqueting hall of the Prussian Landtag, where, on New Year's Day 1919, the 'Communist Party of Germany/Spartacist League' (KPD) was born; it counted, nationwide, about a thousand members, and in Berlin no more than fifty. During the three days that the Founding Congress was in session, it voted to boycott the elections, endorsed Lenin's proposition that the Revolution should continue with the aim of establishing the 'dictatorship of the councils', and very nearly passed a resolution pulling out of every trade union in the country – the trade unions, it was stated, were opposed to the 'council system'. They were. The Revolutionary Shop Stewards, for their part, refused to join the Communists because they disapproved of Liebknecht's 'revolutionary gymnastics'.[45]

Small, grey-haired Rosa Luxemburg attempted to give the Congress a few history lessons based on the unadulterated seventy-year-old principles of Marx and Engels, 'point by point' and prior to the revisionism introduced 'in the year 1895'. In Communist canonical writings on the 'German Revolution', a distinction is made between well-trained revolutionary Marxists in the party and the romantic 'putschist' and 'anarchist' factions, who had learned nothing since the days of Blanqui and the failed Paris Commune of 1871. The 'tactical error' made by the German Communists in the New Year of 1919, it is argued, was that they failed to take heed of the principle of 'democratic centralism', that is, listen to their theoretically trained masters, and chose the route of anarchism instead. The lesson Luxemburg gave in the Prussian banqueting hall was that the 'first phase' of the German Revolution, the November phase, had simply overthrown one capitalist government and replaced it by another. To bring about the 'second phase', the proletarian phase, 'the Ebert–Scheidemann government must be undermined through social and revolutionary mass actions step by step'; she voted with the minority supporting participation in the national elections so as to 'take the National Assembly by storm', yet at the same time advocated a break with the trade unions in order to establish Communist-run 'factory councils' in their place. These would form the pillars of the new revolutionary regime, which Luxemburg said could be accomplished with 'tremendous *speed*'. But, she added with the tone of a saint, 'who among us counts and who cares if our lives last long enough to see this happen?'

Luxemburg's two-phase version of history was consciously modelled after the February and October 'revolutions' in Russia. There was, however, one critical difference: Lenin in 1917 could play the peace card; the

Spartacists in 1919 could not. Their whole campaign was limited in its aspirations to the 'dictatorship of the council system' as opposed to the 'bourgeois democracy' that would necessarily develop out of national elections. This did not make them popular in Germany.

The distinction between Independent Socialists and Spartacists was not clear to anyone living in Berlin in early 1919. Some of the Independents, like Eduard Bernstein and Karl Kautsky, were more moderate than many of the Majority Socialists. Others could be found out on the revolutionary fringe. As with the Spartacists, the peace in the West had undermined their *raison d'être*. One could no longer argue that war was purely a capitalist affair: the war in the East was being prosecuted by Communist troops. Most Independents hailed the Russian success at Riga and agreed with Rosa Luxemburg's anguished remark, expressed in the banqueting hall, 'German and English [military forces] now fight shoulder to shoulder in Riga – this is only a foretaste of further action inside Germany.'[46] It would be a civil war.

Within four days of the Battle of Christmas Eve the three Independent commissars – Emil Barth, Hugo Haase and Wilhelm Dittmann – had walked out of the government, complaining they had not been consulted over the use of armed force or on the early date of the elections, and that the Hamburg Points, reorganizing the military in accordance with the council system, had not yet been executed. Ebert immediately named a new government. He announced that henceforth it would be a 'pure party regime', meaning purely Majority Socialist. Scheidemann and Landsburg were kept on. Rudolf Wissell, a trade-union leader, was brought in to serve as Economics Minister, while Gustav Noske, the man who had negotiated the social peace in mutinous Kiel back in November and had persuaded the sailors not to join their comrades in Berlin in December, was carried into the Chancellery on the shoulders of cheering soldiers to become the Minister of National Defence. 'Of course! Somebody will have to be the bloodhound,' said the bewhiskered hero; 'I won't shirk the responsibility.' The Cabinet gave him a free hand to deal with the problem of order in the capital: 'my authority as Supreme Commander ['*Oberfehlshaber*'] was complete', he tells in his memoirs. Groener was delighted with the appointment.[47]

Another appointment much remarked on at the time was the entry of the professional diplomat Count Ulrich von Brockdorff-Rantzau as Secretary of State at the Foreign Office. At forty-nine, with his monocle and cigarette-holder, he looked the epitome of the Prussian aristocrat – which is precisely what he was. As ambassador to neutral Denmark, the Count had played a pivotal role in German food supplies during the war. He had a reputation for being combative, even stubborn, in his opinions. Like Noske with public order, Rantzau and his experts in the Foreign Office were given complete freedom in the way they dealt with the forthcoming peace conference in Paris; they did not communicate with the Cabinet, and they would have nothing to do with Erzberger's Armistice Commission, the only formal contact Germany had at that moment with the Allies. The Count was convinced that the Paris conference would be dominated by the ideals of Woodrow Wilson, as were most Germans, in so far as they thought of the problem.

On 1 January 1919 Fritz Ebert announced his programme for the national elections, stealing his cue from the political Left: 'Peace, Freedom, Bread!'[48]

The 'bourgeois' parties were beginning to feel a bit left out from the nation's affairs. Count Hermann Keyserling, one of Harry Kessler's friends, thought that this was how things ought to be. He explained himself on New Year's Eve: 'Only socialist policies, contrasting with reactionary conditions among the Western Powers, can again put us in the leading international position.'[49]

There were numerous party rallies, some of them quite bellicose. The German Democratic Party, or DDP, had been active since the elections were announced in mid-December. On the day the Spartacists organized the sailors' funeral, its followers came marching through the Brandenburg Gate singing '*Die Wacht am Rhein*' and holding their black-red-and-gold banners high; it looked as if there was going to be a head-on clash at the corner of Wilhelmstrasse. 'Up with Liebknecht!' screamed the Spartacists. 'Down with Liebknecht!' cried their opponents (who notably abstained from shouting 'Up with' anybody). Then a man in a felt hat was lifted on to the shoulders of his fellow demonstrators to plead that they were the party of order and not disturbance. So they all politely, and quietly, filed away.[50]

In the last hour of 1918 night clouds released a cascade of rain on the city, dampening the sound of the festival cannon and rockets. New Year's Day was cold and clear; but there was no imperial pomp, no grand military parade, as had been the custom up till now. Instead, a huge political demonstration took place 'to protect the religion of the people and not let the socialist regime rob them of it'. The Circus Busch was packed, so an overflow meeting – of around thirty thousand – took place in the Lustgarten. Professor Kunkmann from the Faculty of Theology at the University of Berlin delivered a lecture on 'The Coalition of Evangelical and Catholic Electors in the National Assembly'. At its conclusion, soldiers, Catholic nuns, Lutheran ministers and a flock of the faithful marched in serried ranks down the Linden to demonstrate in front of the Chancellery.[51]

The dispute was over efforts by the Prussian Minister of Education, Adolph Hoffmann, to remove what remained of clerical authority in Prussian schools and to effect, like the republicans in France, a complete separation between Church and State. In the end it was Hoffmann who had to separate himself from the government. Religion was the one issue which held the Centre Party of Matthias Erzberger together. Its leadership in Berlin wanted to rename it the Christian People's Party. But they, too, had to abandon their project. There were so many internal party divisions: the Protestants and Catholics failed to come up with a common electoral programme; the reform-minded group from Mönchengladbach clashed with the dominant conservative faction from Cologne; Rhenish members openly supported the establishment of a Rhenish-Westphalian Republic, separate from Prussia; the Bavarian members did set up their own independent party. As for Erzberger, he was so busy with his Armistice Commission in Spa that he did not have time to provide the kind of energetic party leadership that was so desperately needed. The German Centre Party remained the 'Centre Party', a forum for debate, a planning office for rallies and demonstrations, but not a credible force for government.

The old half-hearted policies of the parties in the imperial era, the incapacity to conceive of anything approaching French or British notions of parliamentary responsibility, remained the norm after November 1918. It was the same culture, supported by the same party machinery. With the new franchise, many of the organizations changed their names to become 'people's parties', to avoid perpetuating their reputation as *Honoratiorenparteien*, or parties of notables. Gustav Stresemann salvaged what he could from his National Liberal Party to establish the German People's Party (DVP), while the Conservatives, aided by the Fatherland Party that had sprung up during the war, organized the German National People's Party (DNVP). The members of these two parties had been openly annexationist during the war, and they showed little enthusiasm for republican institutions born out of defeat. But they had no alternative form of government to suggest.

The idea that a political party existed to build up a majority in parliament, ready to take on the responsibility of government, was utterly foreign to them. Their understanding of a national assembly was of a body in which all the particular interests of Germany should be represented before a central administration that would then somehow have to reconcile them. Government itself was not their problem; the parties went to parliament to represent interests, not to govern. This attitude could be traced back not only to German parliamentarians in Bismarck's Reich but further yet, to the institutions of the old Reich, *das alte Reich*, the Holy Roman Empire of the Renaissance and the Middle Ages, when family, village, corporate guild and city-state had preserved their autonomy under the dynastic protection of of the 'reach'. Certainly, the interests in themselves were no longer the same: Germany, like Western Europe, was a modern society with industrialists, bankers, liberal professions, scientists and academics. But the legal mechanism by which these special interests were represented was very old.

Britain's ancient corporate world had been fully integrated into her parliamentary system. A reading of Keynes shows how this had been achieved in the case of the Treasury and the universities. France had had many violent revolutions, but in every case since 1789 the moving force had been France's old corporate world itself; one only has to consider the geography of revolutionary Paris – Faubourg Saint-Antoine, Belleville, Montmartre, heartland of the guilds. Germany's old corporate world, on the other hand, simply stood to one side and waited for the storm to pass. There was no Belleville or Montmartre in Berlin's revolution. It began with the occupation of the imperial Schloss by sailors imported from Kiel.

Germany was made up of parallel lives and parallel societies that never converged. The only political party that might have provided a liberal and democratic focal point for responsible political forces was the German Democratic Party. The DDP had been founded on 15 November by Theodor Wolff and Georg Bernhard – two journalists, not professional politicians. The whole of the former Progressive Party went over to the Democrats, and the liberal wing of the 'National Liberals' abandoned Stresemann for this new party. Most members of Hugo Preuss's constitutional committee supported it. But the party was already beginning to discover that it had cast its net too wide; its supporters could not agree on whether they wanted a planned national economy or preferred to let the free market do the work, whether foreign policy should consist of a passive acceptance of Allied conditions or should be formulated in terms of a national protest. They could not even agree on the colours of the national flag. Gradually, the founding members were pushed aside and the professional politicians took over.

6

In the south-western suburb of Grunewald, a forested place of hills and lakes and rivers, was a villa belonging to one of the richest men in Germany, Walther Rathenau. Rathenau had designed its simple neoclassical form himself; parts he had decorated with his own hands – hands that were not those of a mere amateur. It was modelled after Prussian architecture of the late eighteenth century – some said it was too Prussian. Its style was graceful, regular and subdued – some said barren. 'Aesthetic enjoyment arises when one becomes aware of an underlying order,' explained Rathenau.[52]

As president of AEG, the huge German electrical conglomerate, and founder in August 1914 of the War Office's Raw Materials Section, which managed the German economy throughout the war, Rathenau was one of the great 'economic men' of the period, comparable in stature to Hoover in the United States and Keynes in England. Like Hoover, he was rich. Like Keynes, he was a philosopher. He had the same zeal for organization as Hoover. He thought art was superior to business, as did Keynes.

But in the winter of 1918–19 Rathenau cut a solitary figure. He had resigned from the Raw Materials Section after serving for only nine months, and had devoted most of his time since then to making speeches and writing. 'Now the void begins,' he wrote glumly on the week he quit office. Colonel House, on a peace mission from neutral America, actually met Rathenau at this moment and was most impressed by him – with his intelligence, his ability to look into the future. 'I wonder how many men in Germany think like him?' he recorded in his diary. 'It saddened me to hear him say he was isolated . . . He wondered if it was he alone who was mad, or all the others.' In October 1915 the London *Times* ran an article that described Rathenau as an 'organizing genius' whose name should be ranked beside those of Falkenhayn and Hindenburg in the German war effort; his Raw Materials Section – 'one of the greatest ideas of modern times' – was what gave the German economy such strength and explained why the Reich's troops could hold out in the West and advance in the East.[53]

The principal forum for Rathenau's speeches in the last years of the war had been the 'Wednesday Club', which brought together around seventy of the leading military, industrial and political leaders in Berlin once a week. Ludendorff and Hindenburg had been seen there. The writing he found difficult. 'I wrestle all day long, and in the evening four pages lie before me. How easy are words and how hard!' he confided to a female friend. He compared his labours to that of a widow who bears a child. 'Such children suffer much from weeping,' he said. 'I do not weep – but I do not laugh much either.'[54]

People who met him at this time noted a craving for friendship, a great babble of intelligent conversation (that went only in one direction), a flurry of rich images and insights into war and peace which were perfectly unique, a yearning for an understanding; but never was a bond struck. He became known as 'the Don Juan of friendships' because his relationships were so fleeting – frequently they were developed during an intense evening at Grunewald only to wither away subsequently. 'The souls of men', he would admit, 'whirl after one another like the stars in their courses, but they cannot leave their orbit and they cannot meet.' This was a 'parallelism', as Rathenau himself called it, that had much in common with the political culture of Germany at the close of the war. Yet in Rathenau's case it was something permanent. No man knew him well. The writer Gerhart Hauptman, the Swedish painter Ernst Norlind and the Prussian staff officer Gustav Steinbömer were frequently mentioned as being his 'closest friends', but this was probably because they so rarely saw him. No woman was intimate with him. He never married. And the one woman who did maintain a regular correspondence with him, Lili Deutsch, the wife of a colleague at AEG – she is the anonymous 'friend' in Harry Kessler's biography of Rathenau – confessed long after his death that 'he was a very sensual man, but I still do not know to this day how the erotic function in him acted'.

Rathenau admitted that he was not like others, and ascribed it to his writing. 'For with me', he told Lili Deutsch, 'the Lord God has set going an experiment which even if it proves a failure – and that seems to me more likely than the opposite – will at least have been an interesting one.'[55]

Few read the works of Rosa Luxemburg in 1918, whereas Rathenau's books and pamphlets were selling, by the end of the war, in tens of thousands. His *In Days to Come* (*Von kommenden Dingen*), which first appeared in 1916, had sold over a hundred thousand copies. At the end of the war, Germany's reading public were not discussing Marxism: they were debating, and quite viciously quarrelling, over the merits of Rathenau's 'experiment'.

Rathenau and Keynes, two of the great economic managers at the time of the war, are well worth comparing. They show that a divergence was occurring in Western thought at the moment of war.

The general decline of religious faith had led Keynes into an introspective moral philosophy which had spurned 'general rules of conduct' and public affairs for more private matters. He placed 'actions which do good' above 'actions which are good'. His theory of probabilities had persuaded him to cast aside grand abstract systems and efforts to predict the distant future: Keynes's economics concentrated on the present and the immediate.

Rathenau went in exactly the opposite direction. Private friendship and intimacy he abandoned – 'my fate is loneliness and I accept it'. He developed a certain scorn for intellectual pursuits, and especially for mathematics: 'The naive error of all philosophy has been its pretension in wanting to penetrate all realms with the aid of intellect, logic, arithmetic, without ever asking if this intellectual thought had absolute value, or even if it represented the mind's unique force.'

While Keynes rejected the Christian ethic that lay behind G. E. Moore's 'general rules', Rathenau fully embraced it, arguing that Christ 'would not speak as a pastor formed at the university' but 'dealt directly with politics and socialism, industry and economics, science and technology'. This is what led Rathenau to elaborate his great system towards which he was sure the entire world was heading. He was the founding father of what a later generation would call 'futurology'.

If Keynes, with his introspective logic, could pursue the happiness principle, Rathenau, looking beyond all horizons, was prepared to accept the consequences of his thought: 'We are not down here to be happy,' he wrote. 'Our way does not lead to happiness but to perfection, it leads to the soul even at the cost of happiness.'[56]

In the last months of the war Rathenau published a number of appeals for support of his system that at the same time summarized, in a declamatory, apocalyptic manner, its major points. They might be compared with J. G. Fichte's *Addresses to the German Nation* that had preceded Prussia's final struggle with Napoleon; the romantic, ascetic Fichte was an author whom Rathenau much admired. The most important of these appeals was *To German Youth (An Deutschlands Jugend)*, appearing in July 1918 just as the tide of Ludendorff's western armies turned into retreat.

'Every night I remember in my heart those who have been killed and those doomed to die, and above all those in distress and those in fear,' he began. He announced that the current crisis would be 'the funeral pyre of

the social structure of Europe, which will never rise again from the flames'.
He described how society would inevitably move on from a lower, intermediary, mechanical stage of life to a higher, more complete, spiritual stage:
to a 'realm of the soul' (*das Reich der Seele*) where 'all the phenomena and
categories of the intellectual world shall cease to exist, including combative
individuality and intellectual science'. None of this could be demonstrated
with facts and figures, and yet, he claimed, nothing was more certain. He
did not promise the establishment of such a paradise on earth for tomorrow.
Strangely echoing the question Clemenceau was always putting to the socialist Jean Jaurès, he noted that one first had to find the men to fit in it. 'Where
are the men?' he asked. New attitudes had to develop. At one time he had
thought this would take a hundred years: now he believed they would
emerge from the war. And somehow they had to be incorporated into the
peace: 'The coming peace will turn out to be nothing but an armistice
and a tale of more wars unending, the grandest nations will sink in decay
and the world in misery unless the peace succeeds in aiding the realization
of these ideas.'[57]

Rathenau did not accept Germany's pursuit of an armistice in October
and was the first to argue in Berlin's press that Ludendorff had lost his
nerve. He called for the creation of a new Ministry of National Defence and
appealed, like Danton in 1792 and Gambetta in 1870, to the people to rise
in a *levée en masse*. 'Let everyone offer himself who feels himself called to
such a task ... All the "Field-Greys", who are today to be met with in our
towns, at the stations and on the railways, must go back to the front ...
The men capable of bearing arms must be combed out of the offices, the
guard-rooms and the depots, in East and West, at the bases and at home.'
Just like Gambetta, he announced that the old imperial age had gone; it
was no longer possible 'to graft the aged and withered tree of Militarism
and Feudalism upon the awakened peoples of the earth'. 'It is not war we
desire but peace; and yet not a peace of abject submission,' he proclaimed.
Ludendorff – more in touch with reality – accepted in principle an abject
submission, then passed the responsibility on to Prince Max.[58]

After the Armistice, Rathenau attempted to found a political party for
all those Germans who did not feel comradeship with the workers' and
soldiers' councils, or with the Council of People's Commissars. He wrote
the programme for the Democratic People's League (the *Demokratischer
Volksbund*), which reflected the absolute ethical values of his writings.
Inheritance would be abolished. Similarly, 'militarism and imperialism,
feudalism and bureacratism are suppressed'. Every German would be guaranteed the right to work and the right to an education. Heavy taxes would
be levied on wealth and income. Finally, his programme declared that 'the
economy is no longer a private matter, but the business of all' – production
would be increased by the suppression of wastage, trade unions would be
governed by the state, enterprises would have to prepare to be nationalized,

imports and the consumption of luxury products would be taxed and restricted, for 'the economy must be rendered more moral and life more simple'.[59]

The programme hardly corresponded to what most of the German middle classes were seeking, and within a few days of its formation the party was dissolved. Rathenau joined the Democrats, the DDP, the party of the non-socialist intellectuals like Preuss and Max Weber. He had plans to run as candidate for the National Assembly in the tiny constituency of Rothenburg-Hoyerswerda, where he chaired the board of directors of a local glass factory, but Ebert's government changed all the constituency borders, so he found himself instead trying to win a nomination in the larger region of Liegnitz: the party would not even allow him to speak. They hated him.

Few people were as rich as Rathenau, few as well known, and few as hated. As he himself confided, in 1918, to Lili Deutsch, 'I have never expected thanks for my work; but no German for decades has been subjected to the amount of enmity which has come instead.'[60]

Within the professional classes, this hatred mounted, like the graph of a simple mathematical equation, with every paragraph and page Rathenau published. His first articles appeared anonymously in the press in the 1890s, when Rathenau was still in his twenties; one detects a soft whisper of contempt. In 1902 he published *Impressions*, a collection of essays under his own name; there is no public comment, but the rumours have turned indignant. Then in 1904 there was *Reflections*, a heavy quarto volume printed on expensive coloured paper; people quietly push it aside with a smile that sighs, 'Ah, another Rathenau book' – there, on the corner of a table, it lies, unread. By 1910 he was writing about economic problems: the hatred becomes passionate. The academics sniggered, businessmen mocked, the interested parties – like the bankers and merchants of the Hansa port towns – grew indignant. When he set up the Raw Materials Section in the War Office there was an outcry: business rivals protested that this was unfair competition; the military bureaucrats refused to accept him as a colleague.

One day he entered his offices to discover that, during the night, wooden partitions had been erected to isolate them from the rest of the building. 'If this man Rathenau *has* helped us, then it is a scandal and a disgrace,' remarked one lieutenant from behind his desk. Rathenau resigned on 1 April 1915, but not before imposing his own successor, Colonel Joseph Koeth.

Henceforth, Rathenau was a marked man. Herbert Hoover might have felt some discomfort as a Baptist in America. Keynes, the son of Nonconformists in England, had to overcome many Establishment prejudices. But the malice Rathenau had to face was of a different order. Rathenau was a Jew in Germany. That, he could never change – 'I believe', he predicted solemnly, 'this attitude will continue to the end of my days.'[61]

7

It was what made Rathenau so fascinating – more fascinating than either Hoover or Keynes. Two men lived in Rathenau: the Prussian and the Jew. As an administrator of the war economy, both through the Raw Materials Section and later through the contacts he maintained in Berlin, he was systematic and at times brutal. Raw materials were seized at home and in the occupied territories; Rathenau was a advocate of annexations in the West, though he opposed Ludendorff's territorial plans in the East. In contrast to his assistant, Wichard von Moellendorff, he was a keen supporter of the Hindenburg Programme, which established an economic dictatorship in all lands controlled by the Reich. In September 1916 he wrote to Ludendorff in support of the deportation of 700,000 Belgians to toil in Germany's armaments factories. Yet, at the very same time, he was writing like a prophet or a man versed in the mysticism of the Kabbalah about the coming new kingdom, the joy of labour and the abolition of the social classes.

'What gives power to my writing', he said, 'is that it does not reek of the midnight oil. It is experienced and lived.'[62] Rathenau's pedigree was not that of a scholar, but that of a hard-nosed industrialist. His father, Emil, had set up a machine factory in a former dance hall on Chausseestrasse, in northern Berlin, where Walther was born in 1867. As a child he used to inspect the engines and admire the roaring forge. But he would also visit his grandparents' home on Viktoriastrasse, by the Tiergarten, where he encountered the remnants of the Jewish salons that had been so active in the Romantic era; he met people who could remember Henriette Herz and Rahel Varnhagen and could describe 'that old fool, Friedrich von Genz' as well as Schiller, the person. When Rathenau spoke of a new 'Stein–Hardenberg age' of political reform and artistic flowering emerging from the Great War he knew what he was talking about: the Romantic era was in his blood. Rathenau loved machinery and Goethe.

The factory suffered serious losses at the time of the Franco-Prussian War, and after the stock-market crisis of 1873 Emil sold it. He went in search of another enterprise. He studied the applied sciences, he visited the world exhibitions of Vienna, Philadelphia and Paris; in 1881 he eventually found what he was looking for: Edison's electric arc-lamp, the article of the future, 'the lamp of the wealthy, but also of the poor, the lamp of the garret and the stable'.[63] Emil Rathenau bought the patent and set up the Allgemeine Elektricitäts Gesellschaft, AEG, which by 1907 was ranked as the largest commercial company in the world.

Like wealthy Jews in Britain and France, the Rathenaus considered themselves fully assimilated within their nation. They celebrated the Christian festivals at home, not the Jewish. Walther quoted the Evangelists rather than the Prophets. But the Rathenaus did not convert – out of pride, it would seem: 'I am a German of Jewish origins,' affirmed Walther in *To*

German Youth. 'My people are the German people, my home is German land, my belief is German belief, which stands above all denominations.'[64]

Two men grew up in Rathenau: Goethe and the scientist. He was determined to exert his independence. He set off to university with the goal of proving he had all the technological expertise of his father, but he did not talk about it. On the day he defended his thesis 'The Absorption of Light by Metals' he was half an hour late for the daily luncheon served at his mother's table, and had to excuse himself profusely – no one knew what he was up to. For ten years he worked in the provinces, as a subordinate technician in a Swiss aluminium factory and then as the manager of a small electrochemical works in dreary Bitterfeld, Prussian Saxony; he accepted no funds from his father. The smells emanating from his experiments in electrolysis were so bad that, one day, all the workers were obliged to abandon the premises. The manager, however, stayed on and worked alone through the night – that is the image we must keep of Rathenau.

When he returned to Berlin in 1899 he joined AEG's board of directors. He did not have the flare of enterprise as did his younger brother, Erich, Emil's favourite; he was more an administrator, a consolidator, the sort of man AEG needed at the time. After Erich's sudden death in 1903, Walther made himself indispensable. He set up electric power stations in Manchester, Amsterdam, Buenos Aires and Baku. He directed the streetcar company in Seville, the mountain-engineering works in East Africa, the electric railways in South America and eighty-four other huge concerns around the planet. AEG had invented a new form of corporate management: 'vertical' and 'horizontal' integration, local autonomy, the co-ordination of the banks with the company's finances, loans that created wealth, a whole after-sales-service sector. The interests of AEG were placed above those of the stockholders: there was little speculation with funds, risks were kept to a minimum, the dividends were tiny. Walther Rathenau's public contempt for Germany's parliament mirrored his attitude towards stockholders' meetings; when he wrote of reconstructing the economic, social and political life of humanity he was reproducing in his imagination the world according to AEG. Or almost.

In 1906 he had a revelation. Disconcerted by the blind utility and purpose of his business activities, burdened by the restraints, he set out on a pilgrimage to discover the material and especially spiritual remnants of ancient civilization. His journey took him to Greece, of course, not Palestine. Like Goethe's trip to Italy, it was a voyage of 'discovery with the soul'. Like the Romantic poet that he was, it seems he was also motivated by the impossibility of realizing his ideal of love with Lili Deutsch. 'More calm and a better frame of mind,' he wrote to her on his arrival in Athens in May. 'Yesterday I spent at the ancient seat of the mysteries: Eleusis. Tomorrow I shall greet the Delphic Oracle. I have much to ask it (including your whereabouts).'[65]

Rathenau was overcome by the sublime grandeur of the landscape, a surrounding nature untouched by the ages, a country teeming with the 'life, mind, blood, light and love' of a 'mysterious Cosmos'. With an able hand, he recorded his first impressions in a sketchbook. The Oracle, he wrote again to Lili Deutsch on 23 May, 'was phantastic and almost magnificent, so that I shall probably have to keep it secret. The drive up to Delphi, the deep, cool ravine and the distant greeting of the sea, quite thrilled me.' The snow-capped Parnassus faced the sea on two sides, bleak and unflinching. In front of him an eagle suddenly started up and rose to the sky. Nobody knows what Rathenau asked the Oracle or what he remarked in the reply. But between views of Delphi and Corinth one finds in his sketchbook a brief note entitled *Breviarium Mysticum*. It lists Rathenau's version of the Ten Commandments:

1. The picture which each man has of the world is the measure of his soul.
2. Many are born with a soul; all can attain one.
3. Everyone who is *bonae voluntatis* is guaranteed a soul.
4. The soul is the mirror image of God.
5. The powers of the soul are threefold: Imagination, Love, Awe.
6. With the Imagination the soul comprehends the world, with Imagination and Love God's creatures, with all three powers God.
7. The soul is disinterested; the intellect is the slave of purpose.
8. In its conflict with the intellect the soul attains to victory, because the intellect defeats its own ends.
9. Art and unconscious creation are the expression of the soul; science and conscious creation the expression of the intellect.
10. The soul derives its nourishment from the urge to life; the intellect from fear of death.[66]

All of Rathenau's subsequent writings are controlled by these ten thoughts. He told Count Harry Kessler on his return to Berlin that the private struggle within him since childhood was over, that he was going to retire from business and write. But he did not retire from business, and he did not begin a serious career in writing until five years later.

Two men lived on in Rathenau, and he could not escape the fact: Prussian and Jew, artist and businessman, mystic and scientist, a creative 'soul' struggling with a mechanical 'intellect'. He wrote in opposites, thus sometimes giving the impression that his work was merely a series of arbitrary declarations – he expected the reader to make the connections. He relied, like an artist, on his intuition, and when contemplating the birth of the soul in the modern world he felt no need for proofs. What appealed to Germans in Rathenau's books was their richness of imagery and their underlying message of hope. Rathenau was an impenitent optimist: things *would* get better.
     Rathenau laid out his great scheme of human progress in a trilogy,

consisting of *Criticism of the Age* (*Zur Kritik der Zeit*, 1912), on the current alienating process of 'mechanization', *The Mechanism of the Mind* (*Zur Mechanik des Geistes*, 1913), which described the rebirth of the people, and *In Days to Come* (*Von kommenden Dingen*, 1916), which focused on the society of the future.

The driving force in history, Rathenau was convinced, was the relentless growth of the world's population. In order to meet the material needs of the people, the effectiveness of human labour had to be enormously increased. This was achieved through organization and technology, the basis of the 'mechanization of the world'. Rathenau thus followed a logic diametrically opposed to that of the Revd Thomas Malthus, who a century earlier had advocated limiting population growth through abstinence. 'The only country which has followed this route, France, is on the point of dying,' noted Rathenau in 1912.[67]

Mechanization, he argued, brought about a revolution in every area of life – mental, social, economic and political. Even the human spirit was altered by specialization and abstraction: it was standardized; it was deprived of surprise and humour. The political state was transformed from a mystical power associated with religion to an armed confederacy for production. Economic organization came to dominate everything else. The power of the state was made subordinate to it. The creative soul of man was crushed in a society uniquely designed for consumption – the satisfaction of material needs.

Rathenau spoke of the globalization of this process, accompanied by an explosion of information. This did not enrich the soul: it impoverished it – images and ideas rushed past in an endless, roaring torrent. Very few of them took hold. Instead, man lost his intimacy with himself and became forgetful – he lost his history. Mechanical methods of work developed and more 'jobs' became available, but they were not the occupations of a craftsman. States became part of a world machine; they lost their identity.

Rathenau's historical process was built, of course, upon two opposing forces; *Mutmenschen* and *Furchtmenschen*, 'men of courage' and 'men of fear' – two images of his inner self. He had first made the distinction back in 1897, when, as 'W. Hartenau', he had published an article, 'Hear, O Israel!', which, if it had been written by a Gentile, would be regarded as racist and anti-Semitic. 'There in the midst of German life is an alien and isolated race of men,' he wrote: 'an Asian horde on the sandy plains of Prussia.' The pressure of population had pushed them there, slaves in the realm of the masters, 'men of fear' among the 'men of courage'. The 'tragedy of the Aryan race' – not of the Jews – was the triumph of the South over the North as a result of waves of migration. The Northern masters defended themselves by maintaining an ancient ethic of courage, which was noble, spiritual, confident, and could be traced back to the likes of Hercules and Ajax. The Southern slaves infiltrated by ruse, 'by the power of fear, of brains and of cunning'. They were utilitarian men, 'men of purpose' (*Zweck-menschen*). They were the ones who established a new industrial civilization. They, the 'men of fear', set the process of mechanization in motion.[68]

W. Hartenau's article, published at the height of the Dreyfus Affair, was not a promising start to a writing career. But when Hartenau became Rathenau he came to some extraordinary conclusions.

The power of mechanization seemed inexhaustible; its grip on work, on leisure, on the arts and on men's souls seemed unloosenable; the logic of globalization, rationalization, and the spreading tentacles of the information industry seemed unavoidable. Yet, in 1912, at the end of his first volume, Rathenau announced that the whole system had already received its death blow.

The world would experience the same kind of revelation of the soul as Rathenau had known before the heights of Parnassus. Ever the optimist, Rathenau was convinced that human nature would undergo a fundamental change. After the long struggle of intuition, imagination and emotion against the mechanical intellect, society would eventually break out into the light and realize the meaning of life. Mechanization itself would lead to a collective, psychological mutation. Modern utilitarian, materialist civilization would sooner or later find a more human culture. The upheaval of war persuaded Rathenau that it was sooner. He could not conceive that such an inhuman process as mechanization could go on for ever. Nowhere in his works is the possibility even considered. It would have represented for him the absolute tragedy, the unimaginable: a plunge into a fathomless, lifeless void.

So his two halves, intuition and intellect, lived on in Rathenau. Instead of a world governed by the forces of fear, he predicted one founded on those of courage: 'Greed dies down, competition ends in love, the intellect is superseded by vision, and scheming ceases.' This is not Marx's communist utopia; it is more Rousseau's ideal world functioning without antagonism in accordance with a 'social contract'. The right of inheritance is curtailed and private incomes are assigned to the community. Rathenau himself speaks of the 'love of Saint Francis, which embraces all creatures including the stars, and, reaching up to heaven, compels God to descend'. Work is transformed into a joy of creation for its own sake and not for the material value it produces.[69]

Rathenau was not a pure mystic. The experience of his two halves guided him: the revelation *and* his knowledge of the German economy, particularly under conditions of war. One can understand how, as a director and then president of AEG, he could gain the impression that mechanization was 'the concentration of the whole world into one compulsory association, into one unbroken society of production and world trade'. Rathenau was at the head of the movement. Obviously the head of the Raw Materials Section, running one of the most vigorous planned economies the world had ever seen, thought the days of anarchy and private enterprise were over – that had been his whole aim. 'Property, consumption and demand are not private matters,' he wrote; that Raw Materials Section had been set up to assure this. Rathenau thought that big businesses, like AEG, would replace private enterprise and lead the way into the more communal, associative way of life; he believed that the transformation would be achieved through a system decentralized not by region, but by economic function. That is how Germany's war economy had been organized. That is how AEG operated.[70]

But Rathenau's remarkable imagination carried him beyond mere observation. He detected trends in the war economy that he was sure would lead to the great transcendental change and establish the 'realm of the soul'. In public opinion, there was a growing contempt for mere riches. In industry, there was a progressive depersonalization of property, as a result of the extension of joint-stock companies and the multiplication of state undertakings (like his own war companies). In politics, the sovereign state was yielding to a more democratic state and one more dependent on outside powers. 'Industry is everybody's business,' said Rathenau. War had shaken the concept of the inviolability of private property.

'In days to come,' he wrote, 'it will be difficult to conceive that the will of a dead man could bind the living; that a man could be allowed to enclose arable land; that, without state authorization, he could leave cultivatable land untilled, demolish and erect buildings, ruin beautiful landscapes, remove or disfigure works of art; ... that he would be justified, provided he paid his taxes, in using his property as he pleased and in employing as many men in whatever work he liked...'[71] In days to come, Rathenau foresaw the disappearance of classes as a consequence of the abolition of 'hereditary oppression' and the disappearance of the privileged ruling caste. All would live by the joy of their creative labour.

One word crops up again and again in Rathenau's writings: 'responsibility'. Men of creative genius and men of great wealth become aware of their 'responsibilities' to the community. A properly functioning society, able to realize a happy end to mechanization, is founded on principles of solidarity and 'responsibility'. The qualities Rathenau associates with courage – like imagination, vision, tenacity and creativity – are often summarized in the word 'responsibility'. With the aid of technology, manual labour becomes more supervisory in nature, thus giving the worker 'responsibility', a share in management. The joy in creation and love of work is driven not by motives of pleasure and profit, or by a taste for luxury, but by a will to power and a desire for 'responsibility'. Technology combines with a revolutionary change in human attitude to raise not just one class but 'industry and society in general to a higher moral plane, to the level of personal responsibility'.[72]

Rathenau not only saw this as a positive social development during the war, as reflected in people's willingness to accept restrictions, but he also thought he could explain the outbreak of war by the earlier lack of social responsibility. He deplored the general quality of world political leadership – though particularly that in Germany – and blamed all nations for allowing a situation of moral and economic chaos to develop. During the war he became an advocate of a European economic community that would include former enemies as well as allies. After the Armistice, he argued that a League of Nations would never work unless a 'League of Industry' were set up alongside.

As early as 1913 he was criticizing 'the indolence of the [German] nation, which is not prepared to fight for its responsibilities and so will be compelled to fight for its security.'[73] By the end of the war he was filled with horror as he watched his nation continue in mad battle against a 'world machine'. Why, then, did he insist on a last-minute *levée en masse*? For the quality of the following peace, he argued, not to prolong the war. What had decided the struggle was not the defeat of the German Army, he claimed, but the defeat of German industrial organization. The most urgent issue in the war had not been military, but rather the clash between two industrial bodies that had divided up the surface of the earth into two powerful state organizations to the exclusion all but a few dwindling enclaves of private enterprise. In the winter of 1918–19 Rathenau prepared to stand on the platform for world order and a transcendental peace, not the private anarchies of the past.[74]

At the very moment of the Armistice, and only a month after his call for a *levée en masse*, Rathenau had written to his old American acquaintance Colonel House. He stated that the Western countries had all had their revolutions, while Germany was only just beginning to undergo one. Against the former 'militarist state', he remarked, 'all resistance was vain'.

'Germany is not guilty,' he went on – he spoke not of Germany's 'war responsibility', but of 'war guilt', a most significant distinction in the case of Rathenau. 'Germany is not guilty,' he said. 'German will was under the hold of a formidable military power, despite all her parliaments. With the revolution, German will is for the first time free, and this will desires peace.'[75]

Would Germany become 'responsible'; would the 'new economy' be realized; would the peace be transcendental? House, at any rate, was highly impressed with Rathenau's letter, and passed it on to his master.

8

In the New Year of 1919 the fragments of the fragments – broken leftovers of the Great War – came into collision at the point where the whole affair had begun: Berlin. Since Christmas, the Kommandatur on the Linden had been eyeing with suspicion the sailors across the canal at the Schloss; they had not yet withdrawn to the Marstall, as promised. The sailors were wondering what Erich Eichhorn's Security Service, across the river in the red-bricked Police Presidium on Alexanderplatz, were up to. The Reich's government in the Chancellery on Wilhelmstrasse was feeling very isolated after the departure of the Independent Socialists; Ebert was still thinking of retreating with his commissars to Weimar or Kassel. On 3 January the Independents withdraw from the Prussian state government on the Linden. The Independents maintained a central office on Schicklerstrasse which had become a debating club between the various strands of the Party. The new German Communist Party (Spartacist League) had its headquarters in Fried-richstrasse, where it argued about Berlin's position in the course of world history: was this still the first (bourgeois) phase in the revolution, the consoli-dation phase, or the second (proletarian) phase? The newspaper offices down on Belle-Allianz Platz, at the southern end of Friedrichstrasse, were little kingdoms in their own right. As for the armed forces in Berlin, there were many; but nobody could truly speak of an army. The Maybug barracks, where the first Berlin mutiny in the November Revolution had occurred, was still populated by troops that as yet had no definite political orientation. The soldiers in the Spandau fortress were clear supporters of Eichhorn's Security Service and Lieutenant Dorrenbach's sailors at the Schloss. So were the troops in nearby Frankfurt-on-Oder. The rapidly growing Free Corps in Moabit, Potsdam and Zossen had, on the other hand, sworn allegiance to the 'Regime'.

There were demonstrations in the streets – Communist, Catholic, and Protestant. There were strikes, mostly for more pay. The Revolutionary Shop Stewards had organized a halt in production at the AEG works in Moabit and had succeeded in closing down the gasworks. But the main talk of the town at New Year was the waiters' strike. Harry Kessler describes sitting down for dinner on New Year's Day when a deputation of waiters entered the restaurant to announce that either management must meet the strikers' demands or the business would be closed down in ten minutes. 'Five minutes later an employee anounced his [the manager's] capitulation. The strikers, with red tabs stuck in their hats and carrying a red flag, left. Blackmail completed, we could return to the matter of food.'[76] On the follow-ing day over a thousand managers and landlords, including Lorenz Adlon, met with representatives of the unions to negotiate a settlement. But many cafés and restaurants in Berlin remained closed in the first days of 1919.

Several newspapers were running a campaign against Eichhorn. The most revealing story was by a correspondent for the 'Political-Parliamentary News Service', an agency close to the government. Eichhorn, it claimed, had been working at a monthly salary of 1,700 marks for Rosta, a Russian service that had been spreading Bolshevik propaganda. Back in November, he had usurped the position of police chief from Eugen Ernst, who had been nominated to the post by the Prussian state government. Since then, it was further stated, he had been cutting telephone and telegraph lines, he had been working in close collaboration with the sailors at the Schloss, he had virtually taken over 'military command' in Berlin since Otto Wels's departure, and he had filled his Presidium and the neighbouring Café Vaterland with artillery and machine-guns. Eichhorn hotly denied the charges. A terrible anger developed among his supporters against the 'lies' of the bourgeois press.[77]

On Saturday, 4 January, the Prussian state government formally dismissed Eichhorn from his post and appointed Eugen Ernst as chief of police in Berlin. But Eichhorn refused to go.

Berlin's broken pebbles and fragments were on the roll.

The first thing Eichhorn did, on receiving notification of his dismissal, was to go round to Schicklerstrasse to appeal for support from his party, the Independent Socialists; they promptly granted it. It just so happened that the Independents' central committee had a meeting with the Revolutionary Shop Stewards that evening at the Police Presidium. The scandalous deed of the Prussian state government now took precedence over all other business. Members of the Communist central committee pledged a qualified support; they were not entirely convinced that the 'second phase' had yet arrived, and carefully avoided calls for the overthrow of the Ebert government. They nevertheless made it clear that this government was the real enemy. 'The Ebert–Scheidemann government has heightened its counter-revolutionary activities with a new contemptible conspiracy,' read a proclamation signed by the Independents, the Stewards and the Communists. 'By this blow directed against the Berlin Police Presidium, the whole German proletariat and the entire German Revolution is to be struck down.' It called for a mass demonstration the next afternoon to defend the 'fate of the Revolution'.[78]

The 'Ebert–Scheidemann government' was only too happy to counter conspiracy theory with conspiracy theory. Henceforth it was 'Spartacus' that was fomenting a *Putsch*. In fact many sides were involved in the uprising of January 1919. At this very moment the Stewards – *'Die Revolutionäre Obleute und Vertrauensleute der Berliner Grossbetriebe'*, or the 'Revolutionary Shop Stewards and Confidence Men of Berlin's Large Factories' – were the most extreme in their demands. But could one name a revolt after them? The phrase does not slip easily off the tongue.

The demonstration that began on Sunday afternoon in the Siegesallee, amid the gaudy marble statues of Prussian margraves, electors and kings, was the largest Berlin had ever seen. The wide avenue was black with people, spreading down towards the Brandenburg Gate and further along the Linden. Here and there a red flag fluttered. Army lorries, with squads of men sporting rifles and machine-guns, were stalled in the human swell. An automobile moved slowly forward: Karl Liebknecht was on his speaking rounds once more.

Karl the Great, Charlemagne, as he was called – to distinguish him from

Karl the Small, Karl Radek, who entered Germany at Christmas to represent Russian Bolshevik interests – moved with crowds as a buoy without mooring would float with the tide; the thumping bands and furling banners flowed eastward past the Schloss on to Eichhorn's red fortress on Alexanderplatz, and so bobbed Liebknecht in his car. A meeting of seventy-one Shop Stewards and Independents was held in the Presidium. Liebknecht and Wilhelm Pieck were the only two Communists present. Ernst, the newly nominated police chief, had the gall to turn up with an assistant, Lieutenant Anton Fischer, who had once headed police intelligence, for Ernst was convinced he could persuade the men inside the building to follow reason and abandon their struggle. He was wrong. What they found was a mobilized camp: wagonloads of machine-guns were on display in the courtyard, trucks arrived from Spandau with further arms, young men gathered about with newly issued rifles. 'But the office is occupied; you can see that with your own eyes, Herr Ernst,' mocked Herr Eichhorn. On learning that Liebknecht and the Shop Stewards were in council upstairs, Ernst and Fischer decided to make a discreet departure.[79]

Participants in the meeting frequently got up from their chairs to wander out on to the balcony and view the chanting crowd. Georg Ledebour spoke for the left-wing Independents, Ernst Däumig for the Shop Stewards, and Eichhorn for himself and against the national elections to be held in a fortnight's time. Liebknecht made another *discours fleuve*. Count Harry Kessler was down there in the multitude. Most of Liebknecht's speech, he said, was unintelligible, and he couldn't be seen because the room behind him was in darkness, but his 'sing-song inflexion' carried over the heads of the crowd right across the square. 'He was like an invisible priest of the revolution, a mysterious but sonorous symbol to which these people raised their eyes. The demonstration seemed half-way between a Roman mass and a Puritan prayer-meeting.'[80]

Surely this was it: the rise of the masses, the insurgence of the proletariat, the 'second phase'. 'Germany is pregnant with the social revolution,' Liebknecht had written in November. Wasn't this the moment of birth? What could be a clearer message than this huge assemblage outside? It looked like one of Ludendorff's armies. What government could stand up against this? The seventy-one who sat inside drafted a proclamation to be distributed that night calling for a second mass meeting on Monday morning and the overthrow of Ebert: 'Forward to the fight for socialism. Forward to the fight for the power of the revolutionary proletariat. Down with the Ebert–Scheidemann government!' They appointed a fifty-three-member Revolutionary Committee with three presidents; Ledebour, Liebknecht and a man called Scholze. Then they drafted another proclamation: 'Comrades! Workers! The Ebert–Scheidemann government has compromised itself. It is herewith declared deposed by the undersigned Revolutionary Committee, the representatives of the revolutionary socialist workers and soldiers

(Independent Social Democratic Party and Communist Party). The under-signed Revolutionary Committee has temporarily taken over governmental affairs.'[81]

But the central committee of the Independent Socialists had not approved. Nor had the Communists' central committee. 'Karl, how could you?' sighed Rosa Luxemburg. Nor was it certain that the majority of the Shop Stewards would support the Revolutionary Committee's inspired initiative. Even more ominous was the assumption it had made about the crowd: nothing proved that it was a united army.

The crowds which appeared the next misty morning would suggest the contrary. During the night, armed bands had taken over most of the major newspaper houses in town and several public buildings, including the Reichs Printing Office – which printed the money which kept Germany turning. Ordinary people felt their livelihoods threatened. There was a sudden concern about the 'freedom of the press' – for it is a peculiar fact that Germany's press during the war years had enjoyed substantial freedom (certainly more than in France, probably more than in Britain). By 11 a.m. on Monday, there were more people in the streets than on Sunday. 'They are made up of the same sort of people, artisans and factory girls, dressed in the same sort of clothes, waving the same red flags, and moving in the same sort of shambling step,' recorded Kessler. But they were jeering at each other, 'and perhaps will be shooting one another down before the day is out'.[82] The army lorries with machine-guns were again rumbling back and forth. The crowds in the Siegesallee applauded Liebknecht. The crowds in Wilhelmstrasse applauded Ebert. Many applauded no one at all. Liebknecht spoke by the Victory Column. Scheidemann, who could never resist a window when the crowd was outside, spoke from the Reichs Chancellery.

During the war, hills and vales had determined the shape of battle. In Berlin, armed, committed men eyed one another across a no man's land of people. The two prizes were the newspaper offices on Belle-Allianz Platz (named to commemorate a Prussian victory at what the British annoyingly called the 'Battle of Waterloo') and Eichhorn's red fortress on Alexanderplatz. They were both surrounded by narrow little alleys and high-roofed dwellings. One would have thought that the Schloss and its neighbouring stables would have made a third strategic point – which is precisely why the Revolutionary Committee moved there late on Sunday night. But the occupying sailors – 'spearhead of the Revolution' – were interested only in their pay, and on Monday afternoon they threw the Committee out. From this moment on, the Committee, like Liebknecht, went wandering in search of a home.

A home in a wide field of battle. The shooting began in front of the rich department store of Wertheim's on Leipziger Platz at two that same afternoon; it quickly spread to Wilhelmsplatz, Potsdamer Platz and down the Linden. Ebert's government proclaimed full emergency powers to deal with the situation; Noske, the National Defence Minister, fled to a girls' school in Dahlem, where he set up military headquarters; the Independent Socialists, at the same time, started negotiations with Scheidemann in the Reichs Chancellery; Scheidemann kept on repeating that there would be no deal until 'freedom of the press' had been restored. The sailors expelled their leader, Lieutenant Dorrenbach, from the Schloss and formally declared themselves 'neutral'.

The 'masses' fled to whatever points of shelter they could find – in shops, in the open apartment-house corridors, behind the advertising pillars and the tables in cafés. The sound of shattering glass accompanied the tat! tat! tat! of machine-guns, the pounding of trench mortars, the blast of grenades. On Monday evening it poured with rain.

Starting a revolution in Berlin's midwinter was not a promising affair. The French had always managed to revolt in May or June, as the sap of life rose – even the Parisian Communards had had the patience to wait for the sun. Berliners chose the depth of nature's depression at a moment of national defeat.

No clear class lines could be drawn in this battle. There was no clean-cut division between soldiers and sailors this time. Nor was it a simple matter of government forces against revolutionaries. Nor of Free Corps against the disintegrating Imperial Army. Some of the violence was merely armed robbery, like the looting of Wertheim's or the ransacking of the main tobacco shops on Unter den Linden. Other incidents were laughable. The War Ministry on Leipziger Strasse was saved by a fast-thinking bureaucrat named Hamburger. Three hundred armed sailors entered the building on Monday and handed Herr Hamburger a piece of paper announcing that the Ebert–Scheidemann government had been deposed and that the Revolutionary Committee was taking over. Hamburger apologized, but noted that the paper had not been signed. The sailors roared off in their lorries in search of a member of the Committee who could sign it; when they returned, the building had been taken over by government forces. Bureaucrats also stalled revolutionary progress in the Reichs Printing Office, held by the workers of Schwarzkopf Industries. They were sitting in the place where the money was made; but the money was lying in cellars which were locked and the revolutionaries didn't have the keys – they were held by the bureaucrats. The workers begged and begged, but those stubborn bureaucrats would not hand them over. And the workers of Schwarzkopf would not break the law. They heaved a sigh of relief when government troops eventually seized the building on Wednesday; the workers wondered how *they* would handle the officials.

On the same day, Lieutenant Ames, the American POW supervisor, staying at the Hotel Adlon, commented on the danger of sticking one's head out of the window: 'In organized warfare, you generally have the satisfaction of knowing the direction of the enemy's fire, but, in the Berlin street fighting, you had no idea from which direction rifle or machine-gun fire might come next.' It was impossible to tell who was fighting for whom. 'I begin to believe the government has only a phantom army,' he commented on Wednesday. 'It never appears.'[83]

The direction of fire was also a problem for Ebert's government. There were bands of armed soldiers and sailors in the barracks of Berlin and Potsdam, but at the moment the violence erupted on Monday, 6 January, nobody knew what side they would take. When Noske left for Dahlem that afternoon he had not yet collected together an army – only two days had passed since his visit to Maercker's Free Corps in Zossen. Supreme Headquarters in Kassel was totally silent.[84] But Ebert got an encouraging sign from local commanders of the barracks, which hurriedly set up a 'garrison council' (*Kommandanturrat*) that brought forward two small forces: one to protect the Reichstag and the area around the Brandenburg Gate, the other stationed on Wilhelmstrasse in front of the Reichs Chancellery.

One of the main points of confusion about 'Spartacus Week' was that the names of government army units evolved with the fighting. Thus the troops responsible for the Reichstag zone were known as the 'Social Democratic Auxiliary Service' (*Sozialdemokratischer Helferdienst*) on Monday, 6 January, but became the 'Reichstag Regiment', one of the Free Corps, after they successfully held off a 'Spartacist' onslaught that Tuesday. As for the newly organized 'Lüttwitz Regiment' out in Potsdam, it soon included several Berlin 'corps'. The 'government forces' were fluid, and were not easy to identify at any given moment. This would explain Lieutenant Ames's confusion.

But there is no doubt that the government's strength was growing hour by hour. Noske describes how his headquarters in the Dahlem girls' school was swiftly transformed into a 'war camp'. Motor pools were organized, a telephone switchboard was set up, and its own radio station went on the air. Not only unemployed soldiers came forward to volunteer their services, but also people of the liberal professions and young students. More ominous for the rebels were the hordes of workers who were turning up to fight for the government. By Wednesday morning, 8 January, Ebert felt confident enought to proclaim that the national elections would take place as planned, in ten days, and that 'the organized power of the people will end oppression and anarchy'. 'The hour of reckoning is near!' his proclamation concluded, and signed off 'The Reich Government!' – with the exclamation mark.[85]

Serious fighting had already taken place outside Wolff's news agency on Belle-Allianz Platz and around the Anhalter and Potsdamer railway stations, with a firing of machine-guns and a lobbing of hand grenades. Whole segments of Eichhorn's Security Service at the Police Presidium defected, placing themselves under the command of the Charlottenburg police headquarters, sympathetic to the government. The sailors at the Schloss had already declared themselves 'neutral'. Liebknecht's 'masses' were beginning to look very thin on the ground.

On Thursday and Friday the air of Berlin resounded with shooting, cannonading and bombing. There was a brief show of sun. The pedestrians, out to enjoy it, made a panicky rush for the side alleys. The editorial offices of the *Rote Fahne*, on Friedrichstrasse, were taken by government troops on Thursday morning. Eichhorn himself withdrew in an armoured car to the Bötzow brewery, also on Friedrichstrasse. The Revolutionary Committee had ceased to function by Friday.

That night, 10–11 January, Major von Hoffmann's Potsdam companies advanced towards the offices of *Vorwärts*. It was a rambling, immensely complex building, with the main offices at the back, behind a courtyard. Hoffmann would have preferred to negotiate with the defendants, who were obviously not going to win. But the government did not want to negotiate, and Major von Stephani's 'Potsdam Free Corps' had got themselves into an excited state of battle-readiness, so there was little alternative: artillery and tanks would have to be used. In the early morning a couple of 10.5 cm howitzers blasted several holes in the façade, a mortar shell virtually split the building in two, a tank smashed through the main door; then the troops advanced with flame-throwers. Around three hundred men surrendered. They were escorted, their hands held to their heads, to the nearby dragoon barracks; some were beaten to death, the others were lined up against a wall and shot.

It poured cold rain all day. Most of rebellious Berlin had already been 'cleaned up' by the time Gustav Noske marched down Leipziger Strasse into the centre of town at the head of his various Free Corps. Accompanied by thumping kettledrums and brass, around three thousand men sang '*Die Wacht am Rhein*' and '*O Deutschland hoch in Ehren*' to an old imperial step. A few pops from rifles could be heard at the bottom of Friedrichstrasse, and the distant stammering of machine-guns occasionally supplemented the patter of rain and the regular rhythm of soldiers' boots – the 'Reichstag Regiment' was finishing off the rebellion in the press houses of Ullstein & Mosse on Belle-Allianz Platz.

There remained the Police Presidium. On Saturday night an armed group took control of the square. The group was under the command of the formerly mutinous 'Maybugs', but was mainly made up – amazingly – of men who had defected from Eichhorn's Security Service four days earlier. In the darkness of Sunday morning, field artillery again went to work, pounding holes in the red-brick headquarters, a building still larger and more complex than the *Vorwärts* offices. By dawn the job was done. Some of the 200-odd defenders were lucky enough to escape over the crooked roofs of the adjoining livery-stable district.

During the fighting, and the week that followed, streets and avenues – sometimes whole quarters – were cordoned off by gun-toting guards. January's dark nights ruled over the days. People remembered how search-lights beamed down empty alleys, making the wet cobbles glisten and the rows of black windows shine for a few seconds like stars. Trams, plunged in darkness, rolled on, throwing off electric sparks which 'crackled like fireworks'.[86]

But then, just round the corner might be found the liveliest scene, a celebration, a festival even. January was theatre season. One could understand why the management of the German Kaiser's Theatre decided to postpone the première of *From Morning to Midnight* for a couple of weeks. Most theatres and opera houses, however, remained open and packed. There was huge applause at a new production of Ibsen's play *Ghosts*.[87]

Post-war, revolutionary Berlin: 'Everybody can say whatever he wishes.'[88] Satirists like George Grosz were having a field day. Berlin was a city of contrasts that engendered pitch-black humour. The Brandenburg Gate had been the site of vicious fighting; between the gilt horses sprouted machine-guns; yet throughout 'Spartacus Week' the Christmas laurel wreaths and red streamers still hung there, along with the banners bearing the motto 'Peace and Freedom'. Boughs of trees and electric cables, shot down by gunfire, littered many of the avenues; wagons of the Fire Department collected the dead and wounded; but people would pick their way through to attend their favourite cabaret. 'The city is mad,' recorded Lieutenant Ames, 'and without the slightest hesitation, men wipe their blood-stained hands and come in from the street battles to the cabarets to dance and drink and dine with women.' 'At four o'clock I was in Friedrichstrasse,' wrote Harry Kessler on 8 January. 'There was a good deal of traffic and a lot of people stood discussing matters in small groups when suddenly there was a sound of shooting from the Unter den Linden end. Yet Leipziger Strasse, except for its closed shops, looked perfectly normal and the big cafés on Potsdamer Platz were open, brightly lit and doing business as usual.' On several of the pillar posts in the centre of town appeared the notice 'Stop it Berlin! Understand! Your dancer is Death!'[89]

9

Colonel Walther Reinhardt, the Minister of War, in a newspaper interview on Sunday, 12 January, stated that militarily Spartacus was defeated. 'What now remains to be done', he said, 'is to undertake measures for order.' The Reich would be holding, on schedule, national elections in a week.[90]

On Monday, Gustav Noske, the Minister of National Defence, issued Secret Order 1A, No. 10, which assigned his troops and Free Corps to various parts of Berlin – a nice, neat military plan to be executed now that the fighting was ended.[91] It was, of course, only partially realized, because he was dealing with a makeshift army in which different fragments competed with one another. (Anton Fischer, whose Republican soldiers had done much of the fighting, was disgusted with the way these novices, the Free Corps, tried to take over.) Noske's mind curiously resembled that of the Spartacists in that he too saw a phase of 'order' inevitably following a phase of 'struggle'. The Spartacists never imposed their 'general strike', the critical element of the proletarian phase of revolution – the tram drivers, for instance, started their strike only on Wednesday but were back at work on Thursday after the government had regained control of its printing office and was able to hand out more money. Noske did not impose 'order'. This can be seen in the kind of troops that made up the 'occupation forces'. Among them was the People's Naval Division, the sailors who lived in the Schloss, the 'spearhead of the Revolution'; they were rearmed and their pay was increased. Berlin was just as divided as it had been in December. Its history did not proceed in phases.

There are no reliable estimates of casualties during the January uprising. Official reports assert that between 150 and 200 lost their lives. The Communists claimed there were well over a thousand dead. When it came back into circulation on 13 January, the Majority Socialist paper *Vorwärts* published a poem:

> Many hundred dead are lying in a row –
> > Proletarians!
> Iron, powder, and lead do not ask if a person belongs to the Right, to the Left
> > or to Spartacus,
> > Proletarians!
> Who has brought violence into the streets?
> > Proletarians!
> Who first took up arms and relied on their results?
> > Spartacus!
> Many hundred dead are lying in a row –
> > Proletarians!
> Karl, Radek, Rosa and companions –
> None of them is there, none of them is there!
> > Proletarians!

A manhunt began. An 'Association for Combating Bolshevism' (founded, it is said, by Russian émigrés) offered rewards of up to 10,000 marks. Emil Eichhorn went into hiding and escaped in a car to Brunswick. Karl Radek was eventually arrested in February and became a prisoner well respected by the government; it needed him for his contacts with Russia.

On Tuesday night, 14 January, Rosa Luxemburg, Karl Liebknecht and a Communist colleague, Wilhelm Pieck, moved from their hiding place in working-class Neukölln to 53 Mannheimer Strasse in the middle-class district of Wilmersdorf. The Guard Cavalry Rifle Division had its headquarters virtually next door, in the Eden Hotel. The three Communist leaders were arrested by a 'citizen guard' the next afternoon and delivered to the hotel.

The circumstances of Wilhelm Pieck's 'escape' remain a mystery. The official story is that he managed to make his getaway while being transported to the Moabit jail. But, according to a German Communist Party report prepared by Hans Kippenberger in 1930, Pieck was permitted to leave the hotel with a letter of protection signed by a military intelligence officer. Kippenberger was murdered in Moscow by Russian Secret Police in 1936. Pieck, on the other hand, was in 1949 named President of the East German Democratic Republic – a post he held until his death in 1960.[92]

Liebknecht and Luxemburg were not so lucky. They were brought, in separate cars, to the Eden Hotel in the evening of 15 January. Soldiers hit Liebknecht with their rifle butts as he entered; he was already bleeding at his interrogation. Then he was led off to prison – at least that was the formal explanation. It was night. As he left the hotel a hefty trooper named Runge clubbed him on the head with his rifle. Liebknecht was carried half-conscious to the waiting car, driven out to New Lake in the Tiergarten, and there shot in the back several times 'while attempting to escape.' His body – that of an unknown man found in the zoological gardens – was delivered to an aid station near the Kaiser Memorial Church in the early hours of the morning.

Runge also clubbed Rosa Luxemburg as she was escorted out of the hotel. She was probably already dead when placed in the back of another waiting car. Lieutenant Vogel emptied his revolver into her head. Her body was thrown over the side of a bridge on the Landwehr Canal, from which it was eventually retrieved in May.

A government investigation into the deaths of the two Communist leaders was held. Private Runge was convicted of 'leaving his post without being properly relieved' and of 'improper use of his weapons'. He spent several months in jail. The judge agreed with court physicians that Lieutenant Vogel was 'psychopathic' – probably the result of his fine war record. He was sentenced to two years' imprisonment. But he never served it – he managed to escape to Holland, and when he returned a few months later Germany was concerned with other matters.[93]

The day before her death, Luxemburg had published a long article, 'Order in Berlin', in the *Rote Fahne*. 'A final and lasting victory in this moment could not be expected,' she stated. Yet she felt the rebellion had played its part in the onward march of history and that the revolution could already proclaim, 'I was, I am, I shall be!'[94]

Count Harry Kessler visited Walther Rathenau at his mother's mansion not long after these events. He found him as talkative as usual – an 'ultra-modernist strumming an old lyre'. Sitting in his damask-covered chair, Rathenau expressed a lot of sympathy for Bolshevism: it was a splendid system, he said, and he was sure that in a century's time it would rule the world. The current problem, he remarked, repeating his earlier idea, was finding the men to put in it. One was still in the age of little men. People had not yet developed a sense of – he returned to his theme – responsibility.

Take Hugo Stinnes, for example, the Ruhr industrialist and the only really important man in Germany. He had made 300 or 400 million marks out of the war, and now he was interested only in his own and his family firm's fortunes.

The Revolution had not yet taken place. In fact nothing had happened at all. But Rathenau was sure that one day it would all change.

He did not believe in death: he thought it was an illusion held by those who could not look at the whole, who could not take in the full scope of history. He quoted the ancients, who compared the end of a person's life to the fall of a leaf: the leaf dies, but the tree goes on living. And if the tree dies, the forest will still carry on. If the forest dies, the earth will surely sprout up something green and fresh. Even if the planet disappears, there will be a thousand others to replace it, all rejoicing in the rays of other suns. 'Nothing organic can die,' claimed Rathenau. 'The conception of dying arises from false observation, through the eye being fixed on the part instead of the whole. Nothing real in the world is mortal.'[95]

Paris in winter

1

On the day when Liebknecht and Luxemburg were murdered, 15 January, Marshal Foch's train rolled in to the old archbishopric town of Trier (or Trèves), now occupied by the Americans, to negotiate with Erzberger and his team the second extension of the Armistice. The main issue on the agenda was food. On 11 November the Allies had insisted on the maintenance of their naval blockade but, at the request of the Germans, had added the clause: 'The Allies and the United States contemplate the provisioning of Germany to such an extent as shall be found necessary.' The blockade, extended into the Baltic as a counter to Russian incursions, was more severe in January than it had been the previous November. No food had yet been delivered.

The problem was payment. In the United States the idea of extending credit to Germans so that they might feed themselves was unacceptable; the warehouses had been stockpiled in preparation for the great American military campaign of 1919 that never took place, and the farmers, during the November elections, had been promised minimum prices for their produce. Would this be on the back of the American taxpayer? If the Germans were to eat American food, they should be made to pay for it.

The French wanted payment for the regions – the cities, the countryside, the industries – that had been devastated by the invader. They knew that the Germans possessed only a limited amount of cash and securities; the French wanted priority placed on the reparation of their own material suffering.

The British wanted payment, too. It was the British Army that had broken the back of the German Imperial Army in the late summer and autumn of 1918. The British Empire had furnished a force of 8.9 million men during the war, and it mourned the loss of 900,000 lives. London and some of the English coastal towns had been bombed, but Canada, Australia and New Zealand were untouched. The price Britain, the Dominions and India had paid was in blood. They had a different understanding of priority in German payments from that of the French. They wanted their 'fair share'.

Foch's train to Trier carried, in January, a team of economic experts to discuss the matter of Germany's hard assets and also to try to mobilize Germany's huge merchant fleet, which was still lying idle in German ports. The Americans were led by Norman Davis, who had come over to Paris to represent the US Treasury at the peace conference. The Comte de Lasteyrie represented the French, and Professor Attolico the Italians. Enjoying a game of bridge with the Americans on the night journey out, as well as during the spare time when the train was parked in Trier, was Britain's representative and chief adviser to the Treasury, John Maynard Keynes.

Military negotiations, under the control of Marshal Foch, were held in one carriage; Davis chaired the financial talks in a second. Shipping negotiations were held separately in the back parlour of a nearby café and did not actually get going until Thursday, the 16th.

'Inquiries were made of the German delegates as to the safety of the Reichsbank's gold and note-issuing plant in view of the Spartacus disturbances,' noted Keynes in his official report to the British Treasury on 20 January. The Allies pressed the Germans to move these further west, if possible to Frankfurt (where they would be within reach of Western armies). The Germans agreed in principle, but they did not think this was the right moment to undertake transfers of gold from Berlin. The gold, they promised, was 'protected by armed guards, machine-guns and gas contrivances'. As for the note-printing plant, they admitted that 'owing to the treachery of the guard' it had been taken over by the Spartacists for a couple of days, but it was now back in the government's possession. However, they thought that 'removal of the plant would present great technical difficulties'.[1]

This was one of the great emotional moments in Keynes's life. Not because of the devastated battlefields which he had just crossed (he appears not to have noticed them). Nor because of the bizarre sight of a medieval German town occupied by the American Third Army. What moved Keynes on 15 January, and during subsequent meetings, was the spectacle of the German delegation, and in particular their leading spokesman, Dr Carl Melchior, a directing partner of the Hamburg bank M. M. Warburg. 'A sad lot they were in those early days, with drawn, dejected faces and tired staring eyes, like men who had been hammered on the Stock Exchange,' Keynes recounted in February 1920 before a private audience of his Bloomsbury friends, who had never supported Britain's war effort and who had reproached Keynes for staying on at the Treasury – the lecture was finally published in 1949, four years after Keynes's death. Keynes described how, on his first day at Trier, he developed 'one of the most curious intimacies in the world' with the man he 'got to love', Dr Melchior: 'From amongst [the delegates] stepped forward into the middle place a very small man, exquisitely clean, very well and neatly dressed, with a high stiff collar which seemed cleaner and whiter than an ordinary collar, his round head covered with grizzled hair shaved so close as to be like in substance to the pile of a close-made carpet.' His eyes gleamed 'straight at us, with extraordinary sorrow in them, yet like an honest animal at bay'.[2]

Keynes had found a secret hero who would weave his way into a story he was developing in his own mind about the aftermath of the war. He already had the main features of the story; it went back to the battles he had waged with America and France over the complex circle of war debts, to his calculations on Germany's limited 'capacity to pay', and to British hopes for a share in the 'reparations'. It also involved the discomfort – one might call it 'guilt' – he had developed within his tiny circle of pacifist Apostles and Bloomsberries. But his story required moral embellishment. Here was the significance, for Keynes, of Trier and Dr Melchior.

The very mundane purpose of his mission was to advance Britain's economic interests. Keynes had noted in a report written the day before, 14 January, that Hoover's food relief programme gave Britain some leverage on the United States. 'The whole position is rather an extraordinary one,' he remarked, 'as the immense surplus of the pig products for which the Americans have to find a market ... exposes them to pressure from us.' Hoover, now running a new Inter-Allied Supreme Council for Relief and Supply, had got himself into an awkward position. 'The underlying motive of the whole thing', explained Keynes, 'is Mr Hoover's abundant stocks of low-grade pig products at high prices which must at all costs be unloaded on someone, enemies failing allies. When Mr Hoover sleeps at night visions of pigs float across his bedclothes.' Keynes thought this was a grand opportunity for Britain to make some ready cash: the Germans would be anxious for food supplies, the Americans were seeking a market, and the British could act as intermediaries. 'It has been suggested by the Americans that we unload on Germany the large stocks of rather low-grade bacon which we now hold and replace these by fresher stocks from America which would be more readily saleable,' reported Keynes. At Trier, Britain would act in concert with the Americans, and the Germans would presumably co-operate. Keynes had a real economic motive to make a hero out of the German with hair like a close-shaved carpet.[3]

A proper hero must be set off against villains, and here the French played an admirable role. The meetings were conducted in English, imperfectly translated into French. The Comte de Lasteyrie, not an articulate man, had difficulty following the proceedings. After one of the sessions, he made angry complaints to Keynes that Norman Davis 'seemed sometimes to set himself up as an arbiter between the French and the German views' – which, given Keynes's comments of the day before, was almost certainly the case. But Keynes was now in a position to portray de Lasteyrie as a symbol of the 'grasping sterility of France', indifferent to the needs of the dignified, defeated German sitting opposite. Keynes later recalled 'I don't believe I have ever ... been so rude to anyone' as he had been to the French count.[4]

De Lasteyrie, however, was not the arch-villain of the piece. That part was reserved for Clemenceau's Minister of Finance – a man named Klotz.

On Sunday, 12 January, in Paris, Hoover's Council for Relief and Supply had adopted the proposal that German payment for Allied food supplies would take priority over all other debts. On Monday, at the Supreme War Council – in front of Wilson, Lloyd George and Clemenceau – Louis-Lucien Klotz said that, while he agreed with the necessity of feeding the Germans, he could not see why German payment for the food should take priority over everything else. Wilson made the rather lame argument that 'the Associated Governments have no money to pay for these supplies, therefore Germany must pay for them'. What he meant was that, having just lost the American elections, he was not sure he could get the necessary appropriation of funds through a hostile Congress – not that the United States did not possess the credit facilities to allow the Peace Conference time to judge the priority of claims on Germany's limited assets. The war had proved that the United States had ample facilities. The warehouses showed that the United States had ample food supplies. Why should the payment for Mr Hoover's pigs and cereals take priority over payment of reparations for the cities, the fields, the homes, the stock, the industries destroyed by Germany's invading armies? Klotz pointed out that 'it was not a question of food supply, it was purely a financial question, and no delay need therefore occur in the supply of food'.[5]

Klotz's argument was so reasonable that Melchior repeated it in Trier the following Wednesday: he asked for credit. A civil war was going on in Berlin: this was hardly an appropriate moment to demand payment for food. But Davis told Melchior that such a credit would be politically and legally impossible: that Germany would do better to use some of its assets now to buy food rather than give them outright to the Allies by way of reparations.[6] Small wonder that the Comte de Lasteyrie was annoyed.

Very little was achieved at Trier. The shipping negotiations held in the café (Keynes reported that E. N. Hurley of the American Treasury 'proved himself an impossible chairman and was guilty of serious indiscretions') went very badly: the German shipowners refused to hand over their vessels to the Allies. Early on Friday morning Foch announced that the Armistice would not be renewed if it was not signed within the hour. The Germans duly signed a document which included a clause pledging food for Germany in exchange for German passenger and cargo ships; the German government would pay for the food according to a predetermined price schedule, and it would be reimbursed for its tonnage. Since, however, the German government exerted no authority over the German shipowners, the boats remained idle in the ports, the Americans and British received no money, and Hoover's foodstuffs were never delivered.

But the German delegation had taken note of the differences developing between the Allies. The British and the Americans appeared, at the moment, to be in a special relationship, while France was cast as the pariah.

Keynes, in his lecture to the Bloomsbury Memoir Club the following year, described Klotz as 'a short, plump, heavy-moustached Jew, well-groomed, well kept, but with an unsteady, roving eye, and his shoulders a little bent with instinctive deprecation'. He admitted that he had not realized, when at Trier, that Dr Melchior was also a Jew.[7]

2

Thanks to Foch's ultimatum, Clemenceau was able to tell Wilson and Lloyd George at 10.30, Friday morning, 17 January, that the Armistice had been renewed for a month and that the Germans had signed 'all the clauses' proposed on the previous Monday.[8] The French were pressed for time. Their armies had achieved a military victory in circumstances they knew could never be repeated; they sought to establish as quickly as possible an internationally guaranteed barrier against a neighbour who would not remain weak for ever. But there were already dissensions among their allies; and the mobilized armies – French, British and American – were getting restless. London's *Punch* published a cartoon showing a hallowed allegory of Peace standing by one of the ornate doors of the Quai d'Orsay and muttering, 'I know I shall have to wait for a while; but I do hope they won't talk too much.'[9] That was the French hope too.

Talks had begun the previous Sunday, within twenty-four hours of Lloyd George's arrival in the city behind walls, Paris. The last international gathering of this kind had been over a hundred years earlier in another walled city, Vienna. There an aristocracy in possession of all Europe had taken over nine months to establish the structure of peace on the Continent. Paris witnessed a new kind of nobility – orators and party leaders, representatives of parliaments and members of a mass press. They would come to a settlement within six months. Yet, though every inhabited continent in the world was involved, half of Europe was beyond their grasp. Never before and never since has an international encounter at this scale ever worked at such speed.

It had been announced on Sunday, 12 January, that the Supreme War Council, which had been running Allied affairs for over a year, was about to meet at the Quai d'Orsay. For everyone then in Paris this represented the beginning of the Peace Conference. Wilson's doctor, Admiral Grayson, was out on the Place de la Concorde that afternoon, just before the meeting opened. He witnessed a most exotic scene. The Western leaders appeared in their cars. There were Japanese and Chinese on the square, 'looking wise and saying nothing'; Arabians could be seen 'in picturesque costume'; the Indian princes wore 'their British uniforms, but with flowing native turbans'.[10]

Twenty-seven nations were represented at the Conference. Most of the delegations were now in Paris. But there was still no formal plan for procedure, nor even had the number of delegates by nation been apportioned.

No central assembly existed. There was no executive administration. Nor was there any indication whether the main subject of discussion would be a treaty with Germany or the affairs of the world.

Each of the four victorious powers had been granted five delegates during the pre-armistice negotiations within the Supreme War Council back in October. At the December meetings in London, Japan was invited to present herself in Paris as a fifth Great Power. Wilson had announced his choice of delegates – which, significantly, included only one Republican – in November; there were already complaints in January that they were not being consulted. Lloyd George drew up his list for the British Empire immediately after the general election; it reflected each of the major political parties in his new Coalition government (which he had set up just before leaving for France), and it included one rotating delegate drawn, according to the subject under discussion, from the Dominion prime ministers. Records show the British delegation in a constant state of communication. Clemenceau revealed his choice only just before the first meeting of the Supreme War Council in January. It was basically a repeat of 'Clemenceau at all the ministries'. What shocked many was the absence of Philippe Berthelot, the best brain at the Quai d'Orsay. Clemenceau's Foreign Minister, Stéphen Pichon – 'fumbling, owl-like'[11] – was the most physically present; André Tardieu was the most brilliant. As secretary-general of the Conference Clemenceau had designated his old friend Paul Dutasta – aimiable but hardly grand. The Japanese delegation was still travelling on the high seas.

Wilson himself had just returned from a disastrous trip to Italy in which he had managed to insult the government, the parliament and the Church. As in London the crowds had applauded, but the President's theory about 'reciprocal feeling' with the people was looking the worse for wear. In Italy the crowds were cheering for their own unexpected military victory, not for Wilson. When he returned to Paris, nobody heard him talk about European leaders lacking the support of their people: Lloyd George had recently been endorsed by a landslide election, Clemenceau had won a large confidence vote in parliament; Wilson had neither the American electorate nor Congress behind him.

War went on in Eastern Europe. While the soldiers, sailors and citizens fought a pitched battle in Berlin, a whirlwind of violence spread through Russia. As the Romanians struggled to rebuild their own ruined country, they sent an army across their borders and overran Transylvania. Italian forces entered Albania and the peninsula of Istria. A Bolshevik coup was in preparation in Hungary. Paderewski, the cultured, gentle pianist, wrote to Colonel House from Warsaw that the Polish situation was 'simply tragic'. 'We have no food, no uniforms, no arms, no munitions.' He asked for artillery and, particularly, German rifle munitions. 'If this action is delayed our entire civilization may cease to exist,' he warned. 'The war may only result in the establishment of barbarism all over Europe.'[12]

Thus the delegates in Paris were caught up in a march of events over which they had little control and which had not slowed since November. There was talk of a 'new order', yet constant reports of old violent chaos.

And there was longing, of course, for peace. '*The Peace Conference*, a magic phrase,' said Clemenceau.[13] Winston Churchill would call it the 'Armistice Dream' – that search for a life more stable, more noble, more beautiful which haunted every thinking man.[14] Harold Nicolson wrote of setting off to Paris under 'the halo of some divine mission'. 'We were preparing not Peace only, but Eternal Peace.'[15]

Westerners wanted to put the horror of war behind them. Only ten weeks earlier British armies had been fighting their way across the Scheldt to Mons and across the Sambre to Maubeuge; the French had entered La Capelle; the Americans had just broken through German defences in the Argonne with their First Army – which had only been inaugurated in August. '*Cette guerre ne doit pas conclure comme les guerres d'autrefois, comme les guerres d'ancien régime*,' said Clemenceau from the Deputies' tribune on 29 December. Not a family in France or in Britain had been untouched by the loss of a relation or a friend. Anyone who took the guided tour out from walled Paris to the 'devastated zones' would return with the thought: 'There has to be a better way of settling disputes.'

Peace in the West had been so sudden. '*La paix en coup de foudre*,' said Clemenceau[16] – which one might liberally translate as 'the peace of short love affairs'. As in love, every development during the next few months was accompanied by a great emotional turmoil. The march of events did not wait for the dreams to catch up. Ideals were hard to realize.

One of the remarkable features of the New Year was the change that had overcome the leading crusader, Woodrow Wilson. After his trips to England and Italy he appeared to lose interest in his Fourteen Points, Four Principles and Five Particulars. This caused a problem for those delegates and counsellors who regarded the Allies as morally bound to these statements by terms of the pre-armistice exchange of notes between Washington and Berlin; it left them headless. It comforted those – all of whom had sat on the Supreme War Council in October – that had treated them as mere guidelines, not practical measures for peace. But Wilson's head had turned to a grander matter, the Covenant of the League of Nations, the 'heir of the Empires', despite warnings from his closest advisers that it would be difficult to get this through the Senate. Rumours spread through the Allied delegations that Wilson would not deliver: 'It was the ghost at all our feasts.'[17]

Wilson had ignored the French peace plan of November as well as a new version put forward by Tardieu in early January. He thus turned his back on a proposition for 'the suspension of all previous special agreements' (i.e. the so-called 'secret treaties' contracted during the war), on the need to place priority on an immediate preliminary treaty with Germany (which would have established the peace), on the distinction between a 'preliminary conference' between Allies and a 'general congress' that would have brought Germany into the talks, and on the idea that the 'four great victorious powers' should, at the preliminaries, decide on the general issues while the 'small powers' would be consulted on 'special affairs' (which would have speeded up procedure). Basically, what Wilson objected to was the plan's use of European historical precedent: he wanted to impose a new global ideal through 'reciprocal feeling' with the peoples.

It was largely on account of Wilson that the world's delegations, when they came face to face in Paris, found that they had no formal plan. But there were some influential people who knew what was needed. One of them was Lieutenant General Maurice Hankey.

Maurice Hankey's astounding talent for note-taking – his ability to reproduce the minutes of long administrative meetings from memory – had been noticed when he was an officer in the Royal Marines; in 1912, at the age of thirty-five, he had been named secretary of the Committee of Imperial Defence. In that post he prepared a 'War Book' that had made it possible for Britain to mobilize in August 1914. 'Without Hankey we should have lost the war,' said Balfour. Hankey became Lloyd George's government secretary. He organized the Imperial War Cabinet, which brought together the Dominion premiers, and used this as a model for the Supreme War Council when it was set up in autumn, 1917. Leather briefcase in hand, Hankey was always there, near his Prime Minister, whether he was in Downing Street, the trenches or Versailles. A real magician, he seemed able to pull out of that case the needed minute, the critical document, on demand.

'The British Empire interested me more than the peace settlement,' Hankey admitted in his memoirs. Nevertheless, he made sure he knew all the tentative plans for the conference by heart. He dismissed the Foreign Office's plan as too ingenious, 'rather resembling a spider's web, with the Supreme Council in the centre, and vast numbers of committees and subcommittees branching out'. Tardieu's scheme was more practical but, all the same, 'over-elaborate'. Why not simply stick to the Supreme War Council?[18]

Hankey managed the conversion of the war council into a peace council in twenty-four hours – an achievement which would determine the administrative structure of the entire conference.

When he arrived in Paris with the Prime Minister late on Saturday evening, 11 January, he learned that urgent decisions were required by Foch for the Armistice renewal, due the following week. A golden opportunity! Call the Supreme War Council in from Versailles. Henry Wilson agreed to collect the military representatives and their four secretaries. The Italian representative was away, and he couldn't find the two British secretaries, but that hardly mattered; the others turned up at the Quai d'Orsay at 2.30, Sunday afternoon. Woodrow Wilson, the prime ministers and the foreign ministers were present. Before the meeting began, Hankey had a few words with Clemenceau; they agreed that it was essential to keep the business of the Armistice renewal separate from any discussion of conference procedure. Foch read a note regarding the Armistice, Wilson made some comments about checking the advance of Bolshevism with food rather than armies, then the meeting adjourned for tea; the military representatives withdrew. A second meeting, with only the civilian leaders attending, started at 4 p.m. with a discussion of the number of delegates that ought to be assigned to the twenty-seven nations: that was the moment the Paris Peace Conference began.[19]

Hankey wrote home the following morning, 'I was too busy to write yesterday, as I was doing *all* the work of the Conference; I had to take single-handed first a Supreme War Council and then a "hush-frocks" conference [Henry Wilson's term for a secret meeting of ministers] – five hours on end. I was working until past midnight, dictating thirty pages of minutes.'[20] Hankey divided these minutes into two separate meetings, the first being that of the Supreme War Council, the second that of the 'Council of Ten' – the term was coined by Hankey on the grounds that this would be a gathering of the prime ministers and foreign ministers of the Five Great Powers. Shortly after midnight Hankey's minutes were distributed to the authorities concerned before anyone else had even begun compiling the record.

So the Council of Ten would meet in the French Foreign Minister's offices at the Quai d'Orsay, where it would act as a steering committee for the Conference. By the end of the week it had made two further decisions that would define its relationship to the other delegations and how it would deal with the world press.

On Monday, 13 January, Wilson – who still thought these were only informal conversations with the European Allies – spoke of a need for an agenda to guide their thoughts. 'It is necessary to move quicksands before we can begin to walk,' he said, and, pulling a slip of paper out of his pocket, suggested a list of five subjects: the League of Nations, reparation, the new states, frontiers and territorial changes, and colonies. 'And', interrupted Lloyd George, 'the responsibility of the authors of the war.' Lloyd George had just received his Attorney-General's interim report on 'Breaches of the Laws of War', which recommended that the ex-Kaiser be prosecuted. Clemenceau responded that 'nothing could be done until the Peace Conference was brought together' and so proposed that all the delegates in Paris be called 'forthwith'. Wilson demurred, arguing that he wanted a complete agreement between the major powers before conferring with the other delegates. Baron Sonnino wanted postponement because the Italian delegation had not yet been appointed. But Clemenceau insisted that 'no further delay should occur in holding the meeting'. His proposal was accepted: a 'Plenary Conference' would be held downstairs in the grand Salle d'Horloge at 2.30 p.m. Saturday, 18 January: the second major institution of the international conference had been established.[21]

Some of the world's best-paid newspaper correspondents had come to Paris. They rode on a wave of rising expectation. During the first years of the war the press had been kept under a tyrannic kind of control by the generals, but as the armies advanced in the last months press restrictions had been loosened; at the war's end, Western newspapers and their proprietors had attained a degree of political power they had never before known. Yet they sought still more. Censorship was lifted in Britain and the United States; it was maintained in France. 'Open covenants openly arrived at,' Wilson had proposed as his Point I; this was surely not going to be a conference like Vienna where public statements had been limited to brief communiqués in Metternich's *Wiener Beobachter*. The foreign correspondents – over five hundred of them in the French capital by the third week of January – thought the Peace Conference would be like reporting on a battle, with its instant drama and life-relating details. But within hours of their arrival they were in despair: they had no stories to tell. On 14 January eleven well-known American correspondents signed a manifesto addressed to Wilson, protesting what they regarded as a 'gag rule' imposed on the Conference. Tumulty, Wilson's secretary, who remained in Washington, cabled on 16 January, 'American newspapers filled with stories this morning of critical character about rule of secrecy adopted for peace conferences, claiming that the first of the Fourteen Points has been violated.'[22]

In fact no such rule of secrecy had been adopted. What had been agreed on in the Council of Ten was a procedure for reporting on negotiations that was the norm for any functioning democratic government. After their first meeting on Sunday, careless talk among advisers had already led to leaks about the apportionment of delegates, German gold reserves, British government views on Russia, and American views on the Adriatic. Some ruling on the press had to be adopted. The Council discussed the problem (along with plenty of others) during the next few days. Wilson kept expressing doubts 'whether anything less than complete publicity would satisfy the American public'. But, as Lloyd George pointed out, that would make decision-making impossible. Peace could not be settled by 'public clamour'. He had just been through a British election which, he said, if it had gone on any longer would have tied his hands with pledges and deprived him of his freedom of action; if every twist and turn in discussions was to be made public, the conference would be turned into something resembling the sixteenth-century Council of Trent that had lasted forty-three years and ended long after the death of its original members.[23]

Clemenceau already had the elements of a solution at the first Sunday meeting. There were, he said, three kinds of conference involved here: informal conversations, the formal preliminary peace conference, and then the general congress. Publicity ought to be graded accordingly. Wilson managed to fudge the distinction between the 'conference' and the 'congress' (it implied the writing of a preliminary treaty and a final treaty – two treaties to be pushed through the US Senate!), but he did finally admit to the difference between 'conversations' between the Great Powers and the 'Conference' to which everyone, including the press, would be admitted. 'The press is well aware that it is excluded from the proceedings of cabinets,' explained Lloyd George. 'Well, this' – he meant the Council – 'is the Cabinet of Nations!' Wilson, who never consulted his own Cabinet, understood the principle. On 17 January, one day before the opening Plenary Conference, a 'memorandum on publicity' was issued to the press stating that 'conversations of the Great Powers are far more analogous to the meetings of a Cabinet than to those of a legislature . . . The vital process [of negotiation] would only be hindered if the discussion of every disputed question were to open by a public declaration . . . It is extremely important that the settlement should be not only just but speedy.'[24]

Thus, within six days, a great chain of relationships had come into being: the small powers and the big powers had been defined, a council and a plenary conference had been created, the reporting to the press was to be determined by the type of meeting that took place. By Friday, the Council was also preparing to set up expert committees broadly identified by Wilson's five-point 'agenda'.

Today, such a complex arrangement would need to be presented with the aid of computer-enhanced, coloured flow diagrams. There were no such things at the time. The system, as Hankey observed, bore a similarity to the British constitution in that it had no statutory basis and was grounded on no plan. 'It was in effect a continuation of the system of conference that had gradually grown up during the war, and had culminated in the Supreme War Council.'[25]

Outside, the rain fell in torrents as the delegates assembled in the Salle d'Horloge – named after a clock that had been ticking at the end of the room since the days when Louis XVI ruled France. Sir George Riddell, the press magnate, had gone round to see the British ambassador, Lord Derby, at ten that Saturday morning. 'Are you going to the opening of the Peace Conference?' he asked. 'No,' replied Derby, 'I have nothing to do with it.' 'I understand you have to summon the delegates,' responded Riddell, somewhat baffled. 'What?' said Derby. 'Now come to think of it, I did receive a communication from the Foreign Office last night.' He looked in his box and there, sure enough, was the letter. Most of the delegates did, in fact, get to the Quai d'Orsay in time for the opening at three.[26]

Selected members of the press were crammed into an ante-room. In the large hall, the delegates sat at long tables, their secretaries and advisers behind them in accordance with a Council decision. A heavy cold had kept Wilson in bed until midday, but he arrived just before Clemenceau. Lloyd George was late; when he entered, Poincaré had already started his speech.

The German Empire, said the French President, had been founded in

Versailles forty-eight years ago to the day; 'born in injustice, it has ended in opprobrium'. He asked the delegates to seek nothing but justice – justice that 'has no favourites', but which first demands 'restitution and reparation for the peoples and individuals who have been despoiled or maltreated', and also 'the punishment of the guilty'. After the speech had been translated into English Poincaré left the room.[27]

Wilson rose to name Clemenceau president of the Conference. House had helped him prepare the speech. 'I would say something regarding Paris as an ancient city, and speak of this event as the crowning glory of her history,' he had advised. That was the gist of Wilson's remarks – this 'ancient and beautiful capital'. (Riddell, at tea with Wilson after the session, noted that the city's coat of arms was a ship bearing the inscription: 'It often rolls but it never sinks.') Lloyd George, in an impromptu seconding address, called Clemenceau 'the grand young man of France'. The confused French interpreter translated it as *'le grand vieil homme'*.[28]

Clemenceau, who had devoted his life to that little word 'justice', made a speech notably more generous than Poincaré's. On 'reparation', he said that the Conference should seek a 'nobler and higher reparation . . . so that the peoples may be able at last to escape from this fatal embrace, which, piling up ruin and grief, terrorizes populations'. And he emphasized what he had always emphasized: the unity of the alliance. 'We have come here as friends; we must leave this room as brothers . . . Everything must yield to the necessity of a closer and closer union among the peoples who have taken part in this Great War. The League of Nations it is here. It is in yourselves; it is for you to make it live; and for that it must be in our hearts.'[29]

The delegates had already received a notice announcing that the 'Order of the Session' would be reparations, 'responsibility for the authors of the war', and 'the international legislation for labour'. Clemenceau explained that the League of Nations would be the subject of the second plenary session, held the next Saturday. In the meantime the delegates were invited to submit their observations in writing to the Secretariat of the Conference on the subjects listed – or on any other subject members 'may think necessary'. Clemenceau paused a moment and then declared, 'As nobody wishes to speak the session is adjourned at 16.35 o'clock!' – and brought his hammer down on the table with such a resounding crash that nobody could possibly say a word.[30]

Nicolson noted in his diary that day that Clemenceau spoke 'like a machine gun'. As the delegates dispersed, there were some whispers about the authoritarian attitude of the Great Powers. Jules Cambon, the veteran diplomat, was heard muttering to an Englishman, *'Mon cher, savez-vous ce qui va résulter de cette conférence? Une improvisation.'*[31]

There would be much improvisation. No international institution existed. No conference of this kind had been called in a hundred years.

Within a week of its creation the Council of Ten had turned its attention to the setting up of the expert committees, so that these could be formally approved at the second plenary session, on 25 January. Once more Hankey played a leading role, drafting with Lloyd George resolutions for the establishment of five committees, concerned with the League of Nations (designed to draw the focus of attention on 25 January), the responsibility of the authors of the war and the enforcement of penalties, reparation for damage (Wilson managed to get deleted the word 'indemnity', included in the original British proposal), international legislation on labour, and international control of the waterways (a phrase more acceptable to Hankey and his British colleagues than 'freedom of the seas').

Many would complain about the delay in the setting up of the territorial committees, which did not take place until the second week of February. But in fact what happened to Italy's borders, and in the Balkans, Greece, Hungary, Romania and Russia – let alone the Middle East, the colonies, Shantung and Japan – was of secondary importance when compared to the one essential committee that was missing: that concerned with the treaty with Germany. Germany's westward thrust across the plain was what had triggered world war. Only a guaranteed accord on this zone could be the basis of world peace. Like fighting in the war, intense diplomatic negotiation had a tendency to become parochial: quickly it would degenerate into arguments about Fiume's suburbs or the Dodecanese. What was needed was a practical point of focus: the peace with Germany. The rest was diversion.

Wilson led the diversion because Wilson sought a global solution: he could not support the idea that the origin and the end of the problem would be Europe. It was Wilson's insistence on his global ideal that made all practical talk so rapidly local. Wilson pulled attention away from what should have been the true focus of the Conference.

Yet how the younger generation, the war generation, loved it. They wanted a reformed humanity, not the old business of power politics. 'Our emotions centred less around the old than around the new,' confessed Nicolson. 'The concepts "Germany", "Austria", "Hungary", "Bulgaria" or "Turkey" were not in the forefront of our minds. It was the thought of the new Serbia, the new Greece, the new Bohemia, the new Poland which made our hearts sing hymns at heaven's gate.'[32] A new Europe, a new world. The moment they stepped into Paris, the junior consultants and experts – the brightest products of the universities – had already laid the ground for their 'disillusionment'. They ignored the one essential matter: peace with the power that had made war on them.

Hankey's creation, the Council of Ten, conducted itself with great ceremony in the Foreign Minister's study, the closed high windows looking out on to a rain-drenched lawn, double doors preventing the entry or exit of sound, a huge log fire heating the air that was already thick with fever. Though Hankey had called it 'the Council of Ten', there would on average be about thirty people present, including secretaries, advisers, and the delegation of the smaller power currently being heard. Clive Day, the young chief of America's 'Balkan Division', once counted fifty-four in the room.[33]

The Congress of Vienna had, in its nine months of existence, witnessed the creation of eight technical committees. The Conference of Paris, in less than six months, saw the creation of 58 committees that had, André Tardieu assures us, 1,646 meetings, their conclusions later being verified by 36 local investigations and then discussed by 3 more general bodies.[34] Normal procedure was for the Council to give a preliminary hearing to territorial and other claims of the various states and then set up an expert committee to report on each claim in detail; the Council, in theory, would then decide the matter on the basis of the committee's report. Because the Council's time was obviously limited, Nicolson complained that the procedure tended to make the expert committee a court of final appeal – a problem that would have most significance when the Conference eventually did get down to drafting the treaty with Germany.

The work went on at such speed. Yet disgruntlement over inaction and delay started on the first day of the Conference and continued throughout it. Most of this was due to a misunderstanding of the organization or to individuals' feelings that their services were not being properly employed. Edith Benham, Wilson's private secretary, records both the President's disappointment and his confusion on being asked, on 12 January, to sit on an 'interallied High Commission' to confer about extending the Armistice. 'Don't wonder in speaking of it that the President said it reminded him of an old ladies' tea party for they all talked and when the Peace Conference finally got under way and they were discussing along very well, a tea table was brought in and they all had tea' – so one intimate witness on Wilson's side recorded Hankey's crucial moment when the Supreme War Council was converted into the Council of Ten. On 21 January, after the first plenary session and while the Council was establishing the first committees, the Canadian Prime Minister, Sir Robert Borden, complained to Lloyd George about the delay in the Conference's work as well as the tendency of the Council to decide everything. 'The Press are getting restless at the apparent inability of the Conference to settle down to the task of making peace,' Nicolson noted in his diary two days later as he prepared his umpteenth report on the Koritsa enclave.[35]

'*Il faut aboutir*,' Clemenceau kept repeating with all the stubbornness he had demonstrated on the front.

For many delegates and their staffs, the pressure of work was intense. 'I am getting a most terrific hustle on,' Hankey wrote home, proudly, on the 22nd. Work conditions were far from ideal. The 207 members of the British delegation were housed in the Hotel Majestic on the Avenue Kléber – which was modern and provided hot water (a luxury for those who had lived in wartime London) – but they worked next door at the Astoria, a former Japanese hospital with bare floorboards that smelt of Lysol. The offices were small and dark. Many suffered from the cold. Miss Mary Hughes, who worked for the head of PID (the Political Intelligence Department), relied on logs that Lord Hardinge, organizing ambassador, filched from some unknown supplier; 'we endeavoured to make fires on the flat hearths, without any small firewood or coal'. Food supplies were very difficult, despite the efforts of Midlands Hotels, the British caterers. But the most distressing feature of that cramped life in Paris was disease. The flu was rampant. The hospital rooms on the top floor of the Majestic were filled to overflowing. Nearly every member of Britain's delegation sniffled or suffered from headaches. Lloyd George referred to the hard conditions when addressing the Commons in April: 'I am doubtful whether any body of men with a difficult task have worked under greater difficulties,' he said. Thinking perhaps of demonstrations by the Confédération Générale du Travail he continued – 'stones clattering on the roof, and crashing through the windows, and sometimes wild men screaming through the key-holes'.[36]

The work was unevenly distributed. In the British delegation it was the political and economic experts who took the lion's share, while Dominion staff seemed less pressed. It had been said in Vienna that the Congress did not work, it danced; so it was for those who had leisure in Paris. Every night in the great hotels the dance bands struck up the tango and the foxtrot. The card game in fashion was no longer whist, it was bridge.

Departmental jealousies were aggravated by the pressure of time and by the fact that the civil servants lived and worked on top of one another. A special flat, with sitting room, was set aside in the Majestic for the men of the Treasury – Keynes, Dudley Ward and Armitage-Smith – though Keynes actually spent the first three weeks of the conference in the South of France, having contracted flu in Trier. The personnel working on the League of Nations got special quarters. But accommodation for others was not as comfortable, and this created bitterness: which department? which floor? One gains the impression from PID's Sir James Headlam-Morley that his principal criticism of the Paris Peace Conference was his dissatisfaction with the floor arrangements.

Several felt they were not being properly consulted. Colonel T. E. Lawrence – Lawrence of Arabia – had no formal position within the British delegation. According to Nicolson, he 'would glide along the corridors of the Majestic, the lines of resentment hardening around his boyish lips: an undergraduate with a chin'.[37] He was not the only one who was resentful.

Hankey himself had to watch out for resenters. Lord Hardinge of Penshurst was expecting to be named secretary of the British delegation. When Lloyd George insisted that Hankey take the job, Hankey became 'thoroughly befogged'. Like Talleyrand during the siege of 1814, he thought the best way to clear his mind was to go out to the city walls. So on Sunday morning,

19 January, he trudged through the rain until he reached an *octroi*, and 'at that dingy spot I saw in a flash the solution'. He took a cab straight back to the Avenue Kléber and proposed that Hardinge become 'Organizing Ambassador', while Hankey accepted the post of 'British Secretary to the Peace Conference'. Everyone was happy save Hardinge.[38]

Hankey had more responsibilities than his title implied. Paul Dutasta, the secretary-general, cheerfully accepted most projects proposed by the former Royal Marine officer, for he had neither the staff nor the space at the Quai d'Orsay to cope with the burgeoning administrative demands being made on him. Hankey offered him the hospitality of his own quarters in the Villa Majestic, just opposite the hotel. Over the next six months this was the nerve centre of Paris.

Just as Friedrich von Genz is remembered as the organizer of the Vienna Congress, so should Maurice Hankey be recognized as organizer of the great Paris Peace Conference.

3

The sun shone down on the Reich that Sunday, 19 January, as the polling booths opened. Germany was the fourth of the belligerent powers – if one counts Poland – to hold national elections in the period of the Armistice. It was one of the prettiest and quietest days of that whole agitated winter. Kessler voted in a bar on the Linkstrasse. 'Cooks, nurses, old ladies, whole families with father, mother, maid, and even small children troop in and take their place in the line,' he noted. 'As undramatic as any natural occurrence, like a rainy day in the country.'[39]

In contrast to the British elections, the turnout was a huge 83 per cent of the new democratic electorate. Only once again in the short history of the Republic would so many participate – in 1932, when the Nazis were manoeuvring for power. The wider franchise brought a few changes to Germany's political landscape. Many groups now called themselves the 'People's Party', including the most conservative. There were fewer academics running, and more representatives of the professions and of business. Interest organizations and labour unions put forward a larger number of candidates. The new system of proportional representation broke down the former regional strongholds of the parties, but, instead of inciting a concern for the great national issues of the time, this merely encouraged the old tendency in German parties to cater to special-interest groups. Corporatism did not fade with the advent of German democracy; it advanced.

In fact the most remarkable feature of the elections of 19 January 1919 was the degree to which they proved the continued existence of the old Germany, the Kaiser's Germany, a Germany that could not recognize any purpose in workers' and soldiers' councils, in 'socialization', in a government of People's Commissars, a Germany that seemed hardly influenced by four and a half years of war and economic hardship. If one compares the results with those of the elections of 1912 (bearing in mind the change in party names) one will note they are almost identical. The Social Democrats were once again the largest party, with 37.9 per cent of the votes going to the Majority branch and 7.6 per cent to the Independents, but they did not have an absolute majority. The largest of the 'bourgeois' parties was, as it had been in 1912, Erzberger's Centre Party with 19.7 per cent of the votes. The DDP and the DVP, which corresponded to the former Progressive and National Liberal Parties, got 19.7 and 4.4 per cent respectively. The DNVP, a transformed Conservative Party, won 10.3 per cent. The Communist boycott of the elections had had no effect at all.

If Ebert, in calling the elections, had sought to broaden the basis of his November government, it was now clear that he would have to do this in co-operation with Germany's political centre. Ultimately Ebert, like Talleyrand at the end of the Napoleonic wars, sought 'legitimacy'. Until the elections, the only legal claim he had to head the government of Germany was Prince Max's offer of the chancellorship on 9 November and the vote, the next day in the Circus Busch, of Berlin's worker's and soldiers' councils; it was no legal claim at all. The election, by placing his party at the forefront, gave Ebert a popular mandate; it also, in sanctioning the pre-war political make-up of the parties, suggested that the German people themselves sought a legitimate government 'consolidated and consecrated by a long succession of years' – as Talleyrand had once put it.

The problem, however, with a substitute imperial regime – an 'Ersatzkaisertum' – was that it risked reviving all the troubles of the old regime: the lack of parliamentary responsibility, the departmentalization of public life, the maintenance of states within the state – like Supreme Command – and, of course, the isolation of the 'monarchy'. It would also be a bitter disappointment for those, particularly from the front, who had put their faith in a new world, who were convinced, like Rathenau, that the old social structures would never rise again from the flames.

The experience of the war had shown the old structures liable to a third danger: the emergence of a totalitarian state. In 1917 Erzberger had built up a new parliamentary majority of Catholic, liberals and Socialists around his 'Peace Resolution'. For the remainder of the war they met in an Inter-Party Committee, but they never managed to create a governing majority. The election results of January 1919 made another Catholic–liberal–Socialist combination inevitable. Could they govern? Would they constitute a real power in Germany?

Supreme Command, still sitting in Kassel, also had a claim to legitimacy. If Ebert had somewhat dubiously inherited the chancellorship from Prince Max, Supreme Command could assert itself as successor to the Kaiser's power, for His Majesty had resigned in Spa, not Berlin, and he had left his last oral instructions with the generals. Besides, after Christmas and the events of January, Ebert owed his existence to Supreme Command.

With the collapse of the old Imperial Army, Supreme Command put its hopes in Noske and his energetic recruitment of the Free Corps. On 19 January – the same day as the elections – Noske issued a decree reducing the soldier's councils to a consultative capacity. Supreme Command, which had been contending the authority of the councils since December, took this as a positive sign that the Minister of National Defence was their man.

The repression, the previous week, of the Spartacist revolt in Berlin did not end the turmoil in Germany. The Revolutionary Shop Stewards reverted to their tactic of strike. On 22 January Berlin was blacked out and all the trams came to a halt because the power stations had gone on strike. The dislocation this caused for the average Berliner was far greater than that of the Spartacus rising; even the cabarets had to close down. Communists and Independents spread their insurgency to other parts of Germany. There was trouble in the ports, the homeland of revolt. During the Berlin rising, an Independent Socialist Republic had been declared in Bremen. Noske was not going to tolerate it, for 'if order were not restored immediately in Bremen, the Government could consider itself lost, for no one would respect it. Any risk was better than that.'[40] After the elections were over Noske sent in the Gerstenberg Division, locally recruited, and, following a series of bloody confrontations, conciliar rule in Bremen came to an end.

For many weeks thereafter the flame of rebellion would rise here and there, and volunteers would be required to stamp it out. The soldiers would enter the reconquered towns in triumphant procession. 'Now we could hope for the future,' said one of the volunteers on subduing Brunswick.[41] It was another form of *ersatz* victory.

The wars in the East intensified. Shortly after the elections a commander in East Prussia reported that what remained of the old army was 'an undisciplined and unruly mass . . . which in every sense gives moral support to enemies of the regime and Fatherland'. Groener, in his memoirs, describes how once again the solution was found in 'volunteer formations', recruited in western Germany but also in large numbers from the German residents of Silesia and Poland. Across the Reich the civilian militias multiplied. A mobile security police that worked for the regional military authorities was created. All these forces were locally recruited – from veterans who couldn't find work, but also from students who had never seen war. By the end of winter they together formed a fighting power of around one million men. Germany, as fast as she demobilized, was being remilitarized by the volunteers.[42]

The chain of command was reorganized; the Free Corps and civil militias were integrated into the regular Army. Supreme Command had not felt so confident in months: it regarded itself as a legitimate instrument of political power in the Reich, the protector of institutions at home against the threat of Bolshevism and a defender of Germany's frontiers – still undefined by the conferees in Paris.

Ebert's government decided to set up the newly elected National Assembly in Weimar for military reasons, not for the liberal culture of Goethe. True, the gabled houses and the grand-ducal palace sheltered memories of enlightened rule, constitutional government and the meditation of playwriters and poets rather than soldiers. But it was the unpoetic Noske who clinched the argument for Weimar: this isolated town of under fifty thousand inhabitants would be easier to defend from insurrectionists than Greater Berlin.

An advance guard of 120 men, picked from Maercker's Volunteer Rifles, was sent into the town on 30 January. Before they reached the central marketplace they were surrounded, disarmed and thrown into prison by a group of Communist rebels. It took Maercker's entire force of 7,000 three days to free their comrades and then dig defensive trenches right round Weimar. The National Assembly opened in the town's New National Theatre on a snowy Thursday, 6 February. The elected representatives owed their security to Maercker's Free Corps.

They sat in the rowed seats of the orchestra stalls; the boxes and the circle were reserved for the public. On the stage, Ebert and the five other People's Commissars sat behind a long table decorated with tulips and carnations. Ebert, looking uncomfortable in his black frock coat, made a strong speech in which he turned over the power of the Commissars to the Assembly and made an important point in foreign policy: if conditions laid down by the 'Entente' were unacceptable to Germany he would break off negotiations.

Kessler, visiting the Assembly three weeks later, described the atmosphere as 'that of a Sunday matinée in a petty court theatre'. He could not imagine anyone like Danton or Bismarck appearing 'in these dainty surroundings'. 'The representatives of all parties, with but few exceptions, belong to the lower middle class,' he went on. 'Dr Allos' cabaret, which is performing here for the entertainment of the Assembly's members, very aptly meets the intellectual demands which the appearance of the Assembly suggests.'[43]

For someone like Count Harry Kessler, the thought of the nation's affairs being taken over by the lower middle classes was unbearable. So it was for Rathenau.

On its second day the Assembly considered two names for the first President of the Republic: Paul Hindenburg and Walther Rathenau. When Hindenburg's name was read out, loud laughter arose from the chairs of the Social Democrats. When it was Rathenau's turn the rollicking developed on the Right – as Rathenau himself put it, there were 'roars and shrieks of laughter. The papers talked of merriment lasting for several minutes, and eye-witnesses related how men and women rocked in their seats with delight at the idea.'[44] Hindenburg did not bat a wooden eyelid at the mockery. Rathenau, on the other hand, was profoundly shocked. He developed a thoroughly unsympathetic attitude towards the National Assembly and parliamentary government in general. Unfortunately for the Republic, the same could be said of many other Germans at the time.

Eventually, on 11 February, the Assembly elected, by 277 out of 379 ballots, Friedrich Ebert as first President of the Republic; he immediately named Scheidemann as Chancellor. Two days later Scheidemann drew up his inevitable government: a combination of Catholics, liberals and Socialists – a group that would have won the approval of Erzberger's Inter-Party Committee two years earlier. It came to be known as the 'Weimar Coalition'.

All three Armistice elections in Europe – in Britain, in Poland and in Germany – had led to wobbling coalitions. Even the United States was now run by a minority government. Political instability might be said to be one of the great consequences of the war. But in each nation the circumstances of instability were different and could be traced back to conditions existing before the war. Germany's coalition arose from a pattern of power that had been in formation during the last decades of the Wilhelmine Reich; potentially, it contained within it all the difficulties the Reich had experienced in those last years, including the chain of circumstances that had eventually pushed her down the road to war in 1914.

On 10 February, Supreme Command relocated for the second time in less than three months. Groener left Kassel that day and, after touring 'the threatened zone' of Bartenstein, Danzig, Oppeln and Kattowitz, arrived on 14 February in his new headquarters at Kolberg on the Baltic coast. From Spa, to Kassel, to Kolberg: nothing symbolized better the march of the war eastward. Kolberg, in Pomerania, was a place that made blood rise within a German soul. Frederick the Great had fought here during the Seven Years War. In 1944 the Nazis would make a coloured epic film out of the defence of Kolberg against Napoleon's Army in 1806. Today the town is called Kołobrzeg, and it is in Poland.

Supreme Command had received no instructions from the government to make this sudden move. At the time it was accomplished, Germany in fact had no government, for Ebert had just passed powers to the National Assembly, which had not yet approved of Scheidemann's coalition. The purpose of the move was clear: to stake Germany's claims in the East, and particularly its claim to Posen, Hindenburg's birthplace. Ebert's provisional government had formally followed a policy of conciliation with the Poles, but Supreme Command had no intention of executing it. Secretly, Hindenburg and his colleagues prepared a strategic plan for the reconquest of Posen. Military action began the moment headquarters were established in Kolberg. General von Bülow invaded Poland with an army of Free Corps and took Kulmsee. A full-scale offensive was ordered on Kattowitz; 'the coal mines', stated Groener, 'should not fall into the hands of the enemy'.[45]

The ambitions of Supreme Command, strengthened by mass volunteer units, went further east than Poland and Silesia. Hindenburg himself had never abandoned his plans for the Eastern annexations as laid down in the terms of the Treaty of Brest-Litovsk the previous year. Perhaps, after a little fighting, Germany and Russia could arrive again at an accord; this would affirm German hegemony in Europe, despite her losses in the West, and would give the Russians (whatever regime came out on top) the recognition they so desperately sought. When Richard Kühlmann had asked Hindenburg, just before the signing of the treaty in March 1918, why he wanted to annex the Baltic states of Estonia, Latvia and Lithuania, the Field Marshal had answered that he wanted to protect his left wing for 'the next war'.[46] His view had not changed. Plans were drawn up to renew the war from bases in Courland, an old site of German intrigue in Eastern Europe, recognizable to anyone who knew the history of the Congress of Vienna.

Supreme Command named General Count Rudiger von der Goltz as commander of German forces in the Baltic. While Supreme Command established itself at Kolberg, von der Goltz entered Mittau, home of the duchesses of Courland, residence of the exiled French court of King Louis XVIII, and now one of the major trading towns of Lithuania. There had already been serious fighting in the area between Germans and the Russian Red Army; the Germans had just blown up the ammunition depot established there. But the tide of war was turning. With the help of Major Bischoff's Brigade of Iron and the Baltic Landeswehr, and a complete restructuring of command – which now included such cold, able, murderous gentlemen as General Hans von Seeckt, Major Werner von Fritsch and Captain Waldemar Pabst, who had made his name at the Battle of Christmas Eve – von der Golz rapidly established a defensive line running north–south from the Latvian coast at Libau down through Lithuania to Kovno. The next great German offensive was simply a matter of timing.

'In alliance with the "White" Russians and under the banner of fighting the Bolsheviks why could not our Eastern politics, which had been blocked by the events of 1918, be achieved in a somewhat altered and more adaptable form?' asked von der Goltz. 'Above all, why could not an economic and political sphere be created next to Russia?' He had been invited in by Ulmanis's Latvian Republic; he had been endorsed by the British Baltic Fleet. But von der Goltz was under no illusion: 'I had four enemies, the Bolshevik Army, the soldiers' councils, the Germanophobe Latvian government, and the Allies. Following sound strategic principles, I determined not to fight them all at once, but instead to fight them one after the other, starting first with the Bolsheviks.'[47]

*   *   *

While the National Assembly, under the protection of Maercker's Volunteer Rifles, was busy establishing a new German government, and Supreme Command prepared for a new Eastern offensive, three British officers – Captains W. S. Roddie, Claude W. Bell and E. W. D. Tennant – arrived in Berlin aboard the 'Armistice Express' to report on conditions in the Reich's capital and the problems of the nation's food supply. Among the several officials they interviewed was Dr Carl Melchior, who had so impressed Keynes at Trier two weeks earlier.[48]

Having passed through war-ravaged Belgium, they had been impressed by the lack of any apparent deforestation in Germany, the sight of land still cultivated, and the large number of goods trains standing idle, many of them piled high with timber. Dr Melchior, however, assured the officers that 'conditions among the poor and the lower-middle class are almost desperate, and the only way to stop the spread of Bolshevism is to send prompt relief in the form of food'. He told them that Germany would go to any lengths to prove her good faith to the Allies in exchange for supplies.

They met a number of army officers who insisted on the terrible effects of the Armistice terms imposed on Germany, being especially outraged at the demand to repair locomotives due to be handed over to the Allies and to restore the machinery they had seized in Belgium and France. Several of the institutions they visited were decorated with portraits of the Kaiser and battle scenes. One former officer of the Guard Regiment, now enrolled in a Free Corps unit, told them, without betraying the slightest malice in his voice, that 'of course Germany would have to have another war as soon as possible, probably within 20 years, as the present situation was unbearable'.

Was it? The three British officers noticed that the Hotel Adlon was well heated and that dinner in the restaurant was good. Other restaurants in town were packed and seemed to suffer from no shortage of foodstuffs, including the meat served on 'meatless' days. 'There was no evidence, whatsoever, of scarcity or want in the outward impressions we got,' they reported. They were struck, even in working-class districts, by the 'mania for dancing' and the number of advertisements for balls. 'The general public', they said, 'seem quite content to enjoy themselves on the edge of a precipice.' On the Friedrichstrasse they were frequently solicited in English by 'ladies of the easy virtue brigade' who appeared 'particularly anxious to forget hostilities'.

After their first few days they became aware of a certain 'bedraggled appearance' about the city. The men were dressed in a 'motley array of untidy uniforms', there was a 'distinct increase in horsed vehicles on the streets during the week'; 'we have not seen or heard a single cat, or seen more than a dozen dogs during the past week'. Major von Schweinitz, their host, told them that this was because 'they have all been eaten and their skins used for leather'.

Dr Bumm of the Board of Health painted a particularly gloomy picture of the effects of underfeeding upon mortality rates among women during childbirth. The officers themselves discovered poor conditions in the orphanages and other institutions where rationing was enforced. No work was getting done, despite the growth in unemployment. The snow in the streets, for instance, was never cleared. 'The masses have actually been mentally affected through insufficient nourishment,' explained Schweinitz.

Maybe. But nowhere did the officers find the outward signs of malnutrition, let alone starvation. The real shortages, they thought, were in coal and in nitrate production – as used in fertilizers, not bombs. These were not on Mr Hoover's list.

It is possible that the three British captains were jaundiced. It is unlikely that the Germans were trying to put on a good show, which would hardly have been in their interest. One is always suspicious of such impressionistic accounts – as when British academics in the Ukraine in the 1930s reported that they saw no hunger. The difference from the Ukraine, however, is that most later studies confirm the British officers' first impressions: Germany was not starving.[49]

4

The Peace Conference in Paris was proceeding at a hectic pace – though civil servants and journalists, expecting the instant emergence of a new era, continually lamented that little was being done. 'For the first fortnight the Conference did practically nothing,' griped Headlam-Morley in a letter to the Foreign Office in London on 3 February. And again, a couple of days later: 'My work here is miscellaneous and disjointed . . . I find it very boring and do it very badly.' Harold Nicolson spent much of this period 'hunting on my own'; he 'snuffed around like a spaniel in the bracken, importantly busy, busily important. I had received no instructions whatsoever from my official superiors: I seldom did.' John Maynard Keynes remained in the Riviera with his friends, recovering from the flu.[50]

The decisions were being made in high quarters. A Reparations Commission, with three subcommittees, had been set up and its members were arguing across polished tables. The League of Nations Commission was already halfway through its labours. The Council of Ten had by now considered a dozen territorial questions and was organizing the territorial commissions to look into the details. Thanks to the efforts of people like Headlam-Morley and Nicolson, most of this detailed business would be completed by the end of February. The speed of work was extraordinary, the problems overwhelming.

The 'Ten' – still referring to themselves as the 'Supreme War Council' whenever the military chiefs were present – met in the French Foreign Minister's private office, to the right of the ante-room on the first floor of the Quai d'Orsay. It had a high domed ceiling from which hung a heavy chandelier; around the walls hung sixteenth-century Gobelin tapestries, mirrors and more gilded, glittering lights – as the afternoon's gloom deepened outside in the garden they would be turned on one by one.

In late January and all through February the Council held 'auditions', during which delegates of the various nations would expound on their complex claims. Clive Day dismissed these meetings as a show: 'for spectacles . . . the Council was very well fitted. The spectacular, however, is always superficial . . .' Charles Seymour likened them to a faculty committee meeting, and there actually was something of a university atmosphere about it all. For instance, when the Ten debated whether they should hear the Romanian delegates or not, President Wilson suggested that 'the British students of the subject, and the Americans, French, Italians, and Japanese if they had a body of students conversant with those things' should talk among themselves first. But neither Balfour nor Clemenceau went along with this.[51]

Churchill, who was in the room on 14 February, described Clemenceau, the Conference president, at his French Regency table as 'grim, rugged, snow-white'. Nicolson spoke of him as bearing 'the half-smile of an irritated, sceptical and neurasthenic gorilla'. He always wore grey gloves, even when writing; a long moustache covered his mouth; his eyebrows shaded his sleepy eyes – on the rare occasions when something interested him he would suddenly open them very wide and lean forward. If he decided the discussion had lasted long enough, he would cry out, *'Objections? . . . Adopté!'* Wilson would frequently get restless, stand up from his desk, and pace up and down the Aubusson carpet, kicking it with his tidy black shoes. Clemenceau often expressed himself in English, fluent but with a decided Gallic accent. Baron Sonnino, in contrast, spoke English like a man from Oxford. Lloyd George was generally considered the most amusing man present at the conferences; he was 'very alert, not knowing very much about things, and generally, I think, not understanding things very exactly'. When translations were needed, Paul Mantoux was the main interpreter; 'he puts more spirit into his translations than the principal puts into his original speech,' noted Seymour. 'To talk through an interpreter was like witnessing the compound fracture of an idea,' said Wilson professorially. The translations at least allowed time for tempers to cool and provided the chance to develop second thoughts.[52]

The experts would sidle through the double doors with their books, their maps, their pouches. In the Council's chamber they would sit directly behind their masters, occasionally interrupting them to give advice. Outside, they and the delegates of the smaller powers would sit on the gilt chairs in the ante-room 'as if awaiting the dentist'. Tea would be served from silver trolleys. The Quai d'Orsay's ante-room became one of the main centres of intrigue and rumour in Paris.

Several factors compelled haste. In the second week of February Lloyd

George would have to return to London for the opening of Parliament, with his victorious new majority. In the third week Wilson was due back in Washington to close the old, lame-duck, Congress. There was also the regular monthly deadline: the renewal of the Armistice with Germany. Each renewal represented a greater challenge than the preceding one; every month the Allies were reminded that they had yet to make peace with their enemy. Clemenceau repeatedly raised the point that 'Armistice is the status of war.'

The next renewal was due on 17 February; it would have to be signed on the 16th; negotiations in Trier would therefore have to take place on the 14th and 15th. Why not make this deadline the date for a 'preliminary peace' with Germany and be done with this shady ambiguity which still hung over, and menaced, the world? That, at any rate, was what the French wanted; they had never really abandoned their plan of November.

Lurking behind all the deadlines and acting as an accelerator on the minds of those who worked in Paris was what came known as the 'race with demobilization'. Life in the Allied armies turned cold and dismal when General Winter crept into their camps. There arose from them an increasingly shrill cry to go home. In January, Francis Woodman, an educational secretary of the YMCA, visited the American camp at Saint-Aignan in the Sologne, within the department of Loir-et-Cher. He described what he saw as a 'sea of mud'. 'I believe we are losing many men in this region from unnecessary exposure,' he wrote. Another infamous camp lay just outside Brest, in Brittany – a pestiferous bog that was the first and last sight many thousands of Americans had of France. With the USS *George Washington* moored in the nearby harbour, this miserable place was frequently brought to the attention of the American President. It made a scandal in the press. 'Hundreds of complaints' were received in Paris about the filthy conditions and the poor treatment of the troops, the abuses 'costing the lives of many American soldiers', according to the *New York Evening Telegram*.[53]

French soldiers were rumoured to be once more on the verge of mutiny. Some of the British forces, so disciplined during the war, did mutiny. On 27 January, Army Ordnance detachments and the Mechanical Transport – not the most obedient section of the Army in the best of times, and one that had seen no fighting – took over the whole port town of Calais. The mutineers persuaded many returning soldiers on the leave-boats to join them, so that by the second day of the revolt there were between 3,000 and 4,000 armed men occupying the city. Most soldiers with fighting experience were now in occupied Germany; it was a situation that curiously mirrored, though on a smaller scale, the one the German Army faced in the last days of the war. Two divisions were recalled from their forward march on Germany and placed under the orders of General Julian Byng, commander of the Third Army, famous at Vimy Ridge, Cambrai, Bapaume and Le Quesnoy.

On the night of 30 January, Byng surrounded Calais with a ring of steel. There could have been a bloodletting as serious as that in Berlin; but reason won out, the leaders of the revolt were arrested, and the men returned to their camps.[54]

Conscript soldiers of the Allied armies were not the only troops suffering from the poor conditions in France. Out on the plains of Champagne over eighty thousand Poles were encamped, the remnants of 'Haller's Army' that, in 1917, had fought its way to the Baltic and from there had been carried in British vessels to the Western Front. A British officer visited their camps in early February and, in a report to Headlam-Morley, drew 'a lamentable picture of the conditions among them'.[55] These Polish soldiers also wanted to go home. They wanted to go home and fight.

Poland blighted the dreams of those who sat in Paris. Though they might look out to blue seas and imagine the establishment of a new world order, they could not stop taking an occasional nervous glance back over their shoulders at the northern plain, from where the war had come, and notice trouble emerging on the far side of Germany. Poland: Napoleon's key to Europe. Poland: it had baffled the American members of The Inquiry. Poland: the Allies had deliberately avoided mentioning it in the Armistice of 11 November, though they had all recognized its right to independence.

The Polish delegates were the first Europeans to be heard in an 'audition' before the Council of Ten. That was on Wednesday, 29 January, just as Byng's three divisions were surrounding the British mutineers in Calais. Roman Dmowski, the Polish Foreign Minister, who had formerly headed the Polish National Committee in Paris, led the delegates. The Prime Minister, Ignace Paderewski, had taken office in Warsaw only eight days before.

Dmowski, according to Hankey's minutes, 'compared Germany to the god Janus. Germany had one face towards the West, where she had made peace, and the other face towards the East, where she was organizing for war. Her troops there were concentrated and out for war. She might have given up the West, but she had not given up her plan for extending her Empire to the East.' The Poles, said Dmowski, would respect all Allied calls for restraint, but he underlined the vagueness of Article 12 in the November Armistice and he pointed out that his country was under threat from three sides, 'first by the Bolsheviks on the East, second by the Ukrainian bands on the South-East [it was even rumoured that the Germans and the Ukrainians had come to some kind of accord], and by Germans on the North-West'. He spoke of massacres in Eastern Galicia and the 'many crimes' committed by German soldiers retreating from the Eastern Front. He noted that the Germans had organized 'a special corps, known as the "Heimatschutz Ost", consisting largely of officers'; he had got the title wrong, but this was one of the only references ever made to the German Free Corps during the Paris Peace Conference.

Dmowski admitted that Poland's frontiers were not clear and recommended that 'we should start from the date 1772, before the first partition' – not that this huge Poland, which included in the east a vast zone of non-Polish-speaking peoples, should define the country's frontiers but that 'this must be the point of departure'. Dmowski provided a novel definition of nationality that did not perfectly conform to Wilson's Points, Principles and Particulars: 'the great need in Eastern Europe was to have established governments'. He also volunteered his own definition of Bolshevism: 'the rule of a despotic organization representing a well-organized class in a country where all other classes were passive and disorganized'. The implication was clear: create a nation without an established government and you will introduce the rule of Bolshevism. Dmowski claimed that neither Lithuania nor the Ukraine was 'advanced enough to be considered a nation'. 'The Ukrainian State at present was really organized anarchy,' he said. Dmowski sought a large Polish state, capable of standing up to both Russians and Germans.[56]

In the meantime, Paderewski in Warsaw persisted in his appeals to Paris for military aid. 'Poland cannot communicate with the civilized world,' he wrote to Colonel House on 4 February. South Galicia continued to be invaded, he reported, 'patrols have been seen in our oil districts', Silesians were being arrested and deported, 'college students, mere children [were being] hanged'. 'People cannot conceive why at this moment of ever growing Eastern danger', he ended, 'no assistance is being given, and General Haller's Army is detained in France.'[57]

The truth is that very few people in walled Paris knew what was going on east of the Rhine. The one permanent formal contact between Germany and the Allies was at Spa, where the Allied Armistice Commission stared at the German Armistice Commission and passed pieces of paper across a table in the Hôtel Britannique. The Ten in Paris obviously had not a clue what kind of government was being set up in Weimar. Clemenceau was impressed by the fact that the National Assembly had opened with the deputies singing *'Deutschland über alles'*; then they placed 'all power in the hands of the accomplices of Wilhelm II'. He noted that the new President Ebert, 'a tailor' (he had in fact been a saddler), had said in his inaugural address, 'We will not accept terms which are too hard.' Clemenceau thought his Chancellor was the aristocratic Brockdorff-Rantzau (who was actually Foreign Secretary). Edith Benham, Wilson's private secretary, noted how the American President would sometimes discuss in the evenings the 'mysterious old-new nations' of Eastern Europe. Experts and civil servants relied on information they could glean from people who had made brief visits east, and more often from emigrants, most of whom had left their country during or before the war. The future historian Lewis Namier, a Polish Jew from a landowning family in Galicia, was an important source for the British Foreign Office. 'Have you been following events in Posen?' Headlam-Morley asked him on 13 February. 'There is a great gap in my knowledge for the period after Christmas' – a serious gap, and one that could not be filled by Namier, who had arrived in England in 1907.[58]

The French were ready to encourage Dmowski in his quest for a large and strong Poland, a useful counterweight to Germany. But their main concern at the moment was Poland's survival. On 22 January Foch had warned the Ten, 'Poland might be suffocated before its birth. It has no bases, no outlets, no communciations, no supplies, no army.' He had presented a plan to occupy, with Allied troops, the crucial railway link between Danzig on the Baltic and Thorn on the old border between German and Russian Poland, and to send in Haller's Army. 'The troops might begin to arrive in three weeks or a month,' he confidently remarked.[59]

But the British and the Americans were not that keen. Lloyd George had his electoral promise to abolish conscript armies in mind; at this very moment he was facing mutiny. Lloyd George's idea was the old idea of a Britain maintaining the world's peace with her Navy; a good peace, in his view, was one that re-established in Europe a self-regulated balance of forces that would give Britain the freedom to move on the seas in tranquil commerce with her Empire: he did not want a military entanglement in Poland. Wilson was committed to his world system, a peace established by self-determined nations. His 'students' had examined the linguistic maps of Poland and were puzzled; they had not yet envisaged how Poland's frontiers could be justly determined. Send in troops now and one might prejudice the whole world system. Thus, though Britain and America were at loggerheads over economic issues, they found they had something in common in Poland: they did not want their soldiers involved.

As a matter of fact, the same principle brought them together on most territorial matters concerning Europe – so much so that informal talks were held between specialists at the Majestic and the Crillon that allowed the two powers to present a united front at the Quai d'Orsay. This would determine the course of the Peace Conference for more than a month. 'The great surprise at the Conference', wrote William Rappard of the Swiss mission to his government, 'has been the Anglo-American *entente cordiale*, on one side, and the very strong Franco-American tension, on the other.'[60] *Entente précaire* would have been a more accurate way of putting it.

Wilson certainly made an attempt to calm French fears about security. In an address to the French Senate on 20 January, and again in front of the Chamber of Deputies on 3 February, he spoke of France standing at the 'frontier of freedom', a country that held guard 'at the chief post of danger'. He evoked the name of Lafayette. He was constantly reiterating that, once the League of Nations was established, no nation, and most particularly France, would remain isolated if it were attacked. Yet he got immensely annoyed at French insistence, officially and in the press, that he visit the devastated regions. 'I regret that they want to make me see red, thinking it will affect me in my deliberations at the Peace Conference,' he told A. G. Gardiner of the London *Daily News*. 'If France had been entirely made a shell hole it would not change the ultimate settlement,' he confessed.[61]

There were other petty annoyances that the President's circle complained about: the postal service was awful, the telephones were impossible, the prices for everything were too high, and, to cap it all, the French were trying 'to work off old gassed horses on us'. The French, for their part, blamed the high prices on the American presence; they thought the Americans were getting arrogant in the hotels and restaurants; they particularly objected to the presence of American Military Police in the district around the Place de la Concorde. On 27 January Harold Nicolson attended a huge luncheon offered by the French press. 'I gathered a vivid impression of the growing hatred of the French for the Americans,' he recorded in his diary, adding ominously, 'Wilson shares this growing unpopularity. Lafayette is becoming a hazy bond of union.'[62]

Some of this seeped through the double doors on the first floor of the Quai d'Orsay.

The Americans did not feel nearly as pressed as the British – facing debt and mutiny – to reduce their military commitments in Europe. Conse-quently, it was Lloyd George who first raised queries about the wisdom of Foch's plan in Poland. He thought that the Polish envoys in Paris had to be immediately told that they should limit their aims to 'indisputably Polish territory' and that it would not be a good idea to send in Haller's Army, because one could not expect the Germans to let men and arms through Danzig that were going to be used to attack them; 'fairness was due even to the enemy', he said.

It was not long before the Americans were supporting the British point of view. Charles Seymour, present during Dmowski's appeal for armed support, noted how Wilson and Lloyd George 'frequently whispered together'. The main gist of the Anglo-American agreement, imposed on the Council by several resolutions passed in the last week of January and the first fortnight of February, was that the Poles were given 'solemn warn-ing' against 'adopting a policy of an aggressive character', which would have 'the worst possible effect' on the decisions of the Conference. Haller's Army remained in France. The fragile government in Warsaw had to satisfy itself with a few Poles released from Italian prisoner-of-war camps.[63]

The Ten – dominated by the *entente précaire* – did, however, send into Poland an 'Inter-Allied Commission' with instructions to insist that 'Polish authorities refrain from all use of force against the German forces' and to present a report as soon as possible on the 'Military question and the Food question'. On the night of 9 February, Headlam-Morley went over to the Gare de l'Est to see the commissioners off. 'They had a beautiful train, Paris to Warsaw, the first time such a train has left Paris,' he told Namier the next day; 'each of the nations had its own car.' Flags were flying from every carriage.[64]

Foch did, in the meantime, pass a stern message through the Armistice Commission in Spa on to German Supreme Command that contained an 'injunction' not to resort to force in Poland. It was the German Commission in Spa that responded – perhaps because Supreme Command was so busy at that moment transferring house to Kolberg. The German government, it asserted, had an 'absolute right to ensure the protection of their subjects within their own territory'; moreover, present events required 'rapid intervention' in view of 'the assassination of German subjects and Pogroms against the Jews'. That was quite a novel argument for the Free Corps marching into Poland: they were the protectors of the Jews.[65]

In fact the Ten knew nothing of Germany's Free Corps. They had difficulty enough in estimating the strength of her regular forces. On 24 January, Foch presented a survey of what forces the Allies would have available on the Western Front up to the end of March, by which time 'preliminaries of peace' were expected to be signed with Germany. According to the various demobilization schedules, there would be somewhere between 80 and 90 Allied divisions in front of Germany, consisting of around 1.8 million men. Half of these would be French, America would still have a force of 450,000 men, while the British Army in France would already be reduced to 350,000. Information provided by the Germans at Spa and Trier suggested the enemy still had 37 divisions along the western line of the Rhine and between 15 and 18 divisions in the East. Foch and his staff calculated, on this basis, that there was a total of between 600,000 and 700,000 men in the German Army. As a matter of fact, with the Free Corps included, Germany had around a million men under arms, and they were in majority not standing on the western line but were marching east. They hardly constituted a united force, however: the names and the numbers of the divisions, corps, regiments and battalions were changing by the day. One could not speak, in reality, of the 'German Army'.[66]

Confronted with Foch's figures, the British developed a plan. Lloyd George had seen that if Germany maintained her forces at this high level Britain would have to keep up her conscript army – and there was trouble now in the barracks of Grove Park and Kempton Park, outside London; at Luton, rowdy troops had just burnt down the town hall. 'Great Britain is not a military nation like France and the people are not disciplined,' observed the Prime Minister. 'Why should Germans keep all these troops under arms?' He complained that Foch had not considered calling on Germany to demobilize. At the February renewal of the Armistice, he proposed, this should be demanded; the renewal should be refused if the Germans did not promise this.

Foch pointed out the enormous problem of imposing demobilization on a large nation like Germany; a demobilization clause would be difficult to enforce; estimates of Germany's actual military strength would always be unreliable. He was reminded of Napoleon's effort at Tilsit in 1807 to limit the Prussian Army to 40,000 men: Prussia simply built up a hidden army of volunteers. 'In a country like Germany it would be very easy for the people to take up arms again,' said the Marshal. 'Should a real leader arise, it would not be difficult for him to reconstruct the armies.' Foch thought it dangerous to allow Allied forces in France and occupied Germany to drop below ninety divisions.[67]

The disagreement between Lloyd George and Foch exposed the underlying tension in the Peace Conference. One side felt that, if economic incentives were offered, Germany could be trusted to reduce her arms; the other could place its faith only in an armed peace.

The economics of the thesis of trust were presented by the Americans. Bliss, Pershing and Wilson had taken on an impartial air during the debate; as Bliss observed, the Americans had no problem at all in maintaining the minimum number of troops required by Foch until summer, by which time the peace would undoubtedly be concluded. What needed to be considered, said Wilson, was that Germany's demobilization was directly linked to her ability to resume her economic life: men were hanging around the army depots simply to be fed. The real problem in Germany was the lack of food and unemployment. 'Sooner or later', insisted Wilson, 'the Allies would be compelled to trust Germany to keep her promises.' A great army of occupation could not be maintained on German soil for ever.

Ultimately, Wilson was right – and nobody, in fact, was prepared to disagree with him. The difference of opinion lay in that 'sooner or later': the Americans wanted an economic settlement with Germany 'sooner'; the French preferred 'later'. Lloyd George continued to press for an imposed disarmament at the February Armistice renewal. The leaders agreed to set up a special committee, chaired by Clemenceau's Minister of Reconstruction, Louis Loucheur, to give more precision to the necessary strength of Allied forces on the Western Front during the Armistice period, and to outline a plan of German demobilization that would be imposed at February's renewal. The committee would have to hurry, because both Lloyd George and Wilson had appointments at home with their parliaments.

By the time Loucheur's committee got back to the Ten to report (incredibly, they were ready in under a fortnight), a movement was afoot to present Germany, at the next renewal, with the final naval and military terms of peace. The French and British military chiefs of staff were behind this, but the plan found considerable support among the politicians in Paris. Yet, far from uniting the Allies in a single purpose, the plan increased the tension between them, for it was motivated by totally contradictory objectives. The French wanted to incorporate the terms into the new Armistice, thereby radically changing it. The Americans wanted to present them after the renewal, to ensure that the Armistice was not altered.

'These continual aggravations of the Armistice put the Allies to a moral disadvantage,' announced Wilson; he said he had a 'strong distaste of the practice of making reiterated demands'.[68] The French were not the slightest bit concerned about issues of morality: they wanted to avoid a reiterated attack from a giant neighbour. The British found themselves seated uncomfortably somewhere between the two sides, fully aware that they had started off the whole affair with their demand for an imposed German disarmament.

There was a chain of logic behind all this that none of the Allies liked. But they could not avoid it. Behind the plan for immediate, final military terms of peace lay the demand for German disarmament. Behind that lay the novel situation in Poland. 'Tell the Germans that an attack on Poland will be followed by an immediate advance of the Allied troops along the entire Western front,' exclaimed Clemenceau, realizing at once the source of the problem. He was not sure that final military terms could be prepared at such short notice, but he did think that the renewal of the Armistice provided an opportunity to act and to show once more the brunt of Allied will – and he was getting immensely annoyed with Wilson's insistence on a contractual peace that tied Allied action to abstractions in the Points, Principles and Particulars. Wilson, he said, was 'putting the question in an academic, theoretical and doctrinal light'. Stop the German military machine now, and for good: that was Clemenceau's chief concern.[69]

As for Loucheur's committee, it recommended that at the time of the next Armistice renewal the Germans be required to reduce their forces to twenty-five infantry divisions and five cavalry divisions, with the amount of war material to be left in German hands being fixed accordingly. It then listed, by category, weapons that the Germans would be required to hand over, basing its calculations on a subtraction of the amount such a force would need from the estimated total weapon stock still existing in Germany. The resulting figures were fancifully accurate – such as the 1,575 field guns that the Germans should yield, the 3,825 machine-guns and the 412,500 rifles. To ensure German compliance, it recommended the military occupation of 'Essen and the principal Krupp establishments, the greater part of the Rheinish-Westphalian coal-fields, and the metallic industries which depend on these'.[70]

The British and American representatives on the committee, however, refused to sign this. When Loucheur made his report to the Supreme War Council, Wilson called it a 'panic programme'. He argued that such extensive additions to the Armistice were not 'sportsmanlike', and again emphasized the need for an economic settlement. With Hankey producing draft resolutions, Lloyd George, still sitting uncomfortably in the middle, desperately sought a compromise between the hardening French and American positions. He proposed that a civilian commission be appointed to negotiate immediately with the Germans the supply of food and raw materials that should be allowed to enter their country; if negotiations did not turn out to the Allies' satisfaction, Foch could then apply pressure at the time of the next Armistice renewal. 'If you stop attacking Poland, we will give you bread, sugar and other supplies' – that was no way to talk with the Germans, retorted Clemenceau; they had to be told that if they attacked the Poles the Allies would march.[71]

Lloyd George had already left for London, Wilson was just about to set off for the United States, and Foch's train was literally waiting in the station to carry him to Trier when the compromise was finally found on 12 February. It was presented in another of Hankey's drafts, put forward by Arthur Balfour: he proposed that renewal of the old Armistice terms be made conditional upon Germany desisting from all offensive operations against the Poles; that the renewal be for a short period, terminable with three days' notice; that Germany be shortly presented with the detailed and final naval, military and air conditions of the 'preliminaries of peace'; and that Germany's food and raw material needs be negotiated when the renewal had been signed.

Clemenceau accepted all these points save the last economic one – 'The Allies', he said, 'would be seen to be offering the Germans an inducement.' Foch set off at once for Trier with instructions to put the economics aside.[72]

5

The Americans' policy of emphasizing the economics of peace had contained one fatal flaw: they refused to discuss economics with the European Allies. The Americans had banned from debate the one issue that worried them all: the question of war debts.

The export of Mr Hoover's grain and pig surpluses to the hungry hordes of Central Europe was a perfectly acceptable subject for talks – a humane one. Hoover himself took a high moral stand, lobbying in the Supreme War Council for at least three resolutions which would relieve the pressure of the naval blockade. 'There is no right in the law of God or man that we should [any] longer continue to starve neutrals now that we have a surplus of food,' he said. He asked Wilson to appeal to 'world opinion' to counter the 'selfish and bureaucratic obstruction' of the Europeans. But the Americans were not willing to exchange views with their 'Associates' on the matter of war debts. They were terrified at the prospect of being drawn into the shaky financial structures of Europe. They were especially nervous about the rumours and reports of various projects designed to relieve the Western Europeans of their financial burdens – veiled attempts at Allied debt redistribution, said the Americans, and then fell silent. 'I find on every side the tendency to force the United States into a position in which it will be assuming a larger part of the indebtedness incurred in the war,' wrote Bernard Baruch to the President. Wilson was 'considerably exercised' by such reports.[73]

One of the most radical proposals at the time came from the pen of John Maynard Keynes. Keynes advised the cancellation all war debts. His final memorandum containing this recommendation is dated 28 March 1919, but the idea was in the air long beforehand. Riddell, for example, refers in his diary to the scheme on 16 February. An early draft can be found in Keynes's papers dated 29 November 1918 – Bonar Law, then Chancellor of the Exchequer, had forwarded a copy to Smuts for consideration in the Imperial War Cabinet.[74]

Having recovered from his flu, Keynes had accompanied Foch to Trier on 12 February as one of the civilian commissioners attending the Armistice renewal. But it is unlikely that he met Melchior or any of the other German commissioners on this occasion, since the Supreme War Council had expressly forbidden the discussion of economic affairs with the enemy: the meeting was to be strictly 'soldier to soldier'; the civilian commissioners were simply there to give advice to Foch and his military team – no more.

The Armistice was renewed for an indefinite period, until such time as the Allies were ready to present Germany with their final military terms (or to break it off altogether and recommence hostilities). Keynes was back in Paris on 17 February, writing to the Treasury in London, 'There is no diminution in the amount of work which still keeps us employed from breakfast to midnight.' He complained of the severe shortage of staff.[75]

Keynes argued that 'entangling alliances or entangling leagues are nothing to the entanglements of cash owing'. He presented tables of war loans advanced by the Allies to one another and their net gains and net losses if total inter-Allied indebtedness, amounting to £3.5 billion, were cancelled. Britain had borrowed £800 million from the United States, but had advanced £1.54 billion to her Allies. France had borrowed £485 million from the United States, and had advanced £365 million to her Allies (almost half of which was to Russia). The debts had created a kind of mad merry-go-round. Italy had borrowed almost as much from the United States as had Britain, yet it was obviously ridiculous to imagine that Italy, in her current poor financial position, could be loaded with the same crushing tribute as Britain. Continuation of the system would have an adverse effect on trade in the whole world. For a generation to come, discontented people in Europe would be paying an 'appreciable part of their daily produce' to 'meet a foreign payment'. If all the Allied debts were cancelled the greatest gainers would be Italy and Russia. France would come out a net winner, with £510 million. Britain and the United States would be net losers. This was not an unjustified redistribution of world capital, thought Keynes. The greatest sacrifice would have to be made by the United States, submitting to a loss of £1,668 million. But then the United States had profited immensely from the war. She had seized twice as many German merchant ships as she had herself lost, and had sequestrated German property in America to a value of $425 billion. She had lost relatively few lives. Her military contribution had been limited to the last months of the war. She had never faced bombardment. The country was a good deal richer than it had been in 1914. Even the farmers had profited. 'The Americans are being allowed a voice in the Peace Conference far beyond what their sacrifices justify,' commented Riddell. 'They might well pay their footing, and bear a larger portion of the cost of the war.'[76] A lot of Europeans agreed with him.

The point that had most immediate consequence in Keynes's argument concerned indemnities – or 'reparations', as Wilson insisted on calling them. In his November draft Keynes proposed that, if war debts were cancelled, Britain 'forgo the whole of her share of the indemnity, *not as against the enemy* from whom it would be claimed, but for herself, placing this sum at the disposal of the Peace Conference'. The idea did not reappear in the March draft, by which time the battle lines on German payments had been scored in furrows across the table. But he did stress that a cancellation would immediately calm some of the extreme demands then being made.

The Americans would not hear any of this. Davis warned Wilson that these 'fascinating plans' of international pooling and guarantees would be 'in effect giving a blank check on the United States'. Wilson assured Davis he was 'on my guard'.[77] So extreme was the attitude of the American delegation that they shied away from all economic discussion, despite their championing an economic settlement with Germany. Their position was utterly contradictory. There would be no economic section in the League of Nations. When poor, hapless Monsieur Klotz proposed setting up a commission for economic questions Wilson rejected it out of hand; the American Congress, he remarked, 'was jealous of being forestalled in commitments on economic matters'.[78] Yet, less than two weeks later, he approved the creation of a Supreme Economic Council. The difference between Klotz's commission and Wilson's council was that Americans chaired all the sub-committees of the latter: Davis on Finance, Hurley on Shipping, McCormick on Blockade Control, and Mr Hoover sitting on Food.

Whatever moral ascendancy the Americans had gained from the Armistice in November they had lost in Paris by February. Moreover, their refusal to discuss finances with the Allies had, just as Keynes pointed out, a harmful effect on business in the Reparations Commission.

Why Lloyd George should have named William Morris Hughes and Lords Cunliffe and Sumner as Britain's representatives on the Reparations Commission is somewhat of a mystery. Hughes, the Australian Prime Minister who had sparked off the calls in Britain and in France for 'total indemnity' back in November, was hardly the kind of person who was going to compromise himself now. He was frequently seen in the ante-room of the Quai d'Orsay, a cigarette tucked behind his ear and a glass of brandy at hand, openly vaunting his extravagant demands. Lord Cunliffe, a sworn enemy of the Treasury since his dismissal as governor of the Bank of England, had always argued that Germany could pay £25 billion – four times the Treasury's most optimistic estimate. Lord Sumner, a noted commercial lawyer, fully endorsed the claim put forward by the Federation of British Industries for the total costs of the war. Lloyd George could have chosen from an array of candidates – if not at the Treasury then at the Board of Trade, or among some of his other colleagues on the Imperial War Cabinet. Perhaps he was showing his contempt for civil servants. Or it might have been a deliberately provocative act in the face of American intransigence – the Americans refused to discuss finances; the British would make maximum demands for indemnity. Keynes would later claim that the three men were brought in 'for electioneering and parliamentary purposes'.[79] At any rate, there they were in the three subcommittees of the Commission: Hughes in 'Valuation of Damage', Cunliffe in 'Germany's Capacity to Pay', and Sumner in 'Methods of Payment'.

Once the British started raising their demands, the French were bound to follow. They were worried less about the fairyland totals demanded of Germany than about the proportion of the actual sum received that would go into the reconstruction of regions methodically and scientifically destroyed during four years of enemy occupation.

Opposing British and French demands in 'Valuation of Damage' was a young American commercial lawyer, John Foster Dulles. Dulles defended the idea of a 'contract' having already been established with the enemy through its acceptance of Wilson's Fourteen Points and the qualification added by the European Allies to the Lansing note of 5 November 1918 – that is: 'compensation will be made by Germany for all damage done to the civilian population of the Allies and their property by the aggression of Germany by land, by sea and from the air'. Dulles argued that this limited demands for reparation to 'all damage directly caused by acts of the enemy.'[80]

Hughes, Cunliffe and Sumner simply did not accept this. By mid-February the Reparations Commission was in total deadlock.

6

Baron Paul Henri Benjamin Balluat d'Estournelles de Constant de Rebecque was, in 1919, an elderly French senator for the department of Sarthe. His list of world achievements was almost as long as his name. In 1907 he had accompanied the senator Léon Bourgeois to the Hague Conference to establish legal restraints on the conduct of warfare and to reinforce The Hague's Court of Arbitration, designed to settle international disputes. He had written many books on disarmament and conciliation. In 1909 he was awarded the Nobel Peace Prize. On 20 January 1919 he wrote to Woodrow Wilson to say that the French people were 'more than grateful' to the United States and to Wilson, but at the same time he pleaded with him to visit the devastated regions.

Wilson replied on Friday, 24 January, that he would bear this in mind. On Saturday, at the second plenary session of the Conference, a Commission for the League of Nations was established. Wilson was named its chairman. The time had at last arrived. On Sunday, the 26th, he set out to inspect the devastated regions.[81]

Several of his economic advisers accompanied him in the seven-car motorcade, including Herbert Hoover. They drove straight to Château-Thierry and Bellau Wood, where Wilson claimed American forces had turned back the German Army. He visited the trench where the Marines had been slaughtered, and at the top of a hill he saw for the first time since his arrival in France a military cemetery. Wilson was totally silent.

Wilson's party then took a train to Reims, where they arrived in a blinding snow storm. Through a horizontal torrent of ice they could pick out silhouettes of broken masonry. 'No one can put into words the impressions received amid such scenes of desolation and ruin,' said Wilson. Reims before the war had had a population of 250,000. Now it was reduced to 3,000, most of whom lived in cellars.[82]

Lloyd George also paid a visit to devastation that day. He went north to Amiens and lunched in the ruined château that had once been Foch's headquarters. On the way back to Paris, Riddell travelled with the new Secretary of War, Winston Churchill, who had come over to France for consultations with the Commission for German Disarmament, which the Ten had just set up.

Their conversation turned to war, peace and the curiously ambivalent situation in which the world now found itself. 'The war is over; I mean the period of joint united effort for a common purpose,' Churchill ruminated, staring out of the car's window at the desolation. 'It will never recur. Now we are all fighting each other again.' He spoke of building up a nation with the gallant men who had fought: 'I want them to form the basis of a great national effort. I want them to combine to make an even greater England.' Riddell answered that nowadays people wanted more than high-sounding phrases: they sought better conditions, and intended to assert themselves. 'Yes,' said Churchill, 'better conditions – cheap houses, higher wages, etc.' Churchill's conception of Britain consists of well-paid, well-nurtured people, managed and controlled by a Winston or Winstons, thought Riddell to himself.

They talked of happiness. Churchill said he had learned much from the war, and that he could speak better and more easily than before it. He gibed at Riddell for his teetotalling and spoke of the merits of strong drink: 'It alters one's outlook on life,' he said. Yet he admitted to being gloomy and abstracted when thinking things out. Riddell commented, 'It does not do to look so. This is a smiling age.' In the old days statesmen could look solemn and stately, but 'today the smile is in fashion – the Lloyd George smile, the Wilson smile, and so on'. Churchill quickly answered that his life had been happy as a whole and that now he was happier than ever.

But he was worried about Russia. Churchill, recorded Riddell, 'spoke much of the Bolshevists, against whom he is very bitter'. He wanted a military intervention with British, French and American volunteers. Riddell did not think British public opinion would support another war that would interfere with Russia's domestic affairs. 'Perhaps,' said Churchill, 'but their view might alter.'

The car passed a lonely little cemetery. 'Poor fellows!' remarked Churchill, 'I wish they had lived to see the end of the war!'[83]

7

Wilson's eloquent speeches of the past year, damning the Old and praising the New, had enchanted multitudes of young people, convinced that the war was bound to bring change. 'I thank God daily that you are where you are,' wrote an admiring former student.[84] Wilson not only promised radical change: he claimed it was already there. 'There is a new world, not ahead of us, but around us,' he told the French Senate on 20 January. 'The whole world is awake, and it is awake to its community of interest.'[85] Sadly for Wilson, the world was waking. The charm was wearing off, his spell was broken. It began to be said that he was working for American national interests, not the world community; that he was a party man – and, moreover, a man whose party had no popular following.

The urgent deadlines of mid-February, set by Lloyd George's and Wilson's departure and the renewal of the Armistice, had pushed the Conference in two directions. One followed the lines of Wilson's global approach; it drove the topics of debate out and out, into the Pacific, the Indian Ocean and the Southern Hemisphere. The other went inward, to focus on Europe's northern plain, and Germany. It was a process peculiarly similar to that of the war: as the will to impose a more global peace grew, so the debate became more parochial.

Wilson dominated the first month of the Conference because the European Allies were his debtors. He intended to follow the global approach. He was inspired by his sense of History, by his inner faith in the deep structure of human time, the grander cause, the interest 'not so much in what happened as in what underlay the happening, not so much in the tides as in the silent forces that lifted them'.[86] When Wilson spoke of the League of Nations as a 'vital thing, not merely a formal thing, not an occasional thing, not a thing sometimes called into life to meet an exigency, but always functioning [in] a vital continuity', he meant that he was setting up something at the very base of the historical process, something global. The theme constantly recurred, both in his public pronouncements and in his more confidential negotiations at the Conference. It was one of the reasons why he refused to grant an interview with the press until the Covenant of the League of Nations was written and accepted. Before committing himself to any details, he first had to have a picture of the whole. 'The only way I can succeed is by working silently, saying nothing,' he confessed to Herbert Swope of the *New York World*.[87]

In effect, Wilson had turned the procedure of the Conference upside down. Instead of focusing on the details of the 'preliminaries' with Germany, as the French had proposed in November, Wilson headed directly for the principles of the final peace. This introduced a delay mechanism into all his negotiations. He would not send even Haller's Army into Poland for fear 'we were going to prejudge the whole Polish questions'. He would not decide on the character of mandates (that is, the administration, under the auspices of the League, of former enemy colonies and territorities), since that had to be left in the hands of 'an Executive of the League of Nations'. This attitude drove Lloyd George and Clemenceau to despair. 'No agreement will ever be reached,' complained Lloyd George. 'It is obviously useless to discuss the claims of the Romanians, the Yugoslavs and others,' observed Clemenceau.[88]

In turning the procedure upside down, Wilson reversed the logic of the agenda. The Ten began their discussion of territorial questions with the Pacific Islands, then moved on to New Zealand's claims on Samoa and Australia's in Timor, then to the pressing question of the pastoral deserts of South-West Africa and French and Belgian interests in equatorial jungles, then up to the Middle East and the Arabian problem, on to the Adriatic and the demands of Montenegrins, Yugoslavs and Italians – and finally to Germany. It was only because of an expanding war that the Poles got an early hearing.

The ironic effect of Wilson's global approach lay in the accumulation of secondary questions, which were then passed on to the experts. This caused confusion in the commissions and dissatisfaction among young, idealistic civil servants. They found themselves, like platoon commanders on the front, fighting with the details of a local landscape without any guidance as to how they might get out of them. 'Dispirited and depressed,' Nicolson entered in his diary on 9 February. 'Walk down to Crillon and go over Greek claims with the Americans.' Nicolson was contracting the flu.[89]

Wilson placed priority on the Covenant of the League of Nations, which he was determined to carry back to America in February. But it was not Wilson who wrote it. It was essentially a compilation of three drafts, all of which had their origin in Britain. One, prepared by a certain Phillimore Committee, had been used by Colonel House in the summer of 1918; the other two, by General Smuts and Lord Robert Cecil (the latter drawing heavily on the earlier Phillimore proposals), had been presented to Wilson while in London. Wilson simply worked as a diligent editor; after dinner in the Murat Palace, Edith Benham would frequently hear the President tapping away at an old typewriter that he kept in his study.

On 3 February, Cecil was furious when Wilson, at the first session of the Commission of the League of Nations, presented a revamped version of a final British draft that Cecil had personally delivered at the Murat Palace the previous weekend. Wilson had consulted no one in revising it. But, recorded Cecil that night, 'I supported all his [Wilson's] most tyrannical proposals, coercing poor [Léon] Bourgeois.' Because of this, and some persuasion from House, Wilson eventually went back to the British draft as a working copy for the Commission. The meetings took place in House's suite at the Hôtel Crillon – 'the scene of the making of the most important human document that has ever been written' noted the Colonel with his usual modesty. Ten meetings and ten days later, on Thursday, 13 February, the Covenant was ready for presentation to the plenary session. 'A memorable day,' wrote the Colonel. Wilson considered '13' his lucky number.[90]

The Covenant was made up of twenty-six articles (double thirteen, noted Wilson) that defined the League's organization and the manner in which it would guarantee the peace. It would have an Executive Council (made up of the five Great Powers and four rotating powers), a Permanent Secretariat and a Body of Delegates (as the general assembly was known). In organization it thus resembled not only the alliance structure of the war but also the formal constitution of the Congress of Vienna of 1814–15. Peace would be maintained, first, by making arms reduction a condition of membership and, second, through forced arbitration of international disputes, backed up ultimately by economic and military measures imposed by the members combined.

A subject of intense debate was the future of the colonies and territories forfeited by the Central Powers in the late war. According to terms of the Covenant, if they were 'inhabited by peoples not yet able to stand by themselves', they would be administered by a 'mandatory power' on behalf of the League. These 'mandatories' would govern according to the principle that 'the well-being and development of such peoples form a sacred trust of civilization'; they would be obliged to report annually to the League on the territories committed to their charge.[91]

There were, of course, no articles dealing with economics. The Covenant did, however, guarantee the 'freedom of transit and equitable treatment for the commerce of all States members of the League'. Wilson told reporters on 14 February that, because in the League of Nations there would be no neutrals, they had eliminated the question of neutral rights during war: 'so, as they say, "there ain't no such" issue as Freedom of the Seas'. The main cause of tension between Britain and the United States during the war had disappeared without as much as a puff of smoke.[92]

An article promised that members would 'endeavour to secure and maintain fair and humane conditions of labor for men, women and children'. But an article guaranteeing the 'free exercise of creed, religion or belief' had to be deleted because at the very last minute the Japanese – who had been silent throughout most of the proceedings – wanted to add 'equal and just treatment' according to race. The Southerner Wilson was attending another meeting when the subject was raised, but it was quite obvious to the Texan Colonel House that he could not place before the American Senate an article that abolished racial discrimination. 'It has taken considerable finesse to lift the load from our shoulders and place it upon the British, but happily, it has been done,' recorded House, with relief, just after the meeting.[93]

The debate over mandates, which had since mid-January occupied half a dozen meetings of the Ten, exposed the problem with Wilson's global approach. It was a giant political red herring, and, as it turned out, a very dangerous one.

Mandates, as originally conceived by General Smuts in 1918, were designed to be applied in Eastern European territories no longer administered by the Russian, German, Austro-Hungarian or Turkish empires – territories that had no obvious national identity. A particular point of focus was 'Yugoslavia', a frontier zone behind the mountains, an area of tension and mixed ethnic loyalties which had been used by German Supreme Command in summer 1914 as its excuse for marching west across the plain into Belgium. 'Jugo Slavia is only a name,' A. G. Gardiner of the London *Daily News* told Wilson at one dinner in January 1918.[94] He was exaggerating. A 'Yugoslav Committee' consisting of Habsburg Southern Slavs had been set up in Italy right at the beginning of the war – they sought their independence. In July 1917 the 'Yugoslavs' signed with the exiled Serbian government in Corfu a declaration that united Slovenes, Croats and Serbs in an independent kingdom under the Serbian Karageorgevic dynasty. The Italians showed an interest only after their Army was defeated at Caporetto. During Ludendorff's offensive they held in their capital a Congress of Oppressed Nationalities, out of which emerged a 'Pact of Rome' – a pledge by Italians and Yugoslavs to support each other's national unity. Faced with German and Austrian aggression, Yugoslav nationalism was something very real. The Habsburg Southern Slavs formally declared their independence from Austria on 29 October 1918. But it was only on 1 December that they proclaimed their union with the Serbs under King Peter I. This made some Allied observers, like Gardiner, suspicious of their territorial ambitions.

Smuts's idea was that, if the Yugoslav union did not hold, a League of Nations mandate could take over – the history of the last five years had demonstrated that the region was too dangerous a zone to leave in a state of perpetual warfare. The same could be said of Poland, Czechoslovakia and parts of the former Russian Empire: if national self-determination did not work here then some other form of authority had to be applied, for over ten million had lost their lives when it had not been.

29   Woodrow Wilson, wearing a top hat and leaning out of the boat, arrives at Brest on 13 December 1918 and looks for a place to land in the Old World

30   The Old World politicians – Foch, Clemenceau (wearing his grey gloves), Lloyd George, Orlando and Sonnino – sit out in the garden of 10 Downing Street on 2 December 1918

The 'economic men': (*left*) (31) John Maynard Keynes; (32) Herbert Hoover of the American Food Administration; (33) Dr Carl Melchior; (34) Louis Klotz, the French Finance Minister; (*right*) (35) Edvard Munch's haunting portrait of Walther Rathenau; (36) Count Brockdorff-Rantzau, chief of the German delegation at Versailles; and (37) Matthias Erzberger or, as the caption of this 1919 cartoon in *Kladderadatsch* described him (with an Anglo-French accent), 'Mr Erzbergère, our current Reichs Finance Minister'

38   The maidens of Dover throw paper flowers at the feet of President Wilson on his arrival in England on 26 December 1918

39   Women voted for the first time in Britain in the General Election of 14 December 1918

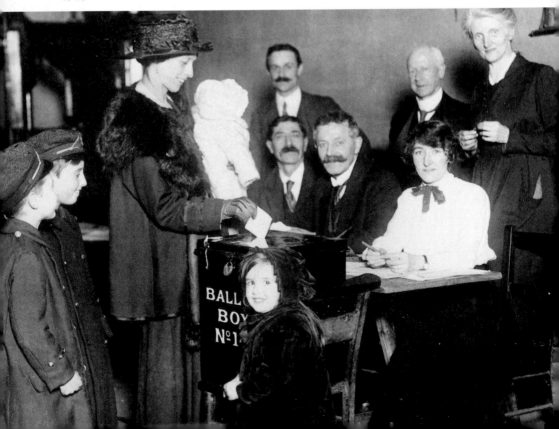

..... *You've seen it through !*

You don't want to talk about it. You don't want to think about it. You just want to lean back and feel that the day you've been dreaming of since that first August of 1914 has come at long last.

It's good to be alive. It's good to be with her. It's good to sit at home, lazily watching the smoke curl up from your Kenilworth Cigarette, and enjoying the flavour of that wonderful golden tobacco that suits the hour so well.

Peace finds Kenilworth Cigarettes unchanged, in size.

Kenilworth Cigarettes are made of mellow golden Virginia leaf yielding a fascinating aroma. They will compare favourably with any Virginian Cigarettes you can obtain, no matter how high the price. Yet Kenilworths only cost 1/4 for 20, 3/3 for 50, 6/6 for 100.

FOR THE FRONT.—*We will post Kenilworth Cigarettes to Soldiers at the Front specially packed in airtight tins of 50 at 2/9 per 100, duty free. Postage 1/- for 200 to 300; 1/4 up to 900.* **Minimum order 200.** *Order through your Tobacconist or send remittance direct to us. Postal Address :—14, Lord Nelson Street, Liverpool.*

Kenilworth Cigarettes

COPE BROS. & CO., LTD.,
LIVERPOOL AND LONDON,
Manufacturers of High-class Cigarettes.

41   During the Great War, sheep were raised in the Bois de Boulogne to feed and clothe Paris

42   People picnicking in the Bois du Boulogne on a Sunday during Ludendorff's offensive of July 1918. The sound of cannon could be heard

43   Statues, monuments and cathedrals were protected against the effects of a German bombardment. This is the statue to Eugène Delacroix in the Luxembourg Gardens

44   A gang of stonebreakers begins demolition of the Paris walls *('les fortifs')* shortly after the signature of the Treaty of Versailles

45   Berlin's civil war: flamethrowers at work in the newspaper district

46   Barbed wire entanglements in eastern Berlin

47 A British Mark V tank, captured during the war, is used to suppress rebellion

48 'Regime-loyal troops' (note the mix of uniforms) fire from behind a roll and bales of paper at the rebel-occupied Mosse newspaper offices

49 Moscow before the war: a view of Ilyinka Street from Red Square. The Upper Trading Rows are on the left; the Middle Trading Rows on the right

50 The fashionable shopping street of Kuznetsky Most (Blacksmith Bridge Street) in the late nineteenth century

51 Moscow after the Revolution: women of the *burzhooi* selling their possessions

52 Citizens, under armed guard, clear rubble in the centre of the city

53   (*above*) At a plenary session of the Peace Conference in Paris, Léon Bourgeois makes practical suggestions regarding guarantees, within the League of Nations, against aggression. In the front row, from left to right: Orlando, Léon Bourgeois (speaking), Jules Cambon, André Tardieu, Louis Klotz and Stéphan Pichon (head slumped in hands). Philippe Berthelot sits behind, between Tardieu and Klotz

54 (*below left*) The 'Four' in Woodrow Wilson's study. From the left: Orlando, Lloyd George, Clemenceau and Wilson

55 (*below*) Ignace Paderewski, Poland's Prime Minister and one of the greatest pianists of his century

56 (*above*) The German delegates receive the terms of the Treaty of Versailles at the Trianon Palace Hotel on 7 May 1919. They are seated between the horseshoe desk with the Czechoslovak delegation to their right and the Chinese delegation to their left. Clemenceau has just begun his brief address. From nearest to furthest: Schücking, Giesberts, Brockdorff-Rantzau, Landsberg, Leinert and Melchior (his head barely visible)

57 (*left*) The battleship *Hindenburg* goes down at Scapa Flow, 21 June 1919. The pennant 'Received' flies from the aft mast in response to Admiral von Reuter's order to scuttle

58 (*right*) 'The Victory Dance' from *Kladderadatsch*, September 1919. Nude Marianne cuts the throat of the dove of peace. Clemenceau's 'death's head' appears from behind the curtains. After Versailles, France was seen as Germany's principal enemy

59   Germans sign the Treaty of Versailles in the Hall of Mirrors, 28 June 1919. The weather was warm and the crowded hall was totally silent, apart from the whir of rolling cameras

60   German officers demonstrate in Kolberg at the moment of signature. The sign reads: 'Immediate release of our prisoners-of-war'

This was a very specific geographical problem. Wilson was impressed with Smuts's idea. In fact he liked it so much that he wanted to apply it to the rest of the world.

Nobody in Paris sought the return of Germany's former colonies to Germany. The cruel treatment of the natives and the establishment of submarine bases that threatened the security of all nations was the official explanation. Wilson wanted all these territories administered by League of Nations 'mandatories'.

The policy brought him into head-on collision with the British Dominion prime ministers. Each one of them had his own version of the 'Monroe Doctrine' that had proclaimed America's sphere of the world barred to foreign interests. Massey of New Zealand explained that his country's occupation of Samoa was a 'life and death matter'. Hughes of Australia said that annexation of New Guinea was nobody else's business. Botha, more polite, could not see why South Africa's takeover of South-West Africa – made up, he said, of primitive herders – should be of interest to anyone but a South African. Wilson, who aboard the *George Washington* had prepared himself for a confrontation with old-style European diplomats, thus found himself faced with colonialists like himself.

The Europeans were in no hurry to help him. The Italians, single-mindedly concerned about the Alps and Istria, totally rejected the idea of mandates; they were delighted to see the focus of discussion shift to the Pacific. The British, their hearts half in Europe and half overseas, used the diversion to avoid making painful military commitments on the Continent; Lloyd George systematically delayed the discussion of European affairs. The French thought mandates an opportunity to weaken American influence at the Conference; 'Bring your savages with you,' Clemenceau urged Lloyd George.

He didn't have to be asked. Australia and New Zealand continued to press for direct annexation. Wilson asked if he was to understand that the two countries had presented an ultimatum to the Conference. 'That's about the size of it, President Wilson,' answered Hughes. 'Australia and New Zealand are trying to block the world,' Wilson grumbled in front of Grayson after the meeting. It was the New World that was committing sin: 'Australia and New Zealand with six million between them can not hold up a conference in which, including China, some twelve hundred million people are represented,' said Wilson.[95]

Old Europe eventually came to his rescue. Lloyd George proposed three classes of mandate ('A', 'B', and 'C'), to be determined by the 'stage of the development of the peoples'. Thus, in the former Turkish Empire the nationhood of several communities had already begun to appear, and the wishes of these communities would have to be the principal consideration of the mandatory. In Central Africa, on the other hand, the mandatory would be more concerned with the 'prohibition of abuses such as the slave trade, the arms traffic and the liquor traffic'. Finally, remote areas like South-West Africa and the South Pacific Islands would be best 'administered under the laws of the mandatory state as integral portions thereof'. When these three distinctions were accepted in early February, a new phrase entered the English language: the 'underdeveloped world'.[96]

Riddell asked Hughes, whom he found sitting in the ante-room after presenting his ultimatum, what he thought the difference was between absolute ownership and a mandate. The Australian answered that there was none.[97]

This might have served as a warning. Faced with Australian intransigence, Wilson became ever more insistent that Germany's Pacific Islands north of the Equator be governed by a mandate. Yes, yes, said the Japanese, who now occupied them, thus controlling about 4 million square miles of ocean. The people of these islands, they reported, were on the whole still in a primitive state and were 'fully contented under the present regime'. The Japanese received a 'C' mandate.

Technicians connected with the American delegation noticed that this might cause some difficulty for American communications with the Orient, most of which passed through old German cables linked with the Island of Yap. Yap was now administered by the Japanese. Walter Rogers, one of the technicians, foresaw 'a rearrangement of the whole cable system of the Pacific'.[98]

Wilson himself observed another problem: the Japanese were now closer to Hawaii than America's Pacific Coast.[99]

Obstinately pursuing his global approach, Wilson had accidentally knocked over Pandora's box in the Pacific.

'We represent as we sit around this table more than twelve hundred million people,' Wilson triumphantly announced in the Salle d'Horloge when he presented the third plenary session with the final draft of the Covenant on Friday, 14 February. He called it a practical document, a human document, one with 'a pulse of sympathy in it'. Several Americans would comment that it was the best speech he had ever made in his life. It ended with an uplifting coda: 'Many terrible things have come out of this war, gentlemen, but some very beautiful things have come out of it.' With the establishment of the League 'we can now live as friends and comrades in a single family'. A family of twelve hundred million, a 'Covenant of fraternity and friendship'.[100]

Hughes stood up and asked whether the session would have an opportunity to discuss the document. Clemenceau told him he could send his comments in writing to the Secretariat's bureau: *'Objections? . . . Adopté!'*

'That was a great performance,' Balfour told Wilson. The President was planning to go straight back to his palace and prepare for his departure that evening. But as he was leaving the great hall with his liegemen cheering about him (House: 'Governor, your speech was as great as the occasion.' Wilson: 'Bless your heart. Thank you from the bottom of my heart'), the Supreme War Council was summoned to an emergency meeting upstairs.

Winston Churchill had just stepped in from the pouring rain. He had been carried by plane from London, and wanted to redirect the Allies' attention back across the European plain – not this time towards Germany, or even Poland, but to the very base of the Continent: Russia.

8

Lloyd George had left Paris one week before, to attend the new Parliament. The miners had just voted to go on strike. Some scaremongers in the press spoke of this as the beginning of the Revolution in Britain. On the day Lloyd George arrived in London, 8 February, 3,000 soldiers in transit from their camps in the North of England to France had marched in a block from Victoria station to Whitehall. They were protesting at their conditions – poor food, bad sleeping quarters, a night spent hanging around on the station's platforms. On Horse Guards Parade they came face to face with a battallion of Grenadiers armed with bayonets. Cavalry surrounded them. The protesting soldiers were thus persuaded to take their breakfast in the nearby Wellington Barracks and then continue their journey to France. Nobody was hurt. But Lloyd George was impressed. He started himself to express fears of revolution. He warned his daughter not to bring her baby to London.[101]

So it was Balfour, not Lloyd George, who introduced Churchill to the Supreme War Council that stormy Friday night of 14 February. The Allies had proposed a truce and a meeting between the various factions now fighting in Russia. Churchill, said Balfour, had come over 'to explain the present views of the British Cabinet'.

Churchill reported that 'great anxiety had been manifested concerning the Russian situation' during a Cabinet discussion the previous day. In view of the imminent departure of President Wilson, he had been sent to Paris to get some policy decision on the matter. The problem was that only the Bolsheviks appeared to be ready to attend the proposed meeting, and they were not showing any sign of a cessation of arms. Churchill, Secretary of War, explained why he had been picked to present this problem in Paris: 'Great Britain has soldiers in Russia who are being killed in action. Their families wish to know what purpose these men are serving. Are they just marking time until the Allies have decided on policy, or are they fighting in campaign representing some common aim?'[102]

Clemenceau said that a matter of such importance could not be settled in so short and unexpected a meeting.

Wilson – who according to Churchill's own account remained standing, 'his elbow resting on Clemenceau's chair' – gave a very frank and simple reply.[103] Not one of the Allies was prepared to reinforce its troops in Russia. Conscripts could not be sent, and it would be hard to find volunteers – and, even if they could be found, 'in some areas they would certainly be assisting reactionaries'. The Allies were facing a 'cruel dilemma': if they remained, their own men would be killed; if they were removed, many Russians could lose their lives. But at some point Allied troops would have to be withdrawn: they could not remain in Russia for ever.

As for a truce and a meeting, Wilson thought that if the various Russian governments existing at the time refused to come to the spot the Allies had designated then the Allies should 'imitate Mohammed, and go to them'. Wilson then left for a quick dinner and boarded a train for Brest.

A need for policy, the 'cruel dilemma', and a vague hope that the solution would present itself in a truce: all this was typical of Western relations with the Eastern base of the Continent.

The history of the proposed truce was itself long and complicated. Allied troops had been sent into Russia to hold up the Eastern Front after the Bolsheviks had made their peace in early 1918 with the Germans; significant support had been supplied by the Czech Legion. But by December 1918 the Germans had fled and the Czechs had saved themselves. On 29 November Balfour had drafted a government memorandum claiming that the Allies had no desire to intervene in Russian domestic affairs: 'it is for the Russians to choose their own form of government'. But, he added, the Allies could not be indifferent to the fate of new anti-Bolshevik administrations scattered around the former Russian Empire and under the shelter of Allied forces. During December these Allied commitments to anti-Bolshevik regimes were strengthened by military accords, and most particularly by an Anglo-French 'Convention' on southern Russia and the Black Sea.

At the same time there were, especially in Britain and the United States, young idealistic civil servants as well as people placed high in government circles who had a certain admiration for the Russian Revolution; some were even ready to believe that the Bolsheviks were leading Russia into a more advanced stage of historical development. In France such people were confined to the opposition, created when the Socialists pulled out of the 'Sacred Union' in 1917. Not so in Britain and the United States. Lloyd George later claimed in his memoirs that, were it not for the dissent of the Ten and the conservative opinion at home, he and Wilson 'would have dealt with the Soviets as the *de facto* Government of Russia'.[104] The Prime Minister was always urging those around him to 'read up the story of the French Revolution' and 'let the Russian people decide for themselves what they wanted'.

Gauging Russian opinion from Western Europe was not a simple task. Paris was the best place to go. There were by now whole districts in Montparnasse and westward, outside '*les fortifs*', at Boulogne-Billancourt where all one heard was Russian, the food was Russian, the music was

Russian, and the signposts were written in the Cyrillic alphabet. Contrary to legend, this was not a camp of reactionaries. The Russian émigrés in Paris somewhat resembled the French 'men of business' who had gathered in Ghent under the umbrella of Louis XVIII at the time of Napoleon's Hundred Days in 1815.[105] True, the Russians' leading figure was the Tsar's last Minister of Foreign Affairs, Sergei Sazonov, but that was only natural – he personally knew all the major diplomats gathered in Paris. Yet, like exiled King Louis, Sazonov performed only one part in a play of many characters. When, in January 1919, the émigrés set up a Russian Political Conference in the hope of gaining some recognition from the Ten, they named Prince Lvov, President of Russia's First Provisional Government, as their chairman, and the Socialist Nicholas Chaikovsky as the main spokesman of their steering committee. Political opinion among the émigrés ranged from imperialist to socialist; though there were not, it is true, many Bolsheviks among them.

Headlam-Morley thought the Ten made a great mistake in 'not sounding the Russians in Paris'. After all, Poland's first recognized government had been the Polish Committee in Paris. The refusal to do as much for Russia came from Lloyd George and Wilson. Almost as soon as the Ten sat down in January the question had arisen of who should represent this vast zone in the East. Sonnino suggested hearing the émigrés, to which Lloyd George retorted, 'We were told they represented every shade of opinion. As a matter of fact, they represented every opinion, except the prevalent opinion in Russia.' Wilson insisted on hearing all parties at once, including the Bolsheviks. This scandalized Clemenceau, for whom the Bolsheviks – like the Germans in Poland – were invaders who should not be rewarded with negotiations; they 'had invaded the Baltic Provinces and Poland'. He was struck by 'the cleverness with which the Bolsheviks were attempting to lay a trap for the Allies'.[106]

On the matter of Russia the Anglo-American *entente précaire* held. The idea of a truce and a meeting in Paris of representatives of 'all the various states in Russia' had been proposed back in December at the Imperial War Cabinet by the Canadian Prime Minister, Richard Borden, as eager as Lloyd George to reduce his military commitments in Europe. Since October, the British and Americans had been putting out feelers to Moscow; by January, serious talks were under way in Stockholm with the Soviet 'commercial attaché for Scandinavia', Maxim Litvinov.

Lloyd George made his appeal to the Ten for an attempt at a truce on 16 January. It was a spellbinding performance. The Allies could pursue one of three policies, he said. One was the military defeat and destruction of Bolshevism: 'Did anyone serious put forward this policy? Was anyone prepared to carry it out?' – it was not a realistic policy. Another was the insulation of Bolshevism, the so-called *cordon sanitaire*: it meant siege, 'that is to say, the blockade of a Russia that had no corn, but a large famished population' – it was an inhuman policy. The only other way he could think of to solve the Russian problem was 'that of asking representatives of the various Russian Governments to meet in Paris after a truce among themselves.'[107]

Clemenceau warned that if representatives of 'Lenin and his gang' came to Paris there would be riots; the Ten would have to host their meeting of the Russian factions elsewhere. Lloyd George and Wilson eventually decided on a tiny island in the middle of the Sea of Marmara. The English called it 'Prince's Island', the Turks 'Prinkipo'. The English remembered it as a holiday resort with luxury hotels and fine views of Europe and Asia; the Turks recalled it as a place where the Byzantine emperors had kept prisoners, their heads shaven, their eyes gouged out. Before the war, Young Turks had transported tens of thousands of rabid dogs from Constantinople to a neighbouring island, where they had been left to devour one another.[108]

The Ten announced their invitation to the Russian factions by radio on 22 January. The meeting would take place at Prinkipo on 15 February, 'provided there is a truce of arms'.[109]

The Russian Political Conference in Paris, infuriated at not being consulted, let it be known that they would not be going to Prinkipo. The anti-Bolshevik governments in Russia, feeling that the Paris Conference was treating them on the same footing as Moscow, equally refused to attend. As for the Bolshevik government, it first demanded a formal invitation and, when this was not forthcoming, stated that it was willing to 'purchase agreement at the price of important sacrifices' – it would recognize Russia's foreign debts, grant mining concessions to Allied business interests, and cede all territories currently held by Allied troops. That is not what the Allies were asking. The Bolsheviks made no mention of a possible ceasefire. Wilson called their language 'rather insulting'.[110]

When Churchill asked the Allies on 14 February, one day before the truce deadline, what policy they had on Russia 'if the Prinkipo meeting were not going to procure a cessation of arms', he already knew the answer: they had none.

Wilson was on his way back home when the Supreme War Council sat down the next afternoon to discuss the problem. It was a critical moment for the peace of Europe, and a critical hour in Winston Churchill's career.

By arrangement with Clemenceau, it was agreed that the French Chief of Staff, General Alby, should begin the meeting with an assessment of the military situation in Russia. He demonstrated that, with the exception of Estonia, the Red Army was advancing on every front. On the other hand the Red Army lacked competent officers, suffered from poor communications, and had little modern equipment. He concluded that 'though numerically inferior, regular Allied troops would easily defeat it'.

Churchill made two proposals. One was 'to carry Prinkipo through to a definite result or get it out of the way' so that the Ten would be free 'for such action as they might wish to take'. He tabled a draft message that extended the deadline for the cessation of fighting by ten days. To avoid wasting any more time, he asked for the simultaneous creation of an Allied Council for Russian Affairs with 'political, economic and military sections, [and] executive powers within limits to be laid down by the present Conference'. Its military section would at once 'draw up a plan for concerted action against the Bolshevists'. Churchill was not asking for expanded military intervention in Russia: he was simply suggesting an investigation into the alternatives available. With the suggested plan 'the Supreme War Council could then make their choice; either to act or to withdraw their troops and leave everyone in Russia to stew in their own juice'.

So: another chance for Prinkipo, and consideration of a joint military plan if the truce did not work. This was hardly the scheme of a mad warmonger. Churchill – who built his history on the study of maps – noted in conclusion that Russia had been the 'counterpoise of Europe' until 1914. If the Allies abandoned her now, within five or ten years Germany would exert 'supreme influence' in the area. Russia, he said, was 'the key to the whole situation': if Russia was not made a living part of Europe, a friend of the Allied powers, 'there would be neither peace nor victory.'[111]

Hankey, who was present, said that 'Churchill's eloquence, enthusiasm and personality produced an electrical effect.'[112] The civilians in the room spoke of abandoning the Prinkipo project altogether. Clemenceau admitted he had always been opposed to it. Balfour said 'he had never been sanguine'. Even House confessed that 'he had never been in favour of the Prinkipo proposal'. But none of them was in a hurry to set up a Council for Russian Affairs. They adjourned in Saturday's twilight.

The weekend was spent in a flurry of meetings, secret encounters and exchanges of coded telegrams between Downing Street and Wilson's boat in mid-Atlantic. House must have known what Wilson knew: the Americans had already decided to withdraw their troops from Russia.[113] But they did not want a public debate on the matter – the Republicans in Congress were calling for withdrawal; the American press campaigned for more involvement – and they did not want even to discuss it with the Allies. Lloyd George in London received an exaggerated account of Churchill's presentation from his private secretary in Paris, Philip Kerr. 'I beg you', Kerr said in his telegram, 'not to commit this country to what would be a purely mad enterprise out of hatred of Bolshevik principles.' The French were not reliable guides, he added, and 'I also want you to bear in mind the very grave labour position in this country.' That Sunday Lloyd George was having dinner with Riddell at his private estate. 'Winston is in Paris,' said the Prime Minister. 'He is a dangerous fellow. He wants to conduct a war against the Bolsheviks. That *would* cause a revolution! Our people would not permit it. Winston has a very excitable brain. He is able, but may go off at a tangent at any moment.'[114]

No one who has read the minutes of Saturday's meeting can conclude this. Clemenceau, Balfour, Sonnino and House, in wanting to abandon Prinkipo altogether, were actually taking a more extreme position than Churchill. It was Lloyd George, in rebellious London, who was excitable, not Churchill.

Lloyd George cabled Kerr, 'I trust he will not commit us to any costly operations.' Kerr showed the telegram to House half an hour before the Supreme War Council met on Monday afternoon. That is what killed the Allied Council for Russian Affairs.[115]

Balfour joined House in opposition to Churchill. Unfortunately the debate – which must have been acriminous – was not recorded in the Council's minutes. Lansing notes rather coolly in a letter to Wilson that Churchill again requested 'an early report as to the practicability of possible joint military action by the associated powers' in Russia and that 'the Americans opposed the adoption of this resolution'. House, writing to Wilson, speaks of the 'extreme position taken by Churchill'. He also reports that 'Clemenceau made an excited speech which Balfour considered offensive and accordingly he answered it rather sharply.'[116]

One can imagine the tone of Clemenceau's 'excited speech'. But was Churchill so extreme? Or were reports of this the reaction of Americans frightened of 'unity of command' and of the British worried about their Continental commitments? The meeting concluded that, rather than set up an Allied council, 'each delegation would consult its military representatives'. In other words, there would be no Allied policy on Russia. 'Dangerous' Churchill had been the scapegoat of those who did not want a policy. On 18 February he returned to London, and the next day, in a speech at Mansion House, he announced, 'If Russia is to be saved, as I pray she may be saved, she must be saved by Russians.' They certainly could not count on the Allies. By 23 February the American commissioners in Paris could sigh with relief, 'Churchill's project is dead and there is little danger that it will be revived again by the Conference.'[117]

Foch, ironically, made his report on the successful renewal of the Armistice in the same room and on the same day that Churchill's proposal was defeated. So the road was now open for the final military terms of peace with Germany. But how were these to be translated into a general European peace without some policy on warring Russia?

Woodrow Wilson, who did not work with maps, assured House that, with the League of Nations an accomplished fact, 'nearly all the serious difficulties will disappear'. He was convinced that his fortnight of successful work on the League of Nations Commission had given the twelve hundred million people of the globe a sense of security, although no international tribunal had been set up (Wilson had a disdain for The Hague), no international army had been formed (Wilson had warned that the American

Senate would never accept one), and anything that approached a real military alliance had been studiously avoided. Ultimately, the guarantee of peace written into the Covenant relied on the exertion of 'world opinion' which, Wilson believed, had been unable to express itself under Europe's system of Old Diplomacy.

Colonel House agreed that, with the grand principles of the League now accepted, the other pieces of the puzzle would swiftly fall into place. 'We'll button up everything in the next four weeks,' he assured the President on the day of his departure. He would have a programme ready for a preliminary peace with Germany before Wilson was back in Paris in early April; this would include a plan for the reduction of Germany's armed forces to a peace footing, the delineation of her boundaries, the amount she would have to pay in reparations, and an agreement on her 'economic treatment'.[118]

The whole of official France was present at the station, its walls decorated with flags, palms and firs, to see the American President off. He stretched out a hand to the Colonel and then fondly embraced him. 'He looked happy, as well indeed he should.'

Grayson, his doctor, thought him tired. Edith Benham, his secretary, described him as 'brain weary'. Yet he must have been pleased by the telegrams from Washington which were handed to him the next morning as he boarded ship. 'Majority of leading papers favourable,' reported one. 'Plain people throughout America for you.' 'The verdict of history will be that this [the Covenant] is the greatest deed done by its greatest man,' read another. 'No man in our history has done so much for humanity,' said a third. Wilson had successfully imposed his global vision on the Conference; the rest was a matter of detail – tiresome detail.[119]

The USS *George Washington* cut a slow path across the winter ocean. The one accompanying battleship, the *New Mexico*, carrying the radio equipment that kept Wilson in touch with the world, developed engine trouble on the fourth day of the voyage. It signalled the President's ship to proceed alone; help would come from another boat, 200 miles away. So the *New Mexico* was left floundering from one grey Atlantic crest to another while the *George Washington* steamed doggedly onward, without radio, without news. That was the day Clemenceau, champion of the 'old system', was shot.

Moscow in winter

1

While President Wilson was temporarily lost out on the heaving Atlantic, a junior member of the American delegation in Paris, William C. Bullitt, was preparing for a trip east to Moscow.

It would be a journey into Europe's war zone. None of the Western powers controlled the area. Nobody could possibly tell, at that moment, what the outcome of the fighting would be. No Westerner even understood the nature of the continuing war, for it bore no resemblance to the Western Front. Eastern Europe was, as a consequence, *terra incognita*, a blank on the map. This was the great difference between the Congress of Vienna of 1815 and the Peace Conference in Paris: at the Congress the delegates had discussed at their leisure the boundaries of all Europe; at Paris, by contrast, half of the Continent was out of bounds for the peacemakers.

The initial purpose of Bullitt's mission to Moscow remains to this day something of a mystery. Bullitt himself claimed he had been ordered to Russia in an effort to renew the Prinkipo proposal. 'It was decided that I should go at once to Russia,' he later told a US Senate hearing, 'to attempt to obtain from the Soviet Government an exact statement of the terms on which they were ready to stop fighting. I was ordered if possible to obtain that statement and have it back in Paris before the President returned to Paris from the United States.'[1] Lincoln Steffens, a journalist who accompanied Bullitt, confirmed that on the train out from Paris he had seen, 'pencilled on a sheet of paper', the seven items Lloyd George's private secretary, Philip Kerr, had drawn up as 'the terms for the Bolsheveki to agree'. 'Colonel House had prepared,' Steffens further asserted, 'Lloyd had planned the visit; and Bullitt's instructions came from House and from the British Prime Minister.'[2]

Asked if his government had been recently approached by the Bolsheviks in Russia, Lloyd George stated in the House of Commons on 16 April, 'We have had no approaches at all except what have appeared in the papers.' He did, however, admit that 'there was some suggestion that a young

American had come back from Russia with a communication'. But Lloyd George feigned ignorance of this. 'It is not for me to judge the value of this communication, but if the President of the United States had attached any value to it he would have brought it before the Conference, and he certainly did not.'[3] Lloyd George was not telling the truth. But neither was Bullitt, nor Steffens.

The Bullitt mission to Moscow was born out of the turmoil among the main Paris delegations produced by Churchill's intervention of 14 and 15 February. As Churchill had put it, Russia was 'the key to the whole situation'; if there was to be a stable peace, Russia would have to resume her old role as 'the counterpoise of Europe'. That whole weekend – while Wilson set off for his boat at Brest – there had been a flurry of secret diplomatic meetings in Paris, private encounters, and a good many coded messages sent across the Channel and the Atlantic. It was as if the Allied governments had suddenly realized that they had no policy on Russia.

They didn't. Since the Armistice of 11 November their policy had been held in limbo, somewhere between support for the anti-Bolshevik governments in Archangel, the Baltic states, Poland, southern Russia and Siberia, and recognition of the new regime in Moscow. While the Americans were furtively disengaging their forces, the French, under Foch, were developing a 'grand plan' for military assistance to the anti-Bolshevik Whites. But only the British had actively committed their forces to Russia.[4]

Wilson had left House groping for a policy. Among the papers of William Wiseman – who was still acting as liaison between British and American policymakers – there is a list of recommendations on how to deal with the Bolsheviks; it seems to have been prepared by advisers during that hectic weekend of consultation. 'Don't say negotiations are broken off' was its first point. 'Issue statement saying Bolsheviks have not complied with conditions for meeting' was the second. It was recommended that the Allies 'now make another statement to clear the issues' and to say that, if the Bolsheviks failed to respond, neighbouring states would be protected from their terroristic armies 'by sending forces to these states'. Lansing personally crossed out this last phrase and replaced it with a nicely vague 'by every means in our Power'.[5]

Lansing also noted in his desk diary on Sunday, 16 February, that he had that day 'talked with House about sending Bullitt to Russia to cure him of Bolshevism'.[6]

On the day after Churchill's last fierce encounter with the Supreme War Council, Lansing – now formally chief of the American delegation – wrote to Bullitt, 'You are hereby instructed to proceed to Russia for the purpose of studying conditions political and economic, therein, for the benefit of the American commissioners plenipotentiary to the peace.'[7] There was nothing about an armistice or terms of peace with the Bolsheviks. Henry White, the token Republican commissioner, later argued that Bullitt had not actually been 'ordered' to Russia, but was simply 'allowed' to go: 'the whole trip was at Bullitt's own instigation'.[8]

Even Colonel House, who, in Bullitt's account, was the person responsible for the 'order',[9] told the other three American commissioners that 'Bullitt was going for information only'.[10] The critical meeting between House and Bullitt was on Monday, 17 February. Whether this was before or after Churchill's appearance at the Supreme War Council cannot be determined (the sole documentary evidence of the date is a scribbled entry in one of Bullitt's note-pads). The only certain element in the story is that the American delegation, and most especially House, had suddenly got very sensitive about Russia. They seemed to be worried that Churchill, with the support of the eager French, was going to pull America into a war with the Bolsheviks. House probably sent Bullitt to Russia to stop this.

Bullitt had for the past year bombarded him with memoranda demanding US recognition of the new Soviet government. In the last couple of months Bullitt had been running a single-handed campaign to send Allied 'missions' into Bolshevik Russia to find out what was going on and to offer armistice terms to its leaders. Nothing came of this until his conversation with House that Monday, the 17th.

According to Bullitt's own account, he came to House with a list of terms that he thought would persuade the Bolsheviks 'to stop their advance and declare an armistice on all fronts'. He presented his list in the form of questions, to which House had replied 'yes'.

The most striking feature about the list is that it is almost exactly the same as the items supposedly drawn up by Philip Kerr as 'the terms for the Bolsheveki to agree.' Kerr later confirmed that he had met Bullitt, but he never mentioned such a list. Kerr, on the telephone all that weekend to report to the Prime Minister his fears about Churchill's intervention, was a very busy man; it is quite possible that Bullitt used with Kerr the same technique as he had applied to House when interviewing him Monday morning. Something even more remarkable about this list is that it corresponds, point by point, to the 'peace terms' approved by Lenin and the Soviet Executive Central Committee only three weeks later. Yet the American President was almost certainly unaware of these points at the time, and it seems highly unlikely that the British Prime Minister had heard about them.

The terms, in all likelihood, originated in Bullitt's own mind. When he left Paris for Russia on 22 February 1919 there seem to have been only four people in the world versed in the supposed American proposals to the Bolsheviks for peace: House, possibly Kerr, Bullitt and his friend Lincoln Steffens, a man with known Bolshevik sympathies. At the age of twenty-eight, Bullitt had embarked on a most extraordinary venture in persuasion. He was one of those rare persons – part diplomat, part confidence man – capable of pulling off such a feat.[11]

*   *   *

The American labour leader Samuel Gompers called Bullitt a 'faddist parlor socialist'. George F. Kennan, who in 1936 replaced Bullitt as US ambassador to Moscow, likened him to the Great Gatsby. He was immensely rich; he never had anything less than a gold piece with which to pay his French taxis, and he carried in his wallet only hundred-dollar bills and thousand-franc notes. He could not imagine playing a subordinate role to anybody; even when presented to the President of the United States he considered himself on an equal footing. 'Romantic, vigorous, at times almost flamboyant, reticence was not a part of Bill's character,' wrote his brother Orville. This was not inconsistent with Kennan's portrayal of Bullitt as a true representative of the 'war generation'; when Kennan compared Bullitt to Scott Fitzgerald's Jay Gatsby he was thinking in particular of his touch of fate, his tendency to burn his candle at both ends, his high hopes and his enormous disappointments. He was part of a generation 'full of talent and exuberance', as Kennan put it, for whom 'the First World War was the great electrifying experience of life'; their ideals were often totally displaced, the politics they pursued were in reality awful, and their ultimate and inevitable disillusionment was very, very bitter.[12]

Bullitt was born in Philadelphia in 1891, but not with a silver spoon in his mouth – it was golden, and studded with diamonds. As a child he was photographed wearing long curls and a Little Lord Fauntleroy suit, and taught to dance the waltz and the cotillion; his family spoke French at the dinner table and told tales of his controversial ancestors: William Christian of the Isle of Man had been hanged, drawn and quartered because of his disloyalty to Cromwell; Fletcher Christian had led the mutiny on the *Bounty*; Patrick Henry was best remembered for his 'Give me liberty or give me death'; and now, over in England, there was his cousin Lady Astor, née Nancy Longhorne, the first woman to take a seat in the House of Commons. Bullitt graduated from Yale in 1912 after his class had voted him 'most brilliant senior'. Professor Chauncey B. Tinker described him as 'one of the most brilliant graduates of this University, a man of keen intellect, wide experience and tireless will'. Following the family tradition, he went up to Harvard Law School. But he did not like the unjust ethics of the place. 'The Divinity School is three blocks to the left,' his teacher told him; Bullitt, typically, left in a huff, never to come back. He got a job at the Philadelphia *Public Ledger*; he was a correspondent in Europe when war broke out, and for the rest of his life he would always regard what he witnessed there as the 'failure of the old diplomacy'.[13]

Bullitt was absolutely convinced he was going to die in the war, even though he never served in the Army. He had avoided this by finding a slot in the Department of State, shortly after America entered hostilities; Bullitt ran his campaign to end the war from behind a desk in Washington. 'What am I going to get killed for?' he asked himself in a diary note early in 1918. He didn't think the ideals of his small circle of American Socialists were worth sacrificing his life for. He certainly didn't want to die for Wilson's Fourteen Points. But there was something he was ready to serve, and serve with a passion: the Russian Revolution.

'I suppose', reflected Bullitt when later interviewed, 'it is the sort of feeling that Wordsworth talks about in his poems on the French Revolution in which he says "Bliss was it in that dawn to be alive, But to be young was very heaven" or something like that.' Every American textbook on the French Revolution quoted Wordsworth. Bullitt, like thousands of the 'war generation', thought of the events in Russia as another French Revolution, making it 'bliss to be alive'. Bolshevik Russia was the hope. It was the big change. It was the reason for fighting. And now it was the explanation for why the war had to stop. 'I know a lot of men who have been in Russia since the Revolution began' – Bullitt was thinking in particular of his friend John Reed, now serving Lenin as Director of Revolutionary Propaganda. 'They are done with Emperors, political emperors, financial emperors and moral emperors. They have exiled the Czar. Taken over the banks and buried Mrs Grundy. As a nation they have become brotherly, open hearted, free from convention and unafraid of life. Is it impossible that the war may end in a similar state of grace in the rest of Europe and America?' He wrote memorandum after unsolicited memorandum to Colonel House in favour of the new revolutionary regime. For instance, on 7 February 1918, 'I do feel sure that Trotsky is the sort of man we need to have in power in Russia and I think that we should do everything possible to strengthen his hands.'[14]

He was furious when America bent to Allied pleas and sent, in August 1918, a few troops out to Siberia. But he thrilled to Wilson's Five Particulars of 27 September – a 'just peace', 'no favourites or separate interests'. 'Never have you voiced more clearly or more simply the hopes which are in the hearts of millions,' he wrote to the President. That was the memorandum that got him on the Paris delegation.[15]

He crossed the Atlantic on the President's ship. 'Attached to the American Delegation' read the name card on his cabin door until halfway across, when rubber and pencil were applied to change the first word to 'Attaché'. Once in Paris, Bullitt's ability to compose memoranda at speed led House to name him Chief of the Division of Current Intelligence Summaries. Bullitt would provide military and political information to the American commissioners every morning, seated on the corner of their beds, watching them shave, or sitting opposite them as they munched on their breakfast. 'So you were practically a clearing house of information for the members of the American mission?' asked Senator Philander Knox during the congressional hearing into his mission the following autumn. 'That is what I was supposed to be,' replied Bullitt.[16] Bullitt used this easy access to the commissioners to push his case for Russia.

Three other Americans accompanied Bullitt on his trip. R. E. Lynch was a naval secretary, who would go only as far as Helsingfors (or Helsinki) in

Finland. Captain W. W. Pettit, a military intelligence officer and Russian expert, was taken along officially as interpreter, but he stopped in Petrograd and never saw Moscow. The man who actually did all the interpreting and arranged most of the introductions was Lincoln Steffens.

Transportation and hotels were organized by the British; there was even a question of having Bullitt's party carried out to Finland by a Royal Navy destroyer. In the end, they caught a boat in London to Norway and then slowly worked their way across Scandinavia to Stockholm, where the American minister, Ira Morris, put them in touch with a Swedish 'Red', Kim Baum. Baum opened the road to Moscow.

Steffens described how Bullitt and Lynch skylarked on the way out; they were 'wrestling and tumbling like a couple of bearcubs'. Steffens thought this was Bullitt's way of not drawing attention to the importance of their mission.[17] At any rate, when Bullitt, Pettit and Steffens arrived in Petrograd on a cold Sunday night, 9 March, things began to get serious. The Soviet Commissar of Foreign Affairs, G. V. Chicherin – a man of high class and culture, like Bullitt – had come up from Moscow to meet them. Steffens explained to Chicherin that it was in the Bolsheviks' interest to co-operate with Bullitt in order to help the Americans and the British win over the hostile French at Paris. Chicherin immediately wired Lenin, who invited the mission down to Moscow. Pettit remained in Petrograd to prepare a report on conditions in the old imperial capital; Bullitt and Steffens took a train to the new Communist capital, the seat of hope for the 'war generation', isolated from the world by five hundred miles of snowfields. 'The Moscow–Petrograd express keeps up to its schedule,' noted Bullitt in his report, 'and on both occasions when I made the trip it took but 13 hours, compared to the 12 hours of prewar days.'[18]

The two Americans were in Moscow for only four days. They were put up in a confiscated palace, centrally heated and supplied with servants. Forewarned of a possible shortage of food, they had brought along their own tinned provisions, to which their Russian hosts added plenty of black bread and 'piles of caviar'. They were treated to opera and the theatre; during one of the performances they actually sat in the Tsar's private box.

Most of their negotiations were with Chicherin and Maxim Litvinov, an old Bolshevik and Deputy Commissar of Foreign Affairs, who had already been in contact with American emissaries in Stockholm at the time of the Prinkipo initiative. Nevertheless, Bullitt did meet Lenin once. While he was waiting for his appointment in the Kremlin, two delegations of peasants were parleying with the Bolshevik leader. One of them, having heard that Comrade Lenin's room was unheated, had come bearing a stove and enough firewood to heat it for three months. Another, learning that he was hungry, had made a journey of several hundred miles to deliver 800 pounds of bread as a gift from their village. Bullitt was impressed. 'There is already a Lenin legend,' he wrote in his report. 'His picture, usually accompanied by that of Karl Marx, hangs everywhere . . . Lenin is regarded as in a class by himself.' Nowhere is it recorded what Bullitt actually discussed with Lenin; all Bullitt himself notes is a general impression: 'Face to face Lenin is a very striking man – straightforward and direct, but also genial and with a large humor and serenity.'[19]

On 14 March, Chicherin and Litvinov handed Bullitt what would become the famous Bolshevik 'peace proposal'. It was signed by Lenin. Chicherin and Litvinov assured him it had been approved by the Executive Central Committee. It was structured like a form, beginning 'The Allied and Associate Governments propose that hostilities shall cease on all fronts in the territory of the Former Russian Empire and Finland . . .' and continuing with blanks left open for the Allied governments to fill in as they wished: the date of the Armistice, the place of a peace conference, its date, and so forth. It consisted of seven points, the words and phrases identical to those Bullitt had proposed to House on 17 February.

According to these terms, all *de facto* governments would remain in control of the territory they occupied at the moment of the Armistice; the Allied economic blockade would be lifted and there would be a reciprocal opening of trade relations; citizens of all the signing states would be granted free passage on member territories; the Allies were to withdraw their troops and all forms of military assistance to 'anti-Soviet governments' which had been set up on territory of the former Russian Empire; a general amnesty was to be proclaimed all round; prisoners of war were to be immediately released; and all existing governments in the former Russian Empire were to recognize their responsibility for payment of the tsarist state's debts to the West.

In all likelihood, Bullitt was the author of these terms. The Bolsheviks had added the paragraph: 'The Soviet Government of Russia undertakes to accept the foregoing proposal provided it is made not later than April 10, 1919.'[20]

Bullitt and Steffens immediately took a train back to Petrograd, picked up Pettit, and, on 16 March, from Helsingfors, telegraphed the terms through to Paris.

As the three men travelled back west they had exalted conversations about the experience, intoxicating one another with their idealism. 'I have seen the future and it works!' exclaimed Steffens.[21] Yes, they had seen hunger and suffering; but it was much better to witness it in Russia than in London, Paris or New York, because in Russia this 'temporary condition of evil' was made tolerable by hope and a plan.

They thus set up in their minds a double standard – one that marked Western political thinking in the years after the Great War. People of Bullitt's 'war generation' could accept evidence of the most extreme forms of suffering in Russia because it was 'temporary' and it was accompanied by hope; in the West, even if hunger and poverty could be proved less important than in Russia, they were a product of the imperialist and capitalist system. Anyway, as Pettit tirelessly pointed out, the misery in Russia had been vastly exaggerated in the Western press.

The double standard applied not only to what they saw with their eyes, but also to what they felt in their souls. As their train trundled past the grey city walls of Paris and came to a halt in the Gare du Nord they sensed, all of a sudden, gladness and relief. Bullitt could not understand this. Why relief? Surely it was wrong to feel glad to be back in capitalist Paris! Steffens explained: they 'had been to heaven' but they 'preferred hell'; 'we were ruined' – 'we could recognize salvation, but could not be saved'.[22]

2

'Russia today is in a condition of acute economic distress,' wrote Bullitt in his formal report to the American delegation. 'Everyone is hungry in Moscow and Petrograd,' he admitted. But, 'the people of Russia are labouring today to establish the system under which they shall live'. Their Communist leaders had an 'almost religious' attachment to their cause. 'I am ready to give another year of starvation to our revolution,' Bullitt quotes one young militant as declaring.[23]

Steffens also wrote a report. 'The organization of life as we know it in America, in the rest of Europe, in the rest of the world, is wrecked and abolished in Russia,' he remarked. He attributed this to the 'destructive spirit' of the Bolsheviks, who wanted to set up an 'economic democracy', not simply a 'political democracy as with us'. They sought 'democracy in the shop, factory and business'. To achieve this, the old system had to be totally destroyed – 'root and branch, fruit and blossom, too'. 'We were convinced', stated Steffens, 'that the Russians have literally and completely done their job.' Now everybody shared poverty – though the children were fed and what trains there were ran on time. Bullitt agreed: 'The food control works well, so that there is no abundance alongside of famine. Powerful and weak alike endure about the same degree of starvation.'[24]

All Western admirers of the Bolshevik Revolution quoted the 'Declaration of the Rights of the Working and Exploited Peoples'. The Bolsheviks had tried to push it through the legally elected Constituent Assembly when it first met in Petrograd on 5 January 1918. But a majority voted against it, so the Bolsheviks cordoned off the Assembly with barricades and pickets, and, when the session finally ended at four o'clock the following morning, they locked the doors; no elected deputy was ever let in again. A few days afterwards the same Declaration was passed by the 'Third Congress of Soviets', packed with Bolsheviks and Left Social Revolutionaries. The Declaration abolished private property and transferred factories, mines, railways and banks to the 'Workers' and Peasants' Soviet Republic'. But the key to what Steffens identified as the Bolsheviks' 'destructive spirit' lay in a clause concerning work: 'With the object of removing parasitical elements of society and of securing industrial organization on a public basis, the obligation of every citizen to work is recognized.' Lenin's war on the bourgeoisie – the *'burzhooi'* in Russian – derived from this.[25]

Lenin demanded a 'war to the death against the rich, the idlers and the parasites'. His party had barely been in power for a month when he openly called for the establishment in every village and town of the means for 'cleansing the Russian land of all vermin, of scoundrel fleas, the bedbug rich and so on'. There would be mass arrests; there would be executions. 'How can you make a revolution without firing squads?' asked Lenin. He espoused the philosophy that it was better to put a hundred innocent people in jail than risk letting a single enemy of the regime go free. 'There is nothing immoral in the proletariat finishing off a class that is collapsing,' confirmed Trotsky: 'that is its right.' Lenin's face beamed when his Commissar for Justice, I. N. Steinberg, suggested that they change the name of his department to the 'Commissariat for Social Extermination'. 'Well put,' said the leader, 'that's exactly what it should be; but we can't say that.' They couldn't say that because the Bolsheviks had an image of a new progressive world order that they had to fashion. The Bolsheviks were masters of the image.[26]

Their chief instrument of war was the All-Russian Extraordinary Commission for Struggle against Counter-Revolution and Sabotage – known as 'the Cheka' for short. It had replaced the Military Revolutionary Committee that had led the Bolshevik *coup d'état* in November 1917. Felix Dzerzhinsky, its Polish director from Vilna – a man who knew all about sadism and torture, having spent most of his adult life in the Tsar's jails – gave a good idea of the service it would provide when it was set up that December: 'Do not think that I seek forms of revolutionary justice,' he told Lenin's new government; 'we are not now in need of justice. It is war now – face to face, a fight to the finish. Life or death!'[27] It was the kind of war that few in the West would ever understand.

But, as the Bolsheviks rightly claimed, it was a popular war. Russia, with its closed castes, its rigid system of government, its narrowly recruited elites, had always possessed a violent counter-culture of social levelling. The peasants wanted to seize the land, the workers wanted control of their workshops, the intelligentsia – a Russian word – turned social thought into dogma. Nearly all Russians were or had been peasants, and they wanted to obliterate that fact, along with the surviving material evidence, from memory. Yet they felt no shame at being poor: rather, they regarded the rich as alien (*chuzhoy*), un-Russian and beyond the pale of known morality. The Cheka's slogan 'Death to the *burzhooi*' struck a popular note in Russia. 'The Bolsheviks are the true symbol of the Russian people,' wrote the historian Iurii Got'e with regret in his diary.[28]

The war with Germany had merely reinforced the cry. The Bolshevik campaign in 1917 for 'Peace, Land and Bread' was not really for peace; it was for a redirection of the war on to an old civil enemy, the *burzhooi*. The Cheka's terror began to spread the moment Trotsky sat down with the Germans at Brest-Litovsk. The Germans invaded Russia in February 1918; they bombed Petrograd on 2 March; the Bolshevik government immediately withdrew to Moscow. It occupied the Kremlin, had 'The Internationale' chime out from the musical clock on the Spassky Tower, and moved the Cheka into the Lubyanka building, the former Russian headquarters of Lloyd's Insurance Company. A new kind of war had begun. In Germany, with the end of hostilities on the Western Front, the war marched East. In Russia that movement can be followed inward into the Continental heart; the war turned civil, and aimed its guns on the *burzhooi*.

But Moscow was special. Moscow did not easily accommodate bureaucrats imported from Petrograd. It never had. Its very isolation had made it a point of resistance – and a most exotic one at that. Visitors before the war were astonished at the architectural mosaic of the town: the old mixed with the new, Asian neighbouring European, Orthodox churches next to the handsome commercial buildings of the Upper Trading Rows. Nicholas II had preferred Moscow to St Petersburg (which had been Russified to 'Petrograd' only at the outbreak of the war with Germany) because of its thousand onion domes, representing 'Holy Russia', untainted by the Western-style administration of the northern capital. Moscow, for him, was a material confirmation of the old Byzantine, autocratic trinity, 'God, Tsar and the People' – no bureaucrats in that.

How ironic it therefore was that this distant and secluded Moscow should become an enclave for the most energetic entrepreneurs of Russia – precisely because the bureaucrats of the Empire had not been there to control them. Central Moscow was bourgeois and nationalistic. After 1905 the combative 'young industrialists' of the Moscow Exchange Society would claim in their newspaper *Utro Rossii* that their town was the true 'city of the Russian bourgeoisie', the centre of 'ancient and free Rus predating the Tsars'.[29]

Before the war, this pugnacious independence was self-evident to any traveller to Moscow. If one stood in the centre of Red Square and looked north-east up Ilyinka Street one would have seen the newly converted Upper Trading Rows on the left and the Middle Trading Rows on the right (monstrous buildings that combined French mansard roofs with Russian window motifs drawn from the time of Ivan the Terrible), the neoclassical Moscow Trade Bank, two-storey beer bars, small retail shops stuffed with imperial regalia, the late seventeenth-century church of St Nicholas (the 'Big Cross', built through the donations of merchants), high side brick walls rented for advertising, and another onion-domed church at the end. The golden cupolas looked like mosques. There were the strange noises of open-air markets, living remnants of medieval bazaars. There was a profusion of colour which might have been borrowed from *The Thousand and One Nights*. Running down through the streets – and looking totally out of place – came the electric trams, installed in 1900 by a company from Manchester.

After 1914 Moscow ran its own war effort, since the central government in Petrograd proved incapable of securing such necessities as food and fuel. Moscow arranged its own loans on the foreign money markets, took the lion's share of 'public services' against a background of rampant inflation, and even conducted its own foreign aid programme, dispatching substantial funds to ravaged communities in Poland and Belgium and to the 'heroic Serbs'. It was in Moscow, under the leadership of Pavel Riabushinsky, that a network of War Industry Committees was organized to counter the power of the magnates of Petrograd's heavy industry, who so scandously cornered all the orders from the tsarist government. Moscow also gave birth, during the war, to the All-Russian Union of Industry and Trade, another important business association. But Moscow's bourgeoisie hardly profited from the war. Rather, small and nationally weak, it was wounded by it – and fatally so. Symbolically, the man who actually handed over the Winter Palace in Petrograd to the armed Bolsheviks was Alexandr Konovalov, the acting prime minister, a Moscow merchant.[31]

Moscow, however, did not yield easily to the Bolsheviks. While Petrograd fell in November[32] 1917 to Bolshevism without a fight – without, indeed, most residents even noticing it – the battle raged in Moscow's streets for ten long days. Under the direction of a 'Committee for Public Safety', military cadets and student volunteers loyal to the Provisional Government took over the Kremlin and succeeded in pushing the Bolshevik forces out into the suburbs. But the Bolsheviks returned with a vengeance. 'It turns out the Bolsheviks have artillery and people who know how to shoot,' wrote Got'e in his diary. Whole quarters in the city centre were torn apart. The Nikitsky Gates, a square to the west of the Kremlin where the Bolsheviks launched their attack, was burned down. One of the Kremlin towers was destroyed. Bombs fell in apartment courtyards. A hand grenade, which came flying through his flat's window, seriously wounded General Alexei Brusilov in the leg – the General had retired from military life after the failure of his last offensive in Galicia. Got'e explains how tenants organized their own guard; all the windows of the building were shattered by a grenade that went off in the entrance and two residents had to be sent to a field hospital: 'I think our present situation can be compared with that of the Parisians in the Commune ... Moscow under six days of shelling by Russian cannons!' Three days later 'armed bands that wear soldiers' uniforms' could be seen everywhere. Red flags flew from their armed lorries, which 'raced down the streets as if they wanted to smash everything in their passage'. As would later be the case in Germany, the spearhead of the revolution was a disintegrating army – led, in this case, by the professionals, the Bolsheviks.[33]

3

In *Doctor Zhivago* Boris Pasternak memorialized winter in Russia at the end of the First World War: 'There were three of them, one after the other, three such terrible winters . . .' He was looking back from a distance of thirty years: 'These three winters which followed one another have now merged into one and it is difficult to tell them apart.' The winters of 1918, 1919 and 1920 – the Years I, II and III of the Russian Revolution – seem to have been 'of the same sort', indistinguishable, inseparable, the whole long period 'dark, hungry and cold, spent in watching the destruction of all that was familiar and the changing of all the foundations of life, and in inhuman efforts to keep hold of life as it slipped out of your grasp'. The novel is about one character's attempt at a homecoming, the renewal of the genuine 'foundations of life' by searching out the hidden, inner secret of art.[34]

Russia brought the war into the home, into the soul. There was no longer any front line, any border between soldier and civilian. Not only was private property abolished, private life itself disappeared. Crossing by train from Poland into Russia in the late 1920s, H. J. Greenwall, a travel writer, noticed a wooden archway marking the empty frontier line. On it was written, 'Soviet Russia abolishes frontiers.'[35] It was more than just territorial boundaries that the new regime had in mind.

Though Russia was a nation of letter-writers, there are few personal journals that record the experience of the first three winters of the Revolution.[36] Diary-keeping was a dangerous activity in Soviet Russia. One must rely on the commentary of visiting foreigners, on the memoirs of émigrés and on the distant recollections of the elderly.

One important source is the French community in Moscow, which might be compared in scale and organization to the Russian community in Paris. The French occupied the quarter north of Kuznetsky Most, Moscow's Piccadilly, where jewellers, florists and fashionable patisseries were clustered together in covered passageways, where well-dressed young couples kept their secret rendezvous. Within the walled French parish, between Lubyanka and Milyutinsky streets, there was a magnificent church, Saint-Louis-des-Français, two schools, an old people's home, a children's home and a house for the curé, who in 1917 was the Abbé J. M. Vidal. Vidal was a great walker – he would think nothing of strolling out to the Garden Ring (Moscow's outer boulevards) and back – and he left a graphic description of what he saw and what happened to his parish during the first three years of Bolshevik rule.[37]

The editor of the French community's *Journal de Russie* was Ludovic Naudeau, who was also Russian correspondent for *Le Temps* in Paris – not favourite reading for the Bolshevik authorities. In July 1918 he was arrested for proposing that Soviet Russia recognize the tsarist debts to the Western powers (though this is exactly what the Bolsheviks offered in answer to the Prinkipo offer of January 1919). He was thrown into the infamous Butyrka

jail, which he discovered was filled with Russian ecclesiastics. After his
release in the following February he spent several days wandering about
Moscow, and left a most vivid account of some of the scenes he encountered
– scenes that are exactly contemporary to the Bullitt visit.[38]

Ivan Bunin, the first Russian to be awarded the Nobel Prize for Literature,
fled to White-occupied Odessa in the summer of 1918. In 1925 his wife
discovered him burning all his diary manuscripts: 'I don't want to be seen
in my underwear,' he told her – the sentiment of many of his countrymen.
But fragments survived; they contain descriptions of his last months in
Moscow, the first of the 'three winters'.[39]

Surely one of the most extraordinary documents to come out of this
period is the diary of Iurii Vladimirovich Got'e. It runs almost daily from
8 July 1917 to 23 July 1922, when Got'e handed it over to Frank Golder, a
representative in Russia for Hoover's American Relief Administration. 'It
will save the materials,' noted Got'e in one of his last entries. Golder duly
shipped the manuscript off to the Hoover Library at Stanford University,
and there it lay in a crumbling postal envelope until it was discovered by
a museum curator in 1982.[40]

Got'e was descended from a French immigrant family, Gautier, that had
kept a fashionable French bookstore on Kuznetsky Most since the eighteenth
century. But Got'e himself abandoned the book trade for the study of history.
He became one of the most prestigious academics of his time, holding
appointments at Moscow University, the Geodesic Institute and the municipal Shanyavsky University; he also directed the Moscow Public Library and
the Rumyantsev Museum, which was housed in a beautiful classical-style
mansion just west of the Kremlin. Got'e was a historian of the positivist
tradition, believing firmly in objective knowledge based on scientific
documentary research. He established his reputation through a study of
eighteenth-century land relations and the rise of the landed gentry in Russia.
Not for him the history of princes and heroes, the sloppy, sentimental stuff
of the earlier Romantic historians. In his first diary entry he admitted, 'I
specifically did not want to write either reminiscences, or reflections, or a
diary, for I have always thought there was quite enough of that rubbish
written without me.' But observing the developments around him – 'to my
great sorrow, shame and humiliation' – he felt obliged to create 'a very
imperfect, very subjective, but nevertheless historical source that may be of
use to someone in the future'.[41]

Day by day Got'e watched and recorded the degradation of life in his
native Moscow. He walked the town in every direction. He noted the details.
He sought, as he put it, to give 'touches' to the general picture of contemporary Russian existence. To read Got'e's diary – never revised, censored or
embellished – is to receive the chill of winter, the Revolution's first 'three
winters'.

*   *   *

It was a 'life of moles', guided by rumour. The only pleasure was to 'rest in one's shells'. A strange feeling overcomes me when I walk about the streets of Moscow – a feeling of death overall, of the termination, irrevocable and inevitable, of all life,' wrote Got'e as the second winter approached. 'I am free of that feeling only when I sit at home, or in the not yet completely looted apartment, or in the museum.' He followed a path that gradually seemed to relieve him of all attachment to things, to comfort, to old company and the like. The only meaningful aim left was to help his wife, Nina, survive. He trudged through the streets of Moscow, 'horror-struck by this dead and murdered city', to find the food that would save her. Everyone he came across appeared to be overcome with fatigue and dismay. On 22 January 1919 he walked west out to the Dorogomilovskaya suburb (now the location of the Kiev station) for milk; he knew a retired carrier there who would do him a favour. 'Everything is closed in moribund Moscow,' he wrote that day. The next morning he was walking east to Myasnitsky Gates, 'to the Samsonov store to get thirty eggs and three pounds of rice'. 'The journey around Moscow during business hours in the morning once again produced a frightening impression on me,' recorded the sober historian – 'it is likely that the invasion of Genghis Khan affected the towns that were subjected to him in approximately the same way: all the windows have been boarded, everything has been killed, everything has stopped.' Since the nationalization of trade, the trading streets of Moscow had come to resemble a cemetery.[42]

From his flat, Got'e would watch it snow. 'Nothing new, all the same haze, the same impending final limit . . . Another snowstorm, as if it wants to cover up everything, as if it wants to destroy all life.' There were no potatoes, and without potatoes the hunger was bound to become more intense. Large fluffed snowflakes hung above the ground, hesitant to make a final settlement. Out on the avenues the snow would descend like a white stage curtain, its lower fringe enveloping pedestrians so that they lost all sense of moving forward and felt instead that they were marking time. A whole city marking time. 'A day without any impressions,' writes Got'e; 'a snowstorm is raging . . .' 'It is as if God himself has definitively withdrawn from us and is showing it to us clearly.' The snow led Got'e and another serious historian, Iakovlev, to talk about where they were actually heading: 'We unanimously decided that everything will gradually die off, the schools will close down, the towns will die of hunger and cold, the railways will stand still, and gorilla-like troglodites will live in the villages, somehow, after the fashion of prehistoric men of the Stone Age.' Superficial 'culture' would have to perish, because the 'Russian people' needed nothing except the crudest satisfaction of its prehistoric needs.[43]

The snow distorted whatever objects were left standing. Out on Strastnaya Square, Pushkin's statue gloomily bowed its head under a white layer of ice. Naudeau noticed that, since his imprisonment, there had been erected a new series of stone effigies to 'reformers' – Spartacus, Marat, Karl Marx, Engels and so on – who snivelled beneath their icicles; on the approach of evening in an unlit park they looked sinister, like phantoms. Phantoms on the war front, phantoms in the city: time was going backwards.

Snow had accumulated in such great piles that many of the streets were impassable; the town no longer possessed the carts, or the drivers, to transport it to the river quays. More snow? 'My wife is being ordered to shovel snow tomorrow – that is yet another touch of contemporary life.'[44]

Among such daily 'touches', Got'e noted the disappearance of electric light. As Rathenau's family had ably demonstrated, electric light was one of the marks of modern civilization. Historians and anthropologists have often emphasized the revolutionary effect the introduction of artificial light had on human behaviour and culture: eating habits were altered, belief in phantoms disappeared, social life was for ever altered; it has even been argued that sexual mores were radicalized because of the demonstrable physical effect that extended daylight has on the age of puberty in animals. Moscow went in the other direction. Moscow fell into darkness.

It was 'like the Middle Ages', said Ivan Bunin. The old porcelain lamps hung uselessly from the ceiling. Oil lanterns could not be used, because there was no oil. No candles were for sale; from animal fats, Muscovites developed substitutes which created a few shadows in a room, gave off an appalling odour and were extinguished by the slightest movement. Walking down one of the alleys in the former commercial centre of Moscow, Naudeau noticed a slight gleam coming from the shop windows, which had been covered with political posters. It evoked, he thought, 'the idea of civilized life stubbornly insisting on giving off a distant glow'. In early March 1918 Bunin emerged from a theatre and saw, through the columns at the entry, 'a blue-black sky with two or three dusky-blue patches of stars'. His return home was like a journey into outer space. He descended 'sepulchrally dark' Nikitskaya Street. 'Four homes rose in the dark green sky. They seemed to be very big, as if making their presence known for the first time. There were almost no passers-by.' Naudeau thought Moscow in February 1919 was no longer Moscow but 'some Siberian village buried beneath mounds of snow'.[45]

People who had lived in Moscow for decades got lost in their own quarters. The streets were not recognizable. Fences had been torn up, barriers had been carted away, wooden homes had been dismantled for firewood. More and more, the streets came to resemble cuttings through a virgin forest. Or ruins in an uninhabited jungle. One would suddenly come up against houses one had never seen before, little Empire houses with garden tables and chairs rotting out on the snow-covered lawn. Bunin: 'I went along an alley that was quiet and completely dark – and I immediately saw some open gates. Behind them was the splendid profile of an ancient house standing deep in the recess of the courtyard, and looking softly dark against a night sky that was totally different from the sky I had seen on the street. In front of this house stood a hundred-year-old tree, its spreading branches looking like a huge tent.' Henri Guilbeaux, a French pacifist who arrived in Moscow five days before Bullitt, was struck by the irregular dark profile of the houses lining the streets that approached the city centre: 'four-storey houses would suddenly be separated by one or more one-storey lodges that would pass by as in a film' – an early Gothic film, the opening scenes of *Dracula*.[46]

The stone and brick of the façades were 'black with soot that has been spat out by little stoves installed in every flat', noted Abbé Vidal. Buildings near the Kremlin bore the marks of bullets and shrapnel. Occasionally an electric torch would light up a narrow apartment-house entrance, revealing the stained walls of its dirty staircase. 'It is impossible to describe the lamentable aspect of great streets, once so lively, so rich in displays of luxury, so brilliant in sumptuous light: Kuznetsky Most, Petrovka, Tverskaya. One would say they are closed-down temples,' mused Vidal. 'It is as if there were a plague,' wrote Got'e.[47]

At the time of Bullitt's visit, the streets were filled with the sounds of a mighty hammering. Between January and March 1919 all the shop signs were ripped down. They could be seen lying in great heaps in the courtyards, or simply abandoned where they had fallen. In the place of a 'Davidov, Founded in 1840' or 'Gregorovich, Father and Sons' – painted in exquisite golden letters – there would be a metal sign, reading in red capitals, 'Tobacconist, No. 50', 'Stationer's, No. 45' or 'Clockmaker's, No. 1'. Four out of five shops were closed and boarded – that is, 'the windows were smashed and the planks, which had been nailed to the panels, had been torn away by frozen passers-by and carried off to their homes'. The former Hotel Metropole was now called 'First House of the Soviets', while the National Hotel had become the 'Second'.

Monsieur Tastevin had somehow managed to hold on to his French bookshop on Kuznetsky Most, and even his sign; his shelves were filled with copies of a red-bound work entitled *A History of the French Revolution*.[48]

Decorations in celebration of the first anniversary of the 'October Revolution' could still be seen in Moscow in February 1919. Naudeau was impressed by what he found painted on the old wooden huts of Okhotny Ryad, once a market for fish, meat and vegetables – a sordid place of smelly public lavatories and pantries. Today it was colourful and empty, a kind of 'commemorative monument to the era when one ate'. There were designs of bright large flowers, overflowing food baskets and allegories of every sort: an 'aesthetic riddle for dinner'. Got'e, by contrast, thought it was all done with dreadful taste: the decorations 'exceed in level of deformity all the German art of the prewar period'.[49]

The theatres were packed. Factories, army barracks and even apartment houses had their own theatres set up by 'Proletkult' – Proletarskaya Kul'tura, the government's 'voluntary' organization for proletarian culture. Moscow's equivalent of Berlin's 'dance with death'? A frenzied rich defiance of misery? Hardly. It was not cabaret. Nor was it London's pantomime. Nor Paris's music halls. People went into Moscow's theatres because they were cold. Naudeau found the Muscovite public 'emaciated, sober in words, dry in gesture, black in dress'. In February 1919 Gorky had two plays being shown; but Charles Dickens had three (*The Cricket on the Hearth*, *A Christmas Carol* and *Little Dorrit*) and Shakespeare one (*Much Ado about Nothing*). The opera Bullitt attended in March was probably Saint-Saëns's *Samson et Dalila*, a 'poem of revolution' as Arthur Ransome – the British compiler of Russian fairy tales – put it the previous month. In the auditorium Ransome noticed 'a good many grey and brown woollen jerseys about, and people were sitting in overcoats of all kinds'.[50]

4

The market economy in Moscow had completely collapsed, partly because of inherent long-term weaknesses, partly because of the war, but primarily because of a fanatical anti-market ideology pursued by the city's new administrators. There were some areas of southern Central Europe – in Austria, and particularly in the Balkans – where, towards the end of the war, the market had been reduced to the rudiments of exchange. But nowhere in Europe outside Russia experienced such a radical closure of commercial networks.

It made a terrible sight. One newspaper reporter who had been on the Western Front remarked that dilapidated, dirty, broken Moscow reminded him of Lille after the Germans had been driven out.[51] The emaciated figures of children could be seen tugging at carts and taxis; not even the Kremlin managed to feed its horses. 'One day,' reported Abbé Vidal, 'I saw in a street a half-dozen bodies of these animals. It was like after a battle, and nobody bothered about them, save the crows and the dogs.'[52]

Two of the evils contributing to economic breakdown had appeared early in the war: the government printed money, and, after the initial mobilization (far more successful than the Germans had ever imagined in their own military plans), the railway system failed. Too much money was chasing after too few goods; Moscow experienced hyperinflation six years before Berlin. It has been estimated that Russia's money supply increased eightfold between 1914 and 1917. True, the war had in the first instance created a small industrial boom. But the burgeoning number of workers in the suburbs of Petrograd and Moscow, and in the 'new towns' of the south, could not turn their money wages into food. After ten-hour shifts in the factories, women set up their stools in the bread queues, which began to appear in Moscow as early as autumn 1915. The price of rye rose in the city by 47 per cent in the first two years of the war, the price of boots went up by 334 per cent, while precious matches increased by 500 per cent. In November 1916 the tsarist government started requisitioning food. Peasants in Russia's central agricultural zone responded by reducing production, since they weren't getting paid. The share of peasant grain sold on the market declined from 16 per cent to 9 per cent; the peasants turned from cash crops (wheat, barley and sugar beet) to subsistence crops (rye, oats and potatoes). This only aggravated the problem in Russia's cities. A siege economy had developed long before the political turmoil of 1917.[53]

Indeed, the crisis predated the war. Urban, commercial civilization was something very fragile in Russia. It was both driven and choked by a growing rural population – one of the great facts of nineteenth-century European economic history. The development of markets relied on a delicate balance that could tip in either direction: towards commercialization, industrial growth and a more varied supply of commodities; or towards autarchy, closure and dearth.

In 1930 Elie Halévy, best known for a monumental *History of the English People in the Nineteenth Century*, published a short book on the origins of the recent war. The war, he argued, 'came to the West from the East; it was forced upon the West by the East'. Halévy – not a historian obsessed by collective anonymous forces; not one to ignore the responsibilities of statesmanship – traced the cause of the diplomatic instability in Central and Eastern Europe to a militant new form of liberalism, a 'democratic nationalism' that rose in revolt against established government. He followed this wave through Japan, China, India and the Ottoman Empire. Its spirit was uncompromising, its message fanatic.[54]

Russia had one foot in this Asiatic world and one foot in Europe. 'Liberalism' was not quite the word to describe this novel nationalist idealism, for the liberalism that Western Europe had realized in the previous century was half economic and wholly urban. Russia could hardly repeat that experience; her urban culture was so recent, and so weak.

'Democratic nationalism' fed both the hopes and fears of peninsular Europe. It incited enormous capital investments. It influenced the strategic thinkers in Germany. Ultimately, it was what pushed Berlin into its catastrophic decision of July 1914 to invade Belgium and France. Russia, since its first advance into the old Commonwealth of Poland back in the 1770s, had always been the 'counterpoise' in Europe. One cannot help but think that Churchill was right to warn that a peace which developed no policy on Russia would not be a peace at all. The dilemma, however, was how to involve undeveloped and barely urbanized Russia.

Moscow well illustrated the problem. Even if they had created the 'city of the Russian bourgeoisie' – a centre of economic pioneers – Moscow's new middle class in 1914 had hardly begun to tap the resources of their own town, let alone the surrounding country. A vast proportion of Muscovites were excluded from the market economy. It is most significant that

Moscow's commercial centre – not the entire administrative area, as in Paris – was surrounded by walls. Before the war, 46 per cent of the turnover of Moscow's trade was conducted in the small area of Kitay-Gorod, 'Stockade City', opposite the Kremlin; another 32 per cent occurred in the neighbouring Bely Gorod, or 'White City'. The densely populated Outer Ring to the north of the Moskva river accounted for only 9 per cent of the turnover, while the whole area to the south of the river added less than 5 per cent. The reason was due to the poor development of city transport: trams stopped at Zemlyanoy Val (the 'Earthen Wall') and the underground, though planned, had to await the arrival of Stalin.[55]

Moscow, a city of 1.6 million inhabitants at the outbreak of the war, was still constrained by its medieval structure – Russian 'medieval', for there had never been trade guilds in the Western sense, the kind of autonomous corporate system that was to save Germany in her hour of crisis. (The principle of private, registered incorporation was introduced into Russia by Mikhail Gorbachev on 4 June 1990.)

Moscow was known as the 'Big Village', because peasants brought their rural life into the city; the city had abjectly failed to carry her civilization to the country. Most of Moscow's 'workers' wore the dress of the Russian heartland – their cotton trousers tucked into high boots, their long shirts hidden under blouses with collars that buttoned on the side, their peaked caps covering the famous peasant 'pudding-bowl' haircut. The women wrapped white calico kerchiefs over their heads. They lived out in the suburbs of Khitrovka or Orekhovo-Zuyevo in ramshackle dormitories that had no sanitation; Moscow's sewers, like the trams, only served one-third of the urban area. Such streets as existed were unpaved and, until the war's crisis, teemed with livestock. The residents held their own open markets, which followed the archaic traditions of the countryside: bargaining, sharp practice, and enormous mark-ups on a tiny inventory.

When the Bolsheviks nationalized trade, this was the system that invaded the city centre – for nobody could actually abolish private marketing. At the corner of many streets, and especially around the railway stations, temporary stands were set up where you could buy a match for 30 copecks or a cigarette at 10.20 roubles; perhaps there were a half dozen eggs for sale, a basket of potatoes, a pound of butter or a bottle of milk. The hat on the head or the tell-tale voice would reveal that many of these vendors were well-educated people who had fallen on hard times. The Sukharevka, an enormous flea market that had been functioning before the war, was still open, despite the odd raid from the Cheka. Lenin complained that in the soul of every Russian there was a 'little Sukharevka'.[56]

The Bolsheviks, with their special view of history, were frightened stiff that they would meet the same fate as the Paris Commune of 1871. According to Marx's analysis of the event, the revolutionary urban Communards had been sabotaged by the surrounding peasant masses – conservative, acquisitive and as conscious of the onward process of history as 'potatoes in a sack'.[57] In January 1919 the Bolshevik government decreed a Food Levy that set regional quotas of supply on all major foodstuffs – grains, vegetables and livestock – according to general needs as defined by the government. The levy had no relationship to harvest production at all. It was more than a measure designed to feed starving cities: it was a war on the countryside, on hoarding, avaricious peasants – the 'battle for grain' as it came to be known.[58]

Commercial relations between the town and the countryside completely broke down. What had begun in 1916 as a peasant withdrawal from the market in answer to the tsarist requisitions now descended into a cycle of violence of a kind that not even Russia had witnessed before. But, again, the Bolsheviks could not actually abolish trade. As a substitute for the conventional market, townsmen went into the countryside to seek out food for themselves. The practice came to be known as 'bagging'; as hard as they tried, the Bolsheviks could not suppress it. An entire factory force might organize the seizure of a train and travel out for several days with tools, scrap metal and fabricated objects (shoe soles made out of conveyor belts, for example) to barter with peasants for food. A black market developed, so that by the time the train was back in Moscow its food wagons would already be nearly empty. Hundreds of miles outside Moscow one would come across these trains, men clinging on to them like grapes on a vine. Guilbeaux, on his way to Moscow in February, passed one of them that had stopped outside Minsk for lack of fuel. While some of the passengers 'looked for water to fill their bottles, others without the slightest embarrassment – necessity makes law – crouched on the running-boards to relieve themselves'.[59]

Because the goods could not move, the people did. Moscow was caught in a general whirl of human movement. The crowds became more varied. Former lawyers and stockbrokers mixed with cabbies, floor-polishers, bath attendants, Tartar rag-and-bone merchants and monks. There were more soldiers drilling on the squares. Naudeau reported hearing, far away down a white and slippery street, the voice of choirs singing the slow melodies of tsarist Russia. Abbé Vidal noticed an increase in the number of Jews, Armenians and Georgians; and there were 'Chinese in Red Army uniforms, who are on the payroll of the dictators'. While Petrograd was being deserted, 'Moscow', wrote Bullitt in his report, 'teems with twice the number of inhabitants it contained before the war.'[60]

He was wrong. The new variety in the crowds led several foreign observers to think that Moscow was growing. In fact between 1918 and 1920 Moscow lost more than half of its population. This was partly due to the spread of epidemics in the autumn and winter of 1918. 'The deadly Spanish flu is spreading everywhere,' noted Got'e on 29 October. It was killing at a respectable Western rate of about a hundred a week. Typhus was doing the work more efficiently; by the end of the year a thousand cases were being reported every week. Yet, if the official records are anything to go by, one must conclude that epidemics were not the major cause of population decline: in 1918 there were only 2,445 deaths ascribed to typhus, cholera and dysentery. The main reason for the decline is that people were fleeing the city en masse. Western academics in the 1960s and 1970s would describe this phenomenon as 'de-urbanization', as if it were some sort of logical phase in the development of Russian society, unrelated to the Bolshevik *coup d'état* of November 1917. But it was the nationalization of all shops and markets, the closure of the main retailing centres, the attempt to ration every commodity through state monopoly, and the forced requisitions that caused it. The figures on Russia's 'de-urbanization' at the end of the First World War are testament to a most terrifying, politically inspired, human catastrophe.[61]

The plunge into hell proceeded in uneven stages, rather as a fated climber, dangling on a cliff face, might watch the fibres of his rope slowly break: first a few threads, then a sudden descent, followed by a moment of stability, then that tearing again. Will rescue come? There are a few seconds of hope. Then back once more to despair. Such a gradual, inevitable, yet unforeseeable rate of fall is described in Got'e's unrevised diary. He knew his flat was going to be taken from him, but he didn't know when; he suspected he was going to be arrested, but he didn't know how or why; he was gnawed by the fear that his wife was going to die – the only other person for whom he lived. He was stoic; he refrained from expressing his feelings; yet, as the descent continued, personal feelings were all that remained in his possession.

'Haze on the general horizon,' he would typically write. What scandalized him was that he, an educated man, could get no information on what was happening in the world or in his town. He was, like most Muscovites, astonished to hear of the Allied victories in October 1918, for he had been led to believe that the Allies had been overrun by Ludendorff's armies. 'It is gratifying that although we have perished, the Germans, too, may end badly,' he noted as the news seeped in. 'All those who really did start the war have been reduced to ashes and are being destroyed,' he recorded on hearing of Austria's collapse. 'It serves them right.' The Armistice barely got a mention: 'A situation without any particular changes: the truce has been concluded, but I still don't know its exact conditions; it seems they are severe.' The official celebrations of the 'October Revolution' were going on at the time – it was 'a sort of Easter night: fireworks were set off for about half an hour at the [the Cathedral of] Christ the Saviour; they probably burned some kind of effigies as well. We were disgusted and didn't go there, despite the proximity.' The Bolsheviks were forecasting that, with the chaos in Central Europe, their revolution would spread. When Got'e picked up rumours of Allied intervention in Russia – 'the Allied fleet has perhaps appeared in the Baltic Sea' – he began to think that rescue would come; it was his brief moment of hope: 'The matter will come clear in 1919; may God grant that we will still be alive.' There is nothing in Got'e's diary about Berlin's Spartacist revolt, save a brief reference, on 18 January, to the murder of Liebknecht and Luxemburg – 'There was a time when I would have been sorry about his arrest, but now I want to say: a dog's death for a dog.' The next day, a Sunday, he was in church: 'A "protest demonstration" over the murder of Liebknecht was taking place at the same time; I didn't see it; they say it was not particularly impressive.' Got'e was aware of the Prinkipo offer and of Chicherin's answer of 4 February ('the whole note is full of the customary Bolshevik lie'); his first thought was that, if there were a temporary lull in the war in Russia, he and his wife might have an opportunity to get out of the country.[62]

But all these snippets of news, including the thought of emigration, were far from Got'e's daily preoccupations, his 'life of a mole'. As if war and the food crisis were not enough for them, the governing officials were taken over by a 'mania for displacement' (Abbé Vidal's term), requisitioning buildings here and there, forcing people out of their homes and imposing cohabitation.

In September 1918 Got'e walked round to Narkompros, the Commissariat of People's Enlightenment, to apply for a 'security certificate' for his flat and for his library. He was told, 'The more such certificates we give out, the less force they have.' In October he had an appointment at the bank 'to eviscerate our safe deposit box, and my brother's box as well'. It took three and a half hours; the 'comrades were polite, but just barely'. When it was all done, Got'e felt a sense of relief: 'that shoe-nail, that splinter that has been sitting there for ten months and causing pain, has been removed'. In November the rent on the flat was raised for the fourth time in the year, and the next day he was warned of eviction: 'military control or counter-intelligence, which has penetrated our house like a cancer tumour, wants to spread further and take over all our front wing'. He prepared to transfer to a 'bivouac' in the back. His landlady was evicted at the end of that month. In December there was a meeting of the 'house tenants' on the 'distribution of the revolutionary tax, for which I was assessed the amount of 2,000 roubles'. In February 1919 he had to 'double up' in the dining room. 'The moving inside our flat has been done,' he reported on the 25th; 'all this is so barbaric and so unnecessary, and so contemporary'. On the 27th: 'I feel light and recall Pecherin's verses about the man sailing on the sea in a canoe; one more anchor cut away, one less hindrance.' Got'e was finally expelled from his home in March. He found a room – another 'bivouac' – in the museum; but he had no firewood, and the moving took time. It was all done by hand, since 'despite our best efforts we are unable to get a single cart either through "cart transport" (as the Bolshevik "central drayage" is called), or independently'.[63]

In addition to his housing problems, Got'e had a number of funerals to attend. On 18 November he was out at the Lutheran cemetery of Vedenskiye Gory to witness the burial of his friend K. A. Wilken. The gravediggers would not bury more than seven bodies a day and would start work only after 1 p.m. Wilken's grave had not been dug deep enough, so the coffin had to be raised from the ground again; the cross at the head of the grave was lost in the process, and the gravediggers were 'rude and disgruntled – a typical manifestation of the Russian Revolution'.[64]

On 1 December he was out in Pushkino village to bury his cousin and childhood friend Volodia Reiman. 'Arkadii Evgen'evich Armand said today that all the old folks will surely pass away this winter,' recorded Got'e. Reiman had been all of forty-seven. On 2 December: 'S. A. Belokurov died. That is an irretrievable loss for the Archive of Foreign Affairs and the Society of History and Antiquities, where he was *everything*.' On 29 December it was the turn of S. F. Fortunatov: 'poor Stepochka lay [in the hospital chapel] still without a coffin in the company of six other deceased, and the ceremony took place in a most difficult and miserable setting'.[65]

Got'e would be seized by periodic bouts of melancholy, as when he looked out on the snow, or contemplated the end of the year 1918, the 'Bolshevik year': 'I haven't had such melancholy as today for a long time; it has been a long time since I perceived so clearly the abyss into which the Russian people have fallen.'[66]

A few streets away Abbé Vidal was watching the destruction of the French parish of Saint-Louis. As with Got'e's home, it did not occur in a day: on the contrary, the descent was made in indeterminate stages, thread by thread. Vidal's image was the Bolshevik 'millipede' which advanced into city quarters, down streets and into houses to install its bureaucrats, its militia and its legions of workers.

The French parish had to make way for the Cheka, which by late 1918 had already taken over most of that quarter of the town. The Cheka needed space: for its prisons, its barracks, its financial, judicial and administrative offices, its transport section, its kitchens and restaurants, its shops, its clubs, its entertainment halls and its reading rooms. The Cheka had been nibbling away at the French parish since January 1918. It first took over the annexe of the consulate and the hospital; its members tore off the doors and the windows, and ripped up the parquet flooring for firewood; they caused such destruction that they were obliged to move into the neighbouring building, a residence. So gradually they advanced. Then, the plunge. In January they requisitioned the main building. Like Got'e, Vidal found himself confined to the corner of a room.

Once requisitioned, the building swiftly deteriorated. Everything disappeared, including the door locks. Nothing could be replaced: there were no shops. Nothing could be repaired: artisans and workers had either been enrolled in the Red Army or had fled – it was said that by 1919 the Bolsheviks had no working class left to lead. The central heating broke down – a disaster for any building in Moscow. The piping burst. Filthy water poured down the central staircase. With the house freezing, the drinking-water supply ceased. Everywhere in Moscow people could be seen trudging about with their buckets seeking out a house with a functioning tap; long queues immediately formed in front of these treasures. No toilets worked, of course: one used the courtyard or the stairwell. When the temperature rose above zero the piles of human filth began to thaw.[67]

The Bolsheviks made war on the country, on the peasantry, on trade, on the shops and the markets, on transport, on the material foundations of urban civilization; they made war on the house, on the home, on the individual, on privacy, on decency – on human 'property' in the full sense of the term.

Such was the picture of Moscow in the winter of the Year II of the Revolution, the season of William Bullitt's mission.

5

'The red terror is over,' wrote Bullitt in his report that March on his return to Paris. He estimated that the 'extraordinary commission for the suppression of the counter-revolution' – he meant the Cheka – had executed around 1,500 people in Petrograd, 500 in Moscow and 3,000 in the remainder of the country: a figure of 5,000 in all, which he contrasted with the 'white terror' which 'in southern Finland alone, according to official figures', had led to the execution without trial of '12,000 working men and women'. He could well have been right on Finland. But he was underestimating the Cheka's victims. Worse still was his assessment of the current situation: the Red Terror was not over. It had only just begun.[68]

The terrible irony of the Western Armistice was that it pushed Russia, at the base of Europe, into a cycle of violence which was to continue and repeat itself right through the so-called 'inter-war period'. At the time of Bullitt's mission a new kind of war was developing in Russia and the surrounding regions – a war that had no 'front'; a new kind of state was being set up in Moscow that had no historical precedent; and a new kind of terror was inaugurated that no Westerner could be expected to understand.

Germany collapsed and retreated in chaos from the Crimea and the Ukraine; she renounced the Treaty of Brest-Litovsk. The Bolsheviks, for their part, had no problem in discarding it. Even at the time of its signature, the previous March, Lenin had called it a 'shameful peace'. He had nonetheless imposed it on his party – to cries of 'Traitor!' and 'Judas!' – because he feared the advancing German armies would destroy the 'socialist workers' government' at its inception. The Bolsheviks needed 'breathing space' he pleaded. Consolidate at home first, then get on with the task of world revolution. 'The bourgeoisie has to be throttled,' he admitted, 'but for that we need both hands free.'[69]

Between the signing of Brest-Litovsk in March and the Armistice of November, the Bolsheviks developed a very special kind of diplomacy. It was designed to embarrass the government sitting on the other side of the table and to stir up the opposition of its people; it was a propaganda exercise, not a negotiation of points between the representatives of sovereign nations. This was not something that well-intentioned Westerners, like William Bullitt, fully grasped. Later the Soviets would call their novel approach to foreign affairs 'demonstrative diplomacy'. Their ultimate aim was world revolution.[70]

Western socialists might interpret the Bolshevik approach to Brest-Litovsk as 'pacifist', which is what the government in Moscow had intended. But the Bolsheviks were not seeking peace. The key word in their vocabulary – as Lenin's biographer Robert Service has pointed out – was not 'peace' but 'struggle': praise for the 'dictatorship of the proletariat', scorn for all forms of socialism hostile to it, eulogies for 'revolutionary justice' *à la* Cheka, incitement of class struggle, struggle against the counter-revolution, and struggle, of course, with the imperialists.[71]

So Brest-Litovsk brought not peace to Russia but, rather, a transformation of the war. This new, transformed, war followed two phases: the first before the Western Armistice, the second after it.

The debate within the Bolshevik party at the time of the Treaty of Brest-Litovsk (3 March 1918) could have been fatal to the Revolution. Nikolai Bukharin's Left Communists resigned from the Executive Central Committee, their leader proclaiming, 'We are turning the party into a dung-heap!' The Left Socialist Revolutionaries, who had lent critical support at the moment of the November takeover of government, also walked out and began fomenting their own revolution. Many of these dissidents had joined the Bolshevik movement out of a conviction that this would lead an international, messianic crusade that would liberate the toilers and the oppressed of the world; to sign a treaty with imperialist Germany now would be to admit defeat. Several of them carried on their 'revolutionary war' with German forces despite the treaty. They allied themselves with the Ukrainian Socialist Revolutionaries and the Borotbist, or Socialist Revolutionary Fighters' Party. Despite its treaty with Moscow, Germany responded by sending in an army to set up its own puppet government in the Ukraine.

But it was not only dissidents who continued the war. The Bolsheviks themselves declared war on the newly independent Ukraine; on 9 February 1918, though negotiations were still under way at Brest-Litovsk, they siezed Kiev. With their violent system of requisitions, they also managed to carry the war into the interior. A flood of refugees moved south. The odd result was that the only cities of the former Russian Empire that grew between 1918 and 1919 were down in the Ukraine, the Don and the southern Volga – one finds descriptions of the chaotic street scenes in the novels of Bulgakov and Sholokhov. Anti-Bolshevik centres of resistance developed there. They also grew in other peripheral areas, such as in the north at Murmansk and Archangel, or in the north-west in Finland and the Baltic states. The first phase of Russia's new war had reduced Bolshevik control in Russia to an area resembling the medieval state of Muscovy.

The pattern of combat up to the time of the Western Armistice was so difficult to define – fighting could spring up here and there; no front lines existed – that governments, in both West and East, tended to underestimate its importance. Even Lenin made the monumental error of declaring, in late February 1918, that 'open civil war' had ended. But the fighting continued, often in the form of skirmishes. The major campaigns of that summer, such as Denikin's advance into the Kuban steppes or that of the 'Komuch' government on the Volga, involved armies of no more than a few thousand.

All this changed after Germany's collapse. The Komuch campaign ended in September 1918 when Lev Trotsky's Red Army took Kazan and Simbirsk, which happened to be Lenin's birthplace. The defenders of the Volga fled eastward to Siberia. Lenin was delighted to hear of the capture of Simbirsk and immediately telegraphed Trotsky to suggest the concentration of 'maximum forces' for the 'accelerated cleansing of Siberia'. Not even a well-equipped Western army would find such a task easy. Lenin was, once again, underestimating the significance of the developing Russian civil war.[72]

At that very moment the great arc of the German armies in France was driven up against the hills of the Belgian Ardennes; the German collapse was inevitable. Ludendorff engineered a new government in Berlin to bear the responsibility of defeat. Prince Max of Baden took up his grim task as acting Chancellor on 1 October.

Lenin might have been no military strategist, but he could understand the meaning of politics. He was quick to see that the events in Berlin implied the end of the temporary suspension in world revolution that had been brought about by Brest-Litovsk. Now it was forward again: Russia, Europe and the world! Germany would provide the essential stepping stone westward across the plain. 'Things have so "accelerated" in Germany that we too must not fall behind them,' Lenin wrote on 1 October to Yakov Sverdlov, chairman of the Central Committee and Lenin's closest collaborator. 'The international revolution has got nearer *over the past week* to such an extent that account has to be taken of it as an event of the days immediately ahead.' The same day, unable to detect exactly where Berlin's political crisis was heading, he addressed another note to both Sverdlov and Trotsky outlining his policy: 'No alliances either with Wilhelm's government or with a government of Wilhelm II + Ebert and the other scoundrels.' This was not only a clear break with Brest-Litovsk – more than a month before the Armistice annulled it – it was also a refusal to collaborate with anything but the extreme Left of German politics. Communist enmity for the European Left, which poisoned the whole 'inter-war' period, was already here. 'We *are beginning* to get ready a fraternal alliance, *grain*, military assistance for the German working masses, for the German labouring millions now that they have started up with their own spirit of indignation,' Lenin went on in the same note. To achieve this step towards the German 'masses' – the term that so obsessed Berlin in the autumn of 1918 – Lenin foresaw a 'tenfold' intensification of requisitioning and a 'tenfold' increase in conscription. In Russia, where peasant revolts were reaching their peak, this could only mean an intensification of war on every front: in every village and in every town that remained within his power. The Bolsheviks were not seeking peace as the war drew to a close in the West. 'All of us shall give our lives in order to help the German workers in the cause of advancing the revolution that has begun in Germany,' stated Lenin in his note.[73]

A Leninist idea, dating back to 1914, of instituting a 'Third International' that would unite Bolshevism with the extremist 'anti-bourgeois' factions of the European Left was revived. It would act as a radical alternative to the Second International, which had been corrupted by all the socialist parties of Europe that had voted, at the outbreak of hostilities, for the 'imperialist' war credits. In late December 1918 Lenin suggested to Chicherin that the new organization might meet 'in Berlin (openly) or in Holland (*secretly*) let's say by 1.ii.1919'; a Third International in Holland or Berlin would offer his partisans another stepping stone west.[74]

Yet, if the Western Armistice reanimated world revolutionary dreams among Bolshevik leaders in Moscow, it also sent out a wave of hope to their opponents now gathering forces on Russia's periphery. The Western fleets began to move again. The Baltic and the Black Sea were opened to Western shipping. For anti-Bolsheviks, Russia began to resume her geographical form at the base of the European peninsula once more; on her southern and northern coasts they could look forward to a supply of food, ammunition – and perhaps even soldiers. Got'e's diary fills with rumours of an 'Allied squadron' in the Baltic. 'The general situation', he writes on 2 December, 'is such that the victors will be obliged to police the world, and there is much evidence to suggest that the entire affair will end not with the triumph of the Bolsheviks, but with a return to order by the will of the cultured countries of the West.' 'What will the coming year of 1919 bring?' he asks himself on 31 December. 'I hope that it will bring some kind of solution.'[75]

At the end of November, French and British troops did land in the Black Sea ports; the French spread north into the Crimea and the Ukraine, the British eastward across the Caucasus to Baku on the Caspian – 'one of the greatest strategic lines in the world' claimed Churchill.[76] But more impressive than their troop commitments was the supply, over the next nine months, of Allied armaments to Bolshevism's opponents: 1 million rifles, 15,000 machine-guns, 700 field guns, 8 million rounds of ammunition. This was approximately what the Soviets managed to produce in the entire year of 1919. In its second, post-Armistice, phase, the Russian civil war involved large conscript armies, massively armed.[77]

Six days after the Armistice there was a *coup d'état* in the Siberian town of Omsk, about 500 miles east of the Urals and 4,000 miles from the nearest seaport. The man who emerged the next morning, 18 November, as 'Supreme Ruler' was an admiral, formerly of the Tsar's Black Sea Fleet, Alexander Kolchak. For the previous eight weeks Omsk had been the site of a Provisional All-Russian Government that claimed to represent the interests of all those opposed to the regime in Moscow. It had been governed by a five-man Directory (its strange model was the corrupt Directory that had ruled France for five years after the Jacobin Terror). General Boldyrev, a member of the government who also acted as commander-in-chief of its army, was probably accurate when he described the atmosphere in Omsk as 'Mexico amidst the snow and ice'.[78] Be that as it may, this government was made up of an alliance of liberals and Right Social Revolutionaries. Whatever slim hope remained of Russia establishing a constitutional democracy died on the day of that coup.

It had been carried out, almost certainly without Kolchak's knowledge, by local Cossacks dismayed at the 'socialist' character of the government.[79] Kolchak had no personal opinion on politics; he was a professional military man who wanted to win the war. The catastrophe in Russia was that the same situation prevailed in Novorossiisk, on the Black Sea, where General Anton Denikin maintained headquarters, and in Archangel in the north, under the Russian General K. E. Miller. No liberals were left.

If a rough parallel can be made, as it often was at the time, between the political character of these anti-Bolshevik towns in late 1918 and centres of French resistance to Paris over a hundred years earlier, one must think of Koblenz in 1792, not Ghent in 1815. Koblenz was the court of generals and princes who wanted to turn the clock back and restore their old privileges. In Ghent the streets teemed with the 'men of business', liberals, who would lead France into the modern era. There was no Ghent in Russia in 1918. The only ideal of the 'Whites' in Omsk, Ekaterinodar and Archangel was to restore old Russia, 'One and Indivisible'. It was not a modern message, and not one that could appeal to independent-minded Ukrainians, Finlanders, Lithuanians and Estonians. Nor was it attractive to peasants of the heartland who now claimed ownership of the soil. Without them, the war would be difficult to win; Napoleon, to his cost, had encountered the problem of skirmishing Russian peasants.

Peasant wars were in full swing throughout much of Russia and the neighbouring states by November 1918. Peasants had stopped paying their taxes and delivering their quotas and were calling for a 'black repartition', an anarchic, even mystical programme aimed at complete freedom from the state through a redistribution of production, land and livestock – the dream of rural folk for generations. They destroyed what was left of the noble estates, and wiped out bourgeois holdings as well as the farms that had been created by the agricultural reforms of the pre-war years. The ideological goals of the conflict were extremely mixed, ranging from 'free soviets' to national liberation movements which could be 'pro-Bolshevik' or 'anti-Bolshevik' or both at the same time. The break-up of the old 'Jewish pale' in the Ukraine and Poland, after the rapid German withdrawal, brought a mass of Jews into the Russian core lands and another element into the fighting – anti-Semitism. Pogroms spread to areas where there had never been any before. The fighting was very brutal; public flogging was reintroduced, the good old Roman tradition of decimation became common, and there was a revival of medieval torture. At the same time one could detect in this extremely localized rural struggle the first signs of a truly twentieth-century style of combat: guerrilla warfare, without fronts, without national colours, without even uniforms to identify the soldiers.[80]

Yet the armies grew. Mass conscription fed both the armies and – with the desertions – the insurgent bands, which had a way of switching sides at whim; this could be caused by a local *coup d'état*, a novel line of propaganda or a sudden new object for revenge. There was an extraordinary accumulation of arms. In the autumn and early winter of 1918 Red Terror had led to the murder of thousands in the Volga and Ural regions, turning this whole eastern zone against the Bolsheviks. In early December Admiral Kolchak, the Supreme Ruler, marched west from Omsk; he crossed the Urals and, on 24 December, captured the critically important industrial town of Perm. The Red Third Army, made up of men recruited at rifle point, virtually disappeared; several of its troops actually joined Kolchak's forces, informing them of the violent hatred for Bolshevism now spreading in the area.

The 'catastrophe of Perm' caused panic in Moscow. In the days leading up to the collapse, Lenin belatedly realized what sort of civil war was developing in Russia; there was no more idle talk about cleansing Siberia. 'The news from near Perm is extremely alarming,' Lenin telegraphed Trotsky on 13 December. 'Danger threatens it. I fear that we have forgotten about the Urals.'[81]

In the weeks that followed, General Krasnov, the Don Cossack leader, pushed northward into the suburbs of Voronezh. General Denikin's Volunteer Army moved into the northern Caucasus. An independent, anti-Bolshevik 'Directory' was set up in Kiev, capital of the Ukraine. By late January Denikin had taken Pyatigorsk, and on 3 February he captured the Chechen capital of Grozny – crucial oil supplies from the Black Sea and the Caspian were now cut off from Moscow.

Yet Foch was right to warn the Supreme War Council in Paris that the Bolsheviks were advancing on all the fronts. That was the curious thing about this new war: *everybody* was advancing. Generals and politicians sitting in Paris had no way of establishing what was happening in Russia: it was *terra incognita*. The Reds took Ufa, in the southern Urals, on 30 December, they had pushed Krasnov out of Tsaritsyn in early February, they seized Kiev; and there was also that small affair of Poland and the Baltic provinces, where Trotsky's army came face to face with what remained of the German armies. Everybody was advancing everywhere.

It was *terra incognita* for the Reds. The Bolshevik leaders were ready to leave Moscow at a moment's notice. As they admitted themselves at the time, they lived and worked in the Russian capital 'sitting on their suitcases'.[82]

6

Before Bullitt left Moscow, his colleague Lincoln Steffens managed to get an interview with Lenin. The walls of the Kremlin, bright red under the winter's sun, resembled the battlements of an Italian fortress; they dominated the centre of the town. The inner courtyards were empty. He was directed to a minor doorway, up a dark staircase, and then down long, deserted corridors to a small office where a young woman worked with a telephone; this was the Kremlin's central telephone service. Lenin had his office next door. It was sparsely furnished. A giant portrait of Karl Marx hung on the wall with a red ribbon dangling round it. The books that Lenin kept on the shelves behind his desk were arranged in alphabetical order.

Lenin was smiling, just as he had been when he received Bullitt. Steffens was hoping that, along with the written agreement handed to them by Chicherin and Litvinov, he could get further assurances from Lenin to take back to Paris. He started by asking him whether, if the borders were opened, Russian propagandists would be prevented from flocking into Europe.

'No,' replied Lenin sharply. Then he leaned back and smiled again. 'A propagandist, you know, is a propagandist. He must propagand. When our propagandists for the revolution won, when they saw the revolution happen, they did not stop propaganding. They went right on propaganding. We had to give them propaganda work to do among the peasants and workers. If our borders are opened, our propagandists will go to Europe and propagand, just as yours will come here and propagand. We can agree not to send them to you, and we can agree that if they do go they shall be subject to your laws but we – nobody can make a propagandist stop propaganda.'

Well, at least he was clear. There was one other point. 'What assurance', asked Steffens, 'can you give that the Red Terror will not go on killing?'

Lenin leaped to his feet in a sudden rage. 'Who wants to ask us about our killings?'

'Paris,' answered Steffens somewhat timidly.

'Do you mean to tell me that those men who have just generalled the slaughter of seventeen millions of men in a purposeless war are concerned over the few thousands who have been killed in a revolution with a conscious aim – to get out of the necessity of war and – armed peace?' He told Steffens not to deny the Terror. Terror, he said, 'served a purpose that has to be served'. As in war, in a revolution there must be unified action, and there were times when that unity had to be forced. Besides, 'we have to devise some way to get rid of the bourgeoisie, the upper classes. They won't let you make economic changes during a revolution any more than they will before one; so they must be driven out.' To carry through the Revolution to its objective, the 'absolute, instinctive opposition of the old conservatives and even of the fixed liberals has to be silenced'.

That was a clear answer too. 'I have seen the future and it works,' Steffens would say on his return to Paris. By then he knew perfectly well what the future held: the Bolsheviks were committed to a propaganda campaign in the West for worldwide revolution and to continuing terror against counter-revolutionaries at home. These were the two basic planks of their programme.[83]

All those who met Lenin in private found him polite and charming. It was not only Bullitt who spoke of him as genial and humorous. Arthur Ransome, who had known Lenin for several years, saw him in February and recorded, 'more than ever, Lenin struck me as a happy man'. He 'tilts his chair this way and that, laughing over one thing or another ... Every one of his wrinkles is a wrinkle of laughter, not of worry.' Ransome thought this was because he was the 'first great leader who utterly discounts the value of his own personality'. Henri Guilbeaux described him as 'lively, jovial, friendly'. Even Ludovic Naudeau, who had just been released from Butyrka jail, was astonished at his simple manners, his dress (he was wearing a woollen cardigan) and the way his face would light up with a smile. 'He is not at all terrible,' Naudeau wrote. He had a guttural laugh; they were talking about the Prinkipo proposal: 'The Isle of the Princes! Ha! ha! Whatever, let's be frank, they had a really funny idea there! The Isle of the Princes! Ha! ha! Why the Isle of the Princes? But there is no one on the Isle of the Princes!' Lenin went on rolling with laughter. Then he got down to discussing the League of Nations. 'A new civilization will finally emerge from all these trials and errors,' he predicted, and suddenly became serious. The archaic English state was dying, Germany was bound to have a revolution; 'the old world can no longer survive – the economic situation arising out of the war will inevitably precipitate its collapse'. Then there was more guttural laughter as he went on about the tastiness of the Soviet experiment. Another laugh, and a garbled version of an English proverb: 'The best proof that the cream tart is tasty is in the eating!' Now, roars of laughter. 'The eyes of the Bolshevik Pope were aflame,' wrote Naudeau; 'the true Lenin showed himself; the wolf suddenly emerged in his mouth, through the skin of the lamb he had until then been dissimulating.' One imagines this was what Steffens witnessed when he courageously raised his little question about Terror; Lenin's sudden rages were famous.[84]

He was not a handsome man. His shoulders were just a little hunched, his head seemed oversized, his ears were small, a slightly squashed nose pushed his cheekbones up, thus narrowing his eyes – those small brown eyes which sparkled with intelligence and could, at times, be so fierce. Simbirsk, where he was born in 1870, the year before the Paris Commune, was on the lower Volga. His paternal grandfather, half Kalmuk, had married a woman wholly so. His mother was the daughter of a baptized Jew who had married into a wealthy Lutheran family from Germany. His great-grandmother had been a Swede. Some have argued that all this foreign blood (hushed up in the Soviet hagiographies written under his successor, Stalin) was what made him so contemptuous of ordinary Russians. But there was another reason. His father had been Inspector of Schools for Simbirsk Province: in Russia, that made him a noble, addressed as 'Your Excellency'. Vladimir Ilyich Ulyanov – who only in 1900 became 'Lenin' (after perhaps the river Lena in Siberia) – passed his childhood on the kind of gentry estate that, as head of the Bolshevik state, he would devote his whole energy to destroying. During his years in political exile before the war, he had made no secret about these noble origins. In 1900, after asking authorization to visit his wife, who was also in exile, permission was granted 'to Vladimir Ilyich Lenin, nobleman by birth'.[85] He lived off his estate's revenue until his mother's death in 1916. He knew nothing of the lives of ordinary Russians, as he later admitted to Maxim Gorky: 'Simbirsk, Kazan, Petersburg, exile – that is all I know.'[86] His exile abroad had lasted seventeen years. Nor did he do much to improve his knowledge on his return in 1917. He never visited the provinces. Once installed in Moscow he rarely ventured outside the Kremlin, particularly after an assassination attempt in August 1918.

In fact Lenin in the winter of 1919 was not that well known to the public. In the dark evening of 19 January he and his sister were being driven by the chauffeur Stepan Gil to Sokolniki on the outskirts of Moscow, where his wife was convalescing from her goitre condition. By a railway bridge their official limousine was stopped by a gang of thieves whom Gil had mistaken for policemen (which is quite possibly what they were). With a gun held at Lenin's temple they emptied his pockets and even robbed him of his Browning pistol. Lenin coolly announced, 'My name is Lenin.' Not only had the thieves failed to recognize him but, worse, this declaration didn't mean anything to them. They continued to rob the others. Then they drove off with the limousine. Lenin, his sister and chauffeur Gil had to walk to Sokolniki. There further humiliation awaited him. Without his pass-card he could not get into the District Soviet, where his wife was waiting for him; nobody could recognize him. It was his wife who came to the rescue. Lenin immediately summoned Dzerzhinsky to Sokolniki to complain about the Cheka's inefficiency. It all ended happily. Within a few days the bandits, or suitable suspects, were rounded up and executed.[87]

Today, next to the Kaiser, Lenin is the figure who comes most quickly
to mind when one thinks of the closing months of the First World War. But
in the winter of 1919 he was hardly a man of international stature; the world
spoke of Wilson, of Lloyd George and of Clemenceau, not of Lenin. Lenin
needed such stature to justify his coup of November 1917; he needed a
world revolution to give his regime, to use Talleyrand's term, 'legitimacy'.
Talleyrand placed civilization at the root of a government's legitimacy. And
so did Lenin – but a 'new civilization'.

It was Lenin's hankering for international stature, and the legitimacy this
would give the Russian Bolsheviks, that made the establishment of the Third
International so urgent. The Communists of the world would come to his
feet. Ebert and Scheidemann sought legitimacy through 'bourgeois elections'; Lenin would attempt it through the Third International.

There was a theory behind this. Two basic themes shaped it: the 'dictatorship of the proletariat' and the idea of 'permanent revolution', both of them
being derivations – some would say distortions – of Marxist thought. Since
1917 Lenin constantly hammered out the point that the 'October Revolution
has realized the dictatorship of the proletariat'. As Martin Malia has recently
observed, this was a metaphysical proletariat: it was made up of intellectuals, organized in a conspiratorial party, who claimed to represent the
exploited workers. One might add that in 1919 the proletariat was even
more metaphysical than it had been two years earlier, since workers, in
hundreds of thousands, were now fleeing the cities for the countryside;
one party member, A. Schliapnikov, poignantly noted at the time that the
Bolsheviks were rapidly becoming 'the vanguard of a non-existent class'.[88]
True, some of this metaphysics could be attributed to a strictly Russian
tradition of 'vanguard' terror advocated by writers like Nikolai Chernyshev-
sky, Sergei Nechaev and Petr Tkachev – all lapped up by Lenin in his youth.
But the idea of a 'dictatorship of the proletariat' is in Marx's own work,
and its most metaphysical feature, the revolutionary vanguard, is already
present in the *Communist Manifesto* of 1848: the Communists, wrote Marx
and Engels, are 'the most advanced and resolute section of the working-class
parties of every country', and 'they have over the great mass of the proletariat the advantage of clearly understanding the line of march'.[89]

The idea of a worldwide revolution must also be imputed to Marx. But the
prophesying about how this was supposed to happen – through 'permanent
revolution' – came from Trotsky, and was based on his observations of the
upheavals in Russia in 1905. Peering through his historical prism, which
divided the ages of man into feudal, capitalist and socialist phases, he spied
a weakness in the Russian centre: the 'bourgeois' and liberal parties had
proved themselves incapable of leading a democratic revolution. So in
Russia one would have to proceed directly from the feudal state to the
socialist state; Russia would have the earliest working-class revolution in
all Europe. Of course, this would need to be led by a highly disciplined

vanguard. And, because this was a country consisting mainly of peasants, the vanguard would have to seek the support of peasants. But peasants did not have the same socialist aims as the vanguard; their ambitions were 'petty bourgeois' – they wanted to own private property, not abolish it. As the Russian vanguard pushed the Revolution towards socialism it would inevitably encounter the opposition of the peasants. The vanguard would thus become dependent on the spread of revolution to the industrial West, where an army of proletarians was waiting for their socialist liberation. Workers of the world unite!

World war helped Lenin add his own prognosis. The European socialist revolution would involve a series of wars, international and civil, that would stretch over many years. In 1914, from his exile in Switzerland, Lenin even predicted a second world war. The Bolsheviks were not pacifists; they encouraged war. This was Russia's chance to be at the hub of a world revolutionary movement. Lenin called on the workers of the world to use their arms against their own governments; 'Let the barricades answer the [imperialist] war.'[90]

Lenin was convinced that war had created a revolutionary situation throughout Europe. He does not seem to have been very troubled by the development of the Armistice in the West. Indeed, he was sure that the imperialist Peace Conference in Paris would succeed only in perpetuating a series of wars that would lead, ultimately, to the socialist revolution.

Lenin repeatedly stated that he did not have a precise schedule for these events. There might be a pause, as in the case of Brest-Litovsk. There might be setbacks, as in the case of the civil war. But he never lost faith in the vanguard role his party played in the spread of worldwide socialist revolution.

Lenin thus laid the legitimacy of the Bolshevik regime upon the validity of two mutually supportive ideas, the 'dictatorship of the proletariat' and 'permanent revolution'. If the Bolshevik party did not represent the proletariat, then there was no point to its seizing power in November 1917. If there was no follow-up in the Western industrial countries, with their sizeable working classes, then the Party could hardly claim to be proletarian. No state, up to that point in the history of the world, had ever made itself hostage to such specific points of theory – not even Savanarola's Florence or the crusader kingdoms of the Middle Ages.

It was not a purely abstract problem. 'Sitting on their suitcases' in Moscow, the Bolshevik rulers were obliged to prove their theory right. There was no turning back; they had blood on their hands. Whatever rudimental 'bourgeois economy' existed in Russia before the war they had wilfully destroyed. No liberal middle way was open to them.

But, despite all their theory, the Bolsheviks had no ideas on how to run a state and no practical thoughts on the management of their devastated economy – which was most ironic for a party whose revolutionary postulations were supposed to be drawn from the laws of economics. While Keynes was developing a major school of economics in Britain, while Hoover was building up the administrative foundations for the largest economy in the world, while Rathenau was speculating on how to apply the lessons of corporate management to politics, all the Bolsheviks could produce was empty slogans like 'maximum unification of the entire economic life of the country in accordance with a single state plan', or 'the greatest centralization of production', or 'full communism, to each according to his needs'.[91]

In the winter of 1919 there was no centralized economy in Russia and no centralized government, and the centralization of the Bolshevik party itself was still only a myth. The names of central agencies were often established before the agencies themselves came into operation. These names were usually contractions, making them sound, to our ears, like postmodern computer companies. 'Sovnarkom', the Council of People's Commissars, became Russia's effective government when in December 1917 it replaced 'Revvoensovet', the Revolutionary Military Council, which had carried out the November coup (called the 'October Revolution' because the old Russian calendar was still being used). The 'Cheka', the Extraordinary Commission for Struggle against Counter-Revolution and Sabotage, was set up at the same time.

Throughout 1918 Lenin and his assistant, Yakov Sverdlov, practically ran the country alone, passing decrees to each other for co-signature without bothering to consult anyone else. Lenin was using his authority as chairman of Sovnarkom, while Sverdlov would sign as secretary of the Party's Executive Central Committee. In 1918 the Central Committee met only infrequently, largely because most of its members were off at war. Zinoviev had been left behind in Petrograd, Stalin was Commissar on the Southern Front, Trotsky was following the fighting from his armed train, and several had been charged with supervising the Red Army's officer corps, which had been recruited from the old tsarist Army. Only six of the Committee's fifteen full members remained in Moscow in the second half of 1918.[92]

This led to complaints within the Party and a growing demand for more active centralization, for both Party and State. In the early months of 1919 the Central Committee met much more frequently at its seat in the former Hotel Metropole, Sverdlov sitting at the presidium ringing his little bell. (A red banner hanging behind him was covered with the usual slogans, like 'Proletariat of all lands, unite.')[93] The Committee set up two inner subcommittees that would supervise business between Committee sessions. This added to the list of postmodern contractions: the 'Orgburo', or Organizational Bureau, took care of internal party problems, while the 'Politburo', or Political Bureau (which in fact had been founded in 1917 but until now had been lying dormant), oversaw political, economic and military policies.

A name was still needed for the territorial fragment of the former Russian Empire that the Bolsheviks were so desperately trying to govern. It had received an official name in the summer of 1918 with the publication in

Izvestiya of the Constitution of the 'Russian Socialist Federal Soviet Republic', or the RSFSR; but this was too much to swallow for most revolutionaries. Besides, the name made the new state specifically Russian, which hardly accorded with the doctrine of 'permanent revolution'. A nationally neutral, memorable contraction had to be found.

It turned up in the form of 'Sovdepiya', (formed on the basis of a contraction of the 'Soviet Deputies' who formally administered the area). No hymn was ever sung to Sovdepiya. It sounded like some abominable forgotten country that Gulliver had crossed in haste during his early eighteenth-century travels. Got'e would gaze out of his window at the snow, the ruined shops, the empty streets, the absence of foreign merchants; 'the process of turning Sovdepiya into a country deprived of any intercourse with the civilized world proceeds unswervingly,' he wrote in his diary, 'a country outside the law'.[94]

Little has been written on Yakov Sverdlov, the man who countersigned Lenin's decrees in Sovdepiya. He had the most extraordinary memory for facts and people, so he felt no need – and nor did he have the time – to write them down; his archives were all in his head. 'Whereas Lenin and a few others provided intellectual guidance for the Revolution,' wrote one Central Committee member, Anatoli Lunacharsky, 'between them and the masses – the Party, the Soviet government apparatus and ultimately all Russia – like a spindle on which it all revolved, like a wire transmitting it all, stood Sverdlov.'[95] His elder brother, Zinovy Peshkov, had joined Kolchak's White government in Omsk (and would later become a close associate of Charles de Gaulle); Sverdlov himself had begun his political career as a Menshevik, not a Bolshevik. But there was no man more loyal to Lenin than Sverdlov. He headed both the Party and the growing state bureaucracy. In the Central Committee he guided debates in favour of his master and drafted many of its organizational reports; it was he who wrote the Constitution of the RSFSR. On the first anniversary of the 'October' Revolution he was photographed in standard Bolshevik dress – black leather jacket and trousers, with a military cap on his head – standing near Lenin at the unveiling of a statue of Marx and Engels. 'The Cheka has made the dictatorship of the proletariat a living reality,' said Lenin that day.[96] There was no more fervent defender of either the 'dictatorship of the proletariat' or 'permanent revolution' than Sverdlov. He led the moves to stamp out heresy, first against the Left Communists at the time of Brest-Litovsk, then against his own Mensheviks and Socialist Revolutionaries. He might truly be called the father of the Red Terror: the link between Lenin and the murder of the Tsar and his family in July 1918 is in Sverdlov.[97] After the attempted assassination of Lenin in the following August it was Sverdlov who temporarily directed the government and started a campaign, within hours of the shooting, for the elimination of Socialist Revolutionaries – the guilt of the prime suspect, the half-blind Fanya Kaplan, who was tortured, executed and cremated in the Kremlin, has never been proven.[98] Historians of twentieth-century terror will always regret that Sverdlov left no archives.

Only one other other Bolshevik leader came close to exercising the authority of Lenin and Sverdlov, and that was Trotsky. Like Sverdlov, Trotsky had been a Menshevik and came over to the Bolsheviks only after the abdication of the Tsar. Unlike Sverdlov, he delighted in dispute and, in public, usually won; Trotsky was the best speaker of all the Bolsheviks, including Lenin. But his power was derived not from his public addresses – in Bolshevik meetings these would be presented as theoretical 'theses' rather than bourgeois speeches – but rather from his position as People's Commissar for Military Affairs. This gave him an independence that no other Bolshevik leader enjoyed. He was rarely in Moscow. A large armoured train – which, with its streamlined gun turrets, steel-plated ammunition carriages and high conical funnels, looked like an engine out of another century – carried the Commissar from one zone of battle to another. He would work within the range of enemy guns. As he explained to his comrades, Marx had provided no theory on how to run a war or how to build up an army. Between January and April 1919, following the disaster of Perm, he doubled the size of the Red Army and recruited the best of the old imperial officers he could find. True, he explained in his military 'theses' published in late February 1919, there was the danger that 'Bonapartism' might arise from his new revolutionary army; but the presence of obstructive, incompetent Bolshevik civilian agents was a great deal more of a threat to the effective defence of the regime than the use of former imperialist 'military specialists'. Several party members took issue with this and formed a counter-faction, the Military Opposition.

Josef Stalin, the chairman of the Revolutionary-Military Council of the Southern Front, was not actually a member of the Military Opposition, but he belonged to the same school of thought: the Party should be commanding the Army, not imperialist officers. In the southern Volga he was constantly intervening in strategic matters. He even claimed merit for the successful defence in autumn 1918 of Tsaritsyn, the strategic city on the Volga linking the Russian heartland with the wheatlands of the northern Caucasus – which is why he would one day change the town's name to Stalingrad. When Trotsky appointed his own regional commander in the area, Stalin began demanding Trotsky's head. Sverdlov stepped in and arranged a compromise. But the feud between Stalin and Trotsky flared up again after Perm, when Stalin demanded a party investigation into the Red Army's military command structure.

The intensity of the struggle suggested that a change was due in the way Sovdepiya was governed. The creation of the Orgburo and the Politburo was yet another sign. 'Iron discipline' and 'strict centralism' might have been the mottoes of Yakov Sverdlov, but for many a keen revolutionary he was not going far enough. 'There is no point in attempting to do the impossible,' Sverdlov would explain. The impossible was exactly what some Bolsheviks sought. The critics began to mock the private partnership that had developed between Lenin and Sverdlov. They called it a 'duumvirate' which failed to permit party supervision of the affairs of state.

The situation was reaching a point of crisis when Lenin called, in late February 1919, for the opening of the Third International. (The term 'Comintern' had not yet entered Soviet vocabulary.) The 'International Workingmen's Organization' had been a scene of socialist infighting ever since its foundation in London in 1864. The First International was torn apart by dogmatic debate between Karl Marx and the anarchist Bakunin over precisely the same issue that was to haunt the Third: the problem of 'state centralism'. The Second International, set up in 1889, ushered in a quarrel between those who demanded strict adherence to a party-led revolution and more liberal-minded 'evolutionists' who were ready to allow society to set the pace of change. This is what had divided Germany's Social Democrats into Majority and Minority wings; the Majoritarians were evolutionists, the Minoritarians tended towards the more revolutionary school of thought. In 1903 the Russian Social Democrats, in a Congress held in Brussels, confused the picture when the 'Majoritarians', or 'Bolsheviks', became the revolutionary branch of the Party, while the 'Minoritarians', or 'Mensheviks', were more evolutionary in their approach.

The Second International had its foundations destroyed by the outbreak of war in 1914. But in February 1919 an attempt was made to re-establish it at a Congress in Berne, Switzerland. Lenin's answer to this was to set up the Third. What he sought was to establish an alternative not only to the evolutionary-minded socialists in Berne, but also to the 'new world order' that was being organized by the Western imperialist bourgeoisie at their Peace Conference in Paris. For the opening of the Third International, Lenin prepared his theses 'on bourgeois democracy and the dictatorship of the proletariat' – it would attack both Western institutions at once.

Typically, the Bolshevik Third International was planned in the strictest secrecy. Noske's brutal suppression of the Spartacist rebellion in January meant that it was not going to be held in Berlin, as Lenin had initially hoped. In response to the murders of Liebknecht and Luxemburg the Bolsheviks lined up four Grand Dukes – Georgi and Nikolai Mikhailovich, Dmitri Konstantinovich and Pavel Aleksandrovich – against a wall in the Peter-and-Paul Fortress and shot them on 27 January – five days after Paris put out its Prinkipo appeal. Lenin then had the complete works of Liebknecht and Luxemburg prepared by his printers in Moscow. It was actually better that events should have followed this course: a living Rosa Luxemburg would have been an embarrassment to Lenin. Even if she had become more radical since her return to Berlin in November, she had never been very keen on the idea of the 'dictatorship of the proletariat' and she had actually voted against the formation of the minuscule German Communist Party at the end of December. Furthermore, the Spartacist defeat handed Lenin a further advantage: an International held in isolated Moscow would give the Bolsheviks complete control.

It was opened in the Courts of Justice, built at the time of Catherine the Great, on 2 March, and would continue until the 6th. Bullitt and Steffens, who arrived in Moscow on the 11th, were apparently totally unaware of it. Only a small room, decorated entirely in red, including the floor, was needed for the thirty-four delegates who attended. There were a Norwegian, a Swede, a Turk, a German Austrian and a Chinese; Mr Finberg represented the 'British Socialist Party' and Mr Reinstein the 'American Socialist Labor Party'. Most significantly, all but four of the delegates were resident in Moscow. One of the four who actually travelled to the Soviet capital was Henri Guilbeaux; he had just been expelled from Switzerland and heard of the International only when Lenin arrived in person at his hotel door and asked him to give a speech. The party Guilbeaux represented had all of a dozen members. Another traveller, Hugo Eberlein, had received a formal mandate from the German Communist Party; besides the Russian Bolsheviks, he was the most important man present.[99]

Lenin started the proceedings with a declaration 'opening the first international communist congress'. Eberlein immediately objected, arguing that this was not an opportune moment – fresh from blood-soaked Berlin he knew what he was talking about – to turn a 'consultative' assembly into a 'full congress'. Lenin had to handle Eberlein carefully, realizing that his German party had a critical role to play in the process of 'permanent revolution'. He calmly explained that the dictatorship of the proletariat was already making significant inroads in different parts of Europe. It had become 'comprehensible to the broad masses' – that word was always on his lips – 'thanks to soviet power in Russia, thanks to the Spartacists in Germany and analogous organizations in other countries such as, for example, the Shop Stewards Committees in England'. Lenin, like Lloyd George, was absolutely convinced that a revolution was about to break out in England: as he put it a week later to Arthur Ransome, 'things have gone further there than in France'. He told the delegates that the British government had recognized workers' councils, or 'soviets', as 'economic organizations' – a piece of misinformation he must have picked up in the Soviet press. 'The temporary defeat in Germany', he went on, 'was less important than this durable triumph.'

So Lenin, in March 1919, had in no way abandoned his hope for a legitimizing world socialist revolution.

On 4 March he delivered his theses 'on bourgeois democracy and the dictatorship of the proletariat'. It was a flat-out attack on 'pure democracy' in capitalist countries, which benefited only the bourgeoisie, and on their 'civic freedoms'. He also launched a sally against the 'Kautskyites' and those

Independent German Social Democrats who had the gall to express doubts about the intentions of Russian soviets and German workers' councils. His main theme was that fraternal Communist parties throughout Europe were converging to collaborate in a worldwide project.

On the 6th, the last day of the congress, Nikolai Osinski, a prominent campaigner for party centralization, delivered his theses on the international situation. It was essentially an attack on the imperialist Conference taking place in Paris (Chicherin had just sent off his note in answer to the Prinkipo proposal). Osinski claimed that the Paris Conference was trampling under-foot the principle of national self-determination – one of the pillars, of course, of the Soviet Federalist Constitution – and, in his analysis, the League of Nations was merely a scheme whereby the United States could challenge British and French colonial interests. The imperialist capitalism that guided the whole Paris Conference would make further armaments races and wars certain. Osinski's theses on the Peace Conference would be repeated by Soviet supporters and apologists for many decades.

That was the first day that the International was mentioned in Soviet newspapers. In the evening a triumphant finale was held in Moscow's Grand Theatre. Lenin, holding his thumbs under his armpits and swaying back and forth on his heels, announced that the Soviet movement was spreading through countries 'such as England' and that the new 'proletarian democracy' was the way of the future. 'The victory of the proletarian revolution around the entire world is guaranteed,' he said. 'At hand is the foundation of an international Soviet republic.' The crowd present all stood up and sang 'The Internationale', in a way, reported Ransome, 'that I have never heard it sung since the All-Russian Assembly when the news came of the strikes in Germany during the Brest negotiations [that is, the Berlin strikes of January 1918]'. The next day was proclaimed a holiday, and a detachment of Trotsky's Red Army marched through Red Square.

'The Bolsheviks have suddenly proclaimed tomorrow the holiday of the Third International,' Got'e entered in his journal on the 6th. 'Somehow, to my shame, I don't understand what that means.' He spent the 7th working on a home-made doorway for his 'bedroom' – 'I have retained the impression that someone was going to the toilet all day behind me in the corridor.' Moscow was plunged into darkness once more that night, except for the Aleksandrovskoe School, which was all lit up: 'they must have been revelling there'.[100]

In a room within the Kremlin, Yakov Sverdlov, thirty-three years old, lay ill on his bed; he had just contracted the dreaded 'Spanish disease'. He drew his last painful breath ten days later. The 'duumvirate' was dead. The mediator between Stalin and Trotsky had gone. The only brake on party centralization had ceased to function.

That week, news reached Moscow that Kolchak had launched a major offensive in the direction of Ufa. Small, starving, isolated Sovdepiya was under threat. The post-Armistice phase of the Russian war – the massive phase – had begun in earnest. 'Everyone is pleased,' wrote Got'e. 'At the same time, hunger is unquestionably growing.'[101]

7

Despite the fact that Bullitt had been on a peace mission to Moscow, neither he nor his two colleagues, Steffens and Pettit, made any mention of war in their reports. No Westerner in early 1919 was fully aware of the scale of the fighting that was developing around the peripheries of 'Sovdepiya' and within the so-called 'successor states' that had replaced three crumbled empires. Yet, if one adds up the toll of casualties in the wars that were fought in Central and Eastern Europe between the Armistice of 1918 and the end of 1922, one will arrive at a figure greater than all war-related deaths in Europe between 1914 and 1918. A recent estimate of casualties in Russia alone during this post-Armistice period proposes a total of 12.6 million lives lost.[102]

Kolchak's armies crossed the Urals in early March and pushed forward on three fronts. To the north, Kolchak hoped to advance by way of Perm (already in his hands), Viatka and Vologda to reach Miller's small force in Archangel and thus link up with the Allies and a closer seaport for critical military supplies. In the centre his objective was Ufa and Kazan, which could open a route to Moscow. In the south he was aiming at the Volga, where he could join Denikin's Volunteer Army and isolate Bolshevik forces in Central Asia. His armies made rapid progress, extending over 400 miles in each direction within a month. He was aided by the break-out of anti-Bolshevik peasant revolts in the provinces of Simbirsk, Samara, Kazan and Viatka. By April he had added well over 100,000 square miles to his territory and was standing, at some points, within twenty miles of the Volga.

In March, the Bolsheviks were busy occupying the Ukraine, with the triple aim of taking over the coal mines in the southern area of the Donbass, of clearing out White forces and, as a directive from Moscow put it, of achieving 'the complete, rapid, decisive annihilation of Cossackdom'. 'The Cains must be exterminated,' was Trotsky's response to the order.[103]

But Kolchak's invasion changed Bolshevik priorities; an army had to be built up to defend the Eastern Front. This gave Denikin an opportunity to break out of his enclave at Rostov, on the mouth of the Don. On 15 March he attacked the Red Eighth Army just south of Lugansk. Which way would he turn? Westward and thus save the lives of tens of thousands in the Ukraine? Or eastward so as to join up with Kolchak's forces on the Volga? Denikin advanced in both directions.

In the meantime General N. N. Iudenich, wartime hero, began assembling behind the protective lakes of Estonia a Russian army made up mainly of prisoners of war who had been released by the Germans in the Baltic. Iudenich's plan was to cross the frontier into Russia and take Pskov, which was at the southern point of Estonia's line of lakes. From there he could march on Petrograd.

'The proletarian slogan must be: civil war,' said Lenin when attacking the socialist pacifists in Switzerland. Now he had it, and more. Even within the frontiers of the former tsarist empire it was a war between different ethnic groups, a patchwork of different nations. But the spiral of violence went wider yet. As the winter of 1919 turned into spring, a score of wars developed from Montenegro in the Balkans, to the coasts of the Black Sea, across the Caucasians, up the Urals, to Archangel in the north, to the Baltic states in the west, and further south in Poland, on her German frontiers, her Czech frontiers, in Galicia, in the Ukraine, and in the area that both Russians and Poles called 'the Borders'. The eastern base of the European peninsula had not yet abandoned war.

Some of these wars resembled Tolstoy's scenes out of the early nineteenth century. Most were fought with cavalry and infantry. A few British tanks (manned by British volunteers) may have appeared north of the Crimea, but they were accompanied by herdsmen from the Kuban. The Polish infantry were dressed in the uniforms of the major power they had last fought for, German, Austrian or Russian; Haller's Army came to be known as the 'Blue Legion' because its troops wore French horizon blue. The Polish 16th Uhlans, from Poznania, went into battle in 1920 wearing their high *rogatywka* hats surmounted by red rosettes; they were equipped with lances, sabres and bayonets, and they charged with a clank and rattle that made them sound like French horsemen at Agincourt. Offensives like those of Kolchak and Denikin ran under their own momentum across vast plains and forests; it has been calculated that by the time Denikin reached his furthest point of advance in October 1919 his front was defended by an average of one man to a mile. That gives a note of caution to the military maps often provided in the histories of the Russian war. Behind the fronts, other minor wars would be going on between factions calling themselves 'Anarchists', 'Greens', 'Grigorevites', 'Makhnovites', 'Sem'novites' and so on; they pursued their own objectives and changed sides whenever they saw fit. Their style of campaign was murderous. Whole villages were wiped out and burnt to the ground. Because of mass desertions, the Red Army developed special techniques for killing its own troops. 'One cannot form an army without repression,' said Trotsky. He introduced the principle of 'decimation' in August 1918, and the following year he set up 'barring detachments' that were placed behind the front and would fire with machine-guns into retreating troops. No one knows how many troops in the Red Army were killed by their own command – except for the official figure provided for 1921, the first year of peace in Russia, when 4,337 soldiers were shot.[104] The worst massacres occurred in the Ukraine, in the Polish–Russian 'Borders', and in the Baltic states of Latvia and Lithuania. Not only Russians were responsible for these.

After the Latvian loss of Riga to the Bolsheviks in late December and the agreement that Ulmanis, the Prime Minister, had (for lack of political alternative) reached with German Supreme Command, General von der Golz set up headquarters in Mitau. By February 1919 German Free Corps were streaming in through the Latvian port of Libau. They were recruited from former units of the old German Imperial Army, from German Baltic émigrés who populated Munich, and from the seaports. The Hamburg Free Corps carried the flag of the ancient Hanseatic League with a pirate's skull-and-crossbones superimposed on it; they grew their hair long, saluted only the officers they knew and liked, and, as far as authority was concerned, 'the only thing that counted was the will of their own *Führer'*.[105] Fragments of the old German Eighth Army added to the strength of von der Golz's Baltic force. Defence lines were built from the coast down through Latvia and on to the Lithuanian capital of Kovno (or Kaunis). On 3 March von der Golz began his drive against the weak Bolshevik forces, pushing them back to the Russian frontier. The German war was marching east again. Within ten days, practically all of Latvia and Lithuania was in German hands. There remained to the Bolsheviks the prize port of Riga.[106]

Through the rest of March and much of April, German Free Corps went on the rampage in search for 'Communists'. Every day in the main public square at Mitau, German firing squads executed suspects by the dozen. The German military commander in the Latvian port of Windau published a proclamation demanding all persons who had worked with the previous Bolshevik government or had served in the Red Army register with his police; failure to register was punishable by execution, and most of those who did register were shot anyway. But that was merely the administrative surface of a wave of slaughter and destruction that swept across the two unhappy Baltic provinces in the early spring of 1919.

The German presence on the western frontiers of 'Sovdepiya' was not limited to the Baltic. Most German forces in the Ukraine and Belorussia had been pulled out in a hurry in November and December 1918, their commanders unwilling and unable to heed the armistice demand to undertake the evacuation only 'as soon as the Allies shall think the moment suitable'. But not every German soldier was withdrawn. In January 1919 there remained a thin grey line over a thousand miles long and, in some places, only fifteen miles wide that dangled like a right-angled key spanner from the southern frontier of Lithuania directly south to Grodno, Brest-Litovsk and Kowel, and then directly east, along the low foothills of the Carpathian Alps to within a hundred miles of Kiev. In other words, this German line formed a barrier across the whole great northern plain south of the Baltic states. It was heavily fortified. In 1918 it had formed the main bastion protecting Germany and Austria from Russian forces. In early 1919, through no deliberate intention of the Germans, it kept Polish forces separate from the Bolsheviks. Not only soldiers were prevented from crossing it:

so too were trains, food supplies, couriers, diplomats and propagandists. *Oberkommando-Ostfront*, or 'Ober-Ost', as this German frontier force was known, ensured Moscow's total diplomatic and political isolation.[107]

It was completely independent from von der Golz's forces in the Baltic; its orders came from General Max Hoffman, who kept a well-staffed command post in Königsberg in East Prussia. Hoffman was hated by the Poles. The appalling massacres committed by marauding German troops in November and December on the river Bug, east of Warsaw, were blamed on him. But as Piłsudki's government in Warsaw watched the developments in the Baltic – first the Soviet advances of December and January, then the rapid deployment of the German Free Corps – they concluded that some kind of accord with Hoffman was needed. On 5 February representatives of the two sides met in the eastern Polish town of Bialystock: the Germans agreed to withdraw the whole of Ober-Ost to the northern region of Suwaiki (in neighbouring East Prussia) while they would let ten Polish battalions cross their lines at Wolkowysk. Four days later the Poles set off. Almost simultaneously detachments from the Western Red Army, with its headquarters in Smolensk, started marching west. They were probably more concerned with the developments in Lithuania than they were about Poles; nevertheless, a collision was now inevitable.

It occurred in the village of Bereza Kartuska at 7 a.m. on Friday, 14 February – oddly enough, the very same day that the plenary session in Paris adopted the Covenant of the League of Nations. Captain Mienicki, commanding the Polish Vilna detachment of fifty-seven men and five officers, overcame a small occupying force of Bolsheviks, taking eighty of them prisoner.[108]

Considered in the context of the two dozen other wars going on at the time, this would seem a puny event. But in fact it marked the beginning of a Soviet–Polish war that would influence the whole course of twentieth-century European history. The vast northern plain area of the Borders – occupied by Lithuanians, Belorussians, Ukrainians and Jews, but hardly any Russians or Poles – was in question. Two ideologies – one national, one socialist – were in struggle. Two sovereign nations were locked in combat. Though Stalin would call this third phase of the Russian Civil War the 'third campaign of the Entente',[109] the one group that exerted virtually no effect on its outcome, and had almost no knowledge of what was happening, was the Allies sitting in conference in Paris. How different this was from Vienna! Here was another great chunk of Europe, of critical strategic importance, that lay outside the influence of the peacemakers.

The Borders – a sparsely populated zone of birch, willow and oak forests, green meadows and heathland, and a network of streams, ponds and canals – held a kind of magical grip on both Poles and Russians. It was a land where myths were built, a country of knights and heroes; it was a stage set for poets. Several of the leading figures in the war that was about to develop had spent their childhood there. Trotsky was born at Yanovka, near Kherson; Karl Radek, who, despite the German military barrier, was constantly commuting between Moscow, Warsaw and Berlin, came from Lvov; Dzerzhinsky was born in Vilna. So too was Poland's President, Józef Piłsudski.

'Wilno' they called the place if you were a Pole; 'Vilnius' if a Lithuanian; 'Vilna' if a Russian. The town was populated by Poles, while the surrounding country was Lithuanian. In the two years since 1917 it had come under eight different regimes – the Tsar's, Kerensky's Provisional Government, German occupation, Soviet rule . . . On 1 January 1919 Polish officers had staged a coup to prevent the local 'Workers' Council' from seizing power; on the 5th a Polish Communist detachment from the Western Red Army overturned the Poles and set up a Soviet government. Piłsudski had his heart set on Vilna, at the northernmost point of the Ober-Ost.

The essence of the Polish national ideal was laid out by the Foreign Minister, Roman Dmowski, before the Council of Ten in Paris on 29 January: the Poles sought a large state, strong enough to stand up to both Russians and Germans. It was a proposal to change the balance of power in Eastern Europe for ever. It was purposely designed to contradict the 1815 settlement at Vienna. Poles could not believe that 'Sovdepiya', invaded from every side, had any future in the concert of nations; Russia would become a secondary power. A new Poland, with its influence stretching, like the old seventeenth-century Polish Commonwealth, from the Baltic to the Black Sea, would be the new power to reckon with – a democratic, parliamentary power. Piłsudski was less scornful about Lithuanians and Ukrainians than Dmowski: if the old Commonwealth were in some way to be revived, it would have to be a democratic federation of nations – Piłsudski always emphasized in his public pronouncements the freedom of choice of the member states; he constantly repeated the new Western ideal of 'self-determination'. Piłsudski was convinced that, given the violence of their recent past, the nations of the Borders, from Finland to the Caucasus, would willingly join in a democratic federation to defend themselves: it was, in effect, an early plan for a Central European Union that would replace the discredited multinational empire of Austria-Hungary.

The Bolsheviks in 'Sovdepiya', on the other hand, were just as convinced that history was on their side, and that the new nation-state was doomed – doomed because it had been built on the false bourgeois premise of nationhood. Nations had no long-term future in the Bolshevik mind; they would wither away under the onslaught of the international socialist revolution. In this context, the Borders and Poland constituted the critical land link though which the Soviet system would be able to spread down the funnel of peninsular Europe and from there overseas to the world. The Borders thus became a land of experiment in 'permanent revolution'. In January, after the capture of Kiev, the Bolsheviks set up a Ukrainian Soviet

Socialist Republic. In February they established the Lithuanian–Belorussian Soviet Republic, soon abbreviated, in the Bolshevik fashion, to 'Lit–Bel'. Private property was abolished, shop signs were torn down, peasants were collectivized, food was requisitioned, and the 'bourgeoisie' were slaughtered. On 12 January, Soviet Supreme Command ordered the start of 'Target Vistula', an operation of 'reconnaissance in depth' as far as the river Niemen and, by February, the Bug. The name of the operation left little doubt that the ultimate object was Warsaw.[110]

But several members of the Central Committee were not keen on the idea of an invasion of Poland; there were too many other wars going on. Better, they thought, to strengthen socialism within one country rather than attempt world revolution now. Lenin and Trotsky were ambiguous on the point. Trotsky would later claim that he had never been in favour of a revolutionary war with Poland; he would say that his idea instead was that revolution would go in the other direction, eastward into the Western empires of Asia and Africa – 'the road to London and Paris lies through Calcutta'.[111] This would certainly be the ideal of Communism after the 1940s. But in 1919 all evidence suggests that both Lenin and Trotsky were expecting their world revolution to begin in the West.

For Piłsudski, an obvious line of defence lay with the White armies of Denikin, Kolchak and Iudenich. Diplomatic soundings were made in February. But the Whites were professional soldiers, not politicians. They couldn't see the point of Polish independence. 'I had absolutely no political objectives,' Kolchak would tell a Bolshevik commission of inquiry after his capture; 'I should not side with any parties.'[112] This included nationalists on the Borders. As for Denikin, he categorically refused to recognize the independence of any state within the frontiers of the old tsarist empire, arguing that this was something for the 'politicians' to consider once a constituent assembly had been set up. Roman Dmowski had approached Sazonov's Russian Political Conference in Paris for their opinion – he got the same response. That was the tragedy of Russia's anti-Bolshevik forces: despite a world war over the issue, they were incapable of recognizing the significance of the principle of nationality.

The Bolsheviks did. They were ready to do anything to prevent an alliance between the Poles and the Whites. The right of national self-determination, after all, had been written into their Constitution. Their philosophy was: Recognize Polish independence, for Poland will disappear anyway after the European revolution. Or, as one of the key figures in Polish–Soviet relations, Julian Marchlewski, put it, 'in the near future all frontiers would lose significance because the revolutionary upheaval in Europe, therefore in Poland as well, was only a matter of time, a matter of a few years'.[113]

Marchlewski was, like Karl Radek and Rosa Luxemburg, a Polish Communist who crossed the land bridge in anticipation of the *grande soirée*. In October 1918 Moscow proposed him as ambassador to the

German-sponsored Regency Council then in Warsaw. He was one of the
founding members of the German Spartacist League. In January 1919 he
illegally entered Berlin with Radek as part of the 'Soviet delegation'. After
the defeat of the Spartacists he fled to the Ruhr, where he stirred up a
violent strike movement among miners and then escaped, disguised among
a group of agricultural workers who were returning to Galicia.

His next point of call was Warsaw, where he arrived in March. He published an article in the Polish socialist paper *Robotnik* urging his countrymen
not to make war on the Soviets, and he offered his services to the Piłsudski
government, offering to act as an intermediary with Lenin. Piłsudski accepted.
Though an undeclared ground war between the Poles and the Soviets was
already under way, periodic meetings between the representatives of the
two governments took place during the next nine months. They were kept
strictly secret because of Piłsudski's fears about the Western Allied reaction.
Throughout this period, Marchlewski was the key player. Marchlewski's
line of argument with Piłsudski's government was that a White victory in
Russia would be a disaster for Poland. Having approached the Whites,
Piłsudski came to the same conclusion: the Soviets would make an enemy
preferable to the Whites.

There developed out of this a novel kind of diplomatic and military
manoeuvring on the strategic Borders which would set the pattern for the
entire inter-war period and which would even partially determine the course
of the Second World War. At times it would look like agreement, at times
it resembled war, and at other critical moments it would become outright
treachery. In the autumn of 1919, Iudenich's White Army would advance
on Petrograd under the stunning silence of the Poles, the Estonians and the
Finns. Without their help his campaign was doomed. At the critical turn of
battle in Volhynia (in the Ukraine) in October 1919, Polish forces deployed
behind the right flank of the Twelfth Red Army halted, thus allowing the
Reds time to annihilate Denikin's forces – painfully, one thinks of Stalin in
1944 holding his troops on the banks of the Vistula as the Nazis moved
into Warsaw.[114]

Marchlewski's negotiations did not imply peace. Even as they were under
way, Piłsudski made his move on Vilna. The town was seized by Polish
cavalry at dawn on 19 April 1919, in a masterful campaign of diversionary
and surprise attacks. Piłsudski entered his birthplace victoriously on the
21st with a proclamation which laid out his plan for a free federation of
nations: 'Now at last, in this land which God seemed to have forsaken,
liberty must reign, with the right of full and unrestricted expression of
aspirations and needs. The Polish Army brings Liberty and Freedom to you
all.'[115]

Lenin responded with a telegram to the Western Red Army headquarters
demanding the town's immediate reconquest. 'The loss of Vilna has
strengthened the Entente still further,' he warned. 'It is essential to ensure

the maximum speed for the recovery of Vilna in the shortest possible time.'[116] Lenin would not allow the bridge to Europe to be closed. Lenin could not imagine a Soviet Russia without the spread of socialist revolution into the industrial West. The legitimacy of his regime was at stake.

Spring 1919

Paris in spring

1

Behind the walls of Paris, the conference commissions and subcommissions were busy drawing up maps, studying rivers and railway lines, and arguing about numbers. On Wednesday morning, 19 February, Harold Nicolson was sitting on the Greek Commission, awaiting the arrival of old Jules Cambon. Cambon was late. At last he poked his wrinkled head around the door and said, 'Clemenceau has been assassinated.'[1]

Clemenceau was being driven from his small flat on the Rue Franklin to the Ministry of War when a young man stepped out of a urinal at the foot of the steep road and, shouting 'I am a Frenchman and an anarchist!', emptied a pistol through the back window of the car. Three bullets pierced Clemenceau's clothing; two only grazed him, but the third hit his shoulder blade and lodged near a lung. The chauffeur raced back to the flat. Clemenceau, seventy-seven and looking a little pale, stepped out of the car on his own and was assisted to his favourite armchair – lying down was painful. 'I was', he gasped, 'on the back seat when I suddenly saw a character pointing his revolver at me. I told myself "*Il va me rater*" ["He's going to miss me"]. Off went the fire crackers and, contrary to my prognosis, I was hit.' he gasped. '*Heureusement! Ils l'ont raté,*' reported *Le Crapouillot*, an old trench journal still in print in February.[2]

Emile Cottin, a twenty-three-year-old carpenter, was condemned to death, but, on Clemenceau's insistence, the sentence was reduced to ten years' imprisonment; he was released in 1924 – an interesting contrast to the fate of Lenin's presumed assailant.

By afternoon Clemenceau was already arguing with his doctors and discussing the business of the Conference with colleagues. André Tardieu found him 'cheerful and making light of the whole matter'.[3]

'Dear, dear, I wonder what that portends,' muttered Arthur Balfour, the British Foreign Secretary, on hearing the news. With Lloyd George in London, Wilson in America and Clemenceau laid low by a bullet, Balfour became the leading figure at the Conference. This period of the negotiations

in Paris – generally known as the 'Balfour phase', the time of 'detailed
work', or the 'period of the Plot', according to the view one takes of the
Conference and the subsequent treaties – lasted around three weeks. By the
second week of March, Lloyd George was back in Paris and Clemenceau
was mobile again (though he had a rasping cough); Wilson would return
on his favourite day of the month, the 13th. For Ray Stannard Baker, who
ran the American press bureau, the three-week interim was a disreputable
time when the diplomats of the Old World set out to destroy the grand
visions of the New. 'No sooner had the President left Paris', he wrote in a
book published three years later, 'than the forces of opposition and discontent began to act. On February 24, resolutions were adopted by the Council
of Ten which, if carried through, would wreck the entire American scheme
for the peace. It was exceedingly shrewd strategy these skilled diplomatists
played. They did not like the League as drafted and they did not want the
Covenant in the Treaty, but they made no direct attack on either proposal.'
For Harold Nicolson, who laboured away in his Greek Commission, it was
a period of 'delay, confusion, overlapping and eventual improvisation'. For
many of the young 'war generation', working in junior positions in Paris,
it was the moment of 'disillusionment'.[4]

In those three weeks of absentee heads of government the Conference
was transformed from the bottom up and the top down. Nearly everyone
present in Paris lived the experience badly. And yet it was necessary. The
enormous gap that had developed between immediate post-war idealism
and the realities of Europe was closed; the spell of the Armistice was
smashed. The main issue was Germany, spanning the great northern plain,
with her western frontiers now forced into peace but her eastern parts
overlapping a zone of war which few peacemakers in Paris could fully
understand and none of them could control.

The transformation of the Conference had begun, shortly before Wilson's
departure, with the realization inside the Council of Ten that German troops
were still fighting a war. The reports filtering through from Poland had
shocked the Allies into action; on 12 February they decided to stop the
monthly renewal of the Armistice terms and, instead, to present Germany
with the detailed and final naval, military and air conditions of the 'preliminaries of peace'. A special commission was created to draft them, and was
expected to get its work done in forty-eight hours. But the generals and
admirals were still hard at work at the time Clemenceau was shot. On 22
February, Balfour told the Ten that 'a general feeling of impatience was
now becoming manifest in all countries on account of the apparent slow
progress in the direction of final peace'. Hankey was called on to prepare
another of his resolutions, which Balfour presented to the Council that same
day; it was resolved that 'without prejudice to the decision of the Supreme
War Council to present naval, military and air conditions of peace to Germany at an early date, the Conference agrees that it is desirable to proceed

without delay to the consideration of other preliminary peace terms with Germany and to press on the necessary investigations with all possible speed'. Both Lansing and House voted for the resolution, along with their European colleagues; and no signal came through from America that Wilson disagreed. All the commissions were ordered to have their reports ready for consideration by the Council of Ten by 8 March. By the time Lloyd George returned on 6 March the order had been given to present these reports in the form of a treaty.

So, under Balfour, Paris had become a hive of activity. On 24 February, Haller's Army finally received instructions to prepare for its embarkation for Poland. Tardieu promised the Ten that same day that military terms for Germany would be ready 'in a few days'.[5] The Reparations Commission, still deadlocked in financial arithmetic, was thrown into a crisis that only a mind of Keynes's calibre could temporarily resolve in early March. Italy, solely concerned with Adriatic matters, objected to Balfour's resolution to concentrate on Germany. Italy, claimed Baron Sonnino, had 'another enemy, Austria, and in fighting her she had borne the full consequences of the war'. What pledges and guarantees were to be made for Italy? The German question was 'the principal and essential question' retaliated Stéphen Pichon, the French Foreign Minister.[6]

Remarkably, most of the commission reports actually were ready and printed up at the Imprimerie Nationale by the deadline of 8 March. Ironically, the one commission which came nowhere near to meeting the deadline was that charged with drawing up the military conditions for Germany. But most of the experts had by now spoken; the time for political decisions had arrived.

Thus, under Balfour, the commissions and subcommissions had been revolutionized. A similar revolution took place at the top, at the place of decision. Europe's international institutions were evolving fast.

The attempt on Clemenceau's life had an immediate impact on the structure of the ruling Council. Even on the day of the incident, both Balfour and House were in the little flat at the top of the Rue Franklin discussing with the French premier the problem of Germany's boundaries. Clemenceau was propped up uncomfortably on an armchair, his reading glasses balanced on his nose, and piles of papers poised on his knees or scattered on the floor about him. Clemenceau was still seeking a wall across the northern plain to protect France from a third German invasion. That wall would be the Rhine. Unlike Foch and Poincaré, he had no ambition to annex the German Rhineland ('Foch wants to do what Napoleon never managed,' he commented). He was ready to recognize a degree of self-determination. What he proposed was a Rhenish republic, independent of Germany. Britain and the United States had gained complete security by impounding the German Navy; France deserved a secure frontier. 'Everything would be done to make [the independent Rhinelanders] contented and prosperous,'

Clemenceau said; they would not even have to pay the indemnity. Despite his wound, he must have been convincing. House immediately sent off an acquiescent report to Wilson.[7]

These informal conversations continued throughout Clemenceau's convalescence. No secretaries were present, no experts sat behind the statesmen, no reporters roamed the corridor. They were intimate, secret; the only record we have of them is in the notes and telegrams Balfour and House sent to their respective governments. When Lloyd George returned in early March and discovered that his arguments over German frontiers were being leaked to Northcliffe's press, he too was won over to the idea of confidential talks. The Council of Ten – where fifty were frequently present in the room – gradually receded into the background. By the end of March, 'Ten' had become 'Four': Clemenceau of France, Lloyd George of Britain, Orlando of Italy, and Woodrow Wilson of America.

The pain this institutional revolution caused within the younger ranks of Paris's peacemakers is recorded in Harold Nicolson's diary, day by day. In February every public building and hotel in town hosted commissions on territorial problems, trade, finance, railways, waterways – issues that were often only vaguely related to the task of drawing up a treaty with Germany. Since the attempt on Clemenceau's life, the streets were bristling with police and detectives. The weather was cold; it rained and snowed. Flu was rife. 'Walk down to Dufayel Club for luncheon,' Nicolson records on 16 February. 'As I cross Champs Elysées, I see coming towards me a British serjeant who looks very strange. I see that he is blubbering, great tears pouring down his cheek. I then recognize him as Walter Wilson, Mark Sykes' orderly, secretary, companion. He comes up to me. He is sobbing hard. He tells me Mark is dying.' Mark Sykes, who in 1916 had organized with his French counterpart, Georges Picot, a treaty that divided the Middle East into spheres of influence, died that night in the Hôtel Lotti. 'I shall miss him – boisterous, witty, untidy, fat, kindly, excitable,' wrote Nicolson the next day. 'I feel glum and saddened.'[8]

Every morning Nicolson was driven by car from the Astoria to the Quai d'Orsay. The Greek Commission – or 'committee', as Nicolson insisted on calling it – met in the Salle à Manger. Droning away in the next room was the Czecho-Slovak Commission, which, after the drawn-out discussions on Medea, the Symplegades and the Arda line in the Salle à Manger, Nicolson regarded as an escape. He once attended an 'audition' before the Council of Ten, on the first floor. Turkhan Pasha, head of the Albanian delegation, made a case for his countrymen; for more than an hour he read, into his henna-dyed beard, from a heap of typewritten pages. 'The Ten chatter and laugh while this is going on. Rather painful.' The whole problem was referred back to the Greek Commission. On rare 'free days' – when no commissions met – Nicolson remained in the Astoria, where the accumulating boxes of documents from the Foreign Office awaited him. 'Work! Work! Work! Work!' 'I am feeling exhausted and unstrung. I lose my temper . . . Come back dead to the world. This is all too much.' 'I come back, as so often now, dispirited, saddened, and one mass of nerves jangled and torn.' 'The strain is appalling.'[9]

On 25 February he learned that all commission reports had to be in by 8 March. Nicolson's Greek report was one of the first to be handed in on that Saturday; 'I take it round, with a feeling of maternal pride, to Hankey.' But that same afternoon he was told that all reports had to be rewritten in 'the form of Treaties'. 'I feel quite dead with it all – and so dispirited.'[10]

Driving the Conference forward was the Western popular press: What were the politicians and the bureaucrats up to? Why wasn't the peace signed yet? Hadn't the guns stopped firing more than three months ago? Nicolson felt the onus of responsibility on his shoulders. He was freqently 'disheartened', 'saddened', and conscious of his 'fallibility'. It was not just the physical strain of his work that exhausted him: there was a moral element too. He had learned everything he could from books, from statistics, from interviews, from proposals and counter-proposals in the commissions; but then, with compasses, rulers, tracing paper and coloured inks, he had to draw his lines: 'there is a definite inarticulate human element behind it all some-where', and he couldn't get it out. The Americans disagreed with the British over what side of the line the Grosse Schütt, on the Slovak frontier, should fall – 'I am *sure* they are wrong and it is heart-breaking to have to support a claim with which I disagree.' Unanimity was the rule in the commission work. If they came up with a majority and a minority report, the Council would ask them to make another effort to reach an agreement. 'Nobody who has not had experience of Committees work in actual practice', commented Nicolson, 'can conceive of the difficulty of inducing a French-man, an Italian, an American and an Englishman to agree on anything. A majority agreement is easy enough: an unanimous agreement is an impossi-bility; or if possible, then possible only in the form of some paralytic compromise.'[11]

The press maintained the pressure. What are they doing? Why the delay? Nicolson became frustrated with the centralization process involved in the drafting of the Treaty. 'It is as though four architects had each designed an entirely different house, and then met round a table to arrive at an agree-ment' – which, in Nicolson's view, was the worst solution; 'even the worst individual design is better than a fusion of four.' Behind the Conference was hidden an expert machine that was marvellous to behold; legal advisers would sometimes intervene and solve a problem 'like electricians fixing a short-circuit'. Some of the best minds in the world were in Paris working on the peace. The real difficulty began when the terms were brought together for consideration by the Council – by politicians 'of no real vision', men 'jealous of the great expert machine'. They 'fiddled'. Nicolson thought 'the whole business is too complex for centralization'. By the end of March, young experts like Nicolson were filled with resentment. 'It will be too awful, if after winning the war we are to lose the peace,' Nicolson wrote, depressed, to a friend on 24 March. Yet the Treaty had not yet been assembled.[12]

Nicolson did have a few moments of pleasure. He set off for a walk through the Forêt de Saint-Germain on Sunday, 23 February, and discovered 'a sense of spring in the black twigs'. On Sunday, 30 March, he was walking in the Val de Chevreuse amid 'snow and sunshine'. On a couple of occasions he attended a party hosted by Boni de Castellane – who was not as rich as before he was divorced and publicly repudiated by Anna Gould. The parties were held in a little house on the Rue de Lille. Leading members of the Russian community attended, and the figure of Philippe Berthelot could be seen creeping around the lighted wax candles. 'Very Congress of Vienna,' commented Nicolson.[13]

On 2 March he dined with Princess Soutzo at the Ritz – 'a swell affair'. After the meal he discovered on a felted bench a thin, grubby, unshaven man, white in his face, holding a cup of coffee in his kid-gloved hands. It was Marcel Proust. Proust asked Nicolson how the commissions of the Conference worked. Nicolson replied that their work usually began at ten o'clock, and the secretaries would sit behind the members. '*Mais non, mais non, vous allez trop vite,*' responded Proust, '*Recommencez. Vous prenez la voiture de la Délégation. Vous descendez au Quai d'Orsay. Vous montez l'escalier. Vous entrez dans la Salle. Et alors? Précisez, mon cher, précisez.*' So Nicolson told him about the handshakes, the maps, the rustle of papers, and the tea in the next room – with macaroons. Proust was delighted. '*Mais précisez, mon cher monsieur,*' he said with a smile, '*précisez, mon cher monsieur, n'allez pas trop vite.*'[14]

Three days later Nicolson was gazing into the puddles on a Parisian pavement; they had taken on the form of international frontiers, salients, ethnic corridors, neutralized channels and demilitarized zones.[15]

2

Two days after the attempt on Clemenceau's life, on 21 February, the head of the Bavarian government, stubby and bearded Kurt Eisner, was crossing the Promenade Platz in Munich in the direction of the Landtag, where he intended to present his resignation. As he turned into Promenade Strasse, a young man, waiting for him, pulled out a pistol and, at point-blank range, shot him twice in the head. Eisner died instantly. His assassin, the twenty-two-year-old Count Anton Arco-Valley, also lay bleeding on the pavement, shot in the neck, mouth and chest by one of Eisner's guards; but he survived to serve a short prison sentence in the Bavarian state prison at Stadelheim – in the same Cell 70 that was to house Adolf Hitler four years later, after the failure of his Beerhall *Putsch*.

Eisner – a drama critic, essayist and poet – had taken over the Bavarian state government with his fellow Independent Socialists on 7 November, when the Wittelsbach dynasty had faded. Working in the once luxuriously furnished apartments of the former Imperial Chancellor, Count von Hertling, he had published the correspondence of Bavaria's Foreign Ministry for the year 1914 with the aim of proving Prussian responsibility for the war: Eisner was hoping the Allies would offer a separate, lenient, peace treaty to Bavaria. But the deterioration of the economy had soon made Eisner unpopular with the Bavarians; 'Out with the Israelite devil!' and 'We want a Bavarian!' cried the demonstrators under his window – Eisner was a Jew, and Prussian. He had responded by organizing a 'Fête of the Bavarian Revolution' in the city opera house; Bruno Walter's orchestra had performed a Beethoven overture and accompanied an aria by Handel, and then Eisner explained his theory of the 'international spirit' as embodied in modern theatre. Nobody was surprised when, in elections for the local parliamentary assembly the following January, Eisner's Independent Socialists won only three seats. Yet Eisner, who had a certain knack for negotiating his way out of difficult corners, managed to remain *Ministerpräsident* until the day of his murder.

His murderer, Count Arco-Valley, a lieutenant in the Bavarian Guards Infantry Regiment, had tried to join the literary and anti-Semitic Thule Society, whose members greeted each other with 'Heil!' and adopted the swastika as their symbol; but the Society had discovered that his mother was a Jew. The rejection had prompted the Count to perform his act on Promenade Strasse.

The assassination set off waves of violence that continued to roll and eddy about Munich until May. On the day it occurred, Eisner's supporters swarmed into the streets, church bells were rung, there were calls for revenge; in the Landtag, Eisner's arch-enemy, Erhard Auer, leader of the Majority Socialists, had just completed a speech on the murder when he found himself facing a butcher's apprentice who, in full view of the horrified Assembly, took careful aim with a pistol and shot Auer out of his chair. The apprentice was shot dead by a soldier. Auer was carried out to a hospital, writhing in pain; he survived. But the Majority Socialists could not stay in Munich. Once a general strike was proclaimed on 27 February, Munich was no longer a place for 'bourgeois' parliamentarians to hang around in. Their newspaper buildings were burnt down. Gun battles broke out in the streets. On the site of Eisner's murder, Count Arco-Valley's sympathizers spread flour scented by bitches in heat so as to attract dogs and make their opponents' shrine a foul-smelling corner of cobble.

The new coalition government of Bavaria had to move to Nuremburg. The German Republic's Defence Minister, Gustav Noske, meanwhile began collecting together an army of Free Corps on Bavaria's borders: Bavaria was not an independent state, and Noske was not going to allow it to become one.[16]

There was violence in Bremen, Mühlheim, Brunswick and Halle. There was talk of Bolshevik takeover in towns and provinces. The National Assembly in Weimar could continue its deliberations only thanks to the circle of steel set up by Maercker's Volunteer Rifles. All Germany was withdrawing into its corporate cells. But that was the difference between Russia and Germany: in Germany those cells existed.

The great wheel of the German economy was still turning. But those who rode upon it were now divided into tiny groups, each one in its own little compartment which, though pivoting with the general movement, was either indifferent or hostile to the one that rode above it or below it. Germany, a departmentalized nation before 1914, was fragmented by the war. More was involved than local revolts against the state. The state itself was divided: Scheidemann's new coalition government in Weimar was built on an unrealizable compromise between nationalists and socialists. Erzberger's Armistice Commission, which faced Allied representatives across a table in Spa, had no communication whatsoever with Count Brockdorff-Rantzau's Foreign Ministry: Germany was developing two separate, uncoordinated policies on the coming Peace Treaty. Managers of banking and industry followed incompatible economic policies. The organized trade unions went in the opposite direction from the disorganized factory shop stewards, who themselves distrusted the workers they claimed to be leading. Agriculture was a world unto itself. Added to all this was a dissolved Imperial Army of young soldiers who were looking for something to do.

One internal division that would have the most significant consequences for the peace in the West was between liberal free-traders and central state planners. It would pit the ideas of Walther Rathenau, an impenitent planner, against those of his successor at the War Office's Raw Materials Section, Colonel Joseph Koeth. When Koeth took charge of the Demobilization Office in November 1918 he began advocating the deregulation of economic controls and the management of the economy by competent private civilians, not state bureaucrats. He had some powerful allies in the bankers of northern Germany, who hated Rathenau and believed that the best guarantee for Germany's future was open trade. Koeth also had an ally in the new Finance Minister, Eugen Schiffer, who joined Scheidemann's government in February 1919. Schiffer was a confirmed economic liberal. When Schiffer presented his budget to the National Assembly on 15 February he made an unprecedented angry attack on the Hindenburg Programme and the manner in which Germany had financed the war.[17] There had been no voice like this in Russia.

The previous December, Wichard von Moellendorff, Rathenau's former colleague at the AEG, had returned to government as Under-Secretary of State of the Reich Economic Office, a body that had been founded in 1917 to plan the transition to peace – at a time when it was assumed that Germany would emerge from the war victorious. In late 1918 Moellendorff was as much an advocate of a centrally planned technocratic rationalization of the economy as he had been when he worked with Rathenau in 1914. For Moellendorff, as for Rathenau, the formation of workers' councils towards the end of the war – even though Germany was by now losing – was a logical step in the direction of economic 'democratization'. Moellendorff, on taking office in December 1918, warned against the short-term day-by-day policy Koeth was following. 'The more distant goal must not be lost sight of,' he said, 'and the future economic system must already be prepared for now.'[18] Moellendorff had been an early defender of the wartime Hindenburg Programme. In the months after the Armistice he still stood by economic planning and corporatist organization. In February he found an ally in the new Economics Minister, the trade-unionist Rudolf Wissell. Between the liberals under Koeth and Schiffer, and the planners under Moellendorff and Wissell – between the Finance Ministry and the Economics Ministry – a great tug-of-war began.

This was not unconnected with the new wave of violence in Germany's cities. The German Communist Party, founded on 1 January, also rode on the great wheel in an isolated compartment, and it did not like the way that wheel was turning. In Weimar, on 24 February, Professor Hugo Preuss presented to the National Assembly a draft constitution that outlined a plan for a strong president and two legislative houses. There was no mention of workers' and soldiers' councils, of 'socialization', of 'economic democracy' or of the rights of the proletariat: this was clearly going to be a bourgeois parliamentary system. The process had to be stopped, said Leo Jogiches, chairman of the Communist Party's Central Committee in Berlin. But how? According to the 'Jogiches Thesis', the kind of sporadic revolts that had occurred in February would never provide the Communists with enough support for a takeover of government. The Communists would never prove a match for Noske's Free Corps. The only chance they had – and they had to take it soon if they were to prevent an institutionalization of the Weimar system – was through a non-violent general strike. The appeal was published in a revived *Rote Fahne* in Berlin on Monday, 3 March. It was no accident that this coincided with the opening of Lenin's Third International in Moscow.

'The dead arise once more,' proclaimed the editorial. Scheidemann's 'Socialist' government was described, with the usual histrionics, as the 'mass executioner of the German proletariat'. Workers and party comrades were asked to cease their labours, but to remain quietly in their factories. And 'Don't let yourself be drawn into pointless shooting.'[19]

Count Harry Kessler was returning from a trip to Weimar when he heard that the general strike had been proclaimed in Berlin. At first it affected only the newspapers. On waking Monday morning, 3 March, he could hear the trams running. Out in the streets he noticed that the government had placarded the walls with posters announcing that socialism 'is here'. Too late, thought Kessler; 'This could be the start of the second revolution.'[20] The trams came to a halt at seven in the evening. Noske proclaimed the next day a state of siege in Berlin, where 'rules of war' would apply. The shooting began on Wednesday.

Kessler was not an impartial observer of Berlin's March Days. In Weimar, Scheidemann's Minister of Police, Eugen Ernst, had warned him that the major conflagration in Berlin was still to come and that 'nothing less than large-scale blood-letting will suffice to quench it'.[21] Kessler, well connected in government circles, had decided to act.

During his last conversation with Rathenau, on 20 February, when Rathenau had explained from his damask armchair what a splendid system Bolshevism was, though it lacked the qualified people to put in it, Kessler had tried to get him to commit himself to some practical kind of programme that would involve workers' councils. He knew, from his writings, that Rathenau could be sympathetic to this. Kessler had already devised his own plan for a League of Nations that would incorporate all of Rathenau's main ideas. In contrast to what he called the 'Paris League of Nations', based on sovereign states, he proposed an organization of international corporations in which labour, in particular, would hold the key. In Kessler's League the supreme power with respect to war, peace and international law would lie with these international corporations, and especially their ability to call for a general strike. Kessler regarded the 'Paris League' as a barely disguised plan by imperialist states to enslave and pauperize their defeated enemies. One could reject it by offering this alternative, better, plan. There were shades of the fated Second International in Kessler's project; it also bore an obvious resemblance to ideas expressed in Rathenau's books. Between Rathenau, Kessler, Moellendorff and Wissell one begins to get an idea of what the economic planners in Germany were actually seeking: they wanted a world of national and international corporatist organizations where the workers' councils would play a leading role. Their schemes contradicted not only plans in Paris, but also the kind of parliamentary democracy currently being set up in Weimar.

Rathenau thought it would be a mistake for Germany to oppose Wilson's League of Nations, since the hatred the world felt for Germany was currently too strong for her alternative plan to have any success. He proposed, instead, that 'we should seek totally unpolitical contacts, forming a sort of *Salon des Refusés* via inter-party conferences, scientific congresses and similar events'; when the inevitable intrigues and divisions appeared in the League, 'then the moment will have come to disrupt it'.[22]

Kessler thought he could get German opposition to the 'Entente' organized much sooner, and went off to Weimar looking for allies. Through Rudolf Nadolny, a diplomat who, during the war, had developed strong links with the Russian Bolsheviks, he was able to establish a plan with Count Brockdorff-Rantzau, the Foreign Minister.

According to Kessler, Rantzau 'seized on my hint that this could prove a way of accommodation with Russia and the Bolsheviks'. Rantzau's grand design was to form an alliance with Russia against the Entente if the terms Paris offered were unacceptable. 'My League of Nations idea', recorded Kessler, 'was obviously attractive to him mainly as a stepping-stone towards Russia.' Rantzau was ready to open up negotiations with the Independent Socialists and even the German Communists; his only real fear was that such a move might prevent the Austrian *Anschluss* ('attachment') with the German Reich (though this was already an accepted principle in Preuss's constitution), and it could provoke the independence of the Rhineland. Rantzau had by now developed the most total contempt for Erzberger and his Armistice Commission in Spa, which seemed to be opening itself up to the liberal bankers of Hamburg and Hanover – hardly the kind of people a slim, neatly dressed Prussian aristocrat like Rantzau would adopt as associates. Gustav Stresemann, the former National Liberal, prepared a dossier for Rantzau that would put Erzberger to shame, proving he had pushed for the annexation of Longwy and Briey in Lorraine even after his so-called 'peace resolution' of July 1917 (which was perfectly true).[23]

Kessler did not hang around long in Weimar. Weimar, for him, was the capital of music, poetry, sculpture and art, not of parliamentary assembly. The appearance of 'taproom and papal conclave politics' in this beautiful town scandalized him; it was like, he said, a 'chimney-stack in the countryside'. He dozed through Preuss's presentation of the draft constitution – 'tedious, colourless, spiritless, ponderous' – and also attended conferences where the main government figures were present: over there was Erzberger 'with his baggy cheeks and sly, sensual lips'; beyond was Scheidemann, presiding 'in his concertina trousers'; while the rotund Professor Preuss listened – 'a sheer monstrosity': the 'three of them constituted the quintessence of German humdrumness.' What a relief it was for the Count to get back to Berlin and start working on Germany's real future![24]

Count Brockdorff-Rantzau also returned to Berlin in a hurry. Kessler immediately started negotiations with the Independent Socialists, like Hugo Haase. German reconstruction, he explained had to be based on the system of workers' councils. Since the government had shown its hostility to that idea, 'Scheidemann, Erzberger and the Centre Party as a whole must be forced to drop out and be replaced by the Independents.' On Tuesday, 4 March, he reported to Rantzau. He told him that the Independents would probably approach him the next day and 'inquire whether he will undertake the government reconstruction, meaning, properly speaking, the *coup d'état*'. Rantzau 'thanked me effusively and said that he will be at my disposal at any time tomorrow'. Wednesday was when the fighting broke out.[25]

So, at the moment of Berlin's most violent post-Armistice revolt, Germany's Foreign Minister was preparing for a *coup d'état* against a government elected by parliament, and to head a regime of Independent Socialists.

The *Berliner Lokal-Anzeiger* later reported that a proclamation of '*der Räte-republik*' ('the Republic of Councils') had been prepared for Sunday, 9 March, but implied that this was the work of 'Spartacus'.[26] In the weeks that followed everybody blamed weak and isolated Spartacus. But if such a proclamation did exist, it is not unreasonable to suppose that Rantzau and his friends knew something about it – a 'Republic of Councils', open to Russia and in defiance of Paris, was on their programme.

Berlin's bloody week was not the product of class struggle; it was a military mutiny. In February 1919 remnants of the old Imperial Army were still returning to Berlin, as they were to other German cities. The Brandenburg Gate was decorated in fresh fir and ribbon; the bands would line up on Pariser Platz, and the soldiers would come marching in. The papers applauded 'our incomparable Army which has resisted half the world for more than four years and remains unbeaten'. On Sunday, 2 March, it was the turn of the 'heroes' of East Africa to come goose-stepping into the square; photographs show the roofs of the surrounding buildings covered with cheering people. At the same time other soldiers departed, for in the East a war was still going on. Throughout the first three months of 1919 regular reports appeared on 'our war with Poland' and photographs were published of Bolshevik atrocities in the Baltic provinces. Trucks, wagons, artillery and tanks queued up with the soldiers at the railway stations to be shipped off East. One body of armed men carried a huge black flag with a white skull and the words '*Freiwilligen-Corps Brüssow von Berlin nach dem Osten*' surrounding it. The white skull-and-crossbones was the symbol of the Free Corps in Berlin (the swastika had not yet made an appearance). It indicated what they were: buccaneers.[27]

In an attempt to keep this mass of soldiers under at least a semblance of control, Scheidemann's new government continued Ebert's policy of jobs, bread and peace at any price. The Reichsbank continued printing money. Schiffer might have preached the importance of fiscal responsibility, but in his budget of February he asked for 25 billion marks and got it.

Welfare fraud became Berlin's number-one problem. In a trade-union report presented to the government in early February it was formally estimated that 25 per cent of the unemployment benefits handed out in Berlin were illegitimate.[28] The real situation was probably worse. A Criminal Division was set up in the city to survey the unemployment offices. But this was grossly insufficient, because the problem was not unemployed workers doubling up their incomes by queueing with their breadbaskets at two or more district centres; it was the syndicates of soldiers, armed with machine-guns, artillery and mortars. The People's Navy Division still held on to the Marstall, next to the Schloss. They had been paid off in January, and thus kept quiet during the Spartacus Week; but now they were demanding more money. All through Berlin there were barracks and buildings under arms that were also demanding money. One of the most famously corrupt organizations was Berlin's Republican Guard (the *Republikanische Soldatenwehr*), which had been set up in November to defend Ebert's regime. No wonder they all supported the 'council system'; it was through the workers' and soldiers' councils that they channelled their fraudulent demands. When it was reported in the last week of February that Scheidemann's government was preparing to abolish the councils in favour of a parliamentary democracy, a cry of dismay swept through military Berlin. The news of Eisner's assassination provided the spark. The *Rote Fahne*'s call for a general strike fanned the flames. But the Communist Party was a spectator of the events that followed.

The strike began on Monday, the 3rd, with the plunder and robbery of stores around Alexanderplatz, though some rich apartment buildings at the Tiergarten were also affected. The Prussian state government had called Noske to Berlin that weekend and named him commander of the armed forces – which meant essentially the Free Corps stationed on the outskirts of the city. In response to the plunder, on Monday afternoon Noske declared Greater Berlin to be in a 'state of siege' in which the 'extraordinary laws of war will be applied'.[29] Up to that time the strike had been mainly confined to newspapers, which had already failed to appear on Sunday, but now the trams ground to a halt. In the night, armed gangs took over around thirty police stations. On Tuesday there was a meeting at the Gewerkschaftshaus at which worker delegates voted their demands. These included recognition of the workers' and soldiers' councils, adoption of the 'Hamburg Points' in the Army, the freeing of all political prisoners, the establishing of a 'Revolutionary Workers' Army', the dissolution of the Free Corps, and the recognition of the 'Soviet regime of Russia'.[30] In other words, virtually all the demands were military in character. Their formulation was the last major act the Communist Party performed during the general strike.

The gunfights began early on Wednesday morning at the Halle Market, when a detachment of the Lüttwitz Regiment ran into a row of loaded rifles held by the Maybugs, whose barracks were nearby. The battle quickly spread to Alexanderplatz, which, with its Police Presidium on the south side of the square, would be the main site of the struggle for the next few days. The Presidium, held by government forces, soon found itself under siege by the combined forces of rebelling Republican Guard, the People's Naval Division, the Maybugs and sundry other armed groups in Berlin. By Thursday the two sides were exchanging heavy-artillery fire and trench mortars. The defenders of the Presidium thought they could hold out until midday with their supply of 50,000 cartridges. Noske ordered aircraft in to provide them with fresh supplies.[31]

Because there were no newspapers, Kessler went out to observe the fighting for himself. 'At the corner of Königstrasse and Neue Friedrichstrasse a fairly phlegmatic crowd stands behind a barrier erected by the Republican Security Guard and listens to the shooting; there is nothing to be seen.

Bullets are whizzing across the Alexanderplatz and from time to time the dull thud of a mortar can be heard.' He thought the 'crowds do not seem very enthusiastic'. He saw the rebel Republican Guard march with their band down Unter den Linden, while on a corner stood Reinhard's Free Corps among their armoured cars and machine-guns. 'The Republicans passed the enemy unchallenged.' The walls of the city were plastered not with revolutionary declarations but with posters asking, 'Who has the Prettiest Legs in Berlin? Caviar-Mousey-Ball, Evening 6 March.' The ball was probably not a great success, because all the city lights went out at six o'clock in the evening. Kessler thought this signalled the beginning of 'a major operation instead of a guerrilla action'.[32]

It did. By Friday, more than 30,000 troops had entered Berlin under Noske's orders; most of them were Free Corps. The defenders of the Police Presidium had been relieved, and the Marstall had been seized from the sailors – they had been machine-gunned as they fled. 'In all Berlin, a sailor's uniform inspires hatred,' noted the *Lokal-Anzeiger* ominously.[33] Members of the Republican Guard tore off their red armbands to hide their identity. The rebel forces retreated east down Frankfurter Allee.

It was here that the Bötzow Brewery stood. Since the Spartacus Week it had come to be known as 'Eichhorn's Fortress', since it was here that Eichhorn had made his last stand in January before his escape. Eichhorn, wisely, never returned to Berlin. But the rebel forces now adopted this imposing building as their final line of defence. The iron railing that surrounded a nearby park was torn up, barbed-wire entanglements were laid between lamp-posts, anti-tank pits were dug, barricades of overturned lorries and wagons were erected; the brewery and neighbouring houses at Strausberger Platz and on Andreasstrasse bristled with machine-guns.

The end of the 'general strike' was pronounced by the *Rote Fahne* on Friday evening, but, because the main battle in Berlin between the Free Corps and rebel militia had little to do with strikers, workers or the Communist Party, the fighting went on through the weekend. On Sunday, Noske issued an order that 'any person who bears arms against government troops will be shot on the spot' – a free hunting licence to the buccaneers, who roared around the streets in their armoured vehicles, the white skull-and-crossbones painted on their sides. Several Berliners began to wonder where the troops' loyalties lay when the Kaiser's flag was hoisted that day above the Schloss.

On Monday there was an unfounded rumour that rebels had massacred seventy of the government's forces at a police station in Lichtenberg. In fact two had been killed in a gun battle. But it was enough to send the Free Corps off on a spree of slaughter. Flame-throwers were brought in along with their tanks and heavy artillery to deal with the last defenders – or anyone who resembled them. The fighting was essentially over by that Monday night, 10 March.

Noske estimated that around 1,200 died in the fighting during the 'week of bloodshed'. Communist sympathizers place the figure at 2,000. Among the dead was Leo Jogiches, the Communist chairman; he was shot in a police station by a detective called Tamshik. By the third week of March, whole sections of Berlin looked like Soissons on the Western Front. There were gaping holes in the buildings, the barricades had been shattered, shells and broken mortar guns lay in the street, the shop signs on the corner hung from a single nail. Lichtenberg, with troops marching down every major avenue, looked like an occupied city.

That Monday night, sailors of the People's Naval Division were instructed to go, the following morning, to their offices at 32 Französische Strasse to receive their pay and demobilization certificates. Their 'paymaster' was Lieutenant Marloh of Reinhard's Free Corps. By midday the place was so densely packed with people that Marloh's detachment was no longer able to handle them. The lieutenant telephoned Reinhard, and Berlin's future SS Oberführer replied, 'Bullets are the best solution.' Marloh picked out twenty-nine sailors at random, lined them up against a courtyard wall, and machine-gunned them. Marloh intended to shoot another 300, but counter-orders came in from an anonymous source.[34]

Kessler speaks of Wednesday, 12 March, as a warm spring day: 'The memory of those who have been shot during the past few days and who can no longer experience this warmth impinges itself, reluctantly, on the mind.' Rumours of more executions spread throughout the remainder of the week. Kessler regarded the shooting at Französische Strasse as 'one of the most abominable civil war crimes'. Yet he was still committed to the idea of a *coup d'état*. The electricity was turned on again. The cabarets, bars, theatres and dance halls were all doing good business.

Surveying the steel-helmeted pickets of Reinhard's brigade the previous week, Kessler had reflected: 'Perhaps one day traditional Prussian discipline and the new socialist one will coalesce to form a proletarian ruling caste which will assume the role of a Rome propagating new brands of civilization at the point of the sword. Bolshevism or any other label will do. The penurious *Junker* officer has always been a sort of prole.' It was not exactly consistent with Rathenau's wartime dreams, but after the experience of bloody March it was easy to follow the train of Kessler's thought.[35]

3

On 4 March, as Berlin entered its week of violence, Allied representatives from Paris sat down with the German Armistice Commission in Spa to negotiate food supplies. Under terms of the Armistice, the Allies had agreed to 'contemplate the provisioning of Germany . . . as shall be found necessary'. That was not meant to imply that they would pay to feed the enemy. The Allies were short of ships, so many of them having been torpedoed by the Germans. Thus it was logical for the Allies to link the supply of food to Germany to the surrender of her merchant ships. The Germans, never convinced that they had actually lost the war, began to take a hard line, treating their merchant ships as bargaining counters for which they demanded American credit in return.

At Spa, the German side was chaired by an under-secretary of state, Dr Otto von Braun, who had already delivered an unbending pronouncement on ships, food and credit when the Armistice was renewed in February. The issue of credit had made the bankers on the German commission very powerful – among them, Dr Carl Melchior of the Warburg Bank in Hamburg.

The Allied side was chaired by a British admiral, George Price Hope, because of the importance of the shipping issue. But several economists and financiers were also included in the team. John Maynard Keynes was there to represent the British Treasury.

Spa had been one of the critical points in the game of diplomatic ping-pong that had been played out during the closing months of the war. So it was to prove at the opening of the negotiations for peace. Keynes described Spa in March 1919 as a haunted place, an empty watering resort where the 'lords of Germany had suffered, in physical seclusion, the decisions of fate'. He slept and dined in Ludendorff's former villa, on the side of a hill, surrounded by black pines. The inside of the villa was still hung with 'vast and hideous imitations of the late German medieval in tapestry and mural decoration, stiff and bare almost to the point of meanness'. Keynes thought the atmosphere Wagnerian.[36]

Keynes's own attitude at Spa had been shaped by a month of conference in Paris. Though he had one of the best apartments in the Majestic, he regarded Paris as an 'awful place'. He was recovering from the flu and felt, like Nicolson, that the 'endless discussions' there were leading nowhere. Though he was the most influential civil servant in the British Treasury, with diplomats and ministers hankering after him, he – like Nicolson – had fallen prey to a sense of powerlessness.

On the day after his arrival in Spa, Keynes descended halfway down the hill, just as Ludendorff had done five months earlier, to the Hôtel Britannique for business. The Allies sat on one side of the table, the Germans on the other. The Germans were unyielding on their ships, their attitude tough; they refused to speak in English, as they had up to now. At one point von Braun, having spoken for a minute or so, paused in the middle of a phrase for the interpretation. But the interpreter was silent: the German had not reached the verb. 'We were wasting our time,' thought Keynes; it was Paris again. He imagined that there must be some way in which to break down the formality of the conference, pierce the barrier of language and get to the truth. 'I looked across the table at Melchior . . .'[37]

A chain of events had brought the Allies and the Germans to Spa. Because of the continuing war between the Poles and the Germans, Lloyd George had demanded, for the February renewal of the Armistice, the imposed disarmament of Germany. Foch had pointed out that the disarmament of an enemy nation was not an easy thing to achieve; it would be easier, he argued, simply to maintain the Allied superiority in armed force. But Lloyd George had promised his electorate the abolition of conscript armies, so he insisted on German disarmament. Wilson was not in as great a hurry to demobilize his armies as Lloyd George; his own electoral concern was the great American agricultural surplus that had been linked to a promise of guaranteed prices to farmers. Wilson therefore took up the economics of German disarmament: he held that the dissolution of German forces was directly related to her ability to resume an economic life. But, while the Americans pressed for a policy that would foster German economic recovery, they refused to discuss with the European Allies the economic issue that worried the Allies most: war debts. The impression the Europeans thus got was that American pressure was applied with the sole aim of selling off to Germany Mr Hoover's surplus of pigs, without committing the United States to opening any further credit either to the Allies or to Germany. Who was going to pay for this sale?

Allied anxiety over American policy was reinforced at the end of February when there was a run on the French franc. On 19 February Keynes, facing a cut-off of American credit to Britain, had informed Klotz, Clemenceau's Minister of Finance, that he would be suspending British wartime subsidies to her Allies. In despair, Klotz and Pichon, the French Foreign Minister, went over to the Hôtel Crillon and appealed to Colonel House for American intervention. The Americans still refused credit, but they managed – where the French had failed – to extract a promise of £2 million from Lloyd George to tide the French over. The French, with the wealthiest corner of their country destroyed by enemy action, wondered why the British had been so niggardly. In their turn, the British – a creditor nation if the loans to her Allies were deducted from her expenses – wondered why wealthy America was refusing help: why should Britain always foot the bill? The Americans rather feebly explained that it was because American credit required the authorization of Congress, now (after the disastrous mid-term elections of November 1918) considered a political impossibility. That was odd, thought the British: Lloyd George had granted his emergency loan without consulting Parliament. American inaction was regarded in Britain as a sign of political frailty.[38]

The currency crisis, combined with the disagreements about German disarmament, not only aggravated the deadlock in the Reparations Commission at Paris, it also led to a total separation of economic issues from military ones – no small development for a conference on peace. Britain, in demanding an imposed German disarmament, had placed herself uncomfortably between partners that had opposite attitudes on how to achieve it: the Americans were ready to trust the enemy; the French were convinced that the only effective peace would be an armed peace. It was the British initiative on disarmament that had led to the decision to prepare final naval and military terms of peace with Germany and to extend the renewal of the Armistice to the moment when these were completed. But where did this leave the financial and economic terms? Deadlocked with the Americans over German war indemnities and cornered on the issue of inter-Allied debts, Britain's first concern was to establish a special relationship with America on the matter of trade.

Since America was unwilling to grant loans to enemy and ally alike, the British Treasury – represented by Keynes in Paris – recommended that German gold reserves should be released to pay for the importation of Hoover's surplus grain and pig products; the food, they proposed, would then be carried to German ports on German merchant ships under the control of the Allies. German ships for American food, paid for with German gold – that was the essence of the British undertaking. The idea was enthusiastically endorsed by the American-controlled Supreme Economic Council in Paris, and particularly by Hoover himself. The plan, if successful, would enable the American government to bypass congressional authorization for credit, get America's agricultural surpluses sold off, and at the same time lighten the burden on British taxpayers.

But the idea was not very popular with the French. They thought the Allies had agreed in London in December that German gold should be reserved for the repair of their devastated regions. In effect, they asked, why should the French pay the bill for the feeding of Germany? Keynes, at the British Treasury, regarded this as an insolent question, ascribing it to their 'narrow intellect', their 'grasping sterility', their Jesuit and Catholic education – Keynes was Low Church, like Hoover. One could afford to pass over French obstruction, thought Keynes: 'It seemed French opposition to the employment of gold must break down in the end, though their faces would have to be saved,' he was to report to his Bloomsbury friends in 1920.[39]

Thus, while the British fought an unremitting battle with the Americans over war indemnities and credit, they threw open a door of friendship on trade. In the face of Germany, Britain took a hard line on disarmament, but was ready to compromise with the enemy on trade. This excited the antagonism of France, on whose soil the most strategically important campaigns of the war had been waged.

This circle of problems had all originated in Allied fears over Germany's continuing war on the Eastern Front. One could not stop Germany from attacking Poland by offering her bread, sugar and pigs, argued Clemenceau. The Americans and the British disagreed with the French premier. That was what initially drove the economic and military issues at the Paris Conference apart.

As for the Germans themselves, riding on their great economic wheel in separate compartments, they could not have presented a less united front.

Nor had they developed much in the way of a policy on how to deal with the West, despite all their talk of the 'psychological method' of diplomacy during the last two years of the war. The Germans were preoccupied with the East and their own domestic affairs.

The ongoing argument, inside Germany, between liberals and planners had created some curious divisions within the ruling classes. The iron and steel producers in the Ruhr had made enemies of machine-builders and other manufacturers by artificially limiting the supply of raw material and then raising prices massively in January and again in February. The manufacturers responded with loud protests against the 'Ruhr magnates', and several came round to supporting the 'socialization' and corporatist programmes of Wissell's Economics Ministry. Many industrialists opposed Schiffer's liberal project of lifting wartime controls. Thus a large section of the German 'bourgeoisie' could be found on the side of the planners and the diplomacy of Brockdorff-Rantzau, who sought an overture to the Bolsheviks in defiance of the West. As for the military, they had long since washed their hands of any responsibility in the negotiations with the West.

German liberals were an educated minority. Moreover, they did not think like liberals in the West. Bankers like Warburg and Melchior had been as nationalist and annexationist as most Germans during the war. But they now argued that Germany's territorial losses made it essential not to restrict trade, since this would simply increase the trend towards separation in lands no longer controlled by the Reich. Germany's recovery, as they saw it, would be determined by her reintegration into the capitalist world.

Liberal bankers had convinced themselves that Wilson, in his Points, Principles and Particulars, had promised Germany a peace based on her capacity to pay and a large-scale international loan. There was nothing in Wilson's vague statements that had ever hinted of such a promise, but the bankers persisted. They deliberately underestimated Germany's capacity to pay in order to keep the bill on indemnities low. They were convinced that their connections could open up the channels of international credit. Politically, they remained in a minority: they could not even count on support from the government in Weimar. But the irony was that America's demand for cash and refusal of credit had temporarily increased the bankers' power during the negotiations with the Allies at Spa: the Germans could now gain credit only through private entrepreneurs – through bankers like Warburg and Melchior, who, through commercial companies and migrant relatives, had established important links with rich America.

Keynes looked across the table at Melchior: the small world of the British Treasury, which excluded all matters political, military and territorial, gazed into the compartment of a German banker. Melchior stared back, 'heavy-lidded, helpless, looking, as I had seen him before, like an honourable animal in pain'.

The morning's conference was adjourned and 'we drifted out towards the urinal to put our coats on'. Keynes pulled Rear-Admiral Hope to one side and whispered, 'May I speak to Melchior privately?' The Admiral was startled but answered, 'Do what you like.' Keynes hung about the hall 'until the French were out of sight'. Then he stealthily climbed the steps of the hotel's central staircase.

A lot of unknown people were hurrying about. Down the stairs came a man whom Keynes recognized as a German secretary. 'I want to speak to Dr Melchior for a moment,' said Keynes. The secretary told him to follow him upstairs and wait on the landing. A few minutes later Melchior appeared. 'May I speak to you privately?' asked Keynes.

Melchior led him down the corridor and into a room where there were three Germans, one battering away on a piano, a second in shirtsleeves bellowing in discordant tenor, a third sprawled on the table. 'Excuse me,' said Melchior, addressing the three, 'but I'd be much obliged if for a few minutes I could have this room for a private conference.' The men roared back at him that this was the hour when music was permitted, then, pointing at his cigarette, told him that smoking was not allowed before five o'clock. 'Here', shrugged Melchior as he turned to Keynes, 'you have a picture of Germany in revolution. These are my clerks.'[40]

Keynes was unaware of what was going on, at that moment, in Berlin. By his own account he was 'quivering with excitement'; Germany was still officially at war with Britain, and his initiative, particularly as a high civil servant of His Majesty's Government, could be regarded as an act of treason. He told Melchior that the British believed his pessimistic assessment of the German economy (Melchior must have smiled to himself) and the urgency of starting the supply of food. The British and the Americans, Keynes assured him, were determined to get the food through, but currently their hands were tied. One of the problems, he explained, was the hard line Germany was taking on ships. The other was French obstruction. If only Melchior could secure a little latitude from Weimar, he 'begged' (Keynes's own word), we could concoct a formula to get the food through and evade the French.

Both men were standing during the interview. Melchior also seemed to be emotionally moved. It was at this moment, Keynes reported, that 'in a sort of way I was in love with him'.

Melchior, who had few friends in Weimar, maintained as deeply pessimistic a tone as he had with the British officers who had visited him in Berlin early in February. It was in part sincerity, in part calculation. He repeated to Keynes much the same story he had told the officers: Germany was collapsing, morality was crumbling, and civilization was growing dim. Melchior and Keynes 'pressed hands', then Keynes rushed off to report to Rear-Admiral Hope.[41]

That afternoon, the formal meeting between the Allies and the Germans was resumed. Keynes sat next to Hope; Melchior sat next to von Braun. Hope took a firm stand, warning Exzellenz von Braun that, if Weimar did not show more flexibility, the negotiations over food could not continue. Keynes recorded with a gibing grin, 'the French derived great satisfaction'.[42]

The representative of the British Treasury was driven back up the hill to Ludendorff's villa. He had a stroll in the pine woods and then sat down for dinner with two British generals. He was just about to retire to bed when a message arrived from the German commission: Weimar could not modify its fundamental position. The Germans were not prepared to deliver their merchant ships.

Keynes claims that it was he who urged the Allied train to leave immediately for Paris: 'We must bring matters to a head and attract the attention of the Great Ones.' They were back in the French capital the next day, Thursday, 6 March, almost at the same time as Lloyd George arrived from London.

Clemenceau had recovered sufficiently to attend the formal conferences once more. Wilson was sailing across the Atlantic on his second official voyage to the Old Continent. Balfour's interregnum in Paris had drawn to a close, and the phase of the Great Ones was about to open. Isolated Moscow was celebrating the Third International. Berlin was bathed in blood.

4

Lloyd George, Clemenceau and House met in the Hôtel Crillon on 7 March for an informal discussion, thereby instituting what became the Council of Four when Vittorio Orlando later joined them. Clemenceau had already set the pattern with the chats in his flat during his convalescence. There was no formal secretariat and so no notes were taken, apart from a few scribblings by Philip Kerr, Lloyd George's private secretary. As a result, the participants could not remember what they had said to each other. This problem was solved only when the polyglot Paul Mantoux was brought in. From 24 March to 28 June he recorded every meeting in French, verbatim.[43]

Their main business was the drafting of the terms of the treaty with Germany, which many had argued should have been the concern of the Conference from the start. House and Lloyd George thought this could be accomplished before the end of March; Clemenceau was more circumspect. One of the predicaments they now faced was the growing detachment of the economic from the territorial and military issues: the economics was becoming abstract; the definition of frontiers lacked a material base.

The Four made an unequal partnership. In terms of sheer economic might, the United States outweighed all the others combined. But many among the Allies considered her military contribution to the war's end minute in proportion to her strength; they were baffled by her subsequent tight-fistedness on credit. And what totally undermined Wilson's credibility in

Paris was his demand, on his return, to revise the Covenant of the League of Nations – something the Allies had never wanted in the German treaty in the first place.

Wilson had spent a very unpleasant fortnight in Washington. His boat had landed in Boston, where he had been greeted by the crowds, but not by Massachusetts's Republican senator, Henry Cabot Lodge. When he got back to the White House he invited, on Colonel House's recommendation, the members of the congressional committees to dinner; the Republicans present complained that the liquor and cigars were not up to the standard of an executive mansion. Lodge made a speech in the Senate criticizing the text of the Covenant and asking his colleagues if they really wanted to endorse a project that guaranteed the independence of every single member state of the League. Wilson responded by holding a luncheon for Democrats, where he spoke in true evangelical form, idealistic and uncompromising. His thinking had not altered since his lectures to the passengers aboard the *George Washington* in December: the peoples of Europe did not trust their own governments, while everyone had confidence in the United States; the League of Nations was the foundation stone of the whole peace – it was the 'heart of the treaty', the 'only machinery', the 'only solid basis of masonry' in it. But the Democrats had been seriously weakened, not only by the mid-term elections, but also by the defection of German-Americans, who did not like what was going on in Paris, and of Irish-Americans, who suspected – correctly, as it turned out – that the text of the Covenant had been written by the British, not the Americans.

Lodge hit back: he introduced on to the floor of the Senate a 'round robin', a defiant declaration signed by thirty-seven Republicans – more than enough to vote down ratification of the Covenant and the treaty. It urged – as the Europeans had been urging since December – that the Conference in Paris get down to the business of a treaty with Germany, and *then* take up 'careful consideration' for a League of Nations. After this the Senate adjourned without voting vital appropriations for the continuation of the American mission in Paris beyond 1 July.

Wilson answered the affront in his traditional manner of 'going to the people'. On the day before he sailed for Europe he appeared arm in arm with the former Republican President, William Taft, on a stage in front of the New York Metropolitan Opera. Taft, however, spoke in praise of Lodge and suggested that several amendments of the Covenant were needed. Wilson, his face angry, his voice hardened, went back to the central 'mechanism' that the Covenant would perform in the treaty. 'When that treaty comes back,' he warned, 'gentlemen on this side will find the Covenant not only in it, but so many threads of the treaty tied to the Covenant that you cannot dissect the Covenant from the treaty without destroying the whole vital structure.' There would be no life in the treaty, he said, if it lacked the League of Nations; 'no man is going to bring back a cadaver with him'.[44]

But Wilson had already realized, within himself, that if his Covenant was going to be anything more than a dead body it would have to be amended. He returned to Paris as a supplicant, not a preacher, to a conference that was at last focusing on the central business of the treaty with Germany.

Aboard the *George Washington* he developed what seemed like a very heavy cold – a chill, a sore throat, sore gums – and remained in bed for half the trip. He accused his doctor of an error of diagnosis. 'I am suffering from a retention of gases generated by the Republican Senators,' he snuffled, 'and that's enough to poison any man.'[45]

Wilson's political embarrassment gave a fresh lease of life to the French. They knew that time was not on their side. They recognized that they could not have withstood the German invader alone – though this is virtually what they had done during the first two years of the war. They placed priority on the steadfastness of the alliance. For the French, the League of Nations was but an extension of this. Clemenceau had no trouble at all in encouraging the two French members of the League of Nations Commission, Léon Bourgeois (who believed that the 'Société des Nations' had been his idea) and Monsieur Larnaude, to obstruct the American campaign for amendment until the French achieved what they wanted: secure frontiers and a military guarantee. In a speech delivered at the Chamber of Deputies, Klotz added another condition: a League of Nations granted the powers of international finance. The idea was promoted in the French press. Unlike the Americans and the British, the French would have been delighted to see economic, territorial and military issues brought together again in one vast project.

The Italians found themselves in an entirely different situation; they had no international project. All that interested them was their frontiers to the north and the east. Lines had been drawn during the negotiations of the secret Treaty of London, when Italy joined the Allies in 1915. But the Allies had in effect abandoned the secret treaties during the pre-armistice negotiations in October 1918. At any rate, the demand that created the greatest passion among all Italians was for the port of Fiume, which lay beyond the most liberal interpretation of the Treaty of London. They wanted lands where the majority of inhabitants were non-Italian – so they were constantly contradicted by the principle of self-determination. The Italians had not a single legal leg to stand on.

The fourth power represented in the Conference's new executive council was that odd conglomerate of nations, colonies and dominions, the British Empire. One eye looked upon Europe, the other veered overseas. Its heart lay in the British electorate, fragmented by the recent collapse of the old two-party system. Great Britain was both a creditor nation and a debtor nation. Her Army had defeated Germany in the last terrible year of the Western conflict. Like France, Britain was ready to take advantage of the American embarrassment. But her aims were not the same. She had security:

she had captured the whole German Navy. She had no territorial ambitions: whatever spheres of influence she sought in the world were now occupied by British armies. She even had money if she played her part well.

Seated between a stubborn Frenchman and a moral American, Britain's Prime Minister had a difficult theatrical role to play. He had no project like the French, no world ideal like the Americans. He might have won a landslide victory in the last election, but he had no party behind him – his huge parliamentary majority could be broken in a day. David Lloyd George, master of pantomime, was entering his golden hour.

In early March the Council of Ten – transforming itself into the Supreme War Council whenever the generals were present – still regularly met at the Quai d'Orsay, though now it sat in Stéphen Pichon's personal cabinet instead of the Conference Chamber opposite. It was a sizeable room all the same, surrounded by great Rubens tapestries of Henri Quatre and Marie de Médicis. On 8 March fifty-nine people were present, among them Keynes.[46]

The delegates were assembled around a steep horseshoe table; their advisers, as usual, crouched behind them. Clemenceau sat inside the table and near the bottom, at his own presidential desk. Foch was at the top, facing the fireplace. To his left were the Americans (including Herbert Hoover), the Japanese (silent, rigid and, by the look of it, unable to understand a word), four uninterested Italians, and, crammed in on the same side, the British. Lloyd George and Lord Robert Cecil were at the table; Keynes and Admiral Hope had taken chairs behind. The French sat opposite. Etienne Clémentel had his brief on trade. The French spokesman for finance and economics was Louis Klotz, who looked very round and bent that day.

Rumour was spreading – thanks largely to Aristide Briand, who wanted his job as premier back – that old Clemenceau was losing his grip. Lloyd George was saying that it now took Clemenceau twenty-four hours to decide things instead of twenty-four seconds, as it did during the war. A bullet in the lung of a seventy-seven-year-old man surely must affect him. Clemenceau, at his desk, had a sad eye.

Many subjects were discussed that Saturday. The blockade in the Adriatic was at last lifted; a Belgian report on the treaty of 1839 was considered; the problem of Latin American states overrepresented on the Economics and Finance Commission was raised. But finally they got down to the matter of ships and food to Germany.

Lord Robert, in a soothing monotone, presented the problem. The surrender of German ships was one issue; the supply of food to Germany was another. The Germans were pledged to the former; the Allies had promised in the Armistice to do the latter. The Germans would have to pay for their food. They could do this through bills of exchange on other countries, through the sale of goods, or through the handover of gold. He didn't say it, but everyone listening at that moment knew it: the whole affair turned on gold.

It took a while for the debate to pick up. The French made a few technical objections to the use of German gold reserves for food. Hoover insisted, against Cecil's initial remarks, that the ship surrender had to be tied to food. The British appealed to the humanitarian spirit and to the threat of Bolshevism in Europe.

Meanwhile, Lloyd George was visibly 'rousing himself'. One always knew when he was about to speak; he would shake his head and fidget in his seat, as if he were going to get up and assault somebody. A little blink of the eyelids. A brief 'Ahem!' Then he would start, with a touch of the Celt in his voice; that yellow material which Lord Robert had just mentioned, for instance, Lloyd George would pronounce 'goold'. 'Goo-oold!'

British soldiers complained that they were occupying a country 'to maintain starvation while the Conference continued to haggle about goo-oold'. He knew that from General Plumer, commander of the British forces in Germany. There were children wandering around the streets half-starved. British soldiers – he shook his head – would not stand that. As long as order was maintained, Germany would act as a breakwater between the Allies and the tide of revolution beyond. But if that breakwater were broken . . . 'I cannot speak for France, but I tremble for my own country.'

Clemenceau lifted his sleepy head. In the Armistice, he responded, no promise had ever been made to feed Germany – 'Almost a promise,' interrupted Arthur Balfour. 'As for Bolshevism,' the old man continued, 'the Germans were using it as a bogey with which to frighten the Allies.' But, he added, his government would be guided by feelings of humanity and Germany must be fed, 'subject to suitable conditions'. Was the Tiger really weakening? Provided the Germans worked for their food – a principle the professed atheist, knowing his Bible, pointed out was in accordance with the teachings of Christ – he said he would even be willing to waive his objection to the use of gold . . .

Just then a messenger entered the room, bearing a telegram from General Plumer. It was like an act of Christ. But it was, of course, the act of David Lloyd George.

'Plumer's cable arrived at the critical moment,' confirmed Lord Riddell in his diary that evening. It came 'while I was seated in the Peace Conference ante-chamber'. Certainly it was not beyond Lloyd George's wild capabilities to have his newspaper friend, Riddell, posted outside the door to ensure that the messenger arrived at the magical moment. The day before, the British Prime Minister had arranged with F. C. Tiarks, a director of the Bank of England and a commercial consultant for the Army of Occupation, to have the telegram sent.

Lloyd George opened the envelope and read aloud its contents. 'Food must be sent into this area by the Allies without delay,' wrote the obedient general. The mortality of women was rising, children were dying, sickness and hunger were spreading. The population in general was in despair. 'The people feel that an end by bullets is preferable to death by starvation.' The bullets were flying aplenty in Berlin that Saturday; this was certain. But the Prime Minister didn't mention the fact. Nobody mentioned it. Attention had been drawn to Plumer.

Clemenceau agreed that food should be furnished. Yet he insisted that the Germans surrender their merchant ships first. The others agreed. Clemenceau wanted Foch to deliver the ultimatum. Lloyd George realized that Foch could make it sound so stiff that the Germans would reject it, as they had at Trier. He switched into humorous mode: stretching out his hands to the Marshal, he said he had such admiration for Foch on the land, but was he equally at home on the sea? They had never travelled across the Channel together. Foch tugged on his moustache and smiled, hinting he had been seasick in the past. Admiral Wemyss, the First Sea Lord, was the man to go. The ultimatum would be delivered by the British.

One item remained: the gold.

Klotz refused to release it, despite Clemenceau's earlier hint. He stood on his little legs and puffed out that the Germans should be allowed to pay for their food in every other way, but not with gold.

'Goo-oold,' replied Lloyd George. Women and children were starving, and here was Monsieur Klotz prating about his 'goo-oold'. He leant forward and held up his hands, like the popular image of a hideous Jew holding a money bag. Klotz was bent over in his seat, silent and shaking. If a Bolshevik state were established in Germany, continued Lloyd George pitilessly, it would erect three statues: to Lenin, to Trotsky, and to ... All round the room people whispered, 'Klotzky.'

Lloyd George turned to Clemenceau and pleaded with him to stop this obstruction – which Clemenceau did, though not without remarking that France had been ruined by war, and now the small guarantees remaining her, a few pieces of gold and securities, were being taken from her.

Keynes was delighted by the spectacle. Monsieur Klotz, he wrote in *The Times* five years later, was 'beaten, almost literally, to the ground by the violence and vivacity of the British Prime Minister's exposure of his folly and incompetence'.[47] Keynes had got his gold.

On 13 March Keynes was in Brussels with Admiral Wemyss, negotiating with the Germans. The Germans were as obstinate as ever. 'Well,' said Rosie Wemyss to Keynes that evening. 'Is this business going to go all right, d'you think? Will they give us the ships?' Wemyss was worried. 'There's got to be no mistake about this, d'you understand? Those are my instructions from the Prime Minister.' Hope had apparently told Wemyss that Keynes had already been in contact with the Germans. 'D'you think', the Admiral went on, 'you could see to it that they don't make any unnecessary trouble? There's got to be no mistake about this, you know.'

At lunchtime the next day Keynes slipped away with a Captain Jack

Grant to the hotel where the Germans were staying. As they entered the lounge, the Germans could be seen, through the glass doors of the dining room, digesting a heavy meal, paper napkins tucked under their chins. Keynes and the Captain hung about until a secretary appeared. 'I want to see Dr Melchior for a moment,' he said. Melchior left his lunch, and the three men took the lift to Melchior's bedroom; the bed was unmade, the chamber pot unemptied, and 'something which seemed like a chemise lay across the bed'. Keynes was blunt: in the afternoon's meeting the Allies would call on von Braun to surrender the ships; nothing could proceed until this was agreed. Melchior's face fell. 'But,' continued Keynes, 'for your own most private information I think it is desirable that you should know what will follow . . .' He told him that the Allies would then be ready to revictual Germany. But the ships had to be promised first, without conditions. 'Can you assure me that von Braun will do this?' Melchior was silent for a moment, and then replied, 'Yes, there shall be no more difficulty about that.'[48]

Within the next two days the details were worked out. On 18 March the first Allied food supplies were rolling into Germany. Old lines of communication, established long before the outbreak of the war, began to open up once more. The trade links of the plain reverted to their ancient pattern. The bankers and the merchant houses counted up their profits again. There was so much to discuss that Keynes managed to persuade the Allies to allow Dr Melchior and his colleagues to move to France as Germany's financial representatives: they were locked up in the Château de Villette, near Compiègne, just north of Paris. Keynes used to motor up there every week for talks.

The ships were delivered; the United States received twice as much tonnage as she had lost in the war.[49] British civil servants transformed themselves into the 'professional suppliers of Germany', as Keynes informed Sir John Bradbury; they seemed unconcerned about the politics of an as yet unsigned treaty. Melchior and his companions were, by early May, no longer the defeated and depressed men Keynes had encountered in Trier back in January: 'They have a backbone again. Their spirits are good and they have an air of being at ease with themselves.'[50]

But the wars in Eastern Europe had still not ended.

5

The final military, naval and air terms of the treaty with Germany went off to the Drafting Commission on 10 March. They were returned to the Supreme War Council on the 17th for further discussion among the heads of government; a hitch had developed over the numbers and the type of army Germany was to be permitted. Lloyd George, who had initiated the whole process by his demand for German disarmament, wanted a long-term-service voluntary army. Foch preferred a short-term conscript army. The debate had the effect of pushing the limit on the size of the German Army down further than anyone had initially intended – to a long-term (twelve-year) volunteer force of 100,000. This was ten times smaller than the actual number of Germans under arms at that time. No one in Paris was apparently aware of the problem of the German Free Corps, though flags of the white skull-and-crossbones flew under the noses of Allied inspectors in Berlin. The Allied military terms were ready for presentation to the Germans by the first week of April.

So it was not at all surprising that Lloyd George and Colonel House expected the whole treaty to be completed well before Easter (20 April). The main hurdle to be overcome was reparations – or 'war indemnities', as the British still insisted on calling them.

The Reparations Commission – with Hughes on 'Valuation of Damage', Cunliffe on 'Germany's Capacity to Pay' and Sumner on 'Methods of Payment' – remained hopelessly deadlocked. On 17 March the three British representatives presented a memorandum to Lloyd George calling on Germany to pay up £1 billion within two years and thereafter to pay annual amounts of £600 million until the year 1961, for interest and sinking fund on the 'remainder of her debt' (which they still estimated at £24 billion). But, the report casually added, they did 'not base our estimate of the annual sum which Germany can pay on statistics', because 'no statistics can really avail'. They had no reliable data. The Americans were pushing in the opposite direction and, but for Allied pressure, would have been happy with no reparations at all. The French, guided by Klotz, were expecting reparations for 'total costs' of the war; Klotz even presented a budget to the Chamber of Deputies based on that assumption. Cunliffe, for one, began to feel most uncomfortable at his Parisian job. 'You are ordered here and ordered there,' he complained to Lord Riddell. 'Do this and do that. But no one ever says, "Good dog!" '[51]

The subject was brought up in front of the Four, but this simply transferred the differences of opinion within the commissions and subcommissions to the heads of government; they were as baffled as the commissions. What was the total amount of damage? How much could Germany pay? How should Germany pay? There was not even agreement on the definition of 'reparations'.

As long as the chain of causes behind it was not broken, the discord would continue. America refused credit, so the European Allies had to cover their debts by a demand on Germany. A critical struggle developed over each nation's share of the total spoil. Lloyd George proposed that 50 per cent go to France, 30 per cent to Great Britain, and 20 per cent to everyone else, including Belgium. France refused to go below 56 per cent.

It was a dizzying, unstoppable merry-go-round. If one nation found its share was insufficient, then the sum total demanded of Germany would have to go up. 'Unless President Wilson was prepared to pool the whole cost of the war, and for the United States to take its share of the whole,' Lloyd George explained to the Imperial War Cabinet, 'he was not in a position to reject our claims for indemnity.'[52] So the sums went up.

The Americans might have been close to the British position on German food and gold, but they were bitter opponents when it came to reparations. They approached the 'obstructive' French.

The link grew out of Balfour's 'interregnum' in February; House had developed a very close friendship with the wounded Clemenceau, whereas he didn't have much to say to Balfour. The American idea was that, if the total claim on Germany were large, France would get a smaller share than if the sum were kept low. In the latter case, priority would be placed on physical damage in the devastated zones – exactly what the Americans understood as 'reparations'. Who knew how much would actually come out of Germany? It would be better for France, argued the Americans, if she aimed at a lower total and a larger share. Moreover, if France could move closer to the American position that the Armistice of November had been a legal contract, based on the Lansing Note of 5 November, then perhaps Wilson could be persuaded to affirm Germany's theoretical liability for the full cost of the war.[53]

This was the origin of the famous 'war guilt' clause. No one in Paris actually spoke of 'war guilt' in the early spring of 1919 – that term was a German invention. The body of experts set up to investigate Germany's violations of international law was formally called the 'Commission on the *Responsibility* of the Authors of the War and the Enforcement of Penalties'. In conversation and correspondence, the British in particular would refer to the subject as 'breaches of the laws of war'. After the Commission submitted its report on 29 March – a report which, while not specifically calling for the trial of the Kaiser, did recommend legal action against the violators of 'usages established among civilized peoples', the 'laws of humanity' and the 'dictates of public conscience' – the Four began their debate of the issue. That they should also set out, at exactly that moment, to solve the reparations problem was no coincidence. Wilson opened the reparations debate on 1 April by saying that they had to prepare for the inevitable German comment, 'At least tell us what the purpose of the reparations will be.' Louis Loucheur, the likeable French Minister of Munitions, began his defence of the French position with the statement: 'Since we accept the principle offered by the American delegation, agreement should be easy.' Both the French and the Americans wanted the reparations chapter of the peace treaty bound up in the language of law.[54]

A real difficulty emerged – one that would haunt the entire twentieth century. What would later be called 'crimes against humanity' did not have a name at the time. Orlando, who was trying to gain points for the untenable Italian position on Fiume, argued that there was no legal precedent for punishing actions outside 'the domestic law of each national entity', a 'subject's obligation towards his sovereign'. Wilson gave a few history lessons – the example of Mary Queen of Scots, of Charles I of England, and of Napoleon – but these hardly supported his case.

Clemenceau was right: they were facing a problem that had no legal precedent, no historical parallel. 'One law dominates all the others,' he said: 'that of *responsibility*. Civilization is the organization of *human responsibilities.*' This lack of precedent to the current situation – 'Was there a precedent in recent generations for the atrocities committed by the Germans during the present war?' – was the Four's best argument. At last an opportunity had arisen to do the unprecedented thing 'in establishing international justice, which up to now has existed only in books'.[55]

'Responsibility', not 'guilt', was the key word. As the debate developed, the four national leaders found themselves struggling over the issue of whether international crimes against humanity were a collective responsibility or should be presented before courts of law as the personal responsibility of those who had given the orders. At Nuremburg in 1945 Allied courts followed the latter course. But reparations demanded from Germany in the 1990s (after a time lapse exceeding even that suggested by Hughes and his colleagues for the reparations of 1919) took the former as their principle. Rathenau had delved into the problem of collective responsibility in his wartime writings. But neither Rathenau nor the Four came up with a clear solution. Nor did any Western thinker in the twentieth century.

The Four eventually pursued both routes, writing them into the final draft of the treaty with Germany. They established the precedent of personal responsibility: 'The Allied and Associated Powers publicly arraign William II of Hohenzollern, formerly German Emperor, for a supreme offence against international morality and the sanctity of treaties.' They also set a precedent on collective responsibility. At the head of the reparations chapter they inserted Article 231: 'The Allied and Associated Governments affirm and Germany accepts the *responsibility* of Germany and her allies for causing all the loss and damage to which the Allied and Associated Governments and their nationals have been subjected as a consequence of the war imposed upon them by the aggression of Germany and her allies.' As Orlando grudgingly admitted to Clemenceau, 'It is history that is taking place here, it is no longer law.'[56]

Britain maintained a low profile during these legal debates – except on the subject of the Kaiser's trial, to which the Prime Minister had committed himself during December's electoral campaign. One might cynically say that this was because Britain had no principles. Britain, indeed, found it extremely hard to salute principles; her policy was at contradiction with itself. To gain her 'fair share' she was obliged to demand a huge total sum from Germany. But, as with her demand for German disarmament, she was reluctant to use force. Britain's aim, said the Prime Minister, was 'to endeavour to secure from Germany the greatest possible indemnity she can pay consistently with the economic well-being of the British Empire and the peace of the world, and without involving an army of occupation for its collection' – a nice little piece of double-talk. A huge indemnity without an army of occupation? 'The economic and financial pressure which we could apply', said Hughes, 'would compel Germany to pay.'[57] Britain placed her faith in her financial houses, not in generals and lawyers. Legal principles were of no great interest to her.

The detail was. In the middle of March, Hughes came up with a magic formula that would substantially increase the bill: German restoration of 'all damage done to the civilian population' – a phrase inserted by the Allies into the Lansing Note of November – was to include separation allowances and invalidity, widows' and orphans' pensions. On this point, Hughes was supported by General Smuts – no extremist, one of the authors of the Covenant, a man much admired by Wilson. Wilson accepted the argument at a meeting of the Four on 1 April.

But many leading British figures in Paris had their private worries about the size of the demands. They included several staff officers, more aware than most that 'Tommy', having fought at the front, wanted to go home and had no desire to play a part in the occupation of Germany. On 18 March, Henry Wilson, Chief of the Imperial General Staff, invited Kerr and Hankey as the only audience to a lecture he delivered on the subject. 'While every exaction on Germany was justified on its merits,' Hankey wrote to Lloyd George the next day, 'the accumulation of these will put Germany in an utterly impossible position.'[58]

That was also the view of most people in the Treasury, headed in Paris by Keynes. The Treasury had no representative on the reparations subcommissions – Lloyd George had an intense distrust of civil servants. But, faced with Hughes's huge demands in his memorandum of 17 March, he did ask Keynes to prepare an alternative report. Keynes, who was still advocating the cancellation of all war debts, came up with a plan for rising annual payments from Germany that would reach a maximum of £400 million a year in 1951–60, yielding a total of £3.8 billion. It was less than a sixth of what Hughes was asking. But Lloyd George did hint to the Americans that he would accept a figure of £5 billion, if only they could get Sumner and Cunliffe to agree.

Lloyd George seems to have been passing through a moderate phase in his reparations policy. This is possibly what encouraged Keynes to put forward other schemes, designed to keep the exactions from Germany down. There was his plan for an across-the-board cancellation of debts, which went back to the previous November. On 11 March, just before leaving for the Brussels negotiations, he recommended that, since no accurate data were available either on the damage inflicted or on Germany's capacity to pay, the treaty should simply avoid fixing the total amount Germany owed; that task could be left to a new 'Reparations Commission' of experts, who would work out the total at a later date. Keynes's initial idea was that, once immediate post-war passions had calmed down, the amount demanded from Germany would be a good deal lower than the kind of figures Hughes was quoting.

This was the plan the Four eventually adopted. It bypassed rather than resolved the problem of the deadlock. The treaty specified no fixed sum; instead, it set up an inter-Allied Reparations Commission that was to assess Germany's total liability by 1 May 1921. And, though the treaty designated a thirty-year period for payment of the debt, it gave the Commission the discretion to prolong this if need be. In addition, Germany was required to pay a large sum in cash (20 billion gold marks, or around £1 billion) before May 1921.

While the Four were deliberating over this thorny issue, Keynes in April was developing another extraordinary project: a 'Scheme for the Rehabilitation of European Credit and for Financing Relief and Reconstruction'.[59] He proposed that the German government issue £1 billion in bonds, one-fifth of which would be used for the purchase of food and materials, while four-fifths would be payable into the reparations account. Interest would be guaranteed jointly by the Central Powers, but would also be underwritten, in certain proportions, by the United States and the Allies. At the heart of the plan, however, lay a hope that the United States would make a loan that would cover the entire bond issue. 'Traded', argued Keynes, 'can only recommence on the basis of credit.' His idea was to remove the obstacles that were now blocking trade and open the power of the bond market – which had already proved itself so significant in the financing of the war. 'It cannot be supposed', he wrote, 'that two great continents, America and Europe, the one destitute and on the point of collapse and the other overflowing with goods which it wishes to dispose of, can continue to face one another for long without attempting to frame some plan of mutual advantage.'

Unfortunately, the United States Treasury envisioned just such a stand-off: no such loan would be available. On 4 May, Keynes complained to Bradbury and to the Chancellor of the Exchequer, Chamberlain, of the 'immediate and violent opposition on the part of Washington'. With America's point-blank refusal to grant a loan, Keynes became disappointed and depressed. 'They would like to assist Germany if they saw a way to do it without helping our reparation schemes,' he noted; 'but France and Italy they would like to see punished.'

Keynes, too, started thinking in terms of national 'responsibility' – not of Germany, but of the United States. 'Washington rejects my proposals', he explained, 'by reason of their strong desire to clear out of European responsibility.'[60]

6

There had been a terrible scene in Downing Street on Friday, 28 February, in the British Cabinet, and it repeated itself when the Cabinet met again the following Tuesday. Though British arms had defeated German forces in the West, though British troops occupied all the former German colonies, though the German Navy was now safely interned in British ports – though Britain's victory at the close of the war had seemed so absolute – the British government could not make up its mind about anything.

Lloyd George had called his Cabinet to discuss a French note that proposed to set up the territories west of the Rhine as a separate Rhenish Republic – something not too dissimilar to the situation that had existed before Castlereagh decided to 'bring Prussia forward' in 1814. Most members of the Cabinet were opposed to the idea, but they could not decide on what kind of military frontier should be established on the Rhine and for how long the area should be occupied. The French wanted to occupy the Saar, as they had in 1814 before Napoleon's escapade in Belgium had caused a revision of the frontiers. The Cabinet were against direct annexation, but they could not decide what should be done with the important coal basin in the area. They could not decide on reparations. They could not decide on Poland. And, when Churchill made an appeal for a firm policy on Russia, they could not decide on that either. While they were meeting, a gloomy report came in from German Agent V.77, who warned that the country was slipping into Bolshevism.[61]

Europe, east of France, seemed a yawning chasm over which Britain had no policy at all. There was, it has to be said, a tradition that had grown up in British politics not to make decisions on the great issues of the moment: let the events speak for themselves, as it were. Keynes describes this attitude very well in several of his portraits of British statesmen at the end of the war. He thought it an admirable quality. Bonar Law, for example, always limited his argument to the pieces 'actually on the board and to the two or three moves ahead which could be definitely foreseen'; it was what made him so difficult to answer in a debate, 'because he nearly always gave the perfectly sensible reply, on the assumption that the pieces visible on the board constituted the whole premises of the argument'. Herbert Asquith was carried to the great offices of state by an 'intellect and rapidity of apprehension' free of 'prejudices and illusion, and an absence of originality and creative power'. He had no fancies to lead him astray; his mind was 'built for the purpose of dealing with the given facts of the outside world.' Then there was Lloyd George himself, a femme fatale in the eyes of Keynes, a 'Welsh witch', an 'enchantress', who simply sang President Wilson's words to a magical tune. Keynes thought Lloyd George went too far in his opportunism. 'Lloyd George is rooted in nothing,' he said; 'he is void and without content; he lives and feeds on his immediate surroundings; . . . he is a prism, as I have heard him described, which collects light and distorts it.'[62]

David Lloyd George was a 'cottage-bred man' from the north of Wales, one of four rare British premiers – along with Disraeli, James Callaghan and John Major – who did not go to a well-known public school, or inherit wealth, or attend one of the 'old universities'. He embodied his country's ambiguities at the close of the war. What did Lloyd George stand for? He cannot be placed easily in a standard political spectrum ranging from Left to Right; the Lloyd George prism embraced all colours. As the fiery orator of the Left in the 1890s he castigated Tories and 'humdrum Liberalism', but once in Parliament and in office he would open his arms to both. Lloyd George was no party man. He was a pacifist during the Boer War – a leading member of the Stop-the-War Committee as well as the League of Liberals against Aggression and Militarism. Yet, despite the disclaimers in his memoirs, he took a warlike attitude towards Germany before 1914 and was a close collaborator of the then Foreign Secretary, Sir Edward Grey; France had no better ally in Parliament, during the years leading up to the war, than Lloyd George.

He was a nationalist. 'As Welsh Liberals we are Imperialists because we are nationalists,' he had written in the early 1890s; Welshmen would die for that national feeling, just as Irishmen would go to the scaffold, or 'wild Nubians' would fall in the sands of the Sahara: 'A government which did not utilize this tremendous force in nature was but a travesty of government after all.'[63] He saw himself as the Parnell of Wales, and he championed the Irish Nationalists as partners in the same cause. But his campaign for Home Rule in Ireland, like his combat for the formal disestablishment of the Welsh Church, fell flat the moment it no longer advanced his political career.

Lloyd George fought for the 'working man': he had a programme that concentrated on redistributing the wealth of Britain, 'trenching' upon the rich and benefiting the poor, and such was the purpose of the 'People's Budget' of 1909, which led to the great constitutional crisis over the House of Lords. He attacked the landowners, 'British Junkers' – a theme he did not forget when he discussed the landowners of Poland in 1919. He defended pensions – a popular concern that found an echo in his demand for reparations. He was one of the best labour troubleshooters Britain has ever known. Yet George Lansbury, editor of the *Daily Herald*, was not the only person to note – as he said to Wilson at the Peace Conference – that 'labour distrusted the Premier because he had failed to keep many of his promises'.[64]

Though Lloyd George worked in the interests of labour, he also happened to be a great friend of businessmen. The dynamic Minister of Munitions of 1915–16 populated his offices with them. He infuriated the generals by bringing Eric Geddes of the North Eastern Railway Company into the War Office in 1915 and, a year later, appointing him Director-General of Military Railways. As Prime Minister, he enraged civil servants by setting up the 'Garden Suburb', a row of temporary shacks in the gardens of 10 and 11 Downing Street, where many a businessman worked.

Was Lloyd George 'The Man Who Won the War'? If he was, he had done it against the advice of most of his generals. Lloyd George was an Easterner, who would commit himself to neither the Western Front nor Gallipoli; after the Somme, he believed the war could be won in the Middle East and ordered a build-up of troops in the Greek port of Salonica, from where they would strike at the heart of the enemy through the mountainous route of Serbia. This won him many friends among Unionists, like Sir Edward Carson and Lord Milner, who thought they could recognize in his strategy the policy of Pitt in the 1790s. Lloyd George, like Carson and Milner, were utterly astonished in late August 1918 when it suddenly became clear to them that the war was being won in France.

The most consistent feature in Lloyd George's politics was outlined in a letter to Margaret Owen, just before he married her in January 1888. 'Men's lives are a perpetual conflict,' he informed her. 'It comes to this, my supreme idea is to get on. To this idea I shall sacrifice everything – except, I trust, honesty.'[65] As it turned out, honesty was the major casualty of the plan.

Behind the plan lay an instinct – one that energized and prompted him, one that gave rhythm to his words: Lloyd George was born into a household of Baptists. Wilson, Hoover, Keynes and Lloyd George all belonged to the same family of Christian Dissenters, and it is interesting to note that Clemenceau's mother was a French Huguenot. Lloyd George might not have lived out his life as an active believer – indeed, it would be more accurate to think of him as a colourful lay preacher constantly haunted by his lack of any faith, a Mr Prendergast, one of Evelyn Waugh's Doubters – but he sang the songs and repeated the sermons. Lord Riddell tells how one evening at dinner in late February 1919 the Prime Minister 'sang Welsh hymns with great vigour, lying back in his chair with he eyes shut. He gave us some stories of Welsh preachers with much dramatic effect – his rendering of some of their sermons very fine.'[66] This drama in his speech was what made him such an accomplished performer: Lloyd George had fire in his belly. Here was the secret of what happened inside him as he 'roused' himself, when he stood up in public and put his 'war paint' on. But if the conflict got too severe, or if it began running against his own interest, that 'war paint' would be speedily removed.

William Dudley Ward, a junior Liberal whip, relates the story of the almost magical way in which Lloyd George could adopt a policy line totally at odds with the one he had been following only minutes earlier. It occurred in Paris at a moment when the Four were discussing the complex question of shipping in the Adriatic. Keynes and Dudley Ward gave Lloyd George a briefing on the subject in the morning and then retired for lunch. Suddenly they realized that their argument was against British interests; they hurtled over to the meeting. Lloyd George was already in full swing. Dudley Ward thought the situation was hopeless. But Keynes wrote down an amazingly brief summary of the new argument on half a sheet of notepaper and passed on to Lloyd George, who glanced at it and proceeded. He seemed to continue along the old line. Dudley Ward looked at Keynes: the situation was hopeless. But gradually the new thought trickled into the Prime Minister's speech; he took plenty of time to make his case, and his conclusion was the diametrical opposite to the case on which he had begun. Nobody else in the room noticed the change. Lloyd George carried the day.[67]

Lloyd George was an omnivorous reader. Lloyd George listened. He could quickly judge if a case was practicable. He always limited himself to the immediate point. He deferred general principles and kept every possible road open. He was a spontaneous actor of British pantomime, whose performance invariably won delighted squeals from his audience.

Lloyd George was sick and tired on his return to Paris in March. The war had turned his hair white, and he had not fully recovered from the flu he had caught the previous autumn. His Tory allies had been giving him trouble during his stay in England. They were claiming that it was they who had won the December elections, not the Prime Minister. Lloyd George threatened to go to the country again. But there was trouble in the collieries, and railwaymen threatened to join the dissent. Odd rumours were coming through of Bolshevik advances in Eastern Europe, and if one listened to the talk of Britain's shop stewards one might easily have thought that Britain was going to be the next country to fall, as Lenin in Moscow was predicting.

There were two by-elections in March, at West Leyton and Liverpool, where the Coalition suffered serious setbacks. The Tories blamed them on the Prime Minister's social programmes. 'I don't intend to play their game,' warned Lloyd George; 'the country is in no mood for delays.' He would push through Parliament his land-acquisitions project for the purpose of cheap housing and have the Conference in Paris finished soon. 'The next five years will be a very trying time for the world,' he told Riddell. 'Civilization in its present form may be severely strained.'[68]

In Lloyd George's civilization, women had a special function: to anoint the wounds and heal the bruises of those men most exposed in the struggle. That task had fallen on the fair shoulders of Frances Stevenson, who had become Lloyd George's secretary in 1912 'on his own terms, which were in direct conflict with my essentially Victorian upbringing'. Their affair was an open secret in Paris. Miss Stevenson speaks in her diary of Lloyd George being 'tired and pale'.

On Thursday, 13 March, the day before Wilson was expected back in Paris, she persuaded the Prime Minister to rest for the morning. In the afternoon they drove down to Fontainebleau together. 'It was a delicious springlike afternoon & the Château looked beautiful.' Primroses and daffodils carpeted the woods and surrounding fields. No wonder Napoleon retired down here when life in Paris got difficult. Fontainebleau was a place for reflection.[69]

Lloyd George was hoping Wilson would join his colleagues in the informal conversations that were under way, and get the 'preliminary treaty' written up in a few days. On Friday afternoon he was at the new 'temporary White House', 11 Place des Etats-Unis, awaiting his arrival. The Prime Minister and the President were going to be neighbours – Lloyd George's flat lay just across the road, on the Rue Nitot – but not for long, hoped Lloyd George. He wanted to tell Wilson how anxious he was to get home and attend to the railway workers' and miners' demands; he couldn't remain in Paris much over a week. But Wilson had changed. He was in a 'very truculent mood', as Cecil put it on his first encounter, 'fiercely refusing to make any concessions to Republican senators'. In the solitude of his ship he had become, if anything, more bitter and determined to push through his world project at any price; he no longer even wanted to amend the Covenant. Lloyd George was furious with him. 'D. says he can think & talk of nothing else but his League of Nations,' noted Frances Stevenson.[70]

As Clemenceau pointed out at a meeting in the Hôtel Crillon that same afternoon, there was surely little point in including the Covenant of the League of Nations in a 'preliminary treaty' with Germany, which was not going to be a member of the League for several years. Wilson's answer to this was that there was not going to be a 'preliminary' treaty. Wilson's insistence on bringing the League of Nations back into the forefront of discussions and inserting the Covenant into the treaty with Germany changed the whole nature of the Conference. Hankey in his notes would still insist that this was a 'preliminary peace conference' that was working on a 'preliminary treaty'. But the 'President was opposed to a preliminary treaty. It would be in his opinion only a waste of time.'[71] Within a week of Wilson's arrival the Conference had lost all appearances of being 'preliminary'.

Lloyd George encouraged this through his intense desire to get back home. All important London was in Paris during Wilson's first week. Asquith was staying at the Ritz. He dashed into the lobby one morning and declared, 'The West Leyton election is the turn of the tide. Things are looking better for us.' When Lloyd George was told this he replied, 'The tide has turned after his ship has gone on the rocks!'[72] Churchill was in town. Bonar Law came over and got a tough lecture from Lloyd George, who said he was not going to bend to Tory pressures: his land-acquisition programme was going to go through quickly; if his Coalition partners didn't like it, then he would appeal to the nation. Lloyd George wanted to be in London and to return to the solid issues of British domestic politics.

Wilson, Clemenceau and Orlando appealed to him to stay. The French were saying that a treaty could be 'signed within the next ten days' which would include just the military and naval and economic conditions. House spoke in terms of 'two weeks'. Lloyd George bowed his head to their appeals. Lloyd George had a plan.

*   *   *

He knew, like the French, that the key to the solution to Allied difficulties was military and economic. The arguments over France's security on her German frontier and over Allied reparations were what had stymied his Cabinet three weeks earlier. Hankey and Kerr – from the 'Garden Suburb' – worked on the problem of French security: offer a military guarantee, they said; work something out with the Americans, who were not keen on a separation of the Rhineland provinces either. Cecil had a private talk with 'truculent' Wilson on 18 March and found him prepared to accept 'something in the nature of an alliance between England and America and France to protect her against sudden aggression', partly because he would never accept a division of Germany along the Rhine. But when Wilson talked to Clemenceau about the proposal he rather spoiled the effect by telling him that such a guarantee amounted to little more than Article X of the Covenant. Nevertheless, the Big Three found they had some common ground on the idea of an Anglo-American military guarantee: Wilson could tie it into his demand for inclusion of the Covenant in the treaty; Clemenceau at last found a response to his one overriding concern, the maintenance of the alliance; and Lloyd George thought he had discovered a way of cutting down the occupying forces in Germany.[73]

On reparations, he already had his solution: no fixed sum in the treaty.

Wilson's activities in the League of Nations Commission were becoming intensely annoying for everybody. Lloyd George complained about his constantly 'reopening questions that have been settled'. Whenever Wilson's name came up, Clemenceau would touch his forehead as if to say that he was a good man, but it didn't all function up there. Even House was getting exasperated. 'The President looked worn and tired,' he noted on Saturday, 22 March. 'He does so much unnecessary work. There was no need for him to sit in the [League of Nations] Committee this afternoon. I could have done it for him.' House thought it was a 'sheer waste of time for him to preside', believed the President's prestige was 'trembling' as a result, and became deeply concerned about 'his future place in history'.[74]

By that time Lloyd George had disappeared for a weekend in sweet Fontainebleau. He told Riddell on Friday that he was going 'to put in the hardest forty-eight hours' thinking I have ever done'.[75] All the main figures of the 'Garden Suburb' were going to enjoy a weekend in the country: Henry Wilson, Cunliffe, Edwin Montagu ('the Assyrian'), Kerr and, of course, 'Hanky-Panky', the unrivalled organizer of mankind, Sir Maurice Hankey.

Saturday's official business was limited to a short and early meeting of the Ten; after less than an hour they adjourned until late on Monday. Wilson spent the afternoon presiding over his League of Nations Commission. Lloyd George and company left for their pleasure outing. To allay suspicion among the delegations and the press, a huge ball was put on at the Majestic that Saturday night. 'A most cosmopolitan crowd,' noted Frances Stevenson in her diary; 'the last touch was put on it when Lord Wimborne arrived with a crowd of wonderful ladies.' As a camouflage to serious business, only Metternich at the Vienna Congress had done better. The public were assured that measures were being taken to stop in the future such invasions of the hotel by revellers – 'otherwise the thing will become a scandal'.[76]

On Sunday, Wilson paid his second formal visit to the devastated regions – this time the area around Soissons. In the morning he looked at what remained of 'Big Bertha', actually one of several enormous cannon the Germans had used to bombard Paris twelve months earlier. The enemy had dynamited the emplacements on their retreat, so that all that was left was torn metal and the great ammunition pits underneath. At his lunch in a half-ruined inn the President's plates rattled when an ammunition dump, a mile away, blew up. Wilson's procession of black cars was stopped before they could enter the western extremity of the Chemin des Dames, because 'we were even then under shell-fire from the exploded projectiles in the burning dump to the north'. Someone had put on quite a show. 'The day has been very instructive to me,' commented Wilson that evening at a press conference in Paris.[77]

Lloyd George and company made a rushed tour of 'the Palace and the sights' on their arrival in Fontainebleau, then everyone was summoned to a private sitting-room in the hotel just opposite the big gates. Lloyd George began by saying that the purpose of the visit was to 'discuss the subject of peace with Germany'. It was going to be a Lloyd George pantomime once again. Each person was assigned a role, as an individual ally, enemy or neutral. Henry Wilson, for example, was assigned both the German and the French points of view; Hanky-Panky got the part of the typical Englishman; Kerr was to act as secretary and editor; Lloyd George would do the summing up. They were given half an hour to prepare, and then, at tea, the performance would begin.

This was how the main ingredients of what would eventually be the Treaty of Versailles were composed. During the half-hour before tea, everyone was left on his own. Hankey went for a quick walk around the palace grounds.

The best two parts were played by Henry Wilson. He turned his military cap back to front, its peak over the back of his neck so that, from the front, he resembled a German officer. Then, with a German accent, he spoke of the threat of Bolshevism to his country.

His next piece was that of a French woman, a shawl over his shoulders, a falsetto Gallic voice. The lady insisted that unenfranchised French women were the real source of public opinion in their country; they had lost so many of their men, they struggled to keep their homes going, they had been occupied by German, British and French troops, their houses were destroyed, their budgets were crippled – they wanted reparation and, especially, punishment of those responsible.

Hankey, as the typical Engishman, spoke of the contribution of sea power to the victory and his distinctive dislike of compulsory military service. The war in the trenches had been a long national agony. Nothing should be conceded to the vague doctrine of 'freedom of the seas'. His country should hold on to the former German colonies and must avoid further military entanglements on the Continent. The 'enormity of their crimes must be brought home to the German people' said Hankey the Englishman, but they also had to be provided 'with the physical force for resisting Bolshevism' – one needed to 'build up the self-respect of the German people so that they may resist the approach of Bolshevism and believe in their own civilization rather than in that which comes from Russia'.[78]

The drafting of a memorandum in two parts – 'Some Considerations for the Peace Conference' and an outline of the peace terms – took up most of Sunday. The group met again in Paris on Monday morning to review Kerr's text, and it was then sent straight round to Clemenceau and Wilson (though it was actually dated Tuesday, 25 March). They had it in their hands before the Ten met, for the last time in their short history, on Monday afternoon.

The preamble, 'Some Considerations', reads like an eighteenth- or early-nineteenth-century essay about grand ideals (one is reminded of Talleyrand's memoranda to the Vienna Congress).[79] 'When nations are exhausted by wars in which they have put forth all their strength,' it opens, 'it is not difficult to patch up a peace that may last until the generation which experienced the horrors of the war has passed away.' The truly hard task is to design a peace that will avoid fresh struggle 'when those who have had practical experience of what war means have passed away'. Averting provocation of the next forgetful generation – 'new Alsace-Lorraines' as Lloyd George would say in conference – was the leitmotif of all that followed. Germany would have to recognize 'responsibility for the origin of the war'; Germany should, however, also be offered the kind of settlement that she could fulfil; the greatest danger was that 'Germany may throw her lot with Bolshevism'. The idea of the treaty must be to offer Europe an alternative to Bolshevism, to provide a 'safeguard to those nations who are prepared for fair dealing with their neighbours, and a menace to those who would trespass on the rights of their neighbours, whether they are imperialist empires or imperialist Bolshevists'.

The terms proposed were divided into seven parts: termination of the state of war, the League of Nations, a territorial section, reduction of armaments, reparation, 'breaches of the laws of war' (on the Kaiser and the individuals responsible) and an economic section. This would be the basic structure of the final treaty.

And a final treaty it clearly was designed to be – not a military or economic 'preliminary': Lloyd George's major concession to the Americans was to put the League of Nations at the head of it. The reparations section was kept open by setting up a 'permanent commission' that would decide later on the actual sum Germany owed the Allies. The security of nations was ultimately to be provided by the League of Nations and a 'limitation of the armaments of all nations'. The memorandum laid out, specifically, that 'there will be no competitive building up of fleets or armies' between 'the British Empire and the United States of America and France and Italy' – 'D. is very annoyed with the American attempt to increase their army & double their navy, while preaching the gospel of the League of Nations,' wrote Frances Stevenson the previous Friday.[80] But, while they waited for the League of Nations to have its full effect on disarmament, French security would be supported by an Anglo-American guarantee: 'As France is naturally anxious about a neighbour who has twice within living memory invaded and devastated her land with surprising rapidity, the British Empire and the United States of America undertake to come to the assistance of France with their whole strength in the event of Germany moving her troops across the Rhine without the consent of the Council of the League of Nations. This guarantee to last until the League of Nations has proved itself to be an adequate security.'

Clemenceau refused to comment on the document when the Four met on Monday and Tuesday, but on Monday, 31 March, he sent Lloyd George his own memorandum. He criticized the idea that the territorial conditions imposed on Germany should be kept moderate – that is, at the expense of Poland and Bohemia – in order to avoid profound feelings of resentment in Germany. According to the Fontainebleau memorandum, the surrender of German colonies was to be total and definitive, the surrender of the German Navy equally total and definitive, and even the surrender of Germany's merchant fleet was going to be total and definitive. All the 'partial and temporary solutions' were apparently reserved for the Continental countries – those who had suffered most from the war. If it were necessary 'to *appease*' Germany, asked Clemenceau, why not offer her 'colonial satisfaction, naval satisfaction, or satisfaction with regard to her commercial expansion'? Why concentrate all the concessions on European territory?[81]

7

Spring brought a fresh spiral of violence to Eastern Europe. Between late March and mid-April Kolchak's forces pushed west towards the Volga, capturing an area larger than Great Britain; but nobody in Paris noticed this advance until more than a month afterwards, by which time Allied support would prove too late. Peasants rose in revolt in the provinces of Simbirsk and Samara to the lovely rural slogan 'Long live the Soviets! Down with the Communists!' Simon Petlioura's Ukrainian nationalists started a reign of terror against Russians of all descriptions, Red and White. The Black Sea port of Odessa was supposed to be the strong point of the French presence in southern Russia, but Clemenceau's policy had been ambiguous ever since the day French troops had landed: 'The inter-Allied action is not of an offensive character,' he wrote to the commander of the Eastern Army on 13 December 1918; 'our aid has the sole aim of assuring the Russians superiority in material over the Bolsheviks.'[82] With fourteen tanks lined round the northern suburbs of the port, four French regiments of the worst quality (brought in from Salonica) along with three Greek regiments and a small unit of Poles protected a population swollen by refugees to over a million. Typhus and starvation undermined morale; Bolshevik propaganda did the rest. After the defences collapsed before the advancing Reds, on 3 April an order came from Paris to evacuate. Odessa became scene of anarchy. French sailors hoisted red flags on their ships, imprisoned their officers, and put out to sea in a sign of union with the Bolsheviks. Lobanov-Rostovsky, a White Russian officer, describes the French 'rolling motor trucks along the breakwater and dumping them into the sea'. Escaping in a Russian steamer, he caught his last sight of Odessa from the deck at night: 'Not a light was visible on shore, but a huge red glare in the sky indicated that fires had broken out all over the city.'[83]

Armies of the 'Succession States', as the states newly formed out of the shattered Russian, German and Austrian empires were known in Paris, were marching out in every direction. Independent Hungary was the one exception. Count Mihály Károlyi – President, Prime Minister and Foreign Minister all rolled into one – had not been able to prevent Czech, Serb and Romanian armies from occupying three-fifths of this former kingdom of the Habsburg crown. A military convention had been drawn up in Belgrade on 13 November, with various demarcation lines. Its severity is often blamed on the French, who had been given the task of policing the area by the Supreme War Council. But there was nothing much that the French could actually do about the division of Hungary: those armies in Hungary were advancing, and the French had few troops available. At first they were lenient with Károlyi's regime, but they could hardly make a stand against Czechs, 'Yugoslavs' and Romanians. At stake was the *cordon sanitaire*, an idea born in the mind of Philippe Berthelot at the Quai d'Orsay. Berthelot wanted to create a corridor of power from the Baltic to the Black Sea that would resist not only Bolshevism but also a repeat performance of German expansionism. The neighbouring states pressed forward, beyond the lines agreed. More lines were drawn. The chiefs of Allied missions in Hungary met and agreed on a 'neutral zone' that would keep the armies separate. But, when the plan was presented to Károlyi as an ultimatum on 20 March, the divided Hungarian government could not agree. Károlyi, who had no political base, handed power over to the Social Democrats, and on 22 March the Social Democrats handed power to a young Bolshevik, Béla Kun. Hungary's 'hundred days' as a Soviet Republic had begun.

The news, rumoured during the weekend, was announced in Paris's newspapers on the morning of Monday 24 March, just as Lloyd George was putting the final touches to his Fontainebleau memorandum. 'At this moment there is a real race between peace and anarchy,' said Wilson when the Four met at three that afternoon, 'and the public is beginning to show its impatience.' He proposed that 'the four of us' take on the most urgent questions, 'such as reparations, the protection of France against aggression and the Italian frontier along the Adriatic coast'. Even Clemenceau agreed: 'it will allow us to speed up the course of business'.[84]

Reparations would be discussed and at least temporarily resolved during three days when Wilson retired to his sickbed in early April. The Italian question was put off until the treaty was practically ready, and, as a result, the Italians nearly missed the signing. What absorbed most of the deliberations in April was the protection of France – France at the west end of the Continent, the west end of the plain, where the outcome of the war had been decided.

The issue was complicated because it involved an agreement on frontiers not just on the west side of Germany – Belgian demands for territory in Luxembourg and Germany, and particularly French demands on the Rhineland – but also the whole eastern side, Bohemia and Poland. It pitted a French idea, the *cordon sanitaire*, against an American idea, 'self determination'. It struck Britain where she was most sensitive, on the idea of her involvement in Europe. It isolated the Italians, who looked only at the Adriatic. It separated idealists, who spoke in universal abstractions, from realists, who read maps. It forced consideration of the origins of the war and the momentum behind the war, what kept it going, what stopped it: the movement of armies across the plain, the exchanges of trade, the settlement of peoples.

The debate on the protection of France began with the most obvious difficulty: that of the Rhineland. This was solved, at least temporarily, in the five days of April (the 14th to the 18th) when Lloyd George was absent, working on his political problems at home. Far more time was devoted to defining the frontiers on the other side of Germany. One area dominated all concerns: flat, frontierless Poland – the 'key to the vault' as Napoleon had put it.

The position each power took in the discussions on the Rhineland would affect its approach to Poland. The Rhineland clause was the longest of all the clauses in the treaty terms proposed in the Fontainebleau memorandum: it confirmed that the area would not be separated from the rest of Germany, though it would have to be demilitarized (meaning not only that no German army could enter it but also that no one in the population could be trained for military service), and it linked this territorial concession for Germany to the Anglo-American military guarantee of France ('in the event of Germany moving her troops across the Rhine'). The Americans in Paris, pushed by House, were already in agreement with the idea of a guarantee and it was actually their proposal that came before the Four on 27 March. It stated that the United States and Britain would 'come immediately to the assistance of France in the case of unprovoked attack by Germany'. That was the slippery expression used by Sir Edward Grey when arranging military talks between Britain and France before the war, for what constituted 'unprovoked attack'? 'I am ready to accept [the idea]', said Clemenceau, 'if aggression is defined as the entry of German forces into the fifty-kilometre zone beyond the Rhine.'[85] Provided Clemenceau's condition was added, France would effectively have her wall across the plain.

But there was wrangling. Foch would not accept the Rhineland as a part of Germany at any price; if the Germans managed to pull off quick raids on the Channel ports, he argued, the Anglo-American guarantee would be next to useless. Lloyd George promised to build a Channel tunnel. He was getting highly annoyed with all this French obstinacy and warned Clemenceau of the basic British dislike of 'Continental commitments' and 'entangling alliances'.[86] The guarantee was becoming dangerously dependent on ratification by the American Senate – which already seemed doubtful – and on the promises of David Lloyd George.

Philip Kerr, Lloyd George's secretary, was one of the staunchest opponents of French plans for a separate Rhineland. This opposition dated back to a small, secret committee which had been set up to study the subject in February, on which Kerr had come into conflict with André Tardieu. Kerr put his entire faith in worldwide disarmament – one can find this philosophy in the Fontainebleau memorandum, which he wrote. By April, disarmament formed the linchpin of British foreign policy, though no one had yet worked out how Britain, without a conscript army, was going to disarm one million Germans (save by vague reliance on 'financial pressures'). The feeling had developed among many British statesmen, who simply reflected a general sentiment in Britain, that Germany would not dare march west again. After such a long and miserable war, people wanted, as Balfour told Clemenceau on 17 March, 'a change in the international system of the world'. At least, in the Western world: if Germany did make a new attempt at expansion, she would concentrate on the chaotic East.[87] For many in Britain, this was something to be welcomed. Germany would not invade France again, Curzon assured the French ambassador in London on 2 April.[88] Lloyd George was delighted to discover that Albert, King of the Belgians, who resented the French presence in Luxembourg, agreed that another German push westward was not likely to happen in a long time; 'Germany won't be very dangerous', His Majesty affirmed, 'before twenty or twenty-five years.'[89]

Not surprisingly, the French managed to patch together the terms on Germany's western frontiers with Colonel House while Lloyd George was in London. Along with the Anglo-American guarantee, House agreed with Clemenceau on 14 April that the Rhineland would be occupied for fifteen years, with a slow withdrawal of forces after five, to ensure that Germany conformed to the treaty. Lloyd George was furious, but there was little he could do about it after House got Wilson's approval the next day.[90]

Lloyd George started nibbling away at the military guarantee. What did 'unprovoked attack' by Germany mean? And, since the American proposal merely spoke of a joint pledge by the USA and 'Great Britain', then the whole 'British Empire' was no longer engaged. There was, furthermore, that little point about American ratification. He refused to commit British troops to the Rhineland for so long. 'All I am asking you for,' replied Clemenceau, 'if absolutely necessary, is to leave me one battalion and a flag.'[91]

A fifteen-year period of occupation went into the treaty.

The bizarre situation in Paris in April was that Lloyd George was now defending the principles of 'Wilsonism' – the new international order, self-determination, justice for all sides – while Wilson himself had apparently joined the camp of military alliances. Since March, he had taken a few steps down from his pulpit. One reason for this was the time he spent seeking amendments on the League of Nations Commission. Another was his health.

Everyone was sniffling in Paris at that time, including the King of the Belgians. On 7 April, Lloyd George had to convoke a meeting of the Four in his bedroom because of a 'slight cold'. But the President seemed to be suffering from something altogether more serious. The heavy cold the President had contracted aboard the *George Washington* just did not go away; Dr Grayson termed it a 'ground-hog case' – a cold that remained buried and inaccessible to his medicines. Wilson became tired and irritable, and, as House explained to Lloyd George, when the President got irritable his irritability remained permanently within him and would never disappear. Shortly after his arrival in Paris, Wilson developed a great deal of pain in his left, blind, eye and nose. Grayson found an abcess developing in his nostril and relieved him after two days. But, while Yugoslav delegates were presenting their case to the Four on 3 April, Wilson was taken violently ill; the conference was summarily adjourned and Wilson went to his room. 'My equatorial zone was considerably upset,' he told Grayson. He had intense pains in his back and stomach, and couldn't control his cough. Grayson announced to the press that the President had 'come very near having a serious attack of influenza' – a strange diagnosis. Today it is thought that he was suffering from some unidentified viral infection. At any rate, three days later he was sitting up in his bed with a 'merry twinkle in his eye', and by 8 April he was back at work. But he remained for the rest of the Conference thin and pale. Baker, the press secretary, spoke of the President as 'toiling terribly' and noticed him tremble as he left meetings.[92]

'He is *worse* today,' Clemenceau reported on 5 April to Lloyd George, who himself was feeling under the weather. Clemenceau doubled up in laughter. 'Do you know his doctor? Couldn't you get round to him and bribe him? . . .'[93]

It was during Wilson's absence that the reparation clauses in the treaty were outlined. As House put it to Clemenceau and Lloyd George within a day of Wilson falling ill, 'it was more important to bring about peace quickly than it was to haggle over details'. Thinking of events in Hungary and Odessa, he said, 'I would rather see an immediate peace and the world brought to order than I would to see a better peace and delay.' Clemenceau and Lloyd George agreed. But the speeding up of decisions within the Four meant that a crowd of commissioners, subcommissioners, delegates, young diplomats and secretaries were going to be brushed aside. Already over-worked and now kept totally in the dark about the direction the Conference was taking, they became increasingly resentful. 'There is some slight evidence today', Baker recorded in his diary on 5 April, 'that peace will be made because peace must be made – a peace written on paper and signed by a few old men.' It was people like Baker who were going to write the history of the Peace Conference.[94]

Lloyd George, disappointed over the Rhineland clauses, still had one card to play: Poland. He might have been ready to offer France a 'guarantee' in return for cutting short the British occupation of Cologne and its surroundings, but he was certainly going to steer clear of any commitment to Poland. British government circles, and particularly the Conservatives, feared the spread of Bolshevism; but they preferred to let the Germans do the job of resisting it rather than commit British aid to Poland and the other eastern 'Succession States' – as the action of Baltic Squadron off Latvia in December had already demonstrated.[95] There was no equivalent of a *cordon sanitaire* in Lloyd George's policy. Poland, in the Prime Minister's mind, was a historical failure. He would often draw the parallel between Poland and Wales; just as landowners had been, in his campaign speeches, the cause of ruin in Wales, so were they in Poland. He saw the Polish government as a clique of greedy feudal landowners who had not fought alongside Britain during the war. When the Ten, backed up by experts of the Polish Affairs Commission, moved towards accepting East Galicia and the town of Lvov (Lemberg) as a part of Poland, Lloyd George took strong exception.

The people of East Galicia were Ukrainian, he said: 'Would France, Great Britain and the United States go to war to maintain Polish rule over them?'[96]

Would the West go to war for Poland? A significant part of the Fontainebleau memorandum was devoted to criticizing the Polish Affairs Commission, which had concluded that Poland should retain complete control of the Baltic port of Danzig and the strategic railway running from there down to Warsaw. On the contrary, argued the memorandum, the Danzig corridor should be drawn 'irrespective of strategic or transportation considerations ... so as to embrace the smallest possible number of Germans.' It proposed, in the finest of Wilsonian terms, that 'as far as possible the different races should be allocated to their motherlands'.[97] Lloyd George told the Four that they should not worry too much about Polish sensitivities; the important matter was 'to avoid anything that would make it difficult for the Germans to sign the treaty'.

France, he said, would make war tomorrow for Alsace if it were contested: 'But would we make war for Danzig?'[98]

Lloyd George wanted to apply the same Wilsonian principles to the new state of Czechoslovakia. No, said Jules Cambon, who was fighting an identical proposal from Lansing and Balfour in the Czechoslovak Commission, if this ethnological criterion were applied they would end up with 'a country as discontinuous as the spots on a panther's skin'. On 4 April, Clemenceau, taking advantage of Wilson's absence, proposed that the Four 'maintain purely and simply the old border between Bohemia and Germany'. Lloyd George, in an astonishingly meek mood that afternoon, accepted this. So the Bohemian Germans on the high hills of the Sudetenland would be included in Czechoslovakia.[99]

But there were no old borders in Poland. The strategic case for a greater Poland had been made by Foch ever since the collapse of the Austrian and German empires. He had frequently rolled out his map before the Supreme War Council to demonstrate that flat Poland and Romania were the gateways to East Central and Central Europe, where military defeat had left a legacy of instability. The river Bug in the north and the river Dnieper in the south could provide ramparts against the Bolsheviks; without a navy, they would be effectively locked in. Poland was the more important of the two because it would also be a rampart against further German expansionism.

At last, in late March, the Four approved the transfer of Haller's Army from France to Poland – through the port of Danzig and down that strategic railway line. Lloyd George, following his new Wilsonian line, objected to the use of force; his policy was to appease the frustrations that give rise to militarism and Bolshevism. 'No man is further than I from the militaristic spirit,' replied Clemenceau, and he had his career to prove it. But Clemenceau thought it insane to ignore strategic considerations in the case of the Danzig corridor: 'If we followed this advice, we would leave a sad legacy to our successors.'[100]

Paris in these early spring days was looking increasingly cosmopolitan. Word had by now reached the most inaccessible corners on the planet that the Great Peace was about to be signed, so that every group which had a complaint or difficulty sent out its delegation: Paris was supposed to solve the miseries of the world.[101] Most of the delegations turned up at Baker's press office on the ground floor of the Hôtel Crillon, for they all wanted to see President Wilson, the prophet. Labour leaders, women's suffrage leaders, Orthodox priests, Arabian princes, handicapped *poilus* and homesick Americans asked for appointments. One day the President of the Armenian Republic turned up and talked about the appalling suffering of his people. But the most striking, and certainly the most colourful, were the strange delegations that came from Central and Eastern Europe. On 31 March a party of Polish peasants from the Orowa and Spisz districts of northern Hungary, 'gayly decorated with red embroidery and high cossack caps of black shaggy fur', came into the office. They wanted the 120,000 Poles of the area incorporated into the New Poland, not Czechoslovakia. Was this the same delegation Wilson met in his home on 11 April? Two 'Galacian [*sic*] peasants, accompanied by a Polish priest and a Polish astronomer', were shown into his office. The peasants were 'garbed in a native mountain costume, which had not been washed since they first put it on, and they smelled very strongly of their herds of goats that they had left in their native hills'.[102]

In his reply to Lloyd George, Clemenceau had argued that nationalism could be a source of strength for the 'Succession States' and need not be limited to the rights of Germans and Bolshevik Russians; but economics and strategy should define their frontiers, not 'self-determination'. In the case of Poland, Wilson followed Clemenceau, not Lloyd George, in an odd reversal of roles. This was because of his academic advisers, like Dr Robert H. Lord of Harvard University, as well as the large Polish-American vote back home. When it was learned by the Four that Haller's Army had travelled to Lvov (Lemberg) to seize East Galicia for Poland there was scandal – but only because of Lloyd George. They dutifully sent telegrams off to Warsaw, but there was not a great deal the Four in Paris could do. Warsaw was at war with Moscow; her troops were defending Vilna against the Red Army, and Lvov to the south would provide a second effective barrier. Who in Paris was going to let Poland become Lenin's bridge?

All the same, Lloyd George was hardly prepared to drop his new cause of 'self-determination' in Poland. He turned to the country's western frontiers and argued in favour of the Germans. On 1 April he defended the idea of Danzig being made a 'free city' like the Hanseatic cities of the Middle Ages; 'they flourished at a time when, it seems, international law was more respected than today'. He also thought that the neighbouring province of Marienwerder, the majority of whose inhabitants were German, should be kept in East Prussia – making Poland's corridor to the sea very narrow indeed. Eventually Wilson persuaded him that the fate of Marienwerder should be decided by a plebiscite. As for the Poles, Lloyd George thought that 'it would be a vain hope to satisfy' them; 'My advice is to decide upon a plan and then to summon the Poles.' Which is exactly what happened.[103]

The terms were drawn up by an expert commission. The Free City of Danzig was to be placed under the authority of the League of Nations, though a customs union would formally attach it to Poland; Marienwerder's future would be decided by plebiscite. After the terms were read out, Ignace Paderewski, the Polish Prime Minister, was introduced to the Four on 9 April. With a high forehead, flowing hair and a flash in his dark eyes, Paderewski looked in every way like the concert pianist he was. 'More often one is disappointed when one meets great men who have been greatly praised,' wrote Frances Stevenson, who lunched with him the next day. But that was not the case with Paderewski. 'There are very few people who have ever impressed me as much as he did. I could have listened to him for hours.'[104]

Paderewski did not see the Middle Ages in the same golden colours as Lloyd George. The Poles, he told the Four, had been familiar with German guarantees – 'scraps of paper' – since the tenth century. He recalled a story of how the Grand Master of the Teutonic Order, having signed a treaty with various Pomeranian and Polish princes of the coastal plains, invited them to dinner and had them all murdered. He rejected the proposal to have a plebiscite in Marienwerder. You could do that, he said, if you were settling differences with friends, but 'not with our enemies'. The Four had fears of a German *irredenta* (or lost, unredeemed, territory)? 'However little is taken from Germany,' he warned them, 'there will always be a *Germania irredenta.*'

Lloyd George tried explaining that what he was proposing was a kind of 'home rule for Danzig'. Danzig, he said, would have 'less autonomy vis-à-vis Poland than Canada has vis-à-vis England'. Lloyd George was always looking overseas, and never into the heart of Europe.

Paderewski did not find this very comforting. Poland, with a population of 25 million, needs Danzig, he said; it was 'a matter of life and death'. Germany, with her 60 million, could do without it; she already had Emden, Bremen, Hamburg, Stettin and Königsberg. Why should the Poles be denied her single port? 'I ask you', he concluded, 'to ponder what I have told you.'

Lloyd George's terms on Danzig and Marienwerder went into the German treaty.

By the time most of the terms had been drafted by the exhausted commissioners – who never had time to compare their notes – the Italians began to fidget for Fiume. Orlando had never said very much during the deliberations of either the Ten or the Four. Hankey's notes often don't even include him in the list of those present, though Mantoux's minutes prove he was attending. But Orlando was getting worried. If this was to be a purely German treaty, how was he going to get his Adriatic demands (territories that had been *Austrian*) discussed by the Four before its signature? Orlando insisted. They were the dominant issue of late April. They were the one issue on which Wilson stood firm for the principle of national self-determination – the President treated the Italians with appalling disdain.

The British and the French were more understanding, and they would have supported Orlando in his demands if he had limited them to the terms of the secret Treaty of London. But Orlando would take nothing less than Fiume. On 22 April the entire Italian delegation left in a huff for Rome. Four became Three.

Under the pressure of a mounting press campaign – most particularly in Lord Northcliffe's *Daily Mail* – on the 'lack of progress' at the Peace Conference, the Four had decided on 13 April to summon German plenipotentiaries to Versailles to receive the 'preliminaries of peace' on 25 April. Why out in Versailles instead of in Paris, where the Conference was being held? There was first a question of French pride: the German Empire had been declared in Versailles' Hall of Mirrors by the victors of the Franco-Prussian War on 18 January 1871 (a declaration which nearly didn't happen owing to an unexpected attack launched that same day by the Parisian National Guard). Second, all the administrative machinery of the Supreme War Council, set up in 1917, was still out there. But the most important reason of them all was that Clemenceau was convinced that there would be riot and revolution in Paris if the Germans appeared in full force – he had been mayor of Montmartre in 1871.

The German reply to the summons arrived on 20 April by telegram: Brockdorff-Rantzau announced that on 25 April the German government 'will send to Versailles three representatives from the Wilhelmstrasse, Herren von Haniel, von Keller and Schmidt, to receive the text of the peace preliminaries and to take it home immediately'.

'We cannot meet with these messengers,' Lloyd George immediately retorted. 'This manner of proceeding would be a sign of insolence.' The Four (as they still were on the 20th) informed the German Foreign Secretary that they would accept only fully accredited plenipotentiaries.[105]

8

Versailles might have been an old city of kings, but the Trianon Palace Hotel, on the edge of the park, was a modern republican building. In the last year of the war, when the Supreme War Council sat there, it had been 'Ritzified': the ceilings were high and white, the corridors long and tiled, and in the large dining room on the north side of the building there was not a picture, a clock or a prancing allegorical statue to be found.

Contrary to legend, an effort had been made not to make the Germans feel too awkward at the presentation of the treaty on 7 May. There was the same kind of horseshoe-table arrangement as had been used by the Ten when they met at the Quai d'Orsay, with secretaries and advisers sitting immediately behind the main participants; a separate table at the base of the horseshoe, the position where Clemenceau habitually sat when he chaired the Council sessions, was now reserved for the Germans. This time

Clemenceau was to sit at the head of the semicircle of tables, with the Americans to his right and the British to his left. The French Prime Minister, when he visited the room with Lloyd George and Wilson two days earlier, had specifically noted that he did not want this separate table to resemble a *banc des accusés*. The problem was fitting in enough space behind it for the forty-five journalists who had been invited at the last minute: the Germans' table had to be moved forward in such a fashion that it was now surrounded by the horseshoe, where the twenty-seven delegations of the Allied and Associate powers were to sit. Germany looked isolated – terribly isolated.[106]

The meeting was set for three o'clock in the afternoon. It was hot, 'like the first day of summer'. In the morning the Three had been in Wilson's Parisian living room discussing the problem of the Austrians and the Adriatic when the door had opened and in came the Italian Prime Minister, slinking like a cat to his own empty chair in the corner. 'We were all too stunned to say anything,' Wilson later reported to his secretary, 'and we acted as though he had never been away.'[107]

The crowds that came to watch the procession of grey, green, khaki, blue and black motor cars roll into the driveway of the Trianon Palace Hotel were no larger than those at a wedding of a local prefect. Clemenceau was among the first to arrive, because the chauffeur of his English Rolls-Royce was one of the fastest drivers in France. Orlando and Sonnino turned up smiling as if nothing had happened. All the Allied delegates were seated by three o'clock, except for the Polish Prime Minister, Paderewski. 'He evidently cannot get it out of his head', noted House in his diary, 'that he is not giving one of his great concerts in which the audience is always supposed to be seated before he enters.' He strode in with great élan, throwing his grey mane back as he took his chair; but the effect was entirely wasted, because the public that day were not waiting for Paderewski.[108]

It is not true that most in the room were unaware of the terms of the treaty: they had been read out in summary form the previous day at a 'secret' plenary session, and an outline had been published in the morning newspapers. Nor were its contents to be a complete surprise to the Germans. Edgar Haniel von Haimhausen of the Foreign Office had described the probable peace conditions before a 'Committee for the Peace Negotiations' that had been set up to co-ordinate activities between the National Assembly, Scheidemann's Cabinet and various interest groups – a committee much needed in fragmented Germany. His predictions were amazingly accurate: the treaty would begin with the establishment of a League of Nations (though he thought Germany would be admitted immediately on the conclusion of the peace); Germany would be completely disarmed, conscription would be abolished, and the entire east bank as well as a zone to the east of the Rhine would be demilitarized; Alsace-Lorraine would be annexed by France, but France would gain only certain economic rights on the Saar; Posen would be annexed by Poland, which would also be granted access to the sea; Germany could not expect the return of her colonies. In fact the only chapter in the treaty that was going to surprise German officialdom was that on reparations.[109]

At two minutes past three, as Paderewski was settling himself down, a French usher in black livery and knee-breeches, with a heavy silver chain around his neck, entered the room and announced, '*Messieurs les délegués allemands*'. Everybody in the room rose in silence.

Count Brockdorff-Rantzau – tall, thin and as white as a ghost – led five other men from his Foreign Office, along with a couple of interpreters, to their special table. The Peace Congress of Versailles – a presentation of the terms before the enemy – had begun.

Rantzau represented a different Germany from that of Dr Melchior, the only serious senior contact the Allies had established up till now. Melchior was a commercial man, and he looked West. Rantzau was exactly the opposite. When he had accepted Ebert's offer of the post of Foreign Secretary on 28 December, during the first wave of violence in Berlin, he had laid down the condition that he be allowed to refuse to sign the West's peace treaty. He was an aristocrat, a cultivated man: a planner, like Rathenau, who looked East; a plotter, like Kessler, who was not commited to the iceberg republic that Ebert and Scheidemann were organizing in Weimar. He was also, on Wednesday, 7 May, a very nervous man. Henry White, the American Republican commissioner, reported after meeting him on his arrival in Versailles the previous week that 'he never saw a greater exhibition of nervousness in a diplomat; that his knees literally knocked together, and White thought that he might at any moment faint'.[110]

Clemenceau stood up and made a brief statement: 'The time has come when we must settle our accounts. You have asked for peace. We are ready to give you peace.' He called it the 'Second Treaty of Versailles'. He outlined the procedure, which in fact had already been described to the German delegation several days beforehand, so there was again no surprise. There would be no oral discussion: all observations by the German delegates would have to be submitted in writing, in English and French translation, within fifteen days. Dr Walter Simons, who ran the German delegation's administrative staff (just as he had when the Germans had negotiated with the Russians at Brest-Litovsk in March 1918), wrote to his wife that Clemenceau 'spoke his introductory words in short staccato sentences which he threw out as if in a concentrated anger and disdain, and which from the very outset, for the Germans, made any reply quite futile'.[111]

Many people were nervous. Mantoux, usually a star performer, was agitated and did not translate Clemenceau's speech into good English. The French officer responsible for the German version did even worse. While this was going on, Paul Dutasta moved from Clemenceau's chair down to the Germans to hand them a printed copy of the 80,000-word treaty; Rantzau stood up and took it with a bow, then sat down, fingered briefly through its pages, and pushed it aside. The two German interpreters were wiping sweat from their brows.

To the astonishment of everyone, Rantzau, still seated, then began to read a long speech in German. Occasionally he would pause, to allow his perspiring interpreters time to translate his comments into English and French, which they did very poorly. Clemenceau had a slight smile on his face. Lloyd George 'roused himself' and, in the process, snapped an ivory paperknife he had in his fingers. Wilson took notes with a pencil. Hughes, the Australian Prime Minister, got up and, in a whisper to Clemenceau, demanded that Rantzau respect etiquette by standing up as he addressed the delegates. Clemenceau merely asked the interpreters, practically inaudible, to move closer to the centre of the room.

Nobody who listened to Rantzau could have maintained any illusions about German penitence or willingness to accept responsibility for the war. He did admit 'the extent of our defeat and the degree of our powerlessness'. He recognized 'the intensity of the hatred which meets us'. But Rantzau was defiant. The whole speech was constructed around the theme of 'war guilt' – the question that had obsessed German government circles since 1916. 'The demand is made that we shall acknowledge that we alone are guilty of having caused the war,' he said with his sharp, metallic voice. 'Such a confession in my mouth would be a lie.' Rantzau belonged to the school of history which emphasizes the role of anonymous forces; in that, his ideas had something in common with Wilson's 'silent forces that lifted the tides'. Perhaps the late German government had contributed something to the war, but the underlying long-term cause was 'the imperialism of all European states'. It is possible that Germany's armed forces 'had sinned in their methods of conducting the war', but so had some of the Allied armies. He admitted injustice had been done to Belgium and he offered to make reparations for this as well as a part of northern France. Yes, 'crimes in war may not be excusable, but they are committed in the struggle for victory', whereas the Allies had continued to commit crimes after the signature of the Armistice, in the form of their blockade – as a result 'hundreds of thousands of noncombatants, who have perished since 11 November, . . . were destroyed coolly and deliberately after our opponents had won a certain and assured victory'. And, instead of clearing up the battlefields of France and Belgium by means of a 'clear and businesslike understanding', the Allies exploited German prisoners of war 'in penal servitude'. He assured the delegates that his team would study the document submitted 'in the hope that our meeting may finally result in something that can be signed by all of us'.[112]

The address had gone through several drafts, and shows parallels with a speech Rantzau had made in April before the National Assembly in Weimar.

Nobody to this day has been able to establish who authored it. Its main points were certainly composed long before the terms of the treaty were known, even to the Four in Paris.

One major influence on the 'war guilt' theme had been an academic organization, the Heidelberger Vereinigung,[113] founded in February 1919 in Professor Max Weber's university home. The principles of the association had been laid down by the former Chancellor, Prince Max of Baden. Prince Max had not been idle since his resignation in November 1918; he lectured in the universities, and cultivated some most important friends. He had never abandoned his belief in the German will, which he was sure would rise out of the ashes. He believed the strength of the national will would determine the success or failure of the German delegation's negotiations with the 'Entente'. In a resolution signed in March, leading professors of history, sociology and law declared 'we believe that all the great powers of Europe who were at war are guilty' and that 'the Allies have no right to pronounce judgement in a case in which they themselves are involved'. Such a conclusion was perfectly consistent with Prince Max's 'psychological method of diplomacy'. It was beautifully abstract, avoided the uncomfortable details, and appealed to a state of mind prevalent among academics in Germany at the time. Several, like Max Weber and Walter Schucking (one of the delegates at Versailles), worked at high levels of government. Many maintained powerful links with the press. These would prove decisive in the days that followed 7 May.

'In the hope that our meeting may finally result in something that can be signed by all of us . . .' Rantzau remained seated as his concluding phrase was translated into a Germanic French and an English that had a pronounced American accent. Clemenceau asked if Rantzau had any further observations to make. Rantzau indicated with a finger that he had none. '*La séance est alors levée!*' declared Clemenceau. The Allied delegates began to break up. '*Restez assis, messieurs,*' pleaded Clemenceau. So they sat down and watched the Germans walk out. At the moment he reached the door, Rantzau briefly stopped, turned round to face the Allies, and lit a cigarette.

Rantzau would maintain to the end of his life that he had deliberately remained seated during his address, that it had nothing to do with his nerves. Simons confirms that the matter was decided just before they entered the hotel. But many independent observers remarked that, while Rantzau held his hands fast to the table, his knees quivered so much that he was physically incapable of standing as he read his long, defiant speech. It is also interesting to note that as he walked, Rantzau, like Talleyrand, had a slight limp.

Notes were exchanged aplenty during the following fortnight. The German experts prepared their demands for amendments that, through a French liaison officer, would end up on the desks of the Allied experts. The Allied refusal to alter the terms would usually come back to the Germans by return courier. Most of the German demands were based on the argument that such-and-such a term was a break in the principles of Wilson's Points, or a breach in the promise of the Lansing Note. Most of the Allied refusals were preceded by a preamble on 'the wanton acts of devastation perpetrated by the German armies', or on Germany's 'aggression and her responsibility' (never 'guilt'). An overwhelming majority of these notes dealt with the clauses on Poland – proving once more the significance of the area.

The Germans asked for an extension. The Allies granted them seven more days. On 29 May the Germans sent the Allies a little book, prepared by German printers who had been rushed to Versailles for the purpose. It warned of dire consequences for the world if the treaty were not revised, and focused its attacks on reparations, the territorial losses – and, of course, the question of 'war guilt'.

But Germany's war against the Treaty of Versailles had by now gone beyond the walls of the experts; it had extended into the press, into the parliament and into the streets of German cities.

9

The events of the next seven weeks, between the presentation of the treaty in early May and its signature in late June, proceeded with such intensity that they ought to be compared with the events of July and August 1914: the outbreak of the Great War. They very nearly did result in new war. But, instead, they brought to the western tip of Europe an outbreak of peace.

The two most important features of these events were the howling campaign against the treaty in Germany and the near defection of Britain from the united Allied front. Fortunately for the peace, Rantzau's delegates in Versailles made one fatal error in their attempt to kill the treaty: they thought it would be Wilson who would defect, not Lloyd George.

The tone of the German campaign was set directly after the presentation by a meeting of all the German delegates and their staff at the Hôtel des Reservoirs – Madame de Pompadour's former home, just down the road from the Trianon Palace Hotel. They voted unanimously to reject the treaty unless it was fundamentally revised; some even recommended the delegation's immediate departure for Germany. In a telegram to Reichs President Ebert they reported that the treaty was 'unfulfillable and unbearable', and insisted that the President use these very words.[114]

Up until now the German press had not paid much attention to the Paris Peace Conference; there were too many civil wars to cover. During the week that the presentation was made in Versailles, Noske's Free Corps captured Munich from a small group of Independent Socialists who had set up a workers' and soldiers' republic. In the process, several thousand lost their lives. There were too many victory parades in Berlin going on. There was not much to say about parliament, on the other hand: the National Assembly in Weimar had not met since 15 April, when it had gone into its Easter recess; what political life remained in the national body was abandoned to committees and caucuses. Civil war, no parliament, but many committees – it was a situation similar to that of November 1918. Ebert, following his sound political instincts, decided the time had come to launch another appeal for national unity.

On 8 May he declared a week of national mourning: the peace conditions had caused 'the most bitter disappointment and unspeakable grief to the entire people'; all public amusements were to be suspended; theatres would show 'only such productions as correspond with the seriousness of these grievous days'. During the fighting, the cabarets and bars had been a place to hide body and soul; at the time of the peace announcement, all that was left was the streets. Scheidemann, the Chancellor, announced that the terms were a 'sentence of death' for Germany. The co-ordinating Committee for the Peace Negotiations summoned the National Assembly to a special session in Berlin on the 12th.[115]

There were huge demonstrations. It was claimed that as many as 200,000 gathered outside the Reichstag on 15 May. Colonial Secretary Johannes Bell, destined to be the man who would actually sign the treaty, addressed a crowd on the future of Germany's colonies in Africa. Ebert assured the masses that the government had no intention of signing the treaty in its present form. But in the Siegesallee a few Communists and readers of the party's *Die Freiheit* called for signing at any price.

The special session of the National Assembly was duly held on the 12th. Dr Wilhelm Kahl, an elderly professor of jurisprudence, evoked the sacred name of Johann Gottlieb Fichte, first rector of the University of Berlin, who had so stirred his students in 1813 that they had descended into the streets and thrown Napoleon and his forces out of town. Scheidemann declared that 'the hand should wither' which signed such a shameful treaty; its terms were 'unacceptable'. Scheidemann was particularly angry with the organization of a Polish corridor – such flouting of the principle of 'self-determination'![116]

The press picked up the message. 'Unacceptable! Unfulfillable! Unbearable!' were the headlines decorating the pillar posts. The words were derived from Scheidemann's speech, which simply reiterated Rantzau's note. In the *Berliner Tageblatt* a correspondent at Versailles reported that 'one of the politicians present characterized the general state of spirit thus: "It is the condemnation to death of Germany."' Who could this politician be but Rantzau?

The newspaper articles published in Berlin never contained details, statistics or a hint of the new frontiers. They were written in the same general terms found in the resolutions of the Heidelberger Vereinigung. The 'Entente' was imperialist, intent on imposing its modern system of 'slavery' on German 'civilization'. Entente 'slavery' was seen as 'infinitely more cruel, more barbarous, more infamous' than that of earlier times; it forced, for example, German prisoners of war to work without wages. The wealth of German commerce would be emptied. Private property could no longer exist. Prussia, after centuries of constructive work, was to be wiped off the map with a mere stroke of the pen.[117]

Disappointment was expressed over Wilson's willingness to accept a 'peace of violence' over a 'peace of justice' (a distinction that had its origin in the Heidelberger Vereinigung). But the anger was aimed at 'England' and France. A notable shift of emphasis in German propaganda took place during the 'week of mourning'. England still had her responsibilities for prolonging the war. 'The "Balkanization" of Europe, which appears in red letters in all the paragraphs of the peace project, is the work of England,' stated the *Vossische Zeitung*. 'She triumphs not only over Germany but also over her own Allies. England triumphs over Europe.'[118] But the theme was no longer *Gott strafe England!* Within days, Germany's first enemy in the world had become France. Versailles had been dictated by 'hyena France'. The French Republic was out for blood; Maid Marianne had gone 'hysterical'. In the cartoons of the period, old, fat John Bull, with his shark's teeth, gave way to a tall, slim, murderous Marianne, with a red Phrygian bonnet on her head and blood on her flimsy white robes.

'One of the first duties of the delegation,' wrote the *Tägliche Rundschau*, 'is to show how heavy was the responsibility of the Entente in the war, in its prolongation and, through that, in its cruelty to humanity. On this subject, our government has a profusion of documents. It is time now to communicate them to the public.'[119] The libraries of Europe and America would be filled with them.

Harry Kessler's diary is blank for this period. 'Since 7 May,' he finally wrote on 12 June, 'I have been so depressed that I was in no mood to write anything.' But Walther Rathenau continued reflecting in his apocalyptic way about society, politics and the problems of 'responsibility'. On 31 May he published in *Die Zukunft* an article called 'The End'. The politicians in Germany, he said, had done a lot a talking since the outbreak of war, and on every major issue they had been proved wrong. They had promised victory, they had said the U-boats would defeat England, they had sworn America would stay out of the war, and when she came in they had announced that Wilson's Principles would save Germany. But their last illusion concerned the peace. They said they would not sign. What then? Germany would be presented with an even worse peace. Rathenau's solution was the most radical of them all: he proposed the abandonment of *all* responsibility. Rantzau, he wrote, should hand over to the enemy governments the duly executed decree dissolving the National Assembly along with the resignation of both the President and his government; he should tell the enemy to take over all sovereign rights of the German Reich, including the whole machinery of government. Let them take on the responsibility of running Germany. 'It would be a case without parallel, the unprecedented downfall of a nation,' wrote Rathenau, 'but at the same time a course compatible with honour and conscience.' The 'Entente', he thought, would soon realize the need for a stable government in Germany 'that could render the country capable of discharging its obligations'. (In a sense, Rathenau was prophetic, for this is exactly what happened in 1945.) Rathenau put his hope in the 'inalienable right of mankind' and the 'clearly predictable march of the events'. As for the last war, it had not brought the revolution that he sought. Because there had been no real revolution, there was no real responsibility. Writing on the first anniversary of the Armistice, he later recognized, 'It was not a revolution. It was simply a collapse. The doors were burst asunder, the warders ran away, and the captive people stood in the courtyard, dazed and helpless.'[120]

Among the first to run away had been the Army. During the May crisis, with every government authority refusing to sign the treaty, the Army was consulted on what to do. Groener, up in Kolberg where he was running his Eastern wars, was summoned to Berlin on 14 May, just as Ludendorff had been summoned from Spa. Groener stated that the Allied attempt to limit German armed forces to 100,000 men was simply 'not discussable' and he demanded that the minimum be set at 350,000 (the number he estimated to be in his *regular army*). The essential issue, the one that had guided him since he had taken over Supreme Command in October, was the 'unity of the Reich'. What Supreme Command actually meant by 'unity' and where it was prepared to fight had been indicated in the shift of its headquarters eastward: as Groener explained in Berlin, the loss of the Rhineland or of Bavaria would be unfortunate, but the loss of the territories in the East would strike at the heart of the Reich.[121]

On his return to Kolberg, Groener came to terms with reality. He made the kind of calculation that Ludendorff, so sure of his power, had never been capable of making. The numbers just did not work out right, despite the strengthening of his forces since January. He would not be able to resist both in the West and in the East; if he turned his troops West to meet the Allies, he could be confronted with an invasion of Poles in the East. A choice had to be made. At that time there was no such thing as 'passive resistance', a doctrine that would be adopted in the Ruhr in 1923. But Groener was comforted by the idea that Britain would not occupy the Rhineland for the sake of the French. So his conclusion was: in the West, sign, because the Allied unity will probably not last; in the East, reserve all forces for the defence of the Reich's 'unity'.[122]

Meanwhile, in Berlin the demonstrations in the streets continued and the press kept up its howl. But the unity of their clamour had broken down. After the Reichstag session of 12 May the Communists and the Independent Socialists took up their banners. 'No more adventurism,' they cried. 'The German government, after the collapse of the old Army has reestablished a NEW MILITARISM,' they proclaimed. 'The Struggle for Peace' was written in red letters on their banderoles. They clashed with the nationalists and the Pan-Germans. In the committee rooms the political debate over whether to sign or not became bitter.[123]

With such pacifist opposition building up on the streets, the centre-Right began to discuss a new theme in the press, that of 'National Bolshevism'. There had already been an inkling of this in the peace projects of Rantzau and Kessler, as well as in the writings of Rathenau. In early March, Kessler, inspired by the sight of Reinhard's steel helmets, had visualized a coalition of 'traditional Prussian discipline' with 'the new socialist one'.[124] During the 'week of mourning', 'National Bolshevism' became a major topic of public debate. For example, Dr R. von Ungern-Sterberg discussed it in the columns of the *Deutsche Allgemeine Zeitung* on 13 May. 'A rapprochement of Germany with Soviet Russia would have as an immediate consequence the stabilization of the situation, currently very shaken,' he wrote. 'We must in the future have economic relations with Russia, our relations should not be compromised by the peace treaty . . . Only England and France could oppose us.'[125] Germany would simply turn her back on the West and rebuild up her empire looking east. It was an idea that pleased the planners. Liberals didn't like it. Scheidemann's government felt uncomfortable with it. *Vorwärts*, which by now was the official government organ, warned that Russia was too poor and too chaotic to be of benefit to Germans. But even in this newspaper the idea won its followers.[126]

In Berlin, there was one brave soul who wanted peace with the West: Matthias Erzberger, the man who had crossed the French line on 7 November. Erzberger, chairman of Germany's Armistice Commission, was one of the few Germans who had actually established a contact with the West; it was through Erzberger's Commission that Melchior had developed his friendship with Keynes. Erzberger detested Rantzau. There was no communication between them. In Scheidemann's Cabinet, Erzberger argued that Rantzau's policy of sending note after note to the Allies was getting nowhere. What would happen if Germany did not sign? Allied armies would enter, north and south Germany would be separated, Poles would invade, and Germany would end up with an even worse treaty than she had now. Erzberger proposed that Germany sign the treaty as presented, with the exception of the 'points of honour', Articles 227 to 231 (the extradition of the Kaiser and his military advisers, and the 'war guilt' clause).[127]

Erzberger was not supported by any other member of the Cabinet. As May turned into June the political situation began to look bleak, as if Rathenau's scenario was going to be fulfilled: the total abdication of German responsibility. Erzberger, in the meantime, had also earned the enmity of the Pan-Germans and the 'National Bolshevists'. 'Erzberger, the defeatist,' they whispered; 'Erzberger, the man who signed the Armistice.'

10

A number of troubling inconsistencies had appeared in the peace policy of David Lloyd George. At the end of March he had enlisted the League of Nations as his charger, yet only a fortnight earlier he had been scoffing at it as a mule that obstructed progress on the treaty. In February he had been the first to advocate the disarmament of Germany, but he had not yet proposed a means of enforcing it. On reparations he had blown hot and cold. 'L. G. spoke of indemnities,' noted Lord Riddell on 5 April, one week after the Fontainebleau memorandum, 'and I thought his tone very changed. Today he said the Germans would have to pay to the uttermost farthing.'[128] His Russian policy depended on which way the White armies blew. He applied the principle of self-determination according to his own taste; it was relevant for Central Europe, but not for Belgium or Italy. Then there was the matter of the treaty itself. He had contributed more than anyone else to its basic form. Yet at the end of May, driven by a veritable hatred he had developed for the Poles, he began to campaign for total revision.

Lloyd George was anything but a weak Prime Minister. He was the most energetic man in Parliament. With the two-party system in complete disarray only he, the non-party man, could have taken leadership of the country. There had been no other man with the stamina to carry the appalling burden of trench warfare in 1916. His very inconsistencies were representative of his island nation, which looked half into Europe and half overseas.

On the other side of the seas lay America, which seemed by language, law and institutions so much more of a natural ally than the powers on the Continent. In London, on 1 May, the Anglo-American Society gave a luncheon at the Calrton Hotel in honour of Mr Josephus Daniels, Secretary of the United States Navy. The Duke of Connaught, representing the King, saluted 'British and American Friendship' and hailed the joint work the British and American navies had done in erecting 'a barrier to protect civilization'. Daniels, in response, claimed the United States Navy flew just one flag – the 'flag of the Anglo-Saxon people fighting for Anglo-Saxon liberties'. 'Hands across the sea and brotherhood with Great Britain,' he ended, raising his glass.[129]

In the month of May, Lloyd George, always sceptical about American intentions, was not convinced by the gesture. Wasn't Daniels's last billion-dollar shipbuilding budget somewhat excessive for 'brotherhood'? The reason for Lloyd George's sudden conversion to the League of Nations was to press for universal disarmament – and, in particular, American disarmament. Brotherhood was not encouraged when, a week later, just as the Allies were sitting down for the presentation of the treaty, the United States laid claim to all German ships interned in her ports. With some of the largest transatlantic liners in the world among them, the acquisition added 654,000 tons to America's ocean-going vessels. It 'will advance this country ten years towards the shipping supremacy of the world' boasted the *New York World*.[130] Many in Britain considered it unjustified, for Britain had lost more than 7.5 million tons in shipping during the war, the United States about 350,000. Britain's one consolation was that she had the entire German Navy – eleven battleships, five battlecruisers, eight light cruisers, and fifty of the latest types of destroyer, or a total of about half a million tons – under her safekeeping. In January, it had all been sent up north, to the Orkneys, where there was a well-protected deep-sea port called Scapa Flow.

As for war debts, if the United States was fraternal it was along the lines of a big brother who refused to pay the bills. Keynes's grand scheme for the 'Rehabilitation of European Credit' got its answer from Wilson on 5 May, at the same time as the naval acquisition was announced. 'Our Treasury and our financial delegates here in Paris', the President wrote, 'are convinced that the plan as presented lacks many elements of economic and financial soundness.' How, he went on, 'can your experts or ours be expected to work our a *new* plan to furnish working capital to Germany, when we deliberately start out be taking away *all Germany's present* capital?'[131] It was a reasonable question, but it addressed only half of the problem: Allied demands for German reparations had grown so huge since the Armistice precisely because the United States had refused to discuss the question of war debts and Allied credit. Keynes thought Wilson's letter 'far too harsh for the human situation facing us',[132] and sank into profound depression.[133] 'The Americans do not really intend to do anything,' he bitterly reported to Bradbury.[134]

Late May and early June in Paris was a time of depressions, resignations and nervous breakdowns. It moulded the state of mind of many a leading figure in the 'generation of disillusionment'.

One of the first to leave Paris despondent was the young William C. Bullitt. He was unhappy that his five-day 'fact-finding' mission to Moscow had not been taken seriously and that Lenin's 'armistice offer' – probably written by Bullitt himself – had not been answered. His one small success had been to get on to a commission that studied the supply of food to Russia. But, since the area was in a state of total war, he did not achieve much here either. On 17 May, as Kolchak's forces marched on Moscow, he resigned. He turned his anger on the whole treaty. 'Russia, "the acid test of good will", for me as for you, has not even been understood,' he wrote in his formal letter to Wilson. 'Unjust decisions of the conference in regard to Shantung, the Tyrol, Thrace, Hungary, East Prussia, Danzig, the Saar Valley, and the abandonment of the principle of the freedom of the seas make new international conflicts certain.' Into this odd and unsavoury pudding Bullitt added the President's own contribution; his manoeuvring 'behind closed doors'.[135] A horrible mixture! The same day Bullitt wrote to House, 'I have come to the conviction that no good ever will issue from a thing so evil.'[136]

Several among the Americans were unhappy. But it was in the British delegation that a real malaise set in. There were many reasons for this. Most of the members were not well housed, they were understaffed and overworked, and they had no sense of direction. The majority disliked the French. The horror of flu stalked every narrow corridor. Great ideals, born during the war, could not stand up to such pressures. Lloyd George consulted more frequently and more widely than any of the other Western leaders. He was a committee man – and the British committees were the best organized in Paris. It had been the British, under Hankey, who had given the Peace Conference form. But the British, under Lloyd George, did not have a policy. On practically every major issue, the Prime Minister's position turned with the winds.

The tensions involved in daily work at the Paris Peace Conference are as difficult to describe as the experience of a soldier on the war front. As in the trenches, the average civil servant, in a tiny, overworked office, never got the 'big view'. Hints of what life was like in the British delegation during May and June are given in Harold Nicolson's diary. With documents and notebooks, he rushes between his offices at the Astoria, the Quai d'Orsay, Balfour's flat on the Rue Nitot and Wilson's residence on the Place des Etats-Unis. He translates German; he draws and redraws maps on the Albanian partition. In the presence of the Allied leaders he feels treated as a child, that no one takes his efforts seriously. He becomes resentful. 'Isn't it terrible, the happiness of millions being decided in that way,' he writes to a colleague in London on 14 May. 'We are all feeling stale and unprofitable,' he enters in his diary on 21 May. He clings to his great wartime ideals: 'I simply long for the moment when I can get away from this disheartening turmoil and start serious work on the League of Nations.' Three days later he is depressed again, writing to his father, 'I am feeling very overworked and dispirited at this hum-bug electioneering sort of peace.' On a few Sundays he manages to get away to Fontainebleau to lie under the lime trees. But the central theme of these seemingly endless weeks of travail is 'accumulated exhaustion', 'general pessimism', 'a feckless day', 'an empty day', 'delay'.[137]

On Friday, 30 May, Maynard Keynes collapsed in a state of nervous exhaustion. 'I am so sick at what goes on that I am near breaking point,' he had told Bradbury on the 27th. 'Partly out of misery for all that's happening, and partly from prolonged overwork, I gave way last Friday and took to my bed suffering from sheer nervous exhaustion,' he told his mother on 1 June. 'I distinctly looked over the edge last week,' he confirmed two days later. He had been intending to resign since at least 14 May, when he spoke of feeling 'worn out' and 'depressed' for the 'last two or three weeks' – in other words, for a period going back beyond the presentation of the treaty. But the Treasury refused to accept his resignation, so he carried on until he was physically no longer able to function. He took a flat on the edge of the Bois de Boulogne, lent to him by a certain Colonel Peel and where he was served by 'an excellent French cook and a soldier servant'. After a week he informed both Bradbury and Norman Davis (of the American Treasury) that 'I am slipping away on Saturday [7 June] from this scene of nightmare, I can do no more good here.' He headed straight for his college at Cambridge.[138]

The 'generation of disillusionment' within the British delegation found many reasons for criticizing the Treaty of Versailles. But the main cause was their own physical exhaustion.

In the last week of May, Lloyd George began backing off from the treaty. He used as a pretext the final German note which arrived, printed and bound, in Allied offices on the 29th. Lloyd George and Riddell, during a dinner together, counted up the words in the first three pages and estimated the full total was about 65,000 words – 'almost as long as a novel', and about as long as the treaty itself.[139] Smuts – whose criticisms of the treaty were giving this South African Boer the reputation of a 'pro-German' – had been arguing since the presentation that the treaty ran against Wilson's Fourteen Points. Several Labour Party members, in particular George Barnes in Paris, were following a similar line. Now they had a book-length German document, filled with compromising quotations from the great American prophet, to support them. Cecil, one of the authors of the League Covenant, admitted that inconsistency with the Fourteen Points was not the only problem; 'Hardinge and his principal assistants [in the Foreign Office] smart under the negligible status to which they have been reduced': the civil servants were in revolt.[140]

Lloyd George called two meetings of the British Empire delegation. The session of 1 June was, according to the Prime Minister himself, 'one of the most remarkable Cabinet Councils ever held by the British Empire.' Nearly the whole British government was there, and all the prime ministers of the Dominions attended. 'The meeting was specially notable for the calm and impartial spirit displayed by every speaker.'[141] They all demanded revision.

Lloyd George, like a kingfisher, picked up every point, digested it, and spat it back in summary form. They should try to get a fixed sum put in the reparations chapter; the period of occupation should be reduced to something like two or three years at a maximum; Germany should be immediately admitted into the League of Nations so that she would be persuaded to reduce her armaments; and the eastern frontiers should be modified – there were too many Germans under Polish rule.

It was the Polish issue that dominated all else. Who, after all, was going to go to war for Poland? 'Poland', said Lloyd George, 'was an historic failure, and always would be a failure, and in this Treaty we were trying to reverse the verdict of history.' Plebiscites would be the solution.[142]

On 3 June, Lloyd George introduced his proposals to the Four, pressing once again the Polish issue. 'I fear that the Poles will use the right of expropriation in order to persecute the Jews,' he said. Wilson objected that most of the areas were sparsely populated and composed of marshes. 'The Highlands of Scotland are also very sparsely populated,' replied Lloyd George – violent Ireland might have been a more appropriate parallel. He claimed that a little more sympathy ought to be shown for the German delegation, since they were not capitalists but represented the Socialists, who were in the majority. His main worry was that the treaty might cause their fall and we could find 'another Moscow in Berlin'.

'It is a little late to say all that,' thought Wilson.[143] He came round to Clemenceau's support. The Americans were actually closer to the French on the matter of reparations. They had plenty of soldiers, and didn't feel anything like the pressure to pull out of Europe in a hurry. And they were in no mood, and never had been, to compromise on naval issues. In fact the only area in the whole negotiations where the Americans and the British had been close was on the question of trade, and that had already been settled. Wilson's sentiment towards the British delegation in May 1919 was not one of brotherhood.

'The time to consider all these questions was when we were writing the Treaty,' Wilson told his own delegation that afternoon, 'and it makes me a little tired for people to come and say now that they are afraid the Germans won't sign.' He was 'very sick' of it. The British, he said, 'are all unanimous, if you please, in their funk'. Some of the most irrational features of the treaty, he argued, had been imposed by the British. Now they wanted to revise it! 'Well,' he concluded, 'the Lord be with us.'[144]

If, instead of trying to separate Wilson from the European Allies, the Germans had concentrated on splitting off 'Lloyd Georgism' from the rest, they might have got a very different treaty: that was Hitler's trick with Lloyd George's successors fifteen years later. But the Germans in the spring of 1919 thought it would be Wilson who would break the front. Wilson stood by Clemenceau, and the front held.

Lloyd George, not one to fall silent, maintained his attack on the treaty for over a week, concentrating his fire on Poland. Paderewski appeared before the Four on 5 June, and Lloyd George had the gall to tell him 'your liberty was paid for with the blood of other people'. The one major concession Lloyd George won was to have a plebiscite in Upper Silesia. 'I cannot hide from you the fact that this decision will be a cruel blow for our people,' Paderewski announced, adding that it was not going to be landowners who suffered – as Lloyd George, with his Welsh model in mind, was assuming – but poor peasants and mineworkers. 'If the results of the plebiscite go against us, it will be a veritable calamity for our people.'[145]

It was a victory of sorts for Lloyd George. The plebiscite that was held in Upper Silesia in March 1921 gave the Germans a majority in three out of every five villages and brought about a new war between German and Polish armies. The League of Nations redivided the area the following

October, which merely increased the appetite of the German *'irredenta'*. Paderewski, by that time, was playing Chopin to the public.

The Allies replied to the German proposals on 16 June 1919. Apart from the eastern frontiers and a promise for a plebiscite in the Saar after fifteen years of French occupation, the treaty was the same as it had been in May. The Germans were given five days to sign. On 20 June the Allies did extend this by another two. Foch ordered a mobilization of the armies on the Rhine.

The German government had returned to isolated Weimar, where Rantzau arrived with his delegation on 18 June. Scheidemann, who had decided he never would sign the treaty, resigned. Ebert attempted to resign, but the Majority Socialist leaders warned him that this would leave Germany in chaos. Rantzau resigned. Ebert asked Gustav Bauer of the Majority Socialists to form a government. Bauer formed a coalition with Erzberger's Centrists and made a statement to the National Assembly, then he resigned. Ebert, desperate, asked Bauer to come back. Which he did. The deadline for a new war in the West was approaching by the hour.

11

Mr B. F. Gribble was a marine artist who had been invited up to the Orkneys to sketch scenes of the German fleet lying at anchor at Bring Deeps, on the north-west side of Scapa Flow. It was an impressive sight, the huge battleships and cruisers moored together in pairs right across the opening of the straits. In the background were the blue-heathered hills of Stromness and Hoy. He had not quite finished his work on Saturday, 21 June, so, instead of joining the British fleet, which sailed out to sea that morning to get in a little torpedo practice, he joined Sub-Lieutenant Leeth on his armed trawler and they motored into Bring Deeps. It was a little before midday when they passed the *Friedrich der Grosse*. The German sailors on board were throwing baggage into small boats roped alongside. 'Do you allow them to go for joy rides?' asked the artist. 'No,' replied Lieutenant Leeth, 'but by jove it looks as if they were.' For a moment he fell grave and silent. The same was going on aboard the *Frankfurt* nearby. The sailors were slinging out their baggage at increasing speed. Some took to the boats. Some jumped into the sea. 'My word,' exclaimed Leeth, 'I've got it. They are scuttling their ships!'[146]

The Lieutenant ordered his men 'to get the cutlasses and rifles ready'. 'Return to your ships at once!' he shouted to the sailors in their boats. 'We have no oars!' they shouted back. 'Here you are then!' screamed Leeth, and he ordered his men to throw out oars. The Germans asked to be taken aboard the trawler. 'Return to your ships at once!' responded Leeth. 'If not, I'll fire on you.'

He opened fire. The Germans could be seen waving white flags. The voice of a German officer could be heard above the rattle of guns: 'You have killed four of my men and we have no arms! I want to look after the men!' There was a pause in the firing. 'You look after them by getting them back to the ships!' shouted Leeth. The German officer: 'We can't go back: they are sinking!' Leeth: 'You must go back and prevent them from sinking!' The German officer: 'It is not our fault! We are carrying out our orders!'

The *Friedrich der Grosse* lurched to its side. The *Brummer* plunged bow first. On the *Hindenburg* the Kaiser's ensign was hoisted, meaning there were still men aboard. In the sea there was a mass of sailors, bobbing up and down in their lifebelts. Some of them tried boarding Leeth's trawler, but one of the crew kept them away with his revolver.

Germans in lifeboats cheered as they watched the ships go down. Gribble noticed that a few of the officers were wearing kid gloves and smoking cigars. Pennants were drifting in the water. Empty lifebelts. Streams of oil.

Not all the ships went down fast. Some, like the *Seyditz*, lay floating on their side like dead grey whales. Leeth was constantly sounding his hooters in order to get other British guardships to come around. They started picking up the freezing men. Two hours passed before the first of the British fleet got back to Scapa Flow from its torpedo practice.

By that time most of the German fleet lay beneath twenty fathoms of water.

That Sunday afternoon on the quarterdeck of HMS *Revenge* – for such was the irony of the name – Admiral Fremantle had German officers and men parade out under an escort of Royal Marines so that he might express his indignation at the deed. 'I take entire responsibility for what has been done,' said Admiral von Reuter in reply.

Was it only his order? The line of command in the German armed forces of 1919 is impossible to trace.

On 28 June 1919, in a stifling Hall of Mirrors, the Treaty of Versailles was signed. A certain Dr Müller and a Dr Bell of the German delegation were the first to affix their names to the thick printed pages of Japanese vellum.

Europe, Europe

1

The wars in Central and Eastern Europe did not stop with the signing of the Treaty of Versailles. Lenin's effort to retake Vilna in the spring of 1919 failed, so the Red Army, equipped with Trotsky's blunt-snouted armoured trains, forced its way into the Ukraine. Denikin's forces retreated south. Petliura's Ukrainian nationalists started negotiating with the Poles, who launched a major invasion of the area in the spring of 1920, grabbing Kiev in early May. It was the eleventh regime the Ukrainian capital had known since the collapse of the Tsarist Empire in February 1917.

But obviously the story did not end there. Tartars, Russians, Ruthenians, as well as Poles, all claimed Kiev to be 'the birthplace of our civilization'. There was an explosion of national enthusiasm within the Russian heartland; even the former imperial commander Marshal Brusilov got caught up in it: he declared that his 'most important task is to engender a sense of popular patriotism', and joined Trotsky's Revolutionary Military Council. Former imperial officers and deserters volunteered for service in tens of thousands. The movement came to be known as 'National Bolshevism', a term the Germans had invented one year before. Kiev was retaken, and by mid-July 1920 the Reds were pouring into Poland. At the Second Congress of the Comintern (as the Third International was now known), held in Petrograd that summer, delegates from every capital in Europe followed the Red Army's advance on large-scale maps while Lenin appealed for the rise of Europe's proletariat. The Polish proletariat did rise – but for Piłsudski, not Lenin. The Russian armies were cut off from their supplies. Stalin's South-Western Army never did get to Lvov. In October it began to snow and the troops dug in: a familiar scenario in the Great War. In the winter, Poles and Russian Bolsheviks negotiated; in March 1921 they signed a treaty at Riga.[1]

Was Riga the end of the European war? It was almost the end of its most significant part, the war on the northern plain. The Russo-Polish war of 1920 was the last major cyclone in the violence, but it triggered off gusts

and eddies elsewhere. One 'minor' war occurred in Upper Silesia, on the
west side of Poland, during the plebiscite that had been initiated by Lloyd
George. German 'residents', many from Bavaria, were brought in, as were
the Free Corps, the Civil Guards, the Military Guards, the Home Defence
units and a special federal Security Police. A secret *Organisation Consul* was
set up in Munich as a kind of general staff designed to co-ordinate these
different units, none of which was formally a part of the *Reichswehr*, or the
'German Army'. In the plebiscite of 21 March 1921, 707,605 men and women
voted for remaining within the Reich, 479,359 voted for union with Poland.
Germany claimed this proved her moral right to the entire province, while
the Poles, with the taste of victory over the Bolsheviks still lingering, insisted
that this proved her right to large parts of it. By May there was serious
fighting. On 20 October the League of Nations, sitting in Geneva, finally
announced a partition, which satisfied no one.

Gusts of violence blew through the Balkans, across Asia Minor and into
the Caucasus. This was in some measure due to the storm in Poland, which
had hindered the western ambitions of the Bolsheviks and turned their
attention south and east. The last of the White forces, under General Peter
Wrangel, were evacuated from the Crimea in November 1920. Two months
earlier the Red Army had seized the oil-rich town of Baku in Azerbaijan.
'The road to Paris and London', wrote Trotsky, 'lies via the towns of
Afghanistan, the Punjab and Bengal.'[2] A Congress of the Peoples of the East
was hosted by the Bolsheviks in Baku that same September; the wealthiest
members of the Asiatic proletariat met in a colourful pageant to hear lectures
on the struggle against Western imperialism. The Bolsheviks supplied arms
to the new nationalist regime in Turkey, and together they cut up Armenia.
The implication of Turco-Russian co-operation was not lost on the Germans,
who looked eastward across Poland with growing resentment.

There was an increase in the incidence of peasant rebellion in central and
southern Russia after 1920. By summer 1921 the destruction of farms, the
requisition of grain and the aridity of nature had created a condition of
mass famine in the Urals, along the Don, in Bashkiria, Kazakhstan, the
southern Ukraine and, most terribly, on the Volga steppe. Villagers, it has
been substantially documented, turned into cannibals.[3]

But Western Europe witnessed peace, if not prosperity. Attention turned
to the old habit of trade; the Reparations Commission, set up by the Treaty
of Versailles, asked of Germany not her punishment, but fiscal responsibility;
and a League of Nations was operating in Geneva.

'Europe is invisible from the Mississippi Valley,' wrote the editorialist of
The Times on 2 March 1921, as Russians and Poles negotiated at Riga and
the Western Europeans prepared a schedule of German payments at a conference in London. The article pointed out that Americans should not be
expected to understand 'Europe', whose 'discontents and wranglings [the

American] knows only as the strange murmurings of a far-off world'.[4]

The *Times* article was right, but it did not go far enough: much of America's misunderstanding of Europe was deliberate. Many of America's leaders, like Hoover, General Pershing and Wilson himself, showed a determination *not* to know about the political and cultural geography of an old peninsula where many nationalities clashed: Europe was feudal, it was ancient, it was not what America was about. If Wilson spoke of 'Europe' with affection, then one knew he was talking about England's Lake Country and the Scottish borderlands, where his ancestors came from. The rest of 'Europe' was very foreign to him. For Wilson, Hoover and Pershing it was America's ideal that mattered, not Europe's material condition. This intentioned, stubborn misunderstanding was what got the American First Army into trouble in the last months of the war. It was what drove Americans to refuse to discuss war debts when in Paris – that was 'Europe's problem', not America's.

Some Americans, on the other hand, did want to talk with Europeans. Colonel House was the most remarkable among them. He earned the ire of the President because of it. Mrs Wilson, in her memoirs, tells how she was shocked at the change in her husband's appearance after his first conference with House on his return to Paris in March 1919. He 'seemed to have aged ten years, and his jaw was set in that way it had when he was making superhuman effort to control himself'. Wilson apparently smiled bitterly at his wife and said, 'House has given away everything I had won before we left Paris. He has compromised on every side.'[5] The memoirs, however, were written twenty years after the event, and Mrs Wilson is not a reliable source. Contemporary documents suggest that the cooling of the relationship was more gradual. House got exasperated with Wilson's obsession with the League of Nations; Wilson was impatient with anyone who placed his priorities elsewhere. By the time the German delegation had arrived in Versailles the two men were barely on speaking terms. When Wilson boarded his train for Brest on 29 June it seemed an effort for him to stare briefly at the little Texan and sternly mutter, 'Good-bye, House.'[6]

Wilson's great battle lay ahead of him – in America, not in Europe. Wilson had never accepted the judgement of European statesmen, European parliaments or even, in the end, the European peoples. The American people, he was convinced, would provide the one solid base from which to launch his world ideal; once he had explained to his people how indispensable the League of Nations was for the peace, the opponents in the Senate would crumble in their embarrassment and the international machinery would be set up.

House had managed to arrange that the first meeting of the League, presided over by Wilson himself, would take place in Washington immediately after the Senate's ratification. House's English friend Sir William Wiseman called on the White House on 18 July, shortly after Wilson's return. 'I ask nothing better', said the President, 'than to lay my case before the American people.' But Wiseman noticed that his face was drawn and grey and twitching.[7]

The senators certainly didn't look as if they were about to capitulate. Philander Knox and Albert B. Fall passed embarrassing amendments. Elihu Root stated that Article X, requiring member states to 'respect and preserve' their fellow members from external aggression, violated the belief that the United States best served the interests of the world by preserving her ideals untarnished by involvement in Europe's quarrels. The President made a poor show when presenting the Treaty of Versailles to Congress on 10 July. He did not even dare mention the Treaty of Guarantee with Britain and France, though it had been stipulated that this should be presented simultaneously; instead, he sent it by courier to the Senate on 29 July. Henry Cabot Lodge prepared his Foreign Relations Committee for hearings. By August, relations between the Senate chairman and the President had descended to the level of a personal feud.

House was the man who had always conciliated Wilson's adversaries. He had done it with such success in Paris that the United States appeared a more reliable partner in the European alliance than Britain. But Colonel House was not in Washington.

Wilson retreated into his 'system'. The ratification of decisions arising out of the six most complex months of diplomatic dialogue the world has ever known became dependent on the text of the Covenant. The more Wilson insisted, the more the Senate resisted, the more dependent the treaty grew.

The logic was utterly mechanical. It was reduced to one item, Article X, on the League's reaction to aggression. 'Article X is the kingpin of the whole structure,' intoned the President, echoing his Princeton days; 'without it the Covenant would mean nothing. If the Senate will not accept that, it will have to reject the whole treaty.'[8] The gauntlet was thrown: surely the Senate would not have the insolence to reject the whole thing.

On 3 September, Wilson set out on the greatest lecture tour of his life. It was a lonely crusade westward, a mirror image of his mission to Europe nine months earlier.

Dr Grayson did not want him to go. Wilson's eyes were red, he complained of 'splitting' headaches, he spent his nights coughing, and had frequent 'asthmatic attacks' during the day. The twitch on the left side of his face was now chronic. He was having trouble with his left arm. His speech became increasingly vague; his confused testimony before Lodge's Foreign Relations Committee on 19 August had shocked everyone, including his friends. Doctors examining Wilson's dossier today estimate a 15 to 45 per cent impairment of the entire person even before he began the trip.[9]

For four weeks the President's train wound its way through America. There was a large group of reporters aboard and a few members of the White House staff; Mr and Mrs Wilson had the last carriage to themselves.

The train passed across the Mid-West, with speaking engagements at Columbus, Ohio, St Louis in Missouri, Kansas City, Des Moines, Omaha, St Paul and Minneapolis. Then it headed over the northern Plains to the Rocky Mountains. Wilson's speeches in the halls of Bismarck and Helena had the same grand swing and rhetorical style that had so moved the world when America entered the war in 1917. There were a few moments when he rambled, the odd phrase that was ungrammatical. The people of Billings, Montana, could not really pick up the connection between Baghdad – in 'Persia' – and the spread of 'Pan-Germanism'.

The train rolled on to the Pacific North-West. More speeches and dinners in Tacoma, in Seattle and in Portland. Down the coast it steamed for a visit to the Bay Area and a rowdy welcome in San Francisco. In San Diego, Wilson returned immediately to his train after dinner instead of spending the evening with his hosts. In Los Angeles he attempted to give the crowds the slip by hiring a taxi instead of using the traditional flag-draped car. After leaving Pueblo, Colorado, on 25 September his train halted for more than an hour while 'Mr and Mrs Wilson took a long walk down a dusty country road by the Arkansas river.'[10] Grayson noted 'a curious drag or looseness' on the left side of Wilson's mouth. The President had made more than forty speeches in three and a half weeks. At nightfall the train turned on to the line for Wichita.

Grayson was woken up by an aide at two o'clock the next morning. He hurried down to the President's private car. Wilson was 'in a highly nervous condition, the muscles of his face were twitching, and he was extremely nauseated'; he had 'a very bad asthmatic attack – the worst that he had had on the trip'. Grayson ordered the rest of his engagements cancelled.[11]

Wilson suffered terribly on the voyage back to Washington. 'I just feel as if I am going to pieces,' he repeated, 'just going to pieces.' Staring out the window, he was completely overcome with emotion; he choked; tears fell from his tired eyes. The train was running so fast that the private car, at the rear, swung from side to side. He was nauseated. At Union Station in Washington he was able to walk without assistance to the automobile awaiting him. He said goodbye to the engineer, the conductor and other train officials; as he descended the platform he turned to wave at the journalists who had accompanied him. The sun – an American sun – was shining with the same brilliance it had had on Armistice Day.[12]

Four days later Wilson was paralysed by a stroke. Grayson diagnosed it, in his daily bulletins to the press, as 'nervous prostration', 'nervous fatigue' or a 'functional', but not organic, 'fatigue neurosis'. The neurological consultant Dr Francis X. Dercum ascribed the paralysis to 'neuresthenia' – a popular disease in the nineteenth century. Both doctors denied that the President was constitutionally disabled. Nevertheless, he lay in his bed for a month, seeing no one save Grayson, the medical experts, a few nurses and Mrs Wilson, who never left the sickroom.

Wilson nearly died in mid-October from a urinary obstruction. Grayson invented a chair back with arms fixed to the bed so that Wilson could perform the simplest government duties. Mrs Wilson read aloud some of the letters he received, passing the reply back to the correspondent; others she kept to herself; and several, evidence suggests, she threw in the waste-paper basket – particularly anything that came from Colonel House. Ray Stannard Baker had lunch with her on 5 November; she looked 'tired & worn after her daily vigil'. She reported that her husband's mind was acute, 'as good as it ever was', but he had not been able to get into the new wheelchair Grayson supplied. Lansing, that same day, wrote how appalled he was by a Thanksgiving Address he had recommended for the President: not a word in it had been changed, and Wilson's signature – written obviously very slowly, with a lead pencil – was 'almost illegible'.[13]

Thanks largely to Lansing and the President's secretary, Joseph P. Tumulty, the executive offices of the government kept turning, the Cabinet met, and most domestic issues – like a coal miners' strike and a veto of Congress's attempt to prohibit the sale of alcohol – were taken care of. But American foreign policy was as paralysed as the President.

As Wilson lay prostrate in the White House, the position up on Capitol Hill over the League of Nations (the sole matter at issue in the treaty) consolidated. The senators were divided into three nearly equal parts: Lodge's intransigent 'reservationists', the Republican 'mild reservationists' and the Democrats. Ratification of the treaty required a two-thirds majority. Every European ally, as well as the British Empire Dominions, had already ratified the treaty. The world awaited America's vote with bated breath.

By early October it looked as if Lodge's group of Republicans was swinging round to a compromise with the moderates. It was the moment for the treaty's defenders to negotiate: the treaty could be saved, but it required revision. All Europeans would have accepted that, as the French ambassador, Jusserand, and the British head of mission, old Sir Edward Grey, made clear.[14]

The great irony of the battle as it shaped up was that Wilson had already accepted Lodge's interpretation of Article X, 'the kingpin of the whole structure', in a note he had sent to the Democratic Senate leader, Gilbert M. Hitchcock: Article X, he confirmed just before embarking on his western crusade, 'leaves each Member State free to exercise its own judgment'. In the United States, that judgement – under the terms of the Constitution – lay ultimately in the Senate.[15] Yet, just two days before his collapse he had declared in Salt Lake City that any amendment to Article X would be a 'knife-thrust to the treaty'.[16] Was there any room for compromise?

Sickness brought out Wilson's worst traits. He became irritable, petulant, jealous of anyone who tried to speak for him or think for him. He heaped vengeance upon his critics, mild and intransigent alike.

One person might have saved him – Colonel House. But House himself was so ill that, when his ship from France arrived in Hoboken on 12 October, he had to be assisted down the gangway: 'a recurrence of the gravel' (kidney stones), he explained to reporters. He remained in his flat in New York, but sent his young assistant, Stephen Bonsal, down to Washington to negotiate with Lodge. A two-thirds majority! Which way would the three parts of the Senate go? Bonsal and Lodge went over the Covenant article by article, with Lodge annotating his copy; he changed roughly forty words and made around fifty insertions – the finished product was milder than anything Lodge had said in public. With these alterations, said Lodge, the Covenant would get through the Senate. Bonsal immediately telephoned House, who let out 'a whoop of joy'. House, on receiving the annotated copy from Bonsal, forwarded it straight on to the White House. It has never been found.[17]

Since September, House had never received answers to his cables and letters from Paris. Two of those letters – one of them containing a critically important plan for resolving European war debts – were opened for the first time when Wilson's papers were handed over to the Library of Congress in 1952. House was most upset when he learned that Mrs Wilson had not informed her husband of his return to America. Baker, after lunching with her on 5 November, was pleased to note in his diary, 'The Colonel's stock has fallen to zero.' Baker was a true believer in the Wilsonian school of thought.[18]

On 6 November Lodge's Committee presented the Senate with fourteen reservations on the Covenant. On the 7th it added a change in the preamble. On the 17th Wilson, who had progressed to his wheelchair, yielded some ground to the 'mild reservationists', but he told Hitchcock that he would veto the treaty if it contained a reservation either on Article X or on the preamble. To avoid this, he urged that the Democrats vote against ratification if these objectionable reservations were included. On 19 November 1919 the Democrats joined Lodge's intransigents and voted the treaty down.

America thus turned her back on Europe. The Treaty of Guarantee, which Wilson had sent in late and on which the French had put so much store, was never even considered at the committee stage; the American Senate had lost all interest in these old frontier matters.

2

Soldiers on the front believed in phantoms; but they would have been astonished to learn that the two great powers to emerge from their sufferings, the United States and Bolshevik Russia, would be governed by ghosts. The inventor of the Wilsonian 'system' of international relations hung on to the White House until March 1921, when he moved out with his wife to a modest home on S Street. Mrs Wilson frequently drove him around Washington in their car. He would sit slumped in the front seat quite unaware of the citizens who waved at him from the pavement. But he did notice soldiers in uniform. On one occasion he saluted 'almost vigorously' a group of them lounging at a street corner. 'Looking back, I could see them staring stupidly at the car,' recorded Stockton Axson, who was sitting in the back seat. 'It was obvious that they had no idea who the broken old man was who had been so attentive to them.'[19] Woodrow Wilson died on 3 February 1924.

The term 'Leninism' first appeared in the Bolshevik press and on the street posters of Moscow in 1923. Lenin was hailed as the great party leader and the head of the state. But Lenin was by this time not even capable of signing his name. He had suffered his first major stroke on 25 May 1922, at the age of fifty-two.

Both Wilson and Lenin appealed to the 'internationalist' spirit of the war generation. They both paid homage to the equally popular idea of national 'self-determination'. That the first idea contradicted the second neither Wilson nor Lenin could admit. In fact the ambivalence is what drove their policies. It pushed Wilson and America into isolation from Europe, because every time events made the contradiction evident Wilson withdrew from his initial position. On the other hand, it impelled Lenin and Bolshevik Russia forward; it increased their ambition not only to enter Europe but to dominate it. 'Internationalism' and national 'self-determination' proved a very seductive mix for the young war generation. That was the crux of 'Leninism'.

At the Second Congress of the Comintern, held in Petrograd in July 1920 as Russian armies swept into Poland, Lenin confirmed the two planks of his doctrine: the 'dictatorship of the proletariat' (an 'iron proletarian centralism' under the control of the Russian Communist Party) and 'permanent revolution' ('armed insurrection' against existing governments with the purpose of replacing them with Communist regimes, preparatory to the establishment of a worldwide Soviet Socialist Republic).[20] He laid down the 'Twenty-one Conditions' for admission to the Comintern; they made all foreign Communists beholden to Moscow. Moscow lost her war with Poland. Peasants throughout Russia rose in revolt. A 'Workers' Opposition' was organized within the heart of the Bolshevik party. There were strikes in Moscow and a sailors' mutiny at Kronstadt, an island off the coast of Petrograd. The border nations went to war. It looked like 1917 all over again, with the Bolshevik leadership playing the part of the Tsar. But the more the Bolshevik leaders lost, the more ambitious they became – and the more murderous.

They held their Tenth Party Conference in March 1921, as they signed with the Poles the Treaty of Riga. The atmosphere was very different from that at the Second Comintern. There were no large-scale maps on the walls – the Russians had lost large swaths of border territory, and had been forced to recognize the independence of the three Baltic states. The mutineers at Kronstadt had established their own independent Revolutionary

Committee. The distribution of rationing cards according to the usefulness of different 'classes' to the state had led to rioting in the cities. The Bolshevik attempt to abolish money had created hyperinflation. Southern Russia faced starvation.

Lenin, in a three-hour speech (neither Bukharin nor Trotsky dared raise a finger), introduced a New Economic Policy. The NEP was an attempt to appease peasants in rebellion. It set up a new tax in kind. Once the peasants had paid their tax – later set at 10 per cent of the harvest – they could sell the remainder of their surplus on the market. Under the NEP, cafés, nightclubs, brothels, banks and even small-scale manufacturers were licensed. Places like Moscow naturally exploded with activity and became populated with 'Nepmen', a disreputable class of nouveaux riches who enjoyed cigars, liquor and women at the expense of everyone else.

Along with the NEP, Lenin got a resolution passed that encouraged the development of local national cultures. 'Indigenization', as it came to be known, was also designed to pacify angry peasants. It made official the status of local languages. It set up schools and colleges for the (Communist) formation of native elites. It introduced a 'federative' idea into the constitution of the Bolshevik state – a concept raised to the level of creed with the foundation of the Union of Soviet Socialist Republics (USSR) in December 1922. Lenin considered these local nationalist concessions especially important for the southern republic of Georgia, which he wanted included in the Union, but where a nasty little war was going on. Not everyone agreed with him, particularly the Georgian Bolshevik Josef Stalin.

The NEP and 'indigenization' certainly represented a retreat from the initial Bolshevik programme. But it was only a tactical one. Lenin himself spoke of the NEP as 'a peasant Brest-Litovsk'. In his long speech to the Tenth Party Congress he explained that the failure of revolution to take hold in Europe left the proletariat no other ally but the Russian peasant. The purpose of the NEP was to forge this new alliance. But the market that it created would be 'socialized', he insisted. Lenin thought the NEP would last 'not less than a decade and probably longer'. Others were more vague. Bukharin told the Third Comintern in July that 'we are making economic concessions in order to avoid political ones'. Zinoviev, the party boss in Petrograd, confirmed the following December that 'the NEP is only a temporary deviation, a tactical retreat, a clearing of the land for a new and decisive attack of labour against the front of international capitalism'.[21]

Europe's first concentration camps[22] were set up at the same time as the NEP. A massive assault on Kronstadt was conducted on 16 March, the day after the Tenth Party Congress closed. Over 10,000 Red troops were killed – including ten congress delegates who participated in the attack – but Kronstadt was taken. Batches of rebel sailors were shot without trial by teenage Komsomols (members of the Communist Youth League, founded in 1919 during the war with Kolchak). On 18 March, the fiftieth anniversary of the Paris Commune, thousands more were shipped out to the island of Solovki in the White Sea – this was the first major Soviet camp. Through the summer and following winter, networks of such camps were organized, the most notorious being SLON, the 'Northern Camps of Special Designation', in the far north, where escape was virtually impossible.

The camps were peopled by prisoners taken during a campaign of mass terror in the countryside that was inaugurated with the NEP. Whole areas of southern Russia and the Ukraine were invaded by Communist forces and units of the Komsomol, equipped with heavy guns, armoured cars, aeroplanes and poison gas. Lenin's new policy was not carrot and stick; it was tax and murder. To this was added the great famine.[23]

Western historians who believe that the Tenth Party Congress of March 1921 opened a new kind of liberal regime in Russia should consider another major proposal the Congress adopted, in addition to the NEP: the ban on factions, a founding principle of the Bolshevik state. It was passed in a secret vote taken on 16 March and was instigated by Lenin's determination to crush the 'syndicalism' of the Workers' Opposition. All party groupings independent of the Central Committee were outlawed; anyone who challenged the Committee's decisions faced the charge of 'factionalism'.

Stalin's rise to power grew directly out of this measure. To ensure that the ban was enforced and that the Workers' Opposition was purged, Lenin created the office of General Secretary of the Party. At the next party congress, in March 1922, Stalin was elected to the post with Lenin's approval. Lenin suffered his first major stroke two months later.[24]

According to Trotsky's memoirs – not perhaps a reliable source – Lenin, in a state of total despair, asked Stalin for poison. Stalin, uncharacteristically honest, consulted the Politburo and Lenin's request for suicide was refused.[25] His recovery was slow, but by September he was back in the Kremlin directing his revolutionary state once more.

Lenin's final struggle was with Stalin – over the question of the foreign-trade monopoly, which Lenin wanted to maintain, and over the explosive issue of nationality rights, especially those of Georgia. The contest drew him into an alliance with Trotsky, and together they attempted to form a 'bloc against bureaucracy'. This, along with his dictated 'Testament' after his second major stroke, in December 1922, has led some historians to conclude that Lenin was planning to liberalize the new Soviet state. But all it really meant was that Lenin, paralysed and thus unable to write, was losing power in a dictatorial bureaucracy that he himself had created. Trotsky, though ruthless and answerable to no one in his army, had no power base in the Bolshevik bureaucracy; he was easily outmanoeuvred by Stalin, the perfect functionary. Lenin was the victim of his own horrible state machinery. Small wonder he had the odd suicidal thought. In the last year of his life he was a virtual prisoner of Stalin.

Lenin died on his country estate of Gorki on 21 January 1924, shortly after his wife, Krupskaya, finished reading to him Jack London's *The Love of Life*. Stalin organized the mass state funeral in Moscow.

3

In 1919, while the Peace Conference was under way, the City of Paris purchased from the French military authorities the twenty-two miles of walls and bastions that surrounded the town. Demolition was begun immediately. But it was a slow process. The walls, with their ditches and breastworks, were between 425 and 440 feet in width; the last stone was removed only in 1932. Beyond the actual fortifications was a military zone *non aedificandi*, designed to allow free fire in the event of battle. It was supposed to be empty of all structures, but wood and cardboard shanty towns had been there for more than half a century, and even a few factories had grown up over time. The 'zone' was divided among thousands of private owners, and parts of it fell within the jurisdiction of the neighbouring communes. The City of Paris wanted to take over the whole area – the fortifications and the 'zone' – because they represented some 3,000 unused acres or the equivalent of a quarter of Paris; the municipality's administrators thought they could do something beautiful with the land. In particular, they were thinking of some kind of grand monument to the war and its sufferings, a model of post-war reconstruction, the realization of all those young dreams for a new world order.

The plans for the area actually went back to the 1880s. In 1903 Eugène Hénard, an urban reformer who, at the turn of the century, had already understood that automobile traffic would be the problem in the city of the future, had proposed an ornamental *'boulevard à redans'*, a motor route landscaped with high buildings, green recesses and parkland. A planning commission set up by the city council in 1913 thought the area would be better used as a site for housing, hospitals, schools and barracks. But it did think this would be an opportunity to 'build grandly and beautifully', so it also presented designs for 'triumphal entrances, grandiose portals, which will immediately announce the universal city, the capital of the artistic world'.

The mood was not so triumphant after the war, in 1919. That year a competition was held to select the best project now that the fortifications had been acquired. The winner, Jacques Greber, proposed that the area and the adjacent 'zone' be used for housing, embellished with formal landscaping, parks and sports grounds. At Porte Maillot there would be a monumental circular plaza.[26]

But the City of Paris had no money, the franc was devalued, there was unemployment and a crisis in housing. To pay for their purchase, the city sold wide areas to private developers. Factories were built, because the owners knew they would be compensated for their eviction. Slum-dwellers moved from one part of the 'zone' to another, collecting an indemnity from the city with each move. The area was infested with corruption and poverty. But, worse than that, there was disease: at Porte de Clignancourt in 1921 forty-seven houses had to be immediately demolished with the break-out of bubonic plague – the 'Black Death'.

The 'zone' became a terrible monument to the Great War, a symbol of 'disillusionment'. 'You would think yourself in a village bombed during the war,' wrote the writer André Warnod after walking around the area in 1930: 'large holes break the walls, and houses are bereft of doors and windows; the road enters the house and becomes part of it'.[27]

The *zoniers* were eventually cleared out – by the authorities of German-occupied Paris in 1940. When the Allies approached the capital in 1944 they found the 'zone' had been turned into an unoccupied desert. It was the Fifth Republic that built the 'Boulevard Périphérique', an autoroute jammed with lorries, cars and leapfrogging white commercial vans: Paris had built herself a new impenetrable wall.

It is often said that Clemenceau won the war but lost the peace – despite his own declared intention to 'win the peace'. Clemenceau himself argued that the peace could not be constructed by one man or one country alone; he stated many times that the defences of France were made up of the bricks of the alliance. 'The alliance in the war has to be followed by the indestructible alliance in the peace,' he repeated. Clemenceau's wall was founded on the 'solidarity of the Allies'.[28]

Clemenceau had treated all other items on the agenda of the Peace Conference as bargaining counters to achieve this. He bargained on territory: unlike Foch and Poincaré, he was no annexationist – 'We have to protect [the Rhinelanders] against Prussian despotism, but we don't have to go into their homes to bring them the revolution. At any rate, it is something I will not do.'[29] He bargained on reparations. He bargained on Russia. He bargained on the Middle East ('Lloyd George has made me a Syrian,' he joked). In every case he had the same end: a British and American commitment on the Western Front. At the Conference, he got it.

Clemenceau admitted that the US failure to ratify the treaty was a catastrophe. He suspected that it was due to an underlying current of American resentment (which could be felt throughout the Conference) that it had been not the Americans who had won the war, but the British and French armies. In the Argonne in the autumn of 1918 the Americans' extraordinary bravery had not been enough to give them a strategic advantage; 'if this miracle had worked', recollected Clemenceau, 'I am pretty much prepared to believe that public opinion would have forced the Senate to vote for the treaty'.[30]

Many of the deputies in the Chamber – of the Left and the Right – thought that Clemenceau, for the sake of his wall of alliance, had given too much away at the Conference. Louis Marin, a moderate, accused him of yielding to the Germans: 'You have reduced us to a policy of vigilance.' Clemenceau retorted that no treaty could do away with vigilance: 'Life is only a struggle. This struggle, you will not suppress it.'[31]

Struggle and the defence of civilization were Clemenceau's leitmotif. 'I take men as they are, the facts as they are: humanity will not change so soon,' he said on 25 September 1919 as the Chamber prepared to ratify the treaty. 'We inscribe "fraternity" and still other things on our walls. I do not believe that since we put them there we feel any more fraternal.'[32]

One had to work with the treaty for what it was, the product of negotiation, not a sacred document. He said, 'What you are going to vote today, it is not even a beginning, it is the beginning of the beginning – a phrase that could be inscribed at the head of every great treaty. 'Enter it well into your heads that this treaty is a set of possibilities and that its success will depend on what you are able to get out of these possibilities.' In other words, don't blame the treaty if things go wrong; have a look at the people who execute it. The treaty was not a text 'as furnished by *notaires* who bind the parties, under the threat of being locked up by the policeman'. The men who inherited the treaty would have to play all the roles – bound party, interpreter, *notaire* and policeman. 'One has to execute this treaty first, this treaty so bad, this treaty which has all the defects of which we are aware. It is the testing stone.'[33]

These words were Clemenceau's political testament. They are not those of a loser.

Clemenceau had announced his intention to resign in December 1919, after the parliamentary elections. He played no active part in the November campaign, and he was probably not enchanted with the composition of the new parliament, dominated by moderate republicans, conservatives and Catholics. The majority called themselves the *Bloc National*; the nation called them the *Chambre à Horizon Bleu* – the equivalent of Britain's 'Khaki' Parliament.

It seems that it was Lloyd George who persuaded Clemenceau, during a visit to London, to run for President in January 1920. Clemenceau presented his candidature at the last minute, made no campaign, and told his closest supporter not to attend a preliminary republican caucus that was held at the Palais de Luxembourg on 10 January. Not surprisingly, all his old enemies united behind Aristide Briand and the caucus voted 408 to 389 for Paul Deschanel, who was disabled by a stroke immediately on becoming President – a third living ghost in the governments of the world. The caucus ballot had not been a formal vote; nevertheless, Clemenceau withdrew his candidature. On 18 January, when the formal vote was taken by the Chamber and the Senate, united in National Assembly, Clemenceau was enjoying lunch in Giverney with his old friend the painter Claude Monet.[34]

A personal saga was developing at that time between Clemenceau and Monet. Clemenceau left no political memoirs save his *Grandeurs et misères d'une victoire*, which he wrote in the last six months of his life in answer to the posthumous memoirs of Foch (whose greatest lifetime error was to die nine months before Clemenceau). Following his resignation he travelled; he rented a wooden bungalow on the coast of the Vendée ('it really is an old shack, you know,' his chauffeur warned his secretary; 'water seeps into the bedrooms, everything is going rotten . . .');[35] he wrote about flowers, Greeks and philosophy; and, as he wrote, he corresponded with Monet. The great painter was going blind.

'Bonsoir Monet,' Clemenceau wrote on 5 December 1925, 'Work, work. It is the most beautiful thing there is in the world. I embrace you, as would have the defunct Encelades, the giant with a hundred arms.'[36] Many factors motivated Clemenceau's friendship with Monet; they had known each other since the 1890s. But what Clemenceau sought now was a memorial to the Great War.

On the day after the Armistice, on 12 November 1918, Monet had in a private letter to Clemenceau offered 'two decorative panels' to the Musée des Arts Décoratifs as 'the only way that I can take part in the Victory'.[37] During the next years the 'two decorative panels' became an epic project of twenty-eight huge paintings, *Les Nymphéas* or *The Water Lilies*. Clemenceau himself described the series as a story of life and death and resurrection – a story of war and peace.[38]

Clemenceau recommended doctors to Monet, he visited him, he consoled him in his letters, but he refused to admit that Monet had a right to delay his work or cancel his contract because of blindness. 'Work, work,' insisted Clemenceau. Monet died on 5 December 1926, exhausted. It is said that at his funeral Clemenceau, bowed in grief, removed with his gloved hands the black shroud on Monet's coffin. 'No, no, no,' he reportedly mumbled – 'not black for Monet.' A photograph shows that Monet was buried under a cloak of many colours.[39]

It is actually outside one's power to honour the dead, claimed Clemenceau, echoing Lincoln's address at Gettysburg; 'We are here to honour ourselves through them, to follow them on the road of sacrifice and devotion where they have so magnificently gone before us.'[40]

There are many memorials to the enormous sacrifices of the Great War, with their inscriptions, their noble statues, their wreaths, their representations of women in mourning. But *Les Nymphéas*, in a silent and peaceful hall in the Orangerie, opened by Clemenceau himself in the year of Monet's death, is the most remarkable of them all.

4

David Lloyd George regretted Clemenceau's departure from politics. Clemenceau was defeated 'by a combination of extremists on the Right and the Left, helped by the many men of no particular convictions whom he had offended in the course of a combative life', said Lloyd George in the final chapter of his *The Truth about the Peace Treaties*. 'He was pre-eminently a man of his word.'[41] One might have thought that the British Prime Minister would have preferred Aristide Briand, who was a kind of French Lloyd George: articulate, charming, a man committed to every political side and theory. But Clemenceau had a uncanny way of keeping Lloyd George on track. During the last year of the war he managed to maintain Britain's engagement on the Western Front, when Lloyd George could very well have gone elsewhere. Why did Clemenceau insist on the presence of French troops in Syria? Because he wanted British troops in Germany, and did not want to see them diverted on some wild Middle Eastern venture. Why did he allow Monsieur Klotz to press so hard on gold and reparations? Because Lloyd George's government was seeking a separate accord with Germany. Why did Clemenceau so vigorously support the Poles in Galicia and Upper Silesia? Because Lloyd George had no commitment at all. After Clemenceau's departure, Lloyd George's policy on Europe fell to pieces.

Signs of this could already be seen in mid-September 1919, when Lloyd George visited Paris and proposed the closure of the Peace Conference, which, it is often forgotten, continued long after the signing of the Treaty of Versailles. A 'Council of the Heads of Delegations' (CHD) now played the role of the Council of Four. There were treaties to be made with Austria, Bulgaria and Hungary. There were many economic problems still to be discussed, and an even greater number of territorial difficulties lay before them. Furthermore, the technical details involved in the establishment of a League of Nations, which had never been considered by Wilson, had to be thrashed out. An international conference of this kind – the only one that existed in the world – was not easy to dismiss.

As in June, the Americans prevented Lloyd George's defection. Frank L. Polk, head of the American delegation, protested and appealed for Wilson's support. He got it. Wilson wired from the American Far West that 'it would be nearly fatal to the whole state of mind of the world if the British were to withdraw'.[42]

But the American part in the alliance was doomed. As a result of the Senate's failure to ratify the treaty, all the American commissioners were instructed to leave Paris. Clemenceau asked Polk who would be left among the Americans. Polk answered, 'No one.' 'Then I will have you immediately arrested,' Clemenceau jokingly replied; he assured Polk it would be for a crime well worthwhile. Clemenceau was less humorous when, discussing Wilson's health problems with the Earl of Derby, the British ambassador, he wondered aloud, 'What on earth is the Lord Almighty doing that he does not take him to his bosom?'[43]

The Conference managed to keep going. After the exchange of ratifications with Germany on 21 January 1920, the CHD passed its functions on to a 'Conference of Ambassadors'. Only when Turkey signed the Treaty of Sèvres on 10 August, that same year, did the Paris Peace Conference formally come to an end.

From then on the guardian of international law was the League of Nations, in Geneva. In structure, it owed a great deal to the institutions that had evolved during the Paris Conference and the Supreme War Council before it. Without the Americans present, most of its business concerned the narrow, violent but nevertheless dynamic little peninsula of Europe. Sir Eric Drummond was the first secretary-general. The post of under-secretary-general went to a Frenchman, Jean Monnet, who would later make his reputation as the 'father of Europe'.

Lloyd George did not like this European League of Nations.

While Lloyd George was busy at his second attempt to withdraw from the alliance that had won the war, Maynard Keynes was in Charleston, Sussex, writing a book with a curious title that would make him a household name, *The Economic Consequences of the Peace*. Since the Armistice, Charleston had become Bloomsbury's main rural retreat. Men and women of a very high-minded society would gather here – 'Cropheads' and 'Bunnies', along with the 'Buggers'. Adrian married Karin, Gerald married Fredegond, James married Alix; Clive's wife, Vanessa, started sleeping with Duncan; Lytton Strachey, key member of the 'Apostles', fell in love with Dora Carrington, though we are assured the relationship was only platonic.

'He is disillusioned,' wrote Virginia Woolf of Keynes. On returning from his ordeal in Paris, he told her that he no longer believed in the stability of things. 'Eton is doomed; the governing classes, perhaps Cambridge too.' Keynes's world seemed to be collapsing.[44]

Keynes turned down various lucrative job offers. He asked King's College to reduce his teaching load, and he resigned from his Girdler lectureship in Cambridge. His main source of income was speculation in foreign currencies, for which he founded his own company – though he would make a serious loss the following year because of measures taken by the German Finance Minister, Matthias Erzberger.

As Keynes told his mother on 25 June (that is, three days before Germany signed the treaty), the main aim of his book was to outline the 'economic condition of Europe as it now is, including a violent attack on the Peace Treaty and my proposals for the future'. By 3 September he was admitting how good this aggression made him feel: 'I haven't lived such a regular life for years and am very well.'[45] He had brought his own two domestics down from London, was served breakfast at eight, and worked on his book until noon; after lunch he read the newspapers and did a little gardening. In this way he got a thousand words written a day. The book was finished in November, the first anniversary of the Armistice.

Several wanted him to tone down the vehemence of his style, including his mother, who found that the last two chapters in particular contained 'too much prophecy of the Jeremiah type'. General Smuts, who had been friendly with him in Paris, pleaded that an attack on the treaty profited no one and advised that it would be 'better to be constructive'. Arthur Salter of the new Reparations Commission warned that he might jeopardize the chances of securing American loans for Europe. But Keynes was committed, as he wrote in an answer to Smuts, to 'violent and ruthless truth-telling'.[46]

There were two main groups exerting an influence on Keynes. One was the members of Bloomsbury, most of them pacifists who would have pulled Britain out of the war in August 1914. The second was the Asquithian Liberals – the 'Squiffites' – who would have withdrawn in 1917. Margot Asquith herself provided warm counsel during the month of August; it was she who urged Keynes to write his character sketches, the most quoted part of the book. But the most important component of the book was Keynes himself. Keynes was pitiless.

The underlying theme of *The Economic Consequences of the Peace* is the primacy of economic issues over all others. 'To what a different future Europe might have looked forward, if either Mr Lloyd George or Mr Wilson had apprehended that the most serious of the problems which claimed their attention were not political or territorial but financial and economic.'[47] The book is a song of praise to the 'economic men' who were appearing on the scene in the aftermath of the war; it is a modern gospel about laws of exchange, the manufacture of wealth and money-making. On economic matters, one never ceases to admire Keynes's clarity and elegance. His theory is very much inspired by the eighteenth-century ideas of the Revd Thomas R. Malthus.[48] European prosperity, argues Keynes, has been built upon a delicate balance between the benefits of trade and the threat of an overgrown population, dependent on supplies from overseas. (Walther Rathenau had made the same point in 1912.) The war broke down that equilibrium; it let loose once again the 'Malthusian devil' which had haunted Europe in the centuries before the development of industry and international trade. Millions of Europeans now faced starvation. The essential matter of the peace was not frontiers, but to get trade moving again. The rest, assumed Keynes, prince of economists, would follow.

But then there was the treaty. 'The disillusion was so complete, that some of those who had trusted most hardly dared speak of it,' wrote Keynes. 'Could it be true? they asked of those who returned from Paris. Was the Treaty really as bad as it seemed?'[49] Keynes's disillusionment lay in the fact that the Big Three had failed to follow his advice. They had broken a contract – the contract made with the Germans at the time of the Armistice. Keynes regarded the Armistice not as a surrender document, but as a binding legal agreement between equal partners. Keynes paid no heed to the continuing war in Germany and to the East. World peace began for Keynes on 11 November 1918, and trade should have started up immediately – in accordance with the 'contract'.

The book hinges on his condemnation of the reparations clauses of the treaty, of their implication that Germany should pay for the full costs of the war and that she should cover the expense of Allied pensions and the like. The clarity of Keynes's prose on this point is so clear: it reminds one of the short, sharp memoranda he sent to the Treasury during his last months of service. Perhaps this is because the book *is* made up of Keynes's memoranda. Whole sections of *Economic Consequences* are simply copied from them, verbatim. Keynes was his own plagiarist.[50]

Regrettably, he omitted his memoranda attacking the American attitude towards war debts and, most particularly, the crucial American refusal to consider his bond plan, which had been the cause of his departure from Paris. Perhaps he was taking heed of Salter's warnings. Or perhaps it was because, during the drafting, he was already in negotiations with Harcourt, Brace & Howe for the American edition.

'If I had influence with the United States Treasury,' he wrote in his book, 'I would not lend a penny to a single one of the present governments of Europe.' The phrase made banner headlines in America, though it contradicted entirely the policy Keynes had been pursuing in Paris. When, in February 1920, a last desperate effort was made to get the Senate to ratify the treaty, extracts from Keynes's book were read out from the floor: America slammed the door on Europe, and bolted it.[51]

Instead of treating Germany as an equal partner, instead of observing their 'contract' (shadows of a *notaire*'s document hang over the pages of Keynes), the Allies aimed, according to the author, 'deliberately at the impoverishment of Central Europe, vengeance'. Keynes called Versailles the 'Carthaginian Peace'. The German edition of *Economic Consequences* was a best-seller.

Keynes attributed the spirit of 'vengeance' in the treaty – and especially the inclusion of war costs (how shocked he was to learn that his friend Smuts had been one of the prime advocates of this) – to a weakness of character among the Big Three. Hence his portraits.

His depiction of Clemenceau is mere caricature. Clemenceau in no way resembled Bismarck; if there was a French Bismarck in Paris at the time it was Raymond Poincaré, Clemenceau's enemy. Clemenceau was not a nationalist; many of his foes in the Chamber were nationalists – even Lloyd George acknowledged that. Clemenceau had no desire at all to turn the clocks back to 1870; 1870 had been a nightmare for Clemenceau, as had been the Second Empire.

One can recognize the features of Lloyd George in Keynes's portrait. Keynes, after all, had worked with him almost on a daily basis since the outbreak of the war. Yet there is more to this sketch of Lloyd George than first meets the eye. Herbert Asquith managed, with suspicious ease, to get it omitted from the first edition. Keynes was not only worried about libel; he was painting a portrait of himself. That was the real inner fury driving the book; the femme fatale was Keynes, not Lloyd George. He had played the role since Eton.[52]

The hidden autobiographical element in *Economic Consequences* emerges even more clearly from Keynes's pages on Woodrow Wilson. An idealistic Cambridge don describes an idealistic Princeton don. Keynes portrayed Wilson as an 'old Presbyterian', which he undoubtedly was; Keynes, with his own Nonconformist background, had all the qualifications to tackle this. When Keynes first saw Margot Asquith in June 1919, he said 'the collapse of Wilson was agonizing'.[53] At the time, it was Keynes who faced physical collapse. Keynes would criticize Wilson for setting down principles 'consistent with every syllable in the Pentateuch'. Keynes had his principles, too: economics. From the beginning to the end of the book one can hear Keynes repeat the Wilsonian phrase 'the kingpin of the whole structure': trade.

'Unless one keeps Keynes's perspective firmly in mind,' writes his biographer Robert Skidelsky, 'the intensity of his denunciations may seem puzzling, even perverse.'[54] Focusing the mind on 'Keynes's perspective' involves the neglect of every other issue. Keynes says nothing on the wars in progress in Central and Eastern Europe. For a Liberal, his brief dismissal of the League of Nations as a 'polyglot debating society' is astonishing. He says nothing on the American responsibility for the reparations merry-go-round, preferring to blame this on the French (though he must have known that the French demands mounted only after the British stake had been laid). He entirely overlooks the significance of the 'war guilt' issue, which haunted Germany for the next two decades. In fact, though he takes a magnanimous stand for the fallen foe, his book contains no information on Germany at all apart from the statistics copied out from his earlier memoranda (statistics derived from Treasury documents of the pre-war era). He has no proposals on how to disarm Germany's marauding private bands. He has nothing to say on European security.

Of course, Keynes would have dismissed these problems as irrelevant to his central theme: trade. Develop trade and the other problems will go away, he argued in his book. This was a Wilsonian, 'kingpin', way of thinking.

'To the formation of the general opinion of the future I dedicate this book,' Keynes concluded. *The Economic Consequences of the Peace* was published on 12 December 1919 and was a best-seller by Christmas. It formed general opinion in Britain for a generation.

Keynes in no way made himself an 'outcast' by leaving the Treasury and writing his book. On the contrary, he became a centre of government attention. He was wined and dined by Treasury officials; he was frequently seen at Westminster in the company of his old colleagues like Austen Chamberlain, Sir Basil Blackett and particularly Sir John Bradbury – Oxford and Treasury – who exercised a critical influence on British policy in the coming years. When they did not see each other, they published mutually supportive letters in *The Times*, which influenced the attitude of many a man in Westminster. The economic debates in the House of Commons during the early months of 1920 give an idea of what an enormous effect Keynes's book had had. Considerable doubts were now being expressed, especially from the opposition benches, about the practicality of the level of reparations expected from Germany.

But there was another influence, besides Keynes, that would change British attitudes to the treaty. In 1920 the British economy entered a serious recession. The traditional manufacturing sectors were having difficulties exporting their wares, unemployment grew at an alarming rate; there were bread lines, and on several occasions mounted police had to disperse groups of the unemployed bearing the red flag. On 16 June, Reginald McKenna, a former Chancellor of Exchequer and now chairman of the London Joint City and Midland Bank, made a speech to a group of accountants in which he argued that exports were Germany's only real source of income, while her 'highly developed manufacturing and commercial power brings her in direct competition with us, more than any other nation in the world'. He demanded that Britain restrict German reparations to raw materials needed by the Allies. It was a very Keynesian proposal.[55]

By 1921 – that critical year, when Russia made her peace with Poland at Riga, when Lenin embarked on the New Economic Policy, and when a plebiscite was held in Upper Silesia – the Treasury officials had composed a series of policy papers which completely altered the British approach on reparations. Lloyd George, in another of his *Truth* books, never acknowledged the influence of Keynes and Bradbury on his thinking, but he did blame his initial reparations policy on the extremism of his 'experts', Sumner and Cunliffe.[56] Members of the Reparations Commission, which had already substantially reduced the sum demanded of Germany from 226 billion gold marks[57] to 132 billion, were warning that Germany was being required to make payments 'beyond capacity'. Bradbury wrote that the total amount demanded was 'ridiculous as well as absurd'. He and his colleages started talking of a 'moratorium'. There were suggestions of granting a loan to Germany. The Treasury officials became extremely worried about Germany's enormous deficits, and they saw the stick of reparations and carrot of the loan as means of imposing fiscal responsibility. Bradbury set the conditions Germany would have to meet for relief on reparations and a loan: an increase in income tax, and controls on capital flow. As a first step, the Treasury officials recommended the calling of an international economic conference. Lloyd George concurred. He spoke of reconstructing 'economic Europe'.

The two pillars of Lloyd George's 'economic Europe' were Russia and Germany. 'We have failed to restore Russia to sanity by force. I believe we can save her by trade,' Lloyd George told the House of Commons on 20 February 1920.[58] Keynes's magic formula let the government avoid tackling the really embarrassing political questions about Russia: Lloyd George simply decided, in Churchill's wicked phrase, 'to grasp the hairy paw of the baboon' and make a deal on trade.[59]

Trade would make the Bolsheviks more human! Ramsay MacDonald, the Labour leader, had seen this in his own publication of 1919, *Parliament and Revolution*. Lenin's government was going to modify its position, he wrote: 'it will commence the work of evolutionary revolution and democratic education, ... it will proceed to carry out a policy of socialization on precisely the same plan as we should do here if a Socialist Party were in power in Westminster'.[60] Which must have been good news for Westminster. Another Labour leader, George Lansbury, attended Moscow's Comintern as the Red Army advanced into Poland. The Bolsheviks, he cabled Lloyd George, were 'first-rate, clear-headed, honest humane men' who were 'doing what Christians call the Lord's work'. Lloyd George confessed to Lord Riddell at the time that 'Lenin is the biggest man in politics. He had conceived and carried out a great experiment.' Lenin was so delighted with the British trade initiative that he expressed his desire to meet Lloyd George.[61]

Negotiations dragged on in London throughout most of 1920. The Anglo-Russian Trade Agreement was signed on 16 March 1921, one week after the Russians made their peace with the Poles and on the very day they launched their final offensive on Kronstadt. In Moscow, Lenin was announcing his New Economic Policy. *The Times* wrote that this proved that Lenin had recognized the failure of Bolshevism; the *Spectator* thought that Lenin had 'admitted the economic collapse of his system'. But these British observers – so sure of the power of trade, so certain that the NEP was the dawn of a new era – should have listened to what Lenin said. 'What we have to do is to get firmly on our feet in order to survive,' he had told the Eighth All-Russian Congress of Soviets in December.[62]

The German delegation that arrived at Victoria station on 28 February 1921 – almost on the same train as the Russians – must have known that the British were eager to reduce the reparations bill and get on with the business of trade: they had only to read the newspapers. But it was clear that this would not be as easy as the Russian agreement. The British had not yet solved their own war-debt problem with America. Indeed, the US Senate had recently aggravated it by passing, on 9 February, a Debt Funding Act, designed to ensure that the United States would be paid every penny owed. Allied war debts were what had made Lloyd George vacillate on reparations.

Connected to this problem were the French demands. Above all the French wanted security, but, despite assurances that Britain would again 'hurry to the help of France if Germany were again to make a wanton attack upon her'[63] it was evident – once again to anyone who read the newspapers – that, without the American guarantee, Britain now had no firm military commitment on the Continent. A second-best alternative for the French was money. Thus a radical reduction of Germany's reparations bill and the achievement of a trade agreement was going to require some dramatic diplomacy – another of Lloyd George's great pantomime acts.

In late January 1921 the Allies had agreed on a total reparations bill of 226 billion gold marks, to be paid over a period of forty-two years. By April, when the Reparations Commission presented its report, as required by the Versailles Treaty, this sum had already been reduced to 132 billion. In May, through an extraordinarily intricate manoeuvre by the British government, the total was in effect reduced to 50 billion: in four months German reparations had been cut by a factor of nearly five.

When the Germans sat down in Lancaster House on 1 March to present their answer to the initial Paris proposals of January, they were expecting some kind of reduction. Through a calculation of compound interest, Walter Simons, the head of the delegation, managed to propose 53 billion in place of the 226 billion. He rounded this down to 50 billion, and then deducted another 20 billion for confiscations the Allies had already made as well as compensation for the German fleet, which the Germans had sunk themselves at Scapa Flow. Thus the Germans were offering total reparations of 30 billion gold marks.[64]

The agenda of the Conference in London also included discussion of war crimes, outstanding territorial problems and German disarmament, but, following the example set by Keynes's book, all these matters were pushed into the background – they were never seriously pursued by the Allies. Lloyd George did, however, put on a show of indignation at Dr Simons's offer. 'The counterproposals mocked the Treaty,' he exclaimed, and he threatened to reimpose economic sanctions and to occupy Düsseldorf, Duisburg and Ruhrort.[65]

While the Conference was in session, a cable arrived from Berlin with a proposal by Walther Rathenau, who since leaving the War Office Raw Materials Section in 1915 had been in the habit of giving private counsel to the government. He recommended that, in the place of reparations, Germany take over the entire Allied war debt to the United States. This intelligent proposal won many admirers in London, and Rathenau immediately came to be regarded as the chief idea-man of Europe. But the plan was doomed because the United States refused to see any connection between German reparations and Allied war debts.[66]

Following the report of the Reparations Commission, a second meeting with the Germans took place in May. Here Lloyd George 'roused himself'. The Treasury had prepared a schedule of payments so complex that nobody could understand it – which was entirely the purpose. Lloyd George stormed up and down; he gave Germany six days to accept the plan.

In its opening article, the plan evaluated the German debt for reparations at the Commission's figure of 132 billion gold marks. The British press and the French took this at face value, but Article 4 of the plan expounded a complicated system of annual payments (of around 3 billion gold marks each year) which, if anybody had added them up, totalled 50 billion – in other words, the same figure Simons had offered in March, without his 'deductions'.

The Germans were puzzled. Their government resigned. The new Chancellor was Josef Wirth, a Centrist from Baden, a planner. The most significant thing Wirth did in his life was to bring Walther Rathenau into his government. Another important achievement of the London Conference of May was that Lloyd George had, without losing face, reduced reparations to a figure comparable to what Keynes had recommended in his Treasury memorandum of November 1918.

Lloyd George still had to set up the great international conference that the men of the Treasury had recommended. First he consulted Rathenau, who came over to London in November 1921. Strongly approving of German actions in Upper Silesia, Lloyd George told Rathenau that he wanted to see a 'strong, healthy, booming Germany'.[67] Then he invited the French Prime Minister, Aristide Briand, a man after his own heart, to talks at Downing Street. For four days before Christmas they discussed the reconstruction of Central and Eastern Europe, the rehabilitation of Russia, the reintegration of Germany into Europe – the 'economic Europe' of Keynes's inspiration. Lloyd George referred to this new Europe as a 'Consortium'. The great conference that was to create it was to take place with the New Year, 1922.

What happened next is really Rathenau's story. But one might note that Briand's government collapsed on the third day of the Cannes Conference in January, and that the Genoa Conference of April turned out to be something very different from what Lloyd George and the men of the Treasury had predicted. Briand's replacement was Raymond Poincaré, the French Bismarck.

A corruption scandal and a venture in the Middle East brought down Lloyd George's government before 1922 was up. Since he had no party behind him, he never entered government again. Through the 1920s and 1930s he was a strong supporter of international trade, which angered adherents of 'imperial preference'. He gave handsome grants from his private 'political fund' (built up from the sale of honours during his premiership) to those with whom he sympathized.

In September 1936 he spent two days at Berchtesgaden in conversation with Adolf Hitler. Hitler, he reported afterwards, 'is a very great man. "Führer" is the proper name for him, for he is a born leader, yes, and a statesman'; Hitler knew how to tackle the problems of unemployment, he had organized an effective welfare programme, and he knew how to stand up for German interests against the unreasonable aspects of the Treaty of Versailles. In late 1937, after the Spanish Civil War had broken out, Lloyd George stated that 'Mussolini is temperamentally an aggressor. I have never thought that Herr Hitler was and I do not believe it now.'[68]

Lloyd George might have become Prime Minister again in May 1940. Though seventy-seven years old, his record suggests he would not have been a British Clemenceau.

5

The German word *'Erfüllung'* means more than 'fulfilment'. The nineteenth-century philosopher G. W. F. Hegel, used it in the sense of consciousness 'becoming', progressing forward to reach ultimately the Supreme Idea – which, like God in the Bible, Hegel never in fact defined. In a Romantic essay of his youth he gave it the opposite meaning: a retreat backwards into origins, a 'homecoming'. The term sometimes carries amorous and sexual overtones. Or it may simply mean the 'execution' of an act. Or a 'realization'. Or an 'overcoming'. It can also imply 'death'. Walther Rathenau actually started emphasizing *Erfüllung* because of the Allies, who spoke of 'enforcing the fulfilment of the treaty'. But Rathenau, well versed in German Romantic philosophy, implied something more mystical on adopting his 'Policy of Fulfilment' (*Erfüllungspolitik*) in 1921.

That was the year Matthias Erzberger was murdered. Though he was a devout Catholic, there had been nothing mystical about Erzberger's politics. 'We do not improve matters by clamouring noisily for "revision of the peace treaty",' he wrote shortly before his death; 'we must rather choose means more appropriate for attaining this end. What are these means? We must, first of all, seek to fulfil all the treaty provisions, however horrible, that can be fulfilled; only in this way can we make the world realize that those provisions that we cannot fulfil are, indeed, objectively impossible.'[69]

Erzberger's proposals were always concrete and detailed. He had spent his life in parliament, and whenever the debates got intense he would jump into the fray with a radiant and carefree manner. He was sometimes even careless. He considered the best defence was the counter-offence. He was a man who lived by making sensational revelations – without always calculating the consequences. When he was cornered he performed poorly; he lost his words, forgot the details, and his round, stocky face would turn white. Foch had observed this in the train at Compiègne.

Erzberger's understanding of 'fulfilment' was much closer to an Allied reading of the policy than Rathenau's. In October 1918 Rathenau had called for a *levée en masse*, while Erzberger prepared to cross the line with a white flag and negotiate. During the crisis of June 1919 Erzberger had argued that the Germans should sign at Versailles, whereas Rathenau had proposed breaking off discussions. Erzberger became the new Minister of Finance in Gustav Bauer's government, following Schéidemann's denunciation of the treaty. His extraordinary aim, given the state of German finances at the time, was to balance the budget: this must have pleased the British Treasury.

The taxes he introduced constituted nothing less than a fiscal revolution.

'We exacted blood but refused to demand sacrifices of property,' he charged.[70] Rushing from one committee to another, he managed to get a war-profits tax, an inheritance tax, a tobacco tax and a land-transfer tax pushed through the Reichstag before the summer recess – a speed of legislation never encountered before in German parliamentary history. Within the next six months he had added a capital-gains tax and an income tax, and had invented the world's first value-added tax. Reich collecting-bureaux were set up throughout the country, and Germany became a centralized state along the lines of the Western model. In 1920 the Reichsmark actually stabilized for a brief moment:[71] Keynes's speculative company in London, counting on German inflation, went bankrupt.

True to style, Erzberger laid his opponents low with crippling revelations. He denounced the Conservative Party, the Pan-Germans and Supreme Command for their illusions about military victory, their annexationism, their U-boat policy and their insistence on maintaining control of Belgium. Using Foreign Office files, he proved the lies behind Ludendorff's 'stab-in-the-back' thesis; he showed the First Quartermaster General had himself been the first to demand an armistice, on 4 October 1918.

Erzberger exposed the plans of some industrialists to exploit Belgium through the help of Karl Helfferich. Helfferich was a brilliant economist – some have even described him as a 'German Keynes'. He was in charge of the Treasury until 1916, and based his entire wartime budget on the assumption that reparations from the defeated enemy would cover expenses. Erzberger's revelations nearly destroyed him. 'Give us back our murdered sons!' shouted the women in the Reichstag galleries at the Conservative deputies.[72]

But Helfferich was not a man to lie low for long. He wrote a series of articles in the press. He countered with his own accusations. 'Erzberger's name very properly stands under the miserable Armistice,' he wrote in his most popular pamphlet. 'Erzberger led us to Versailles . . . Erzberger's name is . . . attached indissolubly to Germany's suffering and Germany's dishonour. Erzberger will soon lead Germany to complete ruin by squandering the little moral, political, and economic capital that has survived her collapse, unless his political power is finally broken.' The campaign became vicious.[73]

There were a few problems that the new reform-minded Erzberger had overlooked. He had been an annexationist himself; in 1916 he had sung in praise of the war's finances; his 'Peace Resolution' of 1917 had assumed a German victory; he had supported Brest-Litovsk. Worse, he had been careless in his personal business affairs. Helfferich accused him of consorting with business, of using insider information, of selling war contracts to the companies he had invested in. The worrying thing for Erzberger was that Helfferich was right.

Erzberger had no choice but to sue Helfferich for libel. The trial, held in the Berlin-Moabit courthouse, was followed by high-society ladies from all parts of the capital: they cheered for handsome Helfferich; they laughed at the corpulent, defensive Minister of Finance. Erzberger called the spectators 'Capitoline geese who thought they could save the Fatherland by their cackling'. In the course of the trial, the prosecutors – trained Prussian civil servants, insulated like Prussian soldiers from the rough-and-tumble of parliamentary life – became convinced that Helfferich's charges were correct. Hate and malice spread to the streets. On 26 January 1920 a demobilized officer, Oltwig von Hirschfeld, stepped up on the running-board of Erzberger's automobile as he was leaving court and shot him in the chest. Erzberger was miraculously saved by his gold pocket-watch. Bleeding profusely, he was carried to hospital. Three days later he was back at his trial.

The judges, on 12 March, found Erzberger guilty of several of Helfferich's accusations, but fined Helfferich 300 marks for libel on the remaining points: it was hardly a victory for the Republic. In a separate trial Hirschfeld was sentenced to jail for a mere eighteen months: this was an incitement to political murder.

The next day Berlin's central streets were filled with the sounds of strutting troops and the roar of tanks; the soldiers, for the first time in the city's history, wore swastikas on their helmets instead of the white skull-and-crossbones. They were the elite forces of the Baltic Free Corps – Captain Hermann Erhardt's Second Marine Brigade, the Third Kurland Infantry Regiment and Bischoff's Iron Division. Bauer's government had ordered their dissolution on 20 February but, instead, the troops had returned to Berlin to dissolve the government. They had entered the city on the very night of the Erzberger verdict.

Wilhelm Groener had, some months earlier, left his command post for a quieter job at the Ministry of Communications. The new commander was General Hans von Seeckt, the very personification of Prussian military discipline. He had a 'rigid, impenetrable face', wrote George Grosz; 'his monocle seemed glued to his face, his grey moustache cut like a brush, his carp mouth arrogantly closed. His incredibly slender waist looked corseted.'[74] Gustav Noske was still Minister of Defence. He telephoned Seeckt and asked him to fulfil the Army's pledge to defend the Republic. 'Troops do not fire on troops,' Seeckt frostily answered.[75] Noske resigned; Bauer and his colleagues fled to Stuttgart. Erzberger, who had relinquished his ministry only the day before, because of the libel verdict, took refuge in the monastery Zum Guten Hirten, to avoid another assassination attempt.

Berlin was now ruled by a military dictatorship – the government of the 'Nationale Vereinigung'. But the East Prussian official Wolfgang Kapp made a comic dictator; and his assistant, General von Lüttwitz, though he had shown resolution when storming the Schloss during the Spartacist rising, proved a useless administrator. All Bauer had to do was to call, from Stuttgart, for a general strike and within five days Kapp's government collapsed. But, having called for a national strike, Bauer then had to face a Communist rebellion in the Ruhr; he had to meekly plead with Seeckt to repress it. The Army complied with its usual haste and ruthlessness.

Meanwhile, in Bavaria, Captain Erhardt had set up his 'secret' *Organisation Consul* – a general staff of the Free Corps – which every government official in Berlin and Weimar knew about and even encouraged. Erzberger's eventual two assassins were members of *Organisation Consul*.

Erzberger was determined to re-enter politics. After all, he was only forty-one and was one of the most brilliant parliamentarians Germany had. He spent a year campaigning with the Christian Trade Unions. On 29 June 1921, just after Josef Wirth had established a new government, he announced that he was going to lead his Centre Party again. His ambition was obviously to play an important part in Wirth's coalition; he even looked like a candidate for Chancellor.

To put his thoughts together, he took a long holiday in the Black Forest in his home state of Baden. In mid-August he moved with his family to Bad Griesbach, at the foot of the Kniebis mountain. The peasant women here still went about in long black dresses and embroidered headwear; the men wore bright-green jackets and brown feathered hats. In the inn, after dinner, the guests sang the old songs of the Fatherland, Erzberger and his family joining in as cheerfully as the others. On the night of 25 August there was a violent storm of thunder and lightning; the electric lights were extinguished; the guests sang by candlelight.

The next morning, a Friday, Erzberger attended a Catholic mass in the local church and then set off for a hike up the Kniebis with his friend Karl Diez. The winding mountain path was shrouded in mist – did a thought of the night he had crossed the line in November 1918 flicker in his mind? There was a faint drizzle, a remnant of the rainstorm the evening before.

As they climbed, they were overtaken by two young men to whom they paid no attention. The route was slippery; Erzberger and Diez decided to turn back. The two strangers had apparently taken a short cut through the wood: they stepped from behind a bush and pulled out revolvers. Erzberger was shot in the chest and forehead at a distance of six inches. With an astonished look on his face he jumped down the steep slope at the side of the path, grabbed at tree roots as he fell, and, when he came to the bottom, attempted to find cover behind a pine – but collapsed. The murderers clambered down the hill, bent over the dying man, and fired three more shots into him.

Diez had tried to fend the men off with his umbrella. He too fell, but was not dead. On dragging himself back to the hotel he encounted a well-dressed lady from Hamburg. She offered him help. But when he told her his story, she exclaimed, 'How could you go walking with a man like Erzberger!'

Diez entered the hotel lobby alone, covered with blood.[76]

*   *   *

Germany's government had no idea how to deal with Lloyd George's puzzling ultimatum of May 1921. Did he mean 132 billion gold marks or 50 billion? It dissolved in confusion, and Josef Wirth became the new Chancellor. Wirth had taken over the Ministry of Finance the previous year, after Erzberger's humiliation in the courts. Like Erzberger, he was a centralizer and a planner. Like Rathenau, he was a bachelor and a lonely man. Early in June, Wirth and Rathenau announced to the Reichstag that they were forming a 'Cabinet of Fulfilment'.

Wirth had met Rathenau in a government commission set up to organize a programme of 'socialization' – a form of economic planning in vogue with the trade unions after Kapp's farcical *'Putsch'*. The commission achieved nothing, but a 'semi-political, semi-intellectual friendship' developed between Wirth and Rathenau. Rathenau was a physicist, Wirth was a mathematician, and 'both of them were interested in philosophy'.[77]

Lloyd George's government in London had not understood what this 'philosophy' implied; all Lloyd George and his colleagues heard and saw was the economics of 'fulfilment', and they were very impressed – especially by Rathenau. They ignored the rest.

Rathenau's popular books had laid out what the 'philosophy' was: a system of opposites, of *Furchtmenschen* and *Mutmenschen*, of 'men of fear' and 'men of courage', of utilitarian men, who had set the process of world 'mechanization' in motion, and creative men, who provided the spiritual alternative. Rathenau's policy of fulfilment included all this.

The contradiction in his thoughts was translated into a contradiction in his actions: between his assertions of peace and his call for a *levée en masse*. In May 1921, when German politics was divided between those willing to accept and those determined to refuse London's ultimatum, Rathenau figured among the refusers – which was one of the reasons why Wirth was so insistent on having him in his government.

Rathenau covered his ambiguous meditation and deeds with 'glistening words', as Eugen Schiffer, Scheidemann's Minister of Finance, put it. The music of his voice was an important part of this. In fact he was quite overcome by its deep, echoing tone himself. On accepting the Ministry of Reconstruction, on 2 June 1921, he explained his *Erfüllungspolitik* before the Reichstag in terms of Beethoven's last string quartet: 'It begins slowly, "Must it be?" and ends with a decisive and powerful "It must be!"' The Reichstag politely applauded.[78]

The 'Ministry of Reconstruction' was itself a strange conception, pervaded by the musical contrasts so typical of Rathenau. It began with a letter he wrote to Erzberger on the day that Weimar's Constituent National Assembly ratified the Treaty of Versailles, 16 July 1919. 'In our present desperate situation,' he advised, 'we must strive to find the central point from which the whole situation *can be unravelled*' – hardly an endorsement of what most Westerners understood by the term 'fulfilment'. 'This point is to be found in Belgium and northern France', he continued; 'that is to say, in the problem of reconstruction.' There was many a good reason why Germany should attempt to limit 'reconstruction' to this devastated zone, but that was absolutely not the aim of the treaty. Rathenau's Policy of Fulfilment was composed in counterpoint.[79]

Throughout the summer of 1921, Rathenau, the Minister of Reconstruction, negotiated with the French over the means of rehabilating the old war front. He proposed the drafting of up to half a million German labourers (not particularly welcome to the people of Flanders and Picardy) and the supply of enough engine driving belts to stretch around the circumference of the globe (not what France's protectionist trade unions were looking for). His total physical accomplishment as Minister was the erection, in a sea of rubble and human poverty, of a score of new wooden sheds.

An element of unreality had crept into the Policy of Fulfilment. And so it was with Rathenau's entire economic programme. As the Reparations Commission shifted from a demand for cash payments to a requirement of fiscal responsibility, Rathenau became indignant. London was even prepared to offer Germany a loan if Germany demonstrated good faith by an effort to balance her budget. Erzberger would have done it. Rathenau refused to do it. The Reichsmark began to edge, disastrously, upwards.

It was most significant that Rathenau and his small party, the Democrats, resigned from Wirth's government over the issue of Poland. Poland was the test. Rathenau did not accept the League of Nation's partition of Upper Silesia. When Rathenau went to London in December 1921 he was a mere private citizen – one who refused to tolerate Western interference in Poland. Lloyd George, concentrating entirely on the economics of his 'Consortium', missed the other side of Rathenau's policy: an accord with the Bolsheviks, 'fulfilment' in the East. It was this that opened the door to German rearmament.

Did Rathenau really intend to rearm Germany? His associates, General Hans von Seeckt and the head of the Foreign Ministry's Eastern department, Baron Ago von Maltzan, certainly did. Rathenau was perhaps manipulated; but he had exposed himself to this by both his thought and his action.

There was, in the first place, his cast of mind. 'National Bolshevism' was an idea born in the press during the heady weeks of May 1919, when Germany woke up to discover that she really had been defeated. The idea was made up of two themes: co-operation with Bolshevik Russia as means of countering the 'Entente', and a German national renewal based on a combination of Prussian discipline with Bolshevik social reform. Both of these themes are expounded at length in Rathenau's writings. He had probably been influenced by the strategic arguments of Supreme Command: in 1914, knock out the West and then proceed to the East; in 1918, make a treaty with Russia and then pound on the West. His ideas of national renewal owed a good deal to his experience as a wartime planner.

Co-operation with Bolshevik Russia had been a German war aim, embodied in the Treaty of Brest-Litovsk. Though annulled by the Treaty of
Versailles, it was still very much present in the spirit of German government
officials. Poland was always the key. In April 1920, as the Red Army prepared to invade Poland, Seeckt and Maltzan negotiated an agreement with
Moscow to set up 'prisoner-exchange offices'. By the following winter Seeckt
had organized the German version, *Sondergruppe R*, assigned to manage 'all
military operations in Russia'; it was financed by huge grants hidden in
Wirth's irresponsible budgets. Wirth himself established the GEFU in the
Ministry of Finance, which, in co-operation with the Russian munitions
industry, produced bombs, tanks and aircraft for Germany. The NEP,
announced by Lenin in March 1921 after his treaty with the Poles, opened
a new phase of collaboration between the 'fulfillers' in Germany and the
Bolsheviks.

That truly was a historic year that began in March, 1921: the Bolsheviks
signed at Riga, the NEP started, the sailors of Kronstadt were shut up in
concentration camps, Germany began a new little war in Upper Silesia,
London proposed a revised payments schedule for reparations, and Wilson,
the invalid, moved out of the White House. It was in 1921 that Rathenau
travelled to London. Lloyd George's idea of an economic 'Consortium' was
a gift to the bomb-makers: what an opportunity this international conference
presented! 'Germany must build up its strength at home and then wait to
strike at the right moment,' Rathenau reported to Seeckt.[80]

With the arrival of the New Year in 1922, Karl Radek, Russian emissary
and surviving Spartacist, undertook a trip to Berlin. On 22 January, Maltzan
showed Wirth the first draft of what would become the Russo-German
Treaty of Rapallo. The Policy of Fulfilment was moving on.

The next stage began with the nomination of a Jew to head Germany's
Foreign Ministry – an unprecedented act. Wirth did it in the secrecy of the
night, on 31 January, shortly after Rathenau's return from Cannes, where the
Allies had agreed to a temporary moratorium on reparations. The industrial
magnates did not want Rathenau as Foreign Minister; Hugo Stinnes, of
Essen's Coal Syndicate and a People's Party deputy in the Reichstag, had
been pushing for Frederic von Rosenberg, a career diplomat currently serving in Vienna. The Nationalists were getting rowdy again. Helfferich was
once more writing articles in the *Deutsche Tageszeitung*, and Count von
Westarp was making bitter speeches in the Reichstag. The winds of violence
in Germany, which since the war had never really settled down, were
whipped up further by the military operations in Upper Silesia.

When he took up the Foreign Ministry, Rathenau was overcome by a
terrible sense of foreboding. He was tormented by the opposing *Mutmensch*
and *Furchtmensch* within him. 'It is late at night and I am thinking of you
with a heavy heart,' he wrote to his tender friend Lili Deutsch within an

hour of accepting the post. 'I stand before this task in deep and earnest doubt. What can a single individual do in the face of this torpid world, with enemies at his back, and conscious of his own limitations and weaknesses?' Count Harry Kessler noticed how Rathenau aged over the next few weeks. He went round to the Foreign Ministry on 20 March and asked how Rathenau was. Rathenau grimaced and pulled a Browning pistol out of his pocket; 'I cannot go about without this little instrument,' he said. Rathenau still regularly attended silent luncheons with his mother in her mansion, not far from the Foreign Ministry. He could not bring himself to tell her that he had accepted the appointment; she learned about it from the newspapers. One day, as they solemnly played with their food, his mother looked up at him and said: 'Walther, why have you done this to me?' Walther humbly replied that he had really been obliged to accept the appointment 'because they couldn't find anyone else'.[81]

The day came when he had to leave Berlin for the great international conference in Genoa. 'It is simply a farewell, for I know that what I have to undertake, whether I will or not, means the breaking of a life,' he wrote to Lili Deutsch. 'I shall return only to be overwhelmed in the abyss.'[82]

In style, the Genoa Conference of 1922 resembled Paris in 1919, only this time both the Germans and the Russian Bolsheviks were present. The Americans were notably absent. The delegations were housed in Renaissance villas and towering eighteenth-century palaces; the narrow gullies of the streets swarmed with journalists from every corner of the planet. Signor Luigi Facta's government – the last constitutional government in Italy before Mussolini marched on Rome – had established in a palace on Piazza della Zecca a central news agency, the 'Casa della Stampa', which supplied a feast of rumour and scandal. World bankers, industrialists, trade unionists, diplomats, politicians and spies fed on it.

Rathenau knew the streets of Genoa well; as a young man he had installed the electric cable cars there. In spare moments he wandered around, unguarded, with his friend Harry Kessler, pointing out vestiges of the Middle Ages and the Renaissance that weren't mentioned in the tourist guides.

As at Paris, a plenary session formally opened the Conference on 10 April. It took place in a medieval hall that was so dark that the glass chandeliers had to be lit even at midday. It was the week of Easter. The premiers and their delegations sat at a horseshoe table, as in 1919. But the new French Prime Minister, Raymond Poincaré, was not there. He had attempted to cancel and then to delay the conference until June; he had managed to keep the discussion of reparations off the agenda – which rather destroyed the purpose of the meeting. All the opening speeches were read from well-prepared texts. Even the French thought Chicherin, head of the Soviet delegation, was reading in Russian until he came to the word '*désarmement*'. Nobody except the Germans knew that when Chicherin and his colleagues had passed through Berlin the previous week they had already got Wirth and Rathenau to agree to the text of a treaty.[83]

Perhaps Lloyd George's suspicions, always acute, were aroused. For the remainder of the week, the hub of the Conference became the 'private conversations' he held in his villa, from which the Germans were excluded. His main aim was to reach an agreement with the Russians, holding out the possibility of a Russian share in the reparations – as had been written into the Treaty of Versailles in Article 116. But it was too late for Lloyd George. The 'Consortium', 'economic Europe', was already dead.

It is quite possible that Rathenau, in his contrary way, was also developing doubts about what his own delegation was getting up to. In his talk with Kessler on 20 March he had acknowledged that his most cordial relations were, first, with the British and then with the French; his worst, he said, were with the Germans. In a long letter he wrote to Ebert a few days after his arrival in Genoa he pointed out that 'the Russian matter holds out more dangers than opportunities for us'.

During that first critical week of the Conference it was Baron von Maltzan who took all the initiatives, not Wirth or Rathenau. Maltzan was most economical in the information he passed on to the Foreign Minister. The Baron was a master of innuendo: he played on the fears of German isolation, he used the rumours spreading out from the Casa della Stampa as though they were strings on his own instrument; he enjoyed the company of both the British and the Russians at his tea table in the Hotel Eden. When he learned on Saturday evening that the 'private conversations' in Lloyd George's villa were deadlocked he didn't breath a word to Rathenau.

At 1.15 a.m. on Easter morning, Adolf Joffe, the former Russian ambassador at Berlin and Spartacist, now a member of the Soviet delegation, called up Maltzan and invited him and his colleagues around to the neighbouring town of Rapallo to sign the treaty between their two countries. Maltzan was delighted. The hour of history had arrived. He donned a black silk dressing gown and went straight round to wake up Rathenau. He found the Foreign Minister in mauve pyjamas, already pacing the floor. 'What,' exclaimed pale Rathenau, turning upon Maltzan as he swung open the door, 'I suppose you bring me the death warrant?'[84]

'No,' replied cool Maltzan; 'news of quite a different character.'

Rathenau, who still had a friendly respect for Britain, wanted to inform Lloyd George immediately. Maltzan, who was now committed to the Russians, said, 'That would be quite dishonourable.' He threatened to resign if Rathenau did tell Lloyd George. The two of them went over to Chancellor Wirth's rooms, and together – Wirth in his nightshirt, Maltzan in his black gown and Rathenau in his mauve pyjamas – they decided to sign the treaty.

So on Easter Sunday, 16 April, Rathenau, Maltzan and two other members of the German delegation drove over to Rapallo. After a brief discussion with Chicherin, Maltzan persuaded Rathenau to go and visit a friend in his villa in Portofino. The villa had no telephone, so Rathenau was not available when Lloyd George, whose suspicions were rising by the hour, called. But he was back in Rapallo at 6.30 sharp to sit down and sign the Soviet–German accord.

Its six terms were quite innocuous, consisting of a mutual repudiation of claims for war costs and damages, and of property claims, a promise to co-operate economically, and a 'most-favoured-nation' clause. It was the signing that counted, not the content. It was announced in the next morning's newspapers.

The French were genuinely furious. Lloyd George 'roused himself'. The Conference actually went on for another month, and eventually broke up when Lloyd George got into a row with the Belgians. The French supported the Belgians and Lloyd George went home, his ambition for an 'economic Europe' deflated, to face another revolt of the Conservatives in his coalition. The Conference had achieved nothing save, as Count Harry Kessler put it, that 'Germany was no longer an outcast.'[85]

The weather in Genoa had been reminiscent of the hard years: cold, misty and gloomy. Rathenau was chilled to the soul. He wrote to Lili Deutsch on 28 April to say that the diplomatic storm induced by the treaty had not yet passed. 'Even nature refuses to be kind,' he reported, gazing from his hotel table. 'I am looking down on a huge green garden full of half-blossoming red and white chestnut trees with a line of mountains beyond, and everything is draped with grey rain-laden wisps of cloud.' The winter, he reflected, 'clings to everything like the war'.[86]

In the spring of 1918, as the armies of Western Europe clashed in their final round, Rathenau had published his apocalyptic open letter *To German Youth*, calling on the young to take the place of mechanistic man, broken in body and soul, and create a *new order*, 'the moral and spiritual rejuvenation of industry'. It was German youth that killed him.

Stubenrauch, Günther, Kern, Fischer and the brothers Techow were all under twenty-five; Stubenrauch, the initiator of the conspiracy, was only seventeen. They were in many ways typical of their generation. They belonged to secret youth groups, they were all connected with the Free Corps, and four of them were members of *Organisation Consul*. They drank together, they plotted in the house of Frau Techow (her husband had been killed in the war), they took target practice from their grey six-seater tourer in Grunewald, only a few hundred yards from where Rathenau lived. Their motives for killing him were vague and predictable: he was a Jew, he was a friend of the Bolsheviks, his Policy of Fulfilment betrayed Germany, and Ludendorff at the Reichtag's Commission of Inquiry (following Erzberger's revelations) had muttered a few words suggesting that 'Rathenau had not wished for victory.' Of the four who actually committed the murder, only one survived to write his memoirs; the three others 'committed suicide' after they had been surrounded by police in their hiding place at Kassel.

In Berlin, Rathenau never accepted police protection, even after Wirth had told him that he had definite evidence of an assassination plot. On receiving Wirth's warning, Rathenau stood motionless before the Chancellor for around two minutes. 'None of us dared break the silence or speak a single word,' Wirth later wrote. 'Rathenau seemed to be gazing on some distant land . . . Suddenly his face and his eyes took on an expression of infinite benevolence and gentleness. With a calm such as I had never witnessed in him . . . he stepped up to me, and putting both his hands on my shoulders said: "Dear friend, it is nothing. Who would do me any harm?" '[87]

It was the third day of summer, 24 June 1922, a real summer's day. An old black car came puttering down the middle of the Königsallee; the weather was so warm and delightful that Rathenau had ordered the hood down. The car 'had one gentleman in the back seat' reported a labourer who was working on a new building nearby; 'one could see exactly what he was like'. The chauffeur slowed down by the tramlines to take a double bend. A big, open, field-grey tourer with four men in smart leather jackets roared past, forcing the chauffeur to swerve. Kern, resting the butt of his submachine-gun in his armpit, opened fire; Fischer tossed in a hand grenade.[88]

Barely a month had passed since the closing session of the Conference at Genoa, when Rathenau had pronounced a speech in his slow and impeccable French. The history of Italy was more ancient than that of most European nations, he remarked. More than one world movement has originated in Italy, he added. Let us hope the people of the earth will again lift up their eyes and their hearts, he entreated. As he changed to Italian, elder statesmen and experienced diplomats, along with journalists and the public, rose to their feet to applaud. In baritone, Rathenau quoted Petrarch: '*Io vò gridando: Pace, Pace, Pace!*'*[89]

---

* 'I go calling: Peace, Peace, Peace!'

Chronology

	General	London	Paris	Berlin	Moscow
1918					
5 January		Lloyd George outlines peace plan			
8 January	Wilson outlines 'Fourteen Points'				
28 January				Chancellor von Hertling cautiously responds to Wilson's Fourteen Points; his speech is followed by a wave of strikes	Red Army established
10 February	Trotsky breaks off negotiations with Germany at Brest-Litovsk				
18 February	German armies march unopposed into Estonia and Ukraine	Representation of the People Act, extending franchise to women			
23 February	Reds seize Rostov				
3 March	Treaty of Brest-Litovsk				Bolsheviks move capital from Petrograd to Moscow
21 March	First of Ludendorff's springtime offensives begins outside Amiens				
23 March			'Big Bertha' (actually several long-range canon) begins three weeks of bombardment		

1918	General	London	Paris	Berlin	Moscow
26 March	Doullens: Allied unity of command agreed				
9 May					Grain monopoly declared
6 June	Czech Legion seize Omsk				
28 June					Decree of Nationalization
6 July					Count Mirbach, German ambassador, assassinated
8 July				Foreign Secretary R. von Kühlmann dismissed for recommending negotiations with Allies	
17 July	Ekaterinburg: Tsar and family murdered				
18 July	Villers-Cotterêts: Mangin's French Tenth Army attacks Crown Prince's forces on their right flank, turning the tide of the war			Rathenau publishes *To German Youth*	
8 August	The German Army's 'black day': Rawlinson's British Fourth Army and Debeney's French First break through between the Avre and the Somme				

13 August	First American Army inaugurated in France	Chancellor von Hertling and Foreign Secretary von Hintze leave for Spa Conference (discussions with Supreme Command)	
15 August	Haig begins reinforcing northern sector of the Somme, opening the greatest battle of the war		
18 August	Denikin's Whites capture Ekaterinodar		
27 August			'Supplementary treaties' signed by Germans and Russians
30 August			Assassination attempt on Lenin
31 August	Police strike		
12 September	American First Army begins Saint-Mihiel offensive		
23 September	Omsk: All-Russian (White) government established		
26 September	Z-Day: joint Allied offensive launched		

1918	General	London	Paris	Berlin	Moscow
28 September				Ludendorff's first plea for an armistice; Hertling and Hintze leave for Spa	
29 September	Rawlinson's Fourth Army crosses the Canal Saint-Quentin; the Hindenburg Line is broken				
1 October		American First Army enmired at Thiaucourt		Prince Max becomes acting Chancellor	
4 October				First German note to Wilson, requesting armistice	
5 October		British forces enter Cambrai			
6 October		Wilson receives first German note	Supreme War Council discusses Turkish armistice; news of German note to Wilson announced		
7 October				Rathenau appeals for *levée en masse*	
10 October		Irish Sea: *Leinster* torpedoed			
17 October		British enter Lille and Douai			

Date			
26 October		Ludendorff dismissed; Groener succeeds as First Quartermaster General	
29 October			Kaiser leaves for Spa
29 October–4 November		Pre-armistice negotiations within Supreme War Council	
31 October	Turkey signs Armistice		
1 November	Kiel: sailors mutiny		
1–3 November	Allied forces cross Scheldt and Sambre Canal; Germany's strategic lateral rail broken; rout of German Army begins		
3 November	Villa Giusti: Austria accepts Allied armistice terms		
3–7 November	American First Army advances to Sedan		
5 November	The 'Lansing Note' – Washington's final note to Berlin		
	American congressional elections		

1918

	General	London	Paris	Berlin	Moscow
7 November	German plenipotentiaries, seeking an armistice, cross Western Front	Australian PM, W. M. Hughes, protests that Dominions not consulted on armistice terms – and particularly war indemnities		Social Democrats present ultimatum that formally demands Kaiser's abdication	
9 November	'False Armistice' in USA	Lord Mayor's Show		Kaiser abdicates Prince Max hands Chancellorship to Ebert	
10 November			Fernand Faure, French journalist, demands Germany pay 'total indemnity'	Council of People's Commissars created	
11 November	Armistice signed near Compiègne	Stock Exchange members sing the 'Doxology' and proceed up Embankment	Mlle Marthe Chenal, sings the 'Marseillaise' on the steps of the Opéra		
13 November	Belgrade: Allied military convention with Hungary				
15 November	International Armistice Commission established at Spa		French peace plan		
16 November		In Central Hall, Westminster, Lloyd George opens election campaign			

Date				
18 November	Omsk: Kolchak named Supreme Ruler			
21 November	Hoover arrives and shows his opposition to the Allied Maritime Transport Council			
23 November	British–French naval detachment lands at Novorossisk			
1 December		Hoover in Paris develops plan for US-run relief programme		
1–3 December	London Conference, attended by the Allied premiers			
6 December	British forces enter Cologne		Chausseestrasse massacre	
10 December				Soldiers' entry and victory parade
13 December	Left bank of Rhine occupied by Allies; Trier: First Armistice renewal			
14 December	General election	Wilson's entry		
15 December	German–Polish diplomatic relations broken			

	General	London	Paris	Berlin	Moscow
1918					
18 December				Congress of Workers' and Soldiers' Councils adopts 'Hamburg Points', creating 'People's Army'	
24 December	Kolchak captures Perm			The Battle of Christmas Eve	
25 December		The 'Great Peace Christmas'			
26 December	Siege of Posen begins	Pantomime season opens			
28 December		Election results announced		Noske named Minister of National Defence and Brockdorff-Rantzau named Foreign Secretary	
29 December	Russian Red Army captures Riga		Clemenceau defends, in the Chamber, the 'old system' of diplomacy		
1919					
1 January				German Communist Party (KPD) founded	
6–12 January				Spartacus Week	
10 January		Lloyd George announces new Coalition government			

Date		
12 January	Supreme War Council opens talks; the informal beginning of the Peace Conference Hankey creates the Council of Ten	Food Levy
15 January	'Russian Political Conference' founded by Russian émigrés	Liebknecht and Luxemburg murdered
16 January		Orgburo established; Politburo reinstated
17 January	Trier: second Armistice renewal	
18 January	First plenary session of the Peace Conference: the official opening	
19 January		Elections for National Assembly
22 January	Ten invite Russian warring parties to Prinkipo	
27 January	Calais: British troops mutiny	
3 February	Denikin captures Grozny	
4 February		Chicherin note, answering Prinkipo offer

1919	General	London	Paris	Berlin	Moscow
5 February	Bialystock: Polish–German accord on Russian borders				Stalin and Dzierzynski report to Central Committee on Perm failure – Trotsky faulted
6 February	Weimar: National Assembly opens		Hoover sets up Supreme Economic Council, under American control		
8 February		Lloyd George in London Troops protest at Whitehall			
11 February	Weimar: Ebert elected President of the Reich				
13 February				Scheidemann's coalition formed – ministerial offices in Berlin	
14 February	Trier: third Armistice renewal, for an indefinite period German Supreme Command moves to Kolberg Bereza Kartuska: Soviet–Polish war begins		Covenant of League of Nations presented at second plenary session Churchill in Paris to discuss Russia Wilson leaves for US		

Date	Events
19 February	Assassination attempt on Clemenceau
21 February	Munich: Kurt Eisner assassinated British inform French of intention to suspend wartime subsidies to Allies; currency crisis begins
22 February	William C. Bullitt leaves for Russia Conference moves to prepare preliminary peace terms with Germany
2 March	Kolchak begins offensive on Ufa Victory parade for East African Corps Third International opens
3 March	Bloody Week begins
4–5 March	Spa: negotiations over German food supplies
6 March	Lloyd George's return
7 March	Premiers' conversations at Hôtel Crillon inaugurate 'Council of Four'
8 March	Lloyd George clashes with Louis Klotz over German gold
10 March	Bullitt arrives

1919	General	London	Paris	Berlin	Moscow
11 March			Keynes recommends avoidance of fixed reparations sum in treaty with Germany		
13–16 March	Brussels: Allies agree to supply food to Germany; Germany agrees to hand over merchant vessels				
14 March			Wilson's return		Bullitt receives 'peace proposal' and leaves
17 March					Sverdlov dies; 'duumvirate' ends
18 March					Eighth Party Congress opens – Party programme on nationalities and on peasants; Lenin defends Trotsky
22–3 March	Béla Kun establishes Soviet Republic in Hungary		Lloyd George's weekend in Fontainebleau		
24 March			Fontainebleau Memorandum (formally dated '25 March')		
27 March			Anglo-American guarantee of French borders discussed by Four		

Date			
3–7 April		Wilson sick	
		Reparation clauses of treaty outlined	
3 April	French evacuate Odessa		
9 April		Paderewski defends Polish cause before the Four	
14 April	Lloyd George in London	House and Clemenceau agree on fifteen-year occupation of Rhineland	
16 April		Lloyd George speaks of Conference at House of Commons	
18 April			Lloyd George in Paris
19 April	Poles seize Vilna		
20 April	Easter Sunday		
25 April			Versailles: arrival of German delegation
1 May		Anglo-American Society honours J. Daniels, US Naval Secretary	
3 May	Free Corps attack and 'cleanse' Munich		
5 May	US unilaterally lays claim to all German vessels interned in her ports		Wilson turns down Keynes's scheme for the 'Rehabilitation of European Credit'

1919	General	London	Paris	Berlin	Moscow
7 May			Versailles: Treaty terms presented to German delegation		
8 May				Ebert declares 'week of mourning' over Versailles terms	
12 May				Special session of National Assembly in Berlin	
14 May				Groener consulted on possible armed resistance to West	
17 May			Bullitt resigns from American delegation		
29 May			Versailles: final German note on Treaty's terms		
30 May			Keynes collapses from exhaustion		
31 May				Rathenau, 'The End' – proposing abandonment of all governmental responsibility to Allies	
1 June			British Empire delegation discusses treaty terms at Lloyd George's residence		

Date		
3 June		Lloyd George presents demands for revision to Four
		Wilson, before American delegation, rejects revision
7 June		Keynes 'slips away'
16 June		Allied reply to final German note
18 June	Scheidemann government resigns; G. Bauer forms government	
20 June		Foch orders mobilization of armies
21 June	Scapa Flow: German Fleet scuttled	
28 June		Versailles Treaty signed
10 September		Treaty of Saint-Germain, with Austria
16 September		Lloyd George in Paris recommends dissolving the Peace Conference
26 September	Wichita, Kansas: Wilson collapses on speaking tour	
14 November	Kolchak abandons Omsk	

	General	London	Paris	Berlin	Moscow
16 November			French legislative elections: success of *Bloc National*		
19 November	Washington: Senate votes down Versailles Treaty				
12 December		Keynes, *Economic Consequences of the Peace* published			
1920					
10 January			Clemenceau resigns		
7 February	Irkutsk: Kolchak executed				
12 March				Conclusion of Erzberger/Helfferich libel trial	
13 March				Kapp *Putsch*	
27 March	British and French evacuate Novorossiisk				
29 March					Ninth Party Congress – Lenin predicts victory of Worldwide Soviet Republic
7 May	Poles occupy Kiev				
4 June			Treaty of Trianon, with Hungary		
5–6 June	Red Army invades Poland				

Date	Event	Event
5–16 July	Spa Conference	
19 July–7 August	Petrograd: second 'Comintern'	
10 August	Treaty of Sèvres, with Turkey; formal end of the Paris Peace Conference	
8 November	Geneva: opening of League of Nations	
14 November	British and French evacuate Wrangel's White forces from Crimea	
22–9 December		Eighth Congress of Soviets – controversy over peasant question and 'War Communism'
1921		
1–7 March	First London Conference – over German reparations	
5 March	Treaty of Riga ends Soviet–Polish war	
16 March	Kronstadt: Red Army attacks mutineers	Anglo-Russian Trade Agreement
21 March	Upper Silesia: plebiscite	Tenth Party Congress adopts NEP and 'ban on factions'

	General	London	Paris	Berlin	Moscow
1920					
30 April–5 May		Second London Conference			
10 May				Josef Wirth becomes Chancellor	
29 May				Rathenau named Minister of Reconstruction	
8 July	Ireland: truce				
26 August	Bad Griesbach: Erzberger assassinated				
16 December		Anglo-Irish Treaty			
1922					
6–12 January	Cannes Conference				
31 January				Rathenau named Foreign Minister	
27 March–2 April					Eleventh Party Congress – after which Stalin named General Secretary of Central Committee
10 April–19 May	Genoa Conference				
16 April	Treaty of Rapallo				
25 May				Lenin's first major stroke	

Notes

PREFACE

1. Samuel Hynes, *The Soldiers' Tale* (New York, 1997), 93–107.
2. Marc Bloch, *French Rural History* (Berkeley and Los Angeles, 1966), xxvii.

THE ELEVENTH HOUR

Beginnings

1. Witnesses speak of a 'medieval' atmosphere on the front. For example, when the French writer Jacques Meyer turned up on the front, fresh out of the Ecole Normale in Paris, he thought the troops showed the 'naivety of their ancestors of the Middle Ages'. 'The war gave the impression of taking us back to a very distant past,' recorded the great medievalist Marc Bloch in a similar vein; he didn't discover the 'collective psychology' of eleventh-century peasants in the archives – he had found it on the front. Jacques Meyer, *Les Soldats de la Grande Guerre* (Paris, 1966), 255–66; Marc Bloch, *Ecrits de guerre, 1914–1918* (Paris, 1997), 169–84; Paul Fussell, *The Great War and Modern Memory* (London, 1975), 114–54.
2. Souvenir hunters tore the white flags to pieces, some of which found their way into museums, others into private collections; one of them was woven into a rather splendid commemorative flag for the 171st Infantry Regiment, now on display at the Villa Pasques in La Capelle.
3. The principal sources used in this section are: *Rapport du Lieutenant-Colonel Ducornez du Centre d'Etudes de l'Infanterie, commandant les avant-postes français à La Capelle le 7 novembre 1918, sur le passage des lignes françaises par les parlementaires allemands du 7 au 9 novembre 1918*, Paris, 22 April 1928, (Syndicat Mixte pour le développement de la Thiérache, La Capelle); le comte de Bourbon-Busset, *Récit de Monsieur de Bourbon-Busset* (transcript of broadcast by the Poste des PTT, 11 November 1935, in private archives of Monsieur Fernand Camart, La Capelle); *L'Illustration*, 16–23 November 1918; General Eugène Debeney, *La Guerre et les hommes* (Paris, 1937), 40; Claude Dufresne, *Ce jour-là* (Paris, 1988), 261–8; Matthias Erzberger, *Souvenirs de guerre* (Paris, 1921); Charles Vilain, *Le 7 novembre 1918 à Haudroy* (Saint-Quentin, 1968)
4. Barbara Tuchman, *The Guns of August* (New York, 1963), 150–2.
5. Erzberger to Falkenhayn, 17 September 1914, and *Der Tag*, 21 October 1914, in Erzberger, *Souvenirs*, xi.
6. Gregor Dallas, *1815* (London, 1996), 196–7.
7. Thomas Mann, 'Reflections of a Nonpolitical Man', in Tuchman, *Guns*, 348.
8. For an excellent critique of the 'historical conditions' school, see Hartmut Pogge von

Strandmann, 'Germany and the Coming of War', in R. J. W. Evans and Hartmut Pogge von Strandmann, eds, *The Coming of the First World War* (Oxford, 1988), 87–123.

9. Ibid., 87.

10. Winston S. Churchill, *The World Crisis, 1911–1918* (London, 1938), I, 37–8. Count Metternich was dismissed from his ambassadorial post in 1912 for predicting that German naval increases would lead to war with Britain by 1915. His illustrious forebear, the Austrian Foreign Minister during the Napoleonic wars, had made a virtue out of weakness. There was no room for a Metternich in the new strong Germany.

11. For the road marker on Jovinus, Tuchman, *Guns*, 234; Blücher's dogs in Marc Blancpain, *La Vie quotidienne dans la France du nord sous les occupations (1814–1944)* (Paris, 1983), 41. Some general comments on Europe's northern plain in my *At the Heart of a Tiger* (London, 1993), 238–40.

12. Quoted by Annette Becker, 'Life in an Occupied Zone', in Hugh Cecil and Peter H. Liddle, eds, *Facing Armageddon* (London, 1996), 638.

13. Naumann quoted by Paul Kennedy, *The Rise and Fall of the Great Powers* (London, 1988), 211.

14. Karl von Clausewitz, *On War* (Princeton, 1976), 87.

15. This, however, is basically the argument of George F. Kennan, *The Fateful Alliance* (Manchester, 1984).

16. Pogge von Strandmann, 'Germany', 114.

17. Books on the 'Origins of the First World War' fill libraries. The classic work is Sidney B. Fay, *The Origins of the World War* (New York, 1966), 2 vols. Jacques Droz, *Les Causes de la Première Guerre mondiale* (Paris, 1973) provides a summary of the early literature. An extremely useful collection of German documents is to be found in Imanuel Geiss, ed., *Juli 1914* (Munich, 1986). Field Marshal Lord Carver, *Twentieth-Century Warriors* (London, 1987), contains good accounts of the formation of the European armies. Recent reviews of war plans and *ante-bellum* international politics can be found in John Keegan, *The First World War* (London, 1998), 27–77, and Niall Ferguson, *The Pity of War* (London, 1998), 31–211.

18. Matthias Erzberger, on a visit to the Vatican in February 1915, raised with the Pope the question of 2,000 Belgian nuns who were reportedly pregnant. He initiated an investigation that was carried out by the 'military administration in Brussels' which asked all Belgian bishops to report on cases of raped nuns in their dioceses. Erzberger was comforted by the response: 'one does not know of a single case of rape committed by German soldiers on the nuns'. Erzberger, *Souvenirs*, 60–1.

19. Tuchman, *Guns*, 347–62; Mark Derez, 'The Flames of Louvain', in Cecil and Liddle, eds, *Armageddon*, 617–29; Lothar Wieland, *Belgien 1914* (Frankfurt, 1984).

20. Becker, 'Occupied Zone', 630–41; on deportations and the 'unemployment problem' in occupied territories, see Erzberger, *Souvenirs*, 232–3.

21. Derez, 'Louvain', 619; Clausewitz, *War*, 4.

22. Nigel H. Jones, *The War Walk* (London, 1983), 10.

23. Churchill, *World Crisis*, I, 39–40; Carver, *Warriors*, 44–6.

24. Grand Admiral Alfred von Tirpitz, *Politische Dokumente*, (Hamburg, 1926), II, 68–73; Fritz Fischer, *Germany's Aims in the First World War* (New York, 1967), 98–106.

25. Dallas, *Tiger*, 435.

26. John Buchan's memoir of the Grenfell brothers, in Samuel Hynes, *The Soldiers' Tale* (New York, 1997), 34–7.

27. Fussell, *Great War*, 116.

28. Bloch, *Ecrits*, 123–4.

29. Erzberger, *Souvenirs*, 360–1.

30. See Rod Paschall, *The Defeat of Imperial Germany* (New York, 1989), 13–14.

31. Siegfried Sassoon, 'The General', in Sassoon, *The War Poems* (London, 1983), 78.

32. Murray McClymont's 1918 parody of 'The General' gives some idea of the depths of bitterness:

> 'Good morning, good morning!' the General said,
> As he passed down the Line with a wound in his head.
> Now, we knew he was wounded by the way that he bled,
> And when he got to the Base the poor bugger was dead –
> (Chorus) HOORAY!

Quoted in Jon Stallworthy, *Wilfred Owen* (London, 1974), 270.
33. Basil Liddell Hart, *History of the World War, 1914–1918* (London, 1934).
34. Jones, *War Walk*, 153–6; Stéphane Audouin-Rouzeau, 'The French Soldier in the Trenches', in Cecil and Little, eds, *Armageddon*, 224.
35. Sassoon, 'Died of Wounds', in *Poems*, 41.
36. Hynes, *Tale*, 39.
37. Tuchman, *Guns*, 242.
38. Dallas, *Tiger*, 447–52, 474–82; Guy Pedroncini, *Les Mutineries de 1917* (Paris, 1967).
39. Peter Simkins, 'The War Experience of a Typical Kitchener Division', and Gary Sheffield, 'Officer–Man Relations, Discipline and Morale in the British Army of the Great War', in Cecil and Liddle, eds, *Armageddon*, 297–313, 413–24.
40. Churchill, *World Crisis*, I, 151.
41. Sassoon, 'In the Pink', in *Poems*, 22.
42. Full text in Siegfried Sassoon, *The Complete Memoirs of George Sherston* (London, 1972), 496.
43. The subject is brilliantly pursued in Pat Barker's *The Regeneration Trilogy* (London, 1996).

Movements

1. Georges Clemenceau, *Grandeurs et misères d'une victoire* (Paris, 1930), 114.
2. Harold Nicolson, *Peacemaking 1919* (Gloucester, Mass., 1984), 49.
3. On the drafting of Wilson's speech, see Charles Seymour (a member of The Inquiry), ed., *The Intimate Papers of Colonel House* (London, 1928), III, 330–52.
4. On the drafting and contents of Lloyd George's speech: David Lloyd George, *War Memoirs* (London, 1933–6), V, 2481–9, 2515–27; Arthur Walworth, *America's Moment* (New York, 1977), 2–3; A. J. P. Taylor, *English History, 1914–1945* (Oxford, 1965), 96–7, 116–17.
5. Stockton Axson (Wilson's brother-in-law), *'Brother Woodrow': A Memoir of Woodrow Wilson* (Princeton, 1993), 201.
6. Edwin A. Weinstein's *Woodrow Wilson: A Medical and Psychological Biography* (Princeton, 1981) is a fairly recent example.
7. Woodrow Wilson's New History, which could sit comfortably in many an academic journal today, is defined in his article 'The Variety and Unity of History', in *The Papers of Woodrow Wilson*, ed. Arthur S. Link et al. (Princeton, 1966–93), XV, 472–91. Wilson's experience as a philosophizing lawyer in Atlanta is recounted by Axson, *'Brother Woodrow'*, 50–6.
8. Axson, *'Brother Woodrow'*, 52.
9. Weinstein, *Wilson*, 14–19, 23; Axson, *'Brother Woodrow'*, 98–9, 108–11, 146–8. Axson put Wilson's radical manner of fleecing the superfluous from his life in a positive light by emphasizing his extraordinary ability to make quick deductions from a small amount of information: 'He lets a few things that he hears construct in his mind many other things which he knows must go with the few things, just as a paleontologist will construct the skeleton of an extinct monster from a few bones.' Axson, *'Brother Woodrow'*, 148.
10. Axson, *'Brother Woodrow'*, 44; Weinstein, *Wilson*, 165–7.
11. Axson, *'Brother Woodrow'*, 85.
12. Ibid., 20–1.
13. Paul Kennedy, *The Rise and the Fall of the Great Powers* (London, 1988), 242–4.

14. Axson, *'Brother Woodrow'*, 132; 'Princeton in the Nation's Service', Sesquicentennial address, 1896, in Wilson, *Papers*, X, 31.
15. A picture of the development of clubland, New York, is in my *At the Heart of a Tiger* (London, 1993), 55–61.
16. Axson, *'Brother Woodrow'*, 140–2.
17. Quoted in Walworth, *America's Moment*, 8.
18. See my *1815* (London, 1996), 266–72.
19. Axson, *'Brother Wilson'*, 193–4.
20. Walworth, *America's Moment*, 11.
21. Ibid., 6.
22. Ibid., 7; Seymour, ed., *House Papers*, III, 334–8, 351–2. The Fourteen Points were:

I. Open covenants of peace, openly arrived at, after which there shall be no private international understandings of any kind but diplomacy shall proceed always frankly and in the public view.

II. Absolute freedom of navigation upon the seas, outside territorial waters, alike in peace and in war, except as the seas may be closed in whole or in part by international action for the enforcement of international covenants.

III. The removal, so far as possible, of all economic barriers and the establishment of an equality of trade conditions among all the nations consenting to the peace and associating themselves for its maintenance.

IV. Adequate guarantees given and taken that national armaments will be reduced to the lowest point consistent with domestic safety.

V. Free, open-minded, and absolutely impartial adjustment of all colonial claims, based upon a strict observance of the principle that in determining all such questions of sovereignty the interests of the populations concerned must have equal weight with the equitable claims of the Government whose title is to be determined.

VI. The evacuation of all Russian territory and such a settlement of all questions affecting Russia as will secure the best and freest cooperation of the other nations of the world in obtaining for her an unhampered and unembarrassed opportunity for the independent determination of her own political development and national policy and assure her of a sincere welcome into the society of free nations under institutions of her own choosing; and, more than a welcome, assistance also of every kind that she may need and may herself desire. The treatment accorded Russia by her sister nations in the months to come will be the acid test of their good will, of their comprehension of her needs as distinguished from their own interests, and of their intelligent and unselfish sympathy.

VII. Belgium, the whole world will agree, must be evacuated and restored, without any attempt to limit the sovereignty which she enjoys in common with all other free nations. No other single act will serve as this will serve to restore confidence among the nations in the laws which they themselves have set and determined for the government of their relations with one another. Without this healing act the whole structure and validity of international law is forever impaired.

VIII. All French territory should be freed and the invaded portions restored, and the wrong done to France by Prussia in 1871 in the matter of Alsace-Lorraine, which has unsettled the peace of the world for nearly fifty years, should be righted, in order that peace may once more be made secure in the interest of all.

IX. A readjustment of the frontiers of Italy should be effected along clearly recognizable lines of nationality.

X. The peoples of Austria-Hungary, whose place among the nations we wish to see safeguarded and assured, should be accorded the freest opportunity of autonomous development.

XI. Rumania, Serbia, and Montenegro should be evacuated; occupied territories restored; Serbia accorded free and secure access to the sea; and the relations of the several Balkan

States to one another determined by friendly counsel along historically established lines of allegiance and nationality; and international guarantees of the political and economic independence and teritorial integrity of the several Balkan States should be entered into. XII. The Turkish portions of the present Ottoman Empire should be assured a secure sovereignty, but the other nationalities which are now under Turkish rule should be assured an undoubted security of life and an absolutely unmolested opportunity of autonomous development, and the Dardanelles should be permanently opened as a free passage to the ships and commerce of all nations under international guarantees.

XIII. An independent Polish State should be erected which should include the territories inhabited by indisputably Polish populations, which should be assured a free and secure access to the sea, and whose political and economic independence and territorial integrity should be guaranteed by international covenant.

XIV. A general association of nations must be formed under specific covenants for the purpose of affording mutual guarantees of political independence and territorial integrity to great and small states alike.

(H. W. V. Temperley, *A History of the Peace Conference of Paris* (London, 1920–4), I, 431–3.)

23. Seymour, ed., *House Papers*, 352–9; John Toland, *No Man's Land* (New York, 1980), 121–5.
24. David Stevenson, *The First World War and International Politics* (Oxford, 1988), 201; Nigel H. Jones, *The War Walk* (London, 1983), 169–75; Toland, *No Man's Land*, 14–23; Rod Paschall, *The Defeat of Imperial Germany, 1917–1918* (London, 1989), 135–9.
25. Matthias Erzberger, *Souvenirs de guerre* (Paris, 1921), 22, 266–7, 297.
26. Ibid., 145–7.
27. The interviews also undermined British strategic thinking in the eastern Mediterranean, which was based on the idea that campaigns in Greece, Palestine and Mesopotamia would serve to 'knock away the props'. In fact Germany could do very well without these 'props'; they were costing her a great deal. Austria, the Ottoman Empire and Bulgaria relied on Germany, not the other way round.
28. Toland, *No Man's Land*, xviii; John Terraine, *To Win a War* (London, 1978), 31–2; Paschall, *Defeat*, 79–80.
29. John W. Wheeler-Bennett, *Brest-Litovsk* (London, 1963), 107–10.
30. D. Stevenson, *International Politics*, 201.
31. Terrainc, *To Win a War*, 141.
32. General P. W. E. Ludendorff, *My War Memories 1914–1918*, (London, 1919), II, 542.
33. Toland, *No Man's Land*, 232, 238; Paschall, *Defeat*, 128–33. The new doctrine was summarized in a pamphlet, *The Attack in Position Warfare* by Captain Hermann Geyer, published by Supreme Command on 1 January 1918. Like all 'new' military doctrines, it had its precedents, notably in the German counter-attack at the end of the Passchendaele campaign in November 1917 and, even more remarkably, in General Robert Nivelle's disastrous offensive on the Chemin des Dames the previous April.
34. Terraine, *To Win a War*, 72; Ludendorff, *Memories*, II, 611.
35. Dallas, *Tiger*, 524–7.
36. Major-General F. Maurice, *The Last Four Months* (London, 1919), 58; Terraine, *To Win a War*, 143.
37. Paschall, *Defeat*, 161–5; Major James G. Harbord, *Leaves from a War Diary* (New York, 1925), 37–8; Terraine, *To Win a War*, 79.
38. F. S. Olivier to his brother, 2 May 1918, in ibid., 67; D. Stevenson, *International Politics*, 202; Clemenceau, *Grandeurs*, 59.
39. Terraine, *To Win a War*, 68; Toland, *No Man's Land*, 196–8 ('maddeniningly mulish' was the comment of the Chief of Imperial General Staff, Sir Henry Wilson); Paschall, *Defeat*, 154–5.
40. Harbord, *Leaves*, 43; James Cooke, 'The American Soldier in France, 1917–1919', in Hugh Cecil and Peter H. Liddle, eds, *Facing Armageddon* (London, 1996), 247.

41. Paschall, *Defeat*, 167–9.
42. Ibid., 155–7.
43. See, for instance, the description of the Second Battle of the Marne by the German officer Rudolf Binding, *A Fatalist at War* (London, 1929), 233–5.
44. Terraine, *To Win a War*, 109, 117, 127.
45. Toland, *No Man's Land*, 313; Binding, *Fatalist*, 242–3.
46. Maurice, *Last Four Months*, 99, 211–14.
47. Winston S. Churchill, *The World Crisis, 1911–1918* (London, 1938), II, 1364.
48. Terraine, *To Win a War*, 105; Harbord, *Leaves*, 223; Eugène Debeney, *La Guerre et les hommes* (Paris, 1937), 17, 24–5.
49. Terraine, *To Win a War*, 100; Toland, *No Man's Land*, 340–51.
50. Gordon A. Craig, *Germany* (Oxford, 1981), 367–8; Admiral Georg Alexander von Müller, *The Kaiser and His Court* (New York, 1964), diary entries for 20 June, 22, 23, 25, 28 July, 2 August 1918, 363, 374–7.
51. Müller, *Kaiser*, 8 August 1918, 377.
52. Harry R. Rudin, *Armistice 1918* (New Haven, 1944), 21–2.
53. At least, according to ibid. Colonel Hans von Haeften of the Military Section of the Foreign Office and responsible for the minutes of at least one of the meetings that followed implied that Hindenburg and Ludendorff were already in Spa by Monday 12 August. See Prince Max of Baden, *The Memoirs of Prince Max of Baden* (New York, 1928), I, 315.
54. Ludendorff, *Memories*, II, 679–89.
55. Prince Max was a brother-in-law of the Kaiser's daughter.
56. Craig, *Germany*, 393; David Blackbourn, *The Fontana History of Germany, 1780–1918* (London, 1997), 487–9; Max of Baden, *Memoirs*, I, 158, 257–9.
57. Ibid., 307–9; Müller, *Kaiser*, 26 June 1918, 366. Müller suggests that Erzberger was intriguing for the downfall of both Kühlmann and Hertling.
58. Prince Max's ambitions for the chancellorship dated from at least 1912. See Max of Baden, *Memoirs*, II, 237.
59. Ibid., I, 119–27, 143–6; Müller, *Kaiser*, 4 July 1918, 368.
60. Report of Major von Schweinitz, and Prince Max to Kaiser, Salem, 15 August 1918, in Max of Baden, *Memoirs*, I, 324, 339.
61. Ibid., 315–16.
62. For this and following paragraphs, Rudin, *Armistice*, 22–5.
63. Max of Baden, *Memoirs*, I, 318.
64. Müller, *Kaiser*, 17 August 1918, 379.
65. Stevenson, *International Politics*, 207.
66. Debeney, *Guerre*, 28.
67. Jones, *War Walk*, 203–4.
68. Siegfried Sassoon, 'Glory of Women', in *The War Poems*, 100.
69. Toland, *No Man's Land*, 349.
70. Terraine, *To Win a War*, 120.
71. Ibid., 124–31; Trevor Wilson, *The Myriad Faces of War* (Cambridge, 1986), 593–9; Debeney, *Guerre*, 39.
72. Churchill, *World Crisis*, II, 1364.
73. Foch–Pershing exchange, in Toland, *No Man's Land*, 394.
74. Terraine, *To Win a War*, 153–4.
75. Paschall, *Defeat*, 180
76. Ibid.
77. Terraine, *To Win a War*, 157–77.

Ends

1. Text of speech in Pierre Renouvin, *L'Armistice de Rethondes, 11 novembre* (Paris, 1968), 365–70; D. Lloyd George, *War Memoirs* (London, 1933–6), VI, 3253–5; see also Arthur Walworth, *America's Moment* (New York, 1977), 16–17.
2. Georges Clemenceau (Senate, 17 September 1918), *Discours de guerre* (Paris, 1968), 219–22.
3. Renouvin, *Armistice*, 41–7; David Stevenson, *The First World War and International Politics* (Oxford, 1988), 223–4; Prince Max of Baden, *The Memoirs of Prince Max of Baden* (New York, 1928), I, 337.
4. Prince Max to Alexander Hohenlohe, January 1918; speech at Karlsruhe, Baden, 22 August 1918; programme of 6 September 1918, in *Memoirs*, I, 198, 328–31, 341–56.
5. Ibid., 355.
6. These phrases are repeated in many reports of October; see Renouvin, *Armistice*, 70.
7. Admiral Georg Alexander von Müller, *The Kaiser and His Court* (New York, 1964), diary entry for 28 September 1918, 396.
8. Ibid., 29 September 1918, 397; General P. W. E. Ludendorff, *My War Memories, 1914–1918* (London, 1919), II, 706–7, 717–24; Renouvin, *Armistice*, 66–71.
9. Max of Baden, *Memoirs*, I, 199, 273–85, 313–14.
10. Ibid., 23, 105, 219, 240, 284, 303, 329.
11. Ibid., 138–40, 304, 324, 351–2.
12. Ibid., 199, 336, 341–6.
13. Renouvin, *Armistice*, 52.
14. There is some conflict in the timing reported by Prince Max. See *Memoirs*, I, 369 and II, 3.
15. The following account is based on ibid., II, 3–47; Ludendorff, *Memories*, II, 717–33; Renouvin, *Armistice*, 59–77; Rudin, *Armistice*, 66–85.
16. See the text of Prince Max's first draft for a speech to the Reichstag, in *Memoirs*, II, 32–9.
17. Walworth, *America's Moment*, 28–9; D. Stevenson, *International Politics*, 220.
18. Walworth, *America's Moment*, 33–4.
19. Account on the composition of Wilson's note in ibid., 19–20, 35; John Toland, *No Man's Land* (New York, 1980), 449–51; Renouvin, *Armistice*, 115. There is some disagreement over the actual moment of the note's arrival in Washington. At any rate, French Intelligence had intercepted and decoded it, and it was on Clemenceau's desk at least twenty-four hours before Wilson was aware of it. Text of the note in Max of Baden, *Memoirs*, II, 64–5.
20. Toland, *No Man's Land*, 439–40.
21. Rod Paschall, *The Defeat of Imperial Germany, 1917–1918* (London, 1989), 181–92; Georges Clemenceau, *Grandeurs et misères d'une victoire* (Paris, 1930), 61.
22. John Terraine, *To Win a War* (London, 1978), 190. On the destruction in Cambrai, see reports in *Le Matin*, 10 October 1918.
23. Terraine, *To Win a War*, 191–2.
24. *Le Matin*, 7 October 1918.
25. Toland, *No Man's Land*, 450; Walworth, *America's Moment*, 20–1; Lloyd George, *War Memoirs*, VI, 3263, 3280.
26. Ibid., 3275–83.
27. Walworth, *America's Moment*, 23–4.
28. Max of Baden, *Memoirs*, II, 20.
29. Erzberger, *Souvenirs*, 370; Ludendorff, *Memories*, II, 730; Max of Baden, *Memoirs*, II, 55–7, 71–3.
30. Max of Baden, *Memoirs*, II, 63, 185, 285.

31. Ibid., 28–9, 43.
32. Ibid., 61–72.
33. Ibid., 76.
34. Ibid., 85–7.
35. André Brissaud, *1918* (Paris, 1968), 386–7.
36. Ferdinand Foch, *Mémoires pour servir l'histoire de la guerre* (Paris, 1931), II, 237.
37. Paschall, *Defeat*, 188–92; Clemenceau, *Grandeurs*, 62–73; Foch, *Mémoires*, II, 247–52.
38. Renouvin, *Armistice*, 114–16, 122–3; Rudin, *Armistice*, 124.
39. House, diary, 14 October, quoted in Toland, *No Man's Land*, 459.
40. The full text of the note is reproduced in Max of Baden, *Memoirs*, II, 87–9.
41. Walworth, *America's Moment*, 25, 33–4.
42. Müller, *Kaiser*, 16 October 1918, 408; Max of Baden, *Memoirs*, II, 89.
43. Pessimists did not become the military commanders of the Great War. In the face of defeat, Foch in 1914, like Haig and Nivelle in 1917, bore a stubborn confidence similar to Ludendorff's in the autumn of 1918. The one exception to the rule was Philippe Pétain, but Pétain was not a man who won wars.
44. Minutes of War Cabinet, 17 October 1918, in Max of Baden, *Memoirs*, II, 102–34.
45. Ibid., 146–61.
46. Full text in ibid., 186–8.
47. Walworth, *America's Moment*, 34.
48. Lloyd George, *War Memoirs*, VI, 3299–3309; Toland, *No Man's Land*, 454–5; Terraine, *To Win a War*, 210–15.
49. Brissaud, *1918*, 394–6; Walworth, *America's Moment*, 44.
50. Ibid., 40–2; Toland, *No Man's Land*, 485.
51. *The Times*, 5 November 1918; Walworth, *America's Moment*, 47–8.
52. Charles Seymour, ed., *The Intimate Papers of Colonel House*, (London, 1928), IV, 156–8, 198–209.
53. Walworth, *America's Moment*, 54.
54. Lloyd George, *War Memoirs*, VI, 3316–20.
55. Toland, *No Man's Land*, 490.
56. Ibid., 506–7; Walworth, *America's Moment*, 56–65.
57. Walworth, *America's Moment*, 51–3; Terraine, *To Win a War*, 219.
58. Walworth, *America's Moment*, 72–3.
59. Text of the 'Lansing Note' in Max of Baden, *Memoirs*, II, 305–6.
60. Müller, *Kaiser*, 10 October 1918, 404; Max of Baden, *Memoirs*, II, 162–3.
61. Max of Baden, *Memoirs*, II, 172–85; Müller, *Kaiser*, 22 October 1918, 410.
62. Ludendorff, *Memories*, II, 761.
63. Ibid., 762–4; Rudin, *Armistice*, 211; and the Kaiser's own account in Müller, *Kaiser*, 412–13.
64. Max of Baden, *Memoirs*, II, 204–5.
65. Ibid., 201–4, 205–6.
66. Müller, *Kaiser*, 27 October 1918, 415.
67. Quotations from Jon Stallworthy, *Wilfred Owen* (Oxford, 1974), 281–3.
68. For an account of the fighting, *Le Matin*, 28 October 1918.
69. Eugène Debeney, *La Guerre et les hommes* (Paris, 1937), 40.
70. Renouvin, *Armistice*, 99–100.
71. Terraine, *To Win a War*, 227–8, 233.
72. *Le Matin*, 27 October 1918; Lloyd George, *War Memoirs*, VI, 3320.
73. Müller, *Kaiser*, 5 and 7 October 1918, 402–3; Max of Baden, *Memoirs*, II, 52; Gordon A. Craig, *Germany (Oxford, 1981), 311.
74. Max of Baden, *Memoirs*, II, 165; Matthias Erzberger, *Souvenirs de guerre* (Paris, 1921), 75.
75. Erzberger, *Souvenirs*, 371; Prince Ernst zu Hohenlohe-Langenburg to Prince Max of Baden, Berne, 25 October 1918, in Max of Baden, *Memoirs*, II, 197–8, 211–14.

76. Max of Baden, *Memoirs*, II, 226–30.
77. James Monroe, fifth President of the United States (1816–24), is remembered in history for his policy of keeping the European powers out of the Western Hemisphere. The 'doctrine' was enforced by the British Royal Navy.
78. Müller, *Kaiser*, 29 October 1918, 416–17.
79. Erzberger, *Souvenirs*, 371–2; Max of Baden, *Memoirs*, II, 240–54.
80. Max of Baden, *Memoirs*, II, 248, 257, 264.
81. The dialogue is reported in a letter the Kaiser sent to a friend, quoted in Terraine, *To Win a War*, 236–7. See also ex-Kaiser William II, *My Memoirs, 1878–1918* (London, 1922), 274–6.
82. Müller, *Kaiser*, 2 November 1918, 418. Prince Max, in his memoirs, defended Scheer's order, arguing that, if executed, it would have made revolution and capitulation a 'psychological impossibility': 'Should our navy suffer a glorious defeat, yes, and even if this last cruise were really to be a "Death Cruise", even then its desirability from a military-political point of view must certainly be conceded. This sacrifice would have been a moral force, capable of putting to shame the many disaffected and despairing folk who would not have been able to escape its influence. I have been justly reminded of Thermopylae.' Max of Baden, *Memoirs*, II, 283.
83. Paschall, *Defeat*, 210–14.
84. On Anzin, see my *At the Heart of a Tiger* (London, 1993), 238–46.
85. Currie in Terraine, *To Win a War*, 238; Philip Gibbs, *Open Warfare* (London, 1919), 1, 3 November 1918, 524–35.
86. *The Times*, 8 November 1918.
87. Guy Chapman, *A Passionate Prodigality*, quoted in Terraine, *To Win a War*, 238.
88. Stallworthy, *Owen*, 283–6.
89. Max of Baden, *Memoirs*, II, 278–9.
90. Ibid., 281.
91. Gordon Brook-Shepherd, *November 1918* (Boston, 1981), 342.
92. Max of Baden, *Memoirs*, II, 296–7.
93. Ibid., 274, 278.
94. Ibid., 292–4.
95. Ibid., 300–6; Erzberger, *Souvenirs*, 375; General Wilhelm Groener, *Lebenserinnerungen* (Göttingen, 1957), 449.
96. *Le Matin*, 8 November 1918.
97. Claude Dufresne, *Ce jour-là* (Paris, 1988), 261–4.
98. Brook-Shepherd, *November 1918*, 344–5; Erzberger, *Souvenirs*, 375–6.
99. Erzberger, *Souvenirs*, 378–9.
100. For the armistice negotiations at Compiègne, ibid., 379–88; Foch, *Mémoires*, II, 546–68; General Jean-Henri Mordacq, *Le Ministère Clemenceau* (Paris, 1930), II, 340–9.
101. Quoted in Brook-Shepherd, *November 1918*, 349–50.
102. Mordacq, *Ministère*, II, 342.
103. Ibid., 344, 352.
104. Erzberger, *Souvenirs*, 383.
105. 'Period' in American.
106. The concessions included an extension in the delay for evacuation from 25 to 31 days, a narrowing of the 'neutral zone' from 40 to 10 kilometres, and a prolongation of the Armistice itself from 30 to 36 days
107. Erzberger, *Souvenirs*, 388.
108. Gunner B. O. Stokes, recollections and letter to parents, 18 November 1918, in Lyn Macdonald ed., *1914–1918* (London, 1988), 307, 315.
109. In Terraine, *To Win a War*, 256.
110. Ibid.

111. Abbé Marcellin Marius Lissorgues, *Notes de l'Aumonier* (Aurillac, 1921), 186–7.
112. *L'Argonnaute*, November 1918.
113. American correspondent quoted in Toland, *No Man's Land*, 548; Grady in L. Macdonald, ed., *1914–1918*, 313. Samuel Hynes, in *The Soldiers' Tale* (New York, 1997), 96, speaks of the Americans as not having yet lost 'their recruiting-office feeling'.
114. Lissorgues, *Notes*, 186.

Autumn 1918

Berlin in autumn

1. *Berliner Tageblatt*, 11 November 1918.
2. Standing before a painting of a Greek statue, she was photographed – presumably on the day of her wedding – in white robes, with white roses dangling languishingly from her ivory hand. Her husband Gebhard, who inherited the title Prince Blücher in 1916, was the great-grandson of Marshal Blücher, who had shared the victory with Wellington at Waterloo. Despite this, the couple were forced to flee England in August 1914. For most of the war they lived in Berlin's Esplanade Hotel. On the morning of 10 November they fled to Dr Mainzer's clinic. For the following, see Evelyn, Princess Blücher, *An English Wife in Berlin* (New York, c. 1920), 11 November 1918, 289–90.
3. *Vossische Zeitung*, 11 November 1918.
4. Ibid., 14 November 1918; *Berliner Morgen-Zeitung*, 14 November 1918 (describing Berlin on the 11th).
5. *Berliner Morgen-Zeitung*, 13 November 1918.
6. *Die rote Fahne*, 9 November 1918.
7. For Germany as a whole, the influenza epidemic of 1918 claimed the lives of 72,721 men and 102,130 women. The highest civilian mortality rates for the entire war were recorded in the months of October and November 1918, the epidemic being largely responsible. See Richard Bessel, *Germany after the First World War* (Oxford, 1993), 39, 224–5
8. Blücher, *English Wife*, 162, 196, 208–9, 250.
9. *Berliner Lokal-Anzeiger*, 12 November 1918.
10. Ibid.
11. Alfred Döblin, *A People Betrayed* (New York, 1983), 5.
12. *Berliner Morgen-Zeitung*, 14 November 1918.
13. Groener to von Payer, Spa, 1 November 1918, in General Wilhelm Groener, *Lebenserinnerungen* (Göttingen, 1957), 443.
14. Ibid., 445.
15. Ibid., 453.
16. Ibid., 451.
17. Ibid., 452.
18. Ibid., 455.
19. Max of Baden, *The Memoirs of Prince Max of Baden* (New York, 1928), II, 313–14.
20. Alexandra Richie, *Faust's Metropolis* (New York, 1998), 142–7, 156–66, 240–1; Giles MacDonogh, *Berlin* (London, 1997), 40–2, 91–2, 109–14.
21. Richard M. Watt, *The Kings Depart* (New York, 1968), 116.
22. Philipp Scheidemann, *Memoiren eines Sozialdemokraten* (Dresden, 1928), II, 295
23. As quoted in ibid., 284–5.
24. Max of Baden, *Memoirs*, II, 329, 334.
25. Ibid., 323–4, 331–2.
26. Scheidemann, *Memoiren*, II, 286–7.
27. *Vorwärts*, 7 November 1918; Max of Baden, *Memoirs*, II, 337.
28. Max of Baden, *Memoirs*, II 323.
29. Prince Max, whose memoirs generally agree with other witnesses, claims that Linsingen

resigned that Friday afternoon (ibid., 338–9). It is clear, however, that he was still acting as district commander on the next critical morning, 9 November.

30. Ibid., 332–3.
31. Groener, *Lebenserinnerungen*, 456.
32. Max of Baden, *Memoirs*, II, 340–3.
33. Blücher, *English Wife*, 278–9.
34. Admiral Georg Alexander von Müller, *The Kaiser and His Court* (New York, 1964), 9 November 1918, 422–3.
35. Scheidemann, *Memoiren*, II, 296.
36. Maurice Baumont, *L'Abdication de Guillaume II* (Paris, 1930), 79–81. Baumont's work, which quotes at length many memoirs and documents, provides an elaborate reconstruction of the events at Spa on 9 November 1918. I have added some details from Groener's memoirs, which would not have been available to Baumont.
37. Ibid., 82–5.
38. Several of Berlin's newspapers reported on the events of 9 November during the following week. Particularly informative on local developments are the articles in the *Berliner Morgen-Zeitung* of 10 and 13 November 1918.
39. Scheidemann, *Memoiren*, II, 280, 292; Max of Baden, *Memoirs*, II, 319.
40. 'Maikäfer' in German. Cassell's translates this as 'cockchafer'; but most English gardeners would call it a 'maybug'. According to *The Oxford English Dictionary*, a 'cockchafer', *Melolontha vulgaris*, is 'a stout broad insect of comparatively large size and greyish chestnut colour' which 'flies with a loud whirring sound'; 'both the perfect insect and the larva are very destructive to vegetation'.
41. *Berliner Morgen-Zeitung*, 10 November 1918.
42. Max of Baden, *Memoirs*, II, 348.
43. Ibid., 349.
44. Prince Max deftly leaves this question of responsibility for the order open; ibid., 352.
45. Ibid., 350–3.
46. On the conference, Baumont, *Abdication*, 88–98; Groener, *Lebenserinnerungen*, 459–61.
47. Grandfather Friedrich von der Schulenburg had played a minor role at the Congress of Vienna, rather like grandson Friedrich's small part in the abdication of the Kaiser. Serious historians, concerned with the important events and global trends of our millennium, might be tempted to brush aside such paltry figures as these. And yet … it is in the touch of their tininess that we feel the secular rhythm. Metternich, at Vienna in 1814, had made an ally of the Saxon envoy, the elder Schulenburg, because Metternich wanted to encourage the idea of a loose German confederation incorporated into a concert of Europe. His rivals in Prussia sought expansion of their small military state on a narrower, nationalist, base: they were interested in a *Nationalbund*, not in being a part of Europe. Grandfather Schulenburg found himself caught between the two conflicting principles, and Saxony – which had been one of the wealthiest states in the old Reich – lost a third of her territory, even if she kept her king. To understand, in a European context, the historical significance of Germany retreating into herself, watch a Schulenburg play.
48. Baumont, *Abdication*, 106.
49. Details of Heye's report, only known later but utterly devastating to the Kaiser's cause, can be found in ibid., 205–38; and Groener, *Lebenserinnerungen*, 457–62. Groener reports these sentences as his own and wonders what might have happened had he maintained his silence and handled the debate more 'cleverly'.
50. Baumont, *Abdication*, III.
51. Ibid., 113–16.
52. Ibid., 123–4.
53. Scheidemann, *Memoiren*, II, 296–7, 303–4, 309–10.
54. Scheidemann provides the sources, but he himself remains sceptical: ibid., 303–5.

55. Max of Baden, *Memoirs*, II, 354–5.
56. Scheidemann, *Memoiren*, II, 304–8.
57. *Berliner Morgen-Zeitung*, 10 November 1918. Description of Reichstag in MacDonogh, *Berlin*, 125–6, Anton Gill, *A Dance between Flames* (London, 1993), 18.
58. In Scheidemann's account, Liebknecht was about to declare his Republic from a balcony of the Schloss. Liebknecht actually did this after four o'clock. But had he already made a proclamation from the rooftop of a car in front of the Reichstag, as the above newspaper article suggests? Heard by a hundred or so, and then reported in the early afternoon's confusion to Scheidemann, this would have made the declaration from the Reichstag's window sill doubly pressing. Scheidemann, *Memoiren*, II, 309–12.
59. Ibid., 312–14.
60. Baumont, *Abdication*, 124–9.
61. Ibid., 135–56; Groener, *Lebenserinnerungen*, 463–5.
62. The initial developments are reported, hour by hour, in the *Berliner Morgen-Zeitung*, 10 and 13 November 1918. The press is not so clear on the following two days of violence. I have tried to balance this with reports from witnesses. The problem with these sources, as well as later historical accounts, is that they are so ideologically motivated. Clearly an independent, fresh study of these critical days would be highly useful.
63. Blücher, *English Wife*, 9 November 1918, 279–82.
64. Müller, *Kaiser*, 9 November 1918, 423.
65. Hedda Adlon, *Hotel Adlon* (Munich, 1955), 108–12. Princess Blücher confirms H. Adlon's timing of the attack on the hotel. See, *English Wife*, 282.
66. See, for instance, *Vossische Zeitung*, 11 November 1918; *Berliner Zeitung*, 13 November 1918; Max of Baden, *Memoirs*, II, 348.
67. Ronald Taylor, *Berlin and Its Culture* (New Haven, 1997), 280.
68. *Berliner Morgen-Zeitung*, 13 November 1918.
69. Ibid.; *Die rote Fahne*, 10 November 1918.
70. *Berliner Morgen-Zeitung*, 13 November 1918.
71. Blücher, *English Wife*, 290–4; Watt, *Kings Depart*, 197–8.
72. Max of Baden, *Memoirs*, II, 363.
73. Baumont, *Abdication*, 159–60.
74. Josef Pilsudski, *The Memories of a Polish Revolutionary and Soldier* (London, 1931), 355.
75. Ibid., 349–53.
76. Ibid., 357.
77. Harry Kessler, *In the Twenties* (New York, 1971), x–xi.
78. Ibid., 6–8 November 1918, 3–6.
79. Pilsudski, *Memories*, 359–60.
80. Ibid.; Kessler, *Twenties*, 8 November 1918, 6.
81. Speech of 3 July 1923 (following the assassination of the recently elected Polish President, Gabriel Narutowicz), in Pilsudski, *Memories*, 366.
82. Quoted in Gordon A. Craig, *Germany* (Oxford, 1981), 402.
83. Döblin, *Betrayed*, 186–7.
84. *Berliner Morgen-Zeitung*, 16 November 1918; Blücher, *English Wife*, Evening, 11 November 1918, 292.
85. *Berliner Tageblatt*, 11 November 1918.
86. C. M. de Talleyrand-Périgord, *Mémoires, 1754–1815* (Paris, 1982), 632; Gregor Dallas, *1815* (London, 1996), 110–11.
87. Some aspects of the problem of legitimacy are discussed in Detlev J. K. Peukert, *The Weimar Republic* (New York, 1989), 5–6, 24–9.
88. Bessel, *Germany*, 73–4, 91–2; B. R. Mitchell, *European Historical Statistics, 1750–1970* (London, 1978), 4.
89. Quoted in Gerald D. Feldman, *The Great Disorder* (New York, 1997), 116

90. *Berliner Tageblatt*, 14 November 1918; Peukert, *Weimar*, 28–9.
91. Feldman, *Great Disorder*, 107
92. Ibid., 90.
93. Ibid., 94, 115.
94. Quoted in John W. Wheeler-Bennett, *The Nemesis of Power* (London, 1953), 11.
95. Groener, *Lebenserinnerungen*, 467.
96. Ibid., 469–70. The two pamphlets quoted here are dated 14 and 19 November.
97. Ibid., 467. Sir John Wheeler-Bennett in *Nemesis*, 20–1, and his *Wooden Titan* (London, 1936), 206–7, mistakenly reports this telephone call as taking place on the evening of the 'revolution', Saturday, 9 November. Wheeler-Bennett's story, repeated by many historians, is taken from Erich Otto Volkmann's *Revolution über Deutschland* (Oldenburg, 1930), 68.
98. *Berliner Morgen-Zeitung*, 19 November 1918.
99. Groener, *Lebenserinnerungen*, 471–2.
100. Karl Epstein, Matthias Erzberger and the Dilemma of German Democracy (Princeton, 1959), 281–3.
101. Samuel G. Shartle, *Spa, Versailles, Munich* (Philadelphia, 1941), 25–6.
102. Groener, *Lebenserinnerungen*, 470–1.
103. Ibid., 473–4; Wheeler-Bennett, *Nemesis*, 29. In public, Hindenburg was more conciliatory about workers' and soldiers' councils. See 'Hindenburg über die A-u-S-Räte', a telegram addressed to 'acting general commanders', published in *Berliner Tageblatt*, 3 December 1918.
104. *Berliner Morgen-Zeitung*, 20 November 1918.
105. Epstein, *Erzberger*, 282.
106. *Berliner Morgen-Zeitung*, 20 November 1918.
107. Shartle, *Spa, Versailles, Munich*, 18–30.
108. Ibid., 30–2.
109. *Vossische Zeitung*, 16 November 1918; *Berliner Lokal-Anzeiger*, 19 November 1918.
110. *Berliner Tageblatt*, 3 December 1918.
111. *Berliner Morgen-Zeitung*, 3 December 1918.
112. *Berliner Lokal-Anzeiger*, 7 December 1918.
113. One reads in that Saturday's *Berliner Tageblatt* (7 December 1918) that 'the large majority of soldiers stand by the side of the Regime and, for the sake of order in the new Republic, are willing to shoot'.
114. Ibid.; *Berliner Morgen-Zeitung*, 8 December 1918.
115. *Die rote Fahne*, 8 December 1918.
116. *Berliner Lokal-Anzeiger, Berliner Morgen-Zeitung, Vossische Zeitung*, 8–11 December 1918.
117. *Berliner Morgen-Zeitung*, 11 December 1918.
118. Ibid.

Paris and Washington in autumn
1. *The Times*, 12 November 1918.
2. Margaret Alice McKenna-Friend, *Mes soixante mois au camp retranché de Paris* (Paris, 1921), 304–5; Marjorie Grant, *Verdun Days in Paris* (London, 1918), 235–6; John F. Macdonald, *Two Towns, One City* (London, 1917), 220–7.
3. B. R. Mitchell, *European Historical Statistics* (London, 1978), 12–14; Eugen Weber, *La France des années 30* (Paris, 1995), 123.
4. Arnold Bennett, *Over There* (London, 1915), 7.
5. S. M., 'Le drame de l'attente', in Camille Clermont, ed., *Souvenirs de Parisiennes en temps de guerre* (Paris, 1918), 229–33.
6. J. F. Macdonald, *Two Towns*, 204–5, 207; Grant, *Verdun Days*, 213–15; Agathe Dyvrande, 'Au Palais', in Clermont, ed., *Souvenirs*, 88–99. Dyvrande notes that in 1918 much of the work at the Palais de Justice – 'empty and sad' – was being conducted by women lawyers,

though the first woman lawyer, Jeanne Chauvin, had been called to the bar only in 1900.

7. Marie-Jeanne Viel, 'L'Armistice du 11 novembre 1918', in Gilbert Guillemenault, ed., *Grandes Heures joyeuses de Paris de la Révolution à nos jours*, (Paris, 1967), 116–17; *L'Œuvre*, 12 November 1918. On Cocteau and Apollinaire, see Vincent Cronin, *Paris* (London, 1994), 15–25.

8. My main sources for this and the following paragraphs are contemporary newspapers, in particular *Le Petit Parisien, Le Matin, Le Temps, L'Œuvre*, and the London *Times*, 8–18 November 1918.

9. In the Senate, after Clemenceau pronounced these last words, a few members on the Right called out, 'Still soldier of God and for that reason soldier of humanity!' Georges Clemenceau, *Discours de guerre* (Paris, 1968), 227–8.

10. Viel, 'L'Armistice', 123.

11. Harold Nicolson, *Peacemaking 1919* (Gloucester, Mass., 1984), 77–8.

12. House and Lloyd George had argued in favour of Geneva. But they had not reckoned on the hostile attitude of the US State Department, which regarded Switzerland as a nest of exiled Eastern European agitators and revolutionaries. Nor had they taken full account of the effect the French ambassador in Washington could have on the mind of the isolated President; on hearing about Lloyd George's campaign for Geneva, Jules Jusserand went round to the White House to warn Wilson that Switzerland was a 'centre of espionage without equal in Europe' and reminded him that it was in Paris that the treaty of 1783, establishing American independence, had been signed. That clinched the matter for the professor of American government: Wilson cabled House on 8 November to say he preferred the French capital, 'where friendly influences and authorities are in control,' to Switzerland, 'which is saturated with every poisonous element and open to every hostile influence in Europe'. See Arthur Walworth, *America's Moment* (New York, 1977), 83–4.

13. It has been calculated that, if there had been no war, the United States would have overtaken total European output by the year 1925; the war advanced this date by six years, to 1919. See Paul Kennedy, *The Rise and Fall of the Great Powers* (London, 1988), 281–2.

14. A succinct summary of French losses, along with diagrams and graphs, can be found in Jean-Jacques Becker and Serge Bernstein, *Victoire et frustrations, 1914–1929* (Paris, 1990), 147–60.

15. Maxime Leroy, *Pour gouverner* (Paris, 1918), quoted in François Monnet, *Refaire la République* (Paris, 1993), 28.

16. Becker and Bernstein, *Victoire et frustrations*, 147–8.

17. Walworth, *America's Moment*, 93–4.

18. Quoted in Alexandre Zévaès, *Clemenceau* (Paris, 1949), 153.

19. Georges Clemenceau, *Vers la réparation* (Paris, 1899), 320; Gregor Dallas, *At the Heart of a Tiger* (London, 1993), 365–9.

20. *L'Humanité*, 7 June 1908.

21. Clemenceau's speech to the Senate, *Journal Officiel*, 22 June 1917

22. Jacques Meyer, *Les Soldats de la Grand Guerre* (Paris, 1966), 221.

23. Jean Martet, *Le Silence de M. Clemenceau* (Paris, 1929), 229; Archives du Sénat, *Auditions de la Commission de l'Armée*, VI, 35 (27 November 1915), and LXXVIII, 8455 (9 May 1917).

24. *L'Homme enchaîné*, 13 June 1917.

25. Georges Clemenceau, *Discours de guerre*, 130–2; Winston S. Churchill, *Great Contemporaries* (London, 1937), 310–11.

26. Guy Pedroncini, *Les Mutineries de 1917* (Paris, 1967), 59.

27. Walworth, *America's Moment*, 92–3.

28. Raymond Poincaré, *Au service de la France* (Paris, 1930–3), X, 409; Richard M. Watt, *Dare Call it Treason* (New York, 1963), 281.

29. *Le Canard enchaîné*, 28 November 1917 – H. P. Gassier's accompanying cartoon shows

Clemenceau as Minister of War, Minister of Justice, Minister of the Navy, Minister of Public Instruction, Minister of Foreign Affairs, etc.

30. An excellent outline of Philippe Berthelot's discreet diplomatic career can be found in Richard D. Challener, 'The French Foreign Office', in Gordon A. Craig and Felix Gilbert, eds, *The Diplomats*, 1919–1939 (Princeton, 1953), 49–85.

31. Poincaré, *Service*, IX, 375, 425.

32. Walworth, *America's Moment*, 99; André Tardieu, *La Paix* (Paris, 1921), 95. See also Harold Nicolson's comments on French preparations, *Peacemaking*, 28.

33. Two drafts of the French plan are in *The Papers of Woodrow Wilson* (Princeton 1966–93), LIII, 85–93, 292–8.

34. E. M. House to W. Wilson, telegram, Paris, 9 November 1918, in ibid., 3–4.

35. H. S. Cummings to W. Wilson, Washington, 4 November 1918; Wilson to Cummings, Washington, 5 November 1918, in W. Wilson, *Papers* LI, 589, 592.

36. On the 'false armistice', see John Toland, *No Man's Land* (New York, 1980), 518–21; Wilson to Robert Bridges, 8 November 1918, in W. Wilson, *Papers*, LI, 640–1.

37. House, diary, 26 October 1919, in Arno J. Mayer, *Politics and Diplomacy of Peacemaking* (London, 1968), 124. In an earlier draft of his appeal, Wilson had written, 'I would be rendered powerless by an adverse judgment.' Homer Stillé Cummings, chairman of the Democratic National Committee, fortunately had the self-damning phrase changed from 'powerless' to 'deplorably impaired'. The final text read, 'I earnestly beg that you will express yourselves unmistakably to the effect by returning a Democratic majority to both the Senate and the House of Representatives. I am your servant and will accept your judgment without cavil, but my power to administer the great trust assigned me by the Constitution would be seriously impaired should your judgment be adverse.' Draft of 15 October 1918, Cummings's comments and the final draft (19 October) in W. Wilson, *Papers*, LI, 343, 380–2.

38. Dan Voorhees Stephens to J. P. Tumulty, Fremont, Nebraska, 9 November 1918, in W. Wilson *Papers*, LIII, 61.

39. *The Sun*, 26 October 1918; T. Roosevelt to H. C. Lodge, telegram, 24 October 1918, in W. Wilson, *Papers*, LI, 455–6.

40. In 1867 Clemenceau, residing in New York, had written a couple of dozen articles for *Le Temps* that sided with Edwin Stanton ('the Carnot of the American war') and Thaddeus Stevens ('the wrath of Robespierre') in their struggle against President Andrew Johnson's scheme of reconstruction. See Dallas, *Tiger*, 69–72.

41. Key Pittman to Wilson, Washington, 6 November; George Creel to Wilson, Washington, 8 November; S. V. Stephens to J. P. Tumulty, 9 November 1918, in W. Wilson, *Papers*, LI, 611–13, 645–6, and LIII, 62.

42. Memorandum of Homer Stillé Cummings, Washington, *c.* 8 or 9 November 1918, in ibid., LI, 646–8.

43. Wilson to Scott Ferris, Washington, 7 November, and to E. A. Woods, 8 November 1918, in ibid., 620, 639.

44. Edith Bolling Wilson, *Memoirs of Mrs Woodrow Wilson* (London, 1939), 202.

45. A Statement, Washington, 11 November 1918, in W. Wilson, *Papers*, LIII, 34.

46. On Tsar Alexander's plans for world peace and his appeal for people's rights, see my *1815* (London, 1996), 20–5, 44–5, 439–3.

47. 'Thanksgiving Proclamation', Washington, 16 November 1918, in W. Wilson, *Papers*, LIII, 95–6.

48. Bernard Baruch to Wilson, Washington, 26 November; Vatican memorandum, 9 November; Remarks to Members of B'nai B'rith, 28 November 1918, in ibid., 16–18, 209, 239–40.

49. Clemenceau telegram to Lloyd George quoted in House to Wilson, Paris, 15 November; Cobb memorandum, Paris, 4 November; House to Wilson, Paris, 14 November; Key

Pittman to Wilson, Washington, 15 November 1918; in ibid., LI, 590–1, and LIII, 71–3, 84–5, 91–3. Also Walworth, *America's Moment*, 116–17.

50. Lansing memorandum, Washington, 12 November; Wilson to House, Washington, 16 November 1918, in W. Wilson, *Papers*, LI, 590–1, and LIII, 96–7.

51. 'Peace Conference', Paris, 15 November 1918, in ibid., LIII, 85–93. The document is a retyped version of House's original telegram, with Wilson's comments typed in red ink. The final draft of the French plan (which included the comments on earlier European congresses and on the Fourteen Points) was delivered by the French ambassador to Lansing on 29 November, but Wilson received it only on 2 December, the day before his departure. He probably did not read it – if he read it at all – until he was on board ship.

52. House to Wilson, Paris, 6 November, in ibid., LI, 606–7. Clemenceau (again, with the speed of negotiations in mind) initially wanted the maximum number of delegates for each nation limited to three, as did some officials of the British Foreign Office.

53. The names of several high-ranking Republicans were put forward, including that of Theodore Roosevelt – he 'seeks to take charge of anything he has a part in, and to take charge in a way thoroughly disloyal to his associates' groused Wilson. House wanted Senator Lodge; Wilson decided to have no senators at all. He explained to his friend Attorney-General Thomas Gregory that 'the Senate was an independent body and that it did not seem fair to influence its free judgment of diplomatic negotiations by appointing Senators'. Not Senator Knute Nelson? not Senator Knox? responded Gregory. 'The appointment of these two men would guarantee the ratification of the Treaty.' Gregory then mentioned the Republicans Elihu Root, William Taft and Governor McCall of Massachusetts, but 'I could see that he drew back a little bit from the suggestion.' Helen Gardner and Anna Howard Shaw were pushing for a woman commissioner. Wilson said it was 'not practicable'. Several wanted a representative from organized labour: the name of Samuel Gompers frequently cropped up. Wilson did not want somebody from a 'special field'. Wilson letters to J. E. Ransdell (Washington, 18 November), to H. H. Gardner (18 November), to A. H. Shaw (18 November) and to F. Morrison (27 November 1918), in ibid., LIII, 117; Gregory memorandum in Charles Seymour, ed., *The Intimate Papers of Colonel House* (London, 1928), IV, 233.

54. Seymour (ed.), *Intimate Papers*, 235.

55. Ibid., 216; 'An Annual Message on the State of the Union', Washington, 2 December 1918 in W. Wilson, *Papers*, LIII, 274–86.

56. H. A. Ash, diary, 2 December 1918, in ibid., 305.

57. Grayson, diary, 4 December 1918, ibid., 313–15; E. B. Wilson, *Memoirs*, 205–6.

58. Grayson, diary, 4 December; Edith Benham, diary, 5 and 8 December 1918, in W. Wilson, *Papers*, LIII, 321, 341.

59. Cary T. Grayson, USS *George Washington*, 12 December; William C. Bullitt, diary, 9 [10] December; Clive Day to Elizabeth Dike Day, 10 December 1918, in ibid., 349–50, 376.

60. R. B. Fosdick, diary, 5 December 1918, in ibid., 321–2.

61. Benham, diary, 9 December 1918, in ibid., 343–4; Cary T. Grayson, *Woodrow Wilson* (New York, 1940), 59; E. B. Wilson, *Memoirs*, 207.

62. E. P. Costigan to Wilson, Washington, 6 December 1918, in W. Wilson, *Papers*, LIII, 328–32.

63. Charles Seymour to his family, USS *George Washington*, 10 December 1918, in ibid., 357.

64. Bowman, memorandum, 10 December; R. B. Fosdick, diary, 11 December; Bullitt, diary, 9 and 11 December 1918, in ibid., 350–6, 365–7.

65. Charles Seymour, *Letters from the Paris Peace Conference* (New Haven, 1965), 32–3, 38.

66. *Le Matin*, 19 November 1918.

67. In an effort to render the devastation comprehensible, the same guide divided the war area into a '*zone chaotique*', west of Tourcoing, Douai, Cambrai, Saint-Quentin and Laon, which had been destroyed during the spring offensives of 1918, and an eastern '*zone de*

destruction systématique', laid to waste by the Germans during their retreat. Towns were flattened, villages were wiped off the map, rich farmland had been transformed into infertile steppe. 'One can clean, clear and rebuild a town, even ruins such as Lens,' noted the guide, 'but one cannot restore to the country its fertility and beauty in a hundred years.' Albert had had a population of 7,400 in 1914; around 250 inhabitants were still there in 1918. In Arras, the gabled Spanish-Flemish houses had been ripped apart and the population had declined from 25,000 to between 2,000 and 3,000. The mines around Lens, which had accounted for one-tenth of French coal production before the war, had all been flooded and the surface installations smashed. Lens itself was just a pile of red-brick rubble. Chemin de Fer du Nord, *Souvenir de la Grande Guerre* (Paris, 1919), I, 3–5, 31–2, 43–7.

68. *Le Matin*, 24 November 1918.
69. Ibid., 19 November 1918. See also reports in *Le Petit Parisien*, 19 and 24 November 1918, and *The Times*, 16 November 1918.
70. *Le Matin*, 28 November 1918.
71. See Alfred W. Crosby, *Epidemic and Peace, 1918* (Westport, Conn., 1976); Jean-Jacques Becker, 'La Grippe espagnole', *L'Histoire*, December 1981, 82–3; Adolph A. Hoenling, *The Great Epidemic* (Boston, 1961); Pete Davies, *Catching Cold* (London, 1999).
72. Symptoms are described in *Le Matin*, 5 November, and *The Times*, 12 November 1918. A graphic picture of the disease is drawn by Willa Cather in her 1922 novel *One of Ours* (London, 1987), 292–319. Hospital report in J.-J. Becker, 'Grippe', 82.
73. Walworth, *America's Moment*, 83.
74. Ibid., 84–5, 257–60; *Le Matin*, 25 November 1918.
75. Walworth, *America's Moment*, 83–4, 260.
76. Ibid., 171; *Le Matin*, 29 November 1918.
77. Wilson, on board the *George Washington*, might have had the French plan in mind when, on 8 December, he remarked to Dr Grayson that he would be returning to the USA before the close of the present US Congress 'to take care of bills', but would then have to go back to Europe, where he expected there to be a 'later conference of the nations of the world to formulate a new international code'. That was certainly what the French plan had proposed in its idea of an international 'congress', following the preliminary Allied 'conference'. Grayson, diary, 8 December 1918, in W. Wilson, *Papers*, LIII, 340
78. House to Wilson, Paris, 12 December 1918, in ibid., 372.
79. House to Wilson, Paris, 9 December 1918, in ibid., 344–5.
80. Herbert Hoover, *The Memoirs of Herbert Hoover* (New York, 1951), I, 294; Walworth, *America's Moment*, 226.
81. E. N. Hurley to Wilson, Paris, 12 December 1918, in W. Wilson, *Papers*, LIII, 372–5.
82. Hoover provides many statistics in his *Memoirs*, I, 300–1, 316–27, and in his *The Ordeal of Woodrow Wilson* (New York, 1958), 88–90. Hoover estimated that in Eastern and Central Europe about 215 million people were, at the end of 1918, in a state of acute famine, while another 185 million people in Allied and neutral countries were urgently in need of overseas food supplies.
83. Walworth, *America's Moment*, 214.
84. Hoover, *Ordeal*, v.
85. Ibid., viii, 8; Hoover, *Memoirs*, I, 206, 324–5.
86. Hoover, *Memoirs*, I, 473–9.
87. Ibid., 279–80.
88. George H. Nash, *The Life of Herbert Hoover* (New York, 1983–8), II, 372.
89. Ibid., I, 1–12.
90. Ibid., 11.
91. Hoover, *Memoirs*, I, 47–51.
92. Ibid., 154.

93. Ibid., 184. Even if one takes as a base the broad period of seventeenth-century crisis, 1560–1660, Hoover's estimates are grossly exaggerated. As in the case of food distribution in general, the relationship of famine to war was vastly more complicated than Hoover's engineering hypothesis suggested. Nevertheless the relationship existed, and Hoover was its pioneer.
94. Ibid., 189, 192.
95. Nash, *Hoover*, II, 371.
96. Hoover, *Memoirs*, I, 286–90, 329–30.
97. Hoover to House, Washington, 13 February 1917, in Hoover, *Ordeal*, 5–6.
98. Hoover to Wilson, Washington, 24 October 1918, in Wilson, *Papers*, LI, 437–9.
99. Hoover to House, Washington, 7 November 1918, in ibid., 635–6.
100. Walworth, *America's Moment*, 217–19.
101. Hoover, *Memoirs*, I, 285.
102. Stephen Roskill, *Hankey* (London, 1970–2), II, 26.
103. House to Wilson, Paris, 27 November 1918, in W. Wilson, *Papers*, LIII, 222–5; House to Balfour, Paris, in Hoover, *Ordeal*, 96–9.
104. Walworth, *America's Moment*, 220.
105. Ibid., 217–23; Hoover, *Memoirs*, I, 340.
106. Ibid., 293.
107. Quoted in Trevor Wilson, *The Myriad Faces of War* (London, 1986), 607.
108. *Le Temps*, 16 December 1918.
109. Ibid., and *Le Matin*, 9–13 December 1918.
110. *L'Humanité*, 12 December 1918.
111. House to Wilson, Paris, 9 December 1918, in Seymour, ed., *House Papers*, IV, 252; Lansing to House, *George Washington*, 10 December 1918; *L'Humanité*, 14 December 1918.
112. *Le Temps*, 16 December 1918.
113. Seymour, ed., *House Papers*, IV, 252.
114. Seymour, *Letters*, 70–4
115. Ibid., 89
116. Ibid., 83–5.
117. For this and the following paragraphs, *Journal Officiel*, Chambre des Députés, Débats, 26–9 December 1918.
118. *La Bataille*, quoted by Pierre Miquel, who reviews press reports on the phrase in *La Paix de Versailles et l'opinion publique française* (Paris, 1972), 60–2.
119. Seymour, *Letters*, 85; Walworth, *America's Moment*, 155.

London in autumn

1. *Morning Post*, 13 November 1918.
2. Churchill's speech in ibid., 26 November 1918. In *The Aftermath* (New York, 1929),1, Churchill adds to his list of successive struggles against military tyranny the victories of the Duke of Marlborough (his great-grandfather) over Louis XIV, though of course this was – significantly – a land campaign on the borders of the Netherlands and France. Speeches of Geddes and Lloyd George in *The Times*, 11 November and 12 December 1918. On the traditional identity of the Royal Navy with world liberties, see Peter Padfield, *Maritime Supremacy* (London, 1999).
3. *Morning Post*, 9 December 1918.
4. Ibid, 3 December 1918.
5. For a vivid account of this arms race – the technology involved as well as the strategic planning – see Robert K. Massie, *Dreadnought* (New York, 1991).
6. Quoted by Bryan Ranft, 'The Royal Navy and the War at Sea', in John Turner, ed., *Britain and the First World War* (London, 1988), 64.
7. The ship went down, during a gale, in less than five minutes. Over 800 men were lost.

The extraordinary story of the few survivors, swept on to a virtually deserted island, is told in the *Morning Post*, 28 December 1918.

8. A. J. P. Taylor, *English History, 1914–1945* (Oxford, 1992), 84.
9. *Morning Post*, 9 December 1918.
10. Ranft, 'War at Sea', 57.
11. Siegfried Sassoon, *The Complete Memoirs of George Sherston* (London, 1972), 317–18; Vera Brittain, *Testament of Youth* (London, 1978), 35–3; Edmund Blunden, *Undertones of War* (London, 1989), 10.
12. Sassoon, *Sherston*, 448–9.
13. Walter Bagehot, *Lombard Street* (London, 1873), quoted in Stephen Inwood, *A History of London* (London, 1998), 476.
14. Michael MacDonagh, *In London during the Great War* (London, 1935), 74–8, 82–4, 266–7, 295–6; Inwood, *London*, 701–4.
15. Pat Barker, *The Regeneration Trilogy* (London, 1996), 495; Brittain, *Testament*, 360, 362.
16. MacDonagh, *London*, 15, 34, 62–4, 91–2, 151, 204, 304–5; Inwood, *London*, 704.
17. Lloyd George speech in *Morning Post*, 18 November 1918; Brittain, *Testament*, 205–32; Francis Sheppard, *London* (Oxford, 1998), 299–300; Trevor Wilson, *The Myriad Faces of War* (London, 1986), 765.
18. J. M. Bourne, *Britain and the Great War, 1914–1918* (London, 1989), 236; MacDonagh, *London*, 118–20, 246.
19. Sassoon, *Sherston*, 484.
20. *The Times*, 29 March 1918; MacDonagh, *London*, 282–4.
21. *Morning Post*, 7 and 11 November 1918.
22. *Daily Mail* and *Morning Post*, 11 November 1918.
23. Ibid., 12 November 1918; *The Times*, 12 November 1918; MacDonagh, *London*, 332–3
24. *The Times* and *Morning Post*, 12 November 1918; Harold Nicolson, *Peacemaking 1919* (Gloucester, Mass., 1984), 8–9. Harold Nicolson claims that 'there was no cheering' – perhaps he had not opened his window at the Foreign Office sufficiently. He also notes that Lloyd George then attempted to leave No. 10 by the back-garden door, which opened on to Horse Guards Parade, but had to retreat from a crowd that 'rushed towards him and patted feverishly at his back'. Nicolson thought this retreat before the hysterical mob most significant and symbolic of Lloyd George's actions in the months to come. It may be true, but to see all this Nicolson must have been watching from a very high window.
25. Jean Moorcroft Wilson, *Siegfried Sassoon: The Making of a War Poet* (London, 1998), 514–26.
26. Robert Graves, *Goodbye to All That* (London, 1981), 240–1; Jon Stallworthy, *Wilfred Owen* (Oxford, 1974), 286–7.
27. Brittain, *Testament*, 456–63.
28. Phylis Constance Iliff, diary, Liddle Collection, Leeds, quoted by Peter H. Liddle, 'Britons on the Home Front', in Hugh Cecil and Peter H. Liddle, eds, *At the Eleventh Hour* (London 1998), 70.
29. A. J. P. Taylor, *English History*, 114; Rolph quotation in Inwood, *London*, 705.
30. *Morning Post*, 12 November 1918.
31. John Turner, 'British Politics and the Great War', in J. Turner, ed., *Britain*, 121; Taylor, *English History*, 67.
32. On the passing of the new franchise bill Vera Brittain, a militant feminist, commented, 'With an incongruous irony seldom equalled in the history of revolutions, the spectacular pageant of the woman's movement, vital and colourful with adventure, with initiative, with sacrificial emotion, crept to its quiet, unadvertised triumph in the deepest night of wartime depression.' Brittain, *Testimony*, 405.
33. Commons session of 7 November, reported in the *Times*, 8 November 1918.
34. Churchill, *Aftermath*, 27.

35. *The Times*, 8 and 9 November 1918.
36. Quoted in David Cannadine, *Aspects of Aristocracy* (London, 1995), 85.
37. Bourne, *Britain*, 180–1; A. J. Stockwell, 'The War and the British Empire', in J. Turner, ed., *Britain*, 39, 42–3.
38. *Morning Post*, 13 and 18 November 1918 (complete text of the letter in the latter number).
39. Ibid., 13 November 1918.
40. Ibid., 18 November 1918.
41. Ibid., 19 November 1918.
42. *The Times* and *Morning Post*, November and December 1918.
43. Socialist historians would later refer to it as the 'Khaki Election', though the real 'Khaki Election' was that of November 1900, in the midst of the Boer War; it was a much more chauvinistic, patriotic affair than that of 1918. Lloyd George may have had something to do with lending the colour khaki to the election of 1918. 'Before the war in the Army you had red coats, and I believe you had blues and buffs,' he said in Newcastle on 29 November. 'The war came, and they all wore one colour. The time has not come yet to return to the old party colours. We dropped the blues and buffs, and during the war we all politically wore khaki. We won the war because we wore only one colour. Could not we do the same again until we have reconstructed this country, rebuilt it? When the summer sun is shining in the blue sky after the storm give the sunshine a chance. When you have got good-will, co-operation, mutual help, a disposition on the part of everybody to do his best, let us trust in them and work together to lift the old land up!' Khaki, for Lloyd George, was the colour of the Coalition, in opposition to what his colleague Winston Churchill called the 'party froth'. Speech reproduced in *The Times*, 30 November 1918.
44. *Morning Post*, 28 November and 13 December 1918.
45. *The Times*, 2 December 1918.
46. On the return of the prisoners of war, see *Morning Post* and *The Times*, November and December 1918.
47. *The Times*, 22 November 1918.
48. Ibid., 28 November 1918.
49. Churchill, *Aftermath*, 28.
50. Ibid., 30–1; *Morning Post*, 30 November, 6 December 1918.
51. *Morning Post* 6, 12, 14 December 1918.
52. *The Times*, 10 December 1918.
53. *Morning Post*, 30 November and 12 December 1918.
54. Robert Skidelsky, *John Maynard Keynes* (London, 1994–5), I, 313, 342, 353.
55. Ibid., 5.
56. Ibid., 269.
57. Ibid., 158–9, 260.
58. John Maynard Keynes, *The Economic Consequences of the Peace*, in Keynes, *The Collected Writings of John Maynard Keynes* (London, 1971), II, 6–7.
59. Skidelsky, *Keynes*, I, 237, 258.
60. Keynes refused permission to publish his talk, explaining that 'it is a great advantage of lecturing that one can say things in a less thought-out form than when one writes . . .Very few lectures stand printing, and I am quite sure this one would not.' A shorthand version, 'The Civil Service and Financial Control', does however appear in Keynes, *Writings*, XVI, 296–307.
61. Skidelsky, *Keynes*, I, 315–27; Keynes to Beatrice Webb, London, 11 March 1918, in Keynes, *Writings*, XVI, 295.
62. Skidelsky, *Keynes*, I, 234, 295; Bruce Kent, *The Spoils of War* (Oxford, 1989), 29; Niall Ferguson, *The Pity of War* (London, 1998), 20–3, 191. According to Trevor Wilson (*The Myriad Faces of War* (Cambridge, 1986), 14) Angell's book was first published in 1909 as *Europe's Optical Illusion*.

63. Keynes to Mrs F. A., London, 24 December 1917, in Keynes, *Writings*, XVI, 266; Ferguson, *Pity*, 318–19, 327; Kent, *Spoils*, 39.

64. Keynes, 'The Financial Dependence of the United Kingdom on the United States of America', 10 October 1916; R. McKenna, 'Our Financial Position in America', 24 October 1916; Bonar Law, Chancellor of Exchequer, to Lord Reading, Ambassador in Washington, 8 May 1918 (Keynes's remarks on the US Treasury being 'small-minded' and seeking Britain's 'financial helplessness' were deleted from the final version), in Keynes, *Writings*, XVI, 197–201; Skidelsky, *Keynes*, I, 339–42.

65. Ferguson, *Pity*, 327; Arthur Walworth, *America's Moment* (New York, 1977), 6–7.

66. Keynes to Sir Basil Blackett, London, 30 January 1918; Bonar Law to Lord Reading, London, 25 March 1918, in Keynes, *Writings*, XVI, 267–72.

67. Herbert Hoover, *The Ordeal of Woodrow Wilson* (New York, 1958), 91–3; William McAdoo to O. T. Crosby, Washington, 14 February 1918; Blackett to Keynes, Washington, 11 April 1918, in Keynes, *Writings*, XVI, 272.

68. For Germany's demands for indemnity, see above, pp. 16, 65. On Allied wartime demands, see Kent, *Spoils*, 19–40.

69. *Morning Post*, 30 November 1918.

70. Kent, *Spoils*, 34–5; *The Times*, 8 November 1918.

71. In his memoirs, Lloyd George explains his appointments to the Committee thus: 'I was so confident that, when men of real practical ability came into contact with the actualities of the problem, they would acknowledge the futility of exaggerated anticipation, that I decided to place on the Committee Mr W. M. Hughes, a believer in high figures, and Mr Walter Long. Walter Long was that kind of politician who gains the confidence of a party with a reputation for caution, sound common sense and moderation, because his utterances never transgress the commonplaces and clichés of that party, and he never startles the public by any originality of thoughts or suggestion, or by an audacity of brilliancy of phrase . . .', *The Truth About the Peace Treaties* (London, 1938), I, 458. See also Kent, *Spoils*, 25–6, 36; *Morning Post*, 13 November 1918; editorial comments by Elizabeth Johnson in Keynes, *Writings*, XVI, 311–12, 336.

72. Keynes to his mother, London, 3 November 1918; L. S. Amery to Bonar Law, London, 26 December 1918, in Keynes, *Writings*, XVI, 338, 383.

73. Lloyd George later blamed Keynes for originating the idea of exacting huge tributes from Germany over a period of years. Keynes replied that the 1916 memorandum was based 'on the assumption that this country would make *no* claim for reparation', that the sum would be limited to 'damage in the territories overrun [by the enemy]'. The memorandum (authored by Keynes and Professor Sir W. J. Ashley) 'The Effect of an Indemnity', 2 January 1916, along with Keynes's comments addressed to Sir Warren Fisher (26 July 1938) and to the *Sunday Times* (30 October 1938), are reproduced in Keynes, *Writings*, XVI, 312–36. Lloyd George's accusing remarks are in Lloyd George, *Peace Treaties*, I, 444–9.

74. The Board of Trade's memorandum on indemnity was initially composed on 17 October 1918 and presented to the War Cabinet on 26 November. Both its figures and its argument bear a resemblance to those of Keynes's 'Notes' of October and his more detailed 'Memorandum' of December. Lloyd George, *Peace Treaties*, 449–54.

75. E. Johnson's account of the report in Keynes, *Writings*, XVI, 336; Kent, *Spoils*, 36–8.

76. 'Notes on an Indemnity', 31 October 1918, and 'Memorandum by the Treasury on the Indemnity Payable by the Enemy Powers for Reparation and Other Claims', December 1918, in Keynes, *Writings*, XVI, 338–83.

77. L. S. Amery to Bonar Law, London, 26 December 1918, in ibid., 383–4.

78. See, for instance, 'The Peace Conference', in *Morning Post*, 28–9 November 1918.

79. Lloyd George, *Peace Treaties*, I, 136.

80. Ibid., 131–3; *The Times* and *Morning Post*, 2 December 1918.

81. Lloyd George, *Peace Treaties*, I, 137–43, 483–7.

82. *The Times*, 21 December 1918; 'Remarks at Humes to American Soldiers', 25 December 1918, in Woodrow Wilson, *The Papers of Woodrow Wilson* (Princeton, 1966–93), LIII, 506.

83. Derby to Balfour, Paris, 2 December 1918, in W. Wilson, *Papers*, 470–2.

84. House, diary, 16 December 1918, in ibid., 401–2.

85. 'Remarks to Representatives of the American Press in Paris', 18 December; Wilson to Herbert B. Brougham, Paris, 17 December; Ray Stannard Baker, 'Memorandum for the President', Paris, 18 December; 'An Address at the University of Paris', 21 December. T. N. Page to Wilson, Rome, 24 December; T. L. Logan to E. N. Hurley, Paris, 23 December 1918, in ibid., 412, 421, 433–6, 461–3, 480–5, 494–6.

86. Lloyd George, *Peace Treaties*, I, 208–9.

87. O. T. Crosby, memorandum, 23 December 1918, in Wilson, *Papers*, LIII, 472–3.

88. Lloyd George, *Peace Treaties*, I, 195; Carter Glass to Wilson, Washington, 19 December; Wilson to Glass, Paris, 23 December 1918, in Wilson, *Papers*, LIII, 441–2, 477–80.

89. Walworth, *America's Moment*, 215–28.

90. House, diary, 17 December 1918, in Wilson, *Papers*, LIII, 417–19.

91. Derby to Balfour, Paris, 20 December 1918, in ibid., 457.

92. *Morning Post* and *The Times*, 27 December 1918.

93. Paul Fussell, *The Great War and Modern Memory* (London, 1975), 191–203.

94. André Tardieu to House, with memorandum, Paris, 24 December 1918, in W. Wilson, *Papers*, LIII, 497.

95. Grayson, diary, 24 December 1918, in ibid., 488–9.

96. Ibid., 26 December 1918, 510; Lloyd George, *Peace Treaties*, I, 179–80; *The Times* and *Morning Post*, 27 December 1918.

97. Grayson, diary, 27 December 1918, in W. Wilson, *Papers*, LIII, 521–2; Lloyd George, *Peace Treaties*, I, 180–3.

98. 'After-Dinner Remarks at Buckingham Palace', 27 December 1918, in W. Wilson, *Papers*, LIII, 522–4.

99. Walworth, *America's Moment*, 151.

100. Indicative of the state of relations between the two countries was the fact that Britain had no resident ambassador in Washington, and the popular American ambassador in London, Walter Page, who had been ill for many months and died in North Carolina just before Christmas, had not yet been replaced.

101. 'An Address at Guildhall', 28 December 1918, in W. Wilson, *Papers*, LIII, 531–3.

102. 'An Address at Mansion House', 28 December; Grayson, diary, 28 December 1918, in ibid., 529, 533–4.

103. Charles Gore, Bishop of Oxford, Wheatley, Oxon., 23 December; Trades Union Congress Parliamentary Committee and the Executive Committee of the Labour Party to Wilson, London, 28 December; Sir George Paish, Pall Mall, 26 December; Asquith to Wilson, Sutton Courtney, Berks., 29 December 1918, in ibid., 487, 514, 535–6, 542.

104. Lloyd George handed Wilson the report by Smuts during the Friday meeting. It is reproduced in ibid., 515–19. A much shorter memorandum on the League, focusing on the prevention of war, had been prepared by the American Secretary of State, Robert Lansing (see ibid., 474–6). Unlike the Cecil and Smuts reports, it does not appear to have been distributed to the Allies. Wilson had only contempt for Lansing.

105. Walworth, *America's Moment*, 149; Lloyd George, *Peace Treaties*, I, 184–202; minutes of the Imperial War Cabinet, 30 December 1918, in W. Wilson, *Papers*, LIII, 558–69.

106. Later political dealings revised this figure upwards to 537 seats. See J. Turner, 'British Politics', 133.

107. Electoral results in *Morning Post*, 30 December 1918; *The Times*, 30 December 1918 and January 1919.

108. Walworth says that Lloyd George, that night, found Wilson 'extremely pleasant' – but

Walworth is actually quoting Lloyd George on his meeting with the President on Friday morning; Walworth, *America's Moment*, 150.

109. 'Remarks in His Grandfather's Church in Carlisle', 29 December; 'Luncheon Address in Manchester', 30 December, and 'Address in Free Trade Hall', 30 December 1918, in W. Wilson, *Papers*, LIII, 541–2; 548–52.

110. Edward Bell, 'Statements made by President Wilson to me on the evening of Saturday, the 28th December, 1918', in ibid., 574–6.

111. Minutes, Imperial War Cabinet, 30 December 1918, in ibid., 565–7.

WINTER 1919

Berlin in winter

1. Knowlton L. Ames, *Berlin after the Armistice* (Chicago, 1919), 77.

2. Ibid., 67; speeches of Hugo Haase, Philipp Scheidemann and Heinrich Scheüch (Minister of War) to the returning troops as well as general description of entries in *Berliner Lokal-Anzeiger*, 11–19 December 1918; Harry Kessler, *In the Twenties* (New York, 1971), 18 December 1918, 36–7.

3. General Wilhelm Groener, *Lebenserinnerungen* (Göttingen, 1957), 473–4. On Hindenburg's letter to Ebert, see above, p. 161.

4. *Berliner Lokal-Anzeiger*, 12, 13, 15 December 1918.

5. Ibid., 20 December 1918.

6. Groener, *Lebenserinnerungen*, 472.

7. *Die rote Fahne*, 16–19 December 1918.

8. Groener, *Lebenserinnerungen*, 475.

9. Kessler, *Twenties*, 21 December 1918, 38.

10. *Die rote Fahne*, 16 December 1918.

11. For instance, editorial in ibid., 9 December.

12. E. O. Volkmann, *Revolution über Deutschland* (Oldenburg, 1930), 152–5. Volkmann's timing and chronology appear to be inaccurate; I have modified these in accordance with reports in the contemporary press.

13. Ibid., 155.

14. *Berliner Lokal-Anzeiger*, 24 December 1918.

15. Volkmann, *Revolution*, 156.

16. Ibid., 157.

17. Ibid., 158.

18. Ibid., 158. Groener writes in his memoirs, 'My intervention . . . happened on the telephone from Wilhelmshöhe [Castle] on the evening of 23 December, after Ebert had sent home troops that had come out for his protection. The officers had rightly grown extremely angry and I also was outraged over the senselessness of these measures, which necessarily took away from the officers the last of their trustworthy men. On my urgent demand Ebert gave his assent to the operation against the People's Naval Division the next day . . .', *Lebenserinnerungen*, 476.

19. See a sailor's report in *Berliner Lokal-Anzeiger*, 24 December 1918 (evening edition).

20. Ibid.

21. Ibid.

22. Groener, *Lebenserinnerungen*, 475.

23. George Grosz, *An Autobiography* (Berkeley and Los Angeles, 1998), 113.

24. Kessler, *Twenties*, 24 December 1918, 41–2; Fischer quoted in Robert G. L. Waite, *Vanguard of Nazism* (Cambridge, Mass., 1952), 3.

25. Kessler, *Twenties*, 25 December 1918; *Vorwärts*, 29 December 1918.

26. *Berliner Lokal-Anzeiger*, 25 December 1918.

27. Ibid., 25 and 27 December 1918. Kessler visited the Schloss on 28 December: 'It was a shock

to be confronted with the dead sailors, some in coffins others on stretchers ... Some relatives, small folk, were having the lids lifted for identification. A stale smell of corpses hung in the cold air.' *Twenties*, 44–5.

28. Ames, *Berlin*, 75.
29. For an assessment of the food situation in Germany at the end of the war, see Richard Bessel, *Germany after the First World War* (Oxford, 1993), 31–41, 195–219; and Gerald D. Feldman, *The Great Disorder* (Oxford, 1997), 99–103.
30. Ibid., 127.
31. Bessel, *Germany*, 97.
32. Feldman, *Great Disorder*, 117.
33. Ibid., 111, 116, 133; Bessel, *Germany*, 92–5.
34. Feldman, *Great Disorder*, 120.
35. Groener, *Lebenserinnerungen*, 476–7.
36. *Berliner Lokal-Anzeiger*, 28 December 1918.
37. Armistice terms in Pierre Renouvin, *L'Armistice de Rethondes, 11 novembre 1918* (Paris, 1968), 418–19.
38. Gustav Noske, *Von Kiel bis Kapp* (Berlin, 1920), 178.
39. Richard M. Watt, *The Kings Depart* (New York, 1968), 375–8.
40. Matthias Erzberger, *Souvenirs de guerre* (Paris, 1921), 214; Kessler, *Twenties*, 14–36.
41. Koeth, in Feldman, *Great Disorder*, 117; 'Erklärung gegen Spartakus' by the Vertreter der Vertraunsräte der Regimenter der Garde-Kavallerie-Schützen-Division, *Berliner Lokal-Anzeiger*, 13 December 1918.
42. Waite, *Vanguard*, 16; Watt, *Kings Depart*, 246–54.
43. Three important books explore the relationship between the arts and violence in Germany: Fritz Stern, *The Politics of Cultural Despair* (Ithaca, 1961); George L. Mosse, *The Nationalization of the Masses* (Berkeley and Los Angeles, 1975); and Modris Eksteins, *Rites of Spring* (London, 1989).
44. Franz Schauwecker, *Im Todesrachen*, quoted in Waite, *Vanguard*, 30–1.
45. Eric Waldman, *The Spartacist Uprising of 1919 and the Crisis of the German Socialist Movement* (Milwaukee, 1958), 149–58; Hans Mommsen, *The Rise and Fall of Weimar Democracy* (Chapel Hill, 1996), 23, 35–6. Speeches delivered at the Founding Congress are reproduced in *Die rote Fahne*, 31 December 1919, and *Berliner Lokal-Anzeiger*, 1–2 January 1919.
46. *Die rote Fahne*, 31 December 1919.
47. Noske, *Kiel bis Kapp*, 68–9.
48. *Berliner Lokal-Anzeiger*, 1 January 1919.
49. Kessler, *Twenties*, 31 December 1918, 47.
50. Ibid., 29 December 1918, 45–6.
51. *Berliner Lokal-Anzeiger*, 2 January 1919.
52. Harry Kessler, *Walther Rathenau* (New York, 1969), 68.
53. House, diary, in Charles Seymour, ed., *The Intimate Papers of Colonel House* (London, 1928), I, 403; *The Times*, 11 October 1915, quoted in Paul Létourneau, *Walther Rathenau, 1867–1922* (Strasbourg, 1995), 150, 174.
54. Letters to Wilhelm Schwaner (2 September 1916) and to Lili Deutsch (undated, *c.* 1918), in Kessler, *Rathenau*, 245, 248–9.
55. The 'Don Juan of friendships' is in James Joll's introduction to Walther Rathenau, *Tagebuch 1907–1922* (Düsseldorf, 1967), 25; Lili Deutsch's confession in Létourneau, *Rathenau*, 37.
56. Walther Rathenau, *An Deutschlands Jugend* (Berlin, 1918), 28, 63, 164.
57. Ibid., 1, 12–14, 69–71, 86.
58. *Vossische Zeitung*, 7 October 1918. For a comparison of Danton and Gambetta, see my *At the Heart of a Tiger* (London, 1993), 116–20.
59. Létourneau, *Rathenau*, 235.
60. Rathenau to Lili Deutsch, in Kessler, *Rathenau*, 139.
61. Rathenau to Emil Ludwig, May 1916, in ibid., 236.

62. *Apology* (1919), quoted in ibid., 141.
63. Professor Riedler, a friend of Emil Rathenau's, quoted in ibid., 11.
64. Rathenau, *Jugend*, 9.
65. For letters and notes at the time of Rathenau's revelation, see Kessler, *Rathenau*, 75–83; Létourneau, *Rathenau*, 77–8, 116–17.
66. Ibid., 77.
67. Walther Rathenau, *La Mécanisation du monde/Die Machanisierung der Welt*, bilingual edition (Paris, 1972), 48–9.
68. Kessler, *Rathenau*, 35–7; Létourneau, *Rathenau*, 72–7, 103–8.
69. Walther Rathenau, *Zur Mechanik des Geistes* (Berlin, 1917), 30–2, 291.
70. Walther Rathenau, *Von kommenden Dingen*, in W. Rathenau, *Schriften und Reden* (Frankfurt-am-Main, 1964), 9, 47, 94–107.
71. Ibid., 48.
72. Ibid., 56.
73. W. Rathenau, 'The Sacrifice to the Eumenides' (1913), quoted by Kessler, *Rathenau*, 163.
74. Ibid., 185–6.
75. Rathenau to House, 10 November 1918, in Létourneau, *Rathenau*, 206–7.
76. Kessler,*Twenties*, 1 January 1918, 51.
77. *Berliner Lokal-Anzeiger*, 1–2 January 1919.
78. *Die rote Fahne*, 5 January 1919.
79. Volkmann, *Revolution*, 172–4. Volkmann incorrectly identifies Fischer as Berlin's military commander, the successor to Otto Wels. Wels's successor, decided after much government debate, was Sergeant Major Klawunde. See *Berliner Lokal-Anzeiger*, 29 December 1918.
80. Kessler, *Twenties*, 5 January 1919, 52.
81. Waldman, *Spartacist Uprising*, 175–6.
82. Kessler, *Twenties*, 6 January 1919, 52.
83. Ames, *Berlin*, diary entry for 7–8 January 1919, 36.
84. So are Groener's memoirs. On the Spartacus uprising, Groener simply has a few words of praise for Noske, the civilian whose task it was to organize a new army. See *Lebenserin-nerungen*, 478.
85. Noske, *Kiel bis Kapp*, 71–2.
86. Kessler, *Twenties*, 11 January 1919, 56.
87. *Berliner Lokal-Anzeiger*, 13 January 1919.
88. Grosz, *Autobiography*, 150.
89. Ames, *Berlin*, 7 January 1919, 36; Kessler, *Twenties*, 8 January 1919, 55; 'Berlin, halte ein! Bestimme dich! Dein Tänzer ist der Tod!' reported in *Berliner Lokal-Anzeiger*, 13 January 1919. Anton Gill develops the theme of dance and plays on the contrast between violence and celebration in *A Dance between Flames* (London, 1993).
90. *Berliner Lokal-Anzeiger*, 13 January 1919.
91. See Noske, *Kiel bis Kapp*, 74–5.
92. See Waldman, *Spartacist Uprising*, 195–6.
93. Waite, *Vanguard*, 62–3; Watt, *Kings Depart*, 272.
94. *Die rote Fahne*, 14 January 1919.
95. Kessler, *Twenties*, 20 February 1919, 70–2; Rathenau, *Mechanik des Geistes*, 177.

Paris in winter

1. Keynes, 'Report on Financial Conversations at Trèves, 15–16 January 1919', in Keynes, *The Collected Writings of John Maynard Keynes* (London, 1971), XVI, 395–6.
2. Keynes, 'Dr Melchior: A Defeated Enemy', in ibid., X, 390–428.
3. Keynes to Sir John Bradbury, Paris, 14 January 1919, in ibid., XVI, 391, 393–4.
4. Keynes, 'Financial Conversations', in ibid., 401; Robert Skidelsky, *John Maynard Keynes* (London, 1994–5), l, 359.

5. Hankey's 'Notes of a Meeting of the Supreme War Council, Quai d'Orsay, 13 January 1919, 2.30 p.m.', in Woodrow Wilson, *The Papers of Woodrow Wilson* (Princeton, 1996–93), LIV, 35–42.

6. Arthur Walworth, *Wilson and His Peacemakers* (New York, 1986), 87.

7. Skidelsky, *Keynes*, I, 360.

8. Council of Ten, Quai d'Orsay, 17 January 1919, in W. Wilson, *Papers*, LIV, 108.

9. Reproduced in Howard Elcock, *Portrait of a Decision* (London, 1972), 42.

10. Grayson, diary, 12 January 1919, in W. Wilson, *Papers*, LIV, 5.

11. Harold Nicolson. *Peacemaking 1919* (Gloucester, Mass., 1984), 120.

12. Ignace Paderewski to E. M. House, Warsaw, 12 January 1919, in W. Wilson, *Papers*, LIV, 32–3.

13. Georges Clemenceau, *Grandeurs et misères d'une victoire* (Paris, 1930), 111.

14. Winston Churchill, *The Aftermath* (London, 1929), 6–12.

15. Nicolson, *Peacemaking*, 32.

16. Clemenceau, *Grandeurs*, 137.

17. Lansing memo, 11 January 1919, in W. Wilson, *Papers*, LIV, 3–4; Nicolson, *Peacemaking*, 196.

18. For this paragraph and the following, Maurice Hankey, *The Supreme Control at the Paris Peace Conference 1919* (London, 1963), 22–5.

19. For Hankey's minutes, see W. Wilson, *Papers*, LIV, 7–26.

20. Hankey, *Supreme Control*, 24.

21. Hankey's 'Notes of a Meeting of the Council of Ten, Quai d'Orsay, 13 January 1919', in W. Wilson, *Papers*, LIV, 43–50.

22. Herbert Bayard Swope and others to Wilson, Paris, 14 January 1919; J. P. Tumulty to C. T. Grayson, Washington, 16 January 1919, in ibid., 54–60, 105.

23. Hankey notes, Council of Ten, 16, 17 January 1919, in ibid., 96, 108–12.

24. Ibid., 12, 17 January 1919, 25–6, 112; 'Memorandum on Publicity', 17 January 1919, in ibid., 121–2.

25. Hankey, *Supreme Control*, 29.

26. George Riddell, *The Riddell Diaries* (London, 1986), 18 January 1918, 252.

27. 'Protocol of Plenary Session, Quai d'Orsay, 18 January 1919', in W. Wilson, *Papers*, LIV, 129.

28. House to Wilson, Paris, 18 January, and Grayson, diary, 18 January 1919, in ibid., 126, 128; Riddell, *Diaries*, 253.

29. 'Protocol,' W. Wilson, *Papers*, LIV, 130–1.

30. Hankey, *Supreme Control*, 42–3.

31. Nicolson, *Peacemaking*, 242.

32. Ibid., 32–3.

33. Clive Day, 'The Atmosphere and Organization of the Peace Conference', in Edward Mandell House and Charles Seymour, eds, *What Really Happened at Paris* (New York, 1921), 23.

34. André Tardieu, *The Truth about the Treaty* (Indianapolis, 1921), 97.

35. Edith Benham, diary, 12 January 1919, in W. Wilson, *Papers*, LIV, 34; Borden to Lloyd George, Paris, 21 January 1919, in Elcock, *Portrait*, 83; Nicolson, *Peacemaking*, 247.

36. Hankey, *Supreme Control*, 29; 'Note on the Diary by Miss Hughes', in Sir James Headlam-Morley, *A Memoir of the Paris Peace Conference 1919* (London, 1972), xlii; Lloyd George, House of Commons, 16 April 1919, in Elcock, *Portrait*, 82.

37. Nicolson, *Peacemaking*, 142.

38. Hankey, *Supreme Control*, 28.

39. Harry Kessler, *In the Twenties* (New York, 1971), 19 January 1919, 60.

40. Gustav Noske, *Von Kiel bis Kapp* (Berlin, 1920), 82.

41. Robert G. L. Waite, *Vanguard of Nazism* (Cambridge, Mass., 1952), 67.

42. General Wilhelm Groener, *Lebenserinnerungen* (Göttingen, 1957), 479; Hans Mommsen, *The Rise and Fall of Weimar Democracy* (Chapel Hill, 1996), 39–40.

43. Kessler, *Twenties*, 24 February 1919, 75.

44. Quoted in Harry Kessler, *Walther Rathenau* (New York, 1969), 265–6.

45. Waite, *Vanguard*, 94–7; Groener, *Lebenserinnerungen*, 479.

46. John W. Wheeler-Bennet, *Wooden Titan* (London, 1936), 126.

47. Quoted in Waite, *Vanguard*, 98–9; Richard M. Watt, *The Kings Depart* (New York, 1968), 382.

48. Captains W. S. Roddie, Claude W. Bell and E. W. D. Tennant, 'Report on a Visit to Berlin, 2nd February 1919 to 11th February 1919', quoted in Gerald D. Feldman, *The Great Disorder* (New York, 1997), 99–102.

49. On the effects of wartime rationing, the continuing Allied blockade and the exaggerated warnings of food shortage in Germany, see ibid., 73–8; Niall Ferguson, *The Pity of War* (London, 1998) 276–81; Richard Bessel, *Germany after the First World War* (Oxford, 1993), 35–40, 196–7, 218–19. Bessel, for example, concludes that 'Germany did not starve as a consequence of the severe wartime problems associated with food, but the shortages made the lives of Germans inside the Reich quite miserable. The most fateful consequences of the food shortages, therefore, were probably upon morale.' He also notes that 'although for some time after the War food continued to be scarce in Germany's cities, and undernourishment widespread, and although the Allied blockade was not lifted until 12 July 1919, Germany's urban population did not starve . . . The history of the demobilization and of the post-war transition is, in large measure, a history of fears.' In his report to the Council of Ten on 29 January 1919 Roman Dmowski, the Polish Foreign Minister, noted that the one area of Poland *not* facing starvation was German Poland (W. Wilson, *Papers*, LIV, 337). Several reports indicate starvation among those denied access to Germany's enormous black market: the residents of orphanages and insanity asylums, and Russian prisoners of war.

50. John Headlam-Morley to John Bailey (Paris, 3 February), and to Mr Koppel (5 February 1919), in Headlam-Morley, *A Memoir*, 18, 21; Nicolson, *Peacemaking*, 104.

51. Day, 'Atmosphere', 19–20; Charles Seymour to his family, Paris, 30 January and 8 February 1919, in W. Wilson, *Papers*, LIV, 382–5, and LV, 34–5; Council of Ten, 30 January 1919, in W. Wilson, *Papers*, LIV, 376.

52. Churchill, *Aftermath*, 173; Nicolson, *Peacemaking*, 254–6; Seymour to family, 30 January 1919 and 8 February 1919, in W. Wilson, *Papers*, LIV, 383, and LV, 35; Grayson, diary, 24 February 1919, in W. Wilson, *Papers*, LV, 244.

53. Francis C. Woodman to W. Wilson, Montrichard (Loir-et-Cher), 18 January 1919, in W. Wilson, *Papers*, LIV, 255–6; Pershing to Wilson, Chaumont, 10 February 1919; Wilson to Pershing, Paris, 13 February 1919; G. F. Close to Pershing, Paris, 13 February 1919, in ibid., LV, 64–5, 149, 151.

54. Churchill, *Aftermath*, 50–1; Arno J. Mayer, *Politics and Diplomacy of Peacemaking* (London, 1968), 326–8.

55. Headlam-Morley to Lewis Namier, Paris, 3 February 1919, in Headlam-Morley, *A Memoir*, 20.

56. Dmowski's presentation before the Ten, 29 January 1919, in W. Wilson, *Papers*, LIV, 335–43.

57. Paderewski to House, Warsaw, in ibid., 480–1.

58. Clemenceau's comments to the Ten, 12 February 1919, in ibid., LV, 99; Benham, diary, 2 February 1919, in ibid., LIV, 432; Headlam-Morley to Namier, 13 February 1919, in Headlam-Morley, *A Memoir*, 29.

59. Supreme War Council, 22 January 1919, in W. Wilson, *Papers*, LIV, 201, 203.

60. William Rappard to Hans Sulzer, Paris, 13 February 1919, in ibid., LV, 152–3.

61. Benham, diary, 20 January, and Grayson diary, 21 January 1919, in ibid., LIV, 175, 178

62. Benham, diary, 31 January 1919, in ibid., 414; Nicolson, *Peacemaking*, 250–1.

63. Supreme War Council, 22 January 1919, in W. Wilson, *Papers*, LIV, 190–204; Charles Seymour to his family, Paris, 30 January 1919, in ibid., 384; Council of Ten, 24 and 29 January, 1 February, in ibid., 247, 334, 418–19.

64. Council of Ten, 1 February 1919, in ibid., 419. Headlam-Morley to Namier, Paris, 10 February 1919, in Headlam-Morley, *A Memoir*, 25.

65. Appendix C of Supreme War Council meeting, 7 February 1919, in W. Wilson, *Papers*, 544–5.

66. Supreme War Council, 24 January 1919, in ibid., 238–9.

67. Ibid., 239–47.

68. Supreme War Council, 8 February 1919, in ibid., LV, 14.

69. Supreme War Council, 12 February 1919, in ibid., 98, 100.

70. Loucheur report, Appendix B, Supreme War Council, 7 February 1919, in ibid., LIV, 538–43.

71. Supreme War Council, in ibid., 534–6.

72. Council of Ten, 12 February 1919, in ibid., LV, 108–9.

73. Hoover to Wilson, Paris, 4 and 7 February 1919; Baruch to Wilson, Paris, 4 February 1919; Vance McCormick, diary, 21 January 1919, in ibid., LIV, 196, 477–80, 558.

74. Keynes, 'The Treatment of Inter-Allied Debt Arising out of the War', 29 November 1918; and Keynes, 'The Treatment of Inter-Ally Debt Arising out of the War', 28 March 1918, in J. Keynes, *Writings*, XVI, 418–28; George Riddell, *Lord Riddell's Intimate Diary of the Peace Conference and After, 1918–1923* (London, 1933), 23.

75. Keynes to Sir John Bradbury, Paris, 17 February 1919, in Keynes, *Writings*, XVI, 404–5.

76. Riddell, *Intimate Diary*, 16 February 1919, 23.

77. Davis to Wilson, Paris, 2 February; Wilson to Davis, Paris, 5 February 1919, in W. Wilson, *Papers*, LIV, 431, 493–4.

78. Council of Ten, 27 January 1919, in ibid., 284–5.

79. Keynes to Austen Chamberlain, London, December 1919, quoted in Skidelsky, *Keynes*, I, 393.

80. 'Principles of Reparation', presented formally by the American Delegation to the President and approved by him on 8 February 1919, in W. Wilson, *Papers*, LV, 31.

81. D'Estournelles de Constant to Wilson, Paris, 20 January; Wilson to d'Estournelles de Constant, Paris, 24 January 1919, in ibid., LIV, 257.

82. Grayson, diary, 26 January; Edith Wilson to John Bolling, Paris, 27 January 1919, in ibid., 278–1, 304–6.

83. Riddell, *Intimate Diary*, 26 January 1919, 15–16; Riddell, *Diaries*, 26 January 1919, 255.

84. Charles McAlpin, New York, 31 January 1919, in W. Wilson, *Papers*, LIV, 411.

85. 'Address to French Senate', 20 January 1919, in ibid., 157.

86. See above, p. 29.

87. Wilson's speech at second plenary session, 25 January; Wilson to Swope, Paris, 7 February 1919, in W. Wilson, *Papers*, LIV, 266, 550–1.

88. Council of Ten, 30 January 1919, in ibid., 354, 357.

89. Nicolson, *Peacemaking*, 260.

90. Robert Cecil, diary, 3 February; House diary, 3 February; House, diary, 13 February 1919, in W. Wilson, *Papers*, LIV, 459–61, and LV, 155.

91. 'Covenant of the League of Nations', in ibid., 164–73.

92. *New York Herald*, 15 February 1919, in ibid., 162.

93. League of Nations Commission, 13 February; House, diary, 13 February 1919, in ibid., 138–40, 155.

94. Benham, diary, 21 January 1919, in ibid., LIV, 197–8.

95. Council of Ten, 30 January; Grayson, diary, 30 January; David Hunter Miller, diary, 30 January 1919, in ibid., 363, 348, 379.

96. 'Draft Resolutions in Reference to Mandatories', 29 January 1919, in ibid., 359–61.

97. Riddell, *Intimate Diary*, 30 January 1919, 17.

98. W. S. Rogers to Wilson, Paris, 30 January 1919, in W. Wilson, *Papers*, LIV, 381.
99. Miller, diary, 30 January 1919, in ibid., 379.
100. Protocol of Plenary Session', 14 February 1919, in ibid., LV, 177–8.
101. Churchill, *Aftermath*, 51–3; Riddell, *Intimate Diary*, 8 February 1919, 21.
102. Supreme War Council, 14 February 1919, in W. Wilson, *Papers*, LV, 180–3; Nicolson describes the rainstorm in *Peacemaking*, 262.
103. Churchill, *Aftermath*, 174.
104. David Lloyd George, *The Truth About the Peace Treaties* (London, 1938), I, 330–1.
105. Gregor Dallas, *1815* (London, 1996), 335–9.
106. Headlam-Morley, *A Memoir*, 25 January 1919, 15; Elcock, *Portrait*, 63; Council of Ten, 21 January 1919, in W. Wilson, *Papers*, LIV, 183–4.
107. Council of Ten, 16 January 1919, in W. Wilson, *Papers*, 99–101.
108. Mayer, *Politics*, 431–2; Churchill, *Aftermath*, 172.
109. Wilson's text, 22 January 1919, in W. Wilson, *Papers*, LIV, 205.
110. 'G. V. Chicherin to the Governments of Great Britain, France, Italy, Japan and the United States of North America, 4 February 1919'; Wilson, press conference, 14 February 1919, in ibid., LV, 161–3.
111. Supreme War Council, 15 February 1919, in Department of State, *Papers Relating to the Foreign Relations of the United States* (Washington DC, 1942–7), IV, 10–21.
112. Hankey, *Supreme Control*, 70.
113. See, for example, T. H. Bliss to N. D. Baker and P. C. March, Paris, 13 February 1919, in W. Wilson, *Papers*, LV, 150.
114. Lloyd George, *Peace Treaties*, I, 371–2; Riddell, *Diaries*, 16 February 1919; the same entry in Riddell, *Intimate Diary*, has been doctored.
115. Churchill, *Aftermath*, 176–7; Mayer, *Politics*, 458.
116. Lansing to Wilson, Paris, 17 February; House to Wilson, Paris, *c.* 17 February 1919, in W. Wilson, *Papers*, LV, 202–4.
117. Churchill, *Aftermath*, 164; American Commissioners to Wilson, Paris, 23 February 1919, in W. Wilson, *Papers*, LV, 232.
118. House, diary, 14 February 1919, in W. Wilson, *Papers*, 193.
119. Telegrams from Tumulty, Filene, and McAdoo, 15 February 1919, in ibid., 197–9.

Moscow in winter

1. William C. Bullitt, *The Bullitt Mission to Russia* (New York, 1919), 33.
2. William C. Bullitt, *For the President, Personal and Secret* (New York, 1972), 4–5.
3. Bullitt, *Mission*, 94.
4. Allied troops in the whole of the ex-tsarist empire totalled, at their height, around 20,000 in the north (around Archangel), 40,000 in the south (around Odessa) and around 50,000 along the whole stretch of the trans-Siberian railway between Vladivostock and Omsk in Siberia. Fourteen different nations were implied, each following their own national interests. The number was tiny by the standards of the day and the troops' plans so chaotic that this could hardly be regarded as an 'imperialist intervention', though this was the theme the Bolsheviks drummed home. The troops were almost entirely paid and supplied by the British government. Yet even the British commitment was half-hearted. Britain's main force in Siberia was Colonel Ward's Middlesex Battalion – otherwise known as the 'Hernia Battalion', on account of the age of the men and their general unfitness for battle. See Richard Pipes, *Russia under the Bolshevik Regime, 1919–1924* (London, 1994), 33, 63–73, 78–83; Orlando Figes, *A People's Tragedy* (London, 1997), 573–5, 650–3.
5. Policy paper reproduced in Arthur Walworth, *Wilson and His Peacemakers* (New York, 1986), 134, n.46.
6. Quoted in Beatrice Farnsworth, *William C. Bullitt and the Soviet Union* (Bloomington, 1967), 193, n.20.

7. Bullitt, *Mission*, 4.
8. Henry White to Henry Cabot Lodge, Washington, 21 November 1919, in Farnsworth, *Bullitt*, 193, n.20.
9. Bullitt, *Mission*, 33.
10. Farnsworth, *Bullitt*, 37.
11. Bullitt, *Mission*, 34–8; Bullitt, *For the President*, 9–10.
12. Gompers comment in Walworth, *Wilson*, 33; Orville H. Bullitt, 'Biographical Foreword', in Bullitt, *For the President*, xxxv–xlv; George F. Kennan, 'Introduction', in ibid., xv–xvi.
13. Farnsworth, *Bullitt*, 4–9.
14. Ibid., 12–17.
15. Ibid., 30.
16. Bullitt, *Mission*, 4.
17. Farnsworth, *Bullitt*, 39
18. Bullitt, *Mission*, 57.
19. Ibid., 64.
20. Ibid., 39–43.
21. Lincoln Steffens, *The Autobiography of Lincoln Steffens* (New York, 1931), II, 798, quoted in Farnsworth, *Bullitt*, 47. Bullitt would claim that Steffens had coined the phrase on the way out to Russia; see Pipes, *Bolshevik Regime*, 67.
22. Farnsworth, *Bullitt*, 47.
23. Bullitt, *Mission*, 49, 60, 69.
24. Ibid., 57, 116–22.
25. 'Declaration of the Rights of the Working and Exploited Peoples', in Morgan Philips Price, *My Reminiscences of the Russian Revolution* (London, 1921), 389–90. On the subsequent drafting of the Soviet 'Constitution' in July 1918, see Robert Service, *Lenin: A Political Life* (Bloomington, Indiana, 1985–95), III, 20–5.
26. Figes, *People's Tragedy*, 524, 536, 630, 643.
27. Ibid., 510–11.
28. Iurii Vladimirovich Got'e, *Time of Troubles* (London, 1988), 8–16 July 1917, 28.
29. *Utro Rossii*, 2 June 1910 and 5 July 1911, quoted by James L. West, 'Pavel Riabushinsky's Utopian Capitalism', in James L. West and Iurii A. Petrov, eds, *Merchant Moscow* (Princeton, 1998), 168.
30. Michael F. Hamm, 'The Breakdown of Urban Modernization', in Michael F. Hamm, ed., *The City in Russian History* (Lexington, Kentucky, 1976), 188–92.
31. James L. West, 'The Fate of Merchant Moscow', in West and Petrov, eds, *Merchant Moscow*, 173–5.
32. Or October in the Old-Style Julian Calendar, which functioned in Bolshevik Russia until 14 February 1918 (New Style).
33. Got'e, *Troubles*, 28 October to 4 November 1917 (Old Style), 72–5; Figes, *People's Tragedy*, 496–7; J. M. Vidal, *A Moscou durant le premier triennat soviétique* (Paris, 1933), 2 November 1917 (OS), 16.
34. Boris Pasternak, *Doctor Zhivago* (London, 1997), 154.
35. H. J. Greenwall, *Mirrors of Moscow* (London, 1929), 15
36. See the commentary and bibliographical notes in Terence Emmons's introduction to Got'e, *Troubles*, 6–10.
37. Vidal, *A Moscou*.
38. Ludovic Naudeau, *En prison sous la terreur russe* (Paris, 1920).
39. Ivan Bunin, *Cursed Days* (Chicago, 1998), ix.
40. Emmons's introduction, Got'e, *Troubles*, 4–5.
41. Ibid., 8–16 July 1917, 28.
42. Ibid., 3, 28 October 1918, 3, 22–3 January 1919, 198, 206, 229, 232–3.
43. Ibid., 21–2, 26 December 1918, 222–4.

44. Naudeau, *En prison*, 217, 221–2; Got'e, *Troubles*, 5 January 1919, 228.
45. Ivan Bunin, *Cursed Days*, 22 February/7 March 1918, 54–5 (Bunin insisted on using the Old Style calendar, despite the reform of February 1918); Naudeau, *En prison*, 215, 218.
46. Bunin, *Cursed Days*, 2/15 March 1918, 65; Henri Guilbeaux, *Du Kremlin au Cherche-Midi* (Paris, 1933), 204.
47. Vidal, *A Moscou*, 139–40; Got'e, *Troubles*, 21 November 1918, 215.
48. Vidal, *A Moscou*, 139; Naudeau, *En prison*, 197–210; Guilbeaux, *Du Kremlin*, 205; Price, *Reminiscences*, 14.
49. Naudeau, *En prison*, 221; Got'e, *Troubles*, 8 November 1918, 211.
50. Naudeau, *En prison*, 216; Arthur Ransome, *Six Weeks in Russia in 1919* (London, 1919), 60–3.
51. C. E. Beschhöfer, *Through Starving Russia* (London, 1921), 16.
52. Vidal, *A Moscou*, 144.
53. Figes, *People's Tragedy*, 297–9.
54. Elie Halévy, *The World Crisis of 1914–1918* (Oxford, 1930). The book is a reproduction of three Rhodes Memorial lectures delivered at Oxford in 1929.
55. Robert Gohstand, 'The Shaping of Moscow by Nineteenth-Century Trade', and Hamm, 'Breakdown', in Hamm (ed.), *City*, 169–78, 191.
56. Vidal, *A Moscou*, 144–5; Beschhöfer, *Starving Russia*, 21–2; Figes, *People's Tragedy*, 623.
57. As a matter of fact, it was the Communards themselves who were the source of their own destruction. See my *At the Heart of a Tiger* (London, 1993), 152–89.
58. On the Bolshevik Food Supplies Dictatorship of 1918 and the Food Levy of January 1919, see Service, *Lenin*, III, 52–6.
59. Guilbeaux, *Du Kremlin*, 203–4.
60. Naudeau, *En prison*, 218; Vidal, *A Moscou*, 145; Bullitt, *Mission*, 58.
61. Figes, *People's Tragedy*, 609–10; Got'e, *Troubles*, 29 October 1918, 207. On Moscow's 'over-population', see Guilbeaux, *Du Kremlin*, 209. On 'de-urbanization', see William L. Blackwell, 'Modernization and Urbanization in Russia', in Hamm (ed.), *City*, 295, 315–19.
62. Got'e, *Troubles*, 1 October, 2, 6, 13, 25 November, 1 December 1918, 18, 19 January, 4 February 1919, 197, 208, 210–11, 213, 216–17, 231–2, 238.
63. Ibid., 28 September, 6 October, 14, 15 November, 29 December 1918, 25, 27 February, 23 March 1919, 196, 199, 213–14, 225, 245, 251.
64. Ibid., 18 November 1918, 214.
65. Ibid., 1, 2, 29 December 1918, 217, 218, 225.
66. Ibid., 30 December 1918, 226.
67. Vidal, *A Moscou*, 83–92.
68. Bullitt, *Mission*, 58. How does one distinguish between the Cheka's victims and, for example, those of the armed Bolshevik bands which penetrated the Don region in the first weeks of 1919 and shot at least 8,000 people? Their leader, Rejngol'd, reported to the Central Committee in Moscow that they were carrying out a 'policy of indiscriminate mass extermination'. Andrea Graziosi, *The Great Soviet Peasant War* (Cambridge, Mass., 1996), 20.
69. Service, *Lenin*, III, 16–18; Figes, *People's Tragedy*, 538–9, 544.
70. Figes, *People's Tragedy*, 538.
71. Service, *Lenin*, III, 87.
72. Lenin to Trotsky, Moscow, 12 September 1918, in ibid., 27.
73. Lenin to Sverdlov, Moscow, 1 October 1918, in ibid., 45–6.
74. Lenin to Chicherin, *c.* late December 1918, in ibid., 47.
75. Got'e, *Troubles*, 2, 31 December 1918, 217–18, 226.
76. Winston Churchill, *The Aftermath* (New York, 1929), 168.
77. Figes, *People's Tragedy*, 652.

78. Ibid., 586.
79. For an account of the coup and Kolchak's unwilling role in it, see Pipes, *Bolshevik Regime*, 39–42.
80. On the peasant wars, the brutality and the mixture of ideologies, see Graziozi, *Great Soviet Peasant War*, 6–37.
81. Service, *Lenin*, III, 49.
82. Ibid., 2, 52.
83. Steffens, *Autobiography*, II, 796–7.
84. Ransome, *Six Weeks*, 81–2; Guilbeaux, *Du Kremlin*, 206; Naudeau, *En prison*, 189–95.
85. Ronald W. Clark, *Lenin* (New York, 1988), 4.
86. Figes, *People's Tragedy*, 386.
87. Service, *Lenin*, III, 98–9. Rumours of this story got through to Got'e, who records it in *Troubles*, 23 January 1919, 233 – along with his entry on Moscow resembling a town invaded by Genghis Khan.
88. Figes, *People's Tragedy*, 610.
89. See Martin Malia, *Russia under Western Eyes* (Cambridge, Mass., 1999), 276–7.
90. Alexandra Kollontai's slogan, in Figes, *People's Tragedy*, 295.
91. Programme of the Eighth Party Congress, March 1919, in Service, *Lenin*, III, 85.
92. Ibid., 60–1.
93. Ransome, *Six Weeks*, 34.
94. Got'e, *Troubles*, 21 December 1918, 223. Got'e often writes of isolation in 'Sovdepiya'. Abbé Vidal speaks of 'Sovdepiya' in the same tone (e.g. *A Moscou*, 84, 86).
95. Quoted in Clark, *Lenin*, 227.
96. Ibid., 383.
97. Figes, *People's Tragedy*, 635–42; Service, *Lenin*, III, 37–8.
98. Ibid., 29–33.
99. On the proceedings of the Third International, see Ransome, *Six Weeks*, 140–50; Guilbaux, *Du Kremlin*, 205–9; Service, *Lenin*, III, 67–72.
100. Got'e, *Troubles*, 6–7 March 1919, 247.
101. Ibid., 15 March 1919, 249.
102. Graziosi, *Great Soviet Peasant War*, 32.
103. Pipes, *Bolshevik Regime*, 80.
104. This might be compared to the 42 soldiers shot after the French mutinies of 1917, and a total of around 300 men executed in the British Army during the entire period of the war.
105. Ernst von Salomon, *Die Geächten*, quoted in Richard M. Watt, *The Kings Depart* (New York, 1968), 380.
106. On von der Golz's Baltic campaign, see ibid, 379–87; Robert G. L. Waite, *Vanguard of Nazism* (Cambridge, Mass., 1952), 97–111.
107. Norman Davies, *White Eagle, Red Star* (London, 1983), 24–5.
108. Ibid., 27.
109. The title of an article Stalin published in *Pravda* in 1920. See Pipes, *Bolshevik Regime*, 7.
110. Davies, *White Eagle*, 26.
111. Quoted in ibid., 67.
112. Quoted in Pipes, *Bolshevik Regime*, 47.
113. Ibid., 90.
114. On Marchlewski's diplomacy, see ibid., 88–95; Davies, *White Star*, 70–2.
115. Davies, *White Star*, 51.
116. Ibid., 53.

SPRING 1919

Paris in spring

1. Harold Nicolson, *Peacemaking 1919* (Gloucester, Mass., 1984), 19 February 1919, 264.
2. *Le Petit Parisien*, 20 February 1919; *Le Crapouillot*, March 1919.
3. Robert Lansing to Woodrow Wilson, Paris, 19 February 1919, in Woodrow Wilson, *The Papers of Woodrow Wilson* (Princeton, 1966–93), LV, 209.
4. Ray Stannard Baker, *Woodrow Wilson and the World Settlement* (New York, 1922), I, xx; Nicolson, *Peacemaking*, 116.
5. Howard Elcock, *Portrait of a Decision* (London, 1972), 131–2.
6. Ibid., 117.
7. Charles Seymour, ed., *The Intimate Papers of Colonel House* (London, 1928), IV, 344–6, 356–8.
8. Nicolson, *Peacemaking*, 16–17 February 1919, 262–3.
9. Ibid., 24, 26–7 February, 6–7 March 1919, 268, 272–3, 279–80.
10. Ibid., 8–9 March 1919, 280–1.
11. Ibid., 24 February, 1 March 1919, 269, 274–5.
12. Ibid., 9, 18, 22 March 1919, 281, 285, 297–8; Nicolson to VSW, 24 March 1919, in ibid., 289.
13. Ibid., 23, 28 February, 30 March 1919, 267, 272, 291.
14. Ibid., 2 March 1919, 275–6.
15. Ibid., 5 March 1919, 277.
16. For Bavaria and Eisner's assassination, see Richard M. Watt, *The Kings Depart* (New York, 1968), 283–95.
17. Gerald D. Feldman, *The Great Disorder* (Oxford, 1997), 132.
18. Richard Bessel, *Germany After the First World War* (Oxford, 1993), 105.
19. *Die rote Fahne*, 3 March 1919.
20. Harry Kessler, *In the Twenties* (New York, 1971), 2–3 March 1919, 78–9.
21. Ibid., 25 February 1919, 76.
22. Ibid., 20 February 1919, 71
23. Ibid., 22, 27 February, 4 March 1919, 73–4, 77, 79–80.
24. Ibid., 21, 24 February, 1 March 1919, 73, 75, 78.
25. Ibid., 4 March 1919, 79–80.
26. *Deutsche Kriegzeitung: illustrierte Wochen-Ausgabe herausgegeben vom Lokal-Anzeiger*, 16 March 1919.
27. Ibid., 16 February, 2, 9 March 1919.
28. Feldman, *Great Disorder*, 119.
29. Gustav Noske, *Von Kiel bis Kapp* (Berlin, 1920), 103–4
30. Ibid., 105.
31. Accounts of the fighting in ibid., 106–12; *Deutsche Kriegzeitung*, 16, 23 March 1919; Robert G. L. Waite, *Vanguard of Nazism* (Cambridge, Mass., 1952), 68–79. Watt's account (*Kings Depart*, 304–8) contains inaccuracies, particularly regarding the fighting around Alexanderplatz.
32. Kessler, *Twenties*, 6 March 1919, 81–2.
33. *Deutsche Kriegzeitung*, 16 March 1919.
34. Waite, *Vanguard*, 75–6.
35. Kessler, *Twenties*, 7, 12, 14, 16 March 1919, 82, 86–9.
36. John Maynard Keynes, 'Dr Melchior: A Defeated Enemy', in Keynes, *The Collected Writings of John Maynard Keynes* (London, 1971), X, 410–11.
37. Ibid., 412–13.
38. Arthur Walworth, *Wilson and His Peacemakers* (New York, 1986), 177–9. Klotz, in his book *De la guerre à la paix* (Paris, 1924), accused Keynes of causing the fall of the franc. Keynes replied in an article in the *Times* on 27 February 1924, in which he pointed out Britain's

desperate need for dollars at the close of the war (while the French, he claimed, had made a windfall through the presence of the American armies purchasing local equipment in francs). Britain extended further credit to France following an Anglo-French agreement on 13 March, so that the total that France had received since January 1919 was over £70 million, exclusive of interest accruing after that date, which amounted to another £110 million. Austen Chamberlain, Chancellor of the Exchequer, 'unpegged' the dollar–sterling exchange rate on 20 March 1919, thereby ending a century on the gold standard, a century of European monetary stability – but this could hardly be blamed on Keynes. For the Keynes–Klotz controversy, see Keynes, *Writings*, XVI, 406–15.

39. Keynes, 'Melchior', in Keynes, *Writings*, X, 409.
40. This quotation from Melchior (ibid., 414) is one of the rare references, in Keynes's *Collected Writings*, to events inside Germany.
41. Ibid., 413–15.
42. Ibid.
43. Paul Mantoux, *Les Délibérations du Conseil des Quatre* (Paris, 1955), 2 vols, translated by A. S. Link and M. F. Boemeke as *The Deliberations of the Council of Four* (Princeton, 1992), 2 vols. Lloyd George, House and Wilson of course spoke in English. Clemenceau would sometimes speak in English, but more frequently he expressed himself in French. Orlando could mumble in French, but whenever the matter of Fiume and the Dalmatian coast was brought up and the passion of 'sacred egoism' rose within him, he launched into a flowing, smiling Italian.
44. Walworth, *Wilson*, 186.
45. Grayson, diary, 11 March 1919, in W. Wilson, *Papers*, LV, 473.
46. For the following, Keynes, 'Melchior', in Keynes, *Writings*, X, 416–23; George Riddell, *Lord Riddell's Intimate Diary of the Peace Conference and After, 1918–1923* (London, 1933), 7–8 March 1919, 29–30.
47. *The Times*, 27 February 1924, in Keynes, *Writings*, XVI, 413.
48. Keynes, 'Melchior', in Keynes, *Writings*, X, 423–6.
49. Riddell, *Intimate Diary*, 26 April 1919, 60.
50. Keynes to Bradbury, Paris, 9 May; Keynes to Bradbury and Austen Chamberlain, Paris, 4 May 1919, in Keynes, *Writings*, XVI, 443.
51. Hughes, Cunliffe, Sumner memorandum, 17 March 1919, in David Lloyd George, *The Truth about the Peace Treaties* (London, 1938), I, 502–4; Cunliffe in Riddell, *Intimate Diary*, 5 April 1919, 47.
52. Lloyd George, *Peace Treaties*, I, 481.
53. R. F. Harrod. *The Life of John Maynard Keynes* (London, 1951), 240–1.
54. P. Mantoux, *Deliberations*, 1 and 2 April 1919, I, 105, 109, 118–23.
55. Ibid., 8 April 1919, 187–95.
56. Ibid., 195. Text of the Treaty of Versailles in H. W. V. Temperley, ed., *A History of the Peace Conference of Paris* (London, 1920–4), 100–336 (Article 231 on p. 214).
57. Lloyd George, *Peace Treaties*, I, 478, 482.
58. Maurice Hankey, *The Supreme Control at the Paris Peace Conference 1919* (London, 1963), 97–8.
59. Keynes, *Writings*, XVI, 429–36. Correspondence with his mother indicates that the report was written during a week Keynes spent in England in mid-April.
60. Keynes to Bradbury and Chamberlain, Paris, 4 May 1919, in ibid., 437–40.
61. Elcock, *Portrait*, 138–41.
62. Keynes, *Writings*, X, 23–4, 33–4, 38.
63. *Carnarvon Herald*, 29 May 1891, and *Pontypridd Chronicle*, 15 January 1892, quoted in Chris Wrigley, *Lloyd George* (Oxford, 1992), 58.
64. Grayson, diary, 24 March 1919, in W. Wilson, *Papers*, LVI, 206.
65. Quoted in Wrigley, *Lloyd George*, 8.

66. Riddell, *Intimate Diary*, 23 February 1919, 25; see also Nicolson, *Peacemaking*, 3 February 1919, 255–6
67. Harrod, *Keynes*, 240.
68. Riddell, *Intimate Diary*, 22 February 1919, 24.
69. Frances Stevenson, *Lloyd George* (New York, 1971), 1 March 1919, 172.
70. Robert Cecil, diary, in W. Wilson, *Papers*, 16 March 1919, LV, 539; F. Stevenson, *Lloyd George*, 14 March 1919, 172.
71. Grayson, diary, 15 March 1919, in W. Wilson, *Paper* LVI, 530.
72. Riddell, *Intimate Diary*, 15 March 1919, 33.
73. Lloyd George, *Peace Treaties*, I, 403; Cecil, diary, 18 March 1919, in W. Wilson, *Papers*, LVI, 81–2.
74. F. Stevenson, *Lloyd George*, 15 March 1919; Riddell, *Intimate Diary*, 16 March 1919, 34; House, diary, 22 March 1919, in W. Wilson, *Papers*, LVI, 180.
75. Riddell, *Intimate Diary*, 19 March 1919, 36.
76. F. Stevenson, *Lloyd George*, 23 March 1919, 175.
77. Grayson, diary, 23 March 1919, in W. Wilson, *Papers*, LVI, 194–200.
78. Hankey, *Supreme Control*, 98–101.
79. Complete text of Fontainebleau memorandum in W. Wilson, *Papers*, LVI, 259–70.
80. F. Stevenson, *Lloyd George*, 21 March 1919, 175.
81. G. Clemenceau, 'General Observations on Mr Lloyd George's Note of March 26th [*sic*]', Paris, 26 March 1919, in Lloyd George, *Peace Treaties*, I, 416–20.
82. Clemenceau to Franchet d'Esperey, Paris, 13 December 1918, quoted in G. Welter, *La Guerre civile en Russie* (Paris, 1936), 76.
83. A. Lobanov-Rostovsky, *The Grinding Mill* (New York, 1935), 334, 338.
84. P. Mantoux, *Deliberations*, 24 March 1919, I, 3.
85. Ibid., 27 March 1919, 42. On an early version of the American proposed guarantee (which followed approaches by the British on 14 March), see House, diary, 20 March 1919, in W. Wilson, *Papers*, LVI, 126.
86. Lloyd George to Clemenceau, Paris, 2 April 1919, in Elcock, *Portrait*, 176.
87. Balfour to Clemenceau, Paris, 17 March 1919, in ibid., 150–1.
88. Ibid., 185.
89. P. Mantoux, *Deliberations*, 4 April 1919, I, 141.
90. 'I went to the Ministry of War to see Clemenceau immediately after the President left,' wrote House on 15 April. 'I said to him "I am the bearer of good news. The President has consented to all that you asked of me yesterday." He grasped both my hands and then embraced me, saying I was his good friend and that he would never forget how much I had done for France.' House, diary, 14 and 15 April 1919, in W. Wilson, *Papers*, LVII, 334–5, 355.
91. P. Mantoux, *Deliberations*, 22 April 1919, I, 318.
92. Grayson, diary, 19, 20 March, 3, 4, 6 April; Baker, diary, 11 April 1919, in W. Wilson, *Papers*, LVI, 85, 10–3, 556–7, 584; LVII, 50, 240. For a more recent assessment of Wilson's sickness, see Edwin A. Weinstein, *Woodrow Wilson* (Princeton, 1981), 328, 338–9.
93. F. Stevenson, *Lloyd George*, 5 April 1919, 178.
94. House, diary, 4 April; Baker, diary, 5 April 1919, in W. Wilson, *Papers*, LVI, 587; VII, 4–5.
95. See above, pp. 287–8
96. Elcock, *Portrait*, 156.
97. Fontainebleau memorandum, in W. Wilson, *Papers*, LVI, 266.
98. P. Mantoux, *Deliberations*, 1 April 1919, I, 108–9.
99. Elcock, *Portrait*, 189–90; P. Mantoux, *Deliberations*, 4 April 1919, I, 144–5.
100. Ibid., 27 March 1919, 34–5.
101. The cosmopolitan crowds of Paris in spring 1919 began to resemble the crowds in Vienna in the autumn of 1814, see my *1815* (London, 1996), 134–42.

102. Baker, diary, 31 March; Grayson, diary, 11 April 1919, in W. Wilson, *Papers*, LVI, 442–3; LVII, 237–8.
103. P. Mantoux, *Deliberations*, 1 April 1919, I, 106–9.
104. F. Stevenson, *Lloyd George*, 10 April 1919, 179.
105. P. Mantoux, *Deliberations*, 20 April 1919, I, 296–7.
106. Grayson, diary, 5 May 1919, in W. Wilson, *Papers*, LVIII, 429–30; *The Times*, 5 and 7 May 1919.
107. Edith Benham, diary, 7 May 1919, in W. Wilson, *Papers*, LVIII, 530.
108. House, diary, 7 May; Grayson, diary, 7 May 1919, in ibid., 502, 520.
109. 'Minutes of the Committee for Peace Negotiations', First Session, 15 April 1919, in Alma Luckau, *The German Delegation at the Paris Peace Conference* (New York, 1941), 182–8.
110. House, diary, 7 May 1919, in W. Wilson, *Papers*, LVIII, 521; see also Wilson's comments on Rantzau's trembling legs in P. Mantoux, *Deliberations*, I, 3 May 1919, 478.
111. Walter Simons to his wife, Versailles, 7 May 1919, in Luckau, *German Delegation*, 119.
112. Speech of Count Brockdorff-Rantzau, Versailles, 7 May 1919, in ibid., 220–3.
113. Its formal title was the 'Arbeitsgemeinschaft für Politik des Rechts', or the 'Association for a Policy of Justice'. See ibid., 46–53.
114. Ibid., 70–1.
115. *Vossische Zeitung*, 9 May 1919.
116. Luckau, *German Delegation*, 96–7.
117. *Berliner Tageblatt*, 8 May 1919, *Kreuz-Zeitung*, 8 May 1919, *Tägliche Rundschau*, 8, 13 May 1919, *Deutsche Tagezeitung*, 8 May 1919, *Frankfurter Zeitung*, 9 May 1919. Cuttings of these articles (and hundreds of others) were collected by Philippe Berthelot's Bureau d'Etudes de la Presse Etrangère at the Quai d'Orsay and arranged in '*cartons verts*'. These are now all deposited at the BDIC in Nanterre. Many of the newspapers quoted here have been studied using this source. See in particular BEPE, 'Allemagne, Mai 1919', F° Delta 789/176/01.
118. *Vossische Zeitung*, 8 May 1919.
119. *Tägliche Rundschau*, 8 May 1919.
120. Kessler, *Twenties*, 12 June 1919, 100; Harry Kessler, *Walther Rathenau* (New York, 1969), 275–8; *The Times*, 9 June 1919.
121. General Wilhelm Groener, *Lebenserinnerungen* (Göttingen, 1957), 492–3.
122. Ibid., 494–6.
123. *Freiheit*, 13 and 20 May 1919.
124. See above, p. 435.
125. *Deutsche Allgemeine Zeitung*, 13 May 1919.
126. Contrast the editorial in *Vorwärts* on 9 May with that of 12 May 1919.
127. Luckau, *German Delegation*, 102–6.
128. Riddell, *Intimate Diary*, 5 April 1919, 48.
129. *The Times*, 2 May 1919.
130. Quoted in ibid., 7 May 1919.
131. Wilson to Lloyd George, Paris, 5 May 1919, in W. Wilson, *Papers*, LVIII, 446–8.
132. Keynes to Philip Kerr, Paris, 10 May 1910, in Keynes, *Writings*, XVI, 441.
133. See two letters to his mother, Paris, 14 May and 1 June 1919, in ibid., 458, 470.
134. Keynes to Bradbury, Paris, 22 May 1919, in ibid., 447.
135. Bullitt to Wilson, Paris, 17 May 1919, in William C. Bullitt, *The Bullitt Mission to Russia* (New York, 1919), 96–7.
136. Bullitt to House, Paris, 17 May 1919, in ibid., 98. Bullitt's passion for the Russian Revolution lasted until the 1930s, when Franklin D. Roosevelt named him ambassador to Stalin's Moscow. After this experience he became a fervent anti-Communist.
137. Nicolson, *Peacemaking*, 330–61.
138. Keynes to Bradbury, Paris, 27 May; Keynes to Mrs Keynes, 14 May, 1 and 3 June; Austen

Chamberlain to Keynes, London, 21 May; Keynes to Norman Davis, Paris, 5 June; Keynes to Bradbury, 6 June 1919, in Keynes, *Writings*, XVI, 458–9, 464, 470–3.

139. Riddell, *Intimate Diary*, 30 May 1919, 83.

140. Cecil to Lloyd George, Paris, 27 May 1919, quoted in Walworth, *Wilson*, 417.

141. Lloyd George, *Peace Treaties*, 1, 688.

142. Elcock, *Portrait*, 270.

143. P. Mantoux, *Deliberations*, 3 June 1919, II, 279–82.

144. Elcock, *Portrait*, 276.

145. P. Mantoux, *Deliberations*, 5 and 14 June 1919, II, 312, 453.

146. For this and the following paragraphs, *The Times*, 23–5 June 1919.

EUROPE, EUROPE

1. Richard Pipes, *Russia Under the Bolshevik Regime, 1919–1924* (London, 1994), 176–93; Orlando Figes, *A People's Tragedy* (London, 1997), 696–703.

2. Quoted in Figes, *People's Tragedy*, 703.

3. Ibid., 776–8.

4. Quoted in David Felix, *Walther Rathenau and the Weimar Republic* (Baltimore, 1971), 128.

5. Edith Bolling Wilson, *Memoirs of Mrs Woodrow Wilson* (London, 1939), 245–6.

6. Arthur Walworth, *Wilson and His Peacemakers* (New York, 1986), 433.

7. Ibid., 531.

8. Ibid., 529–30.

9. Bert E. Park, 'Woodrow Wilson's Stroke of October 2, 1919', in Woodrow Wilson, *The Papers of Woodrow Wilson* (Princeton, 1966–93), LXIII, 639–46.

10. *Denver Post*, 26 September 1919, in ibid., 524.

11. Grayson, diary, 26 September 1919, in ibid., 519.

12. Ibid., 26 and 28 September 1919, 519, 532–3.

13. Ray Stannard Baker, diary, 5 November; Robert Lansing, memorandum, 5 November 1919, in ibid., 618–22.

14. Britain, significantly, had no ambassador in Washington at the time – the 'special relationship' was at its lowest ebb.

15. Wilson to Hitchcock, Washington, September 1919, in W. Wilson, *Papers*, LXIII, ix.

16. *New York Times*, 28 September 1919, in ibid., 529.

17. Stephen Bonsal, *Unfinished Business* (Garden City, NY, 1944), 274–8, 286–7.

18. Edith Wilson to Loulie Hunter House, Washington, 17 October; House to E. Wilson, New York, 22 October 1919, in W. Wilson, *Papers*, LXIII, 580–1, 587–8.

19. Stockton Axson, '*Brother Woodrow*' (Princeton, 1993), 285.

20. Pipes, *Bolshevik Regime*, 183–7.

21. Figes, *People's Tragedy*, 766, 769–70.

22. The term 'concentration camp' was used by the French during the First World War to describe refugee centres. They were often built on a muddy terrain, had poor sanitation, and were homes of infection; but they were not what the term suggests today. Here, the Bolshevik camps of 1921 were the precursors.

23. Figes, *People's Tragedy*, 767–9; Pipes, *Bolshevik Regime*, 382–6, 400–1.

24. Figes, *People's Tragedy*, 764–5; Robert Service, *Lenin: A Political Life* (Bloomington, 1985–95), III, 176–84.

25. Ronald W. Clark, *Lenin* (New York, 1988), 465. Service does not mention the incident, but does give an extensive review of Lenin's health problems since his youth in *Lenin*, III, 256–63. Figes, citing recent sources, lends credence to the story; *People's Tragedy*, 793.

26. Norma Evenson, *Paris: A Century of Change, 1878–1978* (New Haven, 1979), 24–9, 60, 272–5.

27. Quoted in ibid., 207.

28. Chamber speeches of 5 November 1918 and 25 September 1919, in Georges Clemenceau, *Discours de paix* (Paris, 1938), 5, 107.
29. Senate speech, 11 October 1919, in ibid., 271.
30. Georges Clemenceau, *Grandeurs et misères d'une victoire* (Paris, 1930), 61.
31. Chamber speech, 25 September 1919, in ibid., 216.
32. Ibid., 202, 217.
33. Ibid., 207–9, 262.
34. On Clemenceau's 'fall', see Georges Wormser (Clemenceau's secretary at the time), *La République de Clemenceau* (Paris, 1961), 404–6.
35. Jean Martet, *Le Silence de Monsieur Clemenceau* (Paris, 1929), 50, 199.
36. Quoted in George Wormser, *Clemenceau vu de près* (Paris, 1979), 171.
37. Quoted in Michel Hoog, *Les Nymphéas de Claude Monet au Musée de l'Orangerie* (Paris, 1989), 38.
38. Georges Clemenceau, *Claude Monet* (Paris, 1928).
39. Gregor Dallas, *At the Heart of a Tiger* (London, 1993), 560 and photos.
40. Sorbonne address, 2 August 1919, in Clemenceau, *Discours de paix*, 143.
41. David Lloyd George, *The Truth about the Peace Treaties* (London, 1938), II, 1409.
42. Wilson to Lansing, 16 September; Dispatch, 19 September 1919, in Walworth, *Wilson*, 547.
43. Ibid., 556.
44. Virginia Woolf, diary, 8 July 1919, quoted in Robert Skidelsky, *John Maynard Keynes* (London, 1994–5), I, 378.
45. Keynes to his mother, 25 June 1919, in ibid., 376; and Keynes to his mother, 3 September 1919, in Roy Harrod, *The Life of John Maynard Keynes* (London, 1951), 288
46. Skidelsky, *Keynes*, I, 377, 382–3.
47. John Maynard Keynes, *The Economic Consequences of the Peace*, in Keynes, *The Collected Writings of John Maynard Keynes* (London, 1971), II, 92.
48. See Keynes's magnificent essay on Malthus, *Writings*, X, 7–81.
49. Keynes, *Economic Consequences*, in Keynes, *Writings*, II, 24.
50. Ibid., 73–85, 106–85, which are drawn from his memorandum of 26 November 1918.
51. Harrod, *Keynes*, 282, 293.
52. Keynes's portrait of Lloyd George was eventually published in *Essays in Biography*, reproduced in Keynes *Writings*, X, 20–6.
53. Skidelsky, *Keynes*, I, 378.
54. Ibid., 384.
55. Felix, *Rathenau*, 108.
56. David Lloyd George, *The Truth about Reparations and War Debts* (New York, 1932), 11–14.
57. The story of reparations is based on many fairy-tale figures, one of the most imaginative being the 'gold mark', which did not exist in reality; it was based on a calculated pre-war rate of 4 marks to the US dollar (or 20 marks to the British pound). In January 1921 the Reichsmark was quoted at a rate of 64.80 to the dollar; it was at 191.81 the following January, and it would attain a staggering 4.2 trillion during the crisis year of 1923. The causes of German hyperinflation must be traced back to German finances during the war and its aftermath. Contrary to the legend, reparations were not the major factor. See Gerald Feldman's monumental *The Great Disorder* (Oxford, 1997); table on monthly Reichsmark rates to dollar in ibid., 5.
58. Quoted in Clark, *Lenin*, 443.
59. Quoted in Chris Wrigley, *Lloyd George* (Oxford, 1992), 112. Churchill's frequent image of the Bolsheviks as 'apes' and 'baboons' was drawn from Russian Menshevik and Social Revolutionary propaganda, which he had obviously been reading. The Social Revolutionaries were prominent in the struggle against Bolsheviks in Georgia, Azerbaijan and Armenia – an area that interested Churchill.
60. MacDonald quoted at length in Clark, *Lenin*, 432.

61. Ibid., 443–4.
62. Ibid.
63. *The Times*, 3 June 1921, in Felix, *Rathenau*, 105.
64. Bruce Kent, *The Spoils of War* (Oxford, 1989), 123–9.
65. Felix, *Rathenau*, 15.
66. Ibid., 16.
67. Ibid., 113.
68. Wrigley, *Lloyd George*, 138.
69. Quoted by Klaus Epstein, *Matthias Erzberger and the Dilemma of German Democracy* (Princeton, 1959), 380.
70. Ibid., 334.
71. Gerald Feldman points out that there were many other factors also involved in the temporary stabilization of the mark, such as the good harvests of 1920 and 1921; ultimately Erzberger's efforts were doomed because of the burdens inherited from his predecessors, Feldman, *Great Disorder*, 156–218.
72. Epstein, *Erzberger*, 329.
73. Ibid., 353–4.
74. George Grosz, *An Autobiography* (Berkeley and Los Angeles, 1998), 156.
75. Richard M. Watt, *The Kings Depart* (New York, 1968), 506.
76. Epstein, *Erzberger*, 384–7. The two murderers escaped to Hungary on passports supplied by Munich police. Many sections of Germany rejoiced at Erzberger's death. '*Na, da können wir uns ja gratulieren, dass das Schwein endlich tot ist,*' declared Major General von Bering. 'I have taken my best bottle out of the cellar and I'm going to drink to it.' In *Der Erzberger-Mord* (Baden, 1921), 7 – an anonymous contemporary publication which contains many such comments.
77. Harry Kessler's interview of Wirth, in Kessler, *In the Twenties* (New York, 1971), 27 February 1929, 343–4.
78. Felix, *Rathenau*, 81.
79. Ibid., 68; Harry Kessler, *Walther Rathenau* (New York, 1969), 284.
80. Felix, *Rathenau*, 135–6.
81. Kessler, *Rathenau*, 316, 360; Kessler, *Twenties*, 20 March 1922, 154–5.
82. Kessler, *Rathenau*, 319.
83. Felix, *Rathenau*, 138–9.
84. Kessler, *Twenties*, 155; Felix, *Rathenau*, 135–40; Kessler, *Rathenau*, 338–9.
85. Kessler, *Rathenau*, 358.
86. Ibid., 343–4.
87. Ibid., 362.
88. Ibid., 375–7.
89. Ibid., 358; Felix, *Rathenau*, 143–4.

Bibliography

Books dealing with topics relating to the war and the peace of 1914–1922 fill libraries and are published every month. The following list is limited to printed sources I have used in the preparation of *1918*. For newspapers and unpublished documents see the endnotes.

The author and publisher wish to thank the following for permission to reproduce copyright material: extracts from 'The General', 'Died of Wounds', 'In the Pink' and 'Glory of Women', © copyright Siegfried Sassoon, by kind permission of George Sassoon.

Adam, H. Pearl, *Paris Sees It Through: A Diary, 1914–19*. London, Hodder & Stoughton, 1919

Adlon, Hedda, *Hotel Adlon: Das Haus in dem die Welt zu Gast war*. Munich: Kindler, 1955

Ames, Knowlton L., *Berlin after the Armistice*. Chicago: Zucker-Kenworthy, 1919

Audouin-Rouzeau, Stéphane, 'The French Soldier in the Trenches', in Cecil and Liddle, (eds), *Facing Armageddon*, 221–9

——, *A travers leurs journaux: 14–18. Les combattants des tranchées*. Paris: Colin, 1986

Axson, Stockton, *'Brother Woodrow': A Memoir of Woodrow Wilson*, eds. Arthur S. Link et al. Princeton: Princeton University Press, 1993

Baker, Ray Stannard, *Woodrow Wilson and the World Settlement*. 3 vols. New York: Doubleday, 1922.

Barker, Pat, *The Regeneration Trilogy*. London: Viking, 1996

Beaumont, Maurice, *L'Abdication de Guillaume II*. Paris: Plon, 1930

Becker, Annette, 'Life in an Occupied Zone: Lille, Roubaix, Tourcoing', in Cecil and Liddle, (eds), *Facing Armageddon*, 630–41

Becker, Jean-Jacques, 'La Grippe espagnole', *L'Histoire*, December 1981, 82–3

—— and Serge Bernstein, *Victoire et frustrations, 1914–1929*. Paris: Seuil, 1990

Bennett, Arnold, *Over There: War Scenes on the Western Front*. London: Doubleday, 1915

Benoist-Méchin, Jacques, *Histoire de l'armée allemande*. 2 vols. Paris: Albin Michel, 1942–3

Berger, Marcel, and Allard, Paul, *Les Dessous du traité de Versailles*. Paris: Editions des Politiques, 1933

Bernachot, General Jean, ed., *Les Armées alliés en Orient après l'armistice du 1918*. 4 vols. Paris: Ministère d'Etat de la défense nationale, 1972

Beschhöfer, C. E., *Through Starving Russia: Being a Record of a Journey to Moscow and the Volga Provinces in August and September 1921*. London: Methuen: 1921

Bessel, Richard, *Germany after the First World War*. Oxford: Clarendon, 1993

Binding, Rudolf, *A Fatalist at War*. London: Allen & Unwin, 1929

Blackbourn, David, *The Fontana History of Germany, 1780–1918: The Long Nineteenth Century*. London: HarperCollins, 1997

Blackwell, William L., 'Modernization and Urbanization in Russia: A Comparative View'. In Hamm, ed., *The City in Russian History*, 291–330

Blancpain, Marc, *La Vie quotidienne dans la France du nord sous les occupations (1814–1944)*. Paris: Hachette, 1983

Bloch, Marc, *Ecrits de guerre, 1914–1918*, ed. Etienne Bloch. Paris: Armand Colin, 1997

——, *French Rural History*. Berkeley and Los Angeles: University of California Press, 1966

Blücher, Evelyn, Princess, *An English Wife in Berlin: A Private Memoir of Events, Politics and Daily Life in Germany throughout the War and the Social Revolution of 1918*. New York: Dutton, n. d. (c. 1920)

Blunden, Edmund, *Undertones of War*. London: Folio, 1989

Boemeke, Manfred F., Feldman, Gerald D., and Glaser, Elisabeth, *The Treaty of Versailles: A Reassessment after 75 years*. Cambridge: Cambridge University Press, 1998

Bond, Brian, and Cave, Nigel, eds, *Haig: A Reappraisal Seventy Years On*. London: Leo Cooper, 1999

Bonsal, Stephen, *Unfinished Business*. Garden City, NY: Doubleday, 1944

Bourne, J. M., *Britain and the Great War, 1914–1918*. London: Edward Arnold, 1989

Brissaud, André, *1918: Pourquoi la victoire*. Paris: Plon, 1968

Brittain, Vera, *Testament of Youth*. London: Virago, 1978

Brockdorff-Rantzau, Ulrich von, *Dokumente und Gedanken um Versailles*. Berlin: Verlag für Kulturpolitik, 1925

Brook-Shepherd, Gordon, *November 1918*. Boston, Toronto: Little, Brown, 1981

Bullard, Robert Lee, *Personalities and Reminiscences of the War*. Garden City, NY: Doubleday, 1925

Bullitt, William C., *The Bullitt Mission To Russia: Testimony before the Committee on Foreign Relations, United States Senate*. New York: B. W. Huebsch, 1919

——, *For the President, Personal and Secret: Correspondence Between Franklin D. Roosevelt William C. Bullitt*, ed. Orville H. Bullitt. Boston: Houghton Mifflin, 1972

Bunin, Ivan, *Cursed Days: A Diary of Revolution*, trans. and ed. Thomas Gaiton Marullo. Chicago: I. R. Dee, 1998

Cambon, Paul, *Correspondance, 1870–1924*. 3 vols. Paris: Grasset, 1940–6

Cannadine, David, *Aspects of Aristocracy*. London: Penguin, 1995.

Carver, Field Marshal Lord, *Twentieth-Century Warriors: The Development of the Armed Forces of the Military Nations in the Twentieth Century*. London: Weidenfeld & Nicolson, 1987

Cather, Willa, *One of Ours*. London: Virago, 1987

Cecil, Hugh, and Liddle, Peter H., eds, *At the Eleventh Hour: Reflections, Hopes and Anxieties at the Closing of the Great War, 1918*. London: Leo Cooper, 1998

——, eds., *Facing Armageddon: The First World War Experience*. London: Leo Cooper, 1996

Challener, Richard D., 'The French Foreign Office: The Era of Philippe Berthelot', in Craig and Gilbert, eds, *The Diplomats*, 1919–39, 49–85

Chemin de Fer du Nord, *Souvenir de la Grande Guerre: visite des régions dévastées du Nord de la France*. 3 vols. Paris: Touring Club de France, 1919

Churchill, Winston S., *The Aftermath*. New York: Charles Scribner, 1929

——, *Great Contemporaries*. London: Butterworth, 1937

——, *The World Crisis, 1911–1918*. 2 vols. London: Odham, 1938

Clark, Ronald W. *Lenin: The Man Behind the Mask*. New York: Harper & Row, 1988

Clausewitz, Karl von, *On War*, trans. Michael Howard and Peter Paret. Princeton: Princeton University Press, 1976

Clemenceau, Georges, *Claude Monet: Les Nymphéas*. Paris: Plon, 1928

——, *Discours de guerre*. Paris: Presses Universitaires de France, 1968

——, *Discours de paix*. Paris: Plon, 1938

——, *Grandeurs et misères d'une victoire*. Paris: Plon, 1930

——, *Vers la Réparation*. Paris: Stock, 1899

Clermont, Camille, ed., *Souvenirs de Parisiennes en temps de guerre*. Paris: Berger-Levrault, 1918

Cooke, James, 'The American Soldier in France, 1917–1919', in Cecil and Liddle, eds, *Facing Armageddon*, 242–55

Craig, Gordon A., *Germany: 1866–1945*. Oxford: Oxford University Press, 1981

—— and Felix Gilbert, eds, *The Diplomats, 1919–1939*. Princeton: Princeton University Press, 1953

Cronin, Vincent, *Paris: City of Light, 1919–1939*. London: HarperCollins, 1994

Crosby, Alfred W., *Epidemic and Peace, 1918*. Westport, Conn.: Greenwood, 1976

Cross, Tim, *The Lost Voices of World War I: An International Anthology of Writers, Poets and Playwrights*. London: Bloomsbury, 1988

Dallas, Gregor, *At the Heart of a Tiger: Clemenceau and His World, 1841–1929*. London: Macmillan, 1993

——, *1815: The Roads to Waterloo*. London: Richard Cohen, 1996

Davies, Norman, *White Eagle, Red Star: The Polish–Soviet War, 1919–20*. London: Orbis, 1983

Davies, Pete, *Catching Cold: 1918's Forgotten Tragedy and the Scientific Hunt for the Virus that Caused It*. London: Michael Joseph, 1999

Day, Clive, 'The Atmosphere and Organization of the Peace Conference', in House and Seymour, eds, *What Really Happened at Paris*, 15–36.

Debeney, General Eugène, *La Guerre et les hommes: réflexions d'après-guerre*. Paris: Plon, 1937

DeGrote, Gerard J., *Douglas Haig, 1861–1928*. London: Unwin Hyman, 1988

Department of State, *Papers Relating to the Foreign Relations of the United States: The Paris Peace Conference 1919*. 13 vols. Washington DC: US Government Printing Office, 1942–7

Derez, Mark, 'The Flames of Louvain: The War Experience of an Academic Community', in Cecil and Liddle, eds, *Facing Armageddon*, 617–29.

Döblin, Alfred, *Karl and Rosa*, trans. John E. Woods. New York: Fromm, 1983

—— *A People Betrayed*, trans. John E. Woods. New York: Fromm, 1983

Droz, Jacques, *Les Causes de la Première Guerre mondiale: essai d'historiographie*. Paris: Seuil, 1973

Dufresne, Claude, *Ce jour-là: la victoire, 1918*. Paris: Perrin, 1988

Dyvrande, Agathe, 'Au Palais', in Clermont, ed., *Souvenirs*, 88–99

Eksteins, Modris, *Rites of Spring: The Great War and the Birth of the Modern Age*. London: Bantam, 1989

Elcock, Howard, *Portrait of a Decision: The Council of Four and the Treaty of Versailles*. London: Eyre Methuen, 1972

Epstein, Karl, *Matthias Erzberger and the Dilemma of German Democracy*. Princeton: Princeton University Press, 1959

Erzberger, Matthias, *Souvenirs de guerre*. Paris: Payot, 1921

Erzberger-Mord, Der: Dokumente zur Zeitgeschichte. Baden: Unitas, 1921

Evans, R. J. W., and Pogge von Strandmann, Hartmut, eds, *The Coming of the First World War*. Oxford: Clarendon, 1988

Evenson, Norma, *Paris: A Century of Change, 1878–1978*. New Haven: Yale University Press, 1979

Farnsworth, Beatrice. *William C. Bullitt and the Soviet Union*. Bloomington: Indiana University Press, 1967

Fay, Sidney B., *The Origins of the World War*. 2 vols. New York: Free Press, 1966

Feldman, Gerald D., *The Great Disorder: Politics, Economics, and Society in the German Inflation, 1914–1924*. New York: Oxford University Press, 1997

Felix, David, *Walther Rathenau and the Weimar Republic: The Politics of Reparations*. Baltimore: The Johns Hopkins Press, 1971

Ferguson, Niall, *The Pity of War*. London: Penguin, 1998

Figes, Orlando, *A People's Tragedy: The Russian Revolution, 1891–1924*. London: Pimlico, 1997

Fischer, Fritz, *Germany's Aims in the First World War*. New York: W. W. Norton, 1967

Foch, Ferdinand, *Mémoires pour servir l'histoire de la guerre*. 2 vols. Paris: Plon, 1931

Fussell, Paul, *The Great War and Modern Memory*. London: Oxford University Press, 1975

Geiss, Imanuel, ed., *Juli 1914: die europäische Krise und der Ausbruch des Ersten Weltkriegs*. Munich: Deutscher Taschenbuch, 1986

Gibbs, Philip, *Open Warfare: The Way to Victory*. London: Heinemann, 1919

Gill, Anton, *A Dance between Flames: Berlin between the Wars*. London: John Murray, 1993

Gohstand, Robert, 'The Shaping of Moscow by Nineteenth-Century Trade', in Hamm, ed., *The City in Russian History*, 160–81

Got'e, Iurii Vladimirovich, *Time of Troubles: The Diary of I. V. Got'e*, trans. and ed. Terence Emmons. London: I. B. Tauris, 1988

Grant, Marjorie, *Verdun Days in Paris*. London: Collins, 1918

Graves, Robert, *Goodbye to All That*. London: Folio, 1981

Grayson, Cary T., *Woodrow Wilson: An Intimate Memoir*. New York: Holt, Rinehart & Winston, 1940

Graziosi, Andrea, *The Great Soviet Peasant War: Bolsheviks and Peasants, 1917–1913*. Cambridge, Mass.: Ukrainian Research Institute, Harvard University, 1996

Greenwall, H. J., *Mirrors of Moscow*. London: Harrap, 1929

Groener, General Wilhelm, *Lebenserinnerungen*. Göttingen: Vandenhoeck & Ruprecht, 1957

Grosz, George. *An Autobiography*, trans. Nora Hodges. Berkeley and Los Angeles: University of California Press, 1998

Guilbeaux, Henri, *Du Kremlin au Cherche-Midi*. Paris: Gallimard, 1933

Guillemenault, Gilbert, *Grandes Heures joyeuses de Paris de la Révolution à nos jours*. Paris: Gaultier-Langerau, 1967.

Halévy, Elie. *The World Crisis of 1914–1918: An Interpretation*. Oxford: Oxford University Press, 1930

Hamm, Michael F., 'The Breakdown of Urban Modernization: A Prelude to the Revolutions of 1917', in Hamm, ed., *The City in Russian History*, 182–99

——, ed., *The City in Russian History*. Lexington, Kentucky: University Press of Kentucky, 1976

Hankey, Maurice, *The Supreme Control at the Paris Peace Conference 1919*. London: Allen & Unwin 1963

Harbord, Major James G., *Leaves from a War Diary*. New York: Dodd, Mead & Co., 1925

Harrod, Roy, *The Life of John Maynard Keynes*. London: Macmillan, 1951

Headlam-Morley, Sir James, *A Memoir of the Paris Peace Conference 1919*. London: Methuen, 1972

Hoehling, Adolph A., *The Great Epidemic*. Boston: Little, Brown, 1961

Hoog, Michel, *Les Nymphéas de Claude Monet au Musée de l'Orangerie*. Paris: Réunion des Muséees nationaux, 1989

Hoover, Herbert, *The Memoirs of Herbert Hoover*. Vol. I: *Years of Adventure, 1874–1920*. New York: Macmillan, 1951

——, *The Ordeal of Woodrow Wilson*. New York: McGraw-Hill, 1958

House, Edward Mandell, and Seymour, Charles, eds, *What Really Happened at Paris: The Story of the Peace Conference, 1918–1919*, by American Delegates. New York: Scribner, 1921

——, *see also* Seymour, Charles

How to See Paris and the Battlefields: Automobile Tours Organised by Thomas Cooke & Sons. Lille: L. Danel, 1921

Howden Smith, Arthur D., *Mr House of Texas*. New York: Funk & Wagnalls, 1940

Hynes, Samuel, *The Soldiers' Tale: Bearing Witness to Modern War*. New York: Viking, 1997

Inwood, Stephen, *A History of London*. London: Macmillan, 1998

Jedrzejewicz, Waclaw, *Joseph Pilsudski: une biographie*, trans. T. Sas. Lausanne: L'Age d'Homme, 1986
Jenkins, Roy, *Asquith*. London: Collins, 1964
Jones, Nigel H., *The War Walk: A Journey along the Western Front*. London: Robert Hale, 1983
Jünger, Ernst, *The Storm of Steel*. London: Chatto & Windus, 1929

Keegan, John, *The First World War*. London: Hutchinson, 1998
Kennan, George F., *The Fateful Alliance: France, Russia, and the Coming of the First World War*. Manchester: Manchester University Press, 1984
Kennedy, Paul, *The Rise and Fall of the Great Powers: Economic Change and Military Conflict from 1500 to 2000*. London: Unwin Hyman, 1988
Kent, Bruce, *The Spoils of War: The Politics, Economics, and Diplomacy of Reparations, 1918–1932*. Oxford: Clarendon, 1989
Kessler, Harry, *In the Twenties: The Diaries of Harry Kessler*, trans. Charles Kessler. New York: Holt, Rinehart & Winston, 1971
——, *Walther Rathenau: His Life and Work*, trans. W. D. Robson Scott and Lawrence Hyde. New York: Howard Fertig, 1969
Keynes, John Maynard, *The Collected Writings of John Maynard Keynes*, ed. Elizabeth Johnson. Vol. II, *The Economic Consequences of the Peace*; Vol. III. *A Revision of the Treaty*; Vol. X, *Two Memoirs and Other Writings*; Vol. XVI, *Activities 1914–1919 – the Treasury and Versailles*. London: Macmillan, 1971
Kissinger, Henry, *Diplomacy*. London: Simon & Schuster, 1994
Klotz, Louis-Lucien, *De la guerre à la paix*. Paris: Plon, 1924

Lacqueur, Walter, *Weimar, A Cultural History*. London: Weidenfeld & Nicolson, 1974
Lentin, Antony, *Lloyd George, Woodrow Wilson and the Guilt of Germany*. Leicester: Leicester University Press, 1984
Létourneau, Paul, *Walther Rathenau, 1867–1922*. Strasbourg: Presses Universitaires de Strasbourg, 1995
Liddell Hart, Basil, *A History of the World War, 1914–1918*. London: Faber, 1934
Liddle, Peter, 'Britons on the Home Front', in Cecil and Liddle, eds, *At the Eleventh Hour*, 68–83.
Lissorgues, Abbé Marcellin Marius, *Notes de l'Aumonier*. Aurillac: Imprimerie Moderne, 1921
Lloyd George, David, *Family Letters, 1885–1936*, ed. K. O. Morgan. Oxford: Oxford University Press, 1973
——, *The Truth About the Peace Treaties*. 2 vols. London: Gollancz, 1938
——, *The Truth About Reparations and War Debts*. New York: Doubleday, 1932
——, *War Memoirs*. 6 vols. London: Nicholson & Watson, 1933–6
Lobanov-Rostovsky, A. *The Grinding Mill: Reminiscences of War and Revolution in Russia, 1913–1920*. New York: Macmillan, 1935
Luckau, Alma, *The German Delegation at the Paris Peace Conference*. New York: Columbia University Press, 1941
Ludendorff, General P. W. E., *My War Memories, 1914–1918*. 2 vols. London: Hutchinson, 1919

MacDonagh, Michael, *In London During the Great War: The Diary of a Journalist*. London: Eyre & Spottiswoode, 1935
Macdonald, John F., *Two Towns, One City: Paris–London*. London: Grant Richards, 1917
Macdonald, Lyn, ed., *1914–1918: Voices and Images of the Great War*. London: Michael Joseph, 1988

MacDonogh, Giles, *Berlin*. London: Sinclair-Stevenson, 1997
——, *Prussia: The Perversion of an Idea*. London: Sinclair-Stevenson, 1994
McKenna-Friend, Margaret Alice, *Mes soixante mois au camp retranché de Paris (de juillet 1914 à juillet 1919)*. Paris: Tolra, 1921
Malia, Martin, *Russia under Western Eyes: From the Bronze Horseman to the Lenin Mausoleum*. Cambridge, Mass.: Harvard University Press, 1999
Mangin, Louis Eugène, *Le Général Mangin, 1866–1925*. Paris: Lanore-Sorlot, 1986
Mantoux, Etienne. *La Paix calomniée ou les 'Conséquences économiques' de Monsieur Keynes*, pref. Raymond Aron. Paris: Gallimard, 1946
Mantoux, Paul, *The Deliberations of the Council of Four (March 24 – June 28, 1919)*, trans. A. S. Link and M. F. Boemeke. 2 vols. Princeton: Princeton University Press, 1992
Martet, Jean, *Le Silence de Monsieur Clemenceau*. Paris: Albin Michel, 1929
Martin, Benjamin F., *France and the Après Guerre, 1918–1924*. Baton Rouge: Louisiana State University Press, 1999
Massie, Robert K., *Dreadnought: Britain, Germany and the Coming of the Great War*. New York: Random House, 1991
Maurice, Major-General F., *The Last Four Months: The End of the War in the West*. London: Cassell, 1919
Max of Baden, Prince, *The Memoirs of Prince Max of Baden*, trans. W. M. Calder and C. W. H. Sutton. 2 vols. New York: Scribner, 1928
Mayer, Arno J., *Politics and Diplomacy of Peacemaking: Containment and Counter-Revolution at Versailles 1918–1919*. London: Weidenfeld & Nicolson, 1968
Meyer, Jacques, *Les Soldats de la Grande Guerre*. Paris: Hachette, 1966
Milne, James, *A New Tale of Two Cities: Calling Up the Life Adventures of the Great Wartime in London and Paris . . .* London: John Lane, 1923
Miquel, Pierre, *La Paix de Versailles et l'opinion publique français*. Paris: Flammarion, 1972
Mitchell, B. R., *European Historical Statistics, 1750–1970*. London: Macmillan, 1978
Mommsen, Hans, *The Rise and Fall of Weimar Democracy*, trans. Elborg Forster and Larry E. Jones. Chapel Hill: University of North Carolina Press, 1996
Monnet, François, *Refaire la République: André Tardieu, une dérive réactionnaire (1876–1945)*. Paris: Fayard, 1993
Mordacq, General Jean-Henri, *Clemenceau au soir de sa vie*. 2 vols. Paris: Plon, 1933
——, *Le Ministère Clemenceau: Journal d'un témoin*. 4 vols. Paris: Plon, 1930
Mosse, George L., *The Nationalization of the Masses: Political Symbolism and Mass Movements in Germany from the Napoleonic Wars through the Third Reich*. Berkeley and Los Angeles: University of California Press, 1975
Müller, Admiral Georg Alexander von, *The Kaiser and His Court*, ed. Walter Görlitz, trans. Mervyn Savill. New York: Harcourt, Brace & World, 1964

Nash, George H., *The Life of Herbert Hoover*. 2 vols. New York: W. W. Norton, 1983–8
Naudeau, Ludovic, *En prison sous la terreur russe*. Paris: Hachette, 1920
Nicolson, Harold, *Peacemaking 1919*. Gloucester, Mass.: Peter Smith, 1984
Niemann, Alfred, *Kaiser und Revolution*. Berlin: Scherl, 1922
Noske, Gustav, *Von Kiel bis Kapp: Zur Geschichte der deutschen Revolution*. Berlin: Verlag für Politik und Wirtschaft, 1920

Padfield, Peter, *Maritime Supremacy: The Opening of the Western Mind*. London: John Murray, 1999
Paschall, Rod, *The Defeat of Imperial Germany, 1917–1918*. New York: Da Capo, 1989
Pasternak, Boris, *Doctor Zhivago*, trans. Max Hayward and Manya Harari. London: Folio, 1997
Pedroncini, Guy, *Les Mutineries de 1917*. Paris: Presses Universitaires de France, 1967

Peukert, Detlev J. K., *The Weimar Republic*, trans. Richard Deveson. New York: Hill & Wang, 1989

Pilsudski, Josef, *The Memories of a Polish Revolutionary and Soldier*, trans. D. R. Gillie. London: Faber, 1931

Pipes, Richard, *Russia under the Bolshevik Regime, 1919–1924*. London: Harvill, 1994

Playne, Caroline E., *Britain Holds On, 1917, 1918*. London: Alien & Unwin, 1933

Pogge von Strandmann, Hartmut, 'Germany and the Coming of War', in Evans and Pogge von Strandmann, eds, *The Coming of the First World War*, 87–123.

Poincaré, Raymond, *Au service de la France*. Vols. VIII–XI. Paris: Plon, 1930–3

Price, Morgan Philips, *My Reminiscences of the Russian Revolution*. London: Allen & Unwin, 1921

Ranft, Bryan, 'The Royal Navy and the War at Sea', in J. C. Turner, ed., *Britain and the First World War*, 53–69

Ransome, Arthur, *Six Weeks in Russia in 1919*. London: Allen & Unwin, 1919

Rathenau, Walther, *An Deutschlands Jugend*. Berlin: S. Fischer, 1918

——, *La Mécanisation du monde/ Die Mechaniserung der Welt*. Bilingual edition. Paris: Aubier Montaigne, 1972

——, *Schriften und Reden*, ed. Hans Werner Richter. Frankfurt-am-Main: S. Fischer, 1964

——, *Tagebuch 1907–1922*, Ed. Hartmut Pogge von Strandmann. Düsseldorf: Droste, 1967

——, *Zur Mechanik des Geistes*. Berlin: S. Fischer, 1917

Rearick, Charles, *The French in Love and War: Popular Culture in the Era of the World Wars*. New Haven: Yale University Press, 1997

Renouvin, Pierre, *L'Armistice de Rethondes, 11 novembre 1918*. Paris: Gallimard, 1968

Retzlan, Karl, *Spartacus: Aufstieg und Niedergang: Erinnerungen eines Parteiarbeiters*. Frankfurt-am-Main: Verlag Neue Kritik, 1976

Richie, Alexandra, *Faust's Metropolis: A History of Berlin*. New York: Carroll & Graf, 1998

Riddell, George, *Lord Riddell's Intimate Diary of the Peace Conference and After, 1918–1923*. London: Gollancz, 1933

——, *The Riddell Diaries*, ed. John M. McEwen. London: Athlone, 1986

Roberts, John Stuart, *Siegfried Sassoon, 1886–1967*. London: Richard Cohen, 1999

Röhl, John C. G., *The Kaiser and His Court*. Cambridge: Cambridge University Press, 1994

Roskill, Stephen, *Hankey: Man of Secrets*. 3 vols. London: Collins, 1970–2

Rudin, Harry R., *Armistice 1918*. New Haven: Yale University Press, 1944

Sabrow, Martin, *Der Rathenaumord: Rekonstruction einer Verschwörung gegen die Republik von Weimar*. Munich: Oldenburg, 1994

Sassoon, Siegfried, *The Complete Memoirs of George Sherston*. London: Faber, 1972

——, *The War Poems*. London: Faber, 1983

Scheidemann, Philipp, *Memoiren eines Sozialdemokraten*. 2 vols. Dresden: Reissner, 1928

Service, Robert, *Lenin: A Political Life*. 3 vols. Bloomington: Indiana University Press, 1985–95

——, *The Russian Revolution, 1900–1927*. London: Macmillan, 1999

Seymour, Charles, *Letters from the Paris Peace Conference*, ed. Harold B. Whiteman. New Haven: Yale University Press, 1965

——, ed., *The Intimate Papers of Colonel House*. 4 vols. London: Ernest Benn, 1928

Sheffield, Gary, 'Officer-Man Relations, Discipline and Morale in the British Army of the Great War', in Cecil and Liddle, eds, *Facing Armageddon*, 413–24

Sheppard, Francis, *London: A History*. Oxford: Oxford University Press, 1998

Shartle, Samuel G., *Spa, Versailles, Munich: An Account of the Armistice Commission*. Philadelphia: Dorrance, 1941

Simkins, Peter, 'The War Experience of a Typical Kitchener Division: The 18th Division, 1914–1918', in Cecil and Liddle, eds, *Facing Armageddon*, 297–313

Skidelsky, Robert, *John Maynard Keynes*. 2 vols. London: Penguin, 1994–5

S. M., 'Le drame de l'attente', in Clermont, ed., *Souvenirs*, 229–33

Stallworthy, Jon, *Wilfred Owen: A Biography*. Oxford: Oxford University Press, 1974

Steffens, Lincoln, *The Autobiography of Lincoln Steffens*. 2 vols. New York: Harcourt Brace, 1931

Stern, Fritz, *The Politics of Cultural Despair: A Study in the Rise of the Germanic Ideology*. Ithaca: Cornell University Press, 1961

Stevenson, David, *The First World War and International Politics*. Oxford: Oxford University Press, 1988

Stevenson, Frances. *Lloyd George: A Diary*, ed. A. J. P. Taylor. New York: Harper & Row, 1971

Stockwell, A. J., 'The War and the British Empire', in J. Turner, ed., *Britain and the First World War*, 36–52

Stone, Norman, *The Eastern Front, 1914–1917*. London: Penguin, 1998

Story, Somnerville, *Present Day Paris and the Battlefields: The Visitor's Handbook with the Chief Excursions to the Battlefields*. New York: D. Appleton, 1920

Talleyrand-Périgord, C. M. de, *Mémoires, 1754–1815*, ed. Paul-Louis and Jean-Paul Couchard. Paris: Plon, 1982.

Tardieu, André, *La Paix*, pref. Georges Clemenceau. Paris: Payot, 1921.

——, *The Truth About the Treaty*, pref. Colonel Edward M. House. Indianapolis: Bobbs-Merril, 1921 (a version somewhat different from the above)

Taylor, A. J. P. *English History, 1914–1945*. Oxford: Oxford University Press, 1992

Taylor, Ronald, *Berlin and Its Culture: A Historical Portrait*. New Haven: Yale University Press, 1997

Temperley, H. W. V., ed., *A History of the Peace Conference of Paris*. 6 vols. London: Henry Frowde, with Hodder & Stoughton, 1920–4

Terraine, John, *To Win a War: 1918, the Year of Victory*. London: Sidgwick & Jackson, 1978

Thadden, Rudolf von, *Prussia: The History of a Lost State*, trans. A. Rutter. Cambridge: Cambridge University Press, 1987

Tirpitz, Grand Admiral Alfred von, *Politische Dokumente*. 2 vols. Hamburg: Hanseatische Verlaganstalt, 1926

Toland, John, *No Man's Land: 1918, the Last Year of the Great War*. New York: Doubleday, 1980

Tucoo-Chalia, Jean Earnest, *1914–1919: Carnets de route d'un artilleur*. Biarritz: J & D, 1996

Tuchman, Barbara, *The Guns of August*. New York: Dell, 1963

Turner, E. S., *Dear Old Blighty*. London: Michael Joseph, 1980

Turner, John, 'British Politics and the Great War', in J. Turner, ed., *Britain and the First World War*, 117–38

——, ed., *Britain and the First World War*. London: Unwin Hyman, 1988

Vache, Jacques, *Lettres de guerre*. Paris: J.-M. Place, 1989

Vandiver, Frank. 'Haig and Pershing', in Cecil and Liddle, eds, *Facing Armageddon*, 67–78

Vidal, J. M., *A Moscou durant le premier triennat soviétique (1917–1920)*. Paris: Bonne Presse, 1933

Viel, Marie-Jeanne, 'L'Armistice du 11 novembre 1918', in Gilbert Guillemenault, ed., *Grandes heures joyeuses de Paris de la Révolution à nos jours*. Paris: Gautier-Langereau, 1967

Vilain, Charles, *Le 7 novembre 1918 à Haudroy*. Saint-Quentin: Comité de la Victoire et de l'Armistice, 1968

Volkmann, Erich Otto, *Revolution über Deutschland*. Oldenburg: Stallung, 1930

Waite, Robert G. L., *Vanguard of Nazism: The Free Corps Movement in Postwar Germany, 1918–1923*. Cambridge, Mass.: Harvard University Press, 1952

Waldman, Eric, *The Spartacist Uprising of 1919 and the Crisis of the German Socialist Movement: A Study of the Relation of Political Theory and of Party Politics*. Milwaukee: Marquette University Press, 1958

Walworth, Arthur, *America's Moment: 1918, American Diplomacy at the End of World War I*. New York: W. W. Norton, 1977
——, *Wilson and His Peacemakers: American Diplomacy at the Paris Peace Conference, 1919*. New York: W. W. Norton, 1986
Watt, Richard M., *Dare Call It Treason*. New York: Simon & Schuster, 1963
——, *The Kings Depart: The Tragedy of Germany: Versailles and the German Revolution*. New York: Simon & Schuster, 1968
Weber, Eugen, *La France des années 30: tourments et perplexités*. Paris: Fayard, 1995
Weinstein, Edwin A., *Woodrow Wilson: A Medical and Psychological Biography*. Princeton: Princeton University Press, 1981
Welter, G., *La Guerre civile en Russie*. Paris: Payot, 1936
West, James L., 'The Fate of Merchant Moscow', in West and Petrov, eds, *Merchant Moscow*, 173–8
——, 'Pavel Riabushinsky's Utopian Capitalism', in West and Petrov, eds, *Merchant Moscow*, 161–70
West, James L., and Petrov, Iurii A., eds, *Merchant Moscow: Images of Russia's Vanished Bourgeoisie*. Princeton: Princeton University Press, 1998
Wheeler-Bennett, John W., *Brest-Litovsk: The Forgotten Peace, March 1918*. London: Macmillan, 1963
——, *The Nemesis of Power: The German Army in Politics, 1918–1945*. London: Macmillan, 1953
——, *Wooden Titan: Hindenburg*. London: Macmillan, 1936
Wieland, Lothar, *Belgien 1914: Die Frage des belgischen 'Franktireurkrieges' und die deutsche Öffentliche Meinung von 1914 bis 1936*. Frankfurt: Lang, 1984
William II, ex-Kaiser. *My Memoirs, 1878–1918*. London: Cassell, 1922
Williams, Wythe, *Dusk of Europe*. London: Scribner, 1937
Wilson, Trevor, *The Downfall of the Liberal Party, 1914–1935*. London: Collins, 1966
——, *The Myriad Faces of War: Britain and the Great War, 1914–1918*. Cambridge: Polity Press, 1986
Wilson, Edith Bolling, *Memoirs of Mrs Woodrow Wilson*. London: Putnam, 1939
Wilson, Jean Moorcroft, *Siegfried Sassoon: The Making of a War Poet*. London: Duckworth, 1998
Wilson, Woodrow, *The Papers of Woodrow Wilson*, eds Arthur S. Link et al. 69 vols. Princeton: Princeton University Press, 1966–93
Winter, J. M., *The Great War and the British People*. London: Macmillan, 1986
Wormser, Georges, *Clemenceau vu de près*. Paris: Hachette, 1979
——, *La République de Clemenceau*. Paris: Presses Universitaires de France, 1961
Wrigley, Chris, *Lloyd George*. Oxford: Blackwell, 1992

Zévaès, Alexandre, *Clemenceau*. Paris: Julliard, 1949

Index

Compiled by Meg Davies (Registered Indexer, Society of Indexers)